Introduction to
Early Childhood Education

Dedication

Uncountable thanks continue to go to my late husband, Ahmed Essa, whose encouragement, ideas, and wise, steadfast support had always kept me going. In addition, I also dedicate this seventh edition of Introduction to Early Childhood Education *to my new granddaughter, Jordan; my daughter, Fiona; my son, Eugene; my daughter-in-law, Kristie; and my honorary grandsons, Cadel and Keagan.*

7e

Introduction to
Early
Childhood
Education

Eva L. Essa
University of Nevada, Reno

WADSWORTH
CENGAGE Learning·

Australia · Brazil · Japan · Korea · Mexico · Singapore · Spain · United Kingdom · United States

WADSWORTH
CENGAGE Learning·

Introduction to Early Childhood Education,
Seventh Edition
Eva L. Essa

Editor-in-Chief: Linda Ganster

Executive Editor: Mark Kerr

Managing Development Editor: Lisa Mafrici

Developmental Editor: Kate Scheinman

Editorial Assistant: Greta Lindquist

Media Editor: Elizabeth Momb

Brand Manager: Melissa Larmon

Senior Market Development Manager: Kara Kindstrom

Content Project Manager: Samen Iqbal

Art Director: Jennifer Wahi

Manufacturing Planner: Doug Bertke

Rights Acquisitions Specialist: Tom McDonough

Production Service and Composition: Lindsay Schmonsees, MPS Ltd.

Photo Researcher: Sara Golden

Text Researcher: Robin Kristoff

Copy Editor: Debbie Stone

Designer: Norman Baugher

Cover Image: originalpunkt

For product information and technology assistance, contact us at
Cengage Learning Customer & Sales Support, 1-800-354-9706.
For permission to use material from this text or product,
submit all requests online at **www.cengage.com/permissions.**
Further permissions questions can be e-mailed to
permissionrequest@cengage.com.

Library of Congress Control Number: 2012935945

Student Edition:
ISBN-13: 978-1-133-58984-6
ISBN-10: 1-133-58984-7

Loose-leaf Edition:
ISBN-13: 978-1-133-96427-8
ISBN-10: 1-133-96427-3

Wadsworth
20 Davis Drive
Belmont, CA 94002-3098
USA

Cengage Learning is a leading provider of customized learning solutions with office locations around the globe, including Singapore, the United Kingdom, Australia, Mexico, Brazil, and Japan. Locate your local office at **www.cengage.com/global.**

Cengage Learning products are represented in Canada by Nelson Education, Ltd.

To learn more about Wadsworth, visit **www.cengage.com/wadsworth**

Purchase any of our products at your local college store or at our preferred online store **www.CengageBrain.com.**

Printed in the United States of America
2 3 4 5 6 7 19 18 17 16 15

Brief Contents

Contents

Preface

DEAR READER:

With this book, *Introduction to Early Childhood Education*, Seventh Edition, you are embarking on a fascinating journey. The field of early childhood education is a rich and rewarding endeavor for a dedicated person, like yourself, whose aim is to make a difference by working with young children and their families. After reading this book, you will be much more knowledgeable about young children and families, the many components of high-quality early childhood programs, and the role of the professional early childhood educator. What can you expect as you read on?

Who Is this Book for?

This text is intended for current or future professionals who want to learn more about early childhood education. This field encompasses work with children from infancy through age eight. Thus, included in the book is information about infant and toddler programs, programs for preschool-aged children, and before- and after-school programs for young school-aged children. Most of all, this book is for those who plan to or currently teach and care for young children.

Introduction to Early Childhood Education is also relevant for those who work in other capacities in early childhood education programs—administrators, parent education and engagement coordinators, curriculum coordinators, staff training consultants, and others.

Philosophy

This text is built on the underlying philosophy that the early childhood educator's most important task is to provide a program that is sensitive to and supports the development of young children. Only in a child-centered program—in which children are allowed to make choices, the guidelines are clear and logical, activities are planned to meet the needs of the individual children in the group and are sensitive to their cultural and family background, and adults are consistent and loving—will children flourish. A good early childhood experience can contribute immeasurably to helping children become responsible people who care about and show concern for others.

You will see this philosophy reflected throughout the book, in all chapters and on all topics.

Content and Organization

This book is divided into six parts and further subdivided into 16 chapters. The purpose of these six parts is to answer the questions, "*What* is early childhood education?" "*Who* are the people involved in early childhood education?" "*Why* is early childhood education important?" "*Where* is early childhood education carried out?" and "*How* is early childhood education implemented?" (This last question comprises two parts in the text, on curriculum and guidance.) These questions are important ones as you gain insight into all aspects of early childhood education.

Within the 16 chapters, you will learn more about the scope of early childhood education and why it is needed (Chapter 1); the children, families and teachers involved in early childhood education (Chapters 2 to 4); the history leading up to the field today, the theoretic rationale supporting it, and how theory is translated into specific types of programs (Chapter 5); the relevance of accountability, standards, and assessment in carrying out programs (Chapter 6); the importance of the physical environment as the setting of early childhood education programs (Chapter 7); scheduling for and planning the curriculum (Chapter 8); contents of the curriculum as it supports children's creative, physical, cognitive, language, and social development (Chapters 9 to 13); guiding children through daily routines and in group activities (Chapter 14); guiding individual children's social behaviors, including handling challenging behaviors (Chapter 15); and helping children cope with stress in their lives (Chapter 16). These chapters provide a great deal of information about the basic components of early childhood education and working with young children.

From Theory and Research to Practice

Like most fields, early childhood education is built on theoretical ideas, concepts, and research that give it a strong and cohesive foundation. In Chapter 5, several key theories are introduced. Throughout the book, these are referred to with particular emphasis on making them relevant to work with young children. In addition, relevant research studies are cited throughout the text to provide scientific validity to many of the practices and ideas of early childhood education. To help make theoretical and research information meaningful, actual examples of young children and their teachers are frequently provided.

These examples help make the contents of the book, especially theoretical and research information, take on meaning and come alive. As you read through the book and continue to come across names such as Piaget, Erikson, and Vygotsky, you will become familiar with these influential people and their ideas. They are important allies in an introduction to early childhood education because their contributions provide such valuable insights to our understanding of children.

WHAT'S NEW IN THIS EDITION?

You will find that this seventh edition of *Introduction to Early Childhood Education* reflects the latest research, statistics, policy, and changes in the field of early childhood education to provide you with the most current information as you enter the field. Key highlights include:

- In-depth links, in all chapters, to the new *NAEYC Standards* for Professional Preparation Programs. It is possible that you are within a higher-education program that is accredited by an accrediting agency that uses these standards. They specify what one needs to know about early childhood education. At the beginning of each chapter is a listing of the standards met in the chapter. Throughout the chapter is an indication of where each standard is met. Look for the *NAEYC Standards icon* in the margin to alert you to the link between the standards and the book. Finally, on the inside of the front and back covers of the book you will find a chart that indicates where each of the NAEYC Standards is addressed in the book, noted by chapter and page number.

- A new feature, **Brain Storm,** appears in each chapter in this edition. This feature provides information on some of the latest brain development research and discusses how and why this research is relevant to early childhood education practitioners.

- In each chapter one or two videos from the **Education CourseMate appear.** These brief videos, which last from 2 to 8 minutes, will make many of the concepts discussed in the text come alive as they focus on real children and real professionals in the field.

- Extensive discussion and information related to recent developments in the field. These include the **PK-3 Movement** in Chapter 5; the new position statement, **Technology and Interactive Media as Tools in Early Childhood Programs** in Chapters 7

and 9; **Tools of the Mind** in Chapter 11; the new **MyPlate** nutrition program in Chapter 14; **Emotional Intelligence** in Chapter 13; and **Bullying** in Chapter 16.

SPECIAL LEARNING FEATURES

As you begin to use this text, you will appreciate some of its features, which are designed to help the reader master the material as thoroughly and efficiently as possible. As you browse through the book, you will note that its page format is set up with the text on the inside of each page and marginal notations on the outside. Pay close attention to the outside section of each page, for there you will find features that will be of great help to you. In addition to these, other features appear at the end of each chapter. All of these special elements are designed especially for students in a class, such as the one in which you are enrolled.

- **Chapter Opening Questions**—At the beginning of each chapter is a series of questions that will prepare you for encountering the material that will be covered in the chapter.

- **Chapter Opening NAEYC Standards List**—A summary of the standards discussed in each chapter appears at the beginning of the chapter. This listing alerts you to the standards that will be covered in each chapter.

- **NAEYC Marginal Icon**—Throughout the book, you will find a specific icon in the margin of the text wherever NAEYC Standards are discussed in the text.

- **Chapter Opening DAP Quotation**—Each chapter begins with a quotation from the book, *Developmentally Appropriate Practice* (DAP) to underscore the importance of this topic. DAP is one of the most important concepts in the field of early childhood education, and these quotes will help you make the connection between DAP and what you are reading.

- **DAP Marginal Icon**—In addition, in the margins throughout the book you will find a special icon that identifies topics within the text that relate to Developmentally Appropriate Practice.

- **Diversity Marginal Icon**—A diversity icon identifies places in the book where various aspects of this topic are considered. This icon alerts you to the fact that the discussion in the text is relevant to diversity in culture, family structure, language, ability, or gender.

- **Related Videos**—Each chapter leads your attention to one or two videos in the Education CourseMate website. Focused questions tying the video to the text are posed for consideration and can be answered on the website.

- ■ **Key Definitions**—Important definitions of concepts introduced in the book are placed in the outer margin. When you see a new term discussed in the text, it will be highlighted in blue and then defined nearby in the margin. This will help reinforce concepts and reinforce some of the important terminology used in the field of early childhood education. All definitions also appear again, in alphabetical order, at the back of the book in the Glossary and on the Education CourseMate website as flashcards.

- ■ **Key Points**—Also in the margin is, in effect, an outline of the major points of the book. At the beginning of sections and important subsections, you will find a one- or two-sentence summary statement about the key point of that section.

- ■ **Take a Closer Look**—Each chapter provides this special feature, which offers in-depth information about a topic of importance to the field of early childhood education.

- ■ **Stories from the Field**—In each chapter is a feature relating a story from an early childhood practitioner. These stories focus on a subject that is related to the chapter. These firsthand narratives provide insight into what makes working with young children meaningful to professionals.

- ■ **Brain Storm**—This new feature ties the latest brain research to work with young children.

- ■ **Working with Families**—Within each chapter, you will find a section that focuses on one of the important tasks of early childhood teachers—communicating, coordinating, and working with families. These special sections tie the topic of each chapter to the needs and interests of families. These features appear in addition to Chapter 3, which focuses specifically on families of young children. Parents and other family members are a vital and integral part of early childhood programs, and the focus on working with families in each chapter is intended to help highlight and strengthen this element.

- ■ **Chapter Summary**—The main points of each chapter are provided in a brief summary at the end of each chapter for study and review.

- ■ **Key Questions**—Important questions are posed at the end of each chapter to help readers consider the information from the chapter and to explore further its relevance. Some of the key questions suggest activities that will reinforce understanding of the topic.

- ■ **End-of-Chapter Resources**—At the end of each chapter is an updated listings of additional resources, including books, articles, and websites that contain information relevant to early childhood educators in relation to the topic of the chapter.

ACCOMPANYING SUPPLEMENTS

Education CourseMate Website

The Education CourseMate Website to accompany the seventh edition of *Introduction to Early Childhood Education* brings course concepts to life with interactive learning, study, and exam preparation tools that support the textbook. Access an integrated eBook, learning tools including flashcards, quizzes, videos called out in your textbook, and more. The CourseMate icon at the end of each chapter will prompt you to take advantage of the many features provided. You can access the Education CourseMate website at www.cengagebrain.com.

WebTutor™

Jumpstart your course with customizable, rich, text-specific content within your Course Management System. Whether you want to Web-enable your class or put an entire course online, WebTutor™ delivers. WebTutor™ offers a wide array of resources, including media assets, access to the eBook, videos, quizzes, web links, exercises, and more.

Professional Enhancement Booklet

A supplement to accompany this text is the *Introduction to Early Childhood Education Professional Enhancement* booklet for students. This resource, which is part of Wadsworth Cengage Learning's Early Childhood Education Professional Enhancement series and available upon request, focuses on key topics of interest to future early childhood directors, teachers, and caregivers. Students will keep this informational supplement and use it for years to come in their early childhood practices.

Online Instructor's Manual with Test Bank

An online Instructor's Manual accompanies this book. The Instructor's Manual contains information to assist the instructor in designing the course, including a sample syllabus, learning objectives, teaching and learning activities, and additional print and online resources. For assessment support, the updated test bank includes multiple-choice, true/false, and short-answer questions for each chapter.

Online Examview

Available for download from the instructor website, ExamView® testing software includes all the test items from the printed Test Bank in electronic format, enabling you to create customized tests in print or online.

Presentation Slides

Preassembled Microsoft PowerPoint lecture slides for each chapter cover content from the book.

Acknowledgments

Many people have continued to be supportive, facilitating the great commitments of time, energy, and resources that are needed in an undertaking such as the writing and revision of *Introduction to Early Childhood Education.* I gratefully would like to acknowledge their assistance, for without them, the original book through this seventh edition would not have been possible.

Good friends and colleagues such as Melissa Burnham (whose assistance through careful research and insightful comments also was instrumental in development of the section, "Who's Who in Early Childhood Education?" found in Chapter 5), Bill Evans, Alice Honig, Sally Martin, Colleen Murray, Penny Royce-Rogers, Sharon Rogers, Leah Sanders, Sherry Waugh, Bridget Walsh, and many others have offered wonderful ideas and great support. I am particularly grateful to Dr. Alice Honig, Professor Emerita of Syracuse University, for her continued support and friendship and especially her helpful comments and suggestions.

I also want to thank the editorial staff at Cengage Learning who have provided patient support and help in the development and production of this seventh edition—in particular, Mark Kerr and Kate Scheinman. I am particularly grateful for their meticulous editing and attention to detail, which have greatly enhanced this final product.

In addition, I want to recognize the contributions of the early childhood professionals whose experiences can be read in the "Stories from the Field" features that appear in each chapter of this book: Amanda Bonzell, Becky Carter-Steele, Arryell Davis, Wendi Greenless, Jenna Hayes, Maritza Herrera, Natsumi Horsley, Marci Hosier-Behmaram, Colin Kvasnicka, Kathryn Oxoby, Heike Rael, Shari Roberts, Gloria Rodarte, Leah Sanders, Mary Schuster, Jamie Selby, and Courtney Stutzman.

Finally, grateful acknowledgement is given to the following reviewers, who offered numerous, valuable suggestions:

Katherine Abba, *Houston Community College*
Evia Davis, *Langston University*
Marian Everest, *Ventura County Community College*
Josephine Fritts, *Ozarks Technical Community College*
Jill Harrison, *Delta College*
Bridget Ingram, *Clark State Community College*
Jennifer Johnson, *Vance-Granville Community College*
Mary Larue, *J. Sargeant Reynolds Community College*
Rajone Lyman, *Houston Community College–NE*
Lois Silvernail, *Spring Hill College*
Saundra Stiles, *Roane State Community College*

In summary, I wish you, the reader, success as a current or future professional in the field. It is a field that is important and exciting, one that has much potential for growth. Early childhood professionals contribute a great deal to young children, their families, and the profession. Best of luck!

Eva L. Essa
Reno, Nevada

The *What* of Early Childhood Education

Each section of this book focuses on a different aspect of early childhood education, beginning with defining just what this field is. Part I addresses the *what* of early childhood education.

1

The Scope of and Need for Early Childhood Education

DAP The purpose of Developmentally Appropriate Practice is to promote excellence in early childhood education by providing a framework for best practice. Grounded both in the research on child development and learning and in the knowledge base regarding educational effectiveness, the framework outlines practice that promotes young children's optimal learning and development.

Developmentally Appropriate Practice
Copple & Bredekamp, 2009, p. 1

In Chapter 1, you will find answers to the following questions about the scope of and need for early childhood education:

▶ What does Developmentally Appropriate Practice mean for you, as a teacher of young children, and why is it important?
▶ What are the standards to which programs that train early childhood educators are held?
▶ What factors have contributed to the dramatic increase in programs for young children over the past few decades?
▶ What kinds of programs and what ages of children are included in the term *early childhood education*?
▶ How can you provide the best possible program for young children; in other words, what makes for a program of high quality?
▶ What issues have emerged as important ones for the future of early childhood education?

naeyc

NAEYC STANDARDS CONSIDERED IN CHAPTER 1

(See the Standards Correlation Chart on the inside front cover of this book for the titles and description of the standards listed below.)

▶ *Standard 1b:* Understanding the various family and social factors related to the rising need for childcare as part of contemporary influence on early development and learning (pp. 5–6).
▶ *Standard 6e:* Introduction to advocacy as part of professionalism (p. 7).
▶ *Standard 1c:* Familiarity with research-based elements of quality in early childhood programs as these contribute to creating appropriate environments for young children (pp. 16–21).
▶ *Standard 6d:* Being aware of the complexity of the field, and future issues, as part of this complexity (pp. 21–22).

The profession you are exploring through this text and the course in which you are enrolled is **early childhood education.** Just what is this field? What does it encompass? What does it involve? Why is it important? What is its place in today's society? What is its future? There is so much to discuss about early childhood education, so much to share. As you begin learning about this field of study, the answers to some of these questions will gain greater significance and become more focused. This chapter presents an overview of the field of early childhood education. We begin this journey with a brief introduction to two basic principles of the field of early childhood education, Developmentally Appropriate Practice and the Standards for Early Childhood Professional Preparation Programs, such as the academic program in which you are now enrolled. You will see both terms repeated throughout this book, and they will be identified by the DAP icon and the NAEYC icon, appearing in the margin.

early childhood education
Term encompassing developmentally appropriate programs that serve children from birth through eight years of age; a field of study that trains students to work effectively with young children.

DEVELOPMENTALLY APPROPRIATE PRACTICE (DAP)

One of the core concepts of the field of early childhood education that will become increasingly relevant to you is the importance of matching practice with what we know about the development of young children. This fundamental principal is termed **Developmentally Appropriate Practice,** or **DAP** (Copple & Bredekamp, 2009). DAP was developed collaboratively with input from many professionals by the National Association for the Education of Young Children (NAEYC), the largest professional organization of early childhood educators in the country (we will discuss NAEYC more fully in Chapter 4).

DAP is "based on an enduring commitment to act on behalf of children" (Bredekamp & Copple, 1997, p. 8). It reflects NAEYC's mission to promote programs for young children and their families that are of a high quality and that contribute positively to children's development. Decisions about what is good for children are based on a general knowledge of children's development and learning, understanding of each individual child in a group, and familiarity with the social and cultural contexts within which children are being raised.

Throughout the remainder of this text, we will visit and revisit DAP in relation to the various topics we discuss, to emphasize its importance. Let's begin, however, with an examination of early childhood education in terms of why the field has grown so rapidly in the past several decades, what is included in the field, how quality is defined in programs for young children, and what the future might hold.

Developmentally Appropriate Practice (DAP)
Teaching young children by matching practice with what we know about their development.

Key Point ◆◆

A core concept of the profession of early childhood education is Developmentally Appropriate Practice (DAP), ensuring that programs make decisions about what is best for children based on knowledge of children's development and the cultural context within which they are being raised.

NAEYC STANDARDS

A second common thread that you will see throughout this book is the NAEYC Standards for Early Childhood Professional Preparation Programs (2010). NAEYC is the most influential early childhood education organization in our country and, in that capacity, has partnered with other organizations to develop and define criteria that should be met by early childhood education academic programs and the individuals who graduate from these programs. You will read more about this is Chapter 4.

Research shows that when early childhood professionals have specialized training and education, children benefit. These standards describe what early childhood professionals are expected to know and do, defining essential learning outcomes in professional preparation programs and presenting a shared vision of excellence (NAEYC, 2010, p. 9).

It is quite likely that the program in which you are enrolled follows these standards in the classes and other experiences in which students are involved. For this reason, each chapter will begin with an overview of which standards are covered within the chapter. Then, throughout the chapters you will see an icon with a specific reference to the standard that is covered.

THE GROWTH OF EARLY CHILDHOOD EDUCATION

Although the importance and value of education in the early years of life have been acknowledged for more than 2,000 years (Lascarides & Hinitz, 2000), relatively recent factors have brought early childhood education to the forefront of public awareness. Fundamental changes in the economy, family life, public awareness, and public support have had a profound effect on early childhood education. In recent years, newspaper headlines and national magazine covers have directed a spotlight on child care. Much of their focus has been on changes in family life that have brought about the need for child care outside the home. These changes include many complex factors such as a rising cost of living, an increased number of dual-income families, an increase in single-parent families, an increased number of teenage parents, greater mobility as families move more readily to different parts of the country, and a decrease in the impact of the extended family.

The needs of working families are not the only reason early childhood has been a public focus. Over the past several decades, the success of publicly funded programs such as Head Start has shown us that high-quality early educational intervention can help to combat poverty and improve opportunities for children who may be at risk. There has also been increased attention to the needs of special populations of young children, for instance, children who are disabled, abused, or culturally different from the mainstream population. (In each chapter of this book, we will focus on the relevance of early childhood education to such children.) In addition, recent research on the amazingly complex and rapid development of very young children's brains has given us further insight into the importance of the early years. Finally, many professionals are outspoken and eloquent advocates for the rights of children.

BRAIN STORM
IMPORTANCE OF THE BRAIN

In each chapter of this book, you will find this BRAIN STORM feature with information about how early childhood education is related to and is interrelated with the development of young children's brains. At birth, the human brain is still very unfinished, containing millions of brain cells that are waiting to connect to other cells. Such connections are made through experiences and are strengthened as experiences are repeated. This growing network of interconnected cells lays the foundation for lifelong learning; thus, you, as an early childhood teacher, are in an ideal position to support and enhance learning by applying what is known about early brain development (Schiller & Willis, 2008).

Changes in Family Life

DIVERSITY

"Typical" family life has changed considerably since the end of World War II. Demographic information indicates that increasing numbers of women are entering the workforce. No longer do most mothers stay at home to rear their young children. Economic necessity forces many families to rely on two paychecks because one simply does not provide for all of their financial needs. In other families, both parents work because of the desire for personal and professional development rather than because of economic need.

Whereas in 1950 only 12 percent of the mothers of children under six worked (Children's Defense Fund, 2000), by 2008 that number has risen to 61 percent (U.S. Bureau of Labor Statistics, 2008a). This growth in the number of families in which both parents work has dramatically increased the need for child care.

Another family change that has affected the demand for child care is the increase in the number of single parents. The majority of single-parent families are created through divorce. At the beginning of the millennium, 56 percent of the adult population was married and living with a spouse (U.S. Bureau of the Census, 2000). The divorce rate has been steadily increasing, and is almost 15 percent higher now than it was just 30 years ago. The divorced single parent who has custody of the children is probably the mother, although an increasing number of fathers now gain custody or joint custody of their children. Not only will a single parent experience a significant decrease in income and standard of living, but she or he will also, most likely, have to work (or work longer hours) to support the family. Of course, to work outside the home, the single parent needs to find appropriate child care. In addition to the increased number of families headed by a divorced, single parent is a growing number of never-married parents, some still finishing their high school education. Today, far more teenage mothers opt to keep their babies than in past years. These children also need child care while their mothers are at school or work. U.S. Census data note that 67 percent of single mothers and 72 percent of divorced or widowed mothers of children under six work (U.S. Bureau of Labor Statistics, 2008).

A third change in family life is the increasing mobility of many of today's families. Work demands cause some families to move away from relatives who

Key Point ◆◆

Changes in family, such as increasing numbers of women in the workforce and significantly more single-parent families, have resulted in a greater need for child care.

Today, an increasing number of women in their childbearing years are in the workforce. It is estimated that more than 60 percent of mothers of young children work, requiring some form of child care for their children. Experts predict a continuing rise in the percentage of working mothers and children requiring care.

© Cengage Learning

Research has shown that programs such as Head Start offer many positive benefits for children from low-income families.

nuclear family
The smallest family unit, made up of a couple or one or two parents with child(ren).

extended family
Family members beyond the immediate nuclear family; for instance, aunts and uncles, grandparents, and cousins.

might otherwise provide support. Family mobility involving only the small **nuclear family** has contributed to the declining influence of the **extended family,** a network of relatives such as grandparents, uncles and aunts, or adult brothers and sisters beyond the immediate family. On the other hand, a recent report indicates that about 20 percent of young children are, in fact, in the care of their grandparents on a regular basis for some time each week (NACCRRA, 2008a).

Until relatively recently, the most prevalent form of child care was that provided by a relative. Parental and relative care, combined, continue to be most widely used for infants and toddlers, although center care for this age group has been increasing, and is now the norm for almost half of all preschoolers (Capizzano, Adams, & Sonnenstein, 2000). By 2007, nearly two-thirds of all children under age six were in nonparental care, with 36 percent in center-based care (Child Trends Data Bank, 2008). This change in family support is another reason for the increased demand for outside child care.

Changes such as increasing numbers of dual-income families and single-parent families, and a decline in the impact of the extended family, have dramatically raised the demand for child care and brought early childhood education to the forefront of public attention. "Child care is now as essential to family life as the automobile or the refrigerator. . . . [T]he majority of families, including those with infants, require child care to support parental employment" (Scarr, Phillips, & McCartney, 1990, p. 26).

Benefits of Early Childhood Education

The need for child care among working families makes early childhood education a topic of national prominence. However, this need is not the only reason for early childhood education's increasing importance. On a parallel track, there has been extensive discussion and research about the benefits of early education for special populations of children and families. Thus, children from low-income families, children who have grown up with a language other than English, children with disabilities, and children at risk for other reasons have been enrolled in publicly funded programs. This trend has paralleled the increasing diversity of today's families in America. Diversity can be based on numerous elements, including nationality, race or ethnicity, religion, social class, gender, and exceptionality (Robles de Melendez & Beck, 2010). Throughout this book we will consider how early childhood programs reflect and respond to diversity in the children and families they serve. Look for the Diversity icon in the margins, which indicate discussion of an aspect of diversity.

DIVERSITY

Since the mid-1960s, federal, state, and local support has increased as a result of mounting evidence that high-quality early childhood programs can and do make a long-term difference that carries into adulthood. Researchers have concluded that good early childhood programs not only improve the lives of the children and families involved but also result in substantial economic benefits for society. Each chapter of this book includes a feature called, "Take a Closer Look." This feature in Chapter 1 reviews some of the supporting research, especially from the field of economics. Although early intervention programs are expensive, their cost is more than recovered in subsequent years through greater success in school, decreased need for special education, lowered delinquency and arrest rates, and decreased welfare dependence (Barnett, 1996; Schweinhart, 2004; Schweinhart & Weikart, 1997). We will discuss more specific aspects of some of this research in Chapter 5.

Key Point ◆◆
Research has shown that good early childhood education programs have a lasting effect on children from disadvantaged backgrounds.

Child Advocacy

A third factor that has brought early childhood education into the public consciousness is the urgency with which many professionals view the plight of increasing numbers of children and families. Of particular concern are the many families that face abject poverty, lacking the most basic necessities. Yet the social problems reach beyond the needs of the poor, to working parents with moderate incomes who are beset by the scarcity of affordable, high-quality care. Dr. T. Berry Brazelton (1990), a well-known pediatrician and child advocate, concludes that America is failing its children because they are subject to more deprivations than any other segment of society. A large number of children live in poverty. *Yearbook 2011: The State of America's Children* reports that more than 20 percent of children in America are poor and that African American and Latino children are three times as likely to be poor as white children. The poverty rate for children grew by almost 20 percent over the first decade of the new millennium (Children's Defense Fund, 2011).

In its 2011 yearbook on the state of America's children, the Children's Defense Fund expresses deep concern about the number of children who grow up in poverty:

> CDF's *State of America's Children 2011* paints a devastating portrait of childhood across the country. With unemployment, housing foreclosures and hunger still at historically high levels, children's well-being is in great jeopardy. Children today are our poorest age group. Child poverty increased by almost 10 percent between 2008 and 2009, which was the largest single year increase since data were first collected. As the country struggles to climb out of recession, our children are falling further behind. . . . The portrait of continuing and worsening racial and income inequality is clear as we look at the state of America's children today. Rather than moving forward, we are moving backward (Children's Defense Fund, 2011, pp. ix, xiii).

Key Point ◆◆
Many professionals participate in child advocacy, bringing to public and legislative attention the needs of children and families in poverty as well as the need for affordable child care for families with moderate incomes.

Organizations such as the Children's Defense Fund and the National Association for the Education of Young Children actively advocate children's rights. Their frequent lobbying for children's rights through **child advocacy** in the nation's capital has promoted legislation related to child care, mandatory education for children with disabilities, Head Start, health care for poor children, and other vital services.

child advocacy
Political and legislative activism by professionals to urge change in social policies affecting children.

The needs of children and families have come to the attention of both political leaders and the public through the astute efforts of those dedicated to advocating the rights of children, including early childhood professionals. But there is a continuing need to promote a common concern for the welfare of all children. Based on current trends, researchers predict that the problems facing children and families will intensify, the gap between the well-to-do and the poor will widen, and the number of children who grow up in poverty will increase (Children's Defense Fund, 2000).

CHILD CARE—A WISE ECONOMIC INVESTMENT

FOR A NUMBER of decades, some early childhood researchers have argued that high-quality child care is a good economic investment in our country's future. This argument has taken on new urgency in recent years as scientists from a variety of fields try to address some of the many issues that face our nation. The report from an important conference about this topic concludes that: "Investments in quality child care and early education do more than pay significant returns to children—our future citizens. They also benefit taxpayers and enhance economic vitality" (Calman & Tarr-Whelan, 2005, p. 1).

One of the most notable proponents of the importance of public investment in early childhood education is James Heckman, a Nobel Prize–winning economist. Considered among the 10 most influential economists in the world, Heckman launched the Consortium on Early Childhood Development at the University of Chicago in order to bring together leading experts to identify how best to invest in young children in a way that will pay off for society. The consortium's goal is to "identify the most important development opportunities for children five years and younger, and to transform the way society and the business community view investments in early childhood education. We owe it to ourselves and our nation to make this a priority now" (Heckman, as quoted in Harms, 2006b, p. 1).

Heckman's research shows that support for high-quality early childhood programs for disadvantaged children would raise high school graduation rates from 41 to 65 percent and college enrollment from 4.5 to 12 percent. However, if this support were sustained beyond the early years—through the remainder of childhood and adolescence—the combined intervention would result in high school graduation rates of 90 percent and college attendance of 37 percent. The payoff for society would be an improved workforce, the mainstay of the economy. Heckman sees childhood as "a multistage process where early investments feed into later investments. Skill begets skill; learning begets learning" (Heckman, as quoted in Harms, 2006a, p. 1).

Recognition of the importance of the early years has been echoed by other well-known leaders, including the chairman of the Federal Reserve, Ben Bernanke. Bernanke noted,

> Although education and the acquisition of skills is a lifelong process, starting early in life is crucial. Recent research . . . has documented the high returns that early childhood programs can pay in terms of subsequent educational attainment and in lower rates of social problems, such as teenage pregnancy and welfare dependency. The most successful early childhood programs appear to be those that cultivate both cognitive and non-cognitive skills and that engage families in stimulating learning at home. (Bernanke, 2007, pp. 4–5)

The value of early intervention for children living in poverty is not new, however. Much of this recent interest stems from research that was begun many decades ago. Probably the most widely cited study is the Perry Preschool Project, which followed a group of low-income three- and four-year-olds from 1962 to the present day. As children, this group received high-quality early childhood education, augmented by considerable family involvement. A second group of children, who had the same characteristics but did not participate in the early childhood program, has also been followed through the years. The most recent report of these children who had been included in the intervention program and who are now in mid-adulthood shows continuing long-lasting effects of high-quality early education. More of the group who were involved in early education, as compared with those who were not, were employed at age 40, had higher earnings, had graduated from high school, and had significantly fewer arrests. An economic comparison of the cost of early intervention to savings in costs for special education services, welfare, and prison show that for every dollar invested in early care and education there is a $17 savings to society (Schweinhart, Montie, Xiang, Barnett, Belfield, & Nores, 2005).

WHAT IS INCLUDED IN EARLY CHILDHOOD EDUCATION?

We have looked at some of the concerns that have made early childhood education, as one aspect of the needs and welfare of young children, a current issue. But *early childhood education* is a broad term and includes a variety of approaches and programs. We will now examine some of the ways in which this term is used and some of the classifications into which programs can be grouped.

Purpose of Programs

We have already touched on some basic differences in programs that stem from their underlying thrust. The major purpose of many programs is to care for children while their families work. The rapid rise in recent years in the number of children in full-time day care, either in child care centers or in family child care homes, has paralleled the increasing prevalence of working mothers. The primary goal of child care programs is to provide safe and nurturing care in a developmentally appropriate setting for children.

Enrichment is a second aim, prevalent particularly in part-time preschools. Such programs usually include specific activities to enhance socialization, cognitive skills, or the overall development of young children. The underlying notion is that children will benefit from experiences that they may not receive at home; for instance, participating in group activities, playing with a group of age-mates, or learning specific concepts from specially trained teachers. Some programs aim at accelerating aspects of children's development (especially in academic areas) through didactic activities—ones that have high teacher control. Early childhood professionals do not consider such an approach as enriching or as developmentally appropriate (Copple & Bredekamp, 2009; Stipek, Feiler, Daniels, & Milburn, 1995).

A third major purpose, found particularly in publicly funded programs, is compensation. Compensatory programs are designed to make up for some lack in children's backgrounds. The basic philosophy of programs such as Head Start is to provide experiences that will help children enter the mainstream of society more successfully. Such experiences include a range of services that encompass early childhood education, health and dental care, nutrition, and parent education.

These categories, although descriptive of some underlying differences among programs, are not mutually exclusive. Few child care centers are concerned with only the physical well-being and care of children. Most also provide enriching experiences that further children's development. At the same time, preschool programs have to be concerned with appropriate nurturing and safety while the children are in their care. Similarly, compensatory programs are also concerned with enriching experiences and caring for children, whereas child care or preschool programs may serve to compensate for something lacking in the backgrounds of some of the children. In fact, many Head Start programs now are offering wrap-around services to provide extended care for children of working families.

Program Settings

Programs for young children can be divided into home-based and center-based settings. In the United States, when all ages of children are considered, the

Key Point ◆

Early childhood education programs can be defined by their purpose, including child care, enrichment, and compensation for some lack in the children's backgrounds.

Many young children are cared for in family child care homes rather than in center-based care facilities. Typically, family child care homes have children of various ages, spanning infancy through the preschool and primary years.

Key Point ◆◆

Programs are either home-based, such as family child care homes, or center-based, located in a school facility.

family child care homes
Care for a relatively small number of children in a family home that has been licensed or registered for that purpose.

center-based programs
Programs for young children located in school settings; these programs usually include larger groups of children than are found in home-based programs.

Key Point ◆◆

Programs are specially designed for children of varying ages, such as toddlers, preschoolers, and school-age children.

largest number of children cared for in center-based facilities. The National Child Care Information and Technical Assistance Center (NCCIC, 2011) estimates that nearly half of young children are cared for by a relative, about one-fourth are cared for in center-based programs, about 16 percent in a family child care home setting, and the remainder in some other type or arrangement.

Family child care homes are a significant part of the child care market. Because they provide a flexible, home-based care arrangement, it is often convenient for parents (Morissey & Banghart, 2007). In most states, licensing regulations allow for up to six children to be cared for in a family child care home, although there is some variation. Family child care providers are often mothers of young children themselves, and care for their own children along with several others. They tend to serve more infants and toddlers than preschoolers because many families prefer this type of care for younger children while being more likely to select center-based care for preschoolers and primary-school–age children. Studies have concluded that quality is lower in family child care homes than in center-based care. In particular, the quality in unlicensed homes tends to be even lower (Morissey & Banghart, 2007). It is difficult to get accurate information about family child care homes and the children and families who use this form of care because unlicensed homes operate under the radar of licensing agencies.

Center-based programs are located in early childhood centers and usually include larger groups of children than do home-based programs. Center-based programs have had the greatest increase among the types of programs offered in the United States. In the 1960s, only about 6 percent of young children were cared for in centers (Capizzano et al., 2000). By 2006, 60 percent of children were in some kind of center-based care. The number of children in center-based care increases by age, with 28 percent of infants, 43 percent of toddlers, and 78 percent of preschoolers in centers (National Center for Education Statistics, 2008).

Ages of Children

Another way early childhood programs can be grouped is by the age of the children. The classification of early childhood spans from birth to eight years, which includes infants, toddlers, preschoolers, kindergartners, and children in the primary grades. Needless to say, working families need care for children of all of these ages.

INFANTS AND TODDLERS. One of the most dramatic increases in recent years has been in infant and toddler programs. In fact, center-based care for infants and toddlers represents the fastest-growing type of program, though the majority of children under age three are cared for in family child care homes or by a relative (Capizzano et al., 2000; National Center for Education Statistics, 2008). Across the country, child care centers have been converting parts of their facilities to care for infants and toddlers, and many states have incorporated new sections in licensing standards to consider the special needs of this youngest segment of the population.

Not all infant/toddler programs fall under the rubric of child care, however. A number of compensatory programs enroll children from infancy, starting with early parent–child education as a way of intervening in the poverty cycle. Notable is the Early Head Start program for children under the age of three.

PRESCHOOLERS. The largest segment of children in early childhood programs are preschool-age, including youngsters from two or three years of age until they begin formal schooling. Some programs consider the preschool period as beginning at age three; others enroll children once they are out of diapers.

Programs for this age group include a wide variety of options. The majority of preschoolers are in all-day programs that provide care while their families work. Some children attend part-day preschool or nursery school programs for social and educational enrichment. We will examine more specific components of Developmentally Appropriate Practice for preschoolers in later chapters.

KINDERGARTEN AND PRIMARY CHILDREN. Many definitions of early childhood include children up to age eight. Thus, directions for curriculum, teaching strategies, and the environment in kindergartens and primary classrooms derive from what is known about the development and mode of learning of young, school-age children.

Developmentally Appropriate Practice for this age group, just as for earlier ages, involves an integrated approach. **Integrated curriculum** acknowledges the importance of all aspects of human development—social, emotional, physical, cognitive, language, and creative—rather than focusing primarily on the cognitive. It also involves learning experiences that promote all aspects of development rather than separating the day into discrete times, such as for math, reading, physical education, or social studies. Through the use of learning centers (to be discussed in Chapter 7) and projects or themes (Chapter 8), such subjects are fully integrated and each is considered an inseparable part of the other (Copple & Bredekamp, 2009).

BEFORE- AND AFTER-SCHOOL CARE. Young school-age children whose families work full time also require care when they are not in school. This is often provided through before- and after-school programs and full-day holiday and summer care. Such programs generally focus on recreation rather than education, particularly self-directed and self-initiated activities, since the children spend the bulk of their day in school (Bumgarner, 1999).

While many young children are enrolled in such programs, millions of others, labeled **latch-key children,** or **self-care children,** return to an empty home after school. Concerns about the safety, vulnerability, and lack of judgment of young school-age children have prompted an increase in before- and after-school programs. Most states do not set an age limit below which children should not be left alone, though the National SAFEKIDS Campaign suggests age 12 (Database Systems Corporation, 2009).

Sources of Support for Programs

Yet another way of grouping early childhood programs is by the base of their support, especially financial. Many early childhood programs are privately owned,

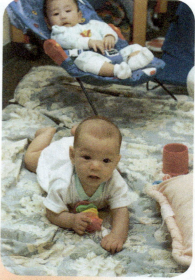

Center-based infant and toddler programs are among the fastest-growing segment of child care programs today.

integrated curriculum
A program that focuses on all aspects of children's development, not just cognitive development.

latch-key children (or self-care) children
School-age children who, after school, return to an empty home because their families are at work.

There are many not-for-profit programs, which are sponsored by entities such as churches, city recreation departments, hospitals, colleges and universities, and YMCA/YWCA organizations. The fact that the sponsor does not operate for-profit gives child care centers sponsored by such groups not-for-profit status.

for-profit businesses, whereas others are not-for-profit enterprises operated through public funds or sponsored by an agency or church. A growing number of early childhood programs are also supported by employers.

FOR-PROFIT PROGRAMS. A majority of child care programs are operated for profit, either as a single, independently owned business or as part of a regional or national chain. For many years, the majority of child care in most American communities was provided by local owners who operated one or two centers. Today, however, child care chains, which have experienced tremendous growth, have moved into virtually every metropolitan area (Neugebauer, 1991). Child care chains are big business! Some even sell stock that is traded on the New York Stock Exchange, deal in mergers and takeovers, and use sophisticated marketing strategies.

NOT-FOR-PROFIT PROGRAMS. In for-profit early childhood programs, what is left over after expenses are paid is considered profit, which goes back to the owner or stockholders. In not-for-profit programs, such monies are incorporated back into the program or are returned to the sponsoring agency. Not-for-profit centers gain that status through incorporation or sponsorship from an entity that is itself not operated for profit. Churches are the most common sponsors of early childhood programs, and other groups, such as YMCAs, YWCAs, city recreation departments, hospitals, colleges, and universities, also are frequently sponsors.

Many religion-sponsored programs came into existence in the 1970s and 1980s. Often, religious buildings included nursery, preschool, or recreational rooms that were used primarily on the day of worship. As the need for child care for working families became a more pressing social concern, many religious groups responded to that need by opening their facilities during the week. Some such programs are affiliated with and incorporate their religion, but many are secular.

EMPLOYER-SUPPORTED PROGRAMS. One of the fastest-growing groups with a stake in early childhood programs are employers. Many companies have found that their interest in the needs and concerns of parent-employees has resulted in a more productive and stable workforce. For the working parents of young children, work and family are not separable and, in fact, often overlap. Child care, in particular, is not just a family issue but is also a concern to employers. Employees with young children, as compared with other workers, more often are late for work, leave work early, miss work altogether, and deal with personal issues while at work. When employers support child care in some way, the result is lower absenteeism, greater stability and loyalty, better morale, decreased stress, and less distraction among their employees.

There are many ways in which employers can support their workers' child care needs. Some large companies have created child care centers in or near the workplace. Another way in which employers help their workers is through arrangements with community child care centers, for instance, through a voucher system or direct subsidies. Such an arrangement can ensure that employees are given priority when child care openings are available.

Other employers provide referral services to help match employees' needs with resources available in the community. Some companies have helped develop and train a community network of family child care homes to meet their workers' needs. A growing trend among employers is to provide more responsive scheduling options, for instance, job sharing or flex-time. Child care is increasingly becoming a benefits option as companies allow their employees to select from a menu rather than providing a common benefits package for all. Some companies, recognizing the significant problem posed by children who are mildly ill, have begun to explore sick-child care options (Galinsky, Bond, & Sakai, 2008) found that nearly half of employers offered some kind of dependent assistance, about one-third offered child care resource and referral services, and 9 percent offered child care at or near the worksite.

As an increasing number of companies provide employer-sponsored child care for their workers, a recent trend has been the rise of employer child care management organizations. Such organizations contract with businesses to provide child care services for their employees. The best known of these management organizations is Bright Horizons Family Solutions, which, in 2008, managed nearly 650 centers across the country, including centers for many of the top American companies (CNN Money.com, 2008).

UNIVERSITY- AND COLLEGE-AFFILIATED PROGRAMS. A sizable group of early childhood programs is linked to higher education. The institution in which you are enrolled may, in fact, have such a program. Some are specifically laboratory or training programs that support student practicums and provide subjects for research; others serve primarily as campus child care centers for the young children of students, staff, and faculty. The trend since the 1980s has been for campus programs to combine these two functions, offering child care to the campus community while using the children and families for practicum and research purposes (Everts, Essa, Cheney, & McKee, 1993).

Such programs are operated either as a campuswide venture or are affiliated with a specific department or unit, for instance, early childhood education, child development, or psychology. Because of the involvement of professional educators, campus programs are generally of high quality, incorporating what has been learned about young children and early childhood programs through research, theory, and professional practice.

> **Key Point** ◆
>
> Early childhood programs affiliated with institutions of higher learning provide training for students, as well as child care for students, parents, faculty, and staff.

Publicly Supported Programs

Another significant supporter of early childhood programs is the public sector, whether it is federal government, state, or local agencies. Head Start is probably the best-known federally supported program. In addition, Child Care and Development Fund block grants allow states to provide child care support for low-income working families. There are also federally subsidized early childhood programs at the more than 400 U.S. military bases around the world. We will discuss Head Start, public school preschools, and military child care in more detail.

HEAD START. In 1964, in response to a growing concern about the perceived disadvantage at which many children from impoverished environments entered elementary school, Project Head Start was initiated. The goal of Head Start was to help break the poverty cycle by providing children and their families with a comprehensive program that would help meet some of their needs. Today, there are Head Start programs in every state and territory, in rural and urban sectors, on Native American reservations, and in migrant areas. Head Start serves nearly 1 million preschoolers (Head Start Program Fact Sheet, 2010); it is estimated

MEETING
MULTIPLE NEEDS

Sometimes finding quality child care is difficult and challenging, especially for new parents. I support parents in their quest for the best possible child care setting for their child by offering resources and referrals. I help parents with their search by providing various options for care as well as finding a good match.

It's especially difficult to find quality child care for infants and toddlers. One wonderful resource for families that some aren't aware of is family child care. Family child caregivers provide a nurturing environment for young children, but are often isolated from other early childhood professionals. Hence, my job is to develop professional support systems for family child care providers through financial assistance, information, monthly child care trainings and visits, program planning, and technical assistance. The services provided help to encourage higher quality in family child

© Theresa Danna Douglas

**Marci, Campus Child Care Connections
Program Coordinator**

care. I also help family child care providers through the process of accreditation, which in turn helps me validate the quality of their individual programs. With this help, there are now several providers in our state who are accredited, and more are currently in the process of becoming so.

Helping parents find the right match for their family is extremely important if the child is to have continuity of care. I need to make sure parents have the right

information so they can be sure they are choosing the best possible child care placement for their child. We try to educate parents and collect all the pertinent information regarding a parent's needs. We provide various brochures, numerous checklists parents use while visiting a center or family child care provider, videos, and conversations with staff. After much discussion, the parents can rest assured they have made the best possible child care choice for their child.

I am confident that by providing family child care providers with access to networks of other providers, they won't feel isolated and alone. They can provide high-quality care for children as well as meet the rising demand for infant and toddler child care slots. This arrangement results in a win–win situation: parents can find the best-quality program for their young children and child care providers are supported in developing high-quality programs.

Key Point ♦

Head Start is the largest publicly supported early childhood program, providing educational, nutritional, health, and parental support to enrolled children and families.

that this figure represents less than half of the eligible children in the country. Altogether Head Start has enrolled more than 27 million children since its inception in 1965 (Head Start Program Fact Sheet, 2010).

Although Head Start is an education program aimed at providing a high-quality early childhood experience for three- to five-year-olds, it also has several other components. An important element is the provision of health care through medical, dental, nutritional, and mental health services for all of its children, recognizing that children who are hungry or ill cannot learn. All children receive medical and dental examinations, immunizations, a minimum of one hot meal and a snack each day, and the services of a mental health specialist if needed.

Family partnership is also an integral element of the Head Start program. Many parents have found employment through the program because it gives them priority for any available nonprofessional Head Start jobs. Another component involves social services for families to provide assistance, information about community resources, referrals, and crisis intervention. Finally, Head Start also serves children with disabilities, following the congressional mandate that at least 10 percent of its children must have a diagnosed disability (Head Start, 1990).

Since 1994, Head Start has also begun to serve children under the age of three. The Early Head Start program provides child development and family services to pregnant women and low-income families with infants and toddlers. Early Head Start was developed in response to the growing recognition of the importance of the earliest years of children's lives and in acknowledgment of the woeful lack of infant and toddler care in most communities. Some Early Head Start programs provide center-based services, while others rely more on home visitation and support. The goals of the program are to enhance children's development (including health, social competence, cognitive and language ability, and resilience); support family development (including parenting, economic self-sufficiency, and family stability); support staff development (for instance, by providing training and educational opportunities); and support community development. About 10 percent of children served by a Head Start program are enrolled in Early Head Start (Head Start Program Fact Sheet, 2010). Early Head Start, like Head Start, mandates continuing staff training and education. Educational requirements for Head Start staff will be discussed in more detail in Chapter 4.

Close to 1 million children are served every year through Head Start programs, but it is estimated that this program serves less than half of eligible children.

DIVERSITY

STATE AND PUBLIC SCHOOL INVOLVEMENT. Current funding for early childhood education programs comes from a wider range of sources than ever before. A majority of states allocate funding out of their budgets for early childhood programs. The number of state-funded prekindergarten programs have increased dramatically over the past two decades. Most of these programs are part-day, part-year programs designed for four-year-olds who are identified as having some risk factors that might keep them from being successful when they start formal schooling. Several states are also moving toward universal access to prekindergarten for all children (Schumacher, Ewen, Hart, & Lombardi, 2005).

Such programs are offered either within public school systems or through a combination of public and private settings. Public schools have, of course, always been the providers of kindergarten and first- and second-grade programs; children in these classes have, by definition, been included in early childhood programs, as a category. Increasingly numbers of school districts are extending their programs to preschoolers. In another way, public schools have, for many years, provided early childhood centers as part of high school or vocational school training programs.

Public school sponsorship of early childhood programs is, of course, subject to the same limited supply of money that constrains other publicly supported programs. Typically, therefore, existing programs serve a limited number of children. In most states, such programs give priority to children who are considered at risk for school failure. Some states specify low-income children, while others indicate that participants have to be Head Start–eligible. This focus on poor children or children at risk is, in large measure, a response to the number of children who are eligible for Head Start but are not included in that program. Some states provide programs for three- as well as four-year-olds, although the majority are structured to serve only four-year-olds. In a few states, prekindergarten programs are designed for children who come from non–English-speaking families. Educators, however, are calling for a broader constituency in public school early childhood programs, one that includes all children rather than only a limited group.

Key Point ◆❖

Increasing numbers of states support early childhood programs, and school districts across the country are offering programs for preschoolers, particularly for those considered at risk for school failure.

CHILD CARE IN THE MILITARY. The U.S. Department of Defense oversees 800 Child Development Centers on military bases around the world (Military .com, 2008). The National Women's Law Center (Pomper, Blank, Campbell, & Schulman, 2004) published a follow-up report on military child care and held up the military as a model for ways to improve civilian child care. The report identified a number of ways that improvements have been brought about in the military child care system to promote high-quality care. These include a certification and inspection system that ensures that programs maintain basic standards; a program accreditation requirement that moves programs to a higher level of quality; and caregiver training and wages that improve staff quality and stability.

DEFINING QUALITY IN EARLY CHILDHOOD PROGRAMS

naeyc

Up to this point, we have discussed early childhood programs in fairly concrete, descriptive terms, looking at characteristics by which programs can be grouped. Programs can and should also be examined in terms of how they best meet the needs and consider the well-being of children. Such considerations are related to quality.

Current research, in fact, focuses on identifying factors that create good early childhood programming for young children. The old questions about whether child care is good or bad for children or what type of care is best are now obsolete; today's research questions seek to find out how to make child care better for young children, providing empirical support for the factors commonly cited as indicators of good programs. The emerging picture tells us that quality in child care is not dependent on single, separable factors but is a result of the presence of and interaction among a variety of complex elements (Essa & Burnham, 2001; NICHD Early Child Care Research Network, 2000a). The research about high-quality early childhood care is also reflected in some important documents that guide the field, for instance Developmentally Appropriate Practice (Copple & Bredekamp, 2009) and the Standards for Early Childhood Professional Preparation Programs (NAEYC, 2010), both of which were introduced earlier in this chapter.

Child–Adult Ratio

child–adult ratio
The number of children for whom an adult is responsible, calculated by dividing the total number of adults into the total number of children.

It has generally been assumed that when caregivers are responsible for large numbers of children, the quality of care is adversely affected. A number of studies have addressed this assumption and found that the ratio significantly affects children's behavior and child–adult interaction (Helburn & Howes, 1996; Howes, 1997).

For instance, when there are larger numbers of children per adult, there is less verbal interaction among adults and children than when the **child–adult ratio** is lower. Teachers in classrooms with lower ratios were more sensitive and responsive to the children than teachers who had more children in their care (Howes, 1997). A significant factor in providing quality care has to do with giving children individualized attention, confirming their unique identity and worth as individuals. When an adult is responsible for a large number of children, that

An optimal ratio of adults to children is one indicator of quality in early childhood programs. A low ratio facilitates interaction and allows for more individualized attention to each child. According to research and the advice of experts, what is an inappropriate ratio for young children? What other factors are important in determining an appropriate ratio?

© Cengage Learning

adult is less able to provide such attention and is more concerned instead with controlling and managing the group.

What is an appropriate child–adult ratio? There is no definitive answer, although the literature does provide some suggested guidelines. For instance, NAEYC suggests a ratio of 3 to 1 for infants, 6 to 1 for toddlers, 8 to 1 for three-year-olds, 10 to 1 for four- and five-year-olds, and 15 to 18 to 1 for children in the primary grades (Copple & Bredekamp, 2009). These ratios are consistent with identified Developmentally Appropriate Practice.

Keep in mind, however, that the child–adult ratio is one variable that inter-acts with other factors, such as group size and teacher qualifications. In France, child–adult ratios are considerably higher than in the United States, but French preschool teachers are highly trained, adequately paid, and accorded greater status and respect than their American counterparts (Howes & Marx, 1992).

Group Size

In the late 1970s, the large-scale National Day Care Study (Roupp, Travers, Glantz, & Coelen, 1979) indicated that group size was one of two consistently important variables that define quality of care for young children. In smaller groups, adults and children interacted more; children were more cooperative, innovative, and verbal; and children earned better scores on cognitive and language tests. Another study summarized that, with a moderate number of children in a group, children seem to demonstrate greater social competence (Clarke-Stewart, 1987b). When caregivers are in charge of large groups of children, however, they tend to be less responsive to the children and provide less social stimulation (Howes, 1983).

Ideal group size cannot really be defined because other variables, including the parameters of the physical environment, need to be considered. The NAEYC, through its Developmentally Appropriate Practice, provides some guidelines for group size (Copple & Bredekamp, 2009). For very young pre-schoolers, the association recommends no more than 12 children per group with two teachers; a maximum group size of 20 children is recommended for four- and five-year-olds.

DAP

TeachSource Video Activity
WATCH•REFLECT•RESPOND

This BBC News Video involves an interview with Dr. Ellen Galinsky about quality in child care. Go to CengageBrain.com and view the video entitled, "The Quality of Child Care," and answer the following questions:

1. Which aspects of quality considered in the text are discussed by Ellen Galinsky?

2. What other indicators of quality does Dr. Galinsky mention?

DAP

Key Point

Research has shown that a moderate group size results in children who are more socially and intellectually competent than those who spend their days in large groups.

Staff Qualifications

Research has given us some indication about teachers who are most likely to provide a high-quality early childhood program. Earlier we discussed how the National Day Care Study (Roupp et al., 1979) found group size to be one of two important quality variables. The other significant variable that emerged from this study was the importance of a staff with specific training in early childhood education and development. Such teachers engaged in more interactions with the children, and the children showed greater social and cognitive abilities as compared with those whose teachers lacked such training. These findings, particularly in relation to children's more advanced cognitive and language ability, have been supported in other research (Burchinal, Roberts, Nabors, & Bryant, 1996; NICHD Early Child Care Research Network, 2000b; Phillipsen, Burchinal, Howes, & Cryer, 1997). In addition, teachers with early childhood training were rated as more positive and less punitive, using a less authoritarian style of interaction with the children (Arnett, 1987).

Key Point ◆◆
Research shows that teachers with specific early childhood training are important for a high-quality program.

Developmental Appropriateness of the Program

Child development theory and research have given us a good understanding of what young children are like and under what conditions they thrive and learn best. From such information, we are able to plan environments, develop activities, and set expectations that are congruent with children's needs and characteristics (Copple & Bredekamp, 2009). Throughout this book—particularly in Chapter 7, which considers how to structure an appropriate environment; Chapters 8 through 11, which examine how various components of the curriculum reinforce development; and Chapters 15 through 17, in which we consider guidance principles—we will focus on Developmentally Appropriate Practice.

In recent years, there has been increasing concern that public education is not adequately preparing children for the challenges of the future. This concern has been accompanied by a push to return to "the basics" in education. Some have interpreted this to include young children, with the idea that an earlier introduction to academics will result in better-prepared and better-educated children.

As we will consider in various contexts in this book, early childhood professionals and researchers have expressed grave apprehensions about this trend, which pushes preschoolers into tasks for which they are not developmentally ready. Young children can learn a lot of material in a mechanistic, rote manner, but if these experiences are meaningless, such information has little relevance. Thus, for an early childhood program to meet quality criteria, it must respect the emerging abilities of young children without imposing inappropriate expectations.

Key Point ◆◆
High-quality programs have developmentally appropriate expectations and activities, and do not push children into inappropriate, accelerated activities.

Child–Adult Interaction

Although many factors contribute to the quality of an early childhood program, perhaps the most important factor on which quality depends is the interaction between the adults and the children. In a good program, adults are involved with children, they are nurturing and responsive, there is ample verbal exchange, and interactions aim to teach, not just to control (Burchinal et al., 2008; Clarke-Stewart, 1987a). A wonderful physical facility, an exemplary child–adult ratio, and a favorable group size would all be negated by uncaring and unresponsive child–adult interactions. It is, after all, the teachers who determine the tone and the character—in effect, the quality—of a program.

Staff Consistency

A serious concern among professionals and families alike is the high rate of staff turnover in early childhood programs, estimated at 41 percent per year in a comprehensive, nationwide study (Whitebook, Howes, & Phillips, 1989). Many young children spend the bulk of their waking hours in child care with adults other than their parents. One important task of the early years is forming a secure attachment relationship to adults. Although their primary attachment is to parents, research has shown that young children certainly do become attached to their caregivers. When children lose an adult with whom they have formed such an attachment, the loss can be profound (Essa, Favre, Thweatt, & Waugh, 1999).

One study found that there is less child–adult interaction in centers with a high teacher-turnover rate (Phillips, Scarr, & McCartney, 1987). This is not surprising when interaction is dependent in part on establishing a relationship, something that takes time to develop. Another study (Howes & Hamilton, 1993) found that toddlers who experienced changes in their primary teachers were more aggressive as four-year-olds. Similarly, McCartney and her co-researchers (1997) found that children who experienced more changes in caregivers during the first year had more behavior problems as preschoolers. In fact, the effects of stable caregivers early in life were still evident when the children were nine years old (Howes, Hamilton, & Phillipsen, 1998). This research supports the importance of a stable, secure relationship between young children and their caregivers.

Respect and Concern for Staff

As we have discussed, a nurturing, well-trained, and consistent staff is important to a quality program, but a reciprocal concern for the well-being of the staff also is needed. Working with young children is a demanding, challenging job. Thus, it is in the best interests of the children, the families, and the employer if staff members receive appropriate pay and benefits and work in a satisfying environment. In such a setting, the needs of the staff are seriously considered, an atmosphere of camaraderie is fostered, autonomy is encouraged in planning an appropriate program for the children, and the physical environment includes space for adults. Chapter 4 will discuss some of the parameters and issues associated with providing such an environment for the staff.

Physical Environment

Even though we will discuss the physical environment of the early childhood program in greater detail in Chapter 7, it is necessary to note here that the physical facility is another important factor that contributes to program quality. In schools that are safe and orderly, contain a wide variety of stimulating equipment and materials, and are organized into learning centers on the basis of similar materials and activities, children demonstrate higher cognitive skill levels

Key Point
Frequent and responsive interaction between adults and children is a necessity for high-quality programs.

Key Point
Staff consistency is important, because high staff turnover has a negative impact on young children.

Key Point
A good staff, which provides an appropriate program for young children, must be respected and nurtured.

Warm, responsive interaction among adults and children is an important element in defining quality in early childhood programs.

and greater social competence, as compared with children in programs that lack these features.

A child-oriented environment conveys to children that this place is meant for them. There are interesting and worthwhile things to do in a child-oriented environment because it was designed with the characteristics, ages, and abilities of the children in mind. A child-centered environment also requires fewer restrictions and prohibitions because it was fashioned specifically for children. This contributes to a positive and pleasant atmosphere. In short, a good environment conveys to children that this is a good place to be, that people here care about them, that these people are able to satisfy their desire to learn and their innate curiosity, and that this is a place in which it is safe to try without fear of failure.

Family Support and Family Engagement

With increasing numbers of children spending many hours per day in child care, families and teachers are, more than ever, partners in many aspects of child-rearing and socialization. Studies have shown that children benefit when the family and the early childhood staff share a common commitment to the best interests of the children, communicate openly, and have mutual respect. However, if there is a lack of communication, so that parents do not know what happened at school and teachers are not informed of significant events in the child's home life, there is a lack of continuity for the child. In Chapter 3 we will explore this home–school link in much greater detail. In addition, at the end of each of the remaining chapters, we will look at the importance of families in relation to the topic of the chapter.

Quality as a Combination of Factors

For the purposes of discussion, we have isolated a number of components that contribute to quality early childhood programming, including child–adult ratio, group size, staff qualifications, developmental appropriateness of the program, child–adult interaction, staff consistency, concern for staff, the physical

A physical environment that is child-centered, organized, and stimulating is integral to the overall quality of a program.

© Cengage Learning

environment, and family involvement. It is important to keep in mind, however, that quality can best be understood and studied as a combination of components. As you further your understanding and knowledge of the field of early childhood education, remember that quality is not defined by a single factor but depends on the complex interaction of a variety of elements in which you, as an early childhood professional, play a key role.

THE FUTURE OF EARLY CHILDHOOD EDUCATION

Up to this point, we have examined social forces that have helped to shape the field of early childhood education, looked at the multifaceted descriptors that define the field today, and examined some qualitative aspects of programs for young children. Let's take a look at some of the factors that have shaped the field as it exists today.

But what lies ahead? Are there more changes in store? Will unresolved social issues be addressed? Will early childhood education become an important force in considering these issues? Lacking the aid of a crystal ball, we might, nonetheless, try to predict what lies ahead by extrapolating from current trends.

> From all economic and social indications, it is reasonable to expect that a high percentage of families will continue to have two parents in the workforce and continue to need care for their young children.

> Employment opportunities in early childhood education will continue to increase. Bureau of Labor Statistics projections indicate that the need for child care workers will increase by 1 percent and for elementary teachers by 16 percent by the year 2018 (U.S. Bureau of Labor Statistics, 2011).

> The number of young children who live in poverty has increased in recent years (Children's Defense Fund, 2011). Federal and state funding for programs such as Head Start and local and state allocations to serve children at risk, along with programs and job opportunities for teachers of young children, have experienced moderate increases over the years. However, the national economic downturn may mean less funding.

> An increasing number of children from families whose first language is not English will be served by early childhood programs, increasing the need for bilingual and bicultural teachers.

> Employer involvement in child care sponsorship is likely to increase as employers recognize the need to provide child care benefits for parents. A shift in the types of program sponsorship, along with new job opportunities, is likely to accompany such a trend.

> Although the number of available positions for early childhood professionals will continue to increase, there are nevertheless grave concerns about the stability of the early childhood workforce. In no other industry is there such a high turnover of employees as in child care.

> As we have discussed, stability of staff is an important element in the quality of early childhood programs because children's trust and attachment to the adults in their lives depends on that stability. As a result, there has been increasing concern about the interplay between the needs of children for quality care, the needs of families for affordable child care, and the needs of early childhood professionals for appropriate compensation and status. We can expect greater focus on these issues in the future.

naeyc

Key Point ◆◆

Economic and social factors point to a continually growing need for early childhood education. These factors include an expected increase in the number of women in the workforce, an increase in the number of children in poverty, and greater employer sponsorship of child care.

Key Point ◆◆

The need for qualified early childhood educators will continue to increase.

Key Point ◆◆

The early childhood profession will continue to address issues related to quality care and the needs of staff.

> In recent years, many states have undertaken initiatives aimed at bolstering the professional development of those who work in the field of early childhood education. We will discuss these initiatives further in Chapter 4.

> It is becoming more and more apparent that our country lacks a cohesive and consolidated social policy within which to consider child and family matters. For instance, a wide variety of agencies initiate, license, administer, and evaluate varying programs for children and families, often relying on disparate philosophies, approaches, and regulations. But, at the same time, because of increased public attention, there also seems to be greater willingness to address such issues with more depth, integration, and forethought.

> As a result, professional organizations are placing greater emphasis on the need to develop a system for financing early childhood education in the United States. Helburn (2003) argues that only the federal government has the ability to provide funding for a cohesive system of child care through which all American children are covered.

> Recent legislation has placed increased emphasis on accountability and assessment of young children, an issue we will discuss further in Chapter 6. Programs that receive federal funding, such as Head Start, have experienced greater pressure to demonstrate that they are making a difference in children's development, particularly in areas related to school readiness.

> Publicly funded programs for young children, including many Head Start, Early Head Start, and kindergarten programs, often are operated only on a part-day basis. Such scheduling is problematic for working parents who need full-day care for their children. Despite limited funding, efforts will need to be made to deliver more wrap-around services that provide extended hours for children who participate in a part-day program such as Head Start and Early Head Start.

> Within the early childhood profession, there is a continued focus on the pluralistic nature of our society and the shrinking world in which children are growing up. Many early childhood programs can be expected to focus more than ever on curriculum based on non-bias and the inclusion of children and families from different cultural, ethnic, linguistic, economic, and religious backgrounds, as well as children with disabilities. We will explore this topic in more detail in Chapter 13.

DIVERSITY

> Finally, because of legislation ensuring that young children with disabilities are included in early education, there will be continued efforts to integrate them into programs with children who do not have disabilities. As we will see in Chapter 2, such inclusive programs benefit everyone involved.

SUMMARY

1. Two central professional concepts in the field of early childhood education are Developmentally Appropriate Practice (DAP), a set of principles about how to teach young children that is based on an understanding of child development and a familiarity with the cultural context within which each child is being raised, and Standards for Early Childhood Professional Preparation Programs.

2. A number of social factors have contributed to the expansion of early childhood programs and have brought early childhood education into the public consciousness. These factors include the following:
   A. Changes in family life such as an increased number of two-earner families and single parents

    B. Growing evidence of the benefits of early education for children living in poverty, children with disabilities, and other children at risk

    C. Child advocacy, which has helped bring the needs of young children and their families to public and legislative prominence

3. There is considerable diversity in the types of early childhood programs; programs vary according to the following factors:

    A. Purpose of programs

    B. Program settings

    C. Ages of the children

    D. Sources of funding support

4. Program quality is one of the most important factors to consider with regard to early childhood programs. The following elements contribute to the quality of early childhood programs:

    A. Child–adult ratio

    B. Group size

    C. Staff qualification

    D. Developmental appropriateness of the program

    E. Quality of adult–child interaction

    F. Staff consistency

    G. Respect and concern for the staff

    H. Quality of the physical environment

    I. Family involvement

    J. Quality as a combination of factors

5. There are trends and projections that suggest what the future holds for early childhood education.

KEY TERMS LIST

center-based programs

child–adult ratio

child advocacy

Developmentally Appropriate Practice (DAP)

early childhood education

extended family

family child care homes

integrated curriculum

latch-key children

nuclear family

self-care children

KEY QUESTIONS

1. If you were given "three wishes" to bring about changes for young children and their families, what would they be? Share these with others in your class. From a combined list, develop several child and family issues that you think child advocates might address.

2. Visit an early childhood program in your community and share this information with other members of your class who have visited different programs. Classify the programs according to their characteristics: for instance, purpose, setting, ages of children served, and source of support. Does your community have a variety of programs? Which types of programs predominate? What family needs are met by these programs?

3. Visit a local Head Start program. What benefits do you see for the children? Talk to a staff member and find out what services are provided for the children and their families.

4. Suppose you were asked by the parent of a young child, "How do I find a good child care program?" What would you answer? How can you help a parent recognize quality indicators?

5. Projections for the future, as we have discussed, indicate an increased need for good early childhood programs. What changes do you think are needed to bring about improvements for children and for early childhood professionals?

ADDITIONAL RESOURCES

Select additional books, articles, and websites on topics discussed in Chapter 1.

Children's Defense Fund. *The state of America's children*. Annually published yearbooks. Washington, DC: The Children's Defense Fund. Also available online at www.childrensdefense.org.

Elkind, D. (1987). *Miseducation: Preschoolers at risk*. New York: Knopf.

Elkind, D. (2001). *The hurried child: Growing up too fast too soon* (3rd ed.). New York: Perseus.

Kagan, S. L., & Cohen, N. E. (1997). *Not by chance: Creating an early care and education system for America's children.* New Haven, CT: The Bush Center in Child Development and Social Policy, Yale University.

HELPFUL WEBSITES

Child Care Information Center:

www.nccic.org

The National Child Care Information Center (NCCIC) is a part of the Child Care Bureau, which, in turn, is part of the federal Administration for Children and Families. It serves as a national clearinghouse and technical assistance center that links parents, providers, policymakers, researchers, and the public to early care and education information. A wealth of helpful and informative data is available through this website.

The Children's Defense Fund:

www.childrensdefense.org

The Children's Defense Fund is one of the most effective and outspoken advocates for the needs and rights of children in America today. Its work includes advocacy related to children's health, welfare, early childhood development, education, family income and jobs, and poverty prevention. Information related to legislation and advocacy activities are found at this website.

Kids Count:

www.aecf.org

The Annie E. Casey Foundation publishes the yearly Kids Count data book, which provides statistics on 10 key measures of child well-being. The report provides national and state-by-state data about the condition of children. This website also provides information about advocacy programs that have experienced success.

Go to **CengageBrain.com** to register your access code for this book's Education CourseMate website, where you will find more resources to help you study. Additional resources for this chapter include TeachSource Videos, glossary flashcards, web links, case studies with critical-thinking questions that apply the concepts presented in this chapter, and more. If your textbook does not include a printed access card, you can go to **CengageBrain.com** to purchase access.

II

The *Who* of Early Childhood Education

Early childhood education is made up of different people. In Part II, we will explore the *who* of this field by examining the characteristics and needs of three groups—children, families, and teachers.

2 | *The Children*

DAP Early childhood practitioners must consider . . .
what is known about child development and learning, . . . what is known
about each child as an individual,
. . . [and] what is known about the
social and cultural contexts in which
children live.

Developmentally Appropriate Practice, Copple &
Bredekamp, 2009, pp. 9–10

In Chapter 2, you will find answers to the following questions about children:

▶ What do all children have in common?
▶ What age-related characteristics distinguish children of different ages, and how does brain development contribute to each child's uniqueness?
▶ Why is play important for all children, and how does play develop?
▶ How can you include children with disabilities in your early childhood program?
▶ What are children who have different abilities like?

NAEYC STANDARDS CONSIDERED IN CHAPTER 2

(See the Standards Correlation Chart on the inside front cover of this book for the titles and description of the standards listed below.)

▶ *Standard 1a:* Knowing and understanding children's characteristics and needs, from birth to age 8 (pp. 27–36).
▶ *Standard 1c:* Recognizing that child development knowledge helps guide selection of strategies for setting positive learning environments (pp. 27–41).
▶ *Standard 4c:* Including a broad range of experiences for children, particularly valuing the importance of play (pp. 36–40).
▶ *Standard 1b:* Understanding the impact of culture and ethnicity on development (p. 41).
▶ *Standard 1b:* Knowing and understanding children's uniquenesses, particularly various disabilities, and how these can affect development (pp. 40–51).
▶ *Standard 1c:* Establishing appropriate learning environments for all children through inclusion (pp. 42–43).
▶ *Standard 2b:* Supporting and engaging families of children with disabilities (pp. 51–52).

At the heart of early childhood education are young children. All the topics we will discuss in ensuing chapters are aimed at gaining a better understanding of children and how, together with their families, we can best facilitate their positive development. Although our focus will be on children, it is always important to keep in mind that they must never be seen in isolation, but rather as part of a family system that provides context and identity through its lifestyle, culture, heritage, and traditions, as emphasized in the DAP guidelines (Copple & Bredekamp, 2009). In this chapter we will take a closer look at children and consider how they should be seen as part of their community and cultural contexts, which shape much of their identity.

CHILDREN—SIMILARITIES

Children who grow up in nurturing environments are generally wonderfully engaging and winning, in part because of the freshness with which they approach all experiences. Most children possess a sense of trust that the world and the people in it are friendly and kind, and they will tackle that world with joy and enthusiasm. The amount of information that children learn in the first few years of life is unparalleled in later learning. At no other time in life will there be such zest and liveliness toward acquiring skills and knowledge.

Our task in working with young children is to provide an environment in which this enthusiasm is nurtured and sustained rather than subdued or even destroyed. Unfortunately, when children are not in nurturing and stimulating environments, they could well lose that sense of freshness and that enjoyment for learning. This is why we will continue to emphasize the importance of engaging in developmentally appropriate practice. Young children are eager to learn, but such eagerness can be battered down if they are frequently overwhelmed by developmentally inappropriate experiences. This is an awesome responsibility for early childhood educators, and it can be met through careful and sensitive study and understanding of the characteristics and needs of young children.

naeyc

DAP

Key Point

The early childhood educator's understanding of child development is vital to providing a supportive and developmentally appropriate program for young children.

Age-Related Commonalities among Children

Although each child is unique, children nonetheless have much in common. All children, including those with disabilities, share the need for nurturing and trustworthy adults, for stability and security, for increasing autonomy, and for a sense of competence and self-worth. Similarly, there are common attributes and skills that characterize children at different ages during the early years. In the course of normal development, children reach developmental milestones in a fairly predictable manner and within a reasonable time range (Allen & Marotz, 2010). Information about development is derived from a body of research that has set norms for children of different ages, which are based on the pioneering research of Arnold Gesell (1880–1961), director of the Yale Clinic of Child Development. According to Gesell, children go through a predictable sequence of development, alternating between broad stages, when they are in balance, and ones during which they are in disequilibrium (Salkind, 2004). Out of this work also came the concept of milestones, important accomplishments during children's development. Much of the information in the following brief overview of some developmental characteristics of infants and one-, two-, three-, four-, five-, and six- to eight-year-olds comes from Arnold Gesell's work. In fact, much of what is considered developmentally appropriate for children at specific ages—the foundation of Developmentally Appropriate Practice—is based on the research of Arnold Gesell.

© Cengage Learning

Children's enthusiasm and eagerness to learn must be nurtured through a supportive environment and by sensitive teachers who understand their development.

INFANTS. The first year of life is crucial in establishing a foundation for all areas of development. Astounding changes mark the first year; within that time, newborns, whose existence is totally dependent on adults, become mobile, communicating 12-month-olds. Professionals who care for infants need a sound understanding of the developmental changes that take place during infancy.

Newborns' earliest movements are reflexive, but quickly develop into more purposeful activity. In addition, their senses operate remarkably well, providing a wealth of valuable information about this new world into which they have been thrust. By the middle of the first year, babies are reaching for and grasping objects, rolling over, and sitting up with support. During the latter half of the year, infants master the pincer grasp (holding objects with the thumb and forefinger), crawling, pulling themselves upright, and perhaps walking alone. Through increasing skill in motor activity and use of all the senses, children learn about and make sense of the world. Socially, infants signal their recognition of significant people, especially parents and caregivers. This burgeoning affinity shifts from following these adults with their eyes to smiling and later to crawling after them. By the end of the first year, babies show strong attachments to parents and caregivers and may show considerable fear or reluctance toward strangers. Infants are amazingly adept at communicating and demonstrate increasing understanding of language. They "converse" with adults through babbling and jabbering long before they can produce recognizable words. First words also appear by the end of the first year, usually relevant to social relationships, especially, "ma-ma" and "da-da" (Allen & Marotz, 2010; Gonzalez-Mena & Eyer, 2012).

Infants need responsive adults who recognize and meet their individual needs in a consistent, nurturing, respectful manner. Caregivers of infants must be extremely sensitive to the importance of establishing a stable relationship through which trust and security are generated. They provide daily routines that are tailored to each child's individual rhythm and needs for care, food, sleep, play, and social interaction. Later, when babies begin to be mobile, caregivers must provide appropriate space for crawling and beginning walking. As discussed in *Developmentally Appropriate Practice in Early Childhood Programs Serving Children from Birth through Age 8*, infants "thrive on responsive caregiving, an engaging environment, and unhurried time to experience the simple joys of being with others" (Copple & Bredekamp, 2009, p. 59). There must be interesting things to explore, yet the environment must also be safe and hygienic (Copple & Bredekamp, 2009).

ONE-YEAR-OLDS. Toddlers, as one-year-olds are also called, have access to an expanding world of wonders to be explored. They gain increasing skills in moving through this world, starting with a lurching, wobbly gait when they first begin to walk and quickly refining their walk so that by the end of their second year their movement is quite smooth and steady and includes running, walking backward, and negotiating stairs. Soon they also begin to combine their newly developed locomotion skill with pushing and pulling objects. They are adept at picking up objects and, with great glee, also love to drop or throw them. Their increasing control over their finger muscles can be seen in their participation at meal times; they enjoy self-feeding finger foods, wielding a spoon, and drinking from a cup, though these endeavors are not always negotiated successfully. They become more independent, wanting to do many things for themselves.

Key Point

Infants rapidly gain skills in all areas of development, relying on information about the world from movement and their senses. They acquire strong attachments to significant adults in their lives; stable, consistent, and loving care is vital for babies.

Key Point

One-year-olds' rapidly growing mobility, coupled with their expanding desire for independence and their curiosity about everything around them, lead them to become avid explorers of their environment. Their growing mastery of language and new ability to mentally represent objects and experiences help them move beyond the here-and-now experiences of infancy.

Language blossoms during the second year, becoming increasingly more intelligible and varied. Vocabulary grows from a few words to an impressive mastery of up to 300 words, and single words soon become two-word sentences. During the second half of the second year, toddlers gain the ability to internally represent objects and events. This is often seen in play, when they imitate the actions of others, engage in simple make-believe play, or dress up. Toddlers have great interest in other children, but their play is characteristically parallel rather than interactive. They focus on their own wants and needs, and yet they also can show remarkable empathy toward other children. Perhaps the greatest challenge for toddlers is the need to reconcile their continuing desire for closeness to their caregivers and their growing need for independence (Allen & Marotz, 2010; Gonzalez-Mena & Eyer, 2012; Honig, 1993).

Caregivers of one-year-olds must continue to provide a safe, consistent, sensitive, loving, and supportive environment. The interactions, conversations, and give-and-take play between caregivers and children contribute immensely to toddlers' development. Caregivers must also be constantly vigilant because toddlers are very curious about everything around them and have very little awareness of safety. DAP tells us that toddlers rely on caregivers who are loving, create an environment that is safe to explore, and provide reassurance to the children that they are safe (Copple & Bredekamp, 2009). The daily schedule provided for one-year-olds is still dictated by individual rhythms and needs, but toddlers begin to exhibit greater similarity in their daily patterns; thus, caregivers may be able to schedule meals and naps for the group, while still remaining sensitive to individual differences (Copple & Bredekamp, 2009).

TWO-YEAR-OLDS. Some early childhood programs incorporate two-year-olds, especially older ones, into preschool groups, whereas others place twos into a separate toddler category. Twos are in a transitional stage, making the move from babyhood to childhood. They are in the process of acquiring and enthusiastically using many new skills, particularly the two that most visibly mark the distinction between baby and child—language and motor control.

Key Point ◆

Two-year-olds, in transition from babyhood to childhood, quickly master many skills. Their growing independence and assertiveness are both a source of enjoyment and a challenge for adults.

During this year, most children increasingly gain body control—in their more self-assured walking and running that has lost its baby stagger and in their new-found finger control that allows them to put together simple puzzles or use eating utensils. At the same time, they experience tremendous language growth. Their growing vocabulary, sentence length, and grammatical forms open up all sorts of possibilities because of this increased communication competence. Self-help skills are also improving during this year, including the achievement of toilet training for the majority of children. Just as important as learning motor, language, and self-help skills is the process of gaining independence through this mastery.

Two-year-olds undertake many activities for their sheer enjoyment rather than to reach a goal. Running is pleasurable in itself rather than as a means of getting somewhere fast; painting means involvement in a sensory process rather than an interest in producing a picture. Activities are also undertaken with enormous enthusiasm. Twos wholeheartedly throw themselves into activities, whether painting, squishing play dough, pouring sand and water, or reading books. They particularly enjoy sensory experiences, using touch, taste, and

© Cengage Learning

Two-year-olds, in transition from babyhood to childhood, are just beginning to master many skills. They need ample opportunity to practice these in a nurturing and safe environment.

smell, as well as sight and sound. Two-year-olds are notorious for their desire to repeat, using newfound skills over and over again. This desire is normal and should be encouraged, for it builds competence and allows children to fully assimilate skills before moving on to new ones.

Two-year-olds are just beginning to gain some social skills, although association with peers is more characterized by playing side by side than by interacting. They generally do not cooperate and share. In fact, young twos, with their limited self-control, may well express their growing independence and self-assertiveness by grabbing a desired toy from a peer or by throwing a tantrum. Tantrums are not uncommon among twos, reflecting, for instance, their limited verbal skills, which are not yet adequate to express what they want. They are also not adept at delaying gratification; they do not have the ability to wait for something they want "right now" (Allen & Marotz, 2010; Copple & Bredekamp, 2009; Trawick-Smith, 2006).

In accordance with DAP, teachers of two-year-olds need to provide a supportive, consistent, and safe environment in which rapidly growing skills can be practiced and mastered. Frequent and enthusiastic praise conveys that adults value the acquisition of skills. Gentle guidance acknowledges children's growing sense of self while helping them develop self-control in relation to others (Copple & Bredekamp, 2009).

THREE-YEAR-OLDS. Three-year-olds have truly left babyhood behind, not only in appearance—with the loss of baby fat—but also in added skills. Increased balance and control are evident in large motor, fine motor, and self-help areas. Threes like to use their new skills by being helpful and wanting to please adults. Their added competence does not mean, however, that they won't occasionally have accidents or revert to earlier behaviors when upset. Overall, however, their characteristic way of responding to school experiences is with enthusiasm and enjoyment.

Key Point ◆

By age three, children are much more adept in motor, self-help, and language skills and are becoming more socially aware of peers. They enjoy helping and pleasing adults.

By three, children's speech is intelligible most of the time and consists of longer sentences. Language becomes much more of a social and cognitive tool. Three-year-olds engage in more extensive conversations, talking with and not just to people, and answering as well as asking questions. In fact, three-year-olds are usually full of questions, constantly asking "Why?" or "What for?" or "How come?" Vocabulary continues to increase dramatically, and grammar becomes more accurate.

This greater language facility helps increase peer interaction among this age group. Three-year-olds are much more socially aware than younger children, and their make-believe play, which began in the previous year by imitating simple personal and home routines, at times includes two or three children. Short-lived friendships begin to form, and children will play with each other as well as near each other. Social problem-solving skills are just beginning to emerge. With guidance, threes may share and take turns, but they still find such behaviors difficult (Allen & Marotz, 2010).

Teachers of three-year-olds need to respect the growing skills and competencies of their charges without forgetting just how recently they acquired them. It is important to maintain patience and good humor, remembering that the enthusiasm with which threes use these skills is not always matched by their accuracy and speed of performance. Because three-year-olds enjoy helping as

Three-year-olds' budding skills allow them to enjoy an ever-widening array of activities and peer interactions.

© Cengage Learning

well as practicing self-help skills, such behaviors should be promoted and valued. The emerging social skills of three-year-olds should be encouraged in an atmosphere in which social exploration is safe and where playing alone or not having to give up a favorite toy is also acceptable. All of these are factors that are congruent with DAP (Copple & Bredekamp, 2009).

FOUR-YEAR-OLDS. Four-year-olds have achieved a maturity and competence in motor and language development that leads them to assume a general air of security and confidence, sometimes bordering on cockiness. "Children test limits in order to practice self-confidence and firm up a growing need for independence" (Allen & Marotz, 2010, p. 142).

Fours seem to be in perpetual motion, throwing themselves wholeheartedly into activities. They have mastered the basics of movement and now eagerly embellish on these. Climbing, pedaling, pumping on a swing, jumping over or off objects, and easily avoiding obstacles when running all contribute to greater flexibility and exploration in play. Four-year-olds like to try to show off with physical stunts. Improved muscle coordination is also evident through more controlled use of the fingers, such as in buttoning, drawing, and cutting with scissors. In addition, many self-care activities have become routines rather than the challenges they were at earlier ages.

The increased competence that leads to noticeable embellishments in motor activities is even more evident in the language area. By age four, most children's language usage has become remarkably sophisticated and skilled. This accomplishment seems to invite new uses for language beyond communication. Fours love to play with language, using it to brag, engage in bathroom talk, swear, tell tall tales, and make up silly rhymes. Four-year-olds are even more persistent than threes in asking questions.

For four-year-olds, peers have become very important. Play is a social activity more often than not, although fours enjoy solitary activities at times as well. Taking turns and sharing become much easier because four-year-olds begin to understand the reciprocal benefits of cooperation. Their imaginative variations of movement and language skills extend into group play, which is usually highly creative and ingenious, touched by their sense of humor.

Key Point

Four-year-olds have achieved considerable mastery in their motor and language abilities. They tend to be quite self-confident, often boasting or showing off. Social play is an important part of their lives.

Four-year-olds need a stimulating environment into which to channel their abundant energy and curiosity.

© Cengage Learning

DAP encourages teachers of four-year-olds to provide an environment in which children have many opportunities for interactions with each other, with adults, and with a wide selection of appropriate and stimulating materials. Because of their heightened social involvements, fours need consistent, positive guidance to help them develop emerging social skills; for instance, in sharing, resolving conflicts, and negotiating (Allen & Marotz, 2010; Copple & Bredekamp, 2009).

FIVE-YEAR-OLDS. Fives are much more self-contained and in control, replacing some of their earlier exuberant behaviors with a calmer, more mature approach. They are competent and reliable, and they take responsibility seriously. They seem to be able to judge their own abilities more accurately than at earlier ages, and they respond accordingly.

Five-year-olds' motor activities seem more poised and their movements more restrained and precise than ever before. They also have a greater interest in fine motor activities, as these children have gained many skills in accurate cutting, gluing, drawing, and beginning writing. This interest is spurred by the new desire to "make something" rather than merely to paint, cut, or manipulate the play dough for the sheer enjoyment of these activities. Five-year-olds' self-reliance extends to assuming considerable responsibility for self-care as well.

Language has also reached a height of maturity for fives; this is exhibited through a vocabulary that contains thousands of words, complex and compound sentence structures, variety and accuracy in grammatical forms, and good articulation. Language increasingly reflects interest in and contact with a broadening world outside the child's intimate family, school, and neighborhood experiences. The social sphere of five-year-olds revolves around special friendships, which take on more importance. By five, children are quite adept at sharing toys, taking turns, and playing cooperatively. Their group play is usually elaborate and imaginative, and it can take up long periods of time (Allen & Marotz, 2010).

Teachers of five-year-olds, after providing a stimulating learning environment and setting reasonable limits, can expect this age group to take on considerable responsibility for maintaining and regulating a smoothly functioning program. Fives need to be given many opportunities to explore their world in depth and assimilate what they learn through multiple experiences. One way in which children can discuss, plan, and carry out ideas stimulated by their experiences is through group projects (Helm & Katz, 2011).

SIX- TO EIGHT-YEAR-OLDS. Before- and after-school programs are designed primarily for young elementary school children of working families. The children in such programs have remarkably mature skills in all areas of development. Physically, they show well-developed and refined motor skills. Their thinking has become much more logical and systematic than it had been during the preschool years, and they are able to recognize and take into consideration the viewpoint of others. The language of school-age children is impressively adultlike, and they love to use these language skills.

Key Point

Five-year-olds, as compared with their younger peers, are much more mature, in control, and responsible. Many skills have been refined, so that at this age children are more interested in projects and activities that result in products.

These five-year-olds had an end product in mind when they began working with the blocks.

School-age children enjoy the camaraderie and close friendship of peers, often of the same sex.

© Cengage Learning

Six- to eight-year-olds exercise considerable independence and are able to follow rules and standards without the need for constant monitoring; yet they certainly still need the nurturance and security of caring adults. They also need the world of peers, within which they often form close friendships. Such friendships are, in most instances, with same-sex peers. For school-age children, play is still an important activity. It is more complex and organized than at earlier ages, incorporating both formal and informal games with rules. At this age, children enjoy projects they can initiate, implement, and carry through to completion, exercising their sense of industry.

Adults who work with six- to eight-year-olds in before- and after-school programs must provide a safe, nurturing climate. Caregivers should provide materials appropriate for the expanding interests of this group and allow children enough independence to pursue these in their own way. At the same time, adults should be available as a resource and to provide guidance and limits. Particularly after school, children also need opportunities to expend energy through large motor activity and games, which adults can arrange (Allen & Marotz, 2010; Click & Karkos, 2010; Trawick-Smith, 2006). DAP reminds us that, although children in the primary years have gained many skills, they continue to learn in active ways, need physical activity to promote both motor and cognitive skills, and need support and opportunities to refine social and language abilities (Copple & Bredekamp, 2009).

Self-Esteem

One thing shared by all children is the need to feel good about themselves. Young children are beginning to form a **self-concept,** perceptions and feelings about themselves gathered largely from how the important people in their world respond to them. One aspect of self-concept is **self-esteem,** children's evaluation of their worth in positive or negative terms (Katz, 2000; Marshall, 2009). Such evaluation can tell children that they are competent, worthwhile, and effective or, alternatively, incapable, unlikable, and powerless. It is particularly noteworthy that children who feel good about themselves seem to be more friendly and helpful toward peers. On the other hand, low self-esteem

Key Point ◆

Six- to eight-year-olds in before- and after-school programs are very independent, though they still need the support and structure provided by caring adults. Their mental abilities allow them to think much more logically and take into consideration the viewpoint of others, which becomes an important factor in their more involved peer relations.

Key Point ◆◆

Positive self-esteem is a need shared by all children and is fostered by adults who convey to children that they are competent and worthwhile.

naeyc

self-concept
Perceptions and feelings children may have about themselves, gathered largely from how the important people in their world respond to them.

self-esteem
Children's evaluation of their worth in positive or negative terms.

The child with good self-esteem has confidence in her ability to succeed and master her environment. What elements of the early childhood environment and what teacher behaviors support and nurture a child's growing sense of who she is and what she can do?

perceived competence
Children's belief in their ability to succeed in a given task.

personal control
The feeling that a person has the power to make things happen.

DIVERSITY

Key Point ◆◆

Recent neurological research underscores the need for stimulation to facilitate the amazing and rapid early learning that takes place, the importance of consistent and nurturing relationships, and the lasting effects of highly negative experiences.

is related to poor mental health, low academic achievement, and delinquency (Marshall, 2009).

A healthy self-concept is vital to all areas of a child's development. Although readiness in the natural progression of development is triggered internally and furthered by appropriate external stimuli, successful mastery of new learning also depends on a child's feelings of competence and ability to meet new challenges. **Perceived competence** reflects the child's belief in his or her ability to succeed in a given task (Marshall, 2009). Successful experiences result in self-confidence that, in turn, boosts self-esteem. Thus, many appropriate yet challenging experiences help the child feel successful, confident, and capable. A key to the development of competence in young children is to provide them with meaningful tasks. Jones (2005) describes the "Big Jobs" she sets for the children in her school; such jobs are useful, helpful tasks that require the cooperation of several people working together. The relevance and usefulness of the tasks give children motivation to solve problems they may encounter and to see the job to its completion. Some examples of Big Jobs include working in the school's garden, moving animal cages to a shady spot, shoveling snow to clear paths, sponging off tables and easels, filling the water table, assembling new furniture, and tightening loose bolts and screws.

The child needs to feel competent and able to face challenges as well as have a sense of **personal control**—the feeling of having the power to make things happen or to stop things from happening. When children generally feel that what happens to them is completely out of their hands, particularly if what happens is not always in their best interest, they cannot develop this sense of control and will tend to see themselves as helpless and ineffective. All children need opportunities to make appropriate choices and exercise autonomy to begin to develop the perception that they have control, which also contributes to their emerging sense of responsibility for their own actions (Katz, 2000).

The early years are crucial in the development of self-concept. Above all, children's positive concepts of themselves reflect healthy parent–child relationships that are founded on love, trust, and consistency. When early childhood teachers enter young children's lives, they also contribute to the formation of that concept. Marshall (2001, 2009) cautions teachers that they must be sensitive to the cultural contexts within which children grow up. Children's self-concept will be enhanced if the values promoted at home and in their school are the same. To do this successfully, teachers must learn about the cultures of the children in their classroom and infuse the curriculum and environment with a variety of materials from these cultures. Stereotypes, prejudice, and discrimination contribute to low self-concept (Katz, 2000).

At the same time, if a child comes to school with a history of abuse or neglect, the teacher's contribution of offsetting negative experiences can help nurture self-esteem. Teachers strengthen children's positive self-esteem if they are sensitive to each child as an individual and to the needs of children for affection, nurture, care, and feelings of competence. Thus, teachers who understand children, know their characteristics, respond to them, and know how to challenge them in a supportive manner contribute to this positive sense of self. In essence, everything the early childhood teacher does has an impact on children's self-concept.

BRAIN STORM
THOSE NEURONS

At birth, the baby's brain contains billions of neurons, which are specialized nerve cells. However, at that time there are few connections among neurons, though once the baby is born, the brain continuously creates connections among brain cells as the infant interacts with and experiences the world. As the child grows, the number of neurons remains relatively stable; but the neurons become bigger and heavier because of the proliferation of the threadlike fibers that form the connections among cells (Graham & Forstadt, 2011).

Myelin is one factor that affects when developmental changes, which are related to identifiable milestones in brain development, occur. Myelin is a white, fatty substance that insulates nerve cells and speeds up the rate at which nerve impulses are transmitted from one cell to another (Shonkoff & Phillips, 2000). The development of new behaviors is facilitated when impulses between cells move more quickly. Myelination, the process by which myelin coats nerve fibers, takes place at different rates in different parts of the brain. Thus, for instance, cells in the area of the brain that controls motor functions related to walking begin to be coated in myelin in the latter part of the first year; myelination thus facilitates the child's mastery of walking. Myelination of the cells involved in the mastery of different skills, therefore, have their own timetable of development.

neurons
The specialized cells of the brain.

myelin
A white, fatty substance that coats nerve fibers in the brain, thereby increasing the speed at which nerve impulses are transmitted from cell to cell.

myelination
The gradual process by which myelin coats brain cells, thus facilitating the development of skills controlled by different parts of the brain as these become myelinated.

The Brain and Children's Development

Another thing that all children share is the link between the fairly predictable sequence of visible development, as previously discussed, and the development of the brain. Over the past few years, the popular media have been full of reports of discoveries about the amazing brain of young children, although scientists caution that some of these claims represent an overinterpretation of the research (Bruer, 1997; Bruer, 2002; Hirsh-Pasek & Bruer, 2007). The rapid-fire development of brain cells in infancy, the amazing learning that takes place in the earliest years, and the potentially lasting effects of negative experiences have all helped to underscore just how important the early years are. The most rapid brain development in relation to sensory and language development takes place during the first year of life, while cognitive development peaks by two to three years of age. Thus, the early years are crucial because the brain is most malleable; the brain's capacity to change decreases with age, especially after three years of age (National Scientific Council on the Developing Child, 2007b; Perry & Szalavitz, 2007; Shonkoff & Phillips, 2000). "The exceptionally strong influence of early experience on brain architecture makes the early years of life a period of both great opportunity and great vulnerability for brain development" (National Scientific Council on the Developing Child, 2007b, p. 1).

There is a sequence of optimal experiences, tied to brain development, which control the mastery of skills in childhood. We have always known that babies follow a specific sequence, first crawling, then standing, walking, running, jumping, and so forth. Brain research has pinpointed the areas of the brain that develop to facilitate learning in motor areas and also in language, cognitive, social, and emotional areas. In addition, different areas of the brain are primarily

naeyc

involved at different ages; the more primitive parts of the brain are dominant during prenatal and early infant development, while increasingly more integrative parts of the brain, such as the cortex and frontal cortex, are involved as the child becomes more mature (Perry & Szalavitz, 2007).

There are times in children's lives that are critical for development. Very young children need to be lovingly touched, held, rocked, and cuddled. They need to experience language, music, and other friendly sounds. They also need ample time and opportunity to play (Steglin, 2005). They need many sensory experiences that stimulate and broaden their repertoire of brain connections. They need to develop a special bond with a small number of significant adults who are positive, responsive, and predictable. In other words, they need to have numerous, repeated positive experiences on which to create templates or internal models of what the world is like. Through such experiences, very young children develop a picture of the world and, most important, build attachment, that special bond that is intimately linked to safety (Perry & Szalavitz, 2007).

When young children do not have such experiences, particularly consistent and predictable care, they cannot fully develop that built-in template for relationships. They do not have that special one or two people who care deeply about them. They may never feel fully safe, because they have not developed a strong, trusting relationship with someone on whom they can totally rely. Such children may grow up never experiencing deep relationships, relating to others only on a shallow level. Lack of a strong, secure attachment to at least one caring adult can result in a child living in an uneasy or stressful state because their needs are never satisfactorily met (Perry & Szalavitz, 2007).

Play

naeyc

Another commonality among all children is the need for play, which serves as a means of learning about and making sense of the world. But more than that, play is essential to all aspects of children's development. DAP underscores that "play is an important vehicle for developing self-regulation as well as for promoting language, cognition, and social competence" (Copple & Bredekamp, 2009, p. 14). Play promotes mastery as children practice skills; it furthers cognitive development as thinking abilities are stretched; it involves language, encouraging new uses; it involves physical activity; it helps children work through emotions; its inventive nature makes it creative; and it is often a socializing event. Beyond all that, it also provides a way for children to assimilate and integrate their life experiences. In no way is play a trivial pursuit, but rather it is a serious undertaking necessary to healthy development for all children. Play is the way children come to understand the world (Steglin, 2005).

DAP

Key Point ◆

Play provides many opportunities for children to practice skills, stretch thinking abilities, work through emotions, socialize, and be creative.

Educators have expressed concern about societal changes that have decreased children's opportunities to play. Opportunities for play in contemporary early childhood classrooms are few, according to Steglin (2005), who makes the case that teachers need to be eloquent advocates for play-based curriculum in the early years. A number of organizations, including the American Academy of Pediatrics (2007) and the Alliance for Childhood (2005), an organization whose membership includes some of the leading advocates for children's healthy development, have expressed concern for the decrease in the amount of time that today's children spend in play. Research also makes strong connections between the quality of play during the early years and children's readiness for school (Bodrova & Leong, 2003). See "Take a Closer Look," for further discussion about the changing nature and opportunities for play and what advocates suggest to change this situation.

WHAT HAS HAPPENED TO CHILDREN'S PLAY?

THERE ALWAYS has been recognition that play is a highly important part of childhood, central in children's lives. "Children have played at all times throughout history and in all cultures" (International Play Association, 2008). But in recent years, the amount of time children spend in play has decreased significantly and the very nature of play itself has changed. A growing number of professionals and organizations are sounding the alarm about the potential harm that can result.

Play benefits children by allowing them "to use their creativity while developing their imagination, dexterity, and physical, cognitive, and emotional strength" (American Academy of Pediatrics, 2007, p. 183). Children learn about their world through play when they can freely explore, practice adult roles, master their fears, and develop confidence and new competencies. The social benefits of play are highly valuable as children work in groups, negotiate and share with others, learn to resolve conflicts, make decisions, and stand up for themselves. In addition, play promotes the development of active and healthy bodies (American Academy of Pediatrics, 2007). Play is also a joyful activity that brings great pleasure to children. A wealth of research underscores the value of play (Saracho & Spodek, 2003; Steglin, 2005).

But the role of play in children's lives has been compromised. One factor has to do with the many children around the world who for a variety of reasons are denied the opportunity to play. These reasons include child labor and exploitation, war and violence, and abject poverty. The United Nations High Commission for Human Rights recognizes that all children have the fundamental right to play, "to be free to explore and discover the physical and social world around them, . . . a key component of preserving community and culture in the broadest sense" (Fronczek, 2004). Article 31 of the United Nation's Convention on the Rights of the Child states that every child has the right to engage in play and recreation activities.

But concerns about children's right to play are increasingly being voiced in relation to children from more affluent and secure backgrounds. "Many of these children are being raised in an increasingly hurried and pressured style that may limit the protective benefits they would gain from child-driven play" (American Academy of Pediatrics, 2007, p. 172). Recess, creative arts, and physical education have been decreased or eliminated for many children as schools face the pressures of meeting requirements of the No Child Left Behind Act of 2001. This act's focus on reading and mathematics potentially has serious implications for children's learning because cognitive capacity is significantly enhanced by physical activity, which often becomes the expendable part of the curriculum. Test taking rather than creative problem solving has become the focus of public education.

In addition, many parents put pressure on their children at early ages to prepare for the future by spending more time on academics and less on free play. Many youngsters engage in a variety of highly scheduled enrichment activities. Although such activities have benefits for children, these are often at the expense of time for play. In addition, children are less likely to be allowed to play outside because of parents' concerns about safety. Thus, children spend far more time indoors than in the past, often in isolated activity with computers or television. Furthermore, contemporary children's toys are much more scripted, further taking away opportunities for imaginative play.

More attention is being focused on the potential harms of this change in children's engagement in play. In 2008, the Public Broadcasting Service produced a documentary, book, and outreach project, "Where Do the Children Play?" One segment of this PBS film examines the suburbs. Explosive growth, massive highways, and distant malls create an isolated environment that does not provide sidewalks or places to ride bikes, walk, or play. As a result, children spend time indoors with electronic media, often by themselves. The film points out that suburban kids—those ironically with the most opportunity in some ways—suffer the greatest health and psychological problems.

▶❚❚ **TeachSource Video Activity**
WATCH • REFLECT • RESPOND

This video provides an overview of the stages of young children's play. Go to CengageBrain.com and view the video entitled, "Young Children's Stages of Play: An Illustrated Guide," and answer the following questions:

1. What do children learn at each stage of play, as shown and discussed in the video?

2. Which types of activities are typical of solitary play and which ones tend to support social play?

Key Point ◆◆

Play can be categorized by its social (six stages) or its cognitive (four stages) characteristics.

STAGES OF PLAY. Play has been of interest to child researchers for many years. Mildred Parten (1932) provided one of the landmark studies, still considered valid today, in which young children's social play was categorized. She found an age-related progression in five types of play and an earliest category that is not really play but observation of others' play. Although children at later ages engage in earlier forms of play, their play is typically more complex than it was when they were younger. Parten's six categories of social play are listed and explained in Figure 2-1.

Figure **2-1**

Parten's Stages of Play

Parten's Categories of Social Play

Types of Play	Definition	Example
Unoccupied behavior	The child moves about the classroom going from one area to another, observing but not getting involved.	*Sebastian wanders to the blocks and watches several children work together on a structure. After a few seconds he looks around, then walks over to the art table, where he looks at the finger painting materials briefly but does not indicate a desire to paint. He continues to wander, going from area to area, watching but not participating.*
Solitary play	The child plays alone, uninvolved with other children nearby. Children at all ages engage in this type of play, although older children's solitary play is more complex.	*Lorraine works diligently at building a sand mountain, not looking at or speaking with the children who are involved in other activities around her.*
Onlooker play	Quite common among two-year-olds, a child stands nearby watching others at play, without joining in.	*Rajeef stands just outside the dramatic play area and watches a group of children participate in doctor play, using various medical props.*
Parallel play	Children use similar materials or toys in similar ways but do not interact with each other.	*Kalie alternates red and blue Legos on a board while Terrance, sitting next to her, uses Legos to build a tall structure. They seem influenced by each other's activity but do not talk to each other or suggest joining materials.*
Associative play	Increasingly evident as preschoolers get older, children interact and even share some of their materials, but they are not engaged in a common activity.	*Several children are in the block area working on a common structure. Jolynne runs a car through an arch she has built at one side of the structure; Arlen keeps adding blocks to the top, saying, "This is the lookout tower," while Akira surrounds the structure with a "fence."*
Cooperative play	Typical of older preschoolers, this is the most social form of play and involves children playing together in a shared activity.	*On arriving at school one day, the children find an empty appliance box in their classroom. At first they climb in and out of the box, but then a few of them start talking about what it might be used for. Jointly, they decide to make it into a house, and their discussion turns to how this could be accomplished. While continuing to discuss the project, they also begin the task of transforming the box, cutting, painting, and decorating to reach their common goal. It takes several days, but the children together create a house.*

These girls are engaged in similar activities, but each is engrossed in her own puzzle and there is little interaction between them. This is typical of parallel play.

© Cengage Learning

Other researchers have viewed play from a different perspective. For instance, Sara Smilansky (1968) proposed play categories based on children's increasing cognitive abilities and measured by how children use play materials. This view is complementary to Parten's classifications because it focuses on a different aspect of play. Smilansky's categories are shown in Figure 2-2.

It is important for teachers to be aware of the different types of play and to recognize that children develop increasing social and cognitive skills as they progress. In particular, this awareness helps set appropriate expectations for young children. For instance, infants need appropriate objects, space, and time for observation, manipulation, and exploration, which helps them learn about the properties of their environment. Toddlers need the kind of toys and props that help them use and integrate their growing ability to mentally represent experiences. Preschoolers need sizable blocks of time to engage in self-selected play and many open-ended materials that lend themselves to exploration and mastery (for instance, clay, blocks, sand and water, and Legos®).

Figure **2-2**

Smilansky's Stages of Play

Smilansky's Categories of Cognitive Play

Types of Play	Definition	Example
Functional play	Characteristic of infants' and toddlers' repetitive, motor play used to explore what objects are like and what can be done with them.	*Clark picks up a block, turns it, and looks at it from all sides. He bangs it on the floor, then picks another block with his left hand and bangs the two blocks together. He alternates striking the blocks against each other and on the floor.*
Constructive play	Involves creating something with the play objects.	*Clark uses blocks to construct a tower. His activity now has a purpose.*
Dramatic play	The child uses a play object to substitute for something imaginary.	*Clark takes four blocks, puts one on each of four plates placed around the table, and says, "Here is your toast for breakfast."*
Games with rules	Involve accepted, prearranged rules in play. This stage is more typical of older children.	*In kindergarten, Clark and a group of peers play the game "Blockhead," agreeing on the game's rules.*

The apparent common goal of these three children suggests that they are engaged in cooperative play.

In addition, time, space, and materials that lend themselves to social play should always be available, including dolls, dress-up clothes, and blocks. School-age children, while appreciating such open-ended materials, also enjoy some simple organized games with rules. It is important, however, to avoid highly competitive activities, which only foster resentment and ill will. We will discuss an alternative, cooperative games, in Chapter 13.

One kind of play, **rough-and-tumble play,** is often mistaken for fighting. Young children may well engage in rough-and-tumble play, which is very physical and vigorous. A number of research studies have shown that this kind of play is natural and can be distinguished by children's laughter and relaxed muscle tone (Carlson, 2011). Inappropriate rough play, on the other hand, often results in tears and includes physical behaviors that are intended to make a child do the bidding of the aggressor by inflicting pain or threatening to do so. "Most children engage in rough play, and research demonstrates its physical, social, emotional, and cognitive value. Early childhood settings have the responsibility to provide children with what best serves their developmental needs" (Carlson, 2011, p. 24). Providing a supportive environment for such play, establishing rules, and supervising are some strategies that help children engage in such play.

rough-and-tumble play
Highly physical play, which should be distinguished from fighting; in such play there is laughter, children's faces reflect enjoyment, and their muscle tone is relaxed.

CHILDREN—UNIQUENESS

Children have many characteristics in common and certainly share basic needs for affection, acceptance, consistency, respect, and appropriate challenges; yet there are many variations among children. The "profiles" of young children presented earlier reflect many common characteristics of these ages, but they will rarely describe any one child. Even while falling within the normal range of development, each child possesses a unique blend of attributes that makes him or her one of a kind.

Temperament

naeyc

temperament
Children's inborn characteristics—such as regularity, adaptability, and disposition—that affect behavior.

Key Point ◆◆

Children have inborn temperaments that contribute to individual uniqueness. Some children are predisposed to be easygoing, whereas others tend to be basically difficult.

Children's unique qualities reflect both inborn and external factors that have molded who they are. Some children are born with an easygoing **temperament;** for instance, they have a moderate activity level, predictable schedule of sleeping and eating, and a positive attitude toward and curiosity in new experiences. Other children have more difficult temperaments and, for example, are more irritable, unpredictable, and more difficult to calm down, as found by Thomas, Chess, and Birch (1968) in their classic study. Although children are born with such temperamental characteristics, these gradually tend to affect the adults around them so that families and teachers may begin to think of children as "difficult" or "easy" and expect and reinforce their behavioral traits. On the other hand, such traits also can be considerably modified by guidance practices (Rothbart & Derryberry, 2002). In turn, then, adults' perceptions of children contribute to children's self-perceptions.

Culture

Children's individuality also is shaped by the cultural, ethnic, religious, and economic background of the family. "Family systems, communication styles, religious preferences, education, parenting practices, and community values all play important roles in shaping a child's unique heritage" (Allen & Marotz, 2010, p. 128b). It is important that early childhood teachers and caregivers be sensitive to family diversity and genuinely value different cultures and backgrounds. Children mirror their primary environment—their home and family—as, of course, they should. If teachers, whether consciously or unconsciously, denigrate what children experience and learn at home, they will convey that the family, including the child, is in some way inferior and undesirable. This would obviously have a detrimental impact on children's self-concept.

CHILDREN WITH DISABILITIES

Some children are born with or acquire conditions that place them outside the typical range of development for their age. They might have a **developmental delay,** meaning that they accomplish tasks in one or more developmental areas at a considerably later age than their peers. Some children are considered **at risk** for delay, with a significant probability that problems will occur if early intervention services are not called into play. Children may be at risk for environmental reasons, such as poverty, or for biological reasons, such as low birth weight (Allen & Cowdery, 2012). With appropriate help, children who have developmental delays may well catch up to age norms. Other children may have a **deficit,** or **impairment,** indicating development that is in some way different (not just slower) from that of most children. Children with hearing or visual deficits, mental retardation, or motor disabilities are part of this category.

It has become more and more evident that children with disabilities benefit from early intervention. In fact, the importance of providing services as early as possible has been underscored by national policies that mandate such services for young children with disabilities. In 1975, Public Law 94-142 (Education for All Handicapped Children Act) was passed to ensure a "free and appropriate public education" for all children with disabilities between the ages of 3 and 21.

DIVERSITY

Key Point ◆◆
Children's uniqueness also derives from the cultural, ethnic, religious, linguistic, and economic background of their families.

DIVERSITY

developmental delay
A child's development in one or more areas occurring at an age significantly later than that of peers.

at-risk children
Children considered to be at risk for developmental delay because of adverse environmental factors, such as poverty or low birth weight.

deficit (or **impairment**)
A problem in development, usually organic, resulting in below-normal performance.

Key Point ◆◆
Children with developmental delays accomplish tasks at an age older than that when their peers accomplish them, whereas the development of children with impairments is in some way different, not just slower.

TeachSource Video Activity
WATCH•REFLECT•RESPOND

This video provides insight into the Individualized Education Plan (IEP) process and the important role of the teacher as an advocate for the child. Go to CengageBrain.com and view the video entitled, "Preschool: IEP and Transition Planning for a Young Child with Special Needs," and answer the following questions:

1. How does the teacher in this video serve as an advocate for Mark?

2. What messages does the teacher convey to the parents and the kindergarten teacher?

Individualized Education Plan (IEP)
Mandated by Public Law 94-142, such a plan must be designed for each child with a disability and must involve parents as well as teachers and other appropriate professionals.

Individualized Family Service Plan (IFSP)
Required by the 1986 Education of the Handicapped Act Amendments for children with disabilities under the age of three and their families; the IFSP, often developed by a transdisciplinary team that includes teachers, social workers, psychologists, and parents, determines goals and objectives that build on the strengths of the child and family.

As part of this law, programs are required to seek the input and involvement of parents, in part articulated through an **Individualized Education Plan (IEP).** The IEP is developed by a team that includes professionals and the parents. A decade later, in 1986, Public Law 99-457 (the Education of the Handicapped Act Amendments) added provisions for children from birth to age five. Specifically, what was referred to as Part H of this law addresses the needs of infants and toddlers with disabilities. It calls for services for children under three who are experiencing or are at risk for developmental delays and requires an **Individualized Family Service Plan (IFSP)** for the child and family, developed by a transdisciplinary team. Public Law 101-476, the Individuals with Disabilities Education Act (IDEA), was passed in 1990, reauthorizing the earlier laws but reflecting a change in philosophy away from labeling children as "handicapped" and referring to them instead as "individuals with disabilities." In 1997, this law was further amended to provide comprehensive services for infants and toddlers (Part C) and preschoolers (Part B). Finally, Public Law 101-336, the Americans with Disabilities Act (ADA), was passed in 1990, assuring all individuals with disabilities, including children, full civil rights, including appropriate accommodations in child care and preschool programs (Cook, Klein, & Chen, 2012). These laws came into being because of the commitment, dedication, and hard work of parents and professionals whose advocacy eventually led to legal remedies for the plight of children with disabilities who, too often, were excluded from the educational system (Deiner, 2010).

Inclusion

least restrictive environment
A provision of Public Law 94-142 that children with disabilities be placed in a program as close as possible to a setting designed for children without disabilities, while being able to meet each child's special needs.

DIVERSITY

Key Point ◆◆

Many early childhood programs integrate children with disabilities. Such inclusion, when carefully planned, provides benefits for all involved.

One of the provisions of Public Law 94-142 is that children with disabilities be placed in the **least restrictive environment.** This means they should be placed in programs that are as close as possible to settings designed for children without disabilities, while remaining appropriate for their unique needs (Allen & Cowdery, 2012; Cook et al., 2012; Winter, 2007). "Inclusion is not merely a place, or an instructional strategy, or a curriculum; it is about belonging, being valued, and having choices" (Allen & Cowdery, 2012, p. 3). This concept has led to the expansion of inclusion—the integration of children with special needs into regular programs. Inclusion is certainly not new, having informally been part of many early childhood programs throughout this century and more formally incorporated over the past several decades into Head Start programs (Cook et al., 2012). It is also important to recognize that inclusion may not be the best alternative for all children with special needs; thus, a decision to integrate a child with special needs into a regular classroom should be made only after careful consideration.

An inclusive program is founded on the premise that young children, both those with and those without a disability, are much more similar than they are different. Children with disabilities can benefit from a good inclusion program by experiencing success in a variety of developmentally appropriate activities, through contact with age-mates who can be both models and friends, and by exposure to the many opportunities for informal incidental learning that take place in all early childhood programs (Deiner, 2010). At the same time, children without disabilities benefit from inclusion by learning that children who are in some way different from them nonetheless have far more commonalities than differences. An increasing number of young children with disabilities are enrolled in early childhood programs (Cook et al., 2012).

Although inclusion has many potential benefits, the benefits do not happen automatically. In other words, inclusion does not simply mean enrolling children with special needs in an early childhood program. Careful planning, preparation, modification, evaluation, and support are necessary for successful inclusion. Early childhood teachers, because they know a great deal about children and how best to work with them, have many skills needed for working with children with disabilities as well. In fact, research has shown that inclusion is most likely to occur when teachers have some formal education in working with children with disabilities (Essa, Bennett, Burnham, Martin, Bingham, & Allred, 2008).

Many children with mild or moderate disabilities are effectively included in early childhood programs. The teacher may work individually with the child in some activities, but the child is a part of the large group in most or all aspects of the program.

But placement of children with special needs in their classes also involves the teachers learning some additional skills. It often means having to acquire and use new teaching strategies, new terminology, and different evaluation tools. It also involves working with a wider range of professionals (for instance, speech and physical therapists or psychologists) and more focused involvement with parents. In addition, early childhood teachers may find themselves with unexpectedly strong emotional reactions, such as pity for the child, anger that the child has to suffer, fear of the disability, or doubt about their own abilities, which they must face and resolve.

One of the keys to successful inclusion is to view each child, whether he or she has a disability or not, as an individual with unique characteristics, strengths, and needs. This involves an attitude that sees a child, not a child with Down syndrome or a child who is blind or a child who stutters. For example, Ted may have Down syndrome but he loves to paint, enjoys listening to stories at group time, and gives terrific hugs. Similarly, Noni's visual impairment does not diminish her enjoyment of the sand table, her budding friendship with Connie, or her ability to make others laugh through her language play. And Manuel, while often tripping over words, can throw and catch a ball accurately. Many times he is the one who notices a colorful butterfly passing or the first buds of spring, and he has a totally winning smile. Working with a group of children means recognizing, encouraging, and building on each child's strengths. In this way, children's self-concept and self-assurance are boosted so they can meet the challenges posed by their disabilities.

Characteristics of Children with Disabilities

It is beyond the scope of this text to discuss in depth such topics as characteristics of children with disabilities, appropriate teaching methods, testing and assessment tools, and the unique needs of the families of children with disabilities. Considerable training is necessary to fully master the skills and information of the relatively new field of early childhood special education. This field combines and integrates the traditional skills of teachers of young children with the specialized expertise of special educators, therapists, and medical personnel. More information about working with children with disabilities, particularly in arrangement of the environment and planning curriculum, is shared in later chapters.

DIVERSITY

naeyc

Most early childhood teachers, however, will inevitably find themselves in one or both of the following situations:

▶ One or more children with disabilities will be included in their class.
▶ They will have concerns about a child who seems to experience consistent difficulties in one or more areas of development.

In the former case, it is important that teachers work with families and specialists to make the inclusion experience successful. In the latter, teachers concerned about a child's functioning need to document their concerns and discuss them with the family, as well as offer some concrete suggestions; for instance, how to begin the referral process so the child is seen by an appropriate specialist. (We will examine methods of observation and assessment in more detail in Chapter 6.) For both of these reasons, it is important that teachers of young children have some basic information about the characteristics of children with special needs.

CHILDREN WITH PHYSICAL DISABILITIES. Children can experience a wide range of motor limitations, from being slightly clumsy to having virtually no muscular control. The causes of such disabilities can stem from orthopedic problems, genetic anomalies, brain dysfunctions, or central nervous system damage. One of the most common motor impairments is cerebral palsy, a central nervous system dysfunction usually caused by lack of oxygen to the brain that can cause children to be uncoordinated and awkward or can leave them with almost no physical control (Paasche, Gorrill, & Strom, 2004). Children with cerebral palsy often face challenges in other areas of development, but the fact that a child is severely impaired physically does not necessarily mean that he is mentally impaired.

Some motor problems can be corrected surgically or with orthopedic aids such as casts, while many others can be improved through systematic physical therapy. For some children, improved functioning can be facilitated through adaptive equipment; for instance, a special chair that supports weak muscles or a wheeled board on which the child can scoot to get around. Generally, specialists make determinations about corrective measures, although early childhood teachers will be able to carry out special procedures or help children adapt to new equipment. It is important to help children feel as independent and involved as possible. Some ways of encouraging independence and involvement include placing materials within their reach, keeping paths accessible to children in wheelchairs or using crutches, and adapting ongoing activities to facilitate as much participation as possible (Cook et al., 2012).

CHILDREN WITH INTELLECTUAL DISABILITIES. When children's intellectual abilities lag significantly behind their chronological age, they are considered to have special intellectual needs (Deiner, 2010). Intellectual functioning is conventionally measured through IQ tests (see Chapter 6 for a fuller discussion), which indicate whether a child's score falls within the average range or is above or below average. Fifty percent of all Americans fall within the average range.

About 85 percent of children with intellectual disabilities are classified as having mild intellectual delays, with IQs between 50–55 and 70–75. Children whose IQs fall between 35–40 and 50–55 are considered to have moderate intellectual delays; this group makes up about 10 percent of children with such disabilities. About 3 percent of children are considered to have severe intellectual delays, with IQs ranging from 20–25 to 35–40. Finally, children whose IQs fall below 20–25, about 2 percent of all individuals with intellectual disabilities, are considered to have profound intellectual delays (Deiner, 2010). "The levels generally indicate the intensity of services that are needed for the child" (Deiner, 2010, p. 336).

Key Point

Motor problems can range from slight awkwardness to no control of motor functions. Special equipment, careful classroom arrangement, and adaptation of activities allow children with motor disabilities to be included.

Key Point

Many children with intellectual disabilities can benefit from inclusive programs. Down syndrome and fragile X syndrome are two relatively common cognitive disabilities.

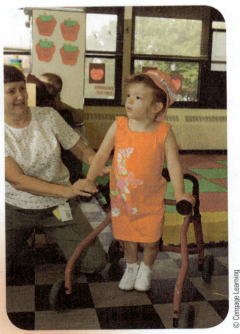

Children with a variety of disabilities are often part of inclusive early childhood programs.

© Cengage Learning

There are many types of intellectual disabilities, stemming from different causes. Two of these are relatively common, and we will briefly discuss them here. Children with **Down syndrome** usually have significant developmental, cognitive, and language delays. They also have some distinctive physical characteristics, including floppy limbs, short stature, a small round head, slanted eyes, and a protruding tongue. Down syndrome children are prone to respiratory infections and frequently have heart abnormalities as well. Such children are usually very affectionate and cheerful and are able to learn adaptive and early academic skills.

Another intellectual disability is **fragile X syndrome,** a disability that occurs far more often in boys than in girls. Delays in all areas of development are usual, and children often have large heads, poor muscle tone, and crossed eyes. Children with fragile X syndrome are sociable but often shy and anxious (Paasche et al., 2004).

Children with intellectual deficits seem to have problems with memory and attention (Deiner, 2010). This has implications for expectations and for strategies used by the teacher. For instance, providing ample opportunity for repetition, many activities that use more than one sensory modality, numerous motor activities that reinforce concepts with action, and an environment that is not overly stimulating and distracting can help children with intellectual deficits focus on activities. Because children with these deficits are usually less mature than their peers, they may need help in joining in the social play of the class. The teacher's assistance can be helpful by modeling appropriate social behaviors to the child and by encouraging other children to be accepting.

Some children are affected by the mother's excessive use of alcohol during pregnancy. **Fetal alcohol syndrome (FAS)** and the less severe manifestation, **fetal alcohol effect (FAE),** can result in a small head and brain, small stature, developmental and language delays, poor impulse control, difficulty in grasping abstract concepts, hyperactivity, distractibility, and sensory/perceptual problems (Harwood & Kleinfeld, 2002; Paasche et al., 2004). It is estimated that 1 out of every 750 children are born with FAS (Burd, Cotsonas-Hassler, Martsolf, & Kerbeshian, 2003). The most effective environment for children with FAS or FAE seems to be one that is structured and predictable. Consistency can help children with FAS and FAE learn the parameters of environment more effectively.

CHILDREN WITH LEARNING DISABILITIES. The term *learning* disability can have many meanings. Such disabilities affect basic learning processes and may be seen in young children who have problems listening, thinking, or speaking; in school-age children, learning disabilities become more apparent when children have difficulties with reading, writing, and math. Learning disabilities are more difficult to diagnose and, therefore, treat in preschool-age children (RTI Goes to Pre-K, 2007). Children with learning disabilities are of average or above-average intelligence; their problem seems to be one of processing information. They often also have problems with motor control, particularly balance, coordination, body image, awareness of space, and directionality (Cook et al., 2012; Deiner, 2010).

CHILDREN WITH ADD OR ADHD. Sometimes, though not always, learning disabilities occur in conjunction with **attention deficit disorder (ADD)** or **attention deficit–hyperactivity disorder (ADHD)** (Paasche et al., 2004). It is important not to confuse the normal activity and exuberance of young children

Down syndrome
A disability in which children have significant developmental, cognitive, and intellectual delays, marked by noticeable physical characteristics such as small head and stature, slanted eyes, and protruding tongue.

fragile X syndrome
A disability in which children have significant developmental, cognitive, and intellectual delays, marked by noticeable physical characteristics such as large head, crossed eyes, and poor muscle tone.

fetal alcohol syndrome (FAS)
Irreversible birth abnormalities resulting from the mother's heavy alcohol consumption during pregnancy. Children are usually mentally challenged and hyperactive and may have small head size, small overall size, and various limb or facial abnormalities.

fetal alcohol effect (FAE)
Not as serious or noticeable as fetal alcohol syndrome, FAE, nonetheless, can leave children at a disadvantage in their ability to learn and reach optimal development.

Key Point

Learning disabilities affect basic learning processes.

attention deficit disorder (ADD)
Difficulty in concentrating on an activity or subject for more than a few moments at a time.

attention deficit–hyperactivity disorder (ADHD)
Manifested by short attention span, restlessness, poor impulse control, distractibility, and inability to concentrate.

TAYLA:
A VERY SPECIAL LITTLE GIRL

Mary, Early Head Start Teacher

Tayla came to our program through Early Intervention Services when she was seven months old. She was small for her age and capable of only eye movement and general hand swipes. We were told that she had monosomy 4Q, a rare disease. She had to be fed by G-tube, had club feet, and had severe palate malformation. She also suffered from respiratory distress and received breathing treatments at home. I had apprehensions when approached with the care of Tayla because she was medically so fragile.

I asked a lot of questions and did as much research about her condition on the Web as I could, but not much information is available. A nearby nursing clinic was brought in for support and emergencies. I continued to be apprehensive, but with daily practice, handling of the G-tube just became a routine. I became more confident with time and took on more of her care, including cleaning and rotating the G-tube, fitting the braces for her club feet, and handling general hygiene needs. I quickly learned to treat Tayla as any other child and include her in all activities to the best of her abilities. This often meant altering the activity a bit, but it made me into a better teacher.

Tayla was a social butterfly who was, for the most part, a happy child. She constantly watched the other children and adults in the room. She would seek out one-on-one care, initiating contact with her eyes and smiles. From the start, we found her to be a master of facial expressions, able to show her mood and communicate effectively. She smiled when the other children in the class vocalized or when my co-teacher and I bantered back and forth. She had the ability to make us laugh.

When she came to our program, she was not capable of vocal communication at all, not even being able to cry. She would breathe harder when she was upset and tears would come to her eyes, but there was no sound whatsoever. As a result, we had to be diligent in using eye contact and observing her, to ensure that we gave her proper care and met her emotional needs. She loved to be touched and held. We often placed her between our legs or touching our legs while sitting on the floor to make physical connection with her.

Tayla thrived at a rate that astounded us all. She had a zest for life. You could see the learning and developmental growth. We all relished every milestone, which had such importance because she had to work 10 times harder to reach a goal. But she made much more rapid progress than we expected. Within four weeks of joining our class, she was able to move her head from side to side and reach up with her hands to grasp a toy. The day she learned to roll over was a big production. We captured the entire sequence on film. Within the same week she scooted across the floor to reach toys and the other children. It was amazing to watch the impact she had on the other children too. They were very empathetic, much more than you would expect of young toddlers. They would automatically look out for Tayla, taking care of her or helping in her care. They would get down on her level to make eye contact or to touch her.

Tayla's feeding needs dictated our classroom schedule. Gradually, she began to eat baby food and food with strong taste. She loved trying new things. Food played an important part in her ability to reach midline and in sensory integration. Tayla liked to paint in her food and used all of her senses to explore. In time she also participated in all classroom activities, including exploring with paint, clay, water, and other materials. She was not left out of any activity.

This progress ended when Tayla was hospitalized for over 8 weeks with respiratory distress and did not return to our class for 11 weeks. At this time, oral feeding stopped and she labored to do the simplest things again. We had taken several steps backwards and had to begin again with the basics. In the coming months, many medical conditions came and went, each with their own challenges.

But that was not what I truly remember about Tayla. I treasure what she taught me and taught the children just with her presence in our classroom. She taught me to love unconditionally, to accept without hesitation each child and his or her own unique abilities, to savor each small accomplishment, to value each struggle, and to covet each small step toward a goal. She taught me how to appreciate the value of a smile, the twinkle in an eye, and how to live each day to the fullest. I appreciate the small things, the quite moments, the one-on-one contact, and above all the gift that each child is. I found myself often personally re-evaluating what is important in life because of the contact I had with Tayla. Tayla was a wonderful teacher!

with ADHD. A child who is truly hyperactive—with a very short attention span, undue restlessness, poor impulse control, inability to concentrate, and great distractibility—needs medical help. Various treatments, particularly psychoactive drugs, have helped many children gain better control over their behavior; however, there is considerable concern in the medical community about the long-term effects of such medications. Be aware that drugs do not cure ADHD but can help children manage their behavior more effectively. The attitude toward the use of drugs has changed over the past several decades, and today, medication is considered best used earlier rather than later (Deiner, 2010). Medication is effective for over 70 percent of children (Landau & McAninch, 1993).

If a child in your class has been diagnosed by a physician as having ADHD and is now taking medication, it is important that you carefully observe how the medication affects the child and report this to the family (Paasche et al., 2004). Particularly for children who spend many hours a day in a child care setting, the teacher's reports can be invaluable. We will discuss various methods of observation, which can help you in this task, in Chapter 6.

CHILDREN WITH VISUAL IMPAIRMENTS. There are varying degrees of visual impairment, with complete sightlessness as the most extreme. However, many children who are considered to have visual impairment are able to see imperfectly, less clearly than a normal person. Some visual impairments, especially if they are caused by a defect of the eye, can be corrected or reduced through surgery or corrective lenses. Others, particularly those stemming from brain or optic-nerve damage, are most likely not correctable (Deiner, 2010).

Children with severe visual impairments are usually identified at an early age. Many children with less serious problems, however, may go undiagnosed, because most children do not routinely go to an ophthalmologist and are simply not aware that something is wrong. It is important to look for signs of potential visual problems. Eyes that are frequently red or watery, have discharge, develop sties, or seem uncoordinated should be checked.

Some behavioral signs may also warn of possible visual problems. These include frequently rubbing the eyes, tilting the head, continually blinking, frowning, squinting, or complaining about headaches or dizziness. It is also important to observe a child carefully who persists in holding a book too close or too far, overestimates or underestimates distances when putting together manipulative toys, loses interest in activities such as group book reading (if this inattentiveness is unusual in other activities), or can't recognize familiar people from a distance. Any of these signs, particularly if they occur in combination with others, are reasons to discuss your concern with the family.

If a child with a severe visual disability is enrolled in your class, there are some approaches you can use to maximize the child's involvement and learning. As with any sensory deficiency, it is important that acuity in the other senses be heightened to help the child learn about the world; thus, the senses of hearing and touch become particularly important. Every new word or concept should be associated with touch. Allow plenty of time for tactile exploration of new objects, particularly relating parts to the whole in more complex items (for instance, pegboard and pegs). Encourage the child to engage in physical activity and talk about what she is doing. Also discuss what you and the other children are doing as it happens. The environment should be free of clutter so the visually impaired child can get around without danger of tripping over an unexpected obstacle. All the children in the class can help maintain an orderly environment. Use auditory and tactile cues to help the child identify various areas of the room

Key Point
Children with mild or moderate visual problems can function well in a regular early childhood program. Children with severe visual impairments will need considerable special assistance.

(the bubbling sound of the aquarium to identify the science area, for instance). A specialist who works with visually impaired children can be a great resource in finding ways to make the child as independent and involved as possible (Cook et al., 2012; Deiner, 2010).

CHILDREN WITH HEARING IMPAIRMENTS. Hearing is very much tied to communication because children learn to understand and talk by listening to and imitating others. As a result, a child with a hearing impairment usually experiences problems in language learning as well. Because language is also a primary tool in acquiring concepts about the world, a child whose language is limited by hearing loss may also experience cognitive problems. Severity of hearing loss, anywhere on the continuum from mild to profound, will affect the corrective measures as well as the strategies a teacher might use. Children with profound hearing loss may have a cochlear implant, a complex electronic device that can provide a sense of sound. Cochlear implants are surgically placed behind the ear. Other children may benefit from hearing aids, which amplify sounds. Some are helped to learn from a combination of methods, including sign language, using whatever hearing capacity they might have, and speech reading skills as part of a **total communication approach.**

Some children with mild hearing loss may not have been identified as having a problem. In addition, ear infections can affect hearing; thus, some children are at risk of losing some of their hearing capacity. Be alert to signs of potential problems. If a child frequently requests that you repeat, often seems not to hear when you speak to her, is inattentive or baffled at group times that require listening, or shows indications that her ears hurt, there may be cause for concern. Monitor such signs more specifically, and then share your observations with the family.

If a child with an identified hearing disability is enrolled in your class, the audiologist or speech therapist can provide guidelines for adapting the program to maximize learning, possibly including some of the suggestions listed here. Before talking to a child with a hearing impairment, make sure that you have the child's attention and wait for eye contact. While talking, always face the child, preferably at eye level, and don't cover your mouth. Whenever appropriate, use body language to augment your words. Also, reduce background noise as much as possible to help the child focus on relevant sounds. Enrich the visual environment of the class by adding as many visual aids as possible; for instance, pictures of the day's routine activities and pictorial labels of classroom materials. If the child is learning sign language, try to learn as many of the signs as possible and help the other children in the class learn some as well (Deiner, 2010).

CHILDREN WITH COMMUNICATION IMPAIRMENTS. Language is a complex process (we will discuss it in more detail in Chapter 12) that depends on a number of interrelated factors. It involves the ability to hear, understand, process information, speak, and articulate sounds so they can be understood by others. Problems in communication can stem from a variety of causes. For instance, a child's language learning might be delayed because of inadequate language stimulation in early life; poor communication could be a symptom of problems with synthesizing information in a meaningful way; or poor articulation might be caused by a malformation in the structure of the mouth. If, as compared with age-mates, a child in your class is particularly difficult to understand, has difficulty understanding what you say, or consistently refuses to talk, there may be a language or speech disability that should be discussed with the family.

© Cengage Learning

Many visual impairments can be corrected or reduced through corrective lenses.

total communication approach
In children with hearing impairments, using a combination of methods such as sign language, speech reading, and hearing aids.

naeyc

Key Point ◆

Children with mild or moderate hearing problems can function well in a regular early childhood program. Children with severe hearing impairments will need considerable special assistance, usually including special equipment.

naeyc

Coordination with the speech therapist can ensure that what is accomplished in therapy is augmented in the early childhood care setting. In addition, a stimulating, consistent, and language-rich environment can encourage the child to use language. Structure activities that will result in success to build the child's sense of confidence. Encourage the child to participate in social activities by encouraging all forms of communication, even if it is nonverbal. When appropriate, create a need for speech; for instance, by "misunderstanding" the child's request made through gestures. Particularly if the child does not talk, maintain relevant commentary. If the child does talk, be a patient listener, giving your undivided attention. Never criticize the child's incorrect speech, or lack of speech, but praise appropriate speech when it occurs.

Communication may also be problematic if a child has little or no command of the English language. However, a child learning English as a second language does not, necessarily, have a language deficit, because the child most likely is fluent in the family's native language. Strategies for helping children become bilingual communicators are discussed in detail in Chapter 12.

CHILDREN WITH EMOTIONAL OR BEHAVIORAL DEFICITS. As an early childhood teacher, you will inevitably be around children whose behavior is out of control at times. Some circumstances or provocations will cause most children to respond in a negative way, such as hitting, using aggressive language, or being destructive. Such occasional behavior is normal and can be dealt with by using suitable guidance techniques. All children need positive guidance to help them gradually develop self-control and acquire appropriate social skills and attitudes toward other people. Because guidance is such an integral part of working with young children, we will devote two chapters to various aspects of guidance, including dealing with problem behaviors (see Chapters 14 and 15).

A small percentage of children have much more severe problems that require intensive therapeutic intervention. One such condition, **autism spectrum disorder,** encompasses several socioemotional conditions that become evident before three years of age and are of unknown origin. Children exhibit a variety of inappropriate behaviors that indicate an inability to read and respond to everyday social cues (Paasche et al., 2004). It is not likely that a severely autistic child would be enrolled in an integrated classroom, but it is highly likely that a child less involved on the autistic spectrum will be in an inclusive class. However, if a child in your class seems particularly distant from or oblivious of others in the class, seems out of touch or disinterested in what is going on, generally reacts with inappropriate emotions or shows no emotion, frequently engages in self-stimulating behaviors, or repeats words rather than responding to them, talk with the family and urge them to seek a professional diagnosis and help (Deiner, 2010).

Some children are emotionally fragile because of life circumstances that put them at risk. Factors such as family and community violence, homelessness, abuse and neglect, and poverty can take a great toll on children's emotional well-being. A consistent, loving, thoughtful environment, provided by the early childhood program, can help give a measure of stability for such children. We will consider how to help children deal with stress in greater detail in Chapter 16.

CHILDREN WITH HEALTH PROBLEMS. A range of chronic health conditions can cause various problems for children. In addition to the physical symptoms of the illness, which are often painful, children with health problems are frequently subjected to scary medical treatment and hospitalizations, may well be excluded from participating in some activities, can be beset by anxiety and

Key Point ◆
The early childhood program can provide a language-rich environment for a child with a communication impairment.

Key Point ◆
Although displaying some behavior problems is normal for young children, some have emotional deficits that require special attention.

autism spectrum disorder
A socioemotional condition of unknown origin in which the child's social, language, and other behaviors are inappropriate and often bizarre.

fears, and are absent from school more than other children. Thus, children with health impairments need special consideration, not only to ensure that their medical needs are met but also to help them cope as effectively as possible with their illnesses.

Children can be beset by many health impairments too numerous to review here, although we will briefly mention one unique group, children who were prenatally exposed to HIV. Children with HIV and AIDS may well be enrolled in early childhood programs, and those who work with them need to understand the characteristics of their illness, how it is transmitted, and precautions that need to be taken, particularly since there are many misconceptions about AIDS. It is important that Universal Precautions, usually spelled out by local or state health codes, are taken.

If a child in your class has been diagnosed as having a chronic health problem, it is important to gather information about the illness. Family members, doctors, and therapists will be the best sources of information because they can give you not only general information about the illness but also information about the child's specific needs. Another source is literature prepared by support or informational organizations related to specific illnesses (for instance, the American Diabetes Association or the Asthma and Allergy Foundation of America). Be particularly aware of preventive measures that need to be taken; for instance, medication or periods of rest. If there is the possibility that the child may suffer an attack, as may happen with asthma or epilepsy, know what steps should be taken. If appropriate, at least one member of the staff should be trained in emergency procedures related to the child's condition.

It is also important to know what information the child has been given about the condition. What you say to the child should agree with what family members or other professionals have told the child. In addition, an open atmosphere allows the child, as well as other children, to discuss fears, concerns, or questions. If a child is frequently absent from school, take steps to ensure that the child continues to feel part of the class. Involve other children in sending get-well messages or telephoning the child (if appropriate), visiting the child at home or in the hospital, and sending school activities that can be done at home (Deiner, 2010).

GIFTED CHILDREN. Recently there has been increasing attention paid to the special needs of another group, those considered **gifted children.** As you read the word *gifted*, you can probably conjure up an image of a child you have come across, one who, in some ways, seemed precocious and talented. Although we often can think of some characteristics of giftedness in specific children, it is much more difficult to define this word because different people have different concepts of its meaning. A broad definition of giftedness would include children whose performance is significantly above average in intellectual and creative areas. At the same time, it is also important to acknowledge that some children have the potential for outstanding performance that may emerge only in a supportive atmosphere.

Children may show a number of traits and abilities that provide clues to their giftedness. They are often precocious in various developmental areas, particularly in language. They may have an unusually large and advanced vocabulary and use it appropriately in conversation on a wide variety of topics; use language in humorous and creative ways by making up elaborate stories, rhymes, and songs; and often begin to read and write earlier than their peers. Giftedness can also be seen in problem-solving ability, as children like to play

---

naeyc

Key Point ◆◆

Children who suffer from chronic illnesses also have special needs.

---

gifted children
Children who perform significantly above average in intellectual and creative areas.

---

naeyc

Key Point ◆◆

Another group with special needs are gifted children, who perform above average in intellectual and creative areas. Such children need a stimulating and challenging environment.

with ideas, come up with unusual solutions, and see more than one view-point. They are generally observant, catch on quickly to new concepts, and have a longer-than-average attention span (Cook et al., 2012; Deiner, 2010). Children displaying such traits usually score significantly above average on intelligence tests, which is one (though certainly not the only) measure of giftedness.

Some children's gift is seen through a special talent in art, music, or another creative area in which they are particularly advanced. One such child, three-year-old Karen, astounded teachers as she drew careful renditions of objects in her environment. On the playground Karen often lay on her stomach on the grass to observe bugs, which she then drew with meticulous detail.

Because gifted children often catch on quickly, they need a wide variety of challenging and rewarding experiences that help them develop positive attitudes about school and learning. At the same time, it is important to keep in mind that gifted young children, although advanced in some areas, are still preschoolers, with the social and emotional needs of those in their age group. Sensitive guidance can help them develop a good sense of self, recognition of individual uniqueness and strengths, and appropriate social interaction skills. The interests of gifted children are similar to those of their age-mates, although they may want to learn more about a topic or delve into it in more depth. Thus, it is important to provide a variety of activities that allow children to enjoy involvement at different levels. At the same time, all of the children will benefit from exposure to novel, diverse, and enriching activities through classroom materials, books, field trips, and class guests.

Some children are considered gifted because of the precocious performance significantly above their age-mates in intellectual or creative areas.

© Cengage Learning

WORKING WITH FAMILIES OF CHILDREN WITH DISABILITIES

Key Point ◆◆

Families of children with disabilities also have some special needs that the early childhood program can help meet.

DIVERSITY

naeyc

All families need support, understanding, and reassurance, something that is particularly true of families with children who have special needs. In addition to dealing with the common multifaceted aspects of parenting, families of young children with disabilities often also experience greater emotional, financial, and physical strains. When a child with a special need is involved in an early childhood program, it is particularly important that open and accepting communication be established between families and teachers.

Effective teachers recognize that a family in which a child with special needs has become a member must make adjustments that could change the family dramatically. They also recognize that each family reacts differently to having a child with disabilities. Responses may well be different, depending on the nature and severity of the child's disability. However, there are numerous other factors that are part of the reaction, factors that can vary considerably, depending on the family's resources and supports. Many variables influence the family's adjustment, including personal characteristics of all family members, stresses associated with having a child with special needs, effective coping skills of the family members, extra demands placed on the family by the child, added expenses of medical treatment, crises associated with the child's disability, fatigue, and many others. Others, including mental health and social service professionals, are often members of a team that can assist the early childhood teacher with working with families of children with disabilities (Gargiulo & Kilgo, 2011; Winter, 2007).

Only relatively recently has the importance of the family in the lives of young children with special needs been legally acknowledged. Both Public Laws 94-142 and 99-457 are very specific in outlining the rights and roles of parents in determining the kinds of educational and therapeutic services their children will receive in programs in which public funding is provided for young children with disabilities. Specifically, these laws outline guidelines for development of an Individualized Education Plan (IEP) for preschoolers and an Individualized Family Service Plan (IFSP) for children under the age of three. Both processes require thorough involvement of families and teachers.

In addition to such legally mandated involvement of families of children with disabilities, families should be included and supported in many other ways. Exchange of relevant information between teachers and families will help both to better understand and work with the child. The school's philosophy of focusing on commonalities rather than on differences among children should also provide support for families. Sometimes families of children with special needs are so centered on the disability that they do not have a clear perspective on the other aspects of the child's development; families can be helped to see just how similar their child is to other children. By recognizing the unique strengths and needs of each family, teachers can be the best possible resource by listening sensitively and openly, offering practical recommendations and support, and helping to maximize each child's potential (Winter, 2007).

SUMMARY

1. Young children are alike in three common areas:
   A. "Profiles" that identify typical traits shared by the majority of children of different ages
   B. The need of all children for positive self-esteem
   C. The need of all children for play as a way of learning about the world
2. Factors that contribute to the wonderful diversity among children include inborn traits and external factors.
3. Some children have specific, special needs that make them unique. The early childhood program can help meet the needs of special children by doing the following:
   A. Ensuring the inclusion of children with and without disabilities into the same program
   B. Recognizing characteristics of children with motor, cognitive, learning, visual, hearing, communication, emotional, and health problems, as well as gifted children

KEY TERMS LIST

at-risk children

attention deficit disorder (ADD)

attention deficit–hyperactivity disorder (ADHD)

autism spectrum disorder

deficit (or impairment)

developmental delay

Down syndrome

fetal alcohol effect (FAE)

fetal alcohol syndrome (FAS)

fragile X syndrome

gifted children

Individualized Education Plan (IEP)

Individualized Family Service Plan (IFSP)

least restrictive environment

myelin

myelination

neurons

perceived competence

personal control

rough-and-tumble play

self-concept

self-esteem

temperament

total communication approach

KEY QUESTIONS

1. Observe several children of the same age. These might be children you work with and know well or children that you are observing for the first time. What traits do they share? How are they similar? Can you draw some conclusions about children of that particular age?

2. As you observe children, identify a child who appears to be self-confident. How does the child express this confidence? Do you see a difference between this child and another who seems less assured?

3. Observe a group of young children at play. Look for examples of the various types of play discussed in this chapter. Do you see a relationship between age and type of play?

4. Think about the same children you observed earlier for Key Question 1 and describe what makes each of them unique. How do they differ? Do you have any indications about what factors underlie these unique characteristics?

5. If you are able, observe an early childhood program in which a child with special needs is integrated. Observe and talk to one of the teachers. What special accommodations have been made for this child? How does the child interact with the other children in the class? How is the child's independence encouraged? Does the child participate in a few, some, or all activities?

ADDITIONAL RESOURCES

Select additional books, articles, and websites on topics discussed in Chapter 2.

Allen, K. E., & Marotz, L. (2010). *Developmental profiles: Pre-birth through age eight* (5th ed.). Clifton Park, NY: Thomson Delmar Learning.

Deiner, P. L. (2010). *Inclusive early childhood education: Development, resources, and practice* (5th ed.). Belmont, CA: Wadsworth, Cengage Learning.

Shore, R. (1997). *Rethinking the brain: New insights into early development*. New York: Families and Work Institute.

HELPFUL WEBSITES

American Academy of Pediatrics:

www.aap.org

The American Academy of Pediatrics' website provides information about issues related to children's health. The Academy is committed to attainment of optimal physical, mental, and social well-being of all children.

Council for Exceptional Children, Division for Early Childhood (DEC):

www.dec-sped.org

This is the official website of the Division for Early Childhood of the Council for Exceptional Children. DEC promotes policies and advances evidence-based practices that support families and enhance optimal development in young children with disabilities or young children who are at risk for developmental delays.

Zero to Three/National Center for Infants, Toddlers, and Families:

www.zerotothree.org

Zero to Three's website advertises itself as the nation's leading resource on the first years of life. It includes a wealth of information for parents and professionals about the growth and development of infants and toddlers.

Go to **CengageBrain.com** to register your access code for this book's Education CourseMate website, where you will find more resources to help you study. Additional resources for this chapter include TeachSource Videos, glossary flashcards, web links, case studies with critical-thinking questions that apply the concepts presented in this chapter, and more. If your textbook does not include a printed access card, you can go to **CengageBrain.com** to purchase access.

The Families

3

In Chapter 3, you will find answers to the following questions about families:

◗ Why is it important to understand family functioning through a theoretical perspective?
◗ What important changes have occurred in American families in recent years?
◗ What needs of families can the early childhood program help to meet?
◗ In what ways can you, as a teacher of young children, include and involve families in your program?
◗ How can you form partnerships with families by involving them in your program?

DAP Developmentally appropriate practices derive from deep knowledge of child development principles and of the program's children in particular, as well as the context within which each of them is living. The younger the child, the more necessary it is for practitioners to acquire this particular knowledge through relationships with children's families.

Developmentally Appropriate Practice, Copple & Bredekamp, 2009, p. 22

NAEYC STANDARDS CONSIDERED IN CHAPTER 3

(See the Standards Correlation Chart on the inside front cover of this book for the titles and description of the standards listed below.)
◗ *Standard 2a:* Knowing families through an understanding of family theory (pp. 56–57, 60).
◗ *Standard 2a:* Understanding characteristics of the changing American family and its needs (pp. 57–63).
◗ *Standard 2b:* Through a variety of strategies, supporting and engaging diverse families through mutually respectful relationships (pp. 58–59).
◗ *Standard 2b:* Understanding and appropriately using a variety of methods of communication with families (pp. 63–71).
◗ *Standard 6e:* Understanding and promoting family empowerment (pp. 60, 62).
◗ *Standard 2c:* Engaging and involving families in their children's learning and education (pp. 71–73).

As we discussed in Chapter 2, children are central in early childhood education. Families have to be considered equally important, however, in part because children are integral members of their family systems, and family values and culture are an inseparable part of children. Families are also at the core of early childhood education because the early childhood staff shares with families the responsibility for socializing young children. It is important to provide for children a sense of continuity between home and school experiences, which can best be ensured through a carefully fostered partnership between the family and the early childhood program (Powell, 1998; Powell & O'Leary, 2009). That effort will be the focus of this chapter.

A THEORETICAL PERSPECTIVE

ecological systems theory
A view of the family as an ever-developing and changing social unit in which members constantly accommodate and adapt to each other's demands as well as to outside demands.

Key Point ◆◆

Ecological systems theory views the family as a dynamic, constantly changing system that interacts with other systems, for instance, those within the community.

microsystem
According to family systems theory, that part of the environment that most immediately affects a person, such as the family, school, or workplace.

mesosystem
According to family systems, the linkages between the family and the immediate neighborhood and community.

Throughout this book, we will review a variety of theories to help you understand more clearly the many aspects of children's development and behavior. It is equally important to understand family functioning from a theoretical perspective. **Ecological systems theory** provides a useful approach to understanding the family as an ever-developing and changing social unit in which members constantly have to accommodate and adapt to each other's demands as well as to demands from outside the family. This theory provides a dynamic, rather than static, view of how families function.

From the perspective of ecological systems theory, the influence that family members have on each other is not one-way but rather is interactive and reciprocal. Furthermore, it is impossible to understand the family by gaining an understanding of its individual members because there is more to the family than the "sum of its parts." It is necessary to view its interaction patterns and the unspoken rules that govern the members' behaviors. Healthy families work well together, communicate often, are able to make effective decisions, and can handle change. In addition, understanding the family means looking at its functioning within the larger context; for instance, the extended family, the community, and the neighborhood. The early childhood center becomes part of that larger context in which families function (Bronfenbrenner & Morris, 1998). Figure 3-1 shows a graphic depiction of the ecological systems.

Each individual's development occurs in a broader ecological context, within different but overlapping systems. The **microsystem** is the most immediate system that affects the individual; it includes the family, classroom, or workplace. These components of the microsystem are linked together in the **mesosystem** through

Figure **3-1**

The Ecological Systems Model

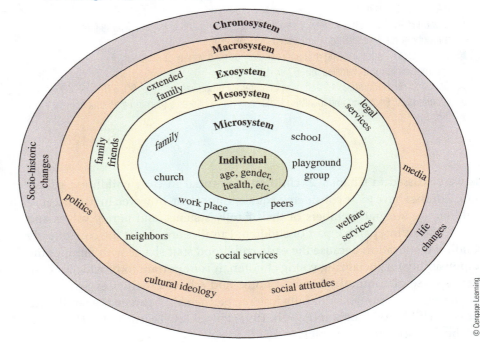

© Cengage Learning

such relationships as family–teacher interaction or employment practices that affect the family (for instance, employer-supported child care or paid maternity leave).

The **exosystem** includes broader components of the neighborhood and community that affect the functioning of the family; for example, governmental agencies or mass media. Finally, the broadest system to affect families is the **macrosystem,** which includes cultural, political, and economic forces. Surrounding all of these systems is the **chronosystem,** which takes into account changes that occur with time, both in terms of changes in the individual and in the historic and cultural context (Bronfenbrenner, 1994; Bronfenbrenner & Crouter, 1983). From such an ecological perspective, the child and family are seen more clearly as part of and affected by many other systems, each of which influences their development and functioning. According to DAP, teachers gain in-depth knowledge about children from their families to "learn about their home and community environment, including its cultural dimensions. This context is critical in making classroom decisions that are appropriate for each child" (Copple & Bredekamp, 2009, p. 45).

Viewing children and families as parts of various systems helps us to avoid seeking simple explanations and to acknowledge the complex interactions that often underlie children's and families' behaviors. We must take time to look at the many factors affecting behavior before jumping to conclusions. It is also important to recognize that families and schools interact to affect children's development in myriad possible directions (Powell & O'Leary, 2009). This perspective makes good communication between home and school an imperative, not a choice. Finally, a systems approach helps us see the interrelatedness of all aspects of children's lives. We cannot assume that the child's home exists in one isolated "compartment," while the school is in another. In the same way, we cannot presume that families' lives can be segmented into isolated facets.

exosystem
According to family systems theory, that part of the environment that includes the broader components of the community that affect the functioning of the family, such as governmental agencies or mass media.

macrosystem
According to family systems theory, the broadest part of the environment, which includes the cultural, political, and economic forces that affect families.

chronosystem
According to family systems theory, this system takes into account the passage of time, both as the individual gets older and in terms of historic changes.

THE CHANGING AMERICAN FAMILY

The family is, and always has been, the most important element in most children's lives. Within the family, children experience the emotional and physical care and sustenance vital to their well-being. But *the family* has no simple definition or boundaries. Whereas several decades ago many young children might have been part of a "traditional" family—working father, homemaker mother, and two or three children—today's youngsters live in any of a wide variety of family configurations. Powell and O'Leary (2009) summarize this change, and its implications for early childhood educators, as follows:

> Sweeping changes in the United States have shaped current ideas about relationships between families and early childhood programs. The growing ethnic, racial, and cultural diversity of the population increases the chances that children will be cared for by adults whose expectations and practices differ from those of the child's family members. Further, profound demographic and economic changes have led to concerns about the adequacy of support systems for families. (p. 61)

In two-earner families, parents often share child care responsibilities.

DIVERSITY

Key Point ◆◆

There is no simple or single definition of the family because families come in many forms.

Family Forms

A family may be made up of one parent and one child or it may be part of an extended family of grandparents, uncles, aunts, cousins, and many other relatives who are in frequent, close contact. Families may have one, two, or more parents; these may be the biological parents, stepparents, adoptive parents, or emotionally rather than legally related caregivers. A single parent may never have been married or may be divorced, separated, or widowed; as part of this group, a sizeable number of young children live with single fathers (U.S. Bureau of the Census, 2011a).

If a family has undergone a divorce, children may live with the same single or remarried parent all of the time, may alternate between two parents who have joint custody, or may live with one parent and see the other for brief times during weekends or holidays. For some children, grandparents or other relatives take on the function of parents. Some divorced parents find alternate living arrangements, perhaps moving back with their own parents, sharing housing with another adult or single parent, or joining in a group housing arrangement. Because of divorce and remarriage, today's children may also acquire various natural and adoptive brothers and sisters, as well as half-siblings, step-siblings, or unrelated "siblings" in less formal family arrangements.

Whatever the family form, a wide range of people can make up a network of significant family members, as defined by emotional as well as legal ties. It is necessary, as a teacher of young children, that you also consider and acknowledge these persons as part of a child's family. Anyone who is important in the child's mind should be considered to be important by you as well.

It is also important to be aware of legal restrictions that might affect children's relationships with adults in their lives. During some divorce proceedings, one parent may file a restraining order against the other, legally limiting or forbidding contact with the child. Although such situations are usually upsetting, it is necessary to be aware of and make appropriate provisions for complying with any legal action.

Key Point ◆◆

Families also differ based on economic, racial, cultural, ethnic, religious, language, and geographic factors.

Other Family Variations

Not only is there great variation in family form and composition, but other characteristics differentiate families as well. Some of these include racial, cultural, ethnic, language, economic, religious, and geographic factors and the sexual orientation of the parents. Such elements affect family customs and traditions and also reflect deeper meanings; for instance, defining values and relationships (Powell & O'Leary, 2009). In some cases, a family's uniqueness includes a mixture of cultures, religions, races, or generations.

Key Point ◆◆

The ethnic makeup of the population of the United States continues to change, with increasing numbers of Hispanic and decreasing numbers of white individuals.

DIVERSITY

INCREASE IN ETHNIC AND CULTURAL DIVERSITY. The ethnic and cultural diversity within the United States continues to change with changing immigration patterns. The proportion of the population that is white, but not Hispanic has been steadily decreasing over the past several decades and is now at 63:7 percent of the total, according to the 2010 U.S. Census (U.S. Bureau of the Census, 2011c). The Hispanic population continues to grow, with Hispanics comprising 16.3 percent of the total population. In addition, nearly 20 percent of the population speak a language other than English at home (U.S. Bureau of the Census, 2011c). Depending on where you live, there are some generalizations that can be made about minority populations. More than 40 percent of the Hispanic population lives in the West, while African Americans contribute the largest share of diversity in the Northeast, the Midwest, and the South. Native American and Asian American populations also are found predominantly in the West. Several states' populations are now more than half made up of minorities (Hobbs & Stoops, 2002). Given this picture, it is highly likely that you will have children and families of a different ethnic, cultural, and language background than your own in your early childhood program. Effective communication is especially important to help both families and teachers achieve mutual understanding and appreciation, which, in turn, will help provide a consistent and positive experience for the children (Powell & O'Leary, 2009).

You can learn about characteristics of various cultural, racial, or religious groups by reading, but it is very important to avoid making large-scale generalizations about a family based on group traits. Families are complex, and only through genuine interest can a teacher get to know them well. Effective and frequent communication helps the teacher become aware of family attributes that can affect the child and family as participants in the early childhood program. (Note that in Chapter 13 we will discuss some guidelines for promoting understanding of cultural and ethnic variations in children and families; in Chapter 12 we will consider some issues in working with children and families who are bilingual or do not speak English at all.)

Families vary widely, something to which the early childhood teacher must be sensitive. Differences in culture, ethnicity, race, religion, language, and family composition are contributing factors. How can you, as the teacher of a diverse group of children, get to know the families and their values?

naeyc

Key Point ◆

Nearly one-fifth of children in America grow up in poverty.

FAMILIES IN POVERTY. Many children living in the United States grow up in poverty. The estimated 19 percent of American children living in poverty includes 34.7 percent of the African American, 30.6 percent of the Hispanic, 31 percent of the Native American, 14.6 percent of the Asian and Pacific Islander, and 15.8 percent of the white children in the country (U.S. Bureau of the Census, 2011b). This means that nearly one-fifth of American children live in families that suffer such severe financial strain that they cannot meet their basic needs. Technically, this figure includes only children who live in families that are considered to be at or below the poverty line. However, a study from the Economic Policy Institute shows that today's families need more than twice that amount to meet basic living expenses. Using this criterion, the number of American children living in poverty jumps to 41 percent (Cottrell, 2010). Furthermore, the poverty rate for children under five years of age is even higher than for older children, at 20.8 percent (Children's Defense Fund, 2008).

Historically, many early childhood education efforts have been aimed at helping economically disadvantaged families, with Head Start and Early Head Start as the most extensive of such antipoverty endeavors. While such programs initially focused almost exclusively on the children, they also emphasize providing strong support to families. This includes information and education, concrete assistance (for instance, providing transportation), and emotional support. Careful research has shown that high-quality early childhood programs, particularly those in which family support has been included, have a dramatic effect, not only in terms of children's later school achievement, but also on their families (Chafel, 1990; Seitz, Rosenbaum, & Apfel, 1985; Zigler & Freedman, 1987).

GAY AND LESBIAN FAMILIES. Another aspect of diversity, for which there is perhaps less recognition than there is for ethnic or cultural diversity, has to do with the sexual orientation of the parents. Early childhood programs often include children whose parents are gay or lesbian partners. In 1990, an estimated 6 million to 14 million children had gay, lesbian, bisexual, or transgender parents (Gates, Badgett, Macomber, & Chambers, 2007), and many young children know that some of their family members or friends are homosexual (Rowell, 2007). Elizabeth Rowell suggests reading children's books that depict families that are gay and lesbian to enhance the curriculum. "Young children from same-sex parent families can recognize themselves, and all are encouraged to talk about the commonalities of happy family lives" (p. 25).

THE NEEDS OF FAMILIES

The fact that a child is enrolled in an early childhood program indicates that the family has a need that the program is able to meet. The most common, and certainly the most obvious, family need is provision of child care while the parents are at work. The proliferation of child care centers and family child care homes in recent decades has been in response to the dramatic increase in the number of working, single-parent, and two-earner-parent families.

But beyond the overall need for responsible and knowledgeable adults to provide care for children while their parents work, families have other needs that the early childhood center can help meet. Some of these have to do with helping the parents, as individuals, meet the demands of their multiple roles. Others revolve around coordination of home and school routines and practices. Keep in mind, however, that although it is an ideal to consider that early childhood teachers can meet everyone's needs—those of children, families, and co-workers—sometimes this is just not possible in actuality. Setting realistic goals within the particular work setting can help establish priorities. There are other community services that may provide for other needs.

Parenthood

We typically view parenthood from the perspective of children's development and how parents facilitate, support, and promote it. Rarely is parenthood seen from the viewpoint of parents and their needs. Erik Erikson (1963), whose theory of human development was one of the first to span adulthood as well as childhood, considers that the most important need of the mature adult in the stage of **generativity** is to care for and nurture others. The tasks of this stage most often are carried out in parenthood, through which the adult is concerned with meeting the needs of the next generation. Implied in this process is growth of the adult as an individual that is separate from the nurturance extended to children. This acknowledgment of adulthood as a period of continued development has also been advanced by other writers (for instance, Gould, 1978; Levinson, 1978; Sheehy, 1976).

Empowerment

When families feel confident and competent in their parenting abilities as well as in their roles as members of the larger community, their children benefit. Unfortunately, some families feel that they are powerless in controlling what happens to them and to their children. An important role that early childhood programs

DIVERSITY

Key Point ◆◆

Early childhood programs also include children whose parents are gay and lesbian.

Key Point ◆◆

One of the most important needs of working parents is for high-quality, reliable care for their young children.

Key Point ◆◆

Many parents are part of Erikson's stage of generativity, in which care and nurture of children is important.

generativity
According to Erik Erikson, the stage of human development in which the mature adult focuses on the care and nurture of the young.

naeyc

THE HIGH PRICE OF CHILD CARE

As you work with families of young children, you will find that for many families in America, the cost of child care is extremely high. Based on data from a government report (Lino, 2008), a report from the National Association of Child Care Research and Referral Agencies, *Parents and the High Price of Child Care: 2008 Update* (NACCRRA, 2008b), reveals some disturbing trends. The report provides details about fees for infant, preschool, and after-school care, including in-center and family child care settings, in all states. It also examines this information in relation to dual-earner and single-parent families. The report ends with recommendations for possible ways to help make high-quality child care more affordable for working families.

Child care is expensive, especially for single-parent families. Infant care costs more than care for preschoolers since the ratio in programs that care for infants must allow for fewer children per caregiver; thus caregiver wages raise the cost of care. The report also found that before- and after-school care, although it is part-time, is just as expensive as child care for preschoolers; as a result, families continue to pay a high price for child care, even after their children enter elementary school. In addition, the report shows some significant increases in child care costs, especially for infant care. The survey also found that the price of child care in a center is going up more than twice as fast as the rate of inflation (NACCRRA , 2008b, p. 6).

The cost of child care is especially difficult to assume for single-parent families. When the average cost for child care is compared to average salaries of singe parents, the proportion that is potentially spent on care for children is very high. If a single parent had two children—for instance, an infant and a four-year-old—the cost of child care becomes unaffordable. Depending on the state, the average price of child care for two children could range from 48 to 102 percent of the median income for single parents. In almost every state, the price for two children comes to more than half of single parents' median household income.

The proportion that families pay for child care in relation to all of their household expenses is also telling. In every region of the country, families spend, on average, more on infant care than they do on food. Monthly child care fees for two children are higher than median rent costs and almost as high as, or in some areas, higher than, monthly mortgage payments. In the great majority of states, the average cost of infant care is higher than tuition at a four-year public college.

Some families turn to family child care, which generally costs less, but the quality of such care is unknown. Many states, the report points out, do not license or monitor family child care providers who care for six or fewer children. In these states, child care homes are not required "to meet health and safety standards, background checks and training requirements" (NACCRRA, 2008b, p. 7).

"As challenging as it is to afford child care, paying for high-quality care (child care accredited by a national organization) is even more difficult" (NACCRRA, 2008b, p. 13). The cost of care in accredited centers can be as much as 30 percent higher than costs in nonaccredited programs. The main reason for this is the lower child-to-staff ratio that is required. Only about 9 percent of centers in the United States are accredited by a professional organization; thus, quality child care is not always easy for families to find.

Affordable, high-quality child care is not readily available in the United States, so many families have to compromise on the care they can afford for their children. The report ends with specific recommendations for increased state and federal investment in child care as well as in measures that would remove barriers and help families find care that is both high quality and more affordable.

Viewing parents and teachers as equals, each contributing relevant information and expertise, helps empower parents.

empowerment
Helping families gain a sense of control over events in their lives.

Key Point ◆◆

A goal of some early childhood programs is to promote empowerment of the families, to help them achieve a sense of control over their lives.

naeyc

Key Point ◆◆

Coordinating the needs of families with the needs of children and the program can be a challenge for early childhood teachers.

can serve for families is to promote **empowerment,** a sense of control or power over events in their lives. This is particularly important as families deal with a variety of agencies and professionals; for instance, school, welfare, and political systems. Professionals can use a wide variety of techniques to help families attain this sense of control, including approaches described in a number of excellent publications, such as Alice Honig's classic *Parent Involvement in Early Childhood Education* (1979).

One of the forces behind the concept of empowerment has been the move toward viewing parents and teachers as equals. Not too many years ago, the pervasive attitude was that professionals were experts, and parents were the passive recipients of their expertise (Powell, 1998). Such a view does not provide parents with the security that they know their child best and that they should be full participants in any decisions that affect the child. Families need to be treated with respect, their opinions should be solicited and taken seriously, and they must be integrally engaged in decisions about the child. In addition, when early childhood professionals give families child development information, they have tools with which to make informed decisions about their children's needs. Thus, involving, consulting with, and providing relevant education for families can have a far-reaching impact by helping them recognize their own importance and competence.

Coordinating Family Needs and the Program

Helping parents reach their potential as effective adults may be a goal in some programs that work extensively with families, particularly those who have limited incomes. In all early childhood programs, there are additional points of contact between families and teachers, at times revolving around seemingly mundane matters, but nonetheless important. A flexible, good-humored attitude can help establish and maintain positive home–school relationships.

Family members' busy lives, or unforeseen events, are sometimes at odds with the schedule and routine of the early childhood center. For instance, one mother expressed concern that the center's afternoon snack, provided at 3:30, was served too late and that the child was not interested in dinner at 5:30. Another parent preferred that her child not take a nap at school, because when he slept during the day, he was just not ready to sleep at home until quite late in the evening. Other problems may keep a parent from arriving until after the center has closed; for instance, car trouble, a traffic jam, or unexpected overtime at work.

All of these situations can cause conflict but also provide an opportunity to evaluate what is best for the child, the family, the other children, and the teachers. Sometimes such predicaments can be resolved fairly easily, but there are times when the needs of the child, the family, or the school directly conflict. There is no simple answer, for instance, to weighing whether a child should take a nap, particularly when he appears to need it, or not take a nap because a delayed evening bedtime keeps his mother from getting the sleep she needs.

Teachers must carefully weigh their own professional judgment of what is best for the child and take into account the child's need for sleep, the potential effect of being sleepy and cranky on the ability to function well at school, and the fact that the child would be treated differently from the other children by not napping (Ethics Commission, 1987). One way of resolving such conflicts—whether it is a matter of discussing naps, snacks, or pick-up time—is communication, our next topic.

COMMUNICATING WITH FAMILIES

Effective, positive communication with families is vital to providing a consistent and congruent experience for young children, but there is no simple formula for ensuring that such contact does indeed take place. Each family is unique and brings to the early childhood program distinctive strengths and needs. Just as the teacher deals with each child as a unique individual by using a variety of teaching and guidance methods, so must a flexible approach be maintained in communicating with families to meet their individual requirements.

There are many bits of information that need to be shared by teachers and the family. For instance, both sides will benefit from discussing the child. In addition, there is often more general information about various aspects of the program that must be shared with families. The type of information to be conveyed often determines the communication method used. Communication, as we will discuss, can be carried out using both individual and group methods. Most early childhood centers use a combination of these approaches.

Individual Methods of Communicating with Families

The best way to get to know each family is through individual interaction and contact. Informally, such contact can take place daily; for instance, when children are dropped off and picked up from school. More formally, scheduled conferences between the teacher and parents or other family members provide an avenue for the exchange of information.

INFORMAL CONTACT WITH FAMILIES. At the beginning and end of each day, at least one teacher should be available to exchange a few words with family members who drop off or pick up their children. Such informal interactions can make teachers more sensitive to the needs of children and families, can establish a mutual trust, can convey a feeling of caring and interest to parents, and can heighten family engagement and engagement in the program. Daily informal contact between teachers and parents is important for another reason when very young children are involved. "During the time the parent is away, the infant is busily going about the business of growing up. Each new achievement . . . should be shared with parents" (Wilson, 1999, p. 90). In addition to being given information about the child's achievements and activities, parents of infants also must be kept informed about their children's routine activities, such as eating, sleeping, and toileting. A form that caregivers fill out throughout each day can help parents see at a glance what the child's day was like.

Because frequent school–family contacts are important, it makes sense to structure the schedule so that staff are free to participate in such exchanges.

▶❚❚ **TeachSource Video Activity**
WATCH•REFLECT•RESPOND

This video provides an overview of the importance of good communication with families. Go to CengageBrain.com and view the video entitled, "Communicating with Families: Best Practice in Early Childhood Settings," and answer the following questions:

1. What are three strategies that you saw in the video that are discussed in Chapter 3?

2. How does the teacher engage and form partnerships with parents?

Key Point ◆◆
Effective home–school communication is important to families, teachers, and children.

Key Point ◆◆
Families and teachers often use the beginning and end of the day as a time for brief, informal communication.

Informal dialogues at the start and end of the day tend to be the most pervasive form of family engagement in early childhood programs (Gestwicki, 2010), especially those primarily involving working parents. In programs for which children arrive by bus or come in car pools, the teacher needs to make an extra effort to maintain contact with families, for instance, through notes or telephone calls (Gestwicki, 2010).

Another informal means of contact with families is through occasional telephone calls. These provide a comfortable way of talking to families, particularly if the calls are made often enough so they do not signal "a problem." Some schools send home "happy notes," brief, personalized notes that share with the family something positive that happened during the day, or use journals that are sent back and forth between home and school with notes from both family and teachers. Some teachers and families use e-mail as a way of touching base. E-mail, however, may not be private; therefore, sensitive information should not be shared in this way (Couchenor & Chrisman, 2011). The Internet provides some other creative means of communication. Some teachers create web pages to post and share information with parents. Others download digital photographs each week and post them on a classroom website that families can easily access.

Olson (2007) offers some fundamental ways in which teachers can create positive relationships with families. She suggests being available to answer parents' questions and letting parents lead the conversation when they have something important to share. She also advises, "be yourself," but stay within personal boundaries while sharing with parents. Another principle is to be trustworthy and keep strictly confidential the information shared by family members. Finally, she advises, "Remember that the relationship is in service of the child's—not your—needs" (Olson, 2007, p. 28).

FORMAL CONTACT WITH FAMILIES. Informal daily contacts between teachers and family members can create a mutually respectful and nonintimidating atmosphere. When teachers and families feel comfortable with each other, communication will more likely be honest. In addition to such day-to-day encounters, more formal opportunities should be structured, when a sizable block of uninterrupted time is set aside for in-depth discussion. Such formal contacts can take the form of a **family–teacher conference** or a home visit.

Such a conference is a regularly scheduled meeting that can satisfy different objectives. It can focus on getting acquainted; sharing information about the child and presenting a "progress report"; or, at the initiation of either teacher or family, solving problems or discussing specific issues. Conferences often have negative connotations for the participants, who may view them as a time to share complaints and problems, even as a "last resort" when all else fails. Nonetheless, routinely scheduled conferences should be positive, affirming, and supportive. Focus on children's natural strengths and characteristics that make them unique (Kersey & Masterson, 2009).

A conference should never be an impromptu event. The teacher needs to be well prepared ahead of time, reviewing relevant information and thinking about how best to present it. In fact, preparing for conferences should be an ongoing process, beginning when the child first enters the program. It is helpful if the teacher is ready with some anecdotes to support what the family is told as well as to convey to them that the teacher knows the child well. It is also important to think through what questions to ask of the family to help the teacher better understand and work with the child.

family–teacher conference
A one-on-one interaction between the child's family and the teacher.

Key Point ◆

More formal family–teacher communication takes place through family conferences and home visits. Both should be planned to facilitate a positive exchange of information.

Regularly scheduled conferences, where teachers and families share information and insights, should be positive and affirming.

© Cengage Learning

At the same time, the teacher should facilitate a relaxed and easy forum for conversation. Sometimes sharing something with the family—for instance, a picture painted by the child or a favorite recipe for play dough—contributes toward creating a positive atmosphere.

Another type of formal individual contact between teachers and family is a **home visit.** Home visits share some of the same objectives and procedures as family–teacher conferences, but they contribute some added benefits as well. A teacher who visits a family at home conveys a sense of caring and interest in the child's world beyond the classroom. Children are usually delighted to introduce their room, toys, pets, and siblings to the teacher and are made to feel very special that the teacher is visiting them at home. Parents can observe firsthand the interaction between the child and the teacher and may become more relaxed with the teacher who has shown this special interest. In addition, teachers can observe firsthand the family's home environment and family–child interactions as a way of better understanding the child's behavior. In some instances, especially once a sense of trust has been established, home visits can become an extremely important source of support; for instance, for teen-aged parents.

Although there are very important benefits in conducting home visits, they are also quite time consuming and may (though certainly not inevitably) intimidate the family. A teacher's commitment to learning as much as possible about the children in the class and their families has to be weighed against the investment of time involved in home visits and the parents' potential anxiety (Gestwicki, 2010).

home visit
A one-on-one interaction between the teacher and the child's family that takes place in the child's home.

WHEN PROBLEMS DEVELOP BETWEEN FAMILIES AND TEACHERS.

Ideally, the family and the teachers cooperate fully to provide congruent, positive experiences for children at home and at school. Unfortunately, there are times when this ideal is not always realized. In fact, family–teacher disharmony is quite common (Galinsky, 1990). Families and teachers may disagree, particularly when they feel rushed and tired or when they are preoccupied with other aspects of their lives. In addition, both may harbor some unacknowledged negative feelings; for instance, disapproval of working mothers, jealousy or competition for the child's affection, or criticism of the other's child guidance approach (Galinsky, 1988, 1990). Although the child is the common

Parents and teachers may, at times, disagree. Communication to help each see the others' point of view can help ease tensions.

bond between family and teachers, there are many other factors that affect their moods and impinge on their interactions. The job stress experienced by the family as well as by teachers can certainly spill over into the brief contact between them as children are dropped off or picked up at school during what Ellen Galinsky calls the "arsenic hour" (1988).

Galinsky (1988) offers some concrete suggestions for working more effectively with parents. She suggests that when teachers become upset with parents, it is often because teachers' underlying expectations are somehow not realized; teachers need to examine whether what they expect is realistic. Similarly, teachers should scrutinize their attitudes toward the parents, looking for hidden resentments or prejudices. Teachers also need to make an effort to see the situations from the parents' point of view, asking themselves how they might feel if they were in the parents' shoes.

It can be very helpful to teachers to develop a support system, whether within their own program or even outside of it, that allows them to express and explore their feelings in an accepting and safe atmosphere. Teachers must also recognize and convey to parents the limits of their role. This includes being familiar with community resources to which parents can be referred when a problem is beyond the scope of the teacher's role and expertise.

There is no simple formula for effective family–teacher communication. The family–teacher relationship is founded on trust and respect that grow out of many small but significant daily contacts. Greeting family members by name; sharing brief, positive anecdotes about their children; writing personalized notes; making phone calls to the family the teacher does not see often; and being sensitive to families' needs all contribute to a good relationship.

Group Methods of Communicating with Families

In addition to personalized, individual contact between families and teachers, early childhood programs generally also use other communication methods for getting information to the families as a group. These methods can serve a functional purpose; for instance, to let families know that the school will be closed the day after Thanksgiving. They may also take on an educational role; for example, to give families insight into an aspect of child development. We will review three such methods—written communiqués, bulletin boards, and meetings.

WRITTEN COMMUNIQUÉS. Newsletters, memos, e-mails, or other written material can be an effective way of getting information to all families. It is, of course, important to match written information to the reading abilities of the families. If many or all of the families in the program are non–English-speaking, for instance, communiqués should be written in the families' primary language.

It is also important that all such materials be neat, attractive, and accurately written. A sloppy, misspelled, and ungrammatical letter conveys that the message

Key Point ◆

There are some strategies that can help when problems arise between families and teachers.

Key Point ◆

Effective methods of communicating with groups of families include newsletters, memos, bulletin boards, and group meetings.

WORKING WITH PARENTS

As the Family Coordinator in my agency, when I talk with someone about how much they enjoy working with children, I always ask them, "Yes, but how do you like working with the parents?" Many people find this more difficult, but I find it absolutely necessary. I think that you cannot truly understand a child and gain a child's trust unless you are able to gain the trust and understanding of that child's family. Even if children are in our care for many hours, they always return to their family, which is where much of learning and development happen. When we are able to work with families and support them in their goals then we can make a huge impact on the lives of the children.

Many families are not connected to their community. They are so busy with work and parenting that they do not have time to participate in their child's education or extracurricular activities. Many families do not know their neighbors, they do not have many friends outside of work, and their extended family may be far away or very busy as well. In order to be able to get parents to participate in program activities, we must be able to connect and build relationships with them so they feel like they are an important part of the program. There are many ways to build this rapport with parents, but

© Theresa Danna Douglas

Jamie, Head Start Family Partnership Coordinator

one way is to talk with parents about their goals. We use the Family Development Matrix to help families learn about their strengths and needs and we then talk with them about what their goals are. Any goal that the parent chooses to work on opens the door for a conversation about what is important for that family and how you can partner with them.

One young mother that I worked with, in talking about her goals, said how much she missed reading for herself. She also did not have any health care for herself and was worried about some health needs that she had and could not address. As we were talking, she also mentioned that she was not involved in any extracurricular activities and had felt isolated since she had become a parent. We talked about all these concerns and wrote up a few

goals to help her get started. One goal that she came up with was to get some audio books and listen to them while she walked in the morning. I provided her with some resources for health care options and encouraged her to come to some of the parent activities. When she arrived at the following month's parent meeting, I was surprised and thrilled. She had a huge smile on her face when she told me that she had been able to get some health care and had seen a doctor regarding her health concerns. She felt great because she was walking more and really enjoyed listening to the books on tape. She admitted to being somewhat nervous about attending the meeting but later stated that she enjoyed herself. She was able to express some pride in herself for the steps she had taken and had gained the confidence to try some new skills. She participates in the program in other ways now and says that she is feeling more connected and willing to volunteer. The more successful this mother can be in accomplishing her goals, the more confident she will be in taking other steps to improve her situation and grow as an advocate for her child. The better we are at reaching out and creating welcoming environments for parents, the more parents will be comfortable in letting us in.

is probably not very important and that the teacher does not care enough about the families to produce a thoughtful document. Today, many schools have access to computers with newsletter design templates or software, which makes it simpler than ever to compose attractively arranged newsletters, check the grammar and spelling, and incorporate graphics.

Many programs produce a regular newsletter that may contain announcements, news of what the teachers have planned for the upcoming time period, new policies, relevant community information, child development research summaries, columns by local experts, and other information of interest to families. A newsletter is only effective if it is read. Thus, its length, the information included, and the writing style need to be carefully considered.

Another form of written communication that can convey a great deal of information to families is a school handbook, which families are given when they enroll their children in the early childhood program. Such a handbook should contain relevant information about school policies and procedures, fees, hours of operation, holidays, sick-child care, birthday routines, and other important matters. At the same time, it should include a clearly articulated statement of the school's philosophy.

BULLETIN BOARDS. Bulletin boards can be a useful means of conveying information, or they can be a cluttered mass of overlaid memos that no one bothers to look at. To be effective, a bulletin board should be attractively laid out, its contents need to be current, and posted items should not compete with each other for attention. Furthermore, if family members know that only current and important items will be posted on a specific bulletin board, they are more likely to pay attention to it.

Bulletin boards can be used for a variety of purposes. They can be informative; for instance, letting families know that the children will be taking a field trip the following week or that a child in the group has chicken pox. Many centers include a notice of the day's activities on a bulletin board, which lets families know the highlights of their child's day. Bulletin boards can also be educational, conveying relevant information in a way that appeals to those who look at it.

At one center, for instance, the teachers wanted to follow up on comments from several parents that their children were just scribbling rather than drawing something recognizable. The teachers wanted to help families understand that children's art follows a developmental pattern. They matted selections of the children's pictures, arranged them attractively on bulletin boards organized by the children's ages, and interspersed the pictures with quotes from experts on children's art. The pictures supported the quotations, thus conveying the messages that children gradually move toward representational art and that there are common steps children go through in their development of art. Many parents commented on how helpful they found this bulletin board message. It proved to be a most effective teaching tool.

A bulletin board can be an effective way to convey information to families as a group. This bulletin board, for instance, is organized and the information is current. What other methods can help ensure good communication with families?

Documentation of children's work and learning are another way that programs communicate with parents. Documentation may take the form of bulletin board displays or smaller daily journal entries, and include such features as photographs, transcriptions of children's words, the teacher's thoughts about the children's work, samples of children's art, and other visible elements. Attention to aesthetic display is important. The content of documentation generally focuses on an aspect of the children's work in the classroom and highlights their thinking about the projects in which they are involved. We will discuss documentation in more detail in Chapter 8.

MEETINGS AND OTHER GROUP FUNCTIONS. Group gatherings can provide another effective way of reaching family members. Such functions can take the form of meetings, the traditional forum for formal family education, or they can be social. In addition, discussion groups may be part of the early childhood program. When planning any kind of group function, however, keep in mind that family members are busy people who will weigh the benefits of attending a school program against other demands on their time. In fact, for some families the pressure of one more thing to do might be so stressful that it would outweigh the advantages of the program. Because each family's needs are different, the early childhood program must facilitate communication in many different ways and be prepared to individualize ways of meeting these needs.

If the director and staff feel that group meetings can serve a positive function in meeting the needs of some of the families, they must ensure that what they plan will interest potential participants. One way to assess what might be relevant to families is to conduct an interest survey. A brief form can solicit preferences about topic choices, time and day, and type of meeting (see Figure 3-2 for a sample Family Interest Survey). If the teachers or the director plan family functions without input from the families, these functions may well fail to match their interests and result in very low attendance (Gestwicki, 2010). Also, families are often more likely to come to a meeting if a meal or snack is included and if child care is provided. However, keep in mind that if children have already spent 9 or 10 hours at the center, adding 2 evening hours may be more than what is reasonable.

BRAIN STORM
PARENTS WANT TO KNOW

A topic that interests many parents is how they can optimize children's learning during the early years. You can help reinforce the importance of the earliest years because of the "explosive growth of the brain . . . and that stimulation acts as a catalyst to brain growth" (Thompson, 2008). In particular, underscore the point that sensitive interaction with adults is what young children need and that such interaction is much more potent for promoting brain growth than the toys, DVDs, and other commercial products marketed for this purpose (Thompson, 2008).

Family get-togethers may focus on having a speaker with expertise on a topic of common interest, or they may revolve around discussion led by a facilitator. It is important to remember that families' shared experiences are a valuable source of information and support. Thus, if the main part of the program includes a speaker, time should also be allocated for discussion.

One particularly enjoyable way of presenting some topics is to illustrate them with slides or videotapes taken of the children at the school. Such subjects as children's play, social development, or developmentally appropriate toys can be enhanced with such visuals. In addition to gaining insight into an aspect of their children's development, families will feel great pride in seeing their youngsters depicted on the screen.

Figure **3-2**

Family Interest Survey

Dear Families:

We would like to plan some family events for this year and want your suggestions.

Please help us by sharing your preferences about the following: (Please rate these as follows: A = yes, definitely interested; B = moderately interested; C = not at all interested.)

1. Type of event:

_____ Family meeting on a specific topic (topic choice below)

_____ Discussion groups on specific topics

_____ Family social function (picnic, dinner, party, and so on)

_____ Fund-raiser to benefit your child's class

2. Topic choice (for meetings or discussion groups):

_____ Child behavior/guidance	_____ Television
_____ Child nutrition	_____ Good toys for children
_____ Learning to read	_____ Balancing family/work
_____ Self-esteem	_____ Brain development
_____ What happens at school?	_____ Child development

3. Best day (circle your choices): M T W Th F Sa

4. Best time:

_____ Lunch time	_____ Afternoons
_____ After work	_____ 7:30–9:00 P.M.

5. Other matters: Will your attendance be influenced by:

_____ Provision of child care   _____ Provision of meals/snack

Thank you for your help!

Small groups are generally more effective than large groups in facilitating participation (Gestwicki, 2010). A common interest can also encourage a more intimate atmosphere for a meeting; for instance, involving families whose children will enter kindergarten or will be moving from the infant room to the toddler program the following year, or involving just the families of children in one class rather than those from the entire early childhood center.

Some centers generate considerable enthusiasm for social events during which families and teachers have the opportunity to exchange information in a relaxed atmosphere. These can include holiday parties, meals, or an open house, and they can involve all family members. One university program sponsored a potluck dinner for families, staff, and student teachers each semester. Prearranged seating ensured that students sat with the families of children they were observing. This event attracted almost all of the families and proved to be enjoyable as well as valuable for all involved.

COMMUNICATING WHEN THERE ARE CULTURAL AND LANGUAGE BARRIERS. Communicating with families from different backgrounds, especially if they speak a language other than English, can be a challenging prospect for many teachers. Communication is more than sharing an understanding of words; it also involves sharing an understanding of ideas. Families are influenced and shaped by their culture, just as we are, and may have unique perspectives on child-rearing and attitudes about children.

DIVERSITY

In their book, *Working with Children from Culturally Diverse Backgrounds*, Klein and Chen (2001) note that one difference in family attitudes revolves around autonomy and obedience. More affluent families tend to value independence, while families with scarce resources value obedience in their children. Some cultures—for instance, Asian cultures—value maintenance of harmony and order, giving the wishes of the individual less importance than those of the family as a whole. Similarly, Hispanic families value conformity and cohesion of the extended family. Gender roles and expectations are also influenced by culture as well as by religion, with traditional roles prevalent in many groups.

As a teacher, it is likely that you will work with children and families from different backgrounds. Kirmani (2007) suggests several strategies that teachers can use to make children and families from other cultures feel welcome. She suggests: (1) using the child's name accurately to preserve the child's sense of self-esteem and convey respect; (2) promoting the child's home language by valuing the child's multilingual skills; (3) including multicultural materials in the environment; and (4) creating inclusive school spaces where families will feel welcome and comfortable. "Numerous studies suggest that when teachers partner with parents and caregivers from minority cultures, teachers gain cultural understanding" (Prior & Gerard, 2007, p. 63) and are therefore better able to help the children succeed.

FAMILY ENGAGEMENT

We have been discussing various ways in which communication between teachers and families can be maintained. However this communication takes place, it implies involvement and engagement on the part of the family. Let's look at family engagement in more detail now.

Family engagement in the early childhood program is more than involvement of families in the program. According to Halgunseth (2009) it implies a continuous, reciprocal, and strength-based relationship and involves six key components:

1. Families are encouraged to participate in decision making about the child's education and serving as advocates for their children.
2. There are many opportunities for two-way communication, and such communication is sensitive to the language spoken by family members.
3. Communication involves collaboration and exchange of knowledge.
4. Children's learning is enhanced because the early childhood program and families work to extend activities from school to home and community.
5. Early childhood professionals and families work collaboratively to establish goals for children.
6. Early childhood professionals are dedicated, trained, and supported in their efforts to fully engage families.

naeyc

Key Point ◆◆

Family engagement in the early childhood program has positive benefits for children, families, and the school.

family engagement
The commitment of families to the early childhood program through a wide variety of options.

Family engagement fits within the ecological systems theory discussed earlier in this chapter, since it supports the idea that children's development and learning take place within a series of systems, including family, school, community, and society.

Ample research has shown that family engagement and involvement have positive benefits for children as well as for families (Dunlap, 2000; Powell & O'Leary, 2009).

It should also be noted that the involvement of families in their children's early childhood programs will vary. While there is a reciprocal relationship between the family and the early childhood program, each providing support and help to the other as they are able, family engagement will vary according to each family's ability to contribute and to its needs. Some families invest a great deal of their time and energy in the program, whereas others need all their resources to cope with the stresses they face. Some families support the program by participating in and contributing time to various school activities; others seek support from the program in facing their personal strains. The early childhood staff must be flexible to be able to recognize each family's capabilities and needs and to set expectations or provide support accordingly.

Families can be involved in their children's programs in many ways. We will look at some of these; specifically, family members as resources, as volunteers in the classroom, and as decision makers.

Families as Resources

Key Point

Family members may serve as resources to the program by contributing special talents, interests, and abilities; they may serve as volunteers or as members of a policy board in a decision-making capacity.

Family members have many talents and abilities to contribute to the program. Many early childhood programs invite parents or relatives to participate on occasions when their job skills, hobbies, or other special expertise can augment and enrich the curriculum. For instance, a teacher may invite Jasmine's mother, who is a dentist, to help the children understand the importance of good dental hygiene and care; the teacher may take the children to visit the bakery owned by Annie Lee's uncle, because the class is discussing foods; she can ask Michael's father to show the children how he makes pottery; or she may invite Ivan's mother and new baby brother when the class talks about babies and growing up. All family members—parents, siblings, grandparents, other relatives, even pets—can be considered part of the program, extending its resource base.

Family members can also help out with maintenance and construction tasks that are part of the program. In some schools, parents routinely take home the dress-up clothes and other classroom items to wash or clean. In others, regularly scheduled clean-up days bring teachers and family members to school on specified weekends to deep clean the facility, materials, and equipment. Family members with carpentry skills may construct or repair equipment. Others may develop learning materials and games at home that will expand the activity options available to the children.

There are other ways in which family members can serve as program resources. For instance, they can help orient new families to the early childhood program, serve as role models, and provide support to other families. Their suggestions and ideas can enrich the program. Family members can also be extremely effective in providing local and state support for legislation that affects children and families. They can help provide program visibility in the community if the school is seeking outside funding. Family support can be a potent force in maintaining a high-quality early childhood program.

Family members, including parents, grandparents, and others, can share their special interest or talents with children in the early childhood program.

© Cengage Learning

Family Members in the Classroom

Family members may also volunteer as teacher aides. Programs such as parent-cooperative preschools require family engagement. In most programs, particularly child care centers, families participate occasionally, or not at all, because parents are usually working while their children are at school.

Having family members in the classroom can have many benefits for children, families, and teachers. Children can benefit from having their parents participate in the classroom, feeling pride and a sense of security as they see their parents and teachers working together. For families, such firsthand experience can provide insight into how their children spend their time at school, a basis for observing their own children in relation to age-mates, and a chance to note guidance techniques used by teachers. Teachers can benefit from the support parents offer, the added pair of hands that can allow expanded activity possibilities, and the opportunity to gain insight into parent–child interactions. Some teachers relish such involvement; others feel skeptical and reluctant, fearing a clash with the parents' child-rearing practices, feeling stress about being under constant observation, or worrying that the children will get overexcited (Gestwicki, 2010).

Family Members as Decision Makers

Some programs ask family members to serve on an advisory or policy board. Head Start and other federally funded programs, for instance, invite parents to participate in parent advisory councils, as outlined by federal regulations. Many not-for-profit child care or preschool centers also require a governing board of which families can be members. Effective decision-making boards can promote a true partnership between families and the school program (Dunst, Trivette, & Hamby, 2006), providing support for the school, empowerment of families, and increased mutual understanding.

FAMILY EDUCATION

All forms of family engagement potentially serve an educational function, as parents have the chance to gain insights into their children's development and the school's program. Often, however, early childhood programs provide specific

family education

Programs aimed at enhancing parent–child relations and improving parenting competence.

Key Point ◆◆

Family education can take many forms to meet the many different needs of families.

family education aimed at enhancing parent–child relations and improving parenting competence. Gestwicki (2010) defines such programs as "specific attempts to offer knowledge and support to parents in hopes of increasing parenting effectiveness" (p. 427). Evaluation of many family education programs aimed at economically disadvantaged families has indicated that such programs can be very effective, although much still remains to be learned through systematic research (Powell, 1998). In addition, there is limited evidence that parent education enhances the parenting skills of middle-class families as well (Harris & Larsen, 1989).

The scope of parent education programs is not easy to capture in a single definition because there is great diversity in the field. Douglas Powell (1986) spells out some of the contrasts in parent education:

> Some programs focus on family–community relations while others teach parents how to stimulate a child's cognitive development. Some programs prescribe specific skills and styles in relating to young children while other programs help parents determine what is best for them. Some programs are designed primarily to disseminate child development information while others attempt to foster supportive relationships among program participants. Some programs are highly structured while others let parents select activities they wish to pursue. In some programs the staff serve as child development experts while other programs adhere to a self-help model with staff in nondirective facilitator roles. There are important differences in the use of professionals, assistants or volunteers, program length (weeks versus years), and program setting (group- versus home-based). (p. 47)

Although family education can take many forms, family get-togethers or meetings are one frequently used forum. The content of such programs can vary widely, determined by family interest and need. Couchenor and Chrisman (2011) suggest some popular topics for family education programs. These include the value of play for young children, Developmentally Appropriate Practice in early childhood programs, positive guidance, limiting television, homework, healthy sexuality development, early brain development, childhood obesity, teaching financial responsibility, bullying, and family engagement in children's education. Finally, the family's involvement in and promotion of children's education includes many areas of interest to families.

SUMMARY

1. Family systems theory is a way of viewing the family as a dynamic unit.
2. The American family has undergone many changes recently. Consider some of these changes by looking at the following:
   A. Variety in family forms
   B. Other factors that contribute to family diversity
   C. Families in poverty
3. Families have specific needs that the early childhood program can address. Consider issues related to family needs, including the following:
   A. The needs of adults in a unique stage of development, separate from their children's development
   B. The need to feel empowered, in control of their lives
   C. Coordination of the needs of the family with the early childhood program

4. Two-way communication between families and the early childhood program is an important element in providing consistency for children. Consider the following methods of communicating with families:

   A. Communicating with individual parents informally, on a day-to-day basis, and formally, through conferences and home visits

   B. Communicating with groups of families through written communiqués, bulletin boards, and meetings

5. Families can be involved in the early childhood program in a number of ways—as resources, in the classroom, and as decision makers.

6. One function of the early childhood program is family education, which can take a variety of forms.

KEY TERMS LIST

chronosystem	family–teacher conference
ecological systems theory	generativity
empowerment	home visit
exosystem	macrosystem
family education	mesosystem
family engagement	microsystem

KEY QUESTIONS

1. Think of your own family history. How has your family changed over the past two (or three or four) generations? Consider maternal employment, divorce, closeness to extended family, and other factors. Compare your family with that of other members of your class.

2. Sometimes the needs of families conflict with those of the program. Which elements of the early childhood program could pose a potential conflict? How might these be resolved? Read "Ethics Case Studies: The Working Mother" in *Young Children,* November 1987, page 16, for insight into the suggestions of professionals to resolve such a conflict.

3. Visit an early childhood program. What evidence of communication with families do you see? Look at bulletin boards, notes, pictures, and other written material. What kind of interaction do you notice between families and teachers? What "messages" about the school's concern for families do they get from this communication?

4. Ask several parents whose children are enrolled in an early childhood program about their contacts with the teachers and the program. What is their overall attitude about contact between home and school? Do they feel it is important or not important … positive or negative … present or absent … supportive or lacking in support? What do they expect from the teachers? Do they feel that communication between families and teachers is important for their children?

5. How can family engagement benefit the early childhood program? List some concrete ways in which families might contribute to the program.

ADDITIONAL RESOURCES

Select additional books, articles, and websites on topics discussed in Chapter 3.

Couchenor, D., & Chrisman, K. (2011). *Families, schools, and communities: Together for children* (3rd ed.). Belmont, CA: Wadsworth, Cengage Learning.

Gestwicki, C. (2010). *Home, school and community relations: A guide to working with parents* (7th ed.). Belmont, CA: Wadsworth, Cengage Learning.

Powell, D. R. (1989). *Families and early childhood programs.* Washington, DC: NAEYC.

HELPFUL WEBSITES

National Parenting Education Network:

www.ces.ncsu.edu/depts/fcs/npen

This website features a network for parent educators that facilitates linkages among practitioners and provides information about best practices and research in the parent education field.

Families and Work Institute:

www.familiesandwork.org

The Families and Work Institute is a nonprofit center for research that provides data about the changing workforce, family, and community in America. Some of the most comprehensive research about work and family issues are available on this website.

Divorceinfo:

www.divorceinfo.com

This website provides a good discussion of the effects of divorce on preschool children, providing information about reactions and behaviors that might occur and ways in which adults can help children whose families are undergoing a divorce.

Go to **CengageBrain.com** to register your access code for this book's Education CourseMate website, where you will find more resources to help you study. Additional resources for this chapter include TeachSource Videos, glossary flashcards, web links, case studies with critical thinking questions that apply the concepts presented in this chapter, and more. If your textbook does not include a printed access card, you can go to **CengageBrain.com** to purchase access.

The Teachers/Caregivers 4

In Chapter 4, you will find answers to the following questions about teachers and caregivers:

- What are the characteristics of a good teacher of young children?
- What kinds of positions are available to you as a professional in the field of early childhood education?
- What paths can teachers-in-training take to become part of the field of early childhood education?
- How do the Standards for Professional Preparation Programs work?
- How are early childhood education programs regulated and held accountable?
- What contributes to professionalism in the field of early childhood education?
- What contemporary issues face the field of early childhood education and what can you contribute toward solutions to these issues?

DAP Whenever you see a great classroom, one in which children are learning and thriving, you can be sure that the teachers … are highly intentional. In everything that good teachers do—creating the environment, considering the curriculum and tailoring it to the children as individuals, planning learning experiences, and interacting with children and families—they are purposeful and thoughtful. As they make myriad decisions, big and small, they keep in mind the outcomes they seek.

Developmentally Appropriate Practice, Copple & Bredekamp, 2009, pp. 33–34

NAEYC STANDARDS CONSIDERED IN CHAPTER 4

(See the Standards Correlation Chart on the inside front cover of this book for the titles and description of the standards listed below.)

- *Standard 6a:* Identifying as an early childhood educator by understanding the characteristics of good professionals; understanding professionalism in early childhood education (pp. 78–80, 88).
- *Standard 6a:* Recognizing the paths through which individuals become early childhood professionals, including training and certification (pp. 84–86).
- *Standard 6c:* Valuing collaboration, for instance, team teaching (pp. 80–81).
- *Standard 6b:* Knowing about and upholding ethical standards (pp. 88–90; Appendix).
- *Standard 6a:* Being aware of and involved in professional organizations (pp. 90–91).
- *Standard 6c:* Engaging in reflective teaching (pp. 91–93).
- *Standard 6d:* Being familiar with current issues and dilemmas facing the field (pp. 93–99).
- *Standards 6e:* Engaging in advocacy for the field (pp. 98–99).

This chapter will focus on you—you as an individual, you as a teacher or caregiver, you as a member of a profession. However, everything discussed in this book is relevant to you as a teacher. You are the one who integrates knowledge about the development of children, about the importance of families, about creating a healthy and stimulating environment, about child-sensitive curriculum planning, and about appropriate and nurturing guidance to provide the best possible care and education for young children. Thus, in this chapter we will explore important aspects of teaching and the profession of early childhood education.

THE EARLY CHILDHOOD TEACHER AND CAREGIVER

naeyc

Key Point ◆

A professional early childhood teacher is distinguished by professionalism, knowledge and standards, judgment, and ability to translate theoretical information into practical application.

early childhood teacher (or early childhood educator)
A specifically trained professional who works with children from infancy to age eight.

caregiver (or child care worker)
Term traditionally used to describe a person who works in a child care setting.

DAP

Respect, patience, and creativity are some of the characteristics thought to be important in good early childhood teachers.

© Cengage Learning

Before beginning a discussion of early childhood teachers, it is important to make some distinctions in terminology. Unfortunately, no universally accepted categories and titles define those who work with young children, although some have been proposed, as we will discuss later. Often labels conjure up stereotypes and do not reflect different educational and experiential backgrounds found in the field.

Throughout this book the terms **early childhood teacher** and **early childhood educator** will be used synonymously. Other terms are also applied to those who work with young children, particularly **caregiver** and **child care worker.** Traditionally, the distinction has been made that a caregiver—for instance, someone who works in a child care center—cares for the physical and emotional needs of infants, toddlers, or preschoolers, whereas the teacher serves an educational function. This is not a particularly appropriate distinction, however, since those who work with young children both educate and nurture as part of their job (Tarrant, Greenberg, Kagan, & Kauerz, 2009).

Certainly the early childhood teacher "cares for" and the caregiver "teaches" young children. Which teacher has not tied shoelaces, wiped noses, or dried tears? And which caregiver has not helped children learn how to zip a coat, assemble a puzzle, or share the tricycle? Teaching and caregiving functions seem not only inherent but also integrally related in both roles to the point at which a distinction is impossible to make (Willer, 1990). The distinction between the teacher and the caregiver, then, is more than a general description of what they do, for their roles certainly overlap. What does distinguish teachers, according to Katz (1984), is their professionalism, the way they use their knowledge and standards of performance. Teachers possess advanced knowledge in child development and early childhood education that they apply when they have to make judgments and decisions on a moment-by-moment basis. At the same time, they also share with other professionals a commitment to maintaining the high standards set by the profession through its organizations. But there really is no simple or single definition of a good teacher of young children.

Characteristics of the Good Early Childhood Teacher

If asked what characteristics a good teacher of young children possesses, most of us would come up with an intuitive list of qualities such as warmth, sensitivity, energy, sense of humor, flexibility, and patience. Some clues about what makes a good teacher of young children can be gleaned from early childhood educators and researchers based on their experience and insight. In a 2008 survey, Laura

Colker interviewed early childhood practitioners to find out what they viewed as important characteristics of effective early childhood teachers. The following 12 characteristics were identified as integral to successful teaching:

1. **Passion.** Most important is having a strong drive, a feeling that you make a difference as a teacher of young children. In fact, in his newest book, *Letters to a Young Teacher* (2007), well-known educator and author, Jonathan Kozol, speaks of the importance of passion in teaching.

2. **Perseverance.** It is important to have strong dedication and willingness to fight for what you believe in and advocate for children's needs as well as for your profession.

3. **Willingness to take risks.** Closely related to the first two characteristics is a willingness to shake up the status quo and take a stand to reach your goals for children and the quality of their education.

4. **Pragmatism.** At the same time, you also need to be able to compromise and know to which battles to devote your energies.

5. **Patience.** This characteristic applies in two ways: patience with the system as you try to bring about changes and patience with the children and families with whom you work.

6. **Flexibility.** Being able to deal with the unexpected and make changes is another quality of successful early childhood teachers.

7. **Respect.** One of the most basic requirements for good teachers is respect for children and families, particularly an appreciation of diversity. Many professionals consider that respectful, healthy relationships between teachers and children are "at the forefront of effective practice" (Gallagher & Mayer, 2008).

8. **Creativity.** Effective early childhood teachers are continually challenged to find creative ways to meet challenges and deal with limited resources.

9. **Authenticity.** This quality refers to self-awareness, knowing who you are and what you stand for.

10. **Love of learning.** In order to inspire children and convey how important learning is, you have to be a committed lifelong learner yourself.

11. **High energy.** It takes a great deal of energy to work with young children and children respond enthusiastically to teachers who have a high level of energy.

12. **Sense of humor.** Learning should be fun; a good sense of humor is an important element of being an effective teacher.

Those who care for infants and toddlers also need special qualities, beyond "liking babies." Balaban (1992) includes in her list of important personal qualities the ability to anticipate and plan; provide an interesting environment; elicit language, problem solving, and play; protect, listen, and watch; smooth "jangled feelings"; comfort; cope; facilitate social interactions; facilitate parent–child separation; and care for the whole family.

Another way of thinking about characteristics of good teachers is in terms of **disposition,** "a tendency to exhibit frequently, consciously, and voluntarily a pattern of behavior that is directed to a broad goal" (Katz, 1993). For many years, Lillian Katz, a longtime leader in the early childhood education field, has written about the importance of dispositions in teachers and as a consideration in teacher education (Da Ros-Voseles & Moss, 2007). The National Council for Accreditation of Teacher Education has mandated that dispositions of teacher candidates should be evaluated (NCATE, 2006). Dispositions of effective

disposition
The tendency to consciously exhibit a set of behaviors that reflect a pattern of good early childhood practice.

teachers have been identified by various authors. Da Ros-Voseles and Moss (2007) share the following five from review of others' writings:

1. Empathy
2. Positive view of others
3. Positive view of self
4. Authenticity
5. Meaningful purpose and vision

While these five dispositions overlap with the characteristics of effective teachers we discussed earlier, they also describe qualities that should be deeply ingrained in a teacher of young children—what Katz (1995) described as habits of mind, not mindless habits.

STAFFING IN EARLY CHILDHOOD PROGRAMS

The early childhood teacher, of course, works within a system along with others who share the tasks of the program. Staff members, from the director to the custodian, contribute toward making the program successful. There can be a variety of staffing patterns depending on the type, size, and philosophy of the program as well as on its funding source. A half-day preschool attended by 15 children may, for instance, be staffed by one owner/teacher and one part-time assistant. However, a not-for-profit child care program in which 160 children are enrolled might involve a board of directors, a director, a curriculum coordinator, a family coordinator, 12 head teachers, 28 full- and part-time assistants, a variable number of volunteers, a secretary, a cook, a custodian, a list of substitute staff, and various community professionals who serve as resource persons.

The distribution and allocation of responsibility also varies in different programs. Some exhibit a hierarchical structure, fashioned as a pyramid, where power trickles down from the top and members in each layer in the structure defer to those above. Thus, in some classrooms that follow this model, one teacher is designated as the head or lead teacher and other staff work under her or him, following that teacher's direction and guidance. Yet, in the early childhood field there is often an alternative to this pyramid structure because of the strong interdependence and interconnectedness among staff members, who frequently make decisions by consensus.

In some programs, classes are co-taught by team teachers who share responsibilities. **Team teaching** is based on a relationship of trust and communication between the two teachers, something that takes time to build. A good team finds many bonuses in this relationship through added flexibility, creativity, problem-solving capabilities, and focus on what each member of the team enjoys most or does best. In addition, the collaboration between the two provides the children with a model for cooperative behavior. Later in this book, you will read about the Reggio Emilia approach to early childhood education. In the programs of Reggio Emilia, Italy, each classroom is run by two teachers who are considered equal and who share responsibility for their classroom (Gandini, 2004).

Whatever the structure, it is sensible to find out before working at a program what the lines of responsibility are in terms of providing direction, feedback, evaluation, and resources. By learning the lines of authority and communication, you, as a teacher, will know whom to seek out for guidance and information, with whom to discuss problems, and where ultimate responsibility for various decisions lies. Whatever the organizational structure of the program,

Key Point ◆
The size and complexity of a program will affect the size and complexity of the staffing pattern.

Key Point ◆
Early childhood programs can have various staffing structures and lines of staff authority and responsibility.

team teaching
An approach that involves co-teaching in which status and responsibility are equal rather than having a pyramid structure of authority, with one person in charge and others subordinate.

In many programs, teachers share responsibility equally for the functioning of the classroom through a collaborative team-teaching approach.

© Cengage Learning

smooth functioning depends in part on a clear understanding of responsibilities and lines of communication and on cooperation among the staff (Click & Karkos, 2010; Sciarra & Dorsey, 2010). We will now briefly examine some of the positions and their responsibilities held by staff members in early childhood programs.

Director

The director performs a variety of tasks, depending on the size and scope of the program. In small programs, the director may double as a teacher for part of the day, whereas in large programs, the role may be purely administrative. This staff member is usually responsible for financial, personnel, policy, and facility decisions; provides community linkages; handles licensing and regulation; and is the ultimate decision maker in the chain of responsibility in all matters that pertain to the program. The job description often also involves staff selection, training, monitoring, and evaluation. In programs that depend on grants and other outside sources of funding, the director may spend much time writing proposals and meeting with influential decision makers. But a director is often also a plumber, a carpenter, and a counselor because she holds the ultimate responsibility for whatever needs to be taken care of.

Key Point ◆

The role of the director will depend on the size and nature of the program.

Teaching Staff

Those who work directly with children may hold a variety of titles. Over the past few years, many states have developed career ladders that define such factors as titles, responsibilities, educational background, and suggested wages for different early childhood positions. While there are commonalities among these career ladders, they are, nonetheless, a reflection of each state's unique approach to career ladder development. Let's now look at two common teaching positions in more depth.

THE HEAD TEACHER. It is the responsibility of the **head teacher,** lead teacher, or master teacher to plan and implement the daily program. This involves knowing each child and family well and individualizing the program to meet the

head teacher
The person in charge of a class who is ultimately responsible for all aspects of class functioning.

Key Point ◆◆

In many programs, head teachers and assistant teachers with distinct responsibilities are identified for each classroom.

assistant teacher

Also called aide, helper, auxiliary teacher, associate teacher, or small-group leader; works under the guidance of the head teacher in providing a high-quality program for the children in the class and their families.

Key Point ◆◆

Most early childhood programs, depending on their size and scope, have some support staff who help with the maintenance and functioning of the program.

specific needs of each. The head teacher usually also takes responsibility for the physical environment of the classroom—setting up equipment, rotating materials, and ensuring a good match between what is available and the children's skill level. The head teacher generally maintains records for the children in the class; is usually involved in family interactions, both informally at the start and end of each day and formally through conferences or meetings; and takes charge of other staff members who work in the class by providing direction, guidance, and feedback.

THE ASSISTANT TEACHER. Also called aide, helper, auxiliary teacher, associate teacher, or small-group leader, the **assistant teacher** works with the head teacher to provide a high-quality program for the children in the class and their families. Depending on the assistant's skill level and experience, this teacher may share many of the head teacher's responsibilities; for instance, participating in curriculum planning, leading large- and small-group activities, being involved in family interactions, and arranging the environment. Because of the assistant teacher's close working relationship with the teacher, open and honest communication and mutual respect are vital between the two. In some schools, an assistant teacher may serve as a "floater," moving among classrooms to help with special activities or during specific times of the day.

Support Staff

Depending on the size and scope of the center, usually some persons serve in a support capacity. These might include (although they certainly are not limited to) persons involved in food preparation, maintenance, and office management.

Large programs often have a cook who is in charge of meal preparation, shopping, and sanitation and maintenance of the kitchen. The cook may also plan meals, if that person has an appropriate background in nutrition, or may participate in classroom cooking projects. A dietitian may serve as a consultant to the program to ensure that children's nutritional needs are appropriately met through the program's meals. In smaller programs, particularly those not serving breakfast, lunch, or dinner, the teaching staff or director may take responsibility for snack planning and preparation.

One of the most important yet difficult tasks of any center serving busy and active young children is maintenance. Daily cleaning, sweeping, vacuuming, sanitizing, and garbage disposal are vital, though usually unpopular, functions. Large programs may have a custodian as part of the staff, whereas others hold contracts with a janitorial service. Often the expense of a maintenance crew or custodian has to be weighed against other important needs, and the teaching staff finds that its responsibilities include many maintenance chores. Most centers compromise by having the staff maintain a modicum of cleanliness and order while a cleaning service is responsible for intermittent deep cleaning of the facility.

Other support staff members take care of office needs. Large programs often have a secretary who maintains records, answers phone calls, manages typing needs, and may handle some accounting tasks. In smaller programs, such tasks may fall to the director. Some programs may employ a part-time accountant or have a receptionist in addition to the secretary. Programs that are part of or housed with other agencies may share custodial and secretarial staff.

Early childhood teaching staff take on a variety of roles and responsibilities, the most of important of which is ensuring the well-being of the children in their care.

© Cengage Learning

Volunteers

Some centers avail themselves of volunteers to help with various aspects of the early childhood program. Volunteers can include parents and other family members, student teachers or interns, members of organizations such as the Junior League, foster grandparents, and other interested community members. To use volunteers most effectively, however, there has to be a well-planned orientation, training, and monitoring component that helps the volunteer understand the program, its philosophy, and its operation. Although volunteers can provide a wonderful additional resource to a program, the reality is that volunteers are not as plentiful as the potential need for them is.

Key Point 🔶

Some programs use volunteers, have a board of directors who are involved in the decision-making process, and call on community professionals to expand the services of the program.

Board of Directors

Particularly in not-for-profit centers, some type of policy making or governing board holds the ultimate responsibility for the program. This board of trustees or **board of directors** may be a very powerful force, making all pertinent decisions that the director then carries out, or it may only be a nominal group, in which almost all decisions are left up to the director. Ideally, a board of directors' role falls somewhere between these extremes (Sciarra & Dorsey, 2010).

Boards of directors are usually made up of community persons who come from a variety of spheres of expertise and influence, most of which are not likely to be related to early childhood education. It is wise, however, to include a child development expert on the board. The director serves as a liaison, helping the board understand the rationale for decisions made on the basis of child development knowledge, while using the board's expertise in areas in which the director is not as well versed. Boards can be very effective in areas such as fiscal management, fund-raising, construction and expansion projects, or the process of lobbying for children's rights.

board of directors
Policymaking or governing board that holds ultimate responsibility, particularly for a not-for-profit program.

Community Professionals

The resources of a center can be expanded through other professionals in the larger community; for instance, health and mental health professionals, social workers, and therapists. In some instances, families are referred to the early childhood program by a community agency; thus, the program and referring agency can work together to maximize the help provided to the

In some programs, community professionals, such as this physical therapist, can expand the services and support provided for children and families.

© Cengage Learning

child and family. In other cases, the early childhood program may help connect families with community agencies and professionals to provide needed services.

TRAINING AND REGULATION IN EARLY CHILDHOOD EDUCATION

naeyc

As we have discussed, many individuals contribute toward providing a good early childhood program through their levels and types of expertise. Such expertise stems from different types of training. In addition, a variety of regulations and quality controls apply to early childhood programs and the personnel who staff them. We will look at training through academic programs and alternative training avenues and then review regulations, licensing, and accreditation of programs.

Academic Teacher Training Programs

Because you are reading this text, you are most likely involved in an academic early childhood program whose aim is to prepare qualified teachers and directors of programs for young children through a combination of coursework and practicum experiences. Such programs exist at two-year associate degree, four-year baccalaureate degree, and postgraduate degree levels. In some states, such programs can lead to state licensure to enable graduates to teach up to second or third grade in public schools. In advanced degree programs, greater depth and more theoretical and research knowledge become

---

BRAIN STORM

HOW IMPORTANT ARE YOU?

Why is it important for you, as an early childhood educator, to have some understanding of how the brain develops? Insights into the amazing brain and its early development, especially because of new technology, are very helpful because they help us to "see" the brain's activity and its power in children's growing mastery of their world. When you provide thoughtful experiences for the young children in your charge, you help strengthen the interconnections among brain cells (neurons) and help these cells grow in size because of the connectors made by these experiences. Rima Shore, in her book, *Rethinking the Brain* (1997, p. ix) gives a great example of a teacher's impact:

A child care provider reads to a three-year-old. In a matter of seconds, thousands of cells in the child's growing brain respond. Some brain cells are "turned on," triggered by this particular experience. Many existing connections among brain cells are strengthened. At the same time, new connections are formed, adding a bit more definition and complexity to the intricate circuitry that will remain largely in place for the rest of this child's life.

You do, indeed, have the potential to exert a profound influence over each child you touch. Your thoughtful, reflective practice can maximize the impact of such moments!

increasingly important topics. As we will discuss below, guidelines for early childhood professional preparation are outlined in standards and position statements from the National Association for the Education of Young Children (NAEYC, 2010).

Child Development Associate Program

In the 1970s, an alternative model for the training of early childhood teachers was initiated through the **Child Development Associate (CDA)** program. Just as successful completion of an academic program leads to a degree, so does successful completion of the CDA program lead to a professional credential as a Child Development Associate. The CDA credential is available for professionals who work with different age groups and in various settings: preschools, infant/toddler programs, family child care, and home visitor programs. More than 200,000 individuals have received a CDA credential. In past years, the majority of CDAs worked in Head Start programs, but the most recent survey of CDAs indicates that more than half of them worked in non–Head Start programs. The National Survey of CDAs (Bailey, 2004) found that over 90 percent remained committed to early childhood education after receiving their credentials, providing an anchor of stability in a field that suffers from a high turnover rate. The CDA is now incorporated into the licensing regulations of 49 states (Bailey, 2004).

An early childhood teacher obtains a CDA credential after a process of application, training, and assessment. A CDA is an early childhood professional who successfully meets the following six goals (Council for Early Childhood Professional Recognition, 2009).

1. Establish and maintain a safe, healthy learning environment.
2. Advance physical and intellectual competence.
3. Support social and emotional development and provide guidance.
4. Establish positive and productive relationships with families.
5. Ensure a well-run, purposeful program responsive to participants' needs.
6. Maintain a commitment to professionalism.

Child Development Associate (CDA)
An early childhood teacher who has been assessed and proven competent through the national CDA credentialing program.

Key Point ◆

In addition to college and university training programs, early childhood professionals can receive training and certification through the national Child Development Associate program.

The T.E.A.C.H. Program

The Teacher Education And Compensation Helps (T.E.A.C.H.) Program is another option in many states for those wishing to enhance their education and training in the field of early childhood education. T.E.A.C.H. was started as part of the early childhood system in North Carolina, with the aim of improving the quality of child care through added education and compensation for those who work with young children; it has now been adopted in a number of other states. Child care teachers and administrators who participate receive education that leads toward a certificate (including CDA) or a degree in early childhood education. In 2008, more than 21,000 teachers had participated in T.E.A.C.H. and 21 states had adopted the Program (Child Care Services Association, 2008). States that have incorporated T.E.A.C.H. in their early childhood system have found that the added monetary investment in the care and education of young children is worth the results in higher quality, an educated child care workforce, lower staff turnover, and increased pay and benefits for staff. Scholarships are provided through the T.E.A.C.H. Program toward the cost of tuition, books, and travel, and a wage increase is built in once a teacher has completed the agreed-upon amount of education. More information is available at www.child careservices.org.

Required Qualifications for Head Start Teachers

A special group of early childhood teachers, those who work in Head Start programs, must meet specific qualifications, although these requirements are applied to programs rather than to individual teachers. As of October 2011, each Head Start and Early Head Start center-based classroom must be staffed by at least one teacher who has an associate, baccalaureate, or advanced degree in early childhood education or a related field. By September 2013, at least 50 percent of Head Start teachers nationwide must have a baccalaureate or advanced degree in Early Childhood Education or a baccalaureate or advanced degree in any subject, and coursework equivalent to a major relating to early childhood education with experience teaching preschool-age children. In addition, all Head Start and Early Head Start aides and assistant teachers must have at least a CDA credential by 2013 (ECLK, 2008).

Regulation and Licensing

Minimum standards for early childhood teachers are generally described in local or state licensing regulations. Some states require little or no training for those who work with and care for young children; others designate more stringent criteria that specify minimum levels of training in early childhood education and child development and appropriate experiences. Keep in mind that minimum standards are just that—minimums. Professional early childhood educators usually far exceed the minimum, and the children in their care, the children's families, the overall early childhood program, and the teachers themselves are the beneficiaries of this professionalism and expertise.

Of course, licensing criteria provide guidelines for far more than teacher qualifications. They can cover a wide range of topics related to health, sanitation, safety, child–adult ratio, group size, acceptable guidance and curriculum practices, meal and sleeping arrangements, and so forth. Minimum standards for various aspects of programs for young children are spelled out by all states, although there is considerable variation in what is deemed acceptable. The National Association for the Education of Young Children, in its position statement, *Licensing and Public Regulation of Early Childhood Programs,* encourages states to adopt requirements that reflect what research tells us about good care for young children and to enforce such regulations vigorously and equitably (NAEYC, 1997). Programs that receive federal funding may need to adhere to specified federal regulations as well. Some programs, particularly those that are part of the public school system, may be regulated by a separate agency with different guidelines and regulations.

Accreditation

To indicate that they strive for a high level of excellence rather than minimum criteria, many early childhood centers have undergone the voluntary accreditation process of the National Academy of Early Childhood Programs, the accreditation division of NAEYC, which started in 1985. In 2008, more than 8,000 programs had been accredited. NAEYC has "reinvented" its accreditation system, which is now a more rigorous process that involves intensive self-study and culminates in a site visit and assessment (NAEYC, 2008b). In recent years, additional accreditation systems other than NAEYC's have been developed. One example is a system developed by the National Association of Child Care Professionals (NACCP). The National Accreditation Commission for Early Care and Education Programs (NAC) is a division of this organization, and includes a growing number of child care programs across the country that have earned NAC accreditation (NACCP, 2008).

Another type of accreditation involves academic programs at colleges and universities. Most colleges of education at four-year institutions are accredited by the National Council for Accreditation of Teacher Education (NCATE, 2006). Many teacher education programs include an early childhood education major, which is accredited by NCATE, in collaboration with NAEYC. Recently, new standards have been adopted, as discussed in more detail below.

NAEYC STANDARDS FOR PROFESSIONAL PREPARATION PROGRAMS

The new standards provide the basis for accrediting a range of higher education programs, including two-year associate degrees, four-year bachelor's degrees, and advanced graduate degrees. As described in the document,

> These standards offer practitioners a framework for applying new knowledge to critical issues. They support important *early learning* goals across settings serving children from birth through age 8. They support critical *early childhood policy* structures including professional credentialing, accreditation of professional preparation programs, state approval of teacher education programs, and state early childhood professional development systems. They apply across degree levels, varying in depth and breadth. (NAEYC, 2010, p. 9)

The standards reflect a set of values shared by early childhood professionals, including diversity, inclusion, respect for families, and reliance on child development principles. The standards also reflect the broad range of settings and ages (birth to 8) that early childhood education encompasses. In particular, they convey a vision for what early childhood educators should possess in terms of knowledge, skills, and dispositions.

There are six standards, each divided further by relevant key elements. When academic programs undergo the accreditation process, they must demonstrate that the programs and students meet the following six standards:

1. Promoting child development and learning
2. Building family and community relations
3. Observing, documenting, and assessing to support young children and families
4. Using developmentally effective approaches
5. Using content knowledge to build meaningful curriculum
6. Becoming a professional (NAEYC, 2010)

Check the Correlation Matrix on the inside cover of this text. It contains a listing of the six standards and their key elements along with an indication of where in this textbook they are discussed. Then, at the start of each chapter you will find a list of standards and key elements addressed within the chapter. In addition, an NAEYC icon, in the relevant places of the text, will further alert you to the link between the standards and the information in this book.

PROFESSIONALISM

This book stresses the importance of the early childhood years, early education, and your role as an early childhood educator. To fully realize that importance, however, you must see yourself as a member of a profession. A profession is different from a job by virtue of some specific characteristics; for instance, a defined code of ethics, a specialized knowledge base involving theoretical principles, specialized training founded on that knowledge base, and universal standards of practice that stem from that knowledge base (Caulfield, 1997).

Those who have written at great length about early childhood professionalism, recognizing that there are many inconsistencies and problems to be faced, do not always agree on the degree to which the field meets the criteria of a profession. Increasing dialogue through conferences and written works has helped to focus more sharply on relevant issues—for instance, low pay and shortage of qualified early childhood teachers—as well as on strategies for combating these (we will discuss some of these later in this chapter). Nonetheless, the expanding concern about professionalism, evident at both national and local levels, should propel early childhood education toward its goals, which include a better definition and greater focus.

Although in many ways the early childhood field has moved toward professionalization, there is concern that professional status is not universally acknowledged by those who work in the field and by the public at large. Those who work with young children need to develop a clearer concept of who they are, what they do, and the importance of their role. At the same time, there is a need for public recognition of the value and status of early childhood educators. As a student embarking on a career in early childhood education, you are in a unique position to develop from the start a sense of professionalism that is furthered by every course you take, every day you spend with children, and every conference you attend. Your competence and recognition of the importance of your role will enhance not only your work with children and families, but also your contributions to the early childhood profession.

Ethics

One of the hallmarks of a profession is its recognition of and adherence to a **code of ethics.** Such a code embodies guidelines for behavior, facilitates decision making, and provides the backing of like-minded professionals when the practitioner takes a "risky but courageous stand in the face of an ethical dilemma"(Katz, 1988, p. 77). Under the leadership of Stephanie Feeney, the NAEYC has adopted a *Code of Ethical Conduct* that delineates ethical responsibilities to children, families, colleagues, and the community and society (NAEYC, 2011).

Teachers who see themselves as professionals share some specific characteristics, such as having specialized training in early childhood education, having a particular knowledge base and theoretical foundation, and adhering to a defined code of ethics.

© Cengage Learning

Key Point ◆◆

The field of early childhood education has a defined code of ethics, adopted by the National Association for the Education of Young Children.

code of ethics
Agreed-upon professional standards that guide behavior and facilitate decision making in working situations.

cultural scripts
Unspoken, and often unconscious, messages that are rooted in our culture and upbringing and tell us how to behave and respond in different situations.

individualism
The general tendency of a cultural group to place greater emphasis on the needs and wants of the individual rather than on those of the group.

collectivism
The general tendency of a cultural group to place greater emphasis on the needs and wants of the group rather than on those of the individual.

CULTURE MATTERS

THE UNITED States is becoming increasingly more diverse and you, as a teacher of young children, will very likely work with children and families from different cultures. We recognize that families bring their unique cultural beliefs and values to the table as they communicate with their children's teachers. We don't, however, always think of the cultural views that we, as teachers, bring to such interactions. We also have a cultural orientation that colors how we view the world. The impact of culture of origin on how children are viewed and on communications between teachers and families is the topic of a recent report from Zero to Three (a national organization that informs, trains, and supports professionals, policymakers, and parents in their efforts to improve the lives of infants and toddlers) entitled, *The Changing Face of the United States: The Influence of Culture on Early Child Development* (Maschinot, 2008).

Cultural values have a profound impact on what we believe, how we behave, and how we react. "Our training in early child development has given us a European American lens that evaluates 'healthy' or 'normal' development from a particular perspective" (Maschinot, 2008, p. 1). The vision of what parents think is important for their children may be very different from what we think is best for children. We have discussed before the importance of cultural sensitivity and will expand on this further.

In the aforementioned publication, *culture* is defined as "a shared system of meaning, which includes values, beliefs, and assumptions expressed in daily interactions of individuals within a group through a definite pattern of language, behavior, customs, attitudes, and practices" (Maschinot, 2008, p. 2). This definition underscores that culture is dynamic and changing, not a static list of traits. It also helps us understand **cultural scripts,** which guide our behavior in different situations and may, in fact, be subconsciously carried out. These cultural scripts are powerful motivators because of their guidance in how to respond to various situations and problems that may arise. The publication further notes that "the key to better understanding other cultures may be the ability to elicit these cultural scripts from families and to be more aware of how our own scripts affect our work" (Maschinot, 2008, p. 3). The author recommends that teachers need to conduct in-depth observations and conversations with families to understand their values.

Perhaps the most important influence on culture is whether it most values **individualism** or **collectivism.** Cultures that value individualism encourage children's independence and assertiveness, whereas cultures that value collectivism are concerned with the well-being of the group more than that of the individual. All of us have a mix of both within us—we are individuals as well as members of a social group—but different societies emphasize one more than the other, and this is reflected in our cultural scripts. One study that measured hundreds of people from 53 societies worldwide found that people in the United States scored highest on individualism among all the countries surveyed. People from Asia and Latin America scored highest on collectivism, while Europeans fell between the two extremes (Hofstede, 1991). Keep in mind that most groups that immigrate to the United Sates are from societies that are far more collectivist and interdependent than is mainstream American culture. Such differences between a child and family's culture of origin and American culture can cause tensions and misunderstandings.

American children are encouraged by their families from very early on to be autonomous, make their own decisions, sleep alone, feed and dress themselves, and be toilet trained at a relatively early age. In collectivistic societies, children are raised to be respectful, self-controlled, dutiful, conforming, empathic, and cooperative. Children are encouraged to rely on others for help with problems rather than finding their own solutions.

Recognizing and understanding such differences helps early childhood teachers work respectfully with children and families from other cultures. "Given that early childhood services are often the first point of contact with mainstream culture for immigrant families and 'minority' families in the United States, it is essential that these services be based on a deeper understanding of the background and lived experiences of the families in our ever-changing culture" (Maschinot, 2008, p. 11).

89

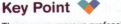

This code recognizes that many of the day-to-day decisions made by those who work with young children are of a moral and ethical nature. Early childhood teachers, for instance, may find themselves in situations with conflicting values in which it is not clear whether the rights of the child, the family, the school, other children in the program, or the teachers are most important. The increasing diversity of the United States can also pose ethical dilemmas as teachers make decisions about what is best for children and their families, especially when there are fundamental differences in values.

A code of ethics provides common principles for dealing with such dilemmas, principles based on the value of childhood as a unique stage of life, on knowledge of child development, on appreciation of the importance of family and cultural ties, on respect for the dignity and value of children and adults, and on helping individuals reach their potential through trusting, positive relationships.

Because children are particularly vulnerable, those who work with them have an important responsibility that is supported and defined by a code of ethics. As you enter the early childhood profession, it is important to read and use NAEYC's *Code of Ethical Conduct*, which you will find in the appendix of this book and which also is available online at www.naeyc.org/files/naeyc/file/positions/Ethics%20Position%20Statement2011.pdf.

In 2011, a Statement of Commitment, which is not part of the Code, was added. This statement is "a personal acknowledgment of the individual's willingness to embrace the distinctive values and moral obligations of the field of early childhood care and education. It is recognition of the moral obligations that lead to an individual becoming part of the profession" (NAEYC, 2011, p. 56).

Professional Organizations

One sign of a profession is the existence of organizations to which members belong and of professional journals that members read. Such organizations and their literature provide its members with support and a sense of common interest and purpose. Early childhood education has several pertinent organizations and journals. We will briefly discuss the two major groups in the field.

1. **The National Association for the Education of Young Children (NAEYC),** the largest early childhood organization, is a powerful voice for children, families, and teachers. NAEYC is dedicated to improving the quality of early childhood programs for children from birth through third grade and their families, improving the working conditions of those who work in such programs, and building public support for high-quality early childhood care and education. Through its history spanning over 80 years, NAEYC has increased in size so that now its diverse membership includes over 100,000 individuals and nearly 450 local, state, and regional groups that are NAEYC Affiliates (NAEYC, 2008b). One of the ways in which NAEYC works toward its goals is through its publications—the bimonthly journal *Young Children*, the quarterly *Early Childhood Research Journal*, and numerous books and other resources. In addition, NAEYC holds an annual conference that is attended by thousands of early childhood professionals each November.

Key Point
There are numerous professional organizations that early childhood students and professionals can join.

National Association for the Education of Young Children (NAEYC)
Largest American early childhood professional organization, which deals with issues related to children from birth to age eight and those who work with young children.

2. **Association for Childhood Education International (ACEI)** is a professional organization that covers a wider spectrum of educational issues by including ages ranging from infancy through early adolescence. It also focuses on international and intercultural issues. The ACEI publishes the journals *Childhood Education* and *Journal of Research in Childhood Education*, and sponsors an annual international conference (ACEI, 2008).

In addition, numerous organizations focus on more specialized groups; for instance, those involved in for-profit child care, Montessori, Head Start, church-sponsored programs, home care (the National Association of Family Day Care), early childhood special education (for instance, the Early Childhood Division of the Council for Exceptional Children), and others. Some organizations concern themselves with very specific age groups of children; for instance, Zero to Three, which promotes the well-being of infants and toddlers. There are regional, state, and local organizations, such as the Southern Early Childhood Association (SECA); branches of the organizations described previously; and some nonaffiliated, local organizations that meet the needs of a group of people in the community.

As a student entering the early childhood profession, you should consider becoming a member of a professional organization. Some colleges and universities have student-member sections of NAEYC or ACEI. By becoming a member, you can keep abreast of new developments, meet and participate in a support network with others in the same field, and attend workshops and conferences at the local, state, or national level. Information about organizations is readily available through your instructor or those who work in the field.

Reflective Teaching

One of the hallmarks of a professional is the ability to be reflective about all aspects of teaching.

Reflection means stepping back from the immediate, intense experience of hands-on work and taking the time to wonder what the experience really means" (Parlakin, 2001, p. 2). It implies being thoughtful about how one approaches a task. It means stopping to think before acting. It also acknowledges that human beings are complex and that all situations cannot be dealt with in one single way. Reflective teaching means not reacting to certain situations in an automatic way because "I've always done it this way."

The NAEYC publication, *When Teachers Reflect* (Tertell, Klein, & Jewett, 1998) considers one reason why reflection is important. With experience, teachers encounter many situations over and over, and eventually become successful in dealing with them. This can apply to a variety of circumstances, for instance, leading group activities, developing curriculums, guiding children's behavior, or interacting with parents. There is comfort in developing successful strategies, but there is also a danger. "The danger in this easy, successful, and routine practice is that it may become more repetitive and routine, less creative and satisfying, and less responsive to the particular child or situation" (Tertell et al., 1998, p. xxiv).

Early childhood educators are often bombarded with quick and easy answers to their work. A wealth of kits, how-to books, and other prototypes provide

REFLECTING ON TEACHING AND LEARNING

I see myself as a teacher and a learner; one role does not exist without the other. I take the risk to know and the risk to change. Becoming a professional educator requires work, training, self-discovery, support, and the belief that the acquisition of knowledge can happen in many ways in many places. I am a career educator who presently works as a coach and mentor in order to share my experience and my certainty that high-quality education is based on a way of thinking and a way of being with children. We are not born teachers; we are born learners. How we teach depends on our values, training, and experience.

My beliefs were shaped by memorable early experiences. My family strongly influenced my values through their respect for teachers and their commitment to lifelong learning. My sweet and thoughtful kindergarten teacher, after noting that I had escaped from school by means of an obscure exit through the fence, didn't reprimand me but redirected my energy into play that encouraged investigation and relationships. I also remember Mrs. Woodcock, my fifth-grade teacher, who used projects, drama, dance, art, and music to make certain that all modes of learning were made available to her students in the implementation of mandatory curriculum.

Numerous adult experiences continued to shape my concepts of teaching and learning. In college I participated in an unconventional internship program that stressed collegiality, was highly supported by the local school district, and encouraged an active role for parents. These created experiences and experiments that supported

© Theresa Danna Douglas

Leah, Coach and Mentor to Early Childhood Teachers

me in finding my style. My study of and visit to the municipal preschools and infant toddler centers of Reggio Emilia, Italy, helped me realize the importance of the voice of children and currently forms the basis of my work—reflective practice with individuals and small groups in order to support change. I also believe that we, as professional educators, can create something better for children within a collaborative climate, one which fosters the satisfaction and pleasure of exchanging ideas with others.

The goal of my current coaching and mentoring role is to help teachers facilitate, document, reflect upon, and plan complexity as they listen to and teach young children. Together we celebrate each small step, which supports new habits. Through encouragement and consideration of the many different possibilities that can be found in each interaction, I build relationships and trust—the foundations upon which I work.

Sometimes I enter the ongoing play of a small group of children to model how to extend their explorations. Another technique I use is parallel observation—where the teacher and I both observe and take notes about a group or an individual child.

Afterwards, we reflect upon the teacher's written notes and discuss how such insight can inform curriculum. In observed ordinary events we often discover extraordinary possibilities.

For instance, one teacher and I observed a group of children using big blocks to create the outline of a waiting room in a doctor's office. One of the builders explained that she had gone with her mother to get a shot. Five children filled the space. Antonio wanted to enter and was told by one of the other children that there was no room. The teacher began get up and intervene but I motioned to her to wait and continue observing. Antonio turned away with a dejected look but then suddenly smiled. He turned and announced, "I am the doctor. I give shots over here." As Dr. Antonio led the group away from the blocks, the teacher smiled. She and I discussed what the boy had done, and planned possibilities for extending this dramatic incident and making it more complex. By attentively observing and listening, this teacher noticed many things about the children, their interests, and the environment.

It is the excitement created by discovery that keeps me in the field of education for young children. When I see the enthusiasm and change that observation, reflection, facilitation, and planning foster in the teachers I coach and mentor, I realize that I made the right career choice. I know that each teacher needs to find her or his own way of being a teacher, just as I did. The resulting style will contain traces of many colleagues and experiences. Each teacher's journey will be unique.

a "one-size-fits-all" approach to curriculum, guidance, parent interaction, and other aspects of the job. More often than not, however, these offer a simplistic, stereotyped method for dealing with complex issues. Reflection requires time because it means reconsidering and rethinking preconceived ideas. But, it results in deeper understanding and much more genuine results that are satisfactory to the children and families as well as to the teacher.

Many college-level early childhood education programs incorporate reflective teaching as part of student learning. You, as a student teacher, may well be encouraged to ask yourself how you feel, what you think, and what others are feeling and thinking. Through such self-awareness, you are able to maximize your learning and offer more thoughtful experiences both for yourself and for the children with whom you work. To work within the principles outlined by DAP requires reflection. DAP is based on the premise that children's development and learning are complex and require thoughtful decisions by the teacher (Copple & Bredekamp, 2009). Some academic programs are incorporating **action research** as part of teacher training. Such research stems from reflection but also adds a way of finding practical solutions to the issues and problems teachers encounter. Stremmel (2002) concludes that "teachers need to be part detectives, searching for children's clues and following their leads, and part researcher, gathering data, analyzing the information, and testing hypotheses" (p. 68). This, he notes, shifts the teacher from someone who simply delivers information to children to a professional who is actively involved in understanding and making a difference in the lives of children.

Some early childhood programs and teacher education programs use coaching to help teachers reach their potential. (See the discussion of coaching in this chapter's "Stories from the Field.") Skiffington, Washburn, and Elliot (2011) suggest a three-phase process, including: (1) a preobservation planning conference to set goals for the children's learning and strategies to meet those goals; (2) observation and analysis, with the coach videotaping the activity and analyzing how it met the goals set in the first step; and (3) a reflective conference in which the coach and teacher watch and discuss the video and the coach asks questions to elicit reflective analysis. "The videotaping that happens in Phase 2 is a very powerful part of the process. ... [It] provides the whole picture: what the teacher did and how the children responded" (Skiffington et al., 2011, p. 13).

> **action research**
> Research carried out by teachers as a way of finding practical solutions to the everyday problems encountered in teaching.

SOME CURRENT ISSUES AND DILEMMAS

Early childhood education is, in many ways, a field of contradictions and extremes. Those who try to define it often find themselves in a dilemma, not clear on what to include and what to exclude. Where does a program fit that barely meets minimum standards, and what about the program that genuinely strives for excellence in meeting the needs of its children and families? Are the kindergarten teacher, the infant care provider, the Head Start teacher, the preschool master teacher, and the home care provider included? Are the preschool teacher who holds a master's degree in early childhood education and the high school graduate who works in a child care center equals in the same field? Can the child care provider who earns minimum wage for the eight hours a day spent caring for children be lumped together with the kindergarten teacher who earns a public school salary for nine months of teaching?

How can the teacher's job description that calls for someone who "likes children" be compared with the one that requires "a degree in early childhood education or child development"? How can the lack of licensing requirements for teachers of young children in many states be reconciled with educators' insistence that those who work with young children need specific training? In fact, is there a good reason to justify why you are enrolled in an academic program while others with no academic training may equally qualify for some positions?

These questions and others are at the heart of the dilemma facing the early childhood profession. We will review some specific issues and look at some possible ways of addressing these. Although we will divide some of these issues into categories such as teacher shortage and low pay, these are not separable concerns that exist independently of each other.

A Historical Perspective

It might be helpful to look at the road traveled by the field of early childhood education to gain a perspective on its current status. Early childhood education today is inextricably linked to the role and status of women in the United States.

Between the mideighteenth and midnineteenth centuries, "womanhood was redefined, its image re-created and re-imagined, its social function reviewed, its links to child rearing and socialization forged, and its authority over the moral and cultural development of the nation rationalized" (Finkelstein, 1988, p. 12). When, in the later half of the nineteenth century, the kindergarten became firmly established as an American institution, women had found their niche in an environment that was not quite domestic, yet not quite public either.

The early-twentieth-century pioneers of the early childhood movement, while building a scientific basis for child study, continued to see women as the guardians of the young, with a specialized role in upholding moral and cultural standards, a noble role that superseded concerns for economic and material comforts. Unfortunately, this legacy of "unselfishness" has followed early childhood educators into the twenty-first century, endowing them with a realization of the importance of their work, yet placing them in a low-paying profession that has low status in our social structure (Finkelstein, 1988).

Teacher Shortage

Over the past several years, increasing attention has been focused on the shortage of qualified early childhood teachers. Employment of child care workers was projected to increase by 18 percent between 2006 and 2016, which is faster than the average for all occupations. A large number of new jobs are expected for child care workers, almost 248,000 over the decade. There is also a shortage of public school teachers, compounding the demand for early childhood staff. The need for elementary teachers is expected to increase by 14 percent by 2016 (U.S. Bureau of Labor Statistics, 2008).

Even more serious than the early childhood teacher shortage is the high rate of turnover among teachers of young children. Whitebook, Sakai, Gerber, and Howes (2001) followed a group of child care center teachers and directors over a six-year period to examine turnover and its impact. The researchers concluded that the child care workforce, including workers employed in

Key Point ◆◆

The history of women over the past two centuries is closely linked with the development of the field of early childhood education.

Key Point ◆◆

The high demand for quality programs for children of working parents, plus the low pay and status of those who work in these programs, have resulted in a serious shortage of early childhood professionals.

The needs of teachers of young children must be an important priority in early childhood programs. Scheduled time and a pleasant place to relax can contribute to teacher satisfaction. What other factors can improve working conditions for teachers of young children?

© Cengage Learning

higher-quality programs, is alarmingly unstable. Of those who participated in the study in 1994, 76 percent were no longer in the same job in 1996, and 82 percent had left their jobs by 2000. They found that the yearly turnover rate averaged 30 percent, ranging from zero to 100 percent, depending on the center. Director turnover was also very high, with over half the centers losing their director by 1996 and two-thirds having a new director by 2000. Only about half of the teachers and directors in the original study stayed in the field of child care.

This high turnover rate appears to be directly related to low pay, illustrated by the inverse relationship between rate of pay and percentage of turnover. Those at the lower end of the pay scale changed jobs at twice the rate of those at the higher end. At the same time, however, there is less turnover among teachers with early childhood training. A follow-up survey of CDAs who had earned their credentials during the preceding five years indicated that more than 90 percent of the respondents continued to teach (Bailey, 2004). Although this does not provide direct evidence that these teachers were still at the same worksite, they at least continued in the profession. However, in the early childhood teaching population at large, a large number of those who work with young children change occupations each year.

High staff turnover takes its toll in several ways. The National Child Care Staffing Study (Whitebook et al., 1989) found that in centers with a high turnover rate, children spent less time in social activities with peers and tended to wander aimlessly. In addition, separation from parents becomes more critical when caregivers change frequently (Galinsky, 1989). Very young children are particularly vulnerable to teacher turnover. Toddlers who lost their primary teacher were found to be more withdrawn and more aggressive two years later (Howes & Hamilton, 1993). Teachers also suffer when their co-workers change frequently because they have to assume the additional burden of orienting and training new staff (Whitebook, 1986).

Resolutions to the issue of high staff turnover, and the related issues of low pay and teacher burnout, are being pursued by professionals and professional organizations. Some of their recommendations will be discussed later in this section.

Low Pay

Key Point ◆◆

Low pay and poor benefits for early childhood teachers are directly tied to the affordability of child care for families.

Staffing shortages would undoubtedly be much less of a problem if early childhood teachers were paid adequate salaries and if they received appropriate recognition and status. For most teachers of young children, however, monetary rewards are not equal to their professional training and value. Although there is a wide variation in pay, early childhood teachers are generally paid poorly.

Low pay feeds into a vicious cycle: Poor pay causes qualified teachers to seek work elsewhere; as a result, jobs are often filled by unqualified staff. They, in turn, reinforce the perception of the low status of early childhood education, which negates the need for higher pay. There is a clear relationship between pay, retention of staff, and quality of programs. Centers that pay higher wages are able to retain qualified teachers and directors. Highly skilled staff stay in their jobs if they earn higher-than-average wages and work with other staff who are also highly trained. Not surprisingly, when there is a significant number of qualified staff in a center who are paid higher-than-average wages, the center is more likely to sustain high quality in its program (Whitebook et al., 2001).

The Center for the Child Care Work Force has been tracking the staffing shortage and teacher turnover for a number of years. Each phase of its study has confirmed that teacher salaries are lower than salaries for other workers with equal education and, in fact, often does not keep pace with increases in the cost of living. Nonetheless, those who remain in their jobs, as well as those who leave for better-paying work, report great satisfaction from working with young children (Whitebook et al., 2001). One report analyzed trends in the early childhood labor market and concluded that the field has changed for the worse since the early 1980s, with fewer staff now having a degree (Belm & Whitebook, 2006).

Another issue tied to low pay is the lack of benefits offered to employees of child care programs. Only 28 percent of child care workers had employer-provided health insurance, according to one large study (Tarrant et al., 2009). The earlier National Child Care Staffing Study found considerable variation in the types of benefits offered. For instance, health benefits were offered by more than 60 percent of nonprofit centers, whereas the percentage dropped to 16, 21, and 24, respectively, for independent for-profit, chain for-profit, and church-sponsored nonprofit child care programs (Whitebook et al., 1989). Generally, early childhood programs sponsored by larger institutions such as hospitals, public school districts, or universities benefit from the policies of their sponsoring agencies. In a similar way, employer-sponsored child care programs often receive their company's benefits package as well.

The reason for the low remuneration earned by early childhood teachers is directly tied to the issue of affordability of child care. Because staff wages and benefits constitute the largest expenditure in early childhood programs, the cost to families is most affected by how much is allocated to that portion of the budget; the higher the teacher salaries, the greater the cost. Part of this balance is the issue of child–adult ratio: The more children per adult, the lower the cost because fewer adults have to be hired. However, high child–adult ratios are associated with higher levels of teacher stress and decreased responsiveness to children (Howes, 1997; NICHD, 1999).

Yet, the answer is not simply a matter of raising the cost of child care charged to families. Although some families can afford to pay higher rates to ensure high-quality care offered by well-trained and well-paid professionals, many others cannot. Two-thirds of employed women are either the sole support of their families or are married to men who earn extremely low wages. Experts contend that the cost families pay for child care includes a hidden subsidy—the low wages teachers receive (Willer, 1990).

Increasingly, professionals argue that early childhood education needs to be publicly subsidized, similarly to the way that elementary, secondary, and higher education are supported. Comprehensive recommendations, such as those in the report *Not by Chance: Creating an Early Care and Education System for America's Children* (Kagan & Cohen, 1997), have been increasingly publicized. In Chapter 1 you read about some of these efforts that come not only from the early childhood field but from other fields as well, such as economics.

Burnout

Intricately tied to staff shortage, staff turnover, and poor salaries is teacher burnout. Burnout is complex, resulting from multiple causes. It is characterized by job dissatisfaction, stress, loss of energy, irritability, and a feeling of being exploited. The **burnout syndrome** involves a person's inability to cope with continuous, ongoing stress, and is accompanied by a loss of energy, purpose, and idealism (Schamer & Jackson, 1996).

Low salaries and minimum benefits contribute to burnout, but so do other factors (Hale-Jinks, Knopf, & Kemple, 2006). Some of these include long working hours, unpaid overtime, time spent outside working hours in curriculum planning or family functions, expectations for maintenance duties, lack of breaks, the constant intensity of working closely with children, high child–adult ratios, and lack of power in the decision-making process. Sometimes a change in working conditions, a seminar, or a support group can help a teacher regain a feeling of commitment and renewal.

Although burnout is a final outcome for some of those who work in early childhood programs, many others find great job satisfaction, which balances some of these negative aspects. The opportunity to contribute to and observe the development of their young charges provides a great source of pleasure to early childhood teachers. In addition, they find other aspects of the job gratifying. These include opportunities for reflection and self-development, satisfying staff relations, job flexibility, a level of autonomy, and staff interdependence (Whitebook et al., 1989).

Men in Early Childhood Education

A somewhat different issue concerns the predominance of females in early childhood education, representing about 97 percent of practitioners (Nelson, Carlson, & West, 2006). There have been, and continue to be, male teachers of young children who have a high commitment to the education and well-being of young children. For some children who grow up in single-parent homes without a father figure, a male teacher can fill a special role. Even more broadly, all children need to know men who are caring and loving (Elicker, 2002).

Yet, men leave the field of early childhood education at an even greater rate than women do. Some male teachers who changed careers reported that they

burnout syndrome
Condition experienced by professionals as a result of undue job stress; characterized by loss of energy, irritability, and a feeling of being exploited.

Key Point
Some early childhood teachers experience burnout.

Key Point
More than 97 percent of early childhood teachers are women, and male teachers leave the field at an even greater rate than female teachers do.

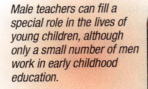

Male teachers can fill a special role in the lives of young children, although only a small number of men work in early childhood education.

© Cengage Learning

were subject to subtle prejudicial attitudes from parents, female co-workers, and administrators. "A major barrier to men becoming early childhood teachers is the pervasive belief in our society and in our profession that men are less able to care for and educate young children than are women" (Cunningham & Watson, 2002). Suspicion that was initially based on vague stereotypes has been intensified by highly publicized cases of sexual abuse in child care settings (Sumsion, 1999).

Theories about why there are so few men in the field have centered primarily on reasons of economics and status (Robinson, 1988). One study, however, indicates that low pay may not be as much a deterrent as formerly thought (Sargent, 2002). Through interviews with a group of men who work in the early childhood education field, Sargent concluded that "men often develop compensatory behaviors to accomplish the objectives of early childhood education in the face of intense suspicion and work expectations not encountered by women" (p. 27).

Professionals within the field need to take active steps to increase the number of men in early childhood education. One specific program that directly addresses the small numbers of men in the field is the Call Me MISTER Program (CMMP) of South Carolina (Cunningham & Watson, 2002; **www .callmemister.clemson.edu**). In recent years, a number of countries have made an effort and provide incentives to recruit men into early education careers (Nelson et al., 2006).

Empowerment and Activism

naeyc

We have raised several urgent issues that face those in the early childhood profession. It is heartening that increasingly more professional and political effort is being devoted to solutions to these issues. Articulate public statements, relevant publications, thoughtful research, and energetic political advocacy and lobbying are making an impact. There is no question that the needs of young children and families, the importance of high quality in child care, and the needs of early childhood teachers are becoming highly visible public matters. From the halls of the Capitol in Washington, DC, to legislative buildings across all of the states, early childhood education and child care have become high priorities. This is, in many ways, an exciting time to be entering the field!

Changes in the current realities of early childhood education can be brought about through joint political action and the empowerment of teachers (Dresden & Myers, 1989). Training for advocacy is being incorporated into higher education programs at all levels, as students learn how policies are made, how the political system operates, and how they can affect it. You may well be taking a public policy course as part of your program of study, something that probably would not have been part of the curriculum 20 years ago. Families are also often enlisted to support public policy endeavors.

What is clear is the resolve of professionals and professional organizations to push for change. Interest in and support for quality child care comes from many sectors both within and outside of the field of early childhood education, including families, teachers, administrators, resource and referral agencies, related service providers, professional organizations, teacher trainers and educators, researchers, civic and religious groups, business and labor organizations, volunteer service organizations, philanthropic organizations and foundations, and civic leaders. A coalition including members of such constituency groups can be a powerful force in addressing such issues.

One of the major challenges of the goal of providing high-quality child care programs is funding and financing. The cost cannot be assumed by families only, but needs to be shared by employers, government, and community organizations. The actual cost of quality early childhood services needs to be estimated, different revenue-generating mechanisms need to be identified, alternative approaches for distributing funds to families must be developed, and coordinated funding initiatives have to be created. Work toward these goals is underway by dedicated and creative professionals who are beginning to address some of the serious issues inherent in the process of changing our current system to the proposed system.

Another challenge is that the governance structure for early childhood education is haphazard and often ineffective. What is needed are more consistent, rational structures, using both state and local boards, that would cover a broad range of topics and have the responsibility for ensuring high-quality, integrated services for children and families. Sharon Lynn Kagan and Kristie Kauzer (2009) argue that the question is not *whether* government should be involved in early education, since it already is at many levels. Instead, the critical question should be how best to make the system work to provide appropriate programs for children and families.

FAMILY SUPPORT FOR THE EARLY CHILDHOOD PROFESSION

In Chapter 3, we discussed the role and responsibility of early childhood teachers toward families. As indicated, the teacher–family relationship is a reciprocal process. While teachers provide many services for families, parents can also be extremely effective advocates for the early childhood education profession. One of the most effective lobbying efforts to promote increased funding allocation for early childhood programs in one state was the appearance of a large group

Key Point ◆

The issues and dilemmas facing early childhood education and its teachers are being addressed through vigorous advocacy and lobbying to help bring about change through political action and empowerment of teachers.

of parents who spoke from their perspective about the importance of that funding. The legislators found the 200 taxpayers who came to promote this bill quite convincing!

Family support, however, does not begin in the political arena. First and most importantly, families must have a sound appreciation of early childhood educators and a clear understanding of the issues they face. Such understanding is promoted in a high-quality program in which teachers act professionally and are articulate about their field. When families recognize that the quality of education and care their children receive is inextricably tied to improving the status and working conditions of their children's teachers and caregivers, they will be better able to help bring about changes.

SUMMARY

1. Early childhood teachers can be described by some identifiable personal characteristics.
2. The staffs of early childhood programs can include a number of individuals in a variety of roles, including the director, teaching staff, volunteers, support staff, board of directors, and community professionals.
3. A variety of training possibilities and regulating entities are associated with early childhood programs.
   A. Early childhood teachers might receive training through academic channels or through the Child Development Associate program.
   B. Early childhood programs are licensed through local or state regulations, which set minimum standards.
   C. Many programs undergo voluntary accreditation through the National Academy of Early Childhood Programs. Four-year and advanced university programs and two-year community college early childhood education programs usually also are accredited, using the NAEYC Standards for Professional Preparation Programs.
4. Professionalism in early childhood education is noted by criteria such as a code of ethics, the existence of professional organizations, and reflective teaching.
5. Although early childhood education presents you with exciting challenges, as a student entering this career, it also presents some issues and dilemmas:
   A. Some of the problems faced by early childhood educators are rooted in the historic antecedents of the field.
   B. Early childhood education faces some serious concerns, including teacher shortage, low pay, burnout, and scarcity of men in the field.
   C. Through advocacy and empowerment of early childhood professionals, these issues are beginning to be addressed.

KEY TERMS LIST

action research

assistant teacher

Association for Childhood Education International (ACEI)

board of directors

burnout syndrome

caregiver

child care worker

Child Development Associate (CDA)

code of ethics

collectivism

cultural scripts

disposition

early childhood educator

early childhood teacher

head teacher

individualism

National Association for the Education of Young Children (NAEYC)

reflection

team teaching

KEY QUESTIONS

1. Imagine that you have been hired as the director of a new early childhood program. What kind of staffing would you want in your program? What positions and staffing structure would help you provide the best program you possibly could?
2. Obtain the requirements for the CDA credentialing process (from your instructor or online at www.cdacouncil.org). Compare these to the ones required by the program in which you are enrolled. What are the points of similarity and the differences?
3. What are the advantages of belonging to a professional early childhood organization? Review several issues of professional journals such as *Young Children* or *Childhood Education* to gain a sense of what organizations such as NAEYC or ACEI have to offer.
4. Talk to several teachers of young children. What do they view as the most rewarding parts of their job? What most frustrates them? Compare their answers with your own goals and expectations.
5. Professional organizations such as NAEYC have been active in advocating for improved working conditions and status for those who work with young children. Review the "Public Policy Report" and "Washington Update" in several issues of *Young Children* to see what kinds of issues are being discussed.

ADDITIONAL RESOURCES

Select additional books, articles, and websites on topics discussed in Chapter 4.

Bowman, B. T., Donovan, M. S., & Burns, M. S. (Eds.). (2001). *Eager to learn: Educating our preschoolers*. Washington, DC: National Academies Press.

Stone, J. G. (2001). *Building classroom community: The early childhood teacher's role*. Washington, DC: NAEYC.

Young Children, the journal published by NAEYC, is an excellent resource for all kinds of early childhood information.

HELPFUL WEBSITES

National Association for the Education of Young Children (NAEYC):

www.naeyc.org

As the largest professional organization in the early childhood education field, NAEYC provides numerous resources to support excellence in programs for young children. Part of the website includes the organization's many position statements on issues of importance. In particular, check out NAEYC's *Code of Ethical Conduct and Statement of Commitment*.

Association for Childhood Education International (ACEI):

www.acei.org

ACEI is an international early childhood organization that is dedicated to supporting the global community in providing optimal education and development of children from birth through early adolescence and to influencing the professional growth of educators who work with these children.

Center for the Child Care Workforce (CCWF):

www.ccw.org

The mission of CCWF is to improve the quality of early care and education for all children by promoting research and policy initiatives. The aim of these is to ensure that the child care workforce is well educated and well compensated and has a voice in the workplace.

Go to **CengageBrain.com** to register your access code for this book's Education CourseMate website, where you will find more resources to help you study. Additional resources for this chapter include TeachSource Videos, glossary flashcards, web links, case studies with critical thinking questions that apply the concepts presented in this chapter, and more. If your textbook does not include a printed access card, you can go to **CengageBrain.com** to purchase access.

III

The *Why* of Early Childhood Education

Early childhood education meets a number of societal needs, as we discussed in earlier chapters. But the importance of this field is also supported by a solid foundation of theory and research, which provides direction to teachers. To address the why of early education, we will consider "Rationale Supporting Early Childhood Education" in Chapter 5 and "Accountability, Standards, and Assessment" in Chapter 6.

5 Rationale Supporting Early Childhood Education

 Developmentally appropriate practice . . . is not based on what we think might be true or what we want to believe about young children. Developmentally appropriate practice is informed by what we know from theory and literature about how children develop and learn. In particular, a review of that literature yields a number of well-supported generalizations, or principles.

Developmentally Appropriate Practice, Copple & Bredekamp, 2009, p. 10

In Chapter 5, you will find answers to the following questions about the rationale that supports early childhood education:

❿ What has been the role and status of children in times past?
❿ Who were the people who shaped our view of young children into what it is today?
❿ What is the relationship of the theories developed to shape that view of children and the kinds of early childhood programs in existence today?
❿ Have these program approaches been supported by research, and what does the research tell us about the effects of early childhood education?

NAEYC STANDARDS CONSIDERED IN CHAPTER 5

(See the Standards Correlation Chart on the inside front cover of this book for the titles and description of the standards listed below.)

❿ *Standard 6a:* Being familiar with the historic roots of the field and knowing about those who helped shape the field to further identify as an early childhood professional (pp. 105–114).
❿ *Standard 1a:* Recognizing the importance of theory in guiding understanding of young children's development and learning (pp. 112–121).
❿ *Standard 4b:* Understanding of underlying theories as these impact effective strategies used in working with young children (pp. 121–131).
❿ *Standard 4b:* Knowing that effective early childhood practices are based on a strong body of research (pp. 131–138).

How we approach the education and care of young children depends, to a great extent, on what we believe children are like. Programs for preschoolers are often structured around some underlying assumptions about the nature of children. For instance, a belief that children learn actively by exploring their environment would result in a different type of early education program

104

than one based on the idea that children learn passively by being taught specific information and skills. Similarly, a belief that children are basically unruly and need strict control so they will learn appropriate behavior would result in a different guidance approach than the notion that children generally strive toward social acceptance from others by conforming to reasonable expectations.

As you continue to learn more about early childhood education, you will begin to see why theory is so important. We will introduce some of the most influential theories in this chapter, although, as you read on, you will begin to realize that the field follows the teachings and beliefs of some theorists more than those of others. What is important about theory is that it provides a framework within which we view children and how they learn. Early childhood educators view children as active learners who learn best by exploring the world around them. Such a belief provides direction for how we structure curriculum, environment, guidance techniques, and all our interactions with children. As you will note, the guiding documents to which we continue to refer, *Developmentally Appropriate Practice in Early Childhood Programs Serving Children from Birth through Age 8* (Copple & Bredekamp, 2009) and the NAEYC Standards for Professional Preparation Programs (NAEYC, 2010), are solidly based on the teachings of key theorists such as Jean Piaget, Erik Erikson, and Lev Vygotsky, all of whom you will meet in this chapter.

We will begin this chapter with a quick trip back in history, as a way of providing you, as an early childhood professional, with an understanding of the path the field has followed to where it is today. After that, we will review key theorists. This historic and theoretical overview will provide the foundation and rationale on which early childhood education has been built.

A LOOK BACK—CHILDREN THROUGH TIME

Key Point ◆

The concept of childhood and the treatment of children through history have always been tied to economic, religious, and social factors.

Interest in the care and education of young children goes back thousands of years. Our Western tradition is traced to ancient Greece, where the writings of philosophers such as Plato and Aristotle reflect a keen sensitivity to the needs of children and the importance of appropriate education in shaping their character. The Greeks saw human development as a transformation from the imperfect state of childhood to the ideal of adulthood (Lascarides & Hinitz, 2000). The Greek tradition, including education for girls as well as for boys, was carried on for several hundred years into the height of Roman times.

Many of the early, enlightened ideas about children were lost, however, during the Middle Ages, when even the concept of childhood seemed to have been misplaced. Children became little more than property and were put to work, for instance, in the fields or tending animals, just as soon as they were big enough. "This period in history was arduous for children" (Lascarides & Hinitz, 2000). Other historians, however, argue that parents during medieval times were intensely concerned with their children and that children were not thought of merely as "little adults" (Classen, 2005). Schools and formal education as a way of passing on cultural traditions had

Early childhood programs have an extensive and rich history, both in the United States and in other parts of the world.

virtually disappeared in Europe except in a few places, such as in Islamic Spain, where learning was highly valued.

Various religious, political, and economic forces provided the impetus for the move out of these Dark Ages, often improving the treatment of children, but at other times exploiting them. Martin Luther, for example, advocated public education for all children in sixteenth-century Germany as a way of promoting religious salvation. In other parts of Europe, some social and political reformers, angered by the injustices that provided an opulent lifestyle for the nobility at the expense of the starving peasants, developed ideas that focused on children and their education as one way of overcoming such inequities.

By the eighteenth century, as the Industrial Revolution swept both Europe and America, the economic search for cheap labor led to the abuse of many children in factories. They were kept at spindles or levers up to as many as 16 hours a day, while being given only minimal food and housing. Such blatant exploitation also led to reforms, eventually including universal public education and laws prohibiting child labor (Lascarides & Hinitz, 2000; Wolfe, 2000).

The twentieth century, while a relatively short period in history, represents an active time in the formation of early childhood education. For one thing, education for all children came to be increasingly accepted, reinforcing the idea that childhood is a separate and important period. Education in the United States, in the eyes of such progressive educators as John Dewey, was a training ground for democracy, a way of equalizing social inequities by imbuing children from a young age with democratic ideals. Philosophers and scientists, who proclaimed the early years as especially relevant, also contributed to the field. Among these, Sigmund Freud focused unprecedented attention on early life experiences as the foundation of personality.

A third contribution came from the development of scientific methods of observation that led to the **child study movement,** out of which grew many university preschool laboratory programs designed to facilitate the careful study of young children. Still another contribution to today's field is the notion of early childhood education as a means to social reform. Important programs were developed throughout this century with the idea of rescuing the poor from poverty. A common purpose motivated those who helped move young children out of factories and into schools at the turn of the century, and those who developed the Head Start philosophy of the 1960s.

Finally, another change that has profoundly affected early childhood education today is the rising need for child care arrangements, which we discussed in Chapter 1. Although recent changes in the economy and family life have brought the proliferation of child care programs available today, such programs are not new. During World War II, many women were required to work and needed arrangements for care of their young children; these arrangements were often publicly subsidized (Braun & Edwards, 1972; Carter, 1987; Greenberg, 1987; Siegel & White, 1982; Weber, 1984).

History and the context of each period have generally determined how children are viewed. Because children are vulnerable and dependent, their image and treatment have been shaped by the needs of the times and by influential thinkers and writers. Today, we view children much more benignly than during many periods in the past. We acknowledge that the childhood years are unique and important, we provide children with special environments, and we promote education as a social and personal necessity. Today's view of children is based, to a greater extent, on theory and research rather than on the religious or political ideas that, in part, dictated the image of children in

Key Point ◆

During the twentieth century, the view of early childhood as an important part of human development was particularly promoted.

child study movement

This movement occurred in the early years of the twentieth century in the United States when many university preschools were established to develop scientific methods for studying children.

the past. Let us now turn to some of the important figures in the historical account of early childhood education. The section that follows will then review influential theorists whose conceptualizations have further refined our ideas of young children.

INFLUENTIAL PEOPLE IN THE HISTORY OF EARLY CHILDHOOD EDUCATION

Many, many individuals have contributed to our current view of young children and their care and education. We will touch on the works of only a few of them. Some developed their ideas because of their direct work with children, often children from families of low socioeconomic status; others' theories emerged out of political and philosophical concerns about the problems of society and how reforms could be brought about. Let us now meet some of the people who have contributed to our views, particularly as these relate to the early years.

Jean-Jacques Rousseau (1712–1778)

Rousseau was not an early childhood educator, but his ideas have certainly influenced the field. As a philosopher writing in the context of the corrupt French society of his time, Rousseau developed the idea that society actually hindered human beings from developing according to their nature. Society, with its hierarchy of the few who were rich and powerful, only imposed misery on the masses, a state that is not natural. Rousseau, in fact, considered anything natural and primitive to be good. Thus, he argued, if children could develop without the artificial trappings of civilization, they would be able to achieve their true potential of being moral and good.

According to Rousseau, young children are innately pure and noble, but they need to be protected from the evil influences of society to maintain this goodness. It is through close contact with nature that they can develop their senses and form their personalities. In a protected rural environment, they learn from what is concrete, not from the abstract, through trial and error and experimentation. Such learning is natural and satisfying, leading to happiness, because children will know nothing of the artificial needs that society creates. Rousseau recognized that children's modes of thinking and learning are different from that of adults and considered good education to be based on the stage of development of the child, not on adult-imposed criteria. A child-centered, uncorrupted education will, eventually, result in adults who are moral and interested in the common good of society.

Rousseau never worked with children—in fact, he actually abandoned all of his own children to foundling homes—but he wrote extensively about his philosophy in his novels and essays. Today, we agree with Rousseau that children have a unique nature that needs to be nurtured and protected. We also recognize the need to provide an appropriate environment for young children, one in which their development can be maximized. Although his highly idealistic view of childhood and human nature was never fully adopted by those who followed Rousseau, he nonetheless had a great influence on later early childhood educators, as we shall soon see (Carter, 1987; Grimsley, 1976; Morgan, 2007; Nutbrown, Clough, & Selbie, 2008; Weber, 1984). Learn more about Jean-Jacques Rousseau in the section, "Who's Who in ECE?" (page 110).

Key Point ◆

Rousseau advanced the notions that children are innately noble and good, that their way of learning is different from that of adults, and that they should be removed from the corrupting influences of society.

Johann Pestalozzi (1746–1827)

Pestalozzi was deeply influenced by Rousseau's ideas about education. He felt that all people, even the poorest, had the right to an education as a way of helping them develop their moral and intellectual potential. He believed in education according to nature and considered that learning for young children is intricately tied to concrete experiences and observation. Unlike Rousseau, however, he stressed the important role of the mother in children's earliest years.

Also unlike Rousseau, Pestalozzi actually worked with children, developing educational methods that are still used today. For instance, he stressed the importance of recognizing individual differences among children and the relevance of children's self-activity rather than rote as the basis of learning.

What made Pestalozzi successful as an educator of young children, however, was his powerful personality and his selfless and passionate dedication and commitment.

> His life was devoted to human relationships, a life of the mind, but more a life of feeling and service. . . . His educational doctrine . . . must be followed with devotion, self-forgetfulness, deep and loving concern for children and for the essence of childhood. (Braun & Edwards, 1972, p. 60)

One of the schools he established became world famous, drawing visitors and students from all over Europe. He is considered to be the first to actually teach young children of preschool age, marking the beginning of the kindergarten movement (Braun & Edwards, 1972; Morgan, 2007; Nutbrown et al., 2008; Ulich, 1967; Weber, 1984). Learn more about Johann Pestalozzi in the section, "Who's Who in ECE?" (page 110).

Friedrich Froebel (1782–1852)

Froebel was one of the visitors at Pestalozzi's school, observing it with some mixed feelings. He greatly admired Pestalozzi's skills but was concerned over his inability to articulate his methods. Froebel, however, was better able to put into words his educational principles. Like his predecessors Rousseau and Pestalozzi, Froebel believed in the interrelatedness of nature and the child's developing mind. He also advocated that education should harmonize with the child's inner development, recognizing that children are in different stages at various ages. He saw childhood as a separate stage that was not just a transition to adulthood but rather a stage with great intrinsic value in its own right.

Froebel also strongly stressed the important role of play in young children's development, not merely as a preparation for adult work. He saw play as a pure and natural mode of learning through which children achieve harmony. Froebel developed a carefully programmed curriculum and specific materials. He is, in fact, credited with developing building blocks, which are now a standard material in early childhood education. His program was centered on play and sensory awareness. Art activities, games, finger plays, songs, blocks, stories, puppet play, planting a garden, and other similar endeavors were part of Froebel's kindergartens (Moore, Campos, Collazo, Maytum, Sampayo, & Sanchez, 2010). His classes were not held in a traditional classroom but rather in a "garden for children," hence the German word **kindergarten** (Braun & Edwards,

1972; Carter, 1987; Morgan, 2007; Nutbrown et al., 2008; Ulich, 1947, 1967; Weber, 1984). Learn more about Friedrich Froebel in the section, "Who's Who in ECE?" (page 111).

Maria Montessori (1870–1952)

A true feminist of her time, Maria Montessori was the first woman to become a medical doctor in Italy. Her interest in psychiatry led her to work with retarded children. She felt that their problems were often educational more than medical, and she proved her point when a number of these institutionalized children easily passed regular school exams after she had worked with them. In 1907, the city of Rome asked Montessori to take charge of a children's day nursery that was attached to a housing tenement for the poor. The housing authorities basically wanted someone who would keep the children off the stairs and prevent them from dirtying the newly painted walls. But Montessori found in this "casa dei bambini" (children's house) the opportunity to explore her teaching methods with children with no retardation.

Montessori's methods were based on the principle that young children learn in a way that is fundamentally different from how adults learn. She was particularly impressed with the great capacity of children to learn so much during the first few years of life. She called this capacity the **absorbent mind,** analogous to a sponge soaking up liquid. She felt that all children have a fundamental, inborn intellectual structure that unfolds gradually as they develop, although individual differences result from different environmental experiences.

If children's absorbent minds are exposed to appropriate learning experiences in the developmental stages, their minds will grow. This is especially true during **sensitive periods,** times when children are most receptive to absorbing specific learning. For instance, during one sensitive period, children are especially receptive to developing sensory perception; during another, they are concerned with a sense of order in their environment; in yet another, their energies focus on coordination and control of movement.

Montessori developed a curriculum that takes advantage of these sensitive periods by making appropriate experiences available to children at times when they are most ready to learn from them. She used the term **prepared environment** to describe this match of the right materials to children's stages of development. Her school included many learning activities that she herself developed to help children acquire skills. Some of these related to **sensory discrimination,** matching and sorting by size, shape, sound, color, smell, or other dimension; others helped children learn practical skills such as polishing shoes or setting a table. More advanced materials were aimed at teaching reading, writing, and math skills through hands-on manipulation.

Much of Montessori's philosophy and approach, particularly her self-correcting materials and strong sense of respect for children, have had an enduring impact on early childhood education. Whether by design in contemporary Montessori schools or by common acceptance in other programs, Montessori's influence is still strongly felt today (Chattin-McNichols, 1992; Gettman, 1987; Lascarides & Hinitz, 2000; Simons & Simons, 1986). Learn more about Maria Montessori in the section, "Who's Who in ECE?" (page 111).

Key Point ◆◆

Montessori, working with children living in the slums of Rome, developed a successful method of early education that is still widely followed today.

absorbent mind
Maria Montessori's term to describe the capacity of young children to learn a great deal during the early years of their lives.

sensitive periods
Maria Montessori's term describing the times when children are most receptive to absorbing specific learning.

prepared environment
Maria Montessori's term to describe the careful match between appropriate materials and what the child is most ready to learn at any given time.

sensory discrimination
Involvement in an activity in which one of the senses is used to distinguish a specific feature or dimension of similar materials; it might include matching or sorting by size, color, shape, sound, smell, or taste.

"Give your pupil no kind of verbal instruction; he should receive none but from experience."

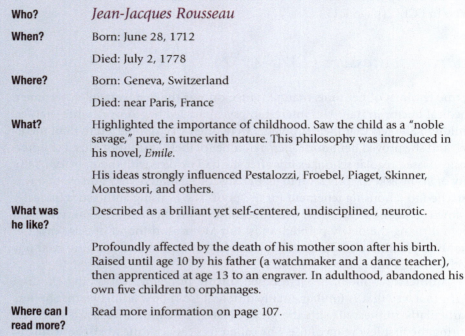

Who?	**Jean-Jacques Rousseau**
When?	Born: June 28, 1712
	Died: July 2, 1778
Where?	Born: Geneva, Switzerland
	Died: near Paris, France
What?	Highlighted the importance of childhood. Saw the child as a "noble savage," pure, in tune with nature. This philosophy was introduced in his novel, *Emile*.
	His ideas strongly influenced Pestalozzi, Froebel, Piaget, Skinner, Montessori, and others.
What was he like?	Described as a brilliant yet self-centered, undisciplined, neurotic.
	Profoundly affected by the death of his mother soon after his birth. Raised until age 10 by his father (a watchmaker and a dance teacher), then apprenticed at age 13 to an engraver. In adulthood, abandoned his own five children to orphanages.
Where can I read more?	Read more information on page 107.

"The first development of thought in the child is very much disturbed by a wordy system of teaching."

Who?	**Johann Pestalozzi**
When?	Born: January 12, 1746
	Died: February 17, 1827
Where?	Born: Zurich, Switzerland
	Died: Brugg, Switzerland
What?	Set the model for what a teacher of young children should be. Much admired for his teaching methods and his concern for poor children. Espoused the need for active learning and education for the whole child. Influenced many contemporaries, especially Froebel, and later educators, even to today.
What was he like?	Considered to be kind, caring, highly sensitive, charismatic, arousing devotion from others.
	A sickly and awkward child, others made fun of him. He did not get along with his peers or his teachers. From an early age, he believed that teaching should be more kind and humane, a belief that was affirmed when he read Rousseau's *Emile*.
Where can I read more?	Read more information on page 108.

Who?	*Friedrich Froebel*
When?	Born: April 21, 1782
	Died: June 21, 1852
Where?	Born: Oberweissbach, Germany
	Died: near Marienthal, Germany
What?	Created kindergarten, literally "garden for children," where play was promoted as the way children learn. Developed early childhood materials, including blocks; materials and activities called "gifts for play."
	Twice visited Pestalozzi's schools; had great influence on the early American kindergarten movement.
What was he like?	Described as a dreamy and restless child and as an idealistic man; was hardworking, dedicated, deeply religious.
	An unhappy childhood, caused by a distant father and uncaring stepmother, led to his resolve to devote his life to making children happy. A bright spot was working in the garden with his father, reflected as a central feature of the kindergarten.
Where can I read more?	Read more information on pages 108–109.

"Play is the highest phase of child development."

Who?	*Maria Montessori*
When?	Born: August 31, 1870
	Died: May 6, 1952
Where?	Born: Chiaravalle, Italy
	Died: Noordwijk-on-Sea, Holland
What?	Developed the Casa dei Bambini, Children's House, for slum children in Rome; developed comprehensive program, including theoretical formulation, materials, curriculum, and child-sized furnishings.
	Influenced by Rousseau, Pestalozzi, Froebel; has had lasting impact through worldwide Montessori schools.
What was she like?	Strong-willed, persistent, ambitious; first woman doctor in Italy; had a mesmerizing personality.
	Even as a child, she had a strong sense of the dignity of every person. A teacher commented disparagingly about the expression in her eyes; from that day on, she never looked this teacher in the eyes. One of her most important lessons is that every human being, even the smallest child, must be treated with respect.
Where can I read more?	Read more information on pages 109 and 122–124.

"The greatest crime that society is committing is . . . wasting money it should spend for its children."

(continued)

"It is human to have a long childhood; it is civilized to have an even longer childhood."

Who?	*Erik H. Erikson*
When?	Born: June 15, 1902
	Died: May 12, 1994
Where?	Born: Frankfurt, Germany
	Died: Harwich, Massachusetts
What?	Psychosocial Theory

Identifies needs of children at different ages/stages, beginning with a need for trust for infants, autonomy for toddlers, initiative for preschoolers, and industry for school-age children; highlights the importance of social interactions in development.

Application: Bank Street Model.

What was he like? Described as thoughtful, energetic, magnetic; a scholarly thinker and prolific writer.

At 18 wandered through Europe as an artist; stumbled on a job as a teacher in a progressive school in Vienna run by Anna Freud. This proved to be the turning point, his introduction to Freud's work and his lifelong involvement with psychoanalytic theory. Later his writings were likened to "works of art," paintings of word pictures with intricate detail and attention.

Where can I read more? Read more information on pages 114–116.

"We should not allow children a completely free rein on the one hand, nor channel them too narrowly on the other hand."

Who?	*Jean Piaget*
When?	Born: August 9, 1896
	Died: September 17, 1980
Where?	Born: Neuchatel, Switzerland
	Died: Geneva, Switzerland
What?	Cognitive Developmental Theory

Intelligence is adaptation to the environment.

Thinking is qualitatively different at each stage: infants and toddlers learn through movement and the senses; preschoolers use symbols to organize ideas; school-agers acquire logical structures of thought.

Application: High/Scope, Reggio Emilia, Bank Street.

What was he like? Precocious, with his first publication at 10, and Ph.D. by 22; constantly searching for answers; always ingenious and inventive in his approach.

Perhaps because his mother was in poor mental health, he developed an interest in psychoanalysis. This soon turned into his lifelong fascination with normal development, especially in the thinking of children.

Much of his theory was developed by careful observation of his own three children.

Where can I read more? Read more information on pages 116–119.

Who?	*B(urrhus) F(rederick) Skinner*
When?	Born: March 20, 1904
	Died: August 18, 1990
Where?	Born: Susquehanna, Pennsylvania
	Died: Cambridge, Massachusetts
What?	Behaviorism

Environment is important in shaping all aspects of behavior. Consistent positive consequences (positive reinforcement) ensure that behavior will be repeated; behavior modification is application of behaviorism.

Application: behavioral approaches like the Bereiter–Engelmann program.

What was he like?	Ambitious, goal-driven, persistent; seen as the "Darth Vader" of psychology by some, as a brilliant innovator by others.

"Fred" Skinner experienced a calm and nurturing childhood. Perhaps his later theory was shaped by childhood experiences, since his Grandmother Burrhus reinforced good behavior with pie, candy, and letting him win at dominoes.

Where can I read more?	Read more information on pages 119–120.

"Teaching is the expediting of learning: A person who is taught learns more quickly than one who is not."

Who?	*Lev Vygotsky*
When?	Born: November 5, 1896
	Died: June 11, 1934
Where?	Born: Orsha, Russia
	Died: Moscow, Russia
What?	Sociocultural Theory

Believed social and historic forces shape intellectual ability: We are the product of our times. Thus, his cognitive theory reflects the Marxist-Leninist philosophy of Russia during his lifetime. Language is a primary tool for conveying society's values.

Application: Reggio Emilia.

What was he like?	An intense yet very social person with the capacity to inspire others; deeply interested in a variety of fields and topics, many of which he mastered.

His childhood friends called him "little professor" because of his academic pursuits; at age 15, he organized stimulating intellectual discussions for his peers. His ability to structure the environment so others could learn contributed to formulation of his ideas about the zone of proximal development.

Where can I read more?	Read more information on pages 121–122.

"Who's Who in ECE?" was compiled with the assistance of Melissa Burnham.

"The maturation of a child's higher mental functions occurs . . . through the adult's assistance and participation."

Other Leaders in America's Early Education Movement

The history of American early childhood education, particularly during the first half of the twentieth century, is filled with stories of determined, creative, strong women whose work helped to lay the groundwork for what the field has become today. One of the founders of the American early childhood education movement was Elizabeth Palmer Peabody, whose efforts led to establishment of the kindergarten. Another leader was Caroline Pratt, who opened the Play School in New York, where young children were "free to be creative and learn through play" (Peltzman, 1998, p. 99). Patty Smith Hill continued work on behalf of kindergartens, unifying and restructuring kindergarten and primary education. Under her leadership, educators began to incorporate into the curriculum what was being learned scientifically about young children. Patty Smith Hill is also important because she founded the organization that eventually became NAEYC.

Lucy Sprague Mitchell was another influential proponent of educational research and its use in designing programs for young children. She is perhaps best known for cofounding what was later to become the Bank Street College of Education, which we will discuss later in this chapter. Another well-known figure in the history of the field is Abigail Adams Eliot, who was one of the founding members of the professional organization that was to become NAEYC. She is among the acknowledged founders of the nursery school movement; Abigail Eliot's strong sense of respect for children permeated her work. Finally, Lucy Wheelock, founder of Wheelock College and a prolific author, lecturer, and activist, was another leading figure in the kindergarten movement. These women and many other individuals helped shaped early childhood education and its predominant underlying philosophy into the field it is today.

INFLUENTIAL THEORISTS OF CHILD DEVELOPMENT

Although many of the predecessors of early childhood education developed a theoretical or philosophical viewpoint about how children develop, it was not until the twentieth century that such ideas were founded on a more empirical base through systematic observations and supporting research. Today, the major way in which we view these different concepts is through theories that are based more on empirical information.

A **human development theory** is a way of describing what happens as individuals move from infancy through adulthood, identifying significant events commonly experienced by all people and explaining why changes occur as they do. It is useful to have a grasp of different theories as you develop your own professional identity and beliefs. This not only gives you a way of assessing your personal values but also offers some alternative views about how children develop and should be treated (Thomas, 1990b). We will now look at just a few of the most influential developmental theorists whose ideas have contributed, directly or indirectly, to the field of early childhood education.

Erik Erikson (1902–1994)

Erik Erikson, beginning his career in the early decades of the twentieth century in central Europe, was a follower of Sigmund Freud. Erikson refined aspects of Freud's theory into his **psychosocial theory.** According to Erikson, each stage of

---

Key Point

The history of early childhood education in America is full of strong, determined women who shaped the field into what it has become today.

human development theory
A way to describe what happens as individuals move from infancy through adulthood, identifying significant events that are commonly experienced by all people, and explaining why changes occur as they do.

psychosocial theory
The branch of psychology founded by Erik Erikson, in which development is described in terms of eight stages that span childhood and adulthood, each offering opportunities for personality growth and development.

development is defined by a conflict, which leads to opportunities for personal growth. These conflicts, in addition to centering on the person alone, also revolve around relationships with others. Erikson's was the first theory that spanned both childhood and adulthood through what he considered to be eight universal stages. The first four are particularly important because they describe significant tasks that occur in the life of the infant and young child. We will focus on those four in detail.

According to Erik Erikson, infants develop a sense of trust if their needs are consistently and predictably met by nurturing caregivers.

1. **Trust vs. Mistrust** (birth through approximately 18 months). The basic theme of infancy is the development of trust. This comes about when children's needs for food, warmth, sleep, and nurturing are met consistently and predictably. This stage revolves around the importance of feeding, although Erikson incorporates all aspects of the baby's existence, including sleep and elimination, in this foundation. The helpless infant must rely on the caregiver to provide satisfaction of needs. When children are not cared for adequately, they develop a sense of mistrust in others and in themselves, and as they move to future stages they see the world as threatening, unpredictable, and hostile.

2. **Autonomy vs. Shame and Doubt** (approximately 18 months through 3 years). Toddlers begin to assert their growing motor, language, and cognitive abilities by trying to become more independent. At the same time, they are still very dependent and must reach a balance between reliance on caregivers and the desire to try new things. One potential conflict revolves around toilet training. Success in this stage means that children have increasing self-control, feel good about their own abilities, and also begin to learn the boundaries of the social world. If children are made to feel ashamed of their efforts, they will develop a sense of self-doubt. In early childhood programs, children need to be allowed to exercise their growing independence within the safety of a loving and supportive environment that does not withdraw bodily cuddles and comforts just because the toddler is mobile and nay-saying!

3. **Initiative vs. Guilt** (approximately 3 to 5 years). Preschoolers' social and physical world expands dramatically in this stage; they are full of curiosity and a desire to try new activities, alone as well as cooperatively with peers. At this age, children enjoy imitating adults, a way of learning about and incorporating adult roles and expectations. Children also acquire an understanding of male and female roles through the subtle expectations of the parent of the opposite sex. If children receive no guidelines or if they are not allowed to explore, satisfy their curiosity, and try new ventures, they will develop a sense of guilt and failure. Thus, in the early childhood setting, it is important to allow children to initiate and try out a variety of experiences and activities and to provide appropriate guidelines within which children can learn the rules and expectations of society.

4. **Industry vs. Inferiority** (approximately age 6 to puberty). By the end of the preschool years, children begin to focus on the development of competence. They like to plan, carry out, and complete projects, unlike younger

Key Point ◆◆

Erikson's psychosocial theory, which spans childhood and adulthood, focuses on specific social tasks that need to emerge for healthy development in each of eight stages.

Trust vs. Mistrust
The first stage of development described by Erik Erikson, occurring during infancy, in which the child's needs should be met consistently and predictably.

Autonomy vs. Shame and Doubt
The second stage of development described by Erik Erikson, occurring during the second year of life, in which toddlers assert their growing motor, language, and cognitive abilities by trying to become more independent.

Initiative vs. Guilt
The third stage of development described by Erik Erikson, occurring during the preschool years, in which the child's curiosity and enthusiasm lead to a need to explore and learn about the world, and in which rules and expectations begin to be established.

Industry vs. Inferiority
The fourth stage of development described by Erik Erikson, starting at the end of the preschool years and lasting until puberty, in which the child focuses on the development of competence.

preschoolers, who are more concerned with the exploratory process of their activities. Children who do not develop an adequate sense of industry will settle for mediocrity and do less than they are able, with a resulting sense of inferiority. Older preschoolers and school-age children should be allowed time, space, materials, and support to engage in the kinds of activities that build a sense of industry.

Erikson describes four other stages that build on the foundations of the ones we have described. Although all stages occur at critical times in development, they never completely disappear. Thus, trust is still important beyond infancy, children continue to struggle with the balance between autonomy and dependency, and initiative and industry are relevant even beyond the early years, though in a more mature form. Erikson emphasizes the importance of play in meeting the tasks of autonomy and initiative during the early years. Erikson's stages highlight some of the important issues for young children and the balance we must provide to help them achieve healthy development (Erikson, 1963; Maier, 1990; Tribe, 1982; Weber, 1984). Gratz and Boulton (1996) suggest that Erikson's stages also provide a suitable framework for teachers of young children to examine and evaluate their own professional development. Learn more about Erik Erikson in the section, "Who's Who in ECE?" (page 112).

Jean Piaget (1896–1980)

One of the most influential forces in early childhood education today is the theory of Jean Piaget. Piaget's **cognitive developmental theory** presents a complex picture of how children's intelligence and thinking abilities emerge. Piaget did not suggest specific educational applications of his work, but educators have transformed his theory, more than any other, into actual models.

Piaget based his theory of cognitive development on his background and training as a biologist. He conceptualized cognitive development as similar to how all organisms function physiologically, adapting to and organizing the environment around them. A common example illustrates our own biological adaptation to the physical environment: If the temperature becomes too warm or too cold, we sweat or shiver to adapt. In a way similar to this physiological adaptation, we also adapt mentally to changes in the environment. At the same time we adapt, we mentally organize what we perceive in our environment so that it makes sense to us.

In a cognitive sense, **adaptation** is involved any time new information or a new experience occurs. A person must adapt to incorporate any new information or experience into the psychological structure. When something new presents itself, however, the existing mental structure is "upset"—put into **disequilibrium**—because this new information or experience does not exactly fit into the old structures.

To return to balance or **equilibrium,** adaptation takes place through the complementary processes of assimilation and accommodation. **Assimilation** occurs when the person tries to make the new information or experience fit into an existing concept or schema. **Accommodation** takes place when the schema is modified or a new concept is formed to incorporate the new information or experience. "Accommodation accounts for development (a qualitative change) and assimilation accounts for growth (a quantitative change); together they account for intellectual adaptation and the development of intellectual structures"

According to Erik Erikson, two-year-olds develop a sense of autonomy through many experiences in which they can feel successful. This helps them to understand and master their world.

© Cengage Learning

naeyc

Key Point ◆◆

Piaget's cognitive developmental theory, one of the most influential on early childhood education, describes how children's thinking is unique in each of four stages.

cognitive developmental theory
The theory formulated by Jean Piaget that focuses on how children's intelligence and thinking abilities emerge through distinct stages.

adaptation
Jean Piaget's term for the process that occurs anytime new information or a new experience occurs.

disequilibrium
According to Jean Piaget, the lack of balance experienced when existing mental structures and a new experience do not fit exactly.

equilibrium
According to Jean Piaget, the state of balance each person seeks between existing mental structures and new experiences.

assimilation
According to Jean Piaget, one form of adaptation, which takes place when a person tries to make new information or a new experience fit into an existing concept.

(Wadsworth, 1984, p. 16). As an example of assimilation and accommodation, imagine a visit by a group of young children to a zoo. Raymond, seeing a panther for the first time, says, "Look, there's a black leopard." He has fit the new animal into an existing mental structure because he is already familiar with leopards and just assumes that the panther is a leopard of a different color. He is using assimilation, making the new information fit into what he already knows. Monique, however, has never visited a zoo and has seen some wild animals only on television or in books. Seeing unfamiliar llamas, she considers what these might be. They resemble horses, but Monique immediately dismisses this category because she knows that horses have smooth hair and shorter necks. She also dismisses camels because she knows they have humps on their backs. She decides finally that this must be an animal she does not know and asks the teacher what it is. Monique is using accommodation, creating a new concept into which this new information can be fitted.

Organization is a process that is complementary to adaptation. While adaptation allows for new information and experiences to be incorporated into existing mental structures, organization defines how such information and experiences are related to each other. Piaget considers that organization is a basic tendency of all human beings. We all strive to organize our experiences to make them understandable, connected, coherent, and integrated. Intelligence is not just a collection of facts but a way of incorporating these into a framework and context that makes sense.

Consider a pedal. By itself it is a small, flat, rectangular item made of plastic. However, in the proper context, fitted on a tricycle, the pedal takes on an entirely different meaning, as it allows the child to turn the wheels that, in turn, make the tricycle move. Organization allows us to expand the visual cues about the pedal to include information about its function as part of a whole.

Piaget called the cognitive structures into which we adapt and organize our environment **schemata** (singular, schema). Schemata are concepts or mental representations of experiences. We constantly create, refine, change, modify, organize, and reorganize our schemata. One popular analogy for schemata is an index card file. Babies are born with only a few "index cards," but as they receive new information through their senses, they have to create new cards to incorporate these experiences. Increasingly, their store of information becomes more complex and they create "dividers" in their files into which information can be categorized and organized through some common features.

Although the formation, adaptation, and organization of new schemata are ongoing processes in cognitive development, that development is typified by distinct abilities at different ages. As a **stage theorist,** Piaget (like Erikson) conceived of qualitatively different characteristics and accomplishments in cognitive ability during various stages of development. Each stage is built on and incorporates the accomplishments of the previous one. Maturation sets limits on when children are capable of achieving specific cognitive abilities.

Thus, the infant, dependent on movement and the senses, learns about the environment through those avenues. By age two, however, a distinctly new ability emerges, the ability for mental **representation** of objects, even though they are not present in the immediate environment. This new ability allows the preschooler to move beyond the limits of the immediate physical environment and include past experiences, imaginary ideas, and symbols. While the preschooler's dramatic acquisition of language skills opens up a world of new possibilities, this age group is still limited by the observable characteristics of objects. Reasoning is not yet logical, although by about seven years of age, children begin

accommodation
According to Jean Piaget, one form of adaptation, which takes place when an existing concept is modified or a new concept is formed to incorporate new information or a new experience.

organization
According to Jean Piaget, the mental process by which a person organizes experiences and information in relation to each other.

schemata
(singular, schema)—According to Jean Piaget, cognitive structures into which cognitive concepts or mental representations are organized.

stage theorist
Any theory that delineates specific stages in which development is marked by qualitatively different characteristics and accomplishments and in which each stage builds on the previous one.

representation
According to Jean Piaget, the ability to depict an object, person, action, or experience mentally, even if it is not present in the immediate environment.

Figure **5-1**

Piaget's Periods of Cognitive Development

sensorimotor period
Piaget's period covering infancy.

Stage 1: Sensorimotor Period (0 to 2 years)
The first period is characterized by motor behavior through which schemata are formed. The child does not yet represent events mentally but relies on coordination of senses and movement, on object permanence development, on learning to differentiate means from ends, and on beginning to understand the relationship of objects in space in order to learn about the environment.

preoperational period
Piaget's period covering the preschool years.

Stage 2: Preoperational Period (2 to 7 years)
Language and other forms of representation develop during this period, although thinking is not yet logical. Development of children's internal mental representations, which allow them to think of objects even if these are not physically present, is the major accomplishment of this period. Children have an egocentric view of the world, in terms of their own perspective. Early classification, seriation, and role-play begin.

concrete operations period
Piaget's period covering the elementary school years.

Stage 3: Concrete Operations Period (7 to 11 years)
The child has internalized some physical tasks or operations and no longer depends only on what is visible, but can apply logic to solving problems. The child now is able to reverse operations (for instance, $5 - 3 = 2$ is the same as $3 + 2 = 5$). The child can also practice conservation—recognize that an object does not change in amount even if its physical appearance changes (stretching a ball of clay into a snake).

formal operations period
Piaget's period covering adolescence.

Stage 4: Formal Operations Period (11 to 15 years)
The final period, rare even in adults, is characterized by sophisticated, abstract thinking and logical reasoning abilities applied to physical as well as social and moral problems.

logical thinking
According to Jean Piaget, the ability that begins to emerge around age seven in which children use mental processes to solve problems rather than relying solely on perceived information.

abstract thinking
According to Jean Piaget, the ability to solve a variety of problems abstractly, without a need to manipulate concrete objects.

object permanence
Part of Jean Piaget's theory, the recognition that objects exist, even when they are out of view; a concept that children begin to develop toward the end of their first year of life.

to apply **logical thinking** to concrete problems. Finally, by adolescence, the young person may be able to apply logic and **abstract thinking** to a wide range of problems.

These changes in thinking ability are the basis for the four periods of cognitive development described by Piaget (Figure 5-1). Although Piaget's stages focus on evolving cognitive abilities, their principles are applied much more widely, to social and moral as well as to physical and mathematical learning.

Early childhood teachers need to be aware of the implications of these stages as they work with young children. Understanding the characteristics and growing abilities of infants in the sensorimotor period is important for infants and toddlers but is also relevant for those who work with preschoolers. For instance, some young preschoolers may not yet have completely grasped **object permanence,** the recognition that an object continues to exist even if it is out of sight. Thus, the toddler who peels off the collage material to re-find the paste underneath is not naughty but is testing a principle that most children grasp during the earlier sensorimotor stage. Similarly, the preschool teacher needs to understand the concrete operations period for the precocious three-year-old who reads and uses deductive reasoning in exhibiting skills usually not seen in children this young. Teachers of school-age children also need to be aware not only of the accomplishments of the concrete operations period but also of the sensorimotor and formal operations periods. An understanding of how children learn, as well as of their characteristics, abilities, and limits is vital to appropriate teaching (Ginsburg & Opper, 1969; Lavatelli, 1970; Piaget, 1983; Saunders & Bingham-Newman, 1984; Thomas, 1990a; Tribe, 1982; Wadsworth, 1984). Learn more about Jean Piaget in the section, "Who's Who in ECE?" (page 112).

B. F. Skinner (1904–1990)

Up to this point, we have considered people whose views are based on a belief that there is an inborn plan according to which children develop. Rousseau, Pestalozzi, Froebel, and Montessori all felt that, given an appropriate environment and understanding adults, children will develop according to nature's plan into healthy, responsible, intelligent adults. Erikson and Piaget likewise believed that development is predetermined and will follow the same stages in each person.

But this view of an innately determined plan is not the only way of viewing human development. An alternative view is that children are not shaped by internal forces but rather by external ones, specifically those emanating from the environment. **Behaviorism** is based on this viewpoint.

B. F. Skinner was one of the behaviorists whose ideas have had widespread influence on all aspects of education, including those encompassing the early childhood years. The application of his theoretical and experimental work can be seen in **behavior modification,** which operates on the underlying principle that behavior can be changed or modified by manipulating the environment, which includes both physical and social components.

Skinner emphasized that almost all behavior is learned through experience. A specific behavior, according to Skinner, can be increased or decreased as a function of what follows it. In other words, if something pleasant or enjoyable consistently happens after the child engages in a specific behavior (the teacher smiles when Jeremy helps to put away the blocks), he is likely to repeat that behavior. Conversely, if something unpleasant or painful follows a behavior (Lars burns his finger when he touches the stove), he is likely not to repeat it. Deliberately attempting to increase or decrease behavior by controlling consequences is called **operant conditioning.**

Skinner used the term **reinforcement** to describe the immediate consequence of behavior that is likely to strengthen it. Whether consciously using the behavioral approach or not, early childhood educators frequently use **positive reinforcement** because of its powerful effect on children's behavior. Teachers of young children are most likely to use **social reinforcers**—for instance, a smile,

naeyc

Key Point ◆◆

B. F. Skinner, one of the important proponents of behavioral theory, emphasized that almost all behavior is learned and can be increased by positive consequences and decreased by negative consequences.

behaviorism
The theoretical viewpoint, espoused by theorists such as B. F. Skinner, that behavior is shaped by environmental forces, specifically in response to reward and punishment.

behavior modification
The systematic application of principles of reinforcement to modify behavior.

operant conditioning
The principle of behavioral theory whereby a person deliberately attempts to increase or decrease behavior by controlling consequences.

reinforcement
In behavioral theory, any response that follows a behavior that encourages repetition of that behavior.

positive reinforcement
Application of a behavioral principle, which includes any immediate feedback (either through tangible or intangible means) to children that their behavior is valued.

social reinforcer
In behavioral theory, a reward that conveys approval through such responses as a smile, hug, or attention.

In B. F. Skinner's theory, behaviorism, behavior is shaped by the environment more than by internal or genetic forces. For instance, when this teacher systematically reinforces the child for correctly identifying the color red, it is more likely that the child will repeat this reinforced behavior.

© Cengage Learning

a hug, attention, or involvement—when they see a child engaging in a behavior they consider desirable.

In addition, systematic attention to behavior and its consequences can be used to encourage new behaviors or eliminate undesirable ones. **Shaping** is the method used to help a child learn a new behavior by teaching it in small steps and systematically reinforcing the attainment of each step. **Extinction** is used to eliminate a behavior that had previously been reinforced by taking away all reinforcement; for example, by totally ignoring the behavior. Extinction, however, is not synonymous with punishment, which is defined as an aversive consequence that follows the behavior. According to Skinner (and early childhood professionals), **punishment** is not an effective way of controlling behavior. To summarize, in all of these methods—reinforcement, shaping, and extinction—it is the manipulation of what immediately follows a behavior that affects it.

To return to what we originally said about the distinguishing feature of behaviorism, behavior is considered to be externally controlled, not driven by internal factors. Because behaviorism has attempted to function as a precise science, **observable behavior** is defined only by what is discernible—for instance, actions and words—rather than by nonobservable factors such as motivation or feelings. Behavior is carefully defined, observed, and graphed by representing the rate or magnitude of a given child's response in measurable units. Examples of such measures might be the number of times a child hits another child or the number of minutes a child plays appropriately with peers.

Elements of behavioral theory are used in many ways in early childhood programs. Particularly in programs for young children with disabilities and some compensatory programs, behaviorist methods have been widely and systematically applied in attempts to teach children specific skills. When the teacher determines exactly what children should learn, those skills can be organized and presented in the form of **programmed instruction.** More pervasive in early childhood education, however, is the use of a number of behavioral techniques such as reinforcement, extinction, or step-by-step shaping. Teachers in many programs, although they do not adhere strictly to all of the theoretical and applied aspects of behaviorism, nonetheless frequently use a number of its techniques (Braun & Edwards, 1972; Bushell, 1982; Peters, Neisworth, & Yawkey, 1985; Sameroff, 1983; Skinner, 1969, 1974; Weber, 1984). Learn more about B. F. Skinner in the section, "Who's Who in ECE?" (page 113).

Lev Semenovich Vygotsky (1896–1934)

All of the previously discussed theorists have focused primarily on the child in explaining how development occurs, although the importance of others, especially the family, is certainly not ignored. Other theorists have given much greater prominence to the importance of the cultural and historical context within which a child is socialized. The Russian psychologist Lev Vygotsky, originator of the **sociocultural theory,** highly stressed the importance of the social environment to development. Vygotsky's ideas have gained greater prominence in recent years, decades after his death, and have spurred considerable interest in cross-cultural studies of child development and child-rearing practices. Vygotsky proposed that social interaction, especially dialogue, between children and adults is the mechanism through which specific cultural values, customs, and beliefs are transmitted from generation to generation.

---

shaping
In behavioral theory, a method used to teach a child a new behavior by breaking it down into small steps and reinforcing the attainment of each step systematically.

extinction
In behavioral theory, a method of eliminating a previously reinforced behavior by taking away all reinforcement; for instance, by totally ignoring the behavior.

punishment
An aversive consequence that follows a behavior for the purpose of decreasing or eliminating the behavior; not recommended as an effective means of changing behavior.

observable behavior
Actions that can be seen rather than those that are inferred.

programmed instruction
A method of teaching in which the teacher determines exactly what the children should learn, devises a sequence of learning activities to teach specific information, and teaches it directly by controlling the information according to children's responses.

sociocultural theory
Originated by Lev Vygotsky, this theory gives prominence to the social, cultural, and historic context of child development.

Vygotsky was particularly intrigued by the question of how young children develop complex thinking. He concluded that the same mechanism through which culture is transmitted—social interaction—is the way in which increasingly more complex thinking develops, as part of learning about culture. Children gain knowledge and skills through "shared experiences" between themselves and adults or older peers. Furthermore, the dialogues that accompany these experiences gradually become a part of children's thinking. Thus, Vygotsky conceived of cognitive development as dependent on, not independent of, social mediation. This view is in contrast to Piaget's, which conceives of the child as gradually becoming more social and less self-focused; in Vygotsky's view, the child is socially dependent at the beginning of cognitive life, and becomes increasingly independent in his or her thinking only through many experiences in which adults or older peers help.

The child acquires new skills and information within what Vygotsky termed the **zone of proximal development (ZPD).** This is the level at which a child finds a task too difficult to complete alone but which, with the assistance and support of an adult or older peer, the child can accomplish. Infants are frequently guided by adults in tasks they have not yet mastered. Many games adults play with infants encourage the baby to increasingly greater participation; many infant motor skills are preceded by periods in which the baby sits, stands, or walks with adult assistance. Similarly, toddlers accomplish many tasks with the guided assistance of adults. Toddlers' one- or two-word sentences, for example, are often extended by adults into a more complete format, which models as well as provides the structure for more elaborate dialogue. Preschoolers also learn many tasks through guided assistance, which, as at earlier and later ages, is adjusted to the child's skill level and gradually withdrawn as the child masters the task. The teacher who tells a child who is struggling to fit a puzzle piece into the frame, "see what happens if you turn the piece around," is working within the zone of proximal development.

Vygotsky's ideas have acquired new relevance in early childhood education. The focus on finding the appropriate zone of proximal development for each child has validated the long-held concern with individualization in early childhood programs. Vygotsky's theory also suggests that, in addition to providing a stimulating environment in which young children are active explorers and participants, early educators need to promote discovery by modeling, explaining, and providing suggestions to suit each child's zone of proximal development (Berk, 1994; Gallimore & Tharp, 1990; Seifert, 1993; Wertsch, 1985). Learn more about Lev Vygotsky in the section, "Who's Who in ECE?" (page 113).

APPLICATION OF THEORIES IN EARLY CHILDHOOD EDUCATION

The work of human development theorists is important to early childhood education if their concepts are translated into practice and methods. In our field, this has happened over the years as a number of **early childhood education models,** founded on a particular theoretical view, were developed. Such models represent a coherent approach to working with young children, including a philosophical and theoretical base, goals, curriculum design, methods, and evaluation procedures. There was a great proliferation of early childhood models in the 1960s and 1970s when educators and researchers were encouraged to develop alternative approaches for Head Start programs. Most models were designed to

Key Point ◆

Vygotsky's sociocultural theory stresses the importance of the social context of development; children's learning is often promoted through assistance from adults or older peers who help the child learn new skills within the zone of proximal development.

zone of proximal development (ZPD)
In Vygotsky's theory, this zone represents tasks children cannot yet do by themselves but which they can accomplish with the support of an older child or adult.

naeyc

early childhood education models
Approaches to early childhood education, based on specific theoretical foundations; for instance, the behavioral, Piagetian, or Montessori view.

Key Point ◆◆

A number of human development theories have been applied to early childhood education through specific models.

examine different ways of helping children at risk for later academic failure to improve their school performance. But models have implications for all children as well (Evans, 1982).

We should not, however, assume that all early childhood programs pursue a carefully prescribed theoretical view. In fact, the majority of programs and teachers of young children probably do not follow a stated philosophical foundation and preference, or they may adhere only to a vaguely recognized theory. An open mind and a practical approach to teaching born out of sensitive observation and interaction with children are, undoubtedly, equally important.

> Often our theories of growth and development, learning and instruction, or optimal teaching application are hidden and not consciously recognized as theories in the usual sense. Good teachers, like all effective professionals, have sets of guiding principles and outcome expectations that may certainly be considered as theories, at least in a general sense. (Hooper, 1987, p. 303)

It is helpful, however, to examine how some specific models have taken the views of a particular theorist (or theorists) and transformed these into program applications. We will examine only five models here, although many alternative approaches exist. These five were selected to illustrate how particular views of child development can be implemented in practice. Included will be a brief overview of Montessori programs as they exist today; the Bank Street approach, which is in part based on the psychosocial view of Erikson; the High/Scope cognitively oriented curriculum, based on Piaget's principles; the Reggio Emilia approach, grounded in part on the theories of Piaget and Vygotsky; and Rudolf Steiner's Waldorf schools.

Montessori Programs

Key Point ◆◆

Today, there is great variation among Montessori programs. The traditional Montessori environment and materials include some unique features; the roles of the teacher and the children's activities differ from those in other types of early childhood programs.

Maria Montessori's ideas and methods gradually found a receptive audience in the United States, where Montessori programs have flourished. Although Montessori is not considered a human development theorist, her program, nonetheless, was based on some carefully considered ideas about how young children grow. Today, a wide range of Montessori programs can be found. Some adhere quite rigidly to the original techniques, whereas others follow an approach that has been adapted to better fit the current social context (Chattin-McNichols, 1992). It is interesting to note that although Montessori devised her program to meet the needs of impoverished children and to help them learn important life skills, Montessori programs today are, for the most part, attended by children from more affluent homes.

THE ENVIRONMENT. If you visit a traditional Montessori classroom, you will soon observe some of the prominent features of such a program, some similar to other types of early childhood settings, and some unique to Montessori. You will quickly notice the sense of order inherent in the room. Child-sized equipment and materials are clearly organized on shelves that are easily accessible to the children. There are distinct areas, each containing materials unique to promoting the tasks to be mastered in that area. The environment is also set up to be aesthetically pleasing, with plants, flowers, and attractive furnishings and materials. The logic, order, and beauty are all integral to the Montessori philosophy.

THE CHILDREN. You will also note children of different ages involved in individual activities, because the essence of a Montessori program is its individualized nature. Children initiate activities and are free to engage in whichever projects they choose, defining a work space for their selected activity on a mat on the floor or on a tabletop. Children are self-directed, working independently or, at times, in twos. Younger children may be learning how to participate in specific activities by observing and imitating their older classmates. The Montessori program is designed as a three-year sequence for children ages three to six.

THE TEACHERS. There is little overt adult control. The teacher's involvement is unobtrusive and quiet. She may be observing from a distance or demonstrating to a child how to use a new material. The teacher does not reinforce or praise children for their work since the activities are intended to be self-rewarding, thus, intrinsically motivating. Montessori teachers learn about the methods and curriculum through an intensive course of study at the graduate level.

THE MATERIALS. As you look more closely at the materials, you will see that they have some special characteristics. Montessori materials are **didactic,** each designed to teach a specific lesson. In addition, they are **self-correcting,** so that the child gets immediate feedback from the material after correctly (or incorrectly) completing a task. Materials are graduated from the simple to the more complex; therefore, children are challenged by progressively more difficult concepts. The materials are carefully and attractively constructed, and usually made of natural materials such as varnished wood.

didactic
A term often applied to teaching materials, indicating a built-in intent to provide specific instruction.

self-correcting
Learning materials such as puzzles that give the child immediate feedback on success when the task is completed.

daily living
Montessori classroom area that focuses on practical tasks involved in self-care and environment care.

sensorial
Montessori classroom area in which materials help children develop, organize, broaden, and refine sensory perceptions of sight, sound, touch, smell, and taste.

conceptual
Montessori classroom area that focuses on academic materials related to math, reading, and writing.

THE CURRICULUM. Different materials fit into each of the three distinct areas of the curriculum. When children first enter a Montessori program, they are introduced to the **daily living** component, in which practical activities are emphasized. Such activities focus on self-help and environmental care skills such as buttoning, brushing hair, watering plants, washing windows, and sweeping.

The second set of activities and materials are **sensorial**—helping children develop, organize, broaden, and refine sensory perceptions of sight, sound, touch, smell, and taste. To foster visual discrimination, for instance, children use the Pink Tower, 10 cubes increasing in size in regular increments of one centimeter, stacked from largest to smallest. A more complex visual discrimination task is involved with the set of color tablets, which require the child to arrange hues of one color from the darkest to the lightest; an even more advanced task might require the child to find the second-darkest hue of each of the seven graded colors when all of the tablets are spread out at random.

The third aspect of the program involves **conceptual,** or academic, materials. The practical and sensorial skills learned in the first two areas have laid the groundwork on which writing, reading, and mathematics is built. Conceptual learning

Montessori programs use special equipment and arrange the classroom into centers that are somewhat different from conventional early childhood areas. How does this equipment for toddler exercises differ from that of a more traditional early childhood program?

© Cengage Learning

activities are concrete and actively involve the child in multisensory ways. Thus, children use their fingers to trace letters cut out of sandpaper, trace letters in cornmeal, or use the Movable Alphabet to manipulate letters to form words. Many of the math materials are based on a decimal system; for instance, the Golden Beads, which come singly or in units of 10, 100, and 1,000. Other activities promote cultural understanding, including maps and animal and plant pictures to identify and classify.

You may notice that some traditional early childhood activities are absent in the Montessori school. Because Montessori programs are reality-based rather than promoting fantasy, you are not likely to find a dramatic play area, a creative art corner, or other activities that invite children to freely use their imagination. You may also note a restriction on how children may use materials. As David Elkind (1983) points out, once children have mastered the use of a particular material in the established manner, they should be free to act on the material and use it freely, in a more experimental way; however, the Montessori method allows materials to be used only in a prescribed procedure. You may also note less emphasis on encouraging language learning.

Montessori schools today vary considerably. Many, in fact, are a blend of the Montessori method and elements of traditional early childhood programs. Relatively little research has evaluated the effectiveness of Montessori programs. Some findings indicate that Montessori children may show greater task persistence and independence, but they appear to score lower on tests of creativity and language development (Chattin-McNichols, 1981; Elkind, 1983; Gettman, 1987; Lillard, 1973; Simons & Simons, 1986; Torrence & Chattin-McNichols, 2000).

The Bank Street Approach

Since the 1920s, New York's Bank Street College of Education has been one of the leading forces in early childhood education in this country. Its **developmental interactionist model** denotes not only that this program is concerned with all aspects of children's development, but also that it places emphasis on interactions, both between the child and the environment and between the cognitive and affective areas of the child's development. In other words, children's development in the cognitive and affective domain is not seen as a separate or parallel function but rather as truly an interactive one.

From such a perspective, this model builds on the works of a variety of theorists, including cognitive theorists such as Piaget, and those who are concerned with the development of **ego strength,** the ability to deal effectively with the environment, such as Erikson. Thus, underlying the program's philosophy is a strong commitment to fostering both intellectual and socioemotional development. Equally important to the acquisition of cognitive skills is the development of self-esteem, identity, competence, impulse control, autonomy, and relationships with other people.

> The school . . . promotes the integration of functions rather than, as is more often the case, the compartmentalization of functions. . . . [It] supports the integration of thought and feeling, thought and action, the subjective and the objective, self-feeling and empathy with others, original and conventional forms of communication, spontaneous and ritualized forms of response. It is part of the basic goal and value system of the school to stimulate individuality and vigorous, creative response. (Shapiro & Biber, 1972, pp. 61–62)

If you were to observe a classroom in which the teachers adhere to the Bank Street philosophy, you would see a program that appears, in most respects, quite similar to a variety of high-quality early childhood programs. The Bank Street approach is considered synonymous with **open education,** a term encompassing programs that operate on the premise that children, provided with a well-conceived environment, are capable of selecting and learning from appropriate activities. The program does not aim to teach children a lot of new concepts, but rather to help them understand what they already know in more depth. Children's own experiences are thus the base of the Bank Street program. Because children come to school with a variety of previous experiences, however, the curriculum must remain open and flexible so each child can build on and expand according to her or his own unique conceptual level.

open education
A program that operates on the assumption that children, provided with a well-conceived environment, are capable of selecting and learning from appropriate activities.

THE ENVIRONMENT. The classroom is arranged into conventional interest areas such as music, art, reading, science, and dramatic play. The purpose of each area is clearly defined by the materials it contains. Many of those materials are handmade, by both teachers and children. Teacher materials are encouraged because they are designed to meet unique and specific needs of the children in the class. Child-made materials may include books that the children have made as part of the reading center or children's collections that are used as tools for counting in the math center.

THE TEACHERS. The Bank Street approach relies heavily on the abilities of competent teachers, who must have a keen understanding of children's development, of each child's individuality, and of how best to structure an environment that will encourage each child to fulfill his or her potential. The teachers' role both in teaching and guidance is to use their sensitivity to recognize nuances in the children and to make changes as appropriate. They recognize the importance of helping the children develop a strong sense of self, exercise their growing autonomy, make an impact on and experience mastery over the environment, make choices, develop a joy in learning, and feel enough confidence to take risks and handle contradictions.

In creating a classroom atmosphere that draws on teachers' understanding of the children, teachers match the types and variety of materials and experiences they provide to children's changing needs. They also understand young children's immature control over their impulses and provide rules that protect and build on positive motivation rather than on arbitrary, authoritarian power. Because each child will bring to school his or her personal experience of interactions with adults, the teachers must build on that experience to develop a meaningful relationship with each youngster (Biber, 1984; Cuffaro, Nager, & Shapiro, 2000; Shapiro & Biber, 1972).

The environment in the Bank Street programs is organized into conventional interest areas. Children learn by interacting within this environment, broadening their previous experiences.

THE CURRICULUM. Because this approach is centered on the idea that the child's development must be viewed as integrated, it also specifies that the curriculum and functioning of the classroom be integrated. To promote learning, curriculum is based on a unifying theme, which serves to help children focus on specific concepts and provides a sense of integration. Children's earliest experiences in the Bank Street classroom are designed to help them understand and master their school environment by participating in activities and chores that contribute to its functioning. Later, learning is extended beyond the classroom to the community to expand the children's understanding of meaningful elements that affect their lives.

The Cognitively Oriented Curriculum

naeyc

A number of programs based on the theoretical precepts of Jean Piaget have evolved over the past several decades. One of those, the cognitively oriented curriculum, was developed by the High/Scope Foundation of Ypsilanti, Michigan, under the leadership of David Weikart (1931–2003). This approach was initially designed in the early 1960s, as part of the Perry Preschool Project, a program for children from impoverished backgrounds, but it has since been adopted more widely, partly through the publication of its carefully outlined curriculum manual, *Educating Young Children: Active Learning Practices for Preschool and Child Care Programs* (Hohmann, Weikart, & Epstein, 2008). In line with Piagetian theory, the cognitively oriented model is based on the premise that children are active learners who construct their own knowledge from meaningful experiences. If you were to visit a cognitively oriented class, you would observe this philosophy in the environment, schedule, and activities and in the children's and teacher's behavior.

Key Point ◆

The cognitively oriented curriculum, based on the theory of Piaget, revolves around activities that help children learn specific cognitive concepts.

THE ENVIRONMENT. The environment is designed to be stimulating but orderly, where children can independently choose from a wide variety of interesting materials. The classroom is divided into clearly defined work areas, each with a specific set of materials appropriate to that area. A cognitively oriented classroom contains at least a housekeeping, block, art, quiet, and large-group area, although there might also be construction, music and movement, sand and water, and animal and plant work areas as well. Accessible, uncluttered storage spaces in each work area are clearly labeled with silhouettes or pictures, facilitating cleanup and promoting a sense of order.

planning time
In the cognitively oriented curriculum, the time set aside during which children decide what activities they would like to participate in during the ensuing work time.

work time
In the cognitively oriented curriculum, the large block of time during which children engage in self-selected activities.

recall time
In the cognitively oriented curriculum, the time when children review their work-time activities.

plan–do–review cycle
The heart of the cognitively oriented curriculum through which children are encouraged to make deliberate, systematic choices with the help of teachers by planning ahead of time, carrying out, and then recalling each day's activities.

THE SCHEDULE. The daily schedule is integral to the philosophy of the cognitively oriented program. Consistency helps children gain a gradual understanding of time. The day begins with a **planning time,** when children decide what activities they would like to participate in during the ensuing work time. A teacher helps each child individually think through what he plans to do, and then records the child's plans. A large block of time is then set aside for **work time,** during which children carry out their plans in self-selected activities, supported and assisted by the teachers.

After work time comes **recall time,** usually carried out in small groups, where children review their work-time activities. This **plan–do–review cycle** is the heart of the cognitively oriented curriculum, helping children make deliberate, systematic choices with the help of the teacher. Additional daily periods include cleanup, considered a learning opportunity; small group time, which typically includes a teacher-planned activity that reinforces a cognitive concept; large-group time for stories, music, games, and other whole-group activities; outside time; and meals and nap, as appropriate to the length of the program day.

THE CURRICULUM. Throughout the day, teachers focus on extending the cognitively oriented curriculum's **key experiences,** a set of eight concepts based on the characteristics and learning capabilities of preoperational children, as discussed by Piaget. (We will consider some of these concepts in more detail in Chapter 11, when we discuss cognitive development and the early childhood curriculum.) The key experiences give the teachers a framework within which to observe each child's individual performance as well as support and extend children's self-initiated activities. The following is a brief description of these eight concepts.

1. Active learning takes place when activities are initiated and carried out by children themselves. It involves learning through all the senses, manipulating and combining materials as a way of discovering their relationships, self-selecting activities and materials, and learning to use equipment and tools.

2. Using language is strongly stressed and encouraged through talking with others about meaningful experiences, describing, expressing feelings, having language written down by a teacher, and playing with language.

3. Representing experiences and ideas—according to Piaget, the hallmark of the preoperational period—allows children to represent the world in nonverbal ways. Key experiences include activities such as recognizing objects through the senses, imitating actions and sounds, role-playing, and drawing or painting.

4. **Classification** begins during the preoperational period as children note similarities and differences among objects. Children are encouraged to investigate and describe the attributes of things, sort and match objects, use objects in different ways, talk about characteristics that some things do not have, and distinguish between "some" and "all."

5. **Seriation,** the ability to arrange objects along some dimension, is promoted by having children make comparisons, arranging objects in order, and matching.

6. **Number concepts** are the basis for mathematical understanding and are built on many concrete experiences. To promote this concept, experiences are planned to encourage children to compare, count, and engage in one-to-one correspondence.

7. **Spatial relationships** are encouraged through assembling and taking things apart, rearranging and reshaping objects, observing and describing things from different perspectives, working with shapes, experiencing and representing the child's own body, locating objects in the environment, and experiencing and describing relative positions and distances.

8. Time is a gradually acquired concept involving both the understanding of time units and sequencing of events in time. Experiences that help children learn such concepts include signals for stopping and starting actions, experiencing and describing different rates of speed and time intervals, observing seasonal changes, discussing future events, planning, representing past events, and describing the order of events (Hohmann et al., 2008; Hohmann & Weikart, 2002).

The cognitively oriented curriculum provides one illustration of how Piaget's theory has been put into practice. Central is the idea that children are active learners who develop appropriate concepts through interaction with the environment. Through a carefully prepared environment and the guidance of knowledgeable teachers, children attain a deeper understanding of the rules

key experiences
In the cognitively oriented curriculum, the eight cognitive concepts on which activities are built.

classification
The ability to sort and group objects by some common attribute or property; for instance, color or size.

seriation
A relationship among objects in which they are placed in a logical order, such as from longest to shortest.

number concepts
One of the cognitive concepts young children begin to acquire, involving an understanding of quantity.

spatial relationship
The relative position to each other of objects and people in space.

that govern the physical and social world (Hohmann et al., 2008; Hohmann & Weikart, 2002; Weikart & Schweinhart, 2000).

The Reggio Emilia Approach

In recent years, increasing attention has been paid by early childhood educators from around the world to the programs established in Reggio Emilia, in northern Italy. The publicly supported early childhood programs of this region, under the guidance and vision of Loris Malaguzzi (1920–1994), have developed an extraordinary curriculum based on many theoretical foundations, Piaget's and Vygotsky's included.

In Reggio Emilia programs, projects are central to the curriculum. This group of children, by observing and learning about the birds in their environment, is engaged in a long-term project. They will continue to explore the topic in depth over time in a variety of ways.

© Cengage Learning

naeyc

Key Point ◆◆

The programs of Reggio Emilia in Italy are carefully designed to foster interactions, exploration, and problem solving; much of the curriculum revolves around projects in which children and teachers thoroughly explore a particular concept or topic in myriad ways over an extended period of time.

THE ENVIRONMENT. The physical space in Reggio Emilia is used to promote an inviting, aesthetically pleasing, comfortable environment in which both human relationships and learning are central. The use of space is designed to encourage communication and nurture relationships. Arrangements encourage collaboration among children, particularly in carrying out projects. Equipment, materials, and activities are arranged to encourage exploration, discovery, and problem solving as well as to offer many choices.

A distinctive feature of each Reggio Emilia school is an *atelier*, a special studio or workshop in which children and teachers have access to a wide variety of resource materials to depict their experiences. The atelier is used to document the children's work; transcripts of their discussions, photographs of their activities, and representations of their projects are carefully arranged to document the process of learning in relation to various projects. These displays provide the children with deeper insights, as they view and review their work and the work of peers, and to teachers and parents, as they consider the learning process of the children through these projects.

▶❚❚ TeachSource Video Activity
WATCH • REFLECT • RESPOND

This BBC News Video provides an introduction to the Reggio Emilia programs. Go to CengageBrain.com and view the video entitled, "The Reggio Emilia Approach," and answer the following questions:

1. Discuss two elements of Reggio Emilia schools shown on this video that you found unique. Why did they catch your attention?

2. What is the commitment of the Reggio Emilia community to the education of young children?

THE TEACHERS. Education, according to Malaguzzi (1993), must be centered on its three important participants—children, teachers, and families. All three must have a sense of well-being if the educational program is to be effective. Teachers in Reggio Emilia schools work in pairs, as co-teachers, who stay with a group of children for three years, from infancy to age three or from three to six. The teachers' role is to be a resource for and, in effect, learning partners with the children. Teachers have the support of a team of pedagogical coordinators and a visual arts teacher. Considerable communication and coordination facilitate the cooperative atmosphere of Reggio Emilia programs. The programs include time for weekly staff meetings and provide ongoing staff development, both of which lead to strong commitment, skill, and a sense of professionalism (Bredekamp, 1993; Gandini, 1993; Malaguzzi, 1993; New, 2000). The Reggio Emilia approach is discussed further in Chapter 8.

THE CURRICULUM. Projects are the central concept around which Reggio Emilia's curriculum revolves. The "Stories from the Field" box gives insight into a project carried out by Amanda, a student teacher.

The project approach allows children, usually in small groups, to explore a concept or topic in depth. Projects can be short or long term, often lasting several months. Because the schedule in Reggio Emilia's schools is flexible and includes large blocks of time for children to work on projects, children can work at a leisurely pace because they are under no time constraints in carrying out their projects. Often the representations of learning in projects are expressed in artwork; but, as George Forman (1993) points out, children move from learning to draw to drawing to learn. Art is a vehicle through which children explore the properties of the concept or topic under study.

The subject or theme of projects can emerge from questions asked by children, ideas proposed by children or teachers, or everyday experiences. Thus, there is no preplanned curriculum beyond the general goals set by the teachers. Projects can revolve around most any topic, ranging from shadows, reflections, caves, and the city when it rains, to designing and building an amusement park for small birds.

Forman cites an example of a project, in which children studied a pervasive feature of their community environment during spring—poppy fields. Children began by drawing the subject, to start thinking about what poppies are like. Teachers and children communicated: They asked questions, examined each others' work, and considered the various aspects of life in a poppy field. After several days of discussing, drawing, and considering questions, such activity was followed by a trip to a poppy field. The children had been immersed in poppies for several days, and were now ready to observe, compare, and ponder some of the questions they had asked. The earlier activity had prepared the children to learn about poppies in greater depth. When they returned to the classrooms and again drew poppies, their creations were much more accurate and dynamic. They were, after all, based on careful redefinition of the subject, or assimilation of new information. Immersion in a topic and a time frame for each project set by the interests of the children, not by the adults, allows for much greater depth of learning.

Waldorf Education

Waldorf schools are the fastest-growing independent educational programs in the world today. These schools are based on the work on Rudolf Steiner (1861–1925), an Austrian philosopher and teacher with distinct ideas about how children should be educated. Many of his ideas are very congruent with those of theorists whose work came after his, such as Piaget. Waldorf schools are set up for preschool as well as elementary and high school students. The schools received their unusual name when Steiner was asked at the end of World War I by a German industrialist who owned the Waldorf Astoria cigarette factory to set up a school for the children of his employees.

THE PHILOSOPHY. Steiner believed that the education of children needs to be of the whole child—what is often referred to as "head, hands, and heart." The program focuses on all areas of development, including spiritual and moral. He further believed that children develop in three distinct stages—from birth to

Key Point ◆

Waldorf schools follow the teachings of Rudolf Steiner, who believed that teaching has to address the whole child, including physical, mental, and spiritual dimensions.

HOW CAN SMALL PEOPLE TAKE PICTURES?

One of my first individual experiences with the project approach came while I was working in a kindergarten classroom with a small group of five- and six-year-olds. I introduced photography to a group of six children, something that has always been a passion of mine and one that I assumed they had minimal experience with. Photography was initially introduced as a new form of art and a passageway for expressing their creativity and individuality through abstract concepts. We began by viewing and discussing the work of famous photographers found in books and magazines, as well as by looking at miscellaneous photographs brought from home. The children primarily focused on the subject matter, labeling it "good" if they could relate the photograph to their daily lives and if the subject matter appealed to them. Black-and-white photography, as well as photographs without people, were initially disregarded or labeled "bad." My hope was that, through further discussion, the children could begin to understand and identify elements of photography that determine a photo's quality and that they would begin to understand that the objects in the pictures are only one aspect of the photo as a whole.

We used both film and digital cameras to explore and photograph our community. Before beginning our "photo walks," the children and I would meet to discuss our route and I would remind them that whenever they felt inspired or found some possible subject matter, they should ask the group to stop and we would wait until they felt they had accurately captured the object or scenery. The cameras were passed between

Amanda, Student Teacher

© Theresa Danna Douglas

children until the roll of film or digital memory was used. I would immediately develop the photographs so that the children could view and discuss their work. The children critiqued their own work and that of the others, making suggestions as to how they could improve or revisit their photographs during our next outing.

As our discussion continued, the elements of photography such as contrast, leading lines, focus, and composition became more prominent in the children's dialogue. While on our first walk along the university's campus, Max and Justin each took photographs that helped to foster the children's knowledge about the leading lines found in different photographs. Aleea pointed to Justin's photo and appropriately explained, "[The water] goes to the building. The lines on the water lead you to the sides and if you connect the whole thing together it leads to the building. What your eye is supposed to look at is the building."

Focus was another element of photography that the children had begun to grasp fully. Referring to a blurry photograph of a dandelion, Nick suggested that Justin "could move the camera away," demonstrating the

creation of further distance between the object and the camera lens.

Justin was the first group member to suggest and display the different angles at which the camera can be held as well as the many ways to use his body to achieve a specific viewpoint and perspective. These discussions led to the understanding of composition, as the children had already discovered many different ways to capture a single subject.

Contrast was the element that dominated most of our conversations, a concept first discovered by Aleea as the group of children discussed the work of famous photographers. As the children discussed their first photographs, Justin claimed, "You can see the contrast a lot better than in color pictures," thus propelling further understanding of contrast in black-and-white photography. This element was added to the children's list of what makes a good photo and was discussed and identified in each of the photographs that the children took.

The children's knowledge, understanding, and appreciation for photography continued to grow with each passing week as they were able to share their ideas with one another and see that they could create and share beautiful black-and-white photographs as well. Their command of the subject matter impressed all who watched the children engage in this form of art. During our first meeting, Justin had asked the group, "How can small people in kindergarten take pictures?" I believe that all of the children have answered this question for anyone who may have asked it or will brave asking it in the future.

6 or 7 years, from 7 to 14 years, and from 14 to 18 years. The characteristics and learning style of children in each stage differ, thus teachers need to provide age-appropriate experiences and hold appropriate expectations in order to promote healthy development.

THE CURRICULUM. Topics and areas of study are presented in experiential rather than abstract ways. Education, according to Steiner, is not merely to instill knowledge but also to make that knowledge meaningful in the context of values, ethics, and a recognition of the humanity of others. Learning is never rushed, as ample time is given to children's activities. A primary goal of this approach is that children develop internal motivation through development of a love of learning. This is expected to stay with children for their entire lives and translate, in adulthood, to being a positive influence in their communities. For all ages of children, the curriculum integrates the arts, practical work, and academics. However, how the curriculum is presented depends on the age of the children.

In the early childhood stage, Waldorf schools consider that children learn best through imitation and example. These children are taught concretely, through movement, whereas children ages 7 to 14 are considered to learn best through artistic and imaginative engagement. Nonetheless, artistic expression is a strong part of the curriculum for all ages, including young children. Play is highly valued, and considerable time is provided for guided free play, both indoors and outdoors. In fact, children's experiences with nature, including weather and seasonal changes, are an important part of the Waldorf approach. This is in line with the emphasis on the rhythms of life, including daily routines and annual festivals and traditions. Another important element of Waldorf schools is language development, which is fostered through songs, poems, movement activities, and stories. Waldorf teachers are proficient storytellers of fairy tales and other favorites from multiple cultural perspectives.

THE ENVIRONMENT. The environments of Waldorf schools are attractive and inviting. The walls are painted in bright colors and children's artwork is abundantly displayed. The environment is arranged to be comfortable and homelike, especially for young children. Buildings and materials are designed with a sense of beauty that is in harmony with the natural surroundings.

A notable feature of Waldorf environments is the use of natural materials. Plastic and other manufactured materials are not found in Waldorf schools. Instead, you will find such items as natural wax crayons, beeswax for use as a modeling medium, dolls and puppets made of natural fabrics, and puzzles and other toys carved out of various kinds of beautiful woods. Waldorf schools recognize and honor children's need to experience nature and natural materials (Association of Waldorf Schools of North America, 2008; Dancy, 2004; Mays & Nordwall, 2006; Nutbrown et al., 2008).

Evaluation of Early Childhood Models

The five models of early childhood programs we have discussed all are based on concepts of how children develop and, to differing degrees, on what is considered developmentally appropriate practice. In the 1960s, when a variety of approaches that might make a difference in the lives of disadvantaged children were explored, other models also were developed. Several of these were based on behavioral theory, most notably the Bereiter–Engelmann model (Bereiter & Engelmann, 1966). The assumption for this model was that children would benefit most from direct instruction and drill in the topics that would be most important when they entered elementary school: math, language, and reading. This approach is considered by most early childhood professionals as developmentally inappropriate because it assumes that children are passive rather than active learners.

The Bereiter–Engelmann program was included in a number of comparative evaluations of early childhood models. Initial studies showed that children in the Bereiter–Engelmann program had significantly improved IQs and achievement test scores. Those scores declined quickly, however, over the next few years, as they also did for children who had been involved in other programs.

The levels of curiosity and inventiveness of the children in the Bereiter–Engelmann model seemed lower than those of youngsters who participated in other types of compensatory programs (Miller & Bizzell, 1983; Miller & Dyer, 1975). In part, this may be because the high level of reinforcement, according to research, tends to decrease the intrinsic interest children may have in learning (Lepper, Greene, & Nisbett, 1973). In other words, once the external motivators for learning were removed, the process of learning may have ceased to hold the children's interest.

Retrospective evaluation of adolescents who had participated in the Bereiter–Engelmann program as preschoolers showed some unexpected outcomes. The youths who had been in a direct instruction program appeared to have higher rates of juvenile delinquency than youths involved in programs in which the major teaching method involved self-selection (Schweinhart, Weikart, & Larner, 1986a). The authors of this study speculated in a subsequent publication (Schweinhart et al., 1986b) that when young children have control over the activities they participate in, they may well develop a greater sense of responsibility and initiative. They point out that development of such traits is crucial in early childhood, as described by such theorists as Erik Erikson (see pages 132–134). Proponents of the direct instructional approach, however, have questioned these conclusions and expressed concern over the research procedures used in these studies (Bereiter, 1986; Gersten, 1986). Thus, the theoretical approach that is used to help children acquire cognitive skills may have some far-reaching effects, but measuring them is not an easy task.

We have explored some different theoretical ideas about how young children develop and learn, and we have examined several models based on these theories. You have undoubtedly recognized by this time that early childhood education is not a single, unified field based on an agreed-upon philosophy. Let us now briefly examine what research tells us about the effects of early childhood education and, where applicable, what role some of these theoretical precepts play in shaping that effect.

RESEARCH SUPPORT FOR EARLY CHILDHOOD EDUCATION

naeyc

A question that must be asked is whether early childhood education makes a difference. As we have already indicated in several contexts, much of the research about the effectiveness of early childhood education has come from the evaluation of programs designed for children from impoverished backgrounds. The result of such research is important in gauging the value of compensatory education, but it also provides us with more general information about early childhood education. In addition, it is important to understand the effect of early childhood education on all youngsters, particularly with the large number of young children enrolled in child care programs. We will look at these two topics separately.

BRAIN STORM
MAKING A DIFFERENCE

Professionals agree that early intervention with families of at-risk children must start in the earliest months and years of life to ensure that these children are provided experiences to support optimal development. Professionals are aware that children of low-income, poorly educated families usually do not attain the same achievement and intellectual levels as children from well-educated and financially stable families. "The recent developments in brain research have provided new insights into why this is so. Parents who are preoccupied with a daily struggle to ensure that their children have enough to eat and are safe from harm may not have the resources, information, or time they need to provide the stimulating experiences that foster optimal brain development" (Hawley & Gunnar, 2000). As a result, very young children who are not spoken to often, who have few playthings, and who have little opportunity to explore their environment may not develop the neural pathways that facilitate later learning. High-quality early intervention programs have been shown to make a difference, so that these children have a chance of reaching their full potential (Hawley & Gunnar, 2000).

The Effects of Early Intervention

The 1960s can be portrayed as a period of great optimism on the part of the educators and psychologists who had a hand in the development of Head Start. As expressed by Edward Zigler, one of the leaders in the Head Start movement:

> Intervention was supposed to impart immediate benefits so that class differences would be eliminated by the time of school entry. Furthermore, many expected that the brief preschool experience would be so potent a counteraction to the deficits in poor children's lives that it could prevent further attenuation in age-appropriate performance and a recurrence of the gap between social classes in later grades. (Zigler & Berman, 1973, pp. 895–896)

Head Start, as we now know, did not live up to that idealistic expectation. Many of the early intervention programs showed some short-term results in improved IQ and achievement scores for the first two years of elementary school (Lee, Brooks-Gunn, Schnur, & Liaw, 1990; Royce, Darlington, & Murray, 1983; Schweinhart & Weikart, 1985). The relatively brief time that

naeyc

Key Point

Research on early intervention programs such as Head Start has shown that they result in long-term, positive effects and cost benefits.

DIVERSITY

children spend in Head Start, however, just cannot make up for the wide variety of social ills that beset the children of poverty. Broader assessments of compensatory programs have demonstrated that early intervention can have important and lasting effects. In a survey of outcome evaluations from a number of early childhood programs for children from low-income families, numerous clear long-term benefits were found (Campbell & Taylor, 1996; Wat, 2007). These include not only IQ gains but also higher test scores and better progress throughout the school years. Children of these programs also were better adjusted, had more positive attitudes, and had a better sense of self. Parents of these children often improved their educational and vocational status and showed reduced incidents of child abuse and neglect. "Early childhood programs clearly do help overcome the barriers of impoverishment" (Campbell & Taylor, 1996, p. 78).

A most interesting set of results comes from the cognitively oriented curriculum, originally called the Perry Preschool Project, which has been one of the most thoroughly researched early childhood programs for children from low-income families. (See also, "Take a Closer Look" in Chapter 1, p. 8.) Follow-up data at adolescence were collected on youngsters who had been enrolled in the program, giving information on their subsequent experiences and functioning within the larger society. When contrasted with a comparable group who had not attended preschool, the cognitively oriented graduates were significantly more likely to have completed high school, experienced job success and satisfaction, and been self-supporting rather than dependent on welfare. They were also less likely to have been arrested, require special education services, or experience a teen pregnancy.

Further follow-up at age 27 of those who had participated in the program as preschoolers showed continued positive results (Schweinhart, Barnes, & Weikart, 1993). Results indicate that, as compared with the control group, these adults had higher earnings, were more likely to own a home, demonstrated a greater commitment to marriage, were less dependent on social services, and had considerably fewer arrests. Most recently, the Perry Preschool Project's results in following the participants to age 40 showed continued differences. Those who had participated in the program as preschoolers continued to have significantly higher earnings and significantly lower arrest rates than those in the control group. Researchers at the High/Scope Foundation estimate that for every dollar invested in the participants when they were children, society gets a $17 return (Schweinhart et al., 2005). This amount represents savings in the juvenile and adult justice systems, remedial education, and welfare. This longitudinal study confirms that a high-quality early childhood intervention program has lifelong positive effects on children as well as for society at large (Schweinhart, 2004).

The Abecedarian Project of North Carolina also has demonstrated long-term positive outcomes for children from backgrounds of poverty. This project followed a group of children from infancy, when they entered the project, into full-time, high-quality child care, through early adulthood. A control group with similar characteristics received no intervention. The children who participated in the early childhood intervention program from infancy to age five had higher cognitive test scores throughout their subsequent schooling. A significant number of the intervention group continued on to higher education. This project underscores the importance of high-quality programming from infancy for children at risk. Such intervention greatly improves the likelihood of later educational success (Bracey, 1996;

Campbell & Ramey, 1994; Ramey, Campbell, Burchinal, Skinner, Gardner, & Ramey, 2000).

Similar, positive long-term results were also found for adolescents who had participated in the Syracuse University Family Development Research Program (FDRP) during their infant and preschool years. Most impressive was the highly significant difference in involvement in the juvenile justice system between these teenagers and a comparable (control) group that had not participated in an early intervention program. Not only had far fewer of the FDRP youngsters been involved in juvenile delinquency, but the severity of the offenses, the number of incidents, and the costs of processing were far lower.

Another finding from this study showed that, particularly for girls, early intervention resulted in better school performance and lower absenteeism during adolescence than was found for the control group. The teachers also rated the FDRP girls, as compared with the control group girls, as having higher self-esteem and self-control (Lally, Mangione, & Honig, 1988). Follow-up studies such as these provide evidence that high-quality early childhood intervention programs can and do make a difference.

Another group considered to be at-risk are children with disabilities. Recall our discussion of children with special needs in Chapter 2. Since parents of children with disabilities have similar child care needs to those for all parents, a growing number of such children are integrated into early childhood programs. Researchers have begun to look at the effect of child care on this group of children. In an extensive review of the research, Odom and his colleagues (2004) concluded that "positive developmental and behavioral outcomes occur for children with and without disabilities in inclusive settings, although as a group, children with disabilities are not as socially integrated as their typically developing peers" (p. 17).

DIVERSITY

The Effects of Early Childhood Programs on Low-Risk Children

Over the past several decades, much of the research in early childhood education has focused on children at risk because of poverty, as we just discussed. More recently, however, researchers have begun to examine the effects of early childhood programs, especially child care, on all children. Since such a large proportion of American children spend much of their time in child care settings, it is important to have a clear picture of how child care impacts their development. The findings of many studies have made a clear link between the quality of child care and children's social, emotional, cognitive, and language development. Some longitudinal studies have also shown that the quality of an early childhood program affects children's later functioning in school. Such findings are particularly alarming. Two large-scale studies (Helburn Culkin, Howes, Bryant, Clifford, Cryer, Peisner-Feinberg, & Kagan, 1995; NICHD Early Child Care Research Network, 2006) found that the majority of young American children, especially infants and toddlers, are in mediocre or inferior early childhood settings.

A number of studies have found that the quality of child care, especially when measured in terms of positive interactions between teachers and children, impacts children's social development. Several studies conducted during the 1980s found that children's emerging socialization is clearly affected by the quality of child care (Clarke-Stewart, 1987b; Phillips, Scarr, & McCartney, 1987).

Key Point ◆◆

Research is showing that high-quality child care has an effect on all aspects of children's development.

Holloway and Reichhart-Erickson (1988) found that a positive teaching style results in children who are more prosocial. In two longitudinal studies, Andersson (1989, 1992) followed children who had been in high-quality infant and child care to ages 8 and 13. At both later ages, children were more socially competent.

Children's emotional and behavioral development also are affected by child care quality. Children's overall behavior is more appropriate in classrooms where teachers use positive teaching techniques (Peisner-Feinberg & Burchinal, 1997). Another study found that preschoolers' emotional expression is much more positive (more smiling and laughing) when caregivers are more engaged and supportive in their interactions with the children than in centers where teachers ignore or minimally interact with the youngsters (Hestenes, Kontos, & Bryan, 1993). Another study found that children who had more positive relations with their teachers in preschool had fewer behavior problems in elementary school; thus, the impact of early school experience reaches well beyond the preschool years (Peisner-Feinberg, Clifford, Culkin, Howes, & Kagan, 1999). As you will recall from Chapter 1, the caliber of child–adult interactions is an important indicator of quality in early childhood programs. Yet another aspect of emotional development—anxiety—has been linked to child care quality as well. Children in inappropriate classrooms show more stress behaviors than those in developmentally appropriate settings (Burts Hart, Charlesworth, DeWolf, Ray, Manuel, & Fleege, 1992; Hyson, Hirsh-Pasek, & Rescorla, 1990).

A number of studies have also linked quality in child care to cognitive and language development. Several studies have found that children enrolled in higher-quality centers are clearly better communicators (McCartney, 1984; Peisner-Feinberg & Burchinal, 1997). The large-scale longitudinal study, the National Institute of Child Health and Human Development Study of Early Child Care and Youth Development, found that higher-quality care predicted higher vocabulary scores (Belsky, Vandell, Burchinal, Clarke-Stewart, McCartney, & Owen, 2007). Another study found that children engage in cognitively more complex play in higher-quality programs (Howes, Smith, & Galinsky, 1995). Howes (1988) discovered that children who had been in high-quality child care earned higher school-skill ratings from their teachers, while Field (1991) found a significant relationship between children's enrollment in a high-quality infant program and their later inclusion in a gifted program in elementary school. Using data from the Early Childhood Longitudinal Study—Kindergarten study, Magnuson, Ruhm, and Waldfogel (2006) found that children who attended preschool entered public school with higher levels of academic skills than children who did not attend an early childhood program. A follow-up study of the children who had participated in a large-scale national study of child care also found that in elementary school those children who had been in higher-quality programs as preschoolers continued to have higher scores in language and math in elementary school (Peisner-Feinberg et al., 1999). Conversely, Howes (1990) found that children in poor-quality child care from an early age were the least task-oriented and most distractible in kindergarten.

It is clear to many early childhood professionals that child care quality has an impact, not only in relation to children's behavior and functioning at the time they are in child care, but potentially for many years later. This is why many professionals urge changes that would improve the overall quality of child care. But bringing about such changes will take considerable commitment from many sectors, including families, child care professionals, employers, and government. It is important that we contribute as positively as possible to the future success of young children. Our research right now tells us that many children are not in high-quality child care settings, and that this compromises not only their current development, but also their chances for a successful future. In fact, placing a priority on the well-being of children should be the most pressing issue of our times. See the "Take a Closer Look" feature for an in-depth discussion of why this is the case.

PK-3—Supporting Continuing Educational Success for Young Children

As we have seen, high-quality early childhood programs have a positive effect on the performance of young children, particularly if they are at risk for failure. Yet, research also shows that such positive effects "often tend to fade out over time as students move through grades 1, 2, and 3" (Kauerz, 2006). In recent years, early childhood advocates have promoted a model that stresses the importance of continuity and alignment among early childhood and early elementary programs.

Typically, there is little or no coordination between these two systems. Yet, professionals are now focusing on the importance of such coordination through the **PK-3 movement** (pre-kindergarten to 3rd grade). They cite a growing body of research that validates the impact of a continuum of learning, starting when children first enter early childhood programs through third grade. Why have these researchers identified the age range from the early years through third grade? We have already discussed the importance of the early years, when brain development is most sensitive to high-quality experiences. At the other end of this range, third grade is when children generally shift from "learning to read to reading to learn" (Kauerz, 2011). This transition in reading skill accompanies what has been called the "fourth-grade slump" (Shore, 2009), when many children, who have not developed strong reading skills, become disengaged from school.

Supporters of the PK-3 movement cite several relevant research strands (Kauerz, 2010). In addition to research about the effectiveness of high-quality learning programs (e.g., Magnuson, Myers, Ruhm, & Waldfogel, 2005), there is also growing evidence that full-day kindergarten improves children's academic achievement (Ackerman, Barnett, & Robin, 2005). Another body of research verifies that even when children attend a high-quality early childhood program or full-day kindergarten, the positive effects of such programs disappear within a year or two. In addition, there is evidence that early elementary classrooms are often developmentally inappropriate and of poor quality (Pianta, Belsky, Houts, & Morrison, 2007; Stuhlman & Pianta, 2009). By combining such research information, the PK-3 concept was developed as a way to address all of these issues through alignment and coordination across all levels. Both Pre-K and elementary school teachers have strengths that can improve the educational experience for all children. Through purposeful communication among teachers at all levels, early childhood educators focus more on intentional instruction, standards, and accountability, while elementary school teachers develop a greater focus on the whole child (socioemotional as well as cognitive) and on the learning environment (Kauerz, 2011). A number of U.S. school districts are implementing this promising approach and finding considerable success, which also has been reflected in a number of studies (Graves, 2006).

naeyc

PK-3 movement
A relatively new approach that stresses the importance of continuity and alignment among early childhood and early elementary programs.

WE NEED PREVENTION, NOT INTERVENTION

"A KEY INGREDIENT in creating the nation's great wealth has long been its willingness to invest in new opportunities for all its children, helping them become productive members of society" (Every Child Matters, 2009, p. 1).

In the "Take a Closer Look" box in Chapter 1 (page 8), you read about the increasing attention that economists and other researchers are giving to the fact that investment in early childhood education is good not only for children but is wise for society at large. For instance, research has shown that investment in young disadvantaged children pays off well; for every dollar invested when children are young, society saves $17 in subsequent years. In a report explaining the economic principles behind the movement to invest in early childhood, the Rand Corporation (Kilburn & Karoly, 2008) seeks to raise awareness of the dismal state of America's children and why investment is vital.

A number of organizations such as the Children's Defense Fund, Kids Count, UNICEF, and others continue to monitor the state of America's children. The report *Homeland Insecurity*, from the group Every Child Matters, paints a bleak picture of the plight of American children. In the preface, the president of Every Child Matters

Education Fund states that "the development of human capital is central to U.S. global competitiveness, increased productivity, caring for an aging population, and fulfilling the moral obligation every generation has to leave the world a better place for the one that follows" (Petit, 2009).

In comparisons with other rich democracies, the United States ranks 20th out of 21 countries in measures of child well-being. The United States ranks lowest in the rate of infant mortality, highest in deaths resulting from child abuse, by far the highest in prison population and homicides, far behind most other rich democracies in percentage of children participating in early childhood programs, and highest in the percentage of cost that parents assume for child care. One of the most striking details is a look at the effectiveness of government intervention on child poverty. In France, for instance, the child poverty rate decreased by 73 percent after government intervention was instituted, while in the United States the decrease was only 18 percent, by far the lowest of any country. The report concludes that such figures illustrate the powerful effect that government policies can have in reducing child poverty, if such policies are strong.

The report also illustrates how much disparity there is among American children because of state policies. Some states are much more proactive on behalf of children than others, as the following examples show. In Massachusetts, 3 percent of children are uninsured, while in Texas that figure is 21.4 percent. In New Hampshire, 8 children per every 100,000 die before age 14, while in Louisiana that figure jumps to 34. Child welfare spending to protect abused children also varies considerably, with Rhode Island spending $181 per capita and South Carolina spending less than $15. There is also a large disparity between the percentage of children enrolled in publicly funded preschool programs by state, with 53 percent of Oklahoma's children involved in such programs as compared with less than 10 percent of Nevada's children.

There is growing urgency, as indicated by reports such as the two discussed above from the Rand Corporation and Every Child Matters, that America's future is inextricably tied to the well-being of its children. All such reports consider the importance of affordable, high-quality early childhood education to be a key ingredient in such an ambitious agenda that better meets the needs of all children.

SUMMARY

1. Early childhood education, although relatively new as a formal system, has antecedents that reach far back in history as ideas about children and how they should be treated were shaped.
2. The writings and work of many individuals through history have contributed to our contemporary ideas about young children and early childhood education.
3. Particularly in this century, a number of theorists have proposed models that help us understand the nature of young children and how best to meet their needs.
   A. Some theorists believe that children's development follows an inborn plan.
   B. Others consider that children's development is affected primarily by external factors.
4. Many theories have been applied to early childhood education through the development of specific program models.
5. Research has proven the effectiveness of early education.
6. The PK-3 movement, which promotes continuity and communication across programs that serve children from birth through third grade, shows promising results for young children.

KEY TERMS LIST

absorbent mind

abstract thinking

accommodation

adaptation

assimilation

Autonomy vs. Shame and Doubt

behaviorism

behavior modification

child study movement

classification

cognitive developmental theory

conceptual

concrete operations period

daily living

developmental interactionist model

didactic

disequilibrium

early childhood education models

ego strength

equilibrium

extinction

formal operations period

human development theory

Industry vs. Inferiority

Initiative vs. Guilt

key experiences

kindergarten

logical thinking

number concepts

object permanence

observable behavior

open education

operant conditioning

organization

PK-3 movement

plan–do–review cycle

planning time

positive reinforcement

preoperational period

prepared environment

programmed instruction

psychosocial theory

punishment

recall time

reinforcement

representation

schemata	social reinforcer
self-correcting	sociocultural theory
sensitive periods	spatial relationship
sensorial	stage theorist
sensorimotor period	Trust vs. Mistrust
sensory discrimination	work time
seriation	zone of proximal development (ZPD)
shaping	

KEY QUESTIONS

1. Historic events have a great impact on our view of children and how we treat them. What social and political events have taken place during your life that have had an impact on young children and their education? Also ask this question of a relative or friend who was born in an earlier era.
2. Observe an early childhood program or interview a teacher or administrator of an early childhood program. What evidence do you see of the influence of one or more theorists (for instance, Piaget or Erikson) or the behaviorists? Ask one of the teachers if he or she draws on any particular human development theories and compare with your observation.
3. What was your earliest school experience? How does it compare with the type of programs you see for young children today?
4. If one is available, observe or interview a teacher or administrator of a Montessori school in your community. How does it differ from other early childhood programs you have seen? How is it similar? What elements of Maria Montessori's original program do you see?
5. Visit or talk with a staff member or administrator of a Head Start program in your community. Which family services and education experiences provided by this program might contribute to the types of long-range positive effects found by the research?

ADDITIONAL RESOURCES

Select additional books, articles, and websites on topics discussed in Chapter 5.

Crain, W. (2005). *Theories of development: Concept and applications.* Upper Saddle River, NJ: Prentice Hall.

Lascarides, V. C., & Hinitz, B. F. (2000). *History of early childhood education.* New York: Falmar Press.

Roopnarine, J. L., & Johnson, J. E. (2009). *Approaches to early childhood education* (5th ed.). Upper Saddle River, NJ: Merrill Prentice Hall.

HELPFUL WEBSITES

Child Development Theories:

www.psychology.about.com
This website provides a brief overview of a number of child development theories, including the ones discussed in this chapter.

High/Scope Educational Research Foundation:

www.highscope.org
Information about the programs, research, and policy initiatives of the High/Scope Foundation are available on this website. High/Scope has used these for more than 40 years to advocate for improved opportunities for all children through high-quality educational programs.

Reggio Emilia:

http://zerosei.comune.re.it
This is the official website of the Reggio Emilia approach to early education.

Go to **CengageBrain.com** to register your access code for this book's Education CourseMate website, where you will find more resources to help you study. Additional resources for this chapter include TeachSource Videos, glossary flashcards, web links, case studies with critical-thinking questions that apply the concepts presented in this chapter, and more. If your textbook does not include a printed access card, you can go to **CengageBrain.com** to purchase access.

6

Accountability, Standards, and Assessment

DAP Assessment of children's development and learning is essential for teachers and programs in order to plan, implement, and evaluate the effectiveness of the classroom experience they provide. . . . In developmentally appropriate practice, the experiences and the assessments are linked. . . ; both are aligned with the program's desired outcomes or goals for children. Teachers cannot be intentional about helping children to progress unless they know where each child is with respect to learning goals.

Developmentally Appropriate Practice,
Copple & Bredekamp, 2009, pp. 21–22

In Chapter 6, you will find answers to the following questions about accountability, standards, and assessment:

▶ Why has accountability of programs for young children become a concern in recent years?
▶ In what ways have standards changed the field of early childhood education?
▶ What is the role of observation in assessment and evaluation, and how can you best carry it out?
▶ What are some of the different kinds of standardized assessments, how do they differ from each other, and how should they be used?
▶ What kind of assessment and evaluation methods should you use?

NAEYC STANDARDS CONSIDERED IN CHAPTER 6

(See the Standards Correlation Chart on the inside front cover of this book for the titles and description of the standards listed below.)

▶ *Standard 3a:* Recognizing the relationship of accountability, learning standards, and assessment (pp. 143–146).
▶ *Standard 3d:* Understanding concerns about misuses of standards and assessment, including NAEYC's Position Statement on assessment, and responsible, ethical use of assessment tools (pp. 143; 156–158).
▶ *Standard 3c:* Knowing about various assessment strategies, including observation, teacher-made assessment tools, and assessment systems (pp. 146–156; 158).
▶ *Standard 3a:* Knowing about standardized tests, their categories, uses, potential benefits, and potential misuses (pp. 152–156).
▶ *Standard 3c:* Using information from assessments to make informed decisions about children and the program (pp. 159–160).
▶ *Standard 3b:* Recognizing the importance of partnering with families and colleagues in relation to assessment (pp. 160–161).

It is important to have a sense of direction and purpose in the program you provide for young children. In recent years, in response to a call for greater accountability, many states as well as professional organizations have developed sets of standards that identify what knowledge, skills, and dispositions children should have gained through their early childhood education experiences. Measurement of whether children have met these standards is achieved through a variety of assessment techniques. We will discuss these interrelated concepts of accountability, standards, and assessment in this chapter.

ACCOUNTABILITY

For many decades now, there has been growing concern over the educational achievement gap among children from different socioeconomic and ethnic backgrounds (Brooks-Gunn, Rouse, & McLanahan, 2007). "Behind these disparities in school-related performance lie dramatic differences in children's early experiences and access to good programs and schools" (Copple & Bredekamp, 2009, p. 2). A variety of initiatives and funding have been devoted to addressing these inequities and, especially over the past decade, have led to a greater call for **accountability.** This means being answerable, especially to those who provide the funds, to ensure that the stated goals are accomplished. All states now have accountability systems that define a common set of indicators of the performance of children and schools (Council of Chief State School Officers, 2008).

In particular, the 2001 No Child Left Behind (NCLB) Act was designed to hold public schools accountable for decreasing the achievement gap among different groups of children. Policies requiring accountability that is tied to future funding affect elementary and secondary education, but they also have more and more of an impact on early childhood education programs. "Critics worry that the practices and measures of some accountability systems are too

naeyc

accountability
Being answerable to the agency or people who fund a program or initiative, ensuring that the funds were well used to reach the stated goals of the program.

BRAIN STORM
MEETING STANDARDS

Pam Schiller and Clarissa Willis (2008) propose that brain research can and should inform how we meet early childhood standards. Here are some strategies:

▶ *Our brains attend to the need for safety and well-being first; therefore attention to providing a safe environment is very important.*

▶ *Research shows that emotions affect memory and brain function; when a person is content, endorphins are released by the brain, enhancing memory. Attention to an emotionally comfortable environment is a must.*

▶ *The brain is more likely to make connections between new and existing knowledge when multiple senses are involved during learning.*

▶ *Brain research shows that children are far more likely to store experiences into long-term memory if hands-on manipulation is involved.*

▶ *New material is integrated into the brain because it relates to something that already has meaning and, therefore, makes sense. Relating to prior knowledge, using graphic organizers, and encouraging children to reflect on what they have learned are ways to help children process new information.*

simple and ignore complications caused by the social barriers poor and inner city children face in performing well on standardized tests. Consequently, many are concerned about the negative features of accountability moving down to affect programs and services for young children" (Council of Chief State School Officers, 2008). See the "Take a Closer Look" box for more in-depth discussion of this concern.

LEARNING STANDARDS FOR CHILDREN

naeyc

learning standards
The expectations for the learning and development of young children across all developmental domains, including physical, cognitive, language, and socioemotional, which are generally published in some kind of document.

content standards
The concepts and skills that children are expected to acquire in relation to their age or grade level and that should be covered in the program or curriculum.

performance standards
The benchmark that describes the level at which children should perform in relation to their age or grade level, measured through some form of test or assessment.

naeyc

In recent years, learning standards for early childhood programs have been established as a way to ensure accountability for programs that are publically funded. All states have developed or are in the process of developing such standards.

We have discussed standards as they apply to teacher education programs and teachers, but standards also have been set for children. Closely tied to accountability are **learning standards** for children. These describe expectations for: (1) the learning and development of young children, including in cognition and general knowledge; (2) language and communication development; (3) physical well-being and motor development; (4) social and emotional development; and (5) approaches to learning. **Content standards** identify the concepts and skills that are to be covered at each age or grade level as part of the curriculum, while **performance standards** describe the expected level that children should reach for their age or grade, as measured through assessments (Bredekamp, 2009).

Standards for children younger than five differ from those for older children because "the primary tasks of young children are to acquire and refine foundational skills—skills that will help them successfully learn the content and information in the later grades" (Gronlund, 2008). Over the past few years, standards have become a widely accepted part of the field of early childhood education, set by individual states as well as by professional organizations such as NAEYC. Head Start also has identified standards through its publication, *The Head Start Path to Positive Child Outcomes* (U.S. Department of Health and Human Services, 2003).

It is important to differentiate between standards and curriculums. A number of authors have noted that standards are not curriculums (e.g., Bredekamp, 2009; Seefeldt, 2005). Bredekamp (2009) points out, however, that many commercial developers of curriculums now design their products to include standards and provide strategies to help children achieve them. Thus, the curriculum is often driven by standards and tied to assessment (which we will discuss in the next section) to measure whether the children are actually reaching the desired outcomes. On the basis of feedback from assessments, teachers can then make needed changes in the curriculum to ensure that children make progress toward the goals set by the standards.

There are both advantages and disadvantages of using early childhood standards. Gaye Gronlund (2008) points out that standards reinforce the great potential for learning in young children, which is supported through quality early childhood programs. Furthermore, standards set general expectations for children at different ages, which help to provide a framework for accountability. She also points out that standards and DAP are not incompatible and can be incorporated into all aspects of children's experiences.

On the other hand, standards can be misused if they are used "cookie-cutter style." Accountability can also have a negative effect if it exerts pressure to set inappropriate expectations. In addition, some teachers may assume that the only way to ensure that children learn the standards is through direct instruction, which is counter to what we know about the importance of exploratory play for children's development. The author also points out that it takes time for teachers to become familiar with the standards and, additionally, that it takes reflective

ARE STANDARDS FOR CHILDREN COMPATIBLE WITH DEVELOPMENTALLY APPROPRIATE PRACTICE?

THE CALL for standards for children has been met with ambivalence and some resistance by early childhood professionals. In part, there is concern that standards assume that children are basically alike; in addition, standards ignore the rich variability that exists among children. "Because young children's development is episodic, uneven, and highly influenced by their prior experiences, early childhood educators tend to believe that no one set of age-related goals can be applied to all children" (Bredekamp, 2009, p. 261). There is further concern that when learning outcomes are specified, the curriculum will be narrowed to meet these.

At the same time, the establishment of a professional guide for those who work with young children, *Developmentally Appropriate Practice in Early Childhood Programs Serving Children from Birth through Age 8* (Copple & Bredekamp, 2009), has provided another set of standards. Central concepts in this document include respect for the whole child, concern for each individual child, play as a major context for development, respect for diversity, and meaningful involvement of families. The values of DAP are congruent with programs that seek to "create a vibrant classroom culture focused on relationships and inquiry" (Curtis & Carter, 2008, p. 9). These values are not compatible, however, with programs that do not respect children's individual pace, learning styles, abilities, and needs; bypass the right of children to engage in child-initiated play; and rely on result-driven standards.

Teachers may see standards as problematic if they work in programs in which activities are primarily child-initiated rather than teacher-directed, engaged learning is valued, teachers see themselves as co-learners with the children, and curriculum revolves around projects that stem from children's interests. Judy Harris Helm (2008) provides insight into how standards can be met as part of a project-focused curriculum. She argues that projects, which are in-depth investigations of a topic of interest to the children, provide for integrated learning experiences that engage children, and that their learning can, therefore, correspond with standards. Furthermore, she states, "learning is easier for children when new information is connected to what they already know, not taught in isolation. Research in early cognition indicates that by the time children are four years old, they have developed a complex, interconnected knowledge base about the world and how it works" (pp. 14–15).

When children investigate a topic that interests them, they often find a need to develop and use the kinds of skills and knowledge listed in standards; their interest in the project topic will help children see the value of skills such as reading, writing, and math when such skills help them in their exploration of the topic (Helm, 2008). In one kindergarten classroom, for instance, children's interest in puppets led to their creation of a puppet performance. Over the three months during which they engaged in this project, the children used literacy skills by writing a play and sending out written invitations to the performance; they used numeracy skills by comparing RSVPs with the number of chairs needed and arranging the classroom to accommodate all their guests; they developed spatial reasoning and motor skills in their construction of a puppet theater; and they developed many social skills as they collaborated, negotiated, and performed before an audience of peers and adults. They met multiple standards through this project by developing skills and knowledge in relation to a topic in which they were intensely interested.

The increasing prominence of standards has also concerned early childhood teachers who highly value children's play. "Play has long had a central role in early childhood education, where it has been viewed as an effective means for promoting all aspects of child development. Many early childhood teachers are concerned that the standards movement and its narrowing of educational goals are pushing aside classroom learning through play in favor of more didactic forms of instruction" (Drew, Christie, Johnson, Meckley, & Nell, 2008, p. 39). These authors, however, consider that play and standards can coexist and that mature forms of play can help children learn the skills delineated in standards. Because play is intrinsically motivating, it provides an ideal vehicle for helping children learn the concepts and academic skills found in standards.

Many early childhood educators have taken the responsibility to ensure that when they adopt learning standards, they do so in a way that supports the development of children through appropriate practice. Respected early childhood advocate and leader, Barbara Bowman, puts it this way: "Standards can help us as educators to clarify where we want to go and give us a yardstick for measuring our success in getting there" (Bowman, 2006, p. 48).

practice for them to integrate standards into good practice. Ultimately, what is important is that early childhood teachers "take good care of young children and help them grow and learn and flourish" (Gronlund, 2008, p. 13).

ASSESSMENT

assessment
A systematic way of gathering information about children's learning and development, through a variety of methods, including observation, tests, portfolios, and other evaluations.

As we have already noted, accountability and standards are closely tied to assessment. **Assessment** is defined by the Council of Chief State School Officers (2008) as "a systematic procedure for obtaining information from observation, interviews, portfolios, projects, tests, and other sources that can be used to make judgments about characteristics of children or programs." Purposes of assessments include the following:

- Promoting children's learning and development
- Identifying children for health and special services
- Monitoring trends
- Evaluating programs and services
- Holding individual children, teachers, and schools accountable

In this section, we will discuss informal and formal types of assessment and the applicability of different approaches; specifically, we will examine observational techniques, teacher-developed rating scales and checklists, and standardized tests. We will also address the potential for misusing evaluation instruments, including the need for sensitivity and care in using them, and the selection of appropriate measures. One way to minimize such potential misuses is to rely on more than one method of assessment through the use of more inclusive, comprehensive assessment systems, which we will consider as well.

Key Point ◆

Observation is an unobtrusive way of gaining information about children.

anecdotal record
A method of observation involving a written "word picture" of an event or behavior.

Observation

One of the most effective informal methods of evaluation is through focused observation. Early childhood teachers use observation as a primary method of gaining insight into the various facets of children's development, at different times and in different contexts (Wortham, 2011). It allows for insight into the processes that children use in learning rather than on milestones or individual facts that are assessed out of context in more formal testing (Dodge, Heroman, Charles, & Maiorca, 2004). Observation can provide us with detailed information about behavior, can help us understand it, and can provide the basis for predicting behavior. One of the most appealing features of observation is that it is unobtrusive and natural. It does not interfere with the child's ongoing activity and behavior, in contrast with more formal tests that require that the child perform specified tasks in an isolated setting.

TYPES OF OBSERVATION. Observation can take a variety of forms. One of the most often used is the **anecdotal record,** a brief description or "word picture" of an event or behavior (Puckett & Black, 2008). A collection of well-written and accurate anecdotes can provide a very descriptive characterization of a child. Anecdotal records come

One of the most effective ways of gaining information about the children in your class is through focused observation.

© Cengage Learning

only from direct observation, are written down promptly and accurately, describe the context of the behavior, are factual rather than interpretive, and can focus either on a typical or an unusual aspect of the child's behavior (Bentzen, 2009; Wortham, 2011).

A **running record** is a more detailed account of a child's behavior over a period of time (Wortham, 2011). Whereas the anecdote focuses on a single event, the running record keeps track of everything that happens during a specified time period, whether it is a half hour or several months.

Such a record can be very useful when you are trying to pinpoint the source of a problem. It was most helpful for getting a handle on the disruptions in one class, where three-year-old Erin seemed to always be at the center of aggressive outbursts. A careful running record, kept over a period of three days, helped the teachers see that Erin was responding to rather subtle taunts from two other children.

One helpful device in keeping a running record is the **ABC analysis,** in which three columns identify the antecedent, behavior, and consequence of incidents (Reynolds & Kamphaus, 2004). This helps you focus not only on the child's behavior, but also on what precipitates and what follows it as well.

Time sampling provides a way of measuring the frequency of a behavior over a period of time (Wortham, 2011). Time sampling is a quantitative method of observation, in that you count how often the behavior occurs at uniform time intervals. You may, for instance, want to know just how often the adults in the classroom attend to Tracy, because you suspect he is often overlooked and neglected. Since you do not have time to observe Tracy all day long, you might determine that every half hour you will spend five minutes watching Tracy, noting every time a teacher attends to or interacts with him. Over a period of a week, you should have a representative sampling of the attention Tracy receives from adults. You might also decide, for purposes of comparison, to observe Sharon at the same time because Sharon appears to get frequent adult attention.

When you want to observe a less frequent behavior, **event sampling** can be used (Wortham, 2011). In this case, you wait until a given behavior occurs and then write a descriptive record of the event. Event sampling can be useful if you have noted that Kareem has periodic crying spells and you have trouble pinpointing the cause. Thus, each time Kareem engages in this behavior, one of the teachers stands back and records carefully what is happening. The ABC method can be very useful in recording such an event because you are trying to get a sense of its causes and consequences (Wortham, 2011).

CHARACTERISTICS OF GOOD OBSERVATIONS. One of the requirements of good observation is that it be objective. Your role as an observer is to be as impartial as possible, to stand back and record what you see rather than what you think the child is feeling or experiencing (Jablon, Dombro, & Dichtelmiller, 2007). Compare the two records in Figure 6-1. What distinguishes one from the other? The first observation tells you how the observer is interpreting the incident; the second describes what is

running record
A type of observation that provides an account of all of the child's behavior over a period of time.

ABC analysis
An observational technique in which the observer records observations in three columns, identifying antecedent, behavior, and consequence.

time sampling
A quantitative measure or count of how often a specific behavior occurs within a given amount of time.

event sampling
A method of observation in which the observer records a specific behavior only when it occurs.

Key Point

Event sampling is used to observe and record only when a specified behavior occurs.

When a behavior such as a tantrum or crying spell occurs infrequently, event sampling is a good observational method to use. Thus, the teacher observes and carefully notes the behavior only when the tantrum or crying event happens.

Figure 6-1

Sample Observations

Observation 1

Letitia comes into the classroom and immediately decides to pick on Erica, whom she doesn't like. She approaches Erica and, in her usual aggressive way, grabs the doll that Erica is playing with. Letitia doesn't really want the doll, she just wants what Erica has. When the teacher sees what has happened, she gets upset with Letitia and makes her give the doll back to Erica. Because of this, Letitia gets really angry and has one of her nasty tantrums, which makes everyone in the class upset.

Observation 2

Letitia marches into her classroom. She looks around for a few seconds, then ambles to the dramatic play area, where Erica is putting a doll into the cradle. Letitia stops two feet in front of the cradle, standing with her legs apart and hands on hips. She watches Erica put a blanket on the doll, then steps right up to it, grabs the doll by an arm, and pulls it roughly out of the cradle. She runs with the doll into the block area and turns around to look back at Erica. As Letitia is running off, Erica yells, "No! I was playing with the doll." Erica looks at Mrs. Wendell, whose eyes move toward the dramatic play area. Erica's shoulders drop and she says in a softer whimper, "Letitia took the doll I was playing with," then starts to cry. As Mrs. Wendell walks toward Letitia, Letitia drops the doll and darts to the art area. Mrs. Wendell catches up with Letitia, holds her by the arm, and urges her back to the block area. She picks up the doll. "Letitia, we need to give this doll back to Erica. She was playing with it." Letitia, her lips pressed together over clenched jaws, pulls away from Mrs. Wendell and throws herself on the floor, kicking her feet and screaming.

Key Point ◆◆

Good observations need to be objective but at the same time be adequately descriptive. A collection of observations can then be combined and interpreted to better understand the child.

happening. Can the first observer really know that Letitia does not like Erica? That the teacher is angry? That Letitia made a conscious decision to pick on Erica?

Another characteristic of good observation is that it is adequately descriptive. Language is a powerful tool that allows us to conjure up a picture of an event. Cohen and Stern, in their classic book, *Observing and Recording the Behavior of Young Children* (1978), provide some helpful suggestions to beginning observers in the use of descriptive vocabulary. The verb *run*, for instance, has many synonyms that can invoke a clearer image of what is being described. Examples include stampede, whirl, dart, gallop, speed, shoot across, bolt, fly, hippety-hop, or dash. Adding descriptive adverbs, adjectives, and phrases will also enliven an anecdote. Although synonyms can add authenticity and life to your observational anecdote, be sure to use the dictionary frequently to ensure that the word you choose actually means what you intend. Can you find some descriptive words in the second example in Figure 6-1 that make the incident come alive?

Good observations also describe nonverbal cues, some of the nuances of body language as well as voice inflection that can give deeper meaning to an anecdote. Children, like adults, share subtle movements of their face and body and shadings of voice that describe common feelings and reactions. Izard (2004), for instance, uses common facial nuances in infants and children to measure emotion. Body language is not easy to read, requiring experience and practice to interpret accurately. As you begin developing observational skills, you might double-check with a more experienced teacher to verify your reading of such nonverbal cues. Again, looking at Figure 6-1, do you see some descriptions of such nonverbal signs?

INTERPRETING OBSERVATIONS. As we have indicated, observational information must be gathered objectively, without inserting personal bias. But there comes a point, once you have gathered a collection of anecdotes, when you can look for patterns (Wortham, 2011). Interpretations, however, should always be kept clearly separate from observations. In reviewing observations that span a period of time, you should be able to find clues to children's unique ways of behaving and responding. When a set of observations shows repeatedly that a child reacts aggressively to conflict, or becomes pleasurably involved in messy media, or talks to adults far more than to other children, you can see a characteristic pattern for that child.

As you interpret observations, keep a clear focus on norms of development for young children. An understanding of the age range within which specific traits and behaviors generally occur (see Chapter 2) will help you interpret observations. Your familiarity with child development, combined with sensitive observation, provide a powerful tool for understanding the children in your care, one that can help you maximize their development. Reflective analysis of your observations can help you identify children's knowledge and skills; it can also help you set goals and direction for the curriculum. "The essence of developmentally appropriate practice is knowing where children are on a continuum of learning and then offering them challenging yet achievable experiences to nudge them on the way" (Dodge et al., 2004, p. 24). Observation should help us know and understand the children we work with because it creates "an attitude of openness and wonder" (Jablon et al., 2007, p. 7). But interpretation should be undertaken cautiously. Human behavior is complex, not easily pigeonholed, and there is the danger of overzealous interpretation when a pattern is more in the mind of the observer than representative of the child.

DAP

SOME OBSERVATIONAL TECHNIQUES. Finding time to observe can be challenging for the busy teacher. Try to develop a pattern and time frame for carrying out observations. It is helpful to carry a pencil and pad in your pocket while working with children to facilitate jotting down some quick notes and then to set aside a few minutes at the end of the day to write up the records.

Thoughtful storage of the information you collect from observations for later use is also important. Computer files, set up for each child, can help organize the information. If a computer or laptop is accessible in the classroom, you can add your notes directly to those files. Alternatively, you can write dated anecdotes on file cards to be kept in a file box with a divider for each child in the class. Another handy storage device for a running record is a loose-leaf notebook with separate pages for each child. A file box or notebook can be kept in a spot that is accessible but ensures confidentiality. Keeping such records can also pinpoint children who are being overlooked when, over a period of time, you find very few or no records on some youngsters.

Early childhood student teachers and, in some programs, teachers may be asked specifically to record observations rather than participate in the class for a period of time. If you are assigned a role as an outside observer rather than as a member of the classroom, the observation will require a somewhat different approach. First, you will have more time to engage in a thorough observation, perhaps to keep a running record. If you are observing in the classroom (rather than from behind a one-way mirror), you should be as unobtrusive as possible so that children's behavior is affected only minimally by your presence. Seat yourself

When recording observations, it is important to note nonverbal cues such as voice inflection or facial expression. These can be revealing. What does this child's body language and expression tell you?

A file box with dividers or a notebook helps organize observations and other information about a child.

Key Point

Checklists and rating scales are ways of checking whether a child or group of children engage in specific behaviors or skills.

checklist
A method of evaluating children that consists of a list of behaviors, skills, concepts, or attributes that the observer checks off as a child is observed to have mastered the item.

rating scale
An assessment of specific skills or concepts that are rated on some qualitative dimension of excellence or accomplishment.

where you are less likely to be noticed, avoid eye contact with children, and dress simply (Wortham, 2011). If children come to you to ask what you are doing, as invariably they will, give a simple answer that does not invite further conversation, for instance, "I am writing."

Teacher-Designed Instruments

Other frequently used, informal methods of evaluation include **checklists** and **rating scales** designed by the teacher. Both types of instruments are based on specific learning objectives or developmental indicators (Wortham, 2011). Checklists and rating scales are prepared in conjunction with observing the children, but results are recorded with a simple check mark or numerical evaluation rather than a lengthy verbal description.

The primary difference between these two is that checklists simply note the presence or absence of a skill or concept, whereas rating scales evaluate the level of attainment (Wortham, 2011). The advantage of such instruments is that they are quick and easy to use, flexible, and very specific to the needs of your situation. However, teacher-designed instruments can be time-consuming to prepare and have to be devised with care and thought to be valid and appropriate.

CHECKLISTS. A checklist lists behaviors, skills, concepts, or attributes and is followed by a space for noting their presence or absence. They can be devised for individual children (Figure 6-2) or for the entire class (Figure 6-3). Some checklists include space for recording multiple observations that can be repeated over a period such as a year (Figure 6-2); others are taken at one point in time (Figure 6-3). If you use a list that includes all the children in the class to get a sense of which children have and which have not mastered specific tasks, do not post such a record in the classroom, where families will see it and make comparisons.

RATING SCALES. Rating scales provide more qualitative information than checklists because they indicate to what extent the child engages in or has mastered a behavior. As a student, you are judged on a rating scale that usually takes the form of letter grades ranging from A (excellent) to F (unsatisfactory), and your cumulative grade point average (GPA) gives a numerical value to all of the ratings (grades) you have received.

The dimensions of ratings applied to children will depend on what you want to measure. You may, for instance, want to determine the frequency of each child's participation in various types of activities (Figure 6-4). In that case you might graph the children on a continuum that goes from "always" to "never" (Wortham, 2011).

Rating scales can also be used to show where a child is in the process of mastering certain tasks. You could, for instance, take the checklist of gross motor skills used in Figure 6-1 and turn it into a rating scale by rating each behavior as follows:

1. Performs task all the time
2. Performs task sometimes
3. Performs task rarely
4. Never performs task

Figure **6-2**

**Checklist of Selected Gross Motor Tasks
(to be completed four times during the year)**

Child: _____

Instructions: Mark with an "X" when task has been mastered.

Behavior	1) ___	2) ___	3) ___	4) ___
Hops on one foot				
Balances on one foot for 5 seconds				
Walks 2-inch balance beam				
Jumps across 12 inches and lands with both feet				
Throws 10-inch ball 6 feet				
Catches 10-inch ball with both arms				
Pumps on swing				
Pedals tricycle				

Date of Observation

Figure **6-3**

Checklist of Selected Gross Motor Tasks for the Entire Class

Date: _____

Instructions: Mark with an "X" when task has been mastered.

Name	Hops	Balance 5 sec	2-inch Beam	12-inch Broad Jump	Throw Ball 6 feet	Catch Ball	Pedal Trike	Pump on Swing

Figure **6-4**

Rating Scale of Frequency of Participation of the Children in Various Classroom Activity Areas

Dramatic Play

Instructions: Rate each child's frequency of participation in the dramatic play area.

Name	Frequency of Interaction				
	Always	Frequently	Occasionally	Seldom	Never

Key Point ◆

Standardized or formal tests are more stringently developed and used, and they must follow specific testing criteria.

naeyc

validity
A characteristic of a test that indicates that the test actually measures what it purports to measure.

reliability
A measure of a test indicating that the test is stable and consistent, to ensure that changes in score are due to the child, not the test.

screening test
A quick method of identifying children who might exhibit developmental delay; only an indicator that must be followed up by more thorough and comprehensive testing.

It may be appropriate to add a "not observed" category to differentiate between a child who cannot perform a task and one who chooses not to engage in the specific behavior while the teacher is observing.

Standardized Tests

Whereas observations and teacher-devised instruments are informal methods of gathering information about children, standardized tests are considered formal assessments. Such instruments are developed by professionals and are distributed commercially. Standardized tests are developed, tested, and refined so they have validity and reliability. **Validity** means that tests measure what they purport to measure. **Reliability** means they are stable and consistent; you know that when a child's score changes, it is because the child has changed, not the test (NAEYC, 2003). When standardized tests are administered, specific standards for testing conditions are delineated to provide uniformity. Over the past few years, the use of standardized tests with young children has increased; thus, we will examine the general categories of such tests and a sampling of specific instruments.

SCREENING TESTS. Screening tests provide a quick method of identifying children who may be at risk for a specified condition; for instance, developmental delay. Screening is not an end in itself but is meant to be followed by more thorough diagnostic testing if the screening instrument shows a possible problem. Most screening tests take about 15 to 30 minutes to administer. They are used by a wide variety of professionals, in addition to early

"Can you catch the ball?" Screening tests are based on several simple tasks that the child is asked to carry out.

childhood educators, including medical and social work personnel. A number of screening instruments have been developed in recent years as a result of the Education for All Handicapped Children Act (Public Law 94-142), which seeks to identify and provide early intervention to young children with disabilities or those at risk for later learning problems (Wortham, 2011).

One widely used screening instrument is the **Denver II** (Frankenburg & Dodd, 1990), for use with infants and children up to age six. Use of the Denver II can be learned relatively quickly. This test, often used by medical as well as early childhood professionals, examines the child's functioning in self-help, social, language, fine motor, and gross motor areas.

Items on the Denver II are scored in relation to a norm. Such **norm-referenced** tests provide a large comparison group for each age against which the score can be compared (Wortham, 2011). For each tested item, the Denver II indicates whether the score of a child is at the 25th, 50th, or 90th percentile or well below or above the functioning of other children who are the same age. If the child fails to accomplish tasks for his or her age group in two or more of the four areas, then more in-depth testing is recommended.

Another widely used screening test is the **Developmental Indicators for the Assessment of Learning (DIAL III)** (Mardell-Czudnowski & Goldenberg, 1998), which screens in the motor, concepts, and language areas. This test, normed for children between the ages of two and six, has separate norms for white and nonwhite children. Like the Denver Developmental Screening Test, this test is easily used with some practice and does not take long to administer.

The **Ages and Stages Questionnaires (ASQ)** (Squires & Bricker, 2009) is an instrument that addresses communication, gross motor, fine motor, and personal-social development in infants and young children. It takes only 10 to 15 minutes for a family member or caregiver to complete. The ASQ system screens for developmental delays at specific ages: 4, 6, 8, 10, 12, 14, 16, 27, 33, 36, 42, 48, 54, and 60 months. Research studies have found this test to be both reliable and valid as a screening tool. Data-management software is available to accompany this assessment tool.

DEVELOPMENTAL TESTS. Frequently, a screening test will indicate the necessity for more complete assessment and is then followed by a more thorough and time-intensive **developmental test.** Such tests measure the child's functioning in most or all areas of development, although some instruments are specific to one or two areas. Various in-depth commercial assessments are available, complete with kits containing the necessary testing materials.

Developmental assessments are usually **criterion-referenced** rather than norm-referenced. Thus, children are measured against a predetermined level of mastery rather than against the scores of a group of children of the same age (Wortham, 2011). The criteria in these tests are based on the test developers' educated understanding of what children can be expected to achieve at various ages.

One widely used developmental test is the **Brigance Diagnostic Inventory of Early Development—Revised** (Brigance, 2004).With some training, early childhood teachers can use this test. It contains subtests for fine motor, gross motor, language, cognitive, and self-help areas; it does not measure social development. Test materials are designed so that a child's progress can be followed in one booklet or recorded in a web-based format over the testing years, from birth to age seven. Testing of many of the items can be incorporated into a

Denver II
A quick test for possible developmental delays in children from infancy to age six.

norm-referenced
A test in which scores are determined by using a large group of same-age children as the basis for comparison, rather than using a predetermined criterion or standard of performance.

Developmental Indicators for the Assessment of Learning (DIAL III)
A developmental screening test for children ages two to six, assessing motor, concept, and language development.

Ages and Stages Questionnaires (ASQ)
Brief tests designed to screen for developmental delays in children from 4 to 60 months.

Key Point

Developmental tests are thorough assessments of children's development in all or several domains.

developmental test
This type of test measures the child's functioning in most or all areas of development, although some such tests are specific to one or two areas.

criterion-referenced
A characteristic of tests in which children are measured against a predetermined level of mastery rather than against an average score of children of the same age.

Brigance Diagnostic Inventory of Early Development—Revised
A developmental assessment tool for children from birth to age seven.

curriculum; therefore, a child does not need to be pulled from the class for the Brigance to be administered.

Another developmental test is the **Assessment, Evaluation, and Programming System (AEPS)** (Bricker, 2003), which links assessment, intervention, and evaluation for children from birth to six years. Teachers use to AEPS to assess and monitor six developmental areas in young children, including fine motor, gross motor, cognitive, adaptive, social communication, and social. The AEPS helps to formulate developmentally appropriate goals, conduct before-and-after evaluations to ensure that interventions are working, and involves families in the whole process. The AEPS also is available in a print version or as a web-based management system.

INTELLIGENCE TESTS. One of the oldest types of standardized assessments is the intelligence test. Such tests have stirred considerable controversy, much of it loaded with emotion because it raises the question of whether intelligence is a fixed biological trait or whether it is malleable and can be raised through an enriched environment. Another volatile controversy about such tests has been the concern over culture bias—that tests are slanted to white, middle-class norms and experiences (Fleege, 1997).

One of the major applications of intelligence tests for young children has been to identify children who fall well below or above the normal range. Classifications of an intellectual disability or giftedness, for instance, are generally set by IQ score ranges. One of the concerns with using IQ scores for young children is that these scores are not particularly predictive of later IQ. Most children's scores change between early childhood and adolescence, and some change considerably (Fleege, 1997).

Such tests are highly structured and must be administered by a psychologist specifically trained in their use. The **Stanford–Binet Intelligence Scale** (Roid, 2003) is a single test with varying tasks for different ages ranging from two through adulthood. The test yields an IQ score; 100 is the average. The Stanford–Binet yields a single, global IQ score, without breaking down results as do some other tests.

READINESS TESTS. The specific purpose of readiness tests—to determine whether a child is prepared to enter a program such as kindergarten or first grade—differentiates them from other types of assessments. Readiness assessments are "a hot topic" because of the increased focus on accountability that we discussed earlier. Readiness is a slippery concept, however, because it is not an innate part of the child but is, rather, a reflection of the values and expectations of the family, the school, the community, and the wider society (Maxwell & Clifford, 2004). Such tests are limited in what they measure, and have been shown to be wrong up to half the time, potentially no more accurate than flipping a coin (Fair Test, 2007). Nonetheless, readiness tests are often used to determine whether a child should be allowed to enter school. In general, however, research has shown that delaying school entry is not in the best interest of children (Marshall, 2003).

One such instrument used extensively by school districts across the country is the **Metropolitan Readiness Test** (Nurss & McGauvran, 1995). It has been criticized, however, because correct answers rely heavily on exposure to specific concepts rather than on innate ability. Unfortunately, the test does not distinguish between a child who has had limited exposure and a child who

---

Assessment, Evaluation, and Programming System (AEPS)
An evaluation instrument for children from birth to six years, which links assessment, intervention, and evaluation in six developmental areas.

Key Point ◆◆
Intelligence tests measure intellectual functioning and are usually highly structured as to how they can be administered and interpreted.

Stanford–Binet Intelligence Scale
A widely used test that yields an intelligence quotient (IQ).

Key Point ◆◆
In recent years, readiness tests have been used increasingly to determine whether children are prepared to enter a specific program such as kindergarten or first grade.

Metropolitan Readiness Test
A test to determine whether a child is prepared to enter a program such as kindergarten.

SELECTING THE RIGHT ASSESSMENT TOOL

Theresa Danna Douglas

Becky, Infant/Toddler Care Coordinator, Early Head Start Program

As part of my job, I work with teachers to provide high-quality early care and education for our infants and toddlers. My job requires me to assist teachers with assessing young children to determine their development and to help plan, implement, and individualize the curriculum. Our Early Head Start program is part of a larger school that serves children from birth through age five. We have five sites and serve approximately 200 children.

Our center has been accredited through the National Association for the Education of Young Children (NAEYC) for more than 20 years. Both Head Start regulations and NAEYC accreditation standards require accountability in the area of assessing young children. As we gathered data for our center's self-assessment prior to our recent reaccreditation, we found that we had two different assessment systems, one for infants and toddlers and one for pre-schoolers and kindergartners. The tool we were using for infants and toddlers wasn't being used uniformly across classrooms, and teachers had a difficult time gathering data for the tool and were uncomfortable using the data to make determinations about development. We decided to look for a system that could be used center-wide and across all of our age groups. As we researched comprehensive assessment systems, we quickly realized that the Assessment, Evaluation, and Programming System for Infants and Children (AEPS) would best meet our needs. AEPS had several advantages over other assessment systems in that it could assess children from birth to 72 months, could evaluate all developmental domains, had an accompanying curriculum to support developmental

goals, and included a newly created computerized database system.

Once we selected the AEPS as our assessment system, we contracted with the publisher to have a trainer conduct two day-long workshops with our staff during our "professional development days." Our center closes four to six times each year for a day to gather all of our teaching staff in one place to learn new strategies to build strong classroom communities. We were lucky that the trainer who came also was one of the developers of the AEPS. She provided great insight into how to use the system, the history of the system, and how to use the accompanying curriculum to set goals for children. After the training, the supervisory staff, including me, worked with teachers individually to implement the system. We decided together on the best methods for gathering data to complete the assessment. Some teachers found it helpful to carry notebooks and pens in their apron pocket so they could spontaneously capture moments of learning in the classroom and have them to use for formal observation time. Since children's conversations are another data source, a few teachers kept a pocket tape recorder handy. Some teachers found that using

sheets of labels they carry on a clipboard lets them document moments during the day. At naptime they peel the label off and stick it in the child's file.

Often for teachers, it is difficult to decide who and when to observe. The supervisory staff brainstormed with teachers about how to choose children so that everyone gets observed throughout the month. Some teachers focus on one child each week and only take notes on that child. Other teachers focus on an area in the classroom to observe each week so they can gather information about several children in specific types of play. Our teachers always have cameras ready to preserve and document activities and children for later use in assessment completion.

Our teachers are action researchers, and the data they collect for assessment helps produce a comprehensive picture of children's strengths, interests, and development in all domains that allows them to plan, implement, and individualize the curriculum. We have found the AEPS useful for so many things in working with our children. In one instance, an AEPS report indicated some delays in social development for one child about whom teachers were concerned. I sat down with the teacher and wrote down her concerns, reviewed the child's present levels of functioning as reported on the AEPS, and planned activities from the AEPS curriculum book to support the child's goals in the area of social development. After a month of implementing the curriculum with a focus on the area of concern, the child is thriving and the teacher feels satisfied and proud that she directly helped this child learn some new skills to help her be socially successful.

Children's ability to answer items on readiness tests depends to a large extent on prior experience. It is important to provide a wide range of experiences to young children so they can continue to expand their understanding of the world that surrounds them.

© Cengage Learning

has actual learning difficulties. The use of these tests has driven many pre-kindergarten programs to incorporate activities designed to prepare children for readiness testing, often at the expense of other appropriate activities, particularly exploratory, hands-on experiences (Schickedanz, Hansen, & Forsyth, 1990).

Head Start Performance Standards

Head Start Program Performance Standards
Federal accountability system for all Head Start programs, requiring that children meet specific outcomes in language, literacy, and math competencies.

In 2003, President Bush announced a new accountability system, in which all Head Start children would be given a national standardized test. The **Head Start Program Performance Standards** were instituted, requiring that children meet specific outcomes in eight general domains containing 27 elements. Programs had to show progress in these standards, especially those that have been mandated by Congress. The mandated domains include language, literacy, and mathematics. Professionals questioned the validity and reliability of such a test, especially since it was intended to be a "high stakes" test, used to evaluate the effectiveness of Head Start (Wortham, 2011). They expressed concern that this push for formal assessment, particularly in academic skills, represents a move away from serving the whole child to a watered-down, skill-based curriculum (Solley, 2007). "Sole reliance on children's cognitive outcomes [is] neither in keeping with the goals of Head Start nor with many definitions of what it means to be ready to succeed in early elementary school" (Raver & Zigler, 2004, p. 58). Meisels and Atkins-Burnett (2004) also expressed concern that items in this test are "rife with class prejudice" (p. 64) and are developmentally inappropriate. They conclude their article in the NAEYC journal, *Young Children*, by saying, "This test is not good early education practice. It is not good public policy. And it is certainly not good for young children" (p. 66).

Key Point ◆

Federal mandates to hold Head Start and other early childhood programs more accountable have led to the development of assessment systems that early childhood educators consider to be inappropriate.

Concerns about Use of Assessment Instruments

naeyc

All informal and formal evaluation methods can give us useful insights into the children in our care. But although using a variety of methods to better understand children has always been an important part of early childhood education, there is a growing concern about potential misuses, particularly of standardized evaluations. The 1980s brought an increased emphasis on testing, particularly as a way of proving that educational goals are being met (Wortham, 2011).

One major concern involves the misuse of readiness tests. With increasing frequency, such tests are being used to decide children's placement; for instance, whether they will be allowed to move on to first grade, placed in a transitional class, or retained in kindergarten or whether they will be admitted to a particular preschool program (Wortham, 2011). Thus, children are often labeled as failures when, in fact, they are expected to conform to inappropriate expectations (NAEYC, 2003). How devastating such practices are on children's self-concepts! Read the eloquent discussion of these concerns in NAEYC's 2003 position statement on *Curriculum, Assessment and Program Evaluation.*

A corollary to this trend is the fact that many early childhood programs have adopted curriculums whose main aim is to prepare children for readiness tests (Bredekamp & Shepard, 1989). Thus, preschool and kindergarten programs promote developmentally inappropriate methods to meet such goals, intensifying the problem of "failures" and children who are "unready" (NAEYC, 2003).

It has long been acknowledged that standardized tests have a variety of limitations. For instance, a test cannot ask every possible question to evaluate what a child knows on a topic; but the fewer questions included, the more the chance that the test just happened to include those for which the child does not know the answers. However, the more items there are on the test, the greater the chance that the child will become restless and disinterested and not give a representative picture of her or his ability.

Another criticism of standardized tests has been that they can be culture-biased, yet test designers have found it impossible to devise tests that are completely culture-free (Wortham, 2011). NAEYC's position statement, *Screening and Assessment of Young English-Language Learners* (2005), can be a valuable guide if you work with children whose native language is not English. In addition, it is very difficult to establish reliable and valid instruments for young children, given the rapid changes that occur in development as well as the normal individual variations among children (NAEYC, 2003). This also calls into question the use of norm groups against which individuals are compared.

In addition to the potential problems with a test itself, there are difficulties in evaluating young children that can affect the accuracy of test results. A number of factors can affect how accurately the test reflects the child's ability. These might include the child's attention and interest, the familiarity (or unfamiliarity) with the surroundings, the trust the child has in the adult tester (or whether the child has even seen this person before), the time of day, the fact that the child slept poorly the night before, or the fact that the mother forgot to kiss the child good-bye. In too many instances, tests are given to young children in large groups, a practice that further decreases reliability (NAEYC, 2003).

If so many problems are inherent in standardized tests, what is the answer to the dilemma of their increasing use with young children? NAEYC (2003) recommends that the relevance of tests be carefully evaluated by administrators:

Key Point

Early childhood professionals have raised some major concerns about the use and misuse of standardized tests, particularly when these lead to developmentally inappropriate practices.

DIVERSITY

Will results from the test contribute to improving the program for the children? Will the children benefit from the test? If the benefits are meager in relation to the cost (expense and time), perhaps the test should not be used. Furthermore, it is recommended that:

- tests be carefully reviewed for reliability and validity.
- tests match the program's philosophy and goals.
- only knowledgeable and qualified persons administer and interpret results.
- testers be sensitive to individual and cultural diversity.
- tests be used for only the purpose for which they were intended.
- no major decision related to enrollment, retention, or placement in a remedial program be made based on only one test, but that multiple sources of information be used for this purpose.

Assessment Systems

naeyc

Key Point

Comprehensive systems of assessment, also called "authentic assessment," focus on the whole child and all aspects of development; such assessments use many different methods and are closely linked to curriculum planning.

authentic assessment
A comprehensive approach to assessment, using multiple methods, which takes into account the whole child and focuses on all aspects of development.

work sampling system
An alternative method of gathering reliable information about young children, using a combination of observations, checklists, portfolios, and summary reports.

High/Scope Child Observational Record (COR)
An alternative method of gathering reliable information about young children; COR uses teachers' notes of observations by classifying them into specific categories.

confidentiality
Requirement that results of evaluations and assessments be shared with only the appropriate family members and school personnel.

Concerns about inappropriate evaluation, such as the ones expressed in NAEYC's position statement on *Curriculum, Assessment, and Program Evaluation* (2003) have led professionals and researchers to suggest some alternative, more comprehensive approaches. Such approaches make a much clearer link between what is being assessed and the early childhood curriculum. The term **authentic assessment** has been coined to reflect this shift. Authentic assessment takes into account the whole child and focuses on all aspects of development. It uses observation and other forms of documentation of the work that children do and how they do it as a basis for educational decisions that affect individual children (Puckett & Black, 2008). Such assessment is ongoing, and it occurs in many contexts and through many different methods. Portfolios are one form of authentic assessment.

One example of a more comprehensive system of assessment is proposed by Meisels (1993). The **work sampling system** combines several types of data over an extended period of time to assess children ages three to eight. Teachers' ongoing observations are recorded either by hand or in a web-based format on developmental checklists. These are categorized into seven domains and include many common, developmentally appropriate activities and expectations. In addition, portfolios of select pieces of the children's work are also compiled, and teachers prepare narrative summary reports at three points during the year. Another alternative testing process is the **High/Scope Child Observational Record (COR),** for children ages 2½ to 6 (High/Scope, 2003). Teachers write brief notes about children's behavior in six categories: initiative, creative representations, social relations, music and movement, language and literacy, and logic and mathematics. These anecdotes are then used to rate children on 30 items, each of which has five levels. The High/Scope Child Observational Record for Infants and Toddlers (2002), for ages six weeks to three years, is also available. Both instruments are available in print and online versions. Alternatives to traditional, often developmentally inappropriate testing methods, the work sampling system and COR offer promise for those who work with young children.

One final note: It is important to keep in mind that any information gathered about children and their families—whether from test results, observations, or something a parent shared—needs to be treated with **confidentiality** and respect.

Selecting and Using Evaluation Methods

We have looked at a number of formal and informal methods of assessment, information that can be mind-boggling considering that we have reviewed only a very small number of the many available commercial instruments. Selecting an appropriate method will depend on how the results are to be used. Tests are designed and used for different purposes, including providing evidence of child or program progress for administrators, teachers, parents, policy-makers, and the general public (Jones, 2004). Assessments also provide opportunities for collaborative and shared decisions among early childhood professionals. We will briefly examine some suggested methods in terms of three purposes of assessment—gaining information: (1) about children, (2) for program planning purposes, and (3) for family feedback. Ideally, these three should work closely together and overlap.

Key Point ◆◆

Evaluation methods can provide valuable information about children, give direction for program planning, and contribute feedback to share with families.

INFORMATION ABOUT CHILDREN. Effective teaching depends on knowing as much as possible about the children in the class; a variety of data-gathering methods can be used, as follows:

❱ Ongoing observation can provide valuable insight into all children, their functioning as part of the class, their growth in all developmental areas, what they particularly enjoy, where they run into difficulties, how they get along with peers and teachers, how they communicate, and so forth.

❱ A screening test, used with all of the children early in the school year, can help identify those who need further diagnostic testing and those who might benefit from specific intervention programs.

❱ A developmental assessment can be given to children whose performance on the screening test indicated a need for further evaluation. Such an assessment should be combined with observation, family interviews, possible professional testing (for instance, by a speech pathologist, audiologist, physical therapist, or doctor), and other sources of information to provide as full a picture of the child as possible. On the basis of a thorough evaluation, it is possible to make better educational and therapeutic decisions about the child's future. Continuing observation and periodic retesting using the developmental assessment can show whether the child is making progress and can pinpoint areas needing further attention.

❱ A collection of the child's work in the form of a portfolio can also contribute to a better understanding of the child's interests and abilities.

INFORMATION FOR PROGRAM PLANNING. One of the main purposes of assessment is to help direct program development. Once you have an idea of strengths and areas that need attention, both for individual children and for the group as a whole, you and your colleagues can plan a prescriptive curriculum (Hendrick & Weissman, 2007). Some useful data-gathering methods include the following:

❱ Information from observations can provide excellent programming direction. You may notice, for example, that the parallel play that predominated earlier in the year is beginning to give way to more and more interactive play (remember our discussion of play in Chapter 2). You might plan activities

One way to assess the ability of all children in a class on a task such as use of scissors, is through systematic observation, recording findings on a checklist.

that require a greater measure of cooperation and set up the class environment to facilitate more social interaction.

▶ Checklists and rating scales allow you to evaluate the functioning of the group of children on tasks that you identify as important. You may, for instance, discover that the majority of your three-year-olds are not able to hold scissors effectively, let alone cut with them. This information tells you that more activities using scissors should be planned to help children acquire this fine motor skill. Similarly, these evaluation devices (as well as observations) will help you determine whether children have successfully met the objectives that you set for specific curriculum units.

▶ Some programs administer either a formal or an informal developmental assessment at specific points of the year to evaluate whether children are meeting the overall goals of the program.

Portfolios of each of the children can provide insight into the children's interests and progress toward meeting program and individual goals.

FAMILY SUPPORT
INFORMATION FOR FAMILY FEEDBACK

All forms of evaluation provide information to share with parents. It is important to examine the child's strengths, not just areas that may be problematic, and it is vital that all information be as accurate, realistic, and unbiased as possible. Data carefully collected over a period of time and thoughtfully evaluated provide the basis for good family-feedback conferences.

There are a number of points to keep in mind when sharing evaluation results with families. In all instances, test results or other evaluation information should never be given in isolation, out of the context of the child's overall nature. Thus, to tell a family that their child is performing below (or, for that matter, above) the norm in fine motor skills is only part of the picture. It is equally important to tell them that their child has excellent social skills, shows leadership qualities, has a delightful sense of humor, seems to particularly enjoy sensory activities, and so forth. Such information does not rely solely on the results of a developmental assessment, which yielded the fine motor score, but is reinforced by observations, anecdotes, and the teachers' reflection about the child.

Another point to remember when sharing evaluation results with families is that you should be able to explain the measures that were applied. Some standardized tests are rather complicated to use, score, and interpret. Be sure that you understand what the test results mean and that you can explain them. It does not help a parent who asks, "What do you mean she scored below the norm?" to be told, "Well, I'm not exactly sure what 'norm' means." If your school uses any kind of standardized test, read its manual carefully, know how the test was constructed, understand how results should be interpreted and used, and be familiar with the terminology.

At the same time, it is also important to keep in mind and convey to families that tests have their limitations. Consider the preceding discussion about the shortcomings of and concerns about tests and let families know that these represent only part of the input used in evaluation. Also remind families, as well as yourself, that children are amazingly flexible and often will experience a quick change or growth spurt in their development that could suddenly modify the test findings. Never present any evaluation results as the definitive information about the child's abilities and functioning. Similarly, let families know that a wide variety of profiles fall within a "normal" range.

Finally, when sharing evaluation results with families, also be prepared to defend the measures you used. A parent may well ask you, "Why did you give this test to my child?" Be able to answer such a question, because it is certainly logical and valid. You need to feel that the test provides valuable information, and you should be able to specify how information will be used. For instance, such measures should help plan relevant learning experiences for the child (Wortham, 2011).

DIVERSITY

EVALUATING THE ENVIRONMENT. A number of instruments are available for assessing the early childhood environment. Such tools are often used for research purposes, but are equally used for self-assessment and program evaluation by teachers and administrators. The most widely used such instrument is the **Early Childhood Environments Rating Scale (ECERS)** (Harms, Clifford, & Cryer, 1998) and its related forms for infant and toddler (ITERS) (Harms, Cryer, & Clifford, 2003), school-age (SACERS) (Harms, Jacobs, & Romano, 1996), and family day-care settings (FDCRS) (Harms & Clifford, 1989). These scales rate all aspects of the physical and social environment and take into account indicators of inclusion and cultural sensitivity. Each scale examines aspects of the environment specific to the age group of children. The ECERS, for instance, includes 43 items under the categories of space and furnishings, personal care routines, language-reasoning, activities, interactions, program structure, and parents and staff. Completing a rating using one of these scales takes about two to three hours.

In addition, a number of states are implementing **Quality Rating and Improvement Systems (QRIS).**

Early Childhood Environments Rating Scale (ECERS)
A widely used assessment of the early childhood environment, used both for research and for program-evaluation purposes.

Quality Rating and Improvement System (QRIS)
Rating of quality of child care programs to help parents make informed choices; implemented in a number of states.

> A QRIS is a set of tools to measure, collect, and disseminate information about the quality of early childhood care and education (ECE) settings, including those based in centers, homes, preschools, and elementary schools. QRIS evaluators rate the quality of these settings through site visits and off-site data collection, eventually boiling their results down to 3- or 4-star reviews that can be used by parents to determine the best places to enroll their children. (Satkowski, 2009)

Does your state have a QRIS system in place?

SUMMARY

1. In recent years, there has been a greater call for accountability in early childhood education programs.
2. In response to this call for accountability, early childhood learning standards have been developed by many states and organizations to spell out knowledge, skills, and dispositions young children should gain.

3. Assessment is an important element in early childhood education and can help determine whether standards are being met.
   A. One of the most widely used methods of evaluation is observation.
   B. Teacher-designed instruments such as checklists and rating scales are another type of assessment.
   C. Many commercially produced standardized tests are used for different purposes.
   D. Although assessment instruments are widely used and even mandated by federal law, there is also considerable concern about their use.
   E. Assessment systems that rely on multiple measures of gathering information about children give a more balanced and authentic picture of their functioning.
   F. Information from evaluations and assessments can be used in different ways.
   G. Environments can be assessed through such widely used instruments as the Early Childhood Environments Rating Scale (ECERS).

KEY TERMS LIST

ABC analysis

accountability

Ages and Stages Questionnaires (ASQ)

anecdotal record

assessment

Assessment, Evaluation, and Programming System (AEPS)

authentic assessment

Brigance Diagnostic Inventory of Early Development—Revised

checklist

confidentiality

content standards

criterion-referenced

Denver II

Developmental Indicators for the Assessment of Learning (DIAL III)

developmental test

Early Childhood Environments Rating Scale (ECERS)

event sampling

Head Start Program Performance Standards

High/Scope Child Observational Record (COR)

learning standards

Metropolitan Readiness Test

norm-referenced

performance standards

Quality Rating and Improvement System (QRIS)

rating scale

reliability

running record

screening test

Stanford–Binet Intelligence Scale

time sampling

validity

work sampling system

KEY QUESTIONS

1. Most states have established Early Childhood Standards. Check whether the Standards are available online or request a copy (your instructor may also be able to obtain copies). Look through these Standards and check for the following: (1) Do the standards seem complete, covering needed elements? (2) Are there areas that do not seem to be covered or adequately covered by the Standards? (3) Would you add or delete anything?
2. With a fellow student, spend about 15 minutes observing the same child. Each of you write an anecdotal observation involving this child for the exact same

period of time. Now compare your two observations. Do they describe the same behaviors, activities, and interactions? Do they convey the same "picture" of this child? If the two observations differ in a significant way, why is this? Are there some subjective elements in either observation that might contribute to this difference?

3. Design a checklist of 10 items to assess social development of a group of preschoolers. How did you decide on which items to include? What resources did you use to put this checklist together? If possible, observe a group of preschoolers and apply this checklist to several of the children.

4. Have you been tested with a standardized instrument? Recall how you felt about the testing situation and the questions asked. What emotional impact did the test have on you? How might young children feel about being tested? What can a tester do to help children perform to their best ability?

5. Given the information from this chapter about the values and potential misuses of evaluation procedures, develop a set of criteria that might guide you, as an early childhood professional, in using assessments in the most effective way. What do you consider to be the three most important benefits of such testing? What should you avoid?

ADDITIONAL RESOURCES

Select additional books, articles, and websites on topics discussed in Chapter 6.

Bentzen, W. R. (2009). *Seeing young children: A guide to observing and recording behavior* (6th ed.). Belmont, CA: Wadsworth, Cengage Learning.

Curtis, D., & Carter, M. (2000). *The art of awareness: How observation can transform your teaching*. St. Paul, MN: Redleaf Press.

McAfee, O., Leong, D. J., & Bedrova, E. (2004). *Basics of assessment: A primer for early childhood educators*. Washington, DC: National Association for the Education of Young Children.

Wesson, K. (2001). The "Volvo effect"—Questioning standardized tests. *Young Children, 56*(2), 16–18.

Wortham, S. (2011). *Assessment in early childhood education* (6th ed.). Upper Saddle River, NJ: Merrill Prentice Hall.

HELPFUL WEBSITES

Alfie Kohn's articles about tests and standards:

www.alfiekohn.org/index.html

Alfie Kohn is an outspoken critic of the standards movement. In this essay and the associated links to the website, Kohn provides both critique and suggestions for bringing about change.

NAEYC's position statement on early childhood *Curriculum, Assessment, and Program Evaluation:*

http://www.naeyc.org/files/naeyc/file/positions/pscape.pdf

This website contains NAEYC's important position statement about assessment in early childhood education programs and its relationship to curriculum and programming.

National Institute for Early Education Research (NIEER):

www.nieer.org

The website of the National Institute for Early Education Research provides reports and information about many timely issues, including federal and state programs for young children. Many of these reports involve issues of assessment and accountability.

Go to **CengageBrain.com** to register your access code for this book's Education CourseMate website, where you will find more resources to help you study. Additional resources for this chapter include TeachSource Videos, glossary flashcards, web links, case studies with critical-thinking questions that apply the concepts presented in this chapter, and more. If your textbook does not include a printed access card, you can go to **CengageBrain.com** to purchase access.

IV

The *Where* of Early Childhood Education

The environment of the early childhood program is an important factor. Just *where* is it that children and their teachers play and work? What elements do we have to keep in mind as we consider the appropriate environment for programs for young children?

7

The Physical Environment

In Chapter 7, you will find answers to the following questions about the physical environment:

- How does the physical environment affect the children in your care and you, as an adult?
- What principles should you use in setting up indoor and outdoor environments for children of different ages and abilities?
- What principles should you use in selecting developmentally appropriate equipment and materials for young children?
- Is it a good idea to add computers for the children's use to the early childhood environment?

NAEYC STANDARDS CONSIDERED IN CHAPTER 7

(See the Standards Correlation Chart on the inside front cover of this book for the titles and description of the standards listed below.)

- *Standard 1c:* Providing both indoor and outdoor environments based on understanding of child development principles (pp. 168–177).
- *Standard 1c:* Structuring environments that are respectful of children and their abilities and meet the needs of different age groups and abilities (pp. 168–173; 177–179).
- *Standard 1c:* Ensuring healthy, safe, and appropriately challenging environments (pp. 198–203).
- *Standard 1c:* Selecting appropriate equipment and materials to support and challenge children (pp. 179–186).
- *Standard 1c:* Knowledge about computers and appropriate software for children's use (pp. 181–183).

Today, many young children spend the bulk of their waking hours in an early childhood program, often in one room for 9 or 10 hours every weekday. They spend some time in the outside play area and occasionally go on excursions into the community, but by and large, for many young children most of the time is spent in a relatively confined space. It is, therefore, very important to maximize this environment, because it has a profound effect on children and their behavior. The early childhood classroom should promote learning and a sense of belonging; the environment should convey positive messages about being in a place that can be trusted, safe, and friendly (Read, 2007).

EFFECTS OF THE PHYSICAL ENVIRONMENT

Take a moment to think about a place where you enjoy spending time. What is it about this place that makes it enjoyable? What are its appealing features? Is it because this place is relaxing and soothing, stimulating and exciting, thought-provoking and challenging, orderly and methodical, comfortable and homey, or colorful and bright? Now think about a place that you do not particularly like, and consider why you are averse to it. It may be that this place is boring, messy, stark, disorganized, dark, or uninviting. Think about spending all day in each of these places. What feelings and attitudes does this idea of each invoke in you? How do you think you would act and react in each place? Can you draw some conclusions about how and why the environment affects you?

Effect of the Environment on Children

The early childhood environment should support the development of children. It has a direct effect on how children behave toward each other. Positive peer interaction is promoted when children are not crowded, when an ample number and variety of items are available, and when socially oriented materials are provided. Classroom arrangement and careful selection of materials also foster cognitive development by providing opportunities for children to classify, find relationships, measure, compare, match, sort, and label. The environment also enhances both fine and gross motor development through a range of appropriately challenging equipment and materials (Dodge, 2004).

KEY POINT ◆

Because children's engagement in activities depends on the environment, teachers need to provide the most appropriate setting to promote positive peer interaction, independence, and self-esteem in children.

Children's growing sense of independence is supported when they can confidently and competently use equipment and when space and materials are arranged so that they can see what is available and make autonomous choices. At the same time, children develop a sense of responsibility when the environment makes it clear how and where materials are to be returned when they finish using them. Children are more productively involved in activities when the purpose of classroom spaces is clearly defined and when materials are developmentally appropriate (Shepherd & Eaton, 1997). Children are also more likely to follow classroom rules when the environment reinforces these; for instance, if it is important for reasons of safety that children not run inside, classroom furnishings should be arranged in a way that makes walking, rather than running, natural.

A pleasant, well-organized environment that provides children with a variety of age-appropriate activity options supports children's development in all domains and enhances learning.

The environment also enhances children's self-esteem when it is designed with their needs and development in mind, when it provides space for personal belongings, and when it promotes competence by allowing children to function independently. In addition, the environment should convey a sense of security and comfort through a friendly, warm, and inviting atmosphere, and through "soft" elements, such as beanbag chairs, carpeting, or sling swings (Curtis & Carter, 2003). The environment also should reflect the culture of the children of the classroom, with appropriate materials and displays that reflect the various cultural and ethnic groups represented by the children and families. Often families are happy to provide materials, as the families in Maritza's Head Start classroom (see "Stories from the Field" box in this chapter).

DIVERSITY

An attractive, aesthetic environment also contributes to children's well-being. The Reggio Emilia program, which was discussed in Chapter 5 and will be considered in more detail in Chapter 8, is noted for the beauty of its architecture, classroom arrangements, and materials. A great deal of thought goes into creating these environments for infants, toddlers, and preschoolers. One of the guiding principles of the Reggio Emilia approach is the importance of a beautifully pleasing environment where children and adults learn together (Gandini, 2004). A beautiful environment is considered a right, not an option, for children. Visitors to Reggio Emilia report that they can see how influential the environment is as they watch engrossed children and engaged teachers interact in these schools. While early childhood education professionals have always understood the importance of a pleasing environment, they often note that they did not fully appreciate just how powerful it can be until they saw beauty in action in Reggio Emilia. After a visit to the schools of Reggio Emilia, Bonnie Neugebauer wrote, "It is beautiful in the way that a home is beautiful. It reflects the stories of the people who live within it and it evolves through a sensitivity to natural beauty—wood, sunlight, plants, colors, comfort" (ExchangeEveryDay, 2008, p. 69).

Effect of the Environment on Teachers

When the environment is set up to maximize children's development, prevent problem behaviors, and promote appropriate behaviors, teachers' well-being will be indirectly supported. More directly, teachers' jobs are made more pleasant if they work in aesthetically pleasing surroundings, if they have a designated space where they can relax and plan, and if their needs are generally taken into consideration. Both personal comfort and professional needs should be supported. Environmental factors such as pleasant temperature, light, color, sound absorption, ventilation, and spatial arrangement can either facilitate or hinder staff in carrying out their jobs. Thus, a carefully arranged environment can help prevent teacher burnout by supporting teachers' goals for the children and by making the worksite a pleasant place to be.

Eisenberg (1997) identifies four categories of space for adults within the early childhood classroom. Appropriate space should be provided for the personal belongings of teachers and volunteers. A small locked area, a coat hook, or space on a shelf can meet this need. Teachers also need space where they can plan and prepare classroom activities; this includes storage for needed materials. A third category for adult space is an area where paperwork can be kept and resource materials such as books and journals can be stored. Finally, there is a need for a designated space for written communication with other adults; for instance, sign-in sheets, messages and information for families, and communiqués among staff members. Eisenberg concludes that a program will be much more harmonious if the adults' needs are considered.

ARRANGING THE INDOOR ENVIRONMENT

As we consider the indoor environment, we must take into account both its fixed features—for instance, the size and shape of the room, placement of windows and doors, and built-in features such as shelves and storage spaces—and movable or semifixed features, such as the arrangement of furnishings and materials, color, and texture (Prescott, 1997).

Fixed Features

Room size will, to a large extent, dictate how many children and how much material can be housed in the space. The maximum number of children allowed in an area is prescribed by licensing regulations. In most states, 35 square feet per child is required, although experts often recommend more. The American Academy of Pediatrics (2002) recommends 50 square feet of space per child. This recommendation is supported by a French study (Legrendre, 2003), which found that less than 54 square feet per child resulted in higher stress levels for children. Phyfe-Perkins (1980) concludes that "crowding of children which provides less than 25 square feet per child for an extended period of time should be avoided. It may increase aggressive behavior and inhibit social interaction and involvement" (p. 103).

The shape of the room has an impact on its arrangement and supervision. A rectangular room seems more adaptable than a square one, and an L-shaped room poses more problems for supervision (Mayesky, 2012).

To some extent, room arrangement will be affected by the amount of natural light available through windows. For instance, color used during art activities is enhanced by clear, bright light; thus, it is desirable to locate the art area near windows. Areas in which children need to attend to close detail, such as the book or language center, should also be located in a well-lighted place. All areas of a room should be well lit, and adequate electric lighting should be provided in places not reached by natural light.

Building materials have an effect on acoustics. Some rooms are constructed with sound-absorbing ceiling, floor, or wall materials, whereas others reverberate with noise. If the room's noise level hinders rather than enhances the children's participation in activities and the communication process, added features such as drapes, carpets, and corkboards can help eliminate much of the noise.

Because many young children's activities are messy, it is important to have water accessible, preferably in the room. Sensory activities, the art center, and cooking projects should be placed near the water source. If there is no running water in or adjacent to the room, an alternative arrangement (for instance, a bucket with soapy water and paper towels) should be close at hand.

If the room contains built-in storage units, the room should be arranged to best use these units. Materials the children use every day—such as, blocks, manipulatives, or art implements—should be placed on shelves that are at the children's level. In addition to built-in storage space, easily reachable portable units should be added as needed. If built-in storage space is above the children's reach, such shelves can be used for teacher materials or items not used every day (Prescott, 1997).

Movable Features

More than a room's fixed features, it is the movable elements that allow you to arrange a well-planned, developmentally appropriate environment for children.

When arranging the classroom, it is best to take advantage of natural features, for instance, placing the art area near a window. What other environmental features will have an impact on how the early childhood classroom is arranged?

KEY POINT ❖

Fixed features of a room—such as its size and shape, placement of doors and windows, built-in storage, and water access—must be considered when arranging the indoor space.

KEY POINT ❖

An early childhood classroom is made more flexible and can meet the needs of young children by thoughtful arrangement of its movable features such as furniture and equipment.

The placement and grouping of equipment and furnishings communicate many messages. They convey the purpose of spaces, set limits on behavior, indicate how many children can comfortably use an area, establish boundaries, invite possible combinations of play through the juxtaposition of areas, and encourage quiet or active involvement. The following are some guidelines for maximizing the effective use of space.

- Children in full-day child care need privacy; thus, places where children can be alone should be provided in the environment.
- Soft areas such as beanbag chairs, pillows, or rugs allow children to snuggle and find comfort.
- Small, enclosed areas promote quiet activities as well as interaction among small groups of children.
- Physical boundaries around areas can reduce distraction, which, in turn, increases attention on activities.
- Large spaces allow for active, large-group activities that are more boisterous and noisy.
- Clearly organized play space and clear paths can result in fewer disruptions and more goal-directed behavior.

Elizabeth Prescott (1997), one of the leading researchers on effective environments for young children, suggests that recurring guidance or curriculum problems can quite often be resolved by rearranging the classroom. She advises teachers to examine classroom pathways from a child's eye level to ensure that they are clearly defined, that all areas have a path leading to them, and that they are not obstructed. Curtis and Carter (1996) also suggest that viewing the room from a child's point of view helps the teacher see whether there are things of interest that pique curiosity within reach of the child, if there is enough room for several children to play together, if there are interesting props to support play, and if there are items that make the child feel at home.

Learning Centers

Indoor space is often organized into **learning centers (also called interest or activity areas),** which combine materials and equipment around common activities. Learning centers can include art, manipulatives, dramatic play, sensory experiences, blocks, music, science, math, computers, books, language arts, woodworking, cooking, and a variety of other areas that fit the unique interests, needs, and characteristics of a group of children and teachers. Available space and materials, ages of the children, and licensing regulations also contribute to decisions about numbers and types of learning centers included in a classroom.

Learning centers allow children to make choices from a range of available, developmentally appropriate activities. A curriculum based on learning centers can be considered responsive to the children because it is designed to meet and respond to their specific needs and experiences. Yet, although learning centers and their activities are generally planned, structured, set up, and facilitated by teachers, the children determine how to engage in and carry out the activity (Sloane, 2000).

When you arrange learning centers, it is important to take into account the size of the activity area. Researchers have found that smaller, more-defined, and secluded areas encourage children to enter more quickly into play, sustain play

KEY POINT ❖

One effective way of arranging the indoor environment is through learning centers that organize materials and equipment around common activities.

naeyc

learning centers (also called interest or activity areas)
Areas where materials and equipment are combined around common activities; for instance, art, science, or language arts.

for longer periods of time, and engage in more complex play (Tegano, Moran, DeLong, Brickey, & Uramassini, 1996). Thus, using all areas of the room, especially odd-shaped ones such as lofts, the area under lofts, and other sheltered nooks, encourages more intense and involved play. Evaluate your classroom to look for all possible areas that can be creatively used as interest areas.

One useful tool in arranging a room into learning centers is to draw a scale model of the classroom, with fixed features such as doors, windows, and built-in furnishings marked. You can then pencil in furniture until you find a workable arrangement. A method that is initially more time consuming but allows more extensive spatial experimentation is to draw and cut out scale models of the furniture and manipulate these on your classroom drawing. Figure 7-1 offers some suggested guidelines to keep in mind when arranging a classroom for preschool or primary school children.

Safety and Health

It is also important to be aware of safety and health considerations when arranging and equipping an early childhood classroom. In fact, a classroom in which safety and health are not of primary concern does not meet the basic needs of children, no matter how well the other indicators of quality might be met. Some guidelines will be spelled out in building codes, fire regulations, health codes, and child care licensing. But beyond these, additional measures can protect children from foreseeable accidents. Each classroom should have at least two exits to be used in case of emergency. Clearly marked emergency exit routes should be posted and familiar to teachers and children alike, and a well-functioning fire extinguisher and smoke detectors should be installed in each room. Carpeting, drapes, and other furnishings should be treated with fire retardants.

Walls and other surfaces should be painted with lead-free paint. Any potentially hazardous substance, such as those used for cleaning or medical purposes, should be stored out of the classroom or in a locked cupboard. Electrical outlets should be covered. Sharp edges should be eliminated from all furniture and built-in storage units. Any lightweight equipment should be backed against a wall or another sturdy surface so it cannot be knocked or pulled over during vigorous play. In addition, a classroom that is carefully arranged with clearly defined learning areas and paths will minimize the number of accidents.

Preventive measures also need to be taken to ensure that the environment is healthy. Cleanliness is an important factor in maintaining a healthy environment. The room should be cleaned every day and the day's accumulated garbage should be removed. Tables should be sanitized before and after meals. Classroom materials should be cleaned at regular intervals. This is particularly important in infant and toddler classes, where children put many things in their mouths. Teachers and children should wash hands frequently, including after toileting or diapering, after messy activities, and before meals or cooking activities. Tissues should be available in the classroom as well, and children and teachers should be encouraged to wash their hands after blowing their noses.

According to DAP, teachers need to provide an environment that ensures children's safety while at the same time helping children do what they are capable of doing for and by themselves.

▶❚ **TeachSource Video Activity**
WATCH • REFLECT • RESPOND

This video provides guidelines for arranging the early childhood environment. Go to CengageBrain.com and view the video entitled, "Preschool: Appropriate Learning Environments and Room Arrangement," and answer the following questions:

1. What strategies did Miss Salazar suggest to Miss Sheila and why did she suggest these?

2. What advice might you give Miss Sheila about her classroom environment?

KEY POINT ◆

Safety should be of primary concern as teachers arrange and equip the classroom.

naeyc

Periodic assessment of the classroom and, if appropriate, rearrangement of learning centers can capitalize on children's changing interests.

Figure **7-1**

Guidelines for Organizing Classroom Space

1. The room arrangement should reflect the program's philosophy. If the program's aim is to foster independent decision making, self-help skills, positive self-concept, social interaction, and more child-initiated than teacher-initiated activities, this should be promoted through room arrangement.
2. Keep in mind the children's ages and developmental levels. As children get older, provide more choices, a more complex environment, and greater opportunity for social play. For young preschoolers, it is best to offer a simple, uncluttered, clearly defined classroom with space for large motor activity. School-age children need more varied materials and flexible space in which they can plan and carry out complex projects.
3. Any environment in which children, as well as adults, spend blocks of time should be attractive and aesthetically pleasing. Thought and care should be given to such factors as the arrangement of furnishings, use of colors and textures, and display of artwork. Plants and flowers added to the classroom can enhance its attractiveness.
4. If children are encouraged to make independent choices, then materials should be stored at a level where children can easily see, reach, and return them.
5. If children are to develop self-help skills, toileting facilities and cubbies for coats and boots should be accessible to them. Access to learning materials also contributes to the development of self-help skills.
6. If the program supports a positive self-concept in children, then there should be individual places for children's belongings, for their projects or art to be saved, and for their work to be displayed.
7. If development of social skills and friendships is encouraged, then the environment should be set up to allow children to participate in activities with small groups of other children without undue interference or disruption.
8. If children are to have many opportunities to select and direct their own activities, then the environment should be set up to offer a variety of activity choices.
9. There should be places for children to be alone if they so wish. Quiet, private spaces can be planned as part of the environment; for instance, a corner with large pillows, a cozy spot in the library area, or a designated rocking chair with cushions.
10. There should be "soft" places in the environment where children can snuggle and find comfort.
11. An environment divided into learning centers should have clearly marked boundaries that indicate the space designated for each given area. Storage shelves and other furnishings can be used to define the edges.
12. Paths to each area should be clear and unobstructed. Children are less likely to use areas that are hard to reach.
13. A pathway to one area should never go through another activity center. This interferes with ongoing play and can cause anger and frustration.
14. Doorways and other exits should be unobstructed.
15. Quiet activities should be grouped near each other, and noisy ones should be placed some distance from these. The block area should not be next to the book area, for example.
16. Group activities that have common elements near each other to extend children's play possibilities. Blocks and dramatic play are often placed next to each other to encourage the exchange of props and ideas.
17. Provide areas for individual, small-group, and large-group activities by setting up different-sized centers.
18. Some areas require more space than others. Block play, for instance, is enhanced by ample room to build and expand block structures.
19. The sizes of various learning centers will, to some extent, convey how many children can play in each area and how active that play should be. Small, cozy areas set natural limits on the number of children and the activity level, whereas large areas send the opposite message.
20. Decrease noise levels by using carpeting or area rugs in noisy centers such as the block area.
21. Place messy activities near a water source.

22. Place activities that are enhanced by natural light near windows. Ensure that all areas are well lit, however.
23. Place tables and chairs in or near centers where tabletop activities are carried out. For instance, tables should be placed in the art and manipulative areas but are not needed in the large block center. Tables scattered through the room can take on an added use during snack time.
24. Consider multipurpose uses for space, especially where room size is restricted. When your room allows for only a limited number of areas to be set aside at any one time, some of these might be used for more than one activity. For instance, the area designated for large-group activities might also be the block area, music center, or place set aside for large motor activity.
25. Some learning centers may not be part of the classroom on a daily basis. Centers such as woodworking, music, or cooking may be brought into the classroom on a less frequent schedule or may be rotated with other areas for specified periods of time.
26. Be flexible in the use of space and open to rearranging it. As children mature and their interests change, so too should the center. Also, if repeated problems arise, try solving these by rearranging the environment.
27. Safety should be an overriding, primary concern in setting up an environment for young children.

Human beings, especially children, are motivated to understand or do what is just beyond their current understanding or mastery. Effective teachers create a rich learning environment to activate that motivation, and they make use of strategies to promote children's undertaking and mastering of new and progressively more advanced challenges. (Copple & Bredekamp, 2009, p. 15)

ARRANGING THE OUTDOOR ENVIRONMENT

Just as the indoor space is arranged with care and thought, considering the children's needs and developmental levels, so should the outdoor environment be carefully designed. The outdoor area should be more than a place where children can let off steam and exercise large muscles. It should also provide opportunities that enhance socialization, cognitive and language development, sensory exploration, creative expression, and an appreciation of nature.

Fixed Outdoor Play Structures

In the early decades of the twentieth century, when the playground movement took root in this country, outdoor play areas were generally equipped with swings, slides, seesaws, and sandboxes, not so different from many playgrounds today. But the design of play structures has also come a long way from such traditional, single-purpose pieces of equipment. Through the efforts of child development specialists, professional playground architects, and commercial equipment developers, far more creative and versatile play structures are now available.

Many of today's playgrounds contain equipment constructed of materials such as tires, cargo nets, railroad ties, telephone poles, large cable spools, barrels, and drainage pipes. Where traditional structures primarily were

KEY POINT

The traditional metal swings and slides of many playgrounds are being replaced by more contemporary playscapes.

Many playgrounds contain conventional metal structures such as this galvanized pipe geodome climber along with metal swings, slides, and climbers. As you read this chapter, you will see that such playgrounds are being replaced by newer "playscapes" and natural environments.

playscapes
Contemporary, often innovative, playground structures that combine a variety of materials.

natural playscapes
A new playground movement that emphasizes a focus on nature; features of the outdoor space are composed of natural materials.

KEY POINT ◆

In recent years, more emphasis has been placed on creating outdoor areas that are aesthetically pleasing and are made up only of natural materials.

constructed of metal, which could become dangerously hot or very cold during weather extremes, new equipment materials include a variety of natural materials, treated wood surfaces, and "space-age plastics" (Solomon, 2005). More contemporary **playscapes** combine a variety of materials and allow for a range of activities. Such equipment must meet standards of safety and developmental appropriateness. Beyond the immovable components of the outdoor space, however, various elements can enhance and expand children's play, as we will discuss.

USE OF "GREEN" PLAYSCAPES. In recent years, a movement to promote **natural playscapes** has emerged (Keeler, 2008). Unlike traditional playground structures, natural playscapes contain a variety of plants, pathways, open areas, sand, water, and structures that promote dramatic and cooperative play. Materials used in the construction of such playscapes are all natural and reflect the local environment. Native plants, from shade-giving trees to flowers and fragrant herbs, are planted throughout the area for aesthetic effect. Pathways are made of varied materials, such as bricks, stepping stones, woodchips, and flagstones, rather than simply of concrete. Playscapes offer enjoyment for all the senses, but they also suggest different ways for children to use the space (Keeler, 2008). In one school where a traditional playground was replaced with a natural playscape, teachers noted how the children's use of the outdoor area changed. The children became much more engaged in creative, cooperative, and imaginative play in their new playscape. Be sure to read the "Take a Closer Look" box for more insight into the importance of nature in children's lives.

Just because equipment is contemporary, however, does not necessarily make it developmentally appropriate or safe. Some guidelines can help ensure that outdoor equipment provides suitable play space for young children.

◗ Because large structures are relatively fixed in the function they serve, they should be complex in design. For example, while including opportunities for a wide range of motor skills, they can also provide some open spaces underneath, which children can use for dramatic play.
◗ Play equipment should provide graduated challenges, offering activities that allow for safe risk-taking for children of different ages and developmental

Today's natural playscapes focus on providing children experiences with nature. Many experts are concerned that children have limited exposure to the natural world and that this is detrimental to healthy development.

IS THERE SUCH A THING AS NATURE-DEFICIT DISORDER?

IN HIS bestselling book *Last Child in the Woods* (2008), Richard Louv makes a compelling case that today's children are seriously disconnected from nature, suffering from what he calls "nature-deficit disorder." He ties this lack of connection to the natural world to many disturbing childhood trends, such as the increase in obesity, attention disorders, and depression. He provides research to support that interaction with nature is crucial for healthy development in childhood.

Louv writes about a time not so long ago when children had opportunities to play freely in woods, fields, creeks, and meadows and enjoy the plants and wildlife they contained.

> For children, nature comes in many forms. A newborn calf; a pet that lives and dies; a worn path through the woods; a fort nested in stinging nettles; a damp, mysterious edge of a vacant lot—whatever shape nature takes, it offers each child an older, larger world. ... In nature, a child finds freedom, fantasy, and privacy: a place distant from the adult world, a separate peace. (p. 7)

The author fondly recalls his own childhood days when he roamed the orchards, fields, and woods near his home. "The woods were my Ritalin. Nature calmed me, focused me, and yet excited my senses" (p. 10).

But over the past few decades, fewer and fewer children have the opportunity to spend part of their childhood outdoors. There are many reasons for this shift. One obvious reason is that so many children spend much of their time plugged into computers, video games, television, and various other electronic devices. The quick pace that envelops many families also contributes to the dearth of time left to devote to playing outdoors; children often have very busy schedules outside of school hours, participating in a variety of lessons and organized activities. Louv cites several studies that document the decrease in discretionary time for unstructured play in the lives of American children between the 1980s and the turn of the century.

According to the author, however, "fear is the most potent force that prevents parents from allowing their children the freedom they themselves enjoyed when they were young. Fear is the emotion that separates a developing child from the full, *essential* benefits of nature. Fear of traffic, of crime, of stranger-danger—and of nature itself" (p. 117). Because of such fears, today's children have a much more restricted area within which they can play than did children in the past. Louv cites statistics that show that phenomena such as child abductions or attacks by wild animals occur quite rarely; yet parents' fear of these keeps many children indoors, where they are subject to different kinds of dangers that are, nonetheless, risky.

"A widening circle of researchers believes that the loss of natural habitat, or the disconnection from nature even when it is available, has enormous implications for human health and child development" (p. 43). The author cites many researchers who declare the therapeutic powers of nature. Spending time in nature leads to stress reduction and the lessening of pressures that can lead to childhood depression. One study concluded that children with more nature near their homes were less likely to exhibit conduct disorders, anxiety, and depression than peers with less nature near their homes. Interaction with nature, especially if it counterbalances sedentary time in front of the TV or computer, is also linked to a lower likelihood of obesity. Finally, Louv makes a powerful argument that nature can help children who exhibit symptoms of attention-deficit disorder; he considers that they suffer from nature-deficit disorder. According to one study discussed in the book, "being close to nature, in general, helps boost a child's attention span" (p. 105).

The author suggest a number of steps that parents, teachers, and child advocates can take to counter the symptoms associated with children's decreasing exposure to nature, including the "leave no child inside" movement. He provides insight into the work of activists who strive to change a legal system that often restricts access to natural areas. Louv also discusses educational reform to encourage more real-world learning. He shares the findings of a model environment-based education program implemented over a 10-year period in 150 schools; students in these schools did exceedingly well on standardized tests and improved grade point averages, outperforming students in more traditional classrooms. The author suggests many more steps that adults can take to help reconnect children with nature. As an early childhood teacher, you should consider how you can help maintain the sense of wonder and joy that young children express about the natural world around them.

175

levels. An outdoor play area used by a range of children could, for instance, include one gently sloped and one taller, more steeply angled slide; balance beams of different widths; or steps as well as ladders leading to raised platforms.

- Play structures should promote social interaction rather than competition among children. Wide slides, for example, encourage two or three children to slide down together; tire swings invite several children to cooperatively pump; and added props encourage dramatic play. At the same time, private places should also be provided to accommodate the times when children want to be alone.

- A final, important factor is the safety of outdoor play equipment. Equipment should be securely anchored to the ground and in good repair, with no sharp edges, broken or splintered elements, or loose nuts and bolts. There should be no openings that could trap a child's head, fingers, hands, or feet. Swing seats should be made of a lightweight material. Safety is also fostered when equipment is of appropriate size; climbing heights should not exceed the reaching height of the children. The surfacing material under swings and climbing structures must also be considered to ensure that children are somewhat cushioned if they fall. In some parts of the country, spiders and other insects like to nest in dark parts of play equipment; for instance, inside tires. Thus, frequent safety checks should be carried out and appropriate measures taken in such cases. If there is frequent rain, tires can also trap water, which then stagnates and attracts mosquitoes; drilling drainage holes into the bottoms of tires can avoid this problem.

Flexible Outdoor Play Components

Although not many adjustments can be made with the large equipment, there are other ways in which the outdoor environment can be arranged to enhance and support children's development. The outdoor play space can be made more exciting and flexible by adding equipment and materials, capitalizing on the natural features of the play space, and creating interest areas.

A variety of movable large equipment components can be added to the outdoor area. When large crates, sawhorses, ladders, ramps, balance beams, tires, pulleys, hollow blocks, or cardboard boxes are provided, children will find a variety of creative ways to incorporate these into their play. Such movable components give children the opportunity to structure and arrange their own environment. McGinnis (2002) suggests "play crates" as a way of extending children's interests in the outdoor environment. Such prop boxes are organized around specific themes, for instance, "a bubble crate, a digging and garden crate, or a boot and funshoe crate" (p. 28).

An outdoor play area should also take advantage of all available natural features. The play yard's physical contours, plants, and surfaces provide potential for enhancing the playground. A small hill can let children experience gathering

Many activities that are commonly considered indoor activities can be carried out on the playground. Sensory tables and art activities, for example, can be accommodated outdoors as well as inside. What other activities, usually restricted to the indoor environment, could also be set up outside?

© Cengage Learning

momentum as they run or roll down, or it can be used as the site for a tunnel. A large, grassy area is ideal for large-group movement, ball toss, or parachute activities.

Trees provide shade; shrubs and flowers add to the aesthetic and sensory pleasures of the yard. A flower, vegetable, or herb garden that the children help tend can provide meaningful science experiences. Multiple surfaces such as fine sand for digging, cement on which to ride tricycles, pea gravel or wood shavings under large equipment, grass to sit on, dirt to make mud with, textured paving stones to touch with hands or bare feet—all add to making the outdoor area a good learning environment.

The playground should also accommodate all indoor curriculum areas; for instance, art, music, science, or story time. Woodworking, sand, water, and other sensory activities are also portable and very suitable additions to the outdoor environment. An outdoor area can also be enhanced by creating defined learning centers that are more permanent, similar to those used indoors.

ENVIRONMENTS FOR INFANTS AND TODDLERS

An environment for infants and toddlers needs to be designed with many of the same guidelines suggested for preschool environments; it must be developmentally appropriate, safe, secure, comfortable, aesthetically pleasing, and appropriately stimulating and challenging. The environment must encourage movement and exploration while meticulously ensuring safety and hygiene. Further, it must be adapted to the needs of very young children by including discrete areas for playing, eating, diapering, and sleeping. Often classrooms for infants and toddlers have features that make them more homelike, for instance, a couch or rocking chair. Remember also that developmental changes are rapid during the first two years of life. The environment must take such changes into account by providing varying levels of stimulation and challenge for different ages (Copple & Bredekamp, 2009; Gonzalez-Mena & Eyer, 2012). Environments for toddlers should be divided into interest or activity areas, according to DAP guidelines, similar to what is suggested for older children (Copple & Bredekamp, 2009).

"Creative [infant and toddler] teachers realize there is almost always a moment to explore the natural world with each child each day" (Williams, 2008). The outdoor environment for infants and toddlers needs to provide opportunities for the unique experiences that are available outdoors while ensuring the children's safety. For very young children in the sensorimotor stage of development (recall the discussion of Piaget's stages of development in Chapter 5), such an environment must encourage basic motor skills and sensory experiences—new sounds, textures, and surfaces. A soft and level surface offers stability and comfort, while shady spaces protect a baby's tender skin. It must allow for a wide range of movement; stimulate the senses; offer novelty, variety, and challenge; and be safe and comfortable. DAP suggests that an outdoor infant/toddler area needs resilient, stable surfaces for babies

An environment for infants should provide many developmentally appropriate social, motor, and cognitive opportunities in which very young children can experience success.

just beginning to be mobile as well as soft areas for infants to lie on quilts. It should include low, soft platforms to climb on, tunnels to crawl through, and low ramps or steps for practicing emerging skills (Copple & Bredekamp, 2009). Multiseat baby buggies allow for outings into the neighborhood with a group of infants or toddlers (Gestwicki, 2010).

ENVIRONMENTS FOR SCHOOL-AGE CHILDREN

School-age children's unique needs should be taken into account in designing environments for them. Many children spend their day in a fairly structured primary classroom; thus, a setting that is more relaxed should be provided for before- and after-school care. The environment should be set up to support opportunities to work alone or be with friends, foster independence, and encourage creative play. In addition, an environment that includes learning centers encourages independent and focused play that helps children feel competent and successful (Gestwicki, 2010). The environment should also provide appropriate space for the kinds of activities that primary school children enjoy, including reading, listening to music, cooking, pursuing projects, playing board games, or doing homework (Bumgarner, 1999).

The outdoor environment also should provide adequate space for the kinds of activities that this age group enjoys. In addition to a variety of traditional play equipment, provide materials that children can use to construct their own equipment (Click & Parker, 2012). There also should be space for children to engage in sports and group games as well as for more individual activities such as riding bicycles, roller skating, or jumping rope (Bumgarner, 1999). Both indoors and outdoors, teachers provide a safe environment with safe boundaries that support children's risk taking, another key concept reinforced by DAP (Copple & Bredekamp, 2009).

ADAPTING THE ENVIRONMENT FOR CHILDREN WITH DISABILITIES

Increasingly, early childhood programs include children with disabilities. It is important, especially when children with different levels of ability are included, to provide a suitable environment in which all children can experience appropriate challenges and successes. Frost (1992) presents a compelling reason why it is important to adapt the early childhood environment for children with special needs. "Play is the vehicle by which children develop and demonstrate competency in dealing with their environment. If a handicapping condition results in play deprivation, the child's competence in interacting with people and objects will also be lacking" (p. 297). Next, we will discuss adaptations for children with physical and visual disabilities.

Children with severe physical limitations need specialized equipment, such as special chairs or bolsters, to help them participate as much as possible in activities. Children who rely on wheelchairs or walkers for mobility, as well as those with other physical limitations, need paths and entries to learning centers that are wide enough for them to maneuver in an unobstructed way throughout the room. Activity opportunities and shelves from which children select materials should be accessible so that these children can be as independent as possible. Similarly, outdoor activities and equipment must

---

DAP

KEY POINT ◆◆

The environment should be adapted in a variety of ways to meet the particular needs of children of different ages and children with disabilities.

DIVERSITY

▶❚❚ **TeachSource Video Activity**
WATCH • REFLECT • RESPOND

This video provides suggestions for toddler classroom environments. Go to CengageBrain.com and view the video entitled, "Creating a Safe Physical Environment for Toddlers," and answer the following questions:

1. Discuss three safety and health practices shown in the video.

2. Which safety practices shown in the video might be modified for four- or five-year-olds? How?

be accessible through modifications such as wide, gently sloped ramps with handrails; raised sand areas; or sling swings that provide secure body support. Modified swings, tricycles, and tables for independent participation in outdoor activities are available and should be provided, if possible (Flynn & Kieff, 2002).

Children with visual impairments require a consistent, uncluttered, and clearly arranged environment that they can recognize through touch. Landmarks such as specific equipment or furniture, and a sensory-rich environment with varying textures, can help blind children orient themselves inside or outside (Frost, 1992). Auditory cues—for instance, wind chimes or bells—can be used to help children locate specific outdoor structures (Flynn & Kieff, 2002).

The environment should always be adapted to children, suited to their unique needs and characteristics. Recognizing that each child is an individual, the play environment should be versatile enough to provide a rich variety of sensory stimuli, opportunities to make and carry out independent choices, and a range of experiences to promote all areas of development in children with varying levels of competence.

A sensitive staff can help make the early childhood experience of children with special needs as beneficial as possible through some appropriate environmental modifications.

DEVELOPMENTALLY APPROPRIATE EQUIPMENT

Early childhood **equipment** refers to furniture and other large items that represent the more expensive, long-term investments in an early childhood facility; **materials** are the smaller, often expendable, items that are replaced and replenished more frequently. Because it is expensive, equipment needs to be acquired carefully.

Basic Equipment

Most early childhood classrooms include a variety of basic equipment. Classroom furniture should include tables, chairs, and cubbies for children's personal belongings. Storage cupboards or shelves can be found within the various learning centers of the classroom on which materials for that area are stored. The dramatic play area should include child-sized kitchen appliances, furniture for doll play, a small table and chairs, storage for dress-up items, and mirrors. Often a sensory table is available in the classroom for sand, water, and other sensory exploration. If the classroom has a woodworking center, a woodworking bench with vises and storage for tools should be included.

Criteria for Selecting Equipment

Some important questions to ask when selecting equipment include the following:

▶ **Does this piece of equipment support the program's philosophy?**
Equipment should promote children's self-esteem and independence, encourage positive social interaction, and support children's development.

naeyc

equipment
Large items, such as furniture, that represent a more expensive, long-term investment in an early childhood facility.

materials
The smaller, often expendable, items used in early childhood programs that are replaced and replenished frequently.

◗ **Is the equipment appropriately sized for the children?** Some pieces of equipment are available in various sizes. For a class of two-year-olds, chairs should be smaller and tables lower than for an older group of preschoolers.

◗ **Is the equipment safe?** When purchasing equipment, it is important to ensure that safety standards are met and that the equipment will withstand long-term use. It must continue to be safe for the expected lifetime of the equipment. Manufacturers of outdoor play structures often provide a safety warranty for such equipment.

◗ **Is the equipment durable?** Early childhood equipment should be well built to withstand hard use by large numbers of children over a period of years. Varnished or plastic surfaces will protect tabletops and shelves. Outside equipment should be finished to resist weathering, rusting, and chipping. It is usually more expensive in the long run to purchase less expensive equipment that is not intended for group use and will have to be replaced sooner.

◗ **Is there room for this equipment?** The size of the classroom or outside play area will dictate how much equipment (and of what size) can be accommodated. A large outside structure that takes up most of the space in a relatively small play yard may be impractical if it leaves little room for other activities. Storage room should be available if a piece of equipment—for example, a water table or woodworking bench—will not be used all the time.

◗ **Can the equipment be constructed rather than purchased?** Sometimes teachers, family members, or community volunteers with carpentry skills can make a piece of equipment at a considerably lower cost than would be required to purchase a commercial equivalent. Ensure that a volunteer carpenter understands your standards for safety and performance. Many exciting play yards have been constructed by family and staff groups; however, if you are considering constructing outdoor equipment, get expert advice to ensure its safety.

Classroom equipment has to be sized appropriately for the children. The chairs and tables in this class of toddlers are smaller than the furnishings in the classrooms of their older peers.

© Cengage Learning

▶ **Is the equipment aesthetically pleasing?** Consider whether a new piece of equipment will fit harmoniously with existing furnishings. When you purchase a new sofa for your living room, for example, you look for something to match the existing decor; in the same way, consider new equipment in the context of the entire classroom.

▶ **Is the equipment easy to clean and maintain?** Classroom items should be relatively easy to sanitize and keep clean. Replacement parts such as bolts or gears should be readily available from the manufacturer.

Computers and Other Technology

Over the past several decades, early childhood programs have increasingly invested in the purchase of computers and software for the children's uses. Toward the end of the 1980s, about one-fourth of early childhood programs had computers; today, the vast majority of facilities have them, although programs that serve children who come from poor families and diverse ethnic groups have less access to such technology (Bowman, Donovan, & Burns, 2001; NAEYC, 2006). A growing number of people (including young children) today have **computer literacy;** in other words, they are knowledgeable about and capable of using a computer. NAEYC and the Fred Rogers Center for Early Learning and Media (2012), in a position statement about media and children, recommend that adults and children also need to develop **digital citizenship,** using media responsibly and ethically.

naeyc

computer literacy
Familiarity with and knowledge about computers.

digital citizenship
The need for adults and children to use media in an appropriate, responsible, and ethical way and to understand the uses, abuses, and misuses of technology.

BRAIN STORM
THE DIGITAL GENERATION

Marc Prensky (2001b) refers to today's children as "digital natives," concluding that their brains work differently from the brains of those of us who did not grow up on a steady dose of computers—whom Prensky calls "digital immigrants." According to Prensky, "It is now clear that today's students *think and process information fundamentally differently* from their predecessors. . . . 'Different kinds of experiences lead to different brain structures,' says Dr. Bruce D. Perry. . . . It is very likely that *our students' brains have physically changed*—and are different from ours—as a result of how they grew up. But whether or not this is *literally* true, we can say with certainty that their *thinking patterns* have changed" (2001, p. 1). It is often argued that young children are entering a world in which familiarity with computers will be a requisite for effective functioning; therefore, exposure to computers and development of some basic computer skills should be part of early childhood programs.

KEY POINT ◆◆

Computers and other electronic media have become a prevalent feature in many early childhood classrooms; in addition, a considerable amount of software has been developed for young children to use. Software must be carefully evaluated for appropriateness.

The new position statement, *Technology and Interactive Media as Tools in Early Childhood Programs Serving Children from Birth through Age 8* (NAEYC, 2012), developed jointly by NAEYC and the Fred Rogers Center for Early Learning and Children's Media, is intended to offer guidance in the use of such media to those

Many early childhood programs today include computers for children's use. Many of the early concerns about computers for young children (for instance, that computers would discourage peer interaction) have been dispelled. What are some advantages and potential problems in using computers in early childhood programs?

software

The "instructions" that direct a computer to perform an activity, usually stored on a disk or directly in the computer; many such programs are available for young children.

working in programs for young children. This position statement notes that "technology and interactive media are here to stay" (p. 2), and must be taken into consideration as part of early childhood education programs. It also cautions that teachers must apply principles of developmentally appropriate practice in the use of such media. Another issue that is emphasized has to do with equity and access. Children from less affluent families need opportunities to learn "technology-handling" skills, which the authors of the position statement consider very similar to "book-handling" skills.

Electronic technology, to which most children are exposed at home as well as at school, is an integral part of twenty-first-century life. Computers and other media can benefit children if they are used appropriately. However, "it is the educational content that matters—not the format in which it is presented" (NAEYC, 2012). Integrating computers into classrooms may make a significant difference in children's developmental gains or it may have no effect at all or actually reduce children's creativity" (Haugland, 2000, pp. 12–13). Computers are not a replacement for children's experiences with real objects and materials but provide opportunities to expand learning (Copple & Bredekamp, 2009).

Research has shown that children can gain knowledge and skills through computer use (Behrmann, 2000; Clements & Samara, 2003). In addition, computers can have positive effects on social interactions among children by bringing them together and can facilitate cognitive and language development. Children engage in more advanced cognitive play, talk about their work, and develop literacy skills.

When should young children be exposed to computers? Haugland (1999) suggests that computers not be used with children younger than three because computers do not "match their learning style" (p. 26). By age three, children have mastered the basic motor, language, and social skills that are requisites for using computers. Haugland (1999) recommends that preschoolers be allowed to explore computers freely, using appropriate software. The International Society for Technology in Education (2007) recommends that by age 5 children should have acquired some basic skills in how to use technology. Children in kindergarten and the early primary grades can use computers in a more structured way, again with developmentally appropriate software. In addition to free-choice computer activities, teachers can also provide some more directed activities that support learning objectives.

Computer **software** refers to the "instructions" that direct the computer to perform an activity. Software is usually stored on a compact disk that is inserted into the computer or can be downloaded onto the computer's hard drive so no disk is needed. The selection of computer software for an early childhood program must follow the same principles as the selection of any developmentally appropriate materials. In an earlier position statement, the NAEYC (2006) underscored the important role of the teachers in evaluating the developmental appropriateness of computer programs. "NAEYC believes that in any given situation, a professional judgment by the teacher is required to determine if a specific use of technology is age appropriate, individually appropriate, and culturally appropriate" (p. 1).

Haugland and Shade (1990) propose 10 criteria for judging developmental appropriateness in selecting computer software for young children.

1. **Age appropriateness**—The concepts taught and methods presented show realistic expectations for young children.
2. **Child control**—The children, as active participants (unlike the computer), decide the flow and direction of the activity.
3. **Clear instructions**—Verbal or graphic directions are simple and precise; written instructions would not be appropriate.
4. **Expanding complexity**—Software begins with a child's current skills, then builds on these in a realistic learning sequence that continues to challenge the child.
5. **Independence**—Children are able to use the computer and software with a minimum amount of adult supervision.
6. **Process orientation**—The intrinsic joys of exploring and discovering are what engage children on the computer. Printouts of completed work can be fun, but they are not the primary objective. Extrinsic rewards such as smiling faces or other reinforcers are not necessary.
7. **Real-world model**—Objects used in software are reliable models of aspects of the world, in appropriate proportion to each other, and in meaningful settings.
8. **Technical features**—Children's attention is best held by high-quality software that incorporates colorful, uncluttered, animated, and realistic graphics as well as realistic sound effects. Software also loads and runs quickly, minimizing waiting times.
9. **Trial and error**—Children have unlimited opportunities for creative problem solving, exploring alternatives, and correcting their own errors.
10. **Transformations**—Children are able to change objects and situations and see the effects of their actions.

Software packages are only one way that media can be used by young children today. The NAEYC Position Statement (2012) comments on the continuing proliferation of technology, such as interactive media, including broadcast and streaming media, a variety of apps, e-books, the Internet, and other formats for delivering content. Many websites are that provide a rich variety of learning opportunities to enhance cognitive and social skills are readily available (Haugland, 2000). There are so many websites available, however, that a teacher must carefully screen and select appropriate ones for use by the children. Information websites, which are often enhanced with sound and video, can be used to help children find answers to questions and build knowledge. Haugland (2000), for instance, discusses a "virtual" trip to the zoo, where children can see and hear the animals (for example, check out a trip to the National Zoo at http://nationalzoo .si.edu/Animals/WebCams/default.cfm?hpout=webcam_link&xtr=).

DEVELOPMENTALLY APPROPRIATE MATERIALS

In addition to the more expensive furnishings and equipment, an early childhood classroom requires a rich variety of play and learning materials. These include the following:

- Commercially purchased items such as puzzles, crayons, or Legos
- Teacher- or family-made games and manipulatives

▶ Commercial or teacher-assembled kits that put together combinations of items for specific dramatic play themes or flannelboard stories

▶ Donated scrap materials for art or construction activities

Montessori equipment
Early childhood learning materials derived from, and part of, the Montessori approach.

One special category of learning resources, **Montessori equipment,** stands out because of its specific attributes and prescribed use. These materials are available through special catalogs for use in Montessori programs. Montessori items are of high quality and design, and their cost is also relatively high. The Montessori philosophy does not recommend that these materials be used by non-Montessori schools, although many eclectic programs stock some of these materials. You may want to review the discussion of Maria Montessori's program and its contemporary counterparts in Chapter 5.

KEY POINT ◆

A wide variety of developmentally appropriate learning materials are available commercially; in addition, many programs also include teacher- or family-made materials. These need to be carefully selected to ensure that they are developmentally appropriate.

Criteria for Selecting Materials

More than ever before, a great selection of early childhood materials is commercially available. Toy and variety stores, as well as catalogs, display variously priced toys and games that often promise to fully educate or entertain young children. In selecting learning and play materials, some specific criteria must be met to ensure their suitability for young children.

1. **Developmentally appropriate**—Materials should match the stage of development of the children. Toddlers just mastering language and locomotion will benefit from play items that encourage vocabulary building, promote a sense of balance, exercise fingers, and feed their burgeoning sense of independence. Older preschoolers and primary children, however, need materials that engage their more refined skills in all areas of development. All early childhood materials, however, should actively involve children, be interesting, and be safe.

2. **Active**—Young children need materials that they can act on. They quickly get bored with items that require no action on their part or that do not

Manipulatives are among the most versatile, open-ended materials because they lend themselves to an infinite variety of uses.

Toddlers who have not yet mastered the social skills involved in sharing should have access to more than one of their favorite play materials.

© Cengage Learning

stretch the imagination. All early childhood materials should promote active involvement and exploration.

3. **Open-ended**—Among the most popular and most frequently used materials are open-ended toys, ones that can be used flexibly and do not dictate how they are to be used. Not all materials in the early childhood program will be open-ended (puzzles, for instance, have only one outcome), but the majority should be.

4. **Give feedback**—As children interact with materials, they should receive feedback on the success of their actions. A completed puzzle tells the child that the pieces have been fitted together correctly; when the "bridge" stays up, the child knows that the blocks were stacked successfully; when there is a place setting for each of the four children at the table in the housekeeping area, they know that they have matched children and dishes appropriately.

5. **Multipurpose**—Materials or combinations of materials should suggest many possibilities for play. Children's problem-solving skills and imaginations will be enhanced by multipurpose materials. Children of different skill levels should be able to use materials successfully.

6. **Safe and durable**—Items purchased for children's use should be sturdy and well constructed. Materials should be of high quality; for instance, hardwood or nonbreakable plastics. Young children should not be given toys that require electricity. All materials should be checked regularly for loose parts, sharp edges, splinters, or chipping paint.

7. **Attractive**—Materials' appearance should be appealing and inviting.

8. **Nonsexist, nonracial**—Materials should convey a sense of equality and tolerance rather than reinforce sexist, racial, or cultural stereotypes.

9. **Variety**—A wide variety of materials that cater to different interests and that meet all developmental needs is necessary. There should be ample materials to develop fine and gross motor skills, exercise cognitive processes, promote language use, encourage socialization, provide outlets for emotional needs, and invite creativity.

10. **Duplicate**—Although variety gives children divergent ways through which they can develop skills, there should also be more than one of some items. Toddlers, who have not yet mastered the art of sharing, especially need the assurance of multiples of popular items.

Teacher- or Family-Made Materials and Resources

KEY POINT

Teachers may develop classroom resource materials; for instance, dramatic play kits, a flannelboard story file, or a song and fingerplay file.

Some of the best early childhood materials are not purchased commercially but are ones that are constructed by an energetic teacher or family members. Homemade materials often are tailored to fit the specific interests or needs of the children. Deb Curtis and Margie Carter (2003), in their book *Designs for Living and Learning: Transforming Early Childhood Environments*, provide numerous ideas for beautiful and unique materials for the classroom.

Teachers also can develop and organize classroom resource materials to facilitate planning and programming. One helpful resource is dramatic play kits, which contain a collection of props for common dramatic play themes. Contained in individual labeled boxes, dramatic play kits can include some of the following items:

▶ **Health theme**—bandages, empty syringes, hospital gowns, stethoscope, empty medicine vials, and similar items donated by local doctors, hospitals, and other health care providers
▶ **Bakery theme**—rolling pins, cookie cutters, baking pans, muffin liners, aprons
▶ **Self-care theme**—small mirrors, combs, toothbrushes, hair rollers, empty shampoo bottles, other cosmetic containers
▶ **Grocery store theme**—empty food containers, cash register, register tapes, bags, play money

Another helpful resource is a flannelboard story file. The flannelboard pieces, a copy of the story, and suggestions for variations can be collected in separate manila envelopes, then labeled and stored in an accessible place. Similar to pulling a book off the bookshelf, flannelboard stories will then be readily available to both teachers and children who wish to use them.

A similar collection of favorites can be put into a song and fingerplay file. One way to do this is to type the most frequently used songs and fingerplays on 5-by-8-inch cards, laminate the cards and punch holes in the upper left corners, alphabetize the cards, and connect the cards with a key ring. This file can be used by new or substitute teachers and can help refresh the memory of teachers who may have forgotten all the words. Newly acquired songs or fingerplays can be added at any time.

Numerous community resources can be tapped for useful materials. Often, scraps can be an early childhood teacher's treasures. Home decorating businesses may be able to contribute color chips and wallpaper or drapery samples. Printing companies may be able to provide trimmings from paper of different colors, sizes, textures, and weights. Carpet sales rooms may make available carpet squares or the heavy inner rolls from carpeting. Businesses that receive copious computer printouts may be able to provide computer printout paper for art and writing projects. Lumber companies are usually willing to share scraps of soft wood or wood shavings. Travel agents may have old travel posters and brochures to contribute. It is a good idea to canvas your community for possible resources. Use of such resources also emphasizes the importance of recycling materials to promote more environmental consciousness.

DIVERSITY

CULTURE AND ENVIRONMENT

Theresa Danna Douglas

Maritza, Bilingual Head Start Teacher

Most of the children in my morning and afternoon classes come from non-English-speaking homes. I have 35 children, and just 3 are native English speakers. I like to respect their cultures, and make the environment reflect the cultures of the children and families. The classroom environment is important for helping children develop their thinking. They need to be able to find connections to what is familiar to them, and their home culture is a large part of that.

At the beginning of each school year, before I know the children and families, I set up the classroom to bring elements from the outside environment into the classroom. The natural environment provides items that are familiar to the children. I bring materials such as rocks, wood, leaves, sticks, plants, and dirt from the outside and place them throughout the classroom. I have found that soon the children also bring in natural items to share.

At the same time, I get to know the children and their interests better. For instance, the children began using the dramatic play area as a grocery store. When I saw their interest, we talked about what else they would need for their store, and soon we began collecting boxes, cans, and other items to be part of the store. I talked with the parents about the children's involvement, and they began to bring in materials for the grocery store. The children also began to find items from other parts of the classroom; for instance, they used materials from the writing center to identify the food boxes. By including learning across the environment, children are able to gain skills in many areas—for example, literacy and math—through projects such as the grocery store.

As I get to know the families better, I begin to invite them to share something of their home culture with the class on special occasions. At Christmas time, one parent worked with the children to make a piñata, explaining why piñatas are part of holiday celebrations in Mexico. Other families contributed small toys and candies to fill the piñata. Another time, parents made a piñata that was filled with folded pieces of paper on which there were different pictures. The children had to share and discuss their picture in a later activity. By sewing patterns around pens and pencils, another parent from Ecuador showed the children how such objects are decorated. We were able to give each child such a decorated pencil for Christmas that year. The parent explained that this was something she did in Ecuador for a living, selling her pencils and pens on the streets. Another parent, from Japan, worked with the children to make kites, which are part of Japanese tradition. She brought special shiny fabric that the children used to make their own kites.

Long after such activities have happened, we keep a memory of them in the classroom. We post photographs of the special activities around the classroom as a reminder. Also, we keep piñata-making materials in the art area and the Japanese kites in the block area, so children can incorporate them into other activities. We put other items into the classroom as well, for example, mariachi instruments in the music area. We also have posters on the walls that are dedicated to each child and his or her family, with descriptions about the family, their country of origin, and such things as their favorite foods. Food is another important aspect of how the children's culture becomes part of the environment. Parents often do cooking activities with the children. One Valentine's Day, a parent helped the children make a special treat—potato-filled flautas. Parents enjoy preparing and eating their favorite dishes with the children.

The environment is very important for making children and families feel comfortable in the classroom. The more the environment reflects the children and what is familiar to them, the better it is.

187

FAMILY ROLE IN THE EARLY CHILDHOOD ENVIRONMENT

DIVERSITY

Families can be active participants in matters related to the early childhood environment. They can contribute in a variety of ways to selecting, modifying, or maintaining various aspects of the environment. Some programs have advisory or policymaking family councils that may be involved in decisions about major purchases or construction. Families also often have a strong commitment to their children's program and are willing to spend a few weekend hours helping to paint, clean, varnish, or construct. Many families contribute to their child's center by making learning materials or contributing recyclables that children can use for creative activities. As noted before, families also can contribute culturally relevant materials for the classroom. As in all areas of the early childhood center's functioning, families can be a tremendous resource in matters related to the environment.

KEY POINT ◆

Parents can be an important resource to the early childhood program in relation to the environment.

SUMMARY

1. The physical environment affects both children and adults.
2. Consider the importance of the indoor environment, focusing on how to use it most effectively to support the development of young children.
3. Consider the outdoor environment, including recent innovations in natural environments, and how to maximize its potential.
4. The environment should be appropriate for the age and ability level of the children. It may need to be adapted to meet the requirements of children with disabilities.
5. Select developmentally appropriate equipment, with particular emphasis on the role of computers in early childhood programs.
6. Consider criteria for selecting appropriate materials for use in early childhood programs.

KEY TERMS LIST

computer literacy

digital citizenship

equipment

learning centers

materials

Montessori equipment

natural playscapes

playscapes

software

KEY QUESTIONS

1. Talk to two or three children who are four or five years old. Ask them what they like about their classroom and playground. Are the features they mention ones that you consider particularly interesting and noteworthy? What do their answers tell you about these children's interests, attitudes, and needs in relation to the environment?
2. Spend some time in an early childhood classroom and attune yourself to the environment. What do you like? What do you dislike? How would it feel to

work all day in this setting? What changes could make this a more pleasant or accommodating environment for adults?

3. Observe a group of children in an outdoor environment. What kinds of activities are the children involved in? Which developmental needs are being met? If you see little involvement in activities that promote one, or several, areas of development (for instance, social, language, cognitive), what changes or additions could be made to bring these about?

4. Browse through one of the many catalogs in which early childhood materials and equipment are advertised. Evaluate several of the items in the catalog according to the criteria outlined in this chapter for selecting equipment and materials. What conclusions can you draw about selecting developmentally appropriate items for young children?

5. If you have access to a computer and early childhood software, try out one early childhood activity on the computer. After you have mastered the activity, evaluate the software according to the criteria presented in this chapter. What do you think young children will learn from the activity? What feature(s) do you think might be appealing, unappealing, or frustrating to preschoolers?

ADDITIONAL RESOURCES

Select additional books, articles, and websites on topics discussed in Chapter 7.

Anderson, G. (2000). Computers in a developmentally appropriate curriculum. *Young Children, 55*(2), 90–93.

Curtis, D., & Carter, M. (2003). *Designs for living and learning: Transforming early childhood environments.* St. Paul, MN: Redleaf Press.

Louv, R. (2008). *Last child in the woods: Saving our children from nature-deficit disorder.* Chapel Hill, NC: Algonquin Books.

HELPFUL WEBSITES

Quality in Child Care Settings—National Network for Child Care:

www.nncc.org

This site provides extensive resources related to child care and early childhood development.

NAEYC's Position Statement, *Technology and Interactive Media as Tools in Early Childhood Programs Serving Children from Birth through Age 8:*

http://www.naeyc.org/files/naeyc/file/positions/PS_technology_WEB2.pdf

Children and Computers—Old Concerns:

http://kidshealth.org/parent/fitness/safety/playground.html

This website includes the Fall/Winter 2000 issue of *Future of Children*, with thought-provoking and well-researched articles about this topic.

How Can We Provide Safe Playgrounds?

http://kidshealth.org/parent/fitness/safety/playground.html

This article from KidSource Online provides helpful tips on how to provide a safe outdoor play environment, how to help children play safely, and what factors make a playground unsafe.

Learning Centers:

www.busyteacherscafe.com/learningcenter/main.htm
This website provides ideas for content and activities that can be provided in learning centers.

Go to **CengageBrain.com** to register your access code for this book's Education CourseMate website, where you will find more resources to help you study. Additional resources for this chapter include TeachSource Videos, glossary flashcards, web links, case studies with critical-thinking questions that apply the concepts presented in this chapter, and more. If your textbook does not include a printed access card, you can go to **CengageBrain.com** to purchase access.

V

The *How* of Early Childhood Education— Curriculum

We will now turn our attention to the *how* of early childhood education, how teachers involve children. In Part V, we will examine the aspects of the early childhood program that deal with the curriculum.

8 Scheduling and Curriculum Planning

 A curriculum is much more than a collection of activities. It provides the framework for developing a coherent set of learning experiences that enables children to reach the identified goals. [The curriculum] must be effective and comprehensive in addressing all the developmental domains and important content areas.

Developmentally Appropriate Practice,
Copple & Bredekamp, 2009, p. 42

In Chapter 8, you will find answers to the following questions about scheduling and curriculum planning in the early childhood program:

▶ What are the major components of a schedule for young children of different ages?
▶ What guidelines can help you develop a developmentally appropriate schedule for children of different ages?
▶ What principles should you use to plan a developmentally appropriate curriculum?
▶ What are the differences between a theme-based and an emergent curriculum?

NAEYC STANDARDS CONSIDERED IN CHAPTER 8

(See the Standards Correlation Chart on the inside front cover of this book for the titles and description of the standards listed below.)

▶ *Standard 4b:* Planning daily schedule and curriculum based on understanding of child development principles and research (pp. 194–218).
▶ *Standard 4a:* Understanding that a well-planned schedule facilitates supportive relationships and interactions (p. 195–196).
▶ *Standard 4c:* Using a variety of teaching approaches rather than always the same techniques during such activities as group times (pp. 195–196).
▶ *Standard 1a:* Planning a daily schedule and curriculum based on sound understanding of child development (pp. 198–207; 208–210).
▶ *Standard 4d:* Engaging in reflective practice about the flexibility of the schedule and to plan curriculum that promotes positive outcomes for the children (pp. 206–207; 213–218).
▶ *Standard 2c:* Understanding the value of family engagement in curriculum planning (p. 218).

A curriculum and activities fit within a schedule, which provides an overall structure for the program. The schedule provides a sequence for the events of the day as well as the length of time various components will last. It also allows for many types of interactions: between child and child, between adult and child, and among small and large groups. In addition, the schedule provides time to do activities in a variety of environments (Hohmann, Weikart, & Epstein, 2008). But more than that, the schedule reflects your program's philosophy, takes into account the needs and interests of the children, and provides the security of a predictable routine for children and teachers.

A curriculum is fitted within the structure of the schedule. Planning the curriculum is at the heart of your program, an opportunity for thoughtfully building on what the children already know, introducing relevant new topics, and creating a positive attitude toward learning. In this chapter we will examine, in detail, guidelines for good scheduling and for effective curriculum planning. As part of the discussion on curriculum planning, we will consider two distinct approaches: the more traditional, theme-based curriculum and the emergent, project-based curriculum.

COMPONENTS OF THE EARLY CHILDHOOD SCHEDULE

Most early childhood programs contain some fairly standard elements. How these components are arranged and how much time is allocated to them reflects the school's, as well as the teachers', philosophy and goals. Consider, for instance, a program in which the children spend the bulk of their time in self-selected activities and one in which the teacher directs and controls most of the day's activities. In the first, the philosophy and goals reflect a respect for the child's growing independence, increasing decision-making skills, and ability to draw what is valuable from the day's experiences. In the second example, the teacher feels a need to supervise the children's experiences closely to ensure that they gain specific skills and information. Both approaches are used, although most early childhood professionals prefer the former, where faith is placed in children's ability to learn and flourish in a well-planned environment. Let us now examine standard components of the early childhood program, keeping in mind that these can be arranged in a great variety of ways.

Activity Time

The largest block(s) of time each day should be reserved for activities from which the children can select. **Activity time,** in many programs, is also called self-selected learning activities, free play, play time, learning center time, or other similar names that connote that the children make choices about the activities in which they engage. This is the part of the schedule in which you insert many of the activities we will discuss in the next few chapters. A wide variety of well-planned activities should reinforce and support the objectives and theme or project of the curriculum. Each day's activities should also provide multiple opportunities for the development of fine and gross motor, cognitive, creative, social, and language skills.

Activity time blocks should last at least 45 minutes (and can be as long as two hours or more) to allow children ample time to survey the options, select an activity, get involved in it, and bring it to a satisfactory conclusion. DAP suggests that extended periods of time of at least one hour be allocated for children to engage in play and projects (Copple & Bredekamp, 2009). Many children will, of course, participate in more than one activity, but others will spend all of their time with one activity.

naeyc

activity time
Largest block(s) of time in the early childhood program day during which children can self-select from a variety of activities.

Key Point ◆
One of the largest time blocks in the early childhood schedule is activity time, during which children select from a variety of developmentally appropriate activities.

DAP

Activity time blocks also allow the teachers to interact with children individually or in small groups. Social guidance, informal conversations, well-timed questions, and careful listening give teachers the chance to learn more about the children in the class, develop relationships, introduce or reinforce concepts, evaluate the children's understanding of concepts, or assess developmental status. It allows for development of personal connections and establishment of warm, nurturing interactions among teachers and children.

When planning the activity time block, consider safety and adequate supervision. Some activities require close attention by an adult, whereas others can be carried out relatively independently by the children. Such activities as cooking and woodworking require constant teacher attention, for example. Water and sand play, other sensory activities, messy media, and blocks also need more attention from adults. For each activity time block, it is important to consider the balance between activities that need more adult guidance and those that are more self-directed, particularly in relation to the number of adults available in the class. It can be easy to lose sight of safety needs in an effort to provide a wide variety of interesting and stimulating activities.

Large-Group Activities

large-group time
(also called circle, story, or group time) Time block(s) during the day when all of the children and teachers join together in a common activity.

Key Point ◆

Large-group times, when teachers and children gather together, can serve a variety of purposes and include many types of activities.

Most programs include one or more times when all of the children and teachers gather together. **Large-group time**—variously called circle, story time, group, meeting time, or other similar names—can be used for many purposes. Some teachers tend to use it in the same way day after day, and others use such times to meet various objectives. Some programs have several group times, each serving a different purpose; for example, morning business (roll call, calendar), story, music/movement, or class meeting.

Group times offer the possibility of meeting a wide variety of objectives. For instance, they provide an excellent opportunity to introduce a new project or curriculum topic or to probe the children's comprehension of concepts and information. They can also be used for discussions, stories and books, songs, fingerplays, movement, socialization, poetry, games, dramatizations, sharing, relaxation exercises, planning and review, calendar or weather, and a host of other activities best carried out with the whole group. Book or story reading is probably the most frequently used group activity, though many other possibilities, which we will consider in the following several chapters, can also be incorporated during group times. Keep in mind that young children are motivated to become readers themselves when they have positive experiences of adults reading aloud to them (Sulzby & Teale, 2003).

As part of a research study (Essa, 2000), six preschool teachers were videotaped and their guidance techniques later analyzed. When children were engaged in self-selected activities, there were almost no behavioral concerns. What became quickly obvious, however, was that the bulk of behavior problems occurred during teacher-led group activities. Teachers were constantly reminding children to sit still, listen quietly, or "keep your hands to yourself." Closer examination of the videotapes showed that there was almost no opportunity for the children to be active participants because the teachers did all the talking, controlled the direction of the activities, and held generally over-long group times. In other words, the group activities, in contrast to the other parts of the curriculum, were not developmentally appropriate.

In traditional programs, group times are almost always teacher-initiated and led, although teachers often seek children's input. In fact, older preschoolers and primary children enjoy and are very competent in leading group activities; for instance, "reading" a familiar book, leading songs, and moving the group into transitions. Such opportunities to take over group leadership should, of course, never be imposed and should be conducted as the child chooses. Early childhood programs, particularly those based on an emergent curriculum approach, use group times in a different way. In keeping with the more egalitarian relationship between adults and children, group times provide opportunities for the genuine exchange of ideas and exploration of topics, and often involve subgroups of children, depending on their interests and involvement in the topic under discussion (Fraser & Gestwicki, 2001).

Some teachers designate meeting time as a chance for children to solve problems. Such meetings provide an opportunity to acknowledge others' positive actions and behaviors as well as to engage in problem solving of issues raised by the children, usually interpersonal conflicts. The teacher acts as facilitator, while the children learn how to resolve interpersonal issues in a productive rather than destructive manner. Class meetings create a very positive sense of community among the children, engender respect, promote cognitive development, and foster problem-solving skills that will be useful for years to come (Vance & Weaver, 2002).

When guiding large-group (as well as small-group) activities, it is important to remember how children learn and what constitutes developmentally appropriate group activities. Children, as active learners, will gain more from activities that allow for their input, include active involvement, and encourage flexible problem solving. Asking children to provide answers for which there is a "right" or "wrong," or "correct" or "incorrect," response does not support their developmental needs and their growing self-esteem.

Small-Group Activities

Some programs include a small-group activity time during which five or six children work with one teacher for a short period, generally 10 to 15 minutes. This can be handled by staggering small groups throughout the program day or by having each teacher take a small group during a designated small-group time block. Usually such times focus on teaching specific concepts and are geared to the abilities and interests of the children in the group (Hohmann et al., 2008). Children are often grouped by developmental level for small-group activities, although Hohmann and his colleagues recommend that small groups represent a cross section of the classroom population to promote cross-learning. In a small-group setting, the teacher has an opportunity to pay close attention to each individual child. As you might expect, careful planning is crucial for successful small-group activity times.

A somewhat different type of small-group activity is an integral part of emergent curriculum programs (Cadwell & Fyfe, 2004). This type of dialogue, although facilitated by the teacher, is not as teacher-directed as the small-group activity previously described. Nonetheless, teachers are full participants in such conversations with small groups of children,

Key Point ◆

During small-group activities, a teacher usually presents a concept to a few children, ensuring that the activity matches their abilities and interests.

© Cengage Learning

In small-group activities, the teacher focuses on a specific concept that is presented to a few children who are at a similar developmental level.

asking open-ended questions, stimulating thinking, and provoking discussion. The purpose of such dialogue is "to explore the children's ideas" (p. 85). What is especially important is that teachers listen carefully to gain insight into the children's process of thinking.

Outdoor Activity

A large time block for outdoor play should be part of the daily schedule. Some adults think of outdoor play merely as a time for children to expend excess energy and for teachers to take a rest. But outdoor time contains far too many valuable opportunities for learning and development to be dismissed in this way. When you think of outdoor play as an integral part of the early childhood experience, it becomes natural to allocate at least 45 minutes to this time block. Keep in mind that outdoor time requires planning in the same way that indoor activity does and that it involves the same kinds of teacher–child interactions. Keep in mind also our discussion in the "Take a Closer Look" box in Chapter 7, about how important it is for children to spend time in natural, outdoor environments.

Just like during activity times, the teacher's role when outside includes setting up a stimulating environment, providing for each child's individual needs, guiding children's behavior, providing a variety of experiences, taking opportunities to clarify concepts, and encouraging exploration and problem solving. In addition, some unique safety concerns require special attention in an outdoor play area. An important skill that you, as the teacher, should develop is the ability to scan, to keep an eye on the entire outdoor play area. It is particularly important to pay attention to the fronts and backs of swings, slides, climbing equipment, tricycles and other wheeled toys, and the area in and around the sandbox.

Time for outdoor play may be affected by the weather, although the weather should never be used as an excuse for not going outside. Children thoroughly enjoy the snow, for instance, if they are properly clothed. Children do not catch cold from playing outside in the winter.

If inclement weather does prevent the children from enjoying outside time, alternative activities should be made available inside so that children can expend energy and engage in large motor activity. Many schools have a selection of large motor equipment, such as tumbling mats or an indoor climbing apparatus, to use on rainy days. If this equipment is in a relatively restricted space, then small groups of children should use it throughout the day rather than having the entire group involved at one time.

Cleanup

It is wise to schedule 10 to 15 minutes, particularly after activity times, for children and teachers to participate in putting the classroom back into order. When cleanup time is included in the daily schedule, it conveys that this is an important component of the program.

Meals

Sharing food provides a unique opportunity for socialization and learning; thus, almost every program includes at least one snack, if not several meals. A three-hour program usually includes a snack time around the halfway point of the day.

Key Point ◆
Large time blocks should be set aside for outdoor activities.

Key Point ◆
Other important components that must be considered in scheduling include cleanup, meals, nap, and transitions.

The timing of meals, however, should be dictated by the children's needs, not by a rigid schedule, especially for infants. If it appears that some children get to school having had breakfast several hours before or not having eaten breakfast at all, then an early morning meal should be provided. An alternative, particularly if children's arrival at school is staggered over several hours, is to have a snack available for a period of time, enabling children to eat as they feel the need to refuel.

Timing of lunch will depend on the ages of the children, the length of time they are at the center, and when morning snack was served. Younger preschoolers may need lunch at 11:30 A.M. and be ready for a nap by noon. How much time is allocated for each of these meals will depend on the children in the group and the type of meal; generally, however, 15 to 20 minutes for snacks and 20 to 30 minutes for lunch is adequate. Most children can comfortably finish a meal in this period of time. We will discuss meals more fully in Chapter 14.

Nap or Rest

In full-day programs, children should have time for sleep or rest during the middle of the day, usually sometime after, though not immediately following, lunch. Allocating one to two hours for this time is usually enough (see Chapter 14 for a more detailed discussion). Also, be aware of your local regulations for rest time, because some states include specific requirements.

Transitions

The times between activities are as important as the activities themselves. Failing to plan how children will get from one area to another—from group to the bathroom to snack, or from cleanup time to putting on coats to going outside—can result in chaos. We will discuss transition techniques in more detail in Chapter 14 in the context of group guidance.

GUIDELINES FOR PROGRAM SCHEDULING

These components of the early childhood day—activity time, large-group activities, small-group activities, outdoor activity, cleanup, meals, nap or rest, and transitions—can be arranged in the daily schedule in a wide variety of ways. Let's examine some guidelines that will help in setting an effective schedule.

Alternating Active and Quiet Times

Children need time both to expend energy and to rest. A useful rule in scheduling is to look at the total time in terms of cycles of activity and rest, boisterousness and quiet, energy and relaxation. Categorize the descriptions of time blocks listed in your daily schedule in terms of active times (for example, activity time, outdoor play, large-group activities that involve movement) and less active times (for example, story, small-group activities, nap, snack).

In applying this guideline, think about providing the opportunity to be physically active after quiet times and to slow down after active involvement. Also consider the total consecutive time that children are expected to sit quietly. Thus, reconsider a schedule in which children sit at a large-group activity from 10:00 to 10:20, then move into a small-group activity from 10:20 to 10:35,

Meals are an important part of the early childhood day, meeting children's nutritional needs and providing opportunities for independence, learning, and socialization.

Key Point ◆

In planning a schedule, it is important to balance times when children are active and when they are quiet.

followed by a snack time until 11:00. Such a schedule ought to include an active break within that hour, rather than having children shift from one relatively inactive period to another. Similarly, when children have been engaged in active exploration, a quieter time should follow. One caution: Do not expect children to move immediately from very active involvement, such as outdoor play, to being very quiet, such as nap time. For such times, plan a more gentle transition that helps children settle down gradually.

Balancing Child-Initiated and Teacher-Initiated Activities

Key Point ◆

There should be a balance between child-initiated and teacher-initiated activities to allow children enough time to make decisions and exercise their growing autonomy.

Key Point ◆

The activity level of the children is an important consideration in making scheduling decisions.

DAP

Key Point ◆

The ages of the children will have an impact on the schedule because older children have longer attention spans and younger children may require more time for some routines.

Most early childhood programs provide large time blocks in which children can make decisions about the activities in which they will participate and how they will carry them out. Most programs also include times when teachers direct activities. Typically, activity time and outdoor time accommodate child initiation, whereas small- and large-group times generally involve teacher initiation. Some functional activities, such as snack, nap, and cleanup, require children to follow the direction of adults and thus do not entail children's initiative. According to DAP, "adult-guided experience proceeds primarily along the lines of the teacher's goals, but is also shaped by the children's active engagement; child-guided experience proceeds primarily along the lines of the children's interests and actions, with strategic teacher support" (Copple & Bredekamp, 2009, p. 17).

A balance between child and teacher control must be carefully considered. When young children are allowed to decide how they will spend their time, they develop qualities such as autonomy, judgment, independent decision making, social give-and-take, initiative, exploration, and creativity. In addition, children are also expected to develop a reasonable amount of compliance, understand the rules of group behavior, and accept the authority and wisdom of adults. Generally, when adults convey respect for and trust in the ability of children to make appropriate decisions, children will reciprocate with enthusiastic participation in adult-initiated activities. Of course, teacher-initiated activities must be developmentally appropriate and engage the interest of the children. Most of the day's activities should, however, be child-selected and allow children to move from activity to activity at their own pace.

Activity Level of the Children

Key Point ◆

Creative scheduling can provide an effective way of working with large groups of children.

By nature, young children are active and must have many opportunities for expending energy. Some children, however, are more active than others. Occasionally, you will find that you have a group in which a large portion is particularly active. If this occurs, a schedule that has worked for you in the past may not serve as well because the needs of the children are different. In such a case, adjusting the schedule as well as the classroom arrangement and the types of activities planned will help the class run more smoothly. You might, for instance, carry out some activities, which are traditionally indoor ones, outside and plan either a longer or an added outdoor time block.

Developmental Level of the Children

As children get older, their attention span noticeably increases; thus, your daily schedule should reflect the group's ages and developmental levels. For older children, plan longer time blocks for small-group, large-group, and activity times. However, younger children require added time for meals, nap, and cleanup. With a group of very young children, you may also want to schedule regular times for toileting; for instance, before going outdoors and before nap.

The length of large-group time can be particularly problematic. The time allocated to such activities will depend on the ages and attention spans of the children. Children can, of course, sit for a longer period of time if the activity captivates their interest; but, generally, a well-paced, shorter group time is more rewarding for all. As the program year progresses, reassess the length of group time and adjust it according to the children's interest.

Group Size

Group size may also influence the schedule. Particularly with a large group of children, creative scheduling can be used to allow for more individualized attention to children. One example is a church-supported child care center where the one large room, in which more than 50 children of varying ages spend the day together, dictates scheduling considerations. Although the children and teachers share the same indoor and outdoor space, the director has created five subgroups of children and teachers who alternate use of the outdoor area, the indoor large motor area, and the wide variety of other learning centers. Thus, while one group is involved in a music activity, another will be outside, while the other groups are engaged in self-selected activities. The children know that they will also have a chance to participate in the other activities because space, teachers, and time blocks are rotated for different groups of children.

Arrival of Children

How children arrive and leave the center—whether over staggered periods of time or at about the same time—has to be taken into account in scheduling. In most child care centers, the early morning period, until most or all of the children are at school, and the late afternoon period, when children start leaving for home, require some special considerations. The arrival or departure of children makes carrying out teacher-initiated activities difficult because the teacher and other children are interrupted frequently and because the arriving or departing children will not get the full benefit of the teacher-led activity. Thus, self-selected activities, in which children can control engagement and disengagement, should be available during such times. In programs in which all the children arrive at the same time, however, the first activity might be a teacher-initiated group time to introduce the plan for the day.

Seasonal Considerations

In geographic locations where the weather varies considerably from season to season, you may want to adjust the schedule according to the time of year. For instance, during winter in a New England child care program, it would be difficult to keep to a schedule that contains three outdoor time blocks when each involves helping children get into and out of their

It is important to consider the children's overall activity level. Sometimes, a particularly active group of children needs additional time outdoors. Alternatively, you may want to plan more activities that let children expend excess energy indoors.

© Cengage Learning

Key Point ◆◆

The schedule also needs to take into account whether all children arrive at school at the same time or whether, as in most child care facilities, their arrival is staggered over a period of time.

 **TeachSource Video Activity**
WATCH • REFLECT • RESPOND

This video provides planning for the daily schedule. Go to CengageBrain .com and view the video entitled, "Preschool and Daily Schedules and Curriculum Planning," and answer the following questions:

1. How does a consistent daily schedule help provide a sense of security for children?

2. Which guidelines discussed in the text for developing a daily schedule were shown in the video?

snowsuits, boots, mittens, and hats. At the same time, a lengthy outdoor time is inappropriate when the temperature is below freezing or, for that matter, when it reaches 100 degrees. Yet once spring or fall arrive and the temperature is balmy, the schedule should allow for longer outdoor time. The weather can certainly affect your schedule, so a flexible approach and attitude are important when working with young children.

SCHEDULING FOR INFANTS AND TODDLERS

naeyc

Scheduling for infants and toddlers takes into account somewhat different factors than does scheduling for preschoolers and older children. In an infant and toddler program, the schedule is initially set by the needs of the children and gradually shifts toward a more uniform schedule, as the children get older. An infant program has to revolve around the eating, waking/sleeping, and elimination patterns of each child. The daily program for each child is uniquely tailored around her or his physiological patterns. As they get older, children begin to eat at times more consistent with adult meals; sleep primarily at night with two daytime naps, then one daytime nap; and regulate their elimination schedule. Thus, by the end of the toddler years, children are ready to enter into a more uniform schedule that applies to the entire group. Babies, however, need to be on a **self-demand schedule**, in which infants communicate what they need and adults respond accordingly (Gestwicki, 2011). One of the best ways to meet the needs of infants and toddlers and to help them make the gradual transition from an individual to a group schedule is to provide a consistent caregiver who remains with them throughout this period, This kind of continuity of care has been shown to promote secure attachment (Essa, Favre, Thweatt, & Waugh, 1999).

Toddlers are in transition from a schedule in which each child's individual needs sets a time frame to one that is more uniform and predictable. A dependable pattern for how the day progresses gives toddlers a sense of security and

self-demand schedule
Infants' schedules are determined by their individual needs, and adults respond appropriately to these.

The schedule may need to be rearranged according to the weather. If winters are severe, it would be difficult to help the entire group get in and out of full snow gear several times a day. Think about your own part of the country. What climatic conditions might affect the schedule during different seasons?

© Cengage Learning

will prevent struggles between adults and children, creating a built-in rhythm that becomes a habit rather than something to be challenged (Gestwicki, 2011). Nonetheless, the toddler schedule still allows for considerable variation, since individual children's needs, especially for rest, will vary. Built-in times for quiet, interspersed with opportunities for children to exercise their boundless energy are also important in a toddler schedule. Finally, plan carefully so that toddlers do not have to wait, since their capacity to wait is not yet well developed. Transitions in which toddlers are helped individually to move to the next activity will be more successful (Gestwicki, 2011).

SCHEDULING FOR SCHOOL-AGE CHILDREN

The guidelines for program scheduling we have already discussed are also relevant to school-age children, but we will mention a few additional elements that are appropriate for this age group. Scheduling for primary school children will vary according to the type of program they are in. Beyond their experiences in kindergarten and the early grades, many children are in some kind of arrangement before school, after school, on holidays, during the summer, or during specific blocks of time if their school follows an alternative calendar. Whatever the time frame, whether part- or full-day, scheduling for this age group needs to take their unique characteristics, experiences, and abilities into consideration. As Carol Gestwicki (2011) points out, children spend six or seven hours every day in an academic setting, with considerable time in teacher-directed activities, so after-school programs should be less schoollike and more like a neighborhood. She further suggests that mixed-age grouping, with an age range of three to four years, facilitates this neighborhood feeling.

A variety of activity choices from which children are free to select should be available. These include opportunities for physical activities, socialization, and creative expression. Breakfast in the morning and snack in the afternoon should also be available for children who are hungry. Large time blocks when children

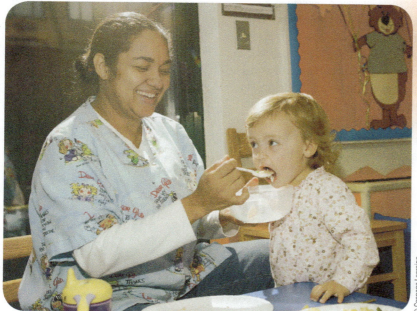

Schedules for infants and toddlers need to be flexible and individualized, revolving around daily routines; in other words, very young children should be on a self-demand schedule.

© Cengage Learning

DAP IN A PUBLIC SCHOOL SETTING

How am I going to blend the DAP philosophies of early childhood education (ECE) with the academic demands of a public school system? This question was much discussed between my fellow students and me as we progressed through our ECE coursework. Now that I am in my second year of teaching kindergarten at a Title 1, K–6 public school, this question is more relevant than ever as I create lesson plans and interact with the children in my classes.

My school district has a list of concepts and skills titled "Critical Content" that needs to be taught throughout the course of the year. Critical Content is based on state standards as well as district standards and is deemed necessary for children to be prepared for first grade. My curriculum is driven by this Critical Content in that I need to ensure that my students master a range of skills in the areas of literacy, reading, writing, math, science, and social studies. My students should read at a specified level, demonstrate specific writing skills, and be able to demonstrate an understanding of addition and subtraction by the time they complete kindergarten. Doesn't sound much like a DAP approach, does it? Fortunately, my district understands that there are many ways to approach the teaching of these skills; not just one prescribed, scripted method.

Theresa Danna Douglas

Kathryn, Kindergarten/EDK (Title 1 Extended Day Kindergarten) Teacher

As the teacher, I have the freedom to decide how I am going to approach the instruction of the Critical Content. Group projects are a way of allowing each to child use existing skills while scaffolding learning in other areas. For example, recently we have had several children absent with a nasty respiratory bug. Kindergarteners' relationships are important and it is stressful for children when their friends are absent for more than one day. During a discussion of their friends' illnesses, several children expressed an interest in learning about germs. This interest led to a short unit with a "project" component. After listening to a relevant Read Aloud, the children decided to create their own representations of germs using a variety of materials. We decided to make a "Germ Book" and used an interactive writing lesson to create the text. Math skills were used to determine the placement of the "germs" on each page. These tasks required teamwork and communication. The book was assembled, laminated, and is now in our class library.

Through this integrated lesson, the children met Critical Content in literacy, writing, math, science, and communication and had experiences in creative representation, social interactions, and fine motor skills. Remember, the driving force of this lesson was taken from the children's interests and classroom relationships.

Sometimes the demands of Critical Content can make scheduling a challenge. Because the attention span of five- and six-year-olds is short, I keep my children moving from table activity to carpet and back again several times. By scheduling frequent movement and changes of activities, fidgeting is reduced and learning is stimulated.

Unlike the upper grades, kindergarten does not have blocks where subjects are taught at a prescribed time. This freedom allows for flexibility. Because I have a group of children with a variety of life experiences, it is important to be flexible with my daily routine. This allows me to meet the diverse needs of my class. Having an ECE background has allowed me to have a better understanding of the children in my class from a developmental point of view. I feel I am working in a positive way to successfully meld DAP with the requirements and expectations of my district.

can engage in activities alone, with a friend, or with a group are needed to support children's growing sense of initiative, independence, and competence. DAP, in fact, suggests that children need ample time to get deeply involved in activities and projects (Copple & Bredekamp, 2009). In addition, in a program that lasts all day, the schedule should provide for alternating times for physical activity and quiet. See Figure 8-4 for a suggested before- and after-school program schedule.

TYPES OF SCHEDULES

Obviously, the schedules of an infant program, a 2½-hour preschool, a child care center, and a before- and after-school program will differ and must be designed to meet the unique needs of the children and teachers. Take the example of two children to illustrate how the program must meet children's needs. David attends a three-hour morning preschool program because his parents want him to have an enriching social and learning experience. He gets up around 7:00, eats breakfast with his parents before his father leaves for work, and plays for an hour or so before his mother takes him to school at the nearby recreation center. At lunch time, his mother picks him up and he has lunch with her and his younger sister Tina, after which he reads or plays with his mother while Tina takes a nap. After dinner, Dad reads the children a story, and they go to bed by 8:00. Rita, who lives with her single mother and two older sisters, has been in child care since she was six weeks old. She gets up at 6:30 and they are out of the house by 7:15, with or without time for breakfast. She spends the day at the child care center, from about 7:45 to 5:30 in the evening. After picking up her sisters, the family stops at the grocery store or sometimes McDonald's, gets home by about 6:30, eats dinner, watches some TV, and goes to bed. Clearly, the two children have very different needs that their respective early childhood programs have to meet.

Although the main scheduling consideration for full-day programs is the needs of the children, the schedule must also take into account the requirements of the staff. Early childhood teachers spend long and difficult hours working with their young charges, a job that can be tiring and frustrating as well as rewarding and energizing. Complementary to the schedule provided for the children has to be a schedule that provides rest, rejuvenation, and planning time for the adults. When the needs of the adults are considered, the children's needs will be met better, and teacher burnout is less likely to occur.

Examples of Schedules

After examining standard components of the early childhood program, guidelines for scheduling, and differences between preschool and child care, you probably have concluded correctly that a daily schedule can be arranged in numerous ways. Figures 8-1, 8-2, 8-3, and 8-4 show four examples of schedules that consider many variables. Of course, any schedule you devise must meet the unique characteristics of your group and children, your philosophy, and your program.

Key Point

The schedule must meet the unique needs of children of different ages, including an individualized schedule for infants and a more flexible schedule with ample time for children to engage in interesting activities for older children.

Key Point

Schedules for various programs (for instance, infant care, preschool, child care, and before- and after-school care) will differ because they meet different needs of the children; the needs of teachers also must be considered in the schedule.

Figure **8-1**

Full-Day Program for a Group of Four- and Five-Year-Olds

7:30–9:00	**Staggered Arrival:** Teachers greet children and talk to parents; self-selected activities such as books, manipulatives, play dough, and blocks.
7:30–8:30	Breakfast available.
9:00–9:20	**Large-Group Time:** Introduction of day's activities; story or discussion related to day's topic.
9:20–10:30	**Activity Time:** Self-selected activities from learning centers, or teacher-planned projects.
10:30–10:40	**Cleanup Time.**
10:40–11:00	**Snack.**
11:00–11:15	**Small-Group Activity:** Teacher-initiated, small-group activity to reinforce specific concepts.
11:15–12:00	**Outdoor Time:** Self-selected activities.
12:00–12:20	**Large-Group Time:** Recap of morning; story; music.
12:20–12:30	**Wash for Lunch.**
12:30–1:00	**Lunch.**
1:00–3:00	**Nap:** Transition to nap and sleep for those requiring a nap.
1:00–1:30	**Rest:** Quiet individual activity for nonsleepers.
1:30–3:00	**Activity Time:** Self-selected activities, both inside and outside; as sleeping children wake, they gradually join others.
3:00–3:20	**Snack.**
3:20–4:00	**Activity Time:** Continued self-selected activities both inside and outside.
4:00–4:10	**Cleanup.**
4:10–4:30	**Large-Group Time:** Closing of day; story; movement activity.
4:30–5:30	**Staggered Departure:** Self-selected activities until all children leave.

Figure **8-2**

Full-Day Program for a Group of Two- to Three-Year-Olds

7:30–9:00	**Staggered Arrival:** Teachers greet children and talk to parents; self-selected activities such as books, manipulatives, play dough, and blocks.
7:30–8:30	Breakfast available.
9:00–9:15	**Large-Group Time:** Introduce day's activities; story.
9:15–10:00	**Activity Time:** Self-selected activities from learning centers, or teacher-planned projects.
10:00–10:15	**Cleanup Time.**
10:15–10:20	**Snack.**
10:20–10:30	**Toileting.**
10:30–11:15	**Outdoor Time:** Self-selected activities.
11:15–11:30	**Large-Group Time:** Story, music, fingerplays.
11:30–11:45	**Wash for Lunch.**
11:45–12:15	**Lunch.**
12:15–2:15	**Nap:** Transition to nap and sleep.
2:15–2:45	**Toileting, followed by Snack.**
2:45–3:30	**Outdoor Time.**
3:30–4:15	**Activity Time:** Self-selected activities.
4:15–4:30	**Cleanup.**
4:30–4:45	**Large-Group Time:** Story, puppets, movement.
4:45–5:30	**Staggered Departure:** Self-selected activities until all children leave.

Figure **8-3**

Half-Day Program for Three- and Four-Year-Olds

8:50–9:00	**Arrival.**
9:00–9:20	**Large-Group Time:** Introduce day's activities; story, music.
9:20–9:40	**Snack.**
9:40–10:30	**Activity Time:** Self-selected activities.
10:30–10:40	**Cleanup.**
10:40–11:00	**Small-Group Activity.**
11:00–11:40	**Outdoor Time.**
11:40–11:55	**Large-Group Time:** Closing and recap of day.
11:55–12:00	**Departure:** Gather belongings; teachers talk to parents briefly.

Figure **8-4**

Before- and After-School Program

6:00–8:30	**Arrival:** Breakfast available, self-selected activities; outdoor play, weather permitting.
8:30	**Board Bus for School.**
3:00–4:15	**Arrival:** Snack available until 4:15; outdoor play, with organized games available.
4:15–4:30	**Large-Group Meeting, Discussion.**
4:30–6:00	**Self-Selected Indoor Activities:** Projects, clubs, activity centers, homework, and so on.

FLEXIBILITY OF THE SCHEDULE

naeyc

The schedule provides the framework within which your program functions. You might think of the schedule as the skeleton and the curriculum and activities as the flesh that fills out and defines the character of the inner structure. A sound skeleton is vital to a healthy body, just as a well-put-together schedule is integral to a well-run program.

The daily schedule also provides security, because it gives the day a predictable order. A good schedule provides the predictability that children need, and they soon learn the sequence of activities. Thus, you can say to a child, "I know you are anxious for your mother to come. After we finish cleaning up, we will go outside. Later, when we come back inside, we will read a story, and then your mother will be here." The child can relate to this temporal time frame because he is familiar with the schedule.

The schedule should also allow for flexibility, rather than being rigidly followed. There are many occasions when the set time frame should be altered. For

Although the daily schedule should be predictable, it also needs to remain flexible. If, for instance, the children seem unusually inattentive and restless at group time, shorten it.

© Cengage Learning

instance, if you find that the children are particularly engrossed in activity time, extend that time and shorten a later time block; the clock should not arbitrarily cut off involved play. If it has been raining relentlessly for two weeks and today is a beautiful, sunny day, plan to spend a large portion of the day outside so everyone can enjoy the nice weather. Similarly, if, despite your best efforts, the children are restless and uninterested in the group activity, shorten the time rather than allowing a negative situation to develop. In other words, use cues from the children—and your judgment—to adapt the schedule if it will improve the flow of the day and better meet the needs of the children. You might also ask the children what changes in the schedule they would suggest. Their insights will surprise you!

Some large early childhood centers, because they have multiple classes that share some common facilities, establish a centerwide schedule. Such a schedule makes flexibility of certain aspects of the day more difficult, but still allows for some latitude. It may not be possible to alter the time allocated for outside play when classes rotate the use of the playground, or of meals if they share a common dining room; however, self-contained parts of the schedule, such as activity or group time, should be adapted as required.

WHAT IS THE CURRICULUM?

naeyc

curriculum
Overall master plan of the early childhood program, reflecting its philosophy, into which specific activities are fit.

Now that we have discussed the daily schedule, let's turn to an examination of the **curriculum**, the content and substance of that schedule. The term *curriculum* has a somewhat different connotation in early childhood than in elementary, secondary, or higher education. In these settings, *curriculum* often refers to a course of study on a specific topic, such as a curriculum in history, social studies, physics, reading, or any other subject. Thus, students typically are in the midst of several curriculums, which are not necessarily connected to each other.

In early childhood, the curriculum tends to be viewed more holistically, and all aspects of the program are integrated and related. Early childhood professionals view the curriculum as integrally tied to a concern for dealing comprehensively with "the whole child," the child's physical, social, cognitive, and emotional development. "This concern for children's overall development is an important distinguishing characteristic of early childhood education that sets it apart from most education for older children [which emphasizes] teaching basic knowledge and skills" (Moravcik & Feeney, 2009, p. 219). The foundation for sound program development is based on research and theoretical knowledge that helps us understand how children learn, what makes for a good learning environment, and what curriculum material is suitable for young children.

Key Point ◆◆

Early childhood professionals view the curriculum as dealing with the "whole child," not focused on only one facet, such as intellectual development.

In particular, the curriculum is founded on the understanding that play is an integral part of children's learning and development and, as such, has to be an integral part of the early childhood curriculum. DAP underscores the importance of play as well. "Play is an important vehicle for developing self-regulation as well as for promoting language, cognition, and social competence" (Copple & Bredekamp, 2009, p. 14).

A recent development in early childhood programming that concerns many professionals is the proliferation of curricula and teaching materials aimed at accelerating young children's development (Copple & Bredekamp, 2009; Elkind,

1987; Olfman, 2003). Advertisements for preschool programs as well as books, kits, and other teaching materials promise parents brighter children, toddlers who read and do math, or future Harvard graduates.

Many accelerated preschool curricula are based primarily on a downward escalation of the curriculum, presenting elementary school tasks and methods to younger children. Elkind (1987) warns that programs that teach reading, math, ballet, or gymnastics to very young children should be considered "miseducation" because they put children at risk for short- and long-term stress and other problems. There is no research-based support for such practices; on the contrary, research tells us that they tend to be damaging.

So, as you begin to think about an appropriate curriculum for young children, where do you turn? It might be helpful to remember that young children are eager, absorbent learners, curious and interested in learning as much about their world as possible. Children are equipped with a drive to explore and discover, an urge to see and feel and hear firsthand, and a thirst for new experiences in both physical and social realms. This suggests that we do not have to force-feed children what we think they should learn. Rather, we can plan a curriculum based on the faith that children's innate interest in their world will lead them to appropriate learning, given a suitable learning environment and knowledgeable, reflective adult guidance. The "Take a Closer Look" box provides a discussion of an international study that compares programs from different parts of the world. Note that these use the kinds of principles we've been discussing.

DIVERSITY

naeyc

Key Point ◆◆

Particularly important is the match between the children's development levels, abilities, needs, and interests and the curriculum. This involves understanding child development principles and knowing the characteristics of each individual child in the group.

Children's Development and Curriculum

What you include in the curriculum must be directly related to the children in your program. A curriculum that does not fit the comprehension level, abilities, needs, and interests of the children is meaningless. To plan an appropriate program requires knowledge about the age group of your class, about family characteristics and backgrounds, and about the individual variations among the children in the class.

First of all, a sound understanding of child development is essential to curriculum planning. A general comprehension of what four-year-olds are like is basic to planning for a class of fours. Not only does such knowledge tell you what to expect of this age group in terms of physical, cognitive, and social ability, but it also helps you understand what interests four-year-olds often share.

Furthermore, the more you know about the backgrounds of the children, the more specifically you can plan a curriculum to meet the characteristics of the group. Any ethnic, cultural, religious, linguistic, or regional factors unique to the group can be incorporated to enhance the curriculum and to help children feel good about their uniqueness.

In addition, your ability to observe children and glean information from your observations will help you in developing an appropriate curriculum for the individuals in the class. Topics and activities must be matched carefully to the general abilities of the children as a group, but variations within the

Having a sound understanding of child development gives you the background to plan developmentally appropriate activities.

© Cengage Learning

EARLY CHILDHOOD CURRICULUM—A GLOBAL PERSPECTIVE

THE TRENDS that are changing American life—including a greater number of dual-earner and single-parent families, increased mobility of families, increasing diversity, and a majority of young children in some kind of early childhood program—have also affected many other parts of the world. Countries across the globe grapple with similar issues as the ones Americans face. Many countries have focused on the importance of high-quality programs for young children, which has led to international discussion and evaluation of early childhood education and care. At the request of education ministers, the Organization for Economic Cooperation and Development sponsored an assessment of various early childhood education approaches, focusing on programs from Italy, New Zealand, Belgium, Sweden, and the United States. The resulting report found interesting similarities and differences among the five included programs (Samuelsson, Sheridan, & Williams, 2006).

The study included the Reggio Emilia programs of Italy, which we discussed in Chapter 5 and will consider in more detail later in this chapter; Te Whāriki of New Zealand, a curriculum grounded in Maori traditions of deep respect for the universe and belief in its interconnectedness; Experiential Education of Belgium, which focuses on the degree of emotional well-being and the level of involvement of the child; the Swedish National Curriculum, a program solidly committed to laying the foundations of democracy; and the High/Scope cognitively oriented curriculum developed in Michigan, which we also discussed in Chapter 5. Each of these programs was deemed to be of high quality, though they differed on various dimensions.

The study defined *curriculum* as a framework or guideline for the overall program, not as a narrowly prescribed sequence of activities. In keeping with this definition, all five programs describe children as active learners with a keen interest in their world. They also share a view of children as having rights and as learning through communication and interaction. In addition, the programs share a belief in the importance of cooperation with parents, viewing the family as a partner in the children's early education. All five also place great emphasis on the need for staff to be reflective in order to develop a deeper understanding of each child and his or her experience. In addition, all programs are described as value-oriented; for instance, the emotional well-being of each person is valued in the Experiential Education program of Belgium, acknowledgement of indigenous values are part of New Zealand's program, and democracy is an underlying value both in the Swedish and Reggio Emilia curriculums. Another similarity among the five programs is the emphasis on teacher competence, acknowledging the research that ties teacher education and training to program quality. Finally, the primary goal of all five curriculums is to give children a good start in life.

While all five programs share many commonalities, including their high quality, the study also found some distinct differences among them. There are variations in how children are viewed. The New Zealand, Swedish, and Italian programs view youngsters as competent children who collaborate with each other and with teachers, while the Belgian and American models view children as having different needs and possibilities at different ages, which teachers enhance through the curriculum. In keeping with this, there is variation on how the teacher is viewed in the educational process. The Italian and New Zealand approach sees children as competent and knowing how to learn, and sees teachers as supporting them in this endeavor; the American and Belgian programs consider that children's competence develops because of interactions with teachers. Another difference among the programs is the degree to which they emphasize the importance of the environment; all acknowledge its role, but while Te Whāriki provides no further details, High/Scope emphasizes that arrangement and organization are significant, Experiential Learning focuses on the correct match between the child's potential and the environmental challenge, and Reggio Emilia describes the environment as a "third teacher," capable of considerable influence in the child's learning. Finally, the programs view assessment in different ways as well. High/Scope, for instance, includes a strong evaluation component while Reggio Emilia views assessment in less traditional way.

The study concludes that all five programs have common values and objectives that are aimed at giving children a good start in life, even if they differ in some aspects. The analysis of these programs also focuses on a vision of what kinds of adults the children in such programs might grow up to be. Whether implicitly or explicitly, they all expect children to grow up as democratic citizens who contribute to their societies, know how to get along with others, and engage in lifelong learning.

group and individual needs must be recognized. If children with disabilities are included in your class, it is particularly important to ensure that your classroom provides an appropriate program for them.

As we continue to reinforce throughout this book, one of the most valuable guides in developing curriculums is NAEYC's *Developmentally Appropriate Practice in Early Childhood Programs Serving Children from Birth through Age 8* (Copple & Bredekamp, 2009). This resource provides a philosophical rationale as well as specific and pragmatic information on appropriate and inappropriate practices when working with young children.

Culture and the Curriculum

Children come to your program with a cultural orientation that reflects their "family's way of living: their values or beliefs, language, patterns of thinking, appearance and behavior" (Jackman, 2009, p. 46). This culture may be different from that of the majority of the class or from yours, as the teacher. It is important, therefore, to include culture carefully and thoughtfully within the curriculum. Rebecca New and Margaret Beneke (2009), in addition to acknowledging the growing diversity among young children, also note that "children in these settings are … distinguished by what they share—a desire to learn in a way that respects their personal lives even as it prepares them to participate in an increasingly global society" (p. 305). We will discuss guidelines for an anti-bias curriculum in more detail in Chapter 13, when we consider socialization through the curriculum.

Types of Curriculum

The early childhood curriculum is the result of both long- and short-term planning. Many programs start with a master plan that covers a sizable period (a

TeachSource Video Activity
WATCH•REFLECT•RESPOND

This video explores curriculum planning and DAP. Go to CengageBrain .com and view the video entitled, "Curriculum Planning: Implementing Developmentally Appropriate Practice in an Early Childhood Setting," and answer the following questions:

1. What three principles of Developmentally Appropriate Practice are shown in this video?

2. How does the video illustrate the importance of play as being central to Developmentally Appropriate Practice?

naeyc

DIVERSITY

BRAIN STORM

LEARNING BY DOING

An important function of a curriculum is to facilitate children's learning in a developmentally appropriate way. Brain research identifies teaching strategies that help children learn and remember relevant and meaningful information and skills. Sousa, in his book, *How the Brain Learns,* (2006) reports the findings of studies that compared retention of learning after 24 hours when different teaching strategies are used. When children learned by doing—by using hands-on activities—they had a 75 percent retention rate. On the other hand, when children learned by hearing the teacher talk about a topic, the retention rate was only 5 percent. Children practicing a new skill initially store this new information in short-term memory, but with repetition, it moves into long-term memory storage. "Continued practice of the skill changes the brain structurally, and the younger the learner is, the easier it is for these changes to occur" (Sousa, 2006, p. 96). It is important that children have ample opportunities to learn by doing, regardless of what kind of curriculum model is used.

year, for instance), and is then filled in with details for shorter segments of time. Such programs generally base the curriculum on a series of themes. In other programs, the curriculum is derived from the interests of the children; planning is generally more spontaneous and flexible in such programs. Such a strategy is called an *emergent curriculum,* and it includes the kind of program used in Reggio Emilia (see Chapter 5) and in other project-based approaches (e.g., Helm & Katz, 2011). In this section, we will discuss both of these widely used approaches.

Themes

naeyc

Many early childhood programs are based on a thematic approach, also called a "traditional" early childhood curriculum (Moravcik & Feeney, 2009). Usually, the teacher decides ahead of time on a series of themes that are relevant to children, which, based on his or her best estimate, would engage their interest. Such themes can range from familiar topics such as family, pets, and the grocery store to more remote ones such as dinosaurs and the night sky. Content of an appropriate early childhood curriculum should be derived from the children's life experiences, based on what is concrete, and tied to their emerging skills. Consider that young children have been part of their physical and social world for only a very short time. They have so much to learn about the people, places, objects, and experiences in their environment. When you give careful consideration to making the elements of the environment meaningful and understandable to children, you need not seek esoteric and unusual topics. Children's lives offer a rich set of topics on which to build a theme-based curriculum, including learning about themselves, their families, and the larger community in which they live (Essa & Rogers, 1992).

Key Point ◆

One method of curriculum planning revolves around themes, which are usually determined ahead of time by the teacher. Themes should be derived from the children's life experiences, including the children themselves, their families, and the community.

naeyc

CHILDREN AS THE FOCUS OF THE CURRICULUM. The most crucial skills with which young children can be armed to face the future are feelings of self-worth and competence. Children are well equipped for success if they are secure about their identities, feel good about themselves, and meet day-to-day tasks and challenges with a conviction that they can tackle almost anything. The curriculum can foster such attributes by contributing to children's self-understanding and providing repeated reinforcement and affirmation of their capabilities, individual uniqueness, and importance.

Self-understanding comes from learning more about oneself—one's identity, uniqueness, body, feelings, physical and emotional needs, likes and dislikes, skills and abilities, and self-care. Children enjoy learning about themselves, so a focus on children as part of the curriculum can and should take up a significant portion of time. It is important, however, to ensure that planned activities are age-appropriate so they contribute to both self-understanding and positive self-esteem. Two-year-olds, for instance, are still absorbed in learning to label body parts; thus, activities that contribute to sharpening this language skill are appropriate. Older

Appropriate curriculum is based on the children's interests, abilities, and experiences. The children's fascination with animals can be encouraged as they learn about their needs through helping to take care of the classroom pet.

© Cengage Learning

preschoolers and school-age children, however, are more interested in finer details. For example, they enjoy examining hair follicles under a microscope or observing how the joints of a skeleton move in comparison to those of their own bodies.

THE FAMILY AS THE FOCUS OF THE CURRICULUM. The family is vitally relevant to children and provides another rich basis for curriculum topics. We can help children build an understanding and appreciation of the roles of the family, similarities among families, the uniqueness of each family, different family forms, the tasks of families, and relationships among family members. Similarly, an examination of the children's family homes, means of transportation, food preferences, celebrations, parental occupations, and patterns of communication also provide appropriate curriculum topics. You might invite family members to come into the classroom and share special knowledge and talents. In addition, children as well as teachers might bring photographs of their families to share.

Themes that focus on the family contribute to children's feelings of self-esteem and pride. They can share information about something central to their lives, while at the same time expanding their understanding of the family lives of the other children. While such learning strengthens children's emerging socialization, it also contributes to cognitive development. Teachers help children make comparisons, note similarities and differences, organize information, and classify various aspects of family structure. Such comparisons need to be nonjudgmental and value each child's family.

THE COMMUNITY AS THE FOCUS OF THE CURRICULUM. Children's awareness of their world can particularly be expanded through themes related to the community. Young children have had experience with numerous aspects of their community, especially shopping, medical, and recreational elements. The community and those who live and work in it can certainly extend the walls of your program and offer a wealth of learning opportunities and curriculum material.

From the community and the people who work in it, children can learn about local forms of transportation; food growing, processing, and distribution; health services, including the role of doctors, nurses, dentists, dental hygienists, health clinics, and hospitals; safety provisions such as fire and police departments; communications facilities, including radio and television stations, newspapers, telephone services, and libraries; and local recreational facilities, such as parks, zoos, and museums. Children can visit an endless variety of appropriate places through field trips. (In Chapter 14, we will discuss field trips in more detail.) In addition, community professionals can be invited to visit your class to share information and tools of their professions with the children.

You can help children begin to build an understanding of the community as a social system by focusing on the interrelatedness of the people who live and work in your area. For instance, people are both providers and consumers of goods and services—the dentist buys bread that the baker produces, and the baker visits the dentist when he has a cavity.

In addition, the larger physical environment of the area in which you live provides a setting worth exploring with the children in your class. Your approach will vary, depending on whether your community is nestled in the mountains, by the ocean, or in the midst of rolling plains. Most young children living in

Kansas, for instance, will not have experienced the ocean. It is difficult to convey what the ocean is like to someone who has never seen it, and this is particularly true for children who rely on concrete, firsthand experience. Therefore, it makes little sense to plan a unit on "the ocean" when it is more than 1,000 miles away. Instead, focus on what is nearby and real in the environment, on what children have some familiarity with and can actually experience.

DEVELOPING WRITTEN PLANS FOR A THEME-BASED CURRICULUM

As we discussed earlier, the curriculum can be viewed as a comprehensive master plan. Once this larger curriculum is in place, units that cover shorter periods of time, daily lesson plans, and individual activities can be developed to fit into the curriculum. We will examine each of these elements. Also keep in mind that curriculum development must be a reflective activity through which teachers thoughtfully and intentionally plan experiences that promote positive outcomes for children.

Planning the Overall Curriculum

Key Point ◆

A written overall curriculum or master plan for a relatively long period of time, such as a year, will facilitate further planning.

The preceding discussions—curriculum is based on enhancing the total development of children, it is founded on a good understanding of children, and it derives its content from children's life experiences—provide direction for curriculum planning. Many programs develop a master plan that spans a typical cycle of time—in most instances, this is a year—and defines some broad topics you wish to cover. Putting together a curriculum master plan requires thoughtful consideration. It should provide a flexible guide, which gives general direction for the year but also allows for input from the children and personalization to reflect the character of the class and its individual children and teachers as the year progresses.

Units

Key Point ◆

Units that revolve around specific themes bring the larger curriculum down to a manageable size for planning and should follow a progression based on how children learn.

Units bring the broad curriculum outline down to a manageable size and provide unifying themes around which activities are planned. A unit can last any length of time, from a day or two to a month or more. It may seem practical to make all units fit into a one-week framework, but keep in mind that it should be the complexity, interest-value, and relevance of the topic to the children that dictate how much time is spent on a unit. Furthermore, the length of units should be flexible so that you can spend more time if the topic intrigues the children or cut it short if the children seem ready to move on. A brief outline of steps in the development of a unit can be found in Figure 8-5.

Planning a unit should begin by carefully considering objectives. What is it that you want the children to learn about the topic? What concepts, skills, and information can this unit convey? Most important, are these relevant, age-appropriate, and of interest to the children and will the children enjoy them? Children have to be the starting point for planning.

A unit should begin with an introduction through which the theme is initially presented. The length of time spent on the introductory component

Figure **8-5**

Steps in Planning a Unit

1. Identify appropriate objectives.
2. Introduce the new theme through review of familiar aspects of the topic.
3. Introduce new information.
   ▶ First concretely, such as through a field trip
   ▶ Through activities that recall the new experience, such as drawing pictures or dictating stories
   ▶ Creative representations of the new experience, such as through art, dramatic play, or blocks
4. Summarize and evaluate.
   ▶ Bread is baked at the bakery.
   ▶ The baker is the person who bakes bread.
   ▶ Many loaves of bread are baked at the bakery (mass production).
   ▶ Bread is made up of many ingredients.
   ▶ Bread is taken by trucks to grocery stores, where it is sold to people such as those in the children's families.

will depend on the length of the unit and on how new the topic is to the children. Often, the introduction takes place during a large-group discussion time.

Introductory components will generally focus on a review of the children's familiarity with the subject or closely related areas and will allow for evaluation of what the children already know about the topic. Thus, if you plan a unit on the topic "bread," you can discuss, for instance, types of bread with which the children are familiar, the food group in which bread belongs (assuming you have already spent time discussing nutrition and the basic food groups), the process of baking (for those children who have helped their family make bread), and the different ways in which bread is used in meals.

Once the topic is introduced, new ideas or information can be presented logically and sequentially. New material should always be presented first in a concrete manner. This often takes the form of a field trip, but concrete experiences can be brought into the classroom through objects or guests. In the case of the bakery unit, you may want to plan a field trip to a local bakery at the beginning of the unit so the children can see how bread is made; however, some in-class experiences with bread baking can be a wonderful preparation for a trip to the bakery. In either case, it cannot be emphasized enough that any new concept should begin with the concrete, with first-hand experience.

Once children have had a chance to observe and learn through firsthand experience, they can begin to assimilate this information through subsequent activities. After the field trip, children should have opportunities to factually represent what they observed by talking about and dictating accounts of the visit to the bakery, drawing pictures of what they saw on the field trip, kneading bread dough, and otherwise recalling and

© Cengage Learning

Follow-up activities help reinforce and clarify concepts learned on the field trip. After a visit to the bakery, the children are now kneading bread dough that will be baked in the school kitchen. How does such an activity reinforce what was learned at the bakery?

replicating their visit. This factual recounting allows children to fix the experience in their minds.

Children can begin to use new information in creative ways once it has been integrated into their existing memory and experiential store. They can play with the information through activities such as art, dramatic play, puppets, or blocks. This element of the unit offers a wide variety of possibilities that children can approach in their unique ways.

Finally, a unit is ended through a summarizing component. Children and the teacher review the major features of the unit and what was learned. The teacher can also engage in a final evaluation of how well the children have met the objectives.

Lesson Plans

lesson plans
The working documents from which the daily program is run, specifying directions for activities.

Daily **lesson plans** provide the working documents from which a program is run. A lesson plan is fitted into the structure set by the schedule, as discussed earlier. At a minimum, the lesson plan describes each activity planned for that day, objectives for activities, and the time frame within which they are carried out. In addition, it can give information about which teacher will be in charge of the activity, in what part of the classroom each activity is to be carried out, and what materials are needed. Lesson plans can take many forms, but they should be complete enough so that any teacher can pick one up and know for any given day what activities are planned and why they are planned.

Key Point ◆◆

Daily lesson plans, by specifying activities and objectives, provide the working documents from which the program is run.

Activities

The smallest element of curriculum planning is the activity, the actual play in which the children will be involved. It is important to be aware of the objectives of a given activity as well as to think through how the activity will be carried out so that the children will gain the knowledge and skills you would like them to acquire.

emergent curriculum
An alternative to the theme-based curriculum; topics are developed based on the interests of the children.

project approach
A curriculum that expands children's learning through in-depth exploration of topics that are of interest to children and teachers.

EMERGENT CURRICULUM

Over the past several decades, considerable attention has been focused on the programs of Reggio Emilia in northern Italy (see Chapter 5). Many American schools have, in turn, adapted the lessons learned from the Reggio approach to their own programs. This alternative approach to a more traditional theme-based curriculum is often called an **emergent curriculum** because it emerges out of the interests of the children. In addition, American educators have re-focused attention on the **project approach**, which dates back several decades (Helm & Katz, 2011; Moravcik & Feeney, 2009) and shares many of the features that make Reggio Emilia's programs unique. The project approach, like Reggio Emilia programs, expands children's and teachers' learning through in-depth exploration of topics of interest to children and teachers.

There are a number of integral components of an emergent curriculum that are particularly relevant to the programs of Reggio Emilia. Among these are the image of the child, the environment, the projects that make up the emergent "curriculum," and documentation (Gandini, 2004). Also vital is the role of the

Key Point ◆◆

An alternative to traditional, teacher-controlled curriculum planning is the emergent curriculum, which is based on in-depth exploration of topics of interest to children and teachers. The centerpiece of such a curriculum is long-range projects, which engage children's interest and enjoyment of learning and flexibly follow the interests that emerge out of the children's and teachers' investigations.

teacher as a reflective collaborator with children and colleagues. We will examine these elements of the emergent curriculum in this section.

Image of the Child

One of the most basic principles of the programs of Reggio Emilia is the importance of viewing children as competent and strong rather than as needy and weak. "All children, each one in a unique way, have preparedness, potential, curiosity, and interest in engaging in social interaction, in establishing relationships, and in constructing their learning while negotiating with everything in their environment" (Gandini, 2004, p. 16). This image of children ensures that teachers' expectations and interactions are highly appropriate. Recognizing their abilities, adults respect and encourage children's ideas and thoughts and use these as the basis for the curriculum. Teachers learn from children by carefully observing and listening to them. This sense of co-learning places children and teachers on an equal plane. Children are seen as powerful learners who are strong and competent, with a desire to experience their world and communicate with others, right from birth (Rinaldi, 2001). Visitors to Reggio Emilia remark on the visible evidence of how children are viewed as they observe highly competent, self-directed infants, toddlers, and children in action.

© Cengage Learning

A classroom project on using recycled materials led one four-year-old to make a whimsical self-portrait out of a variety of items that might have been discarded. Soon other children also created self-portraits, each coming up with a unique depiction of himself or herself. The children spent many weeks collecting and exploring ways to use recycled materials.

naeyc

The Environment

naeyc

Children deserve, and require, a thoughtfully planned, beautiful environment, what Lella Gandini (1993) calls an "amiable school" (p. 6). The environment sends the message that each classroom is a place where children and adults are "engaged together in the pleasure of learning" (Gandini, 1997, p. 18); thus, the environment is considered the "third teacher" (Saltz, 1997). The environment is very carefully arranged to be welcoming and aesthetically pleasing. Light, texture, color, and form all are carefully used to extend and expand learning (Ceppi & Zini, 1998). Furthermore, the environment is arranged to respect children's innate curiosity, drive to explore, and need to interact.

One of the unique aspects of Reggio Emilia environments is the inclusion of an art studio (atelier) as part of each school. This space includes a wealth of resource materials and media through which the children can express their learning. Art is considered an integral part of symbolic learning, a way for children to construct their ideas (Gandini, Hill, Cadwell, & Schwall, 2005). In the atelier, children are encouraged to draw or sculpt what they have been thinking about as a way of explaining and clarifying their thinking process. Anyone who has seen the Reggio Emilia exhibit "The Hundred Languages of Children," which has been touring the United States for several decades, marvels at the beauty and sophistication of the artwork of Reggio Emilia's children. Their art comes out of careful observation and thoughtful reflection about the topics and issues they are working on.

The Emergent Curriculum: Projects

naeyc

Much of what goes on in classrooms that use an emergent approach is similar to the types of activities that take place in any high-quality early childhood program. Children engage in a wide range of self-selected appropriate activities such as with blocks, manipulatives, art materials, dramatic play props, books, and other materials. They interact with each other and with adults in a variety of meaningful ways. It is in the emergence of curriculum, however, that such programs differ from other, more traditional programs.

Ideas for curriculum content come from observation of children's interests and activities, not from what the teachers think the children should learn (Curtis & Carter, 1996). One of the hallmarks of the emergent approach is that teachers truly listen to and reflect on what the children convey. Teachers meet with small groups of children and engage in serious dialogue about things that are important to the children (Cadwell & Fyfe, 2004). Through open-ended questions, teachers can gain great insight into what matters to the children. Such discussions are frequent and ongoing. Children are encouraged to ask questions, and they find answers to these questions through their own exploration and investigation (Helm & Katz, 2011).

There are numerous examples of how children's ideas are converted into a curriculum, many of which have been documented in articles, books, and films. One classic example comes from Reggio Emilia, following a suggestion by the children that the birds in their school's yard would appreciate an amusement park. This idea has been documented in a video, "An Amusement Park for the Birds" (Forman & Gandini, 1994), which follows the project from its initial mention to its culmination four months later. Continued discussion and observation by the teachers shaped the activities of this project to keep the interests and enthusiasm of the children in focus. Topics such as the building of a town (Bayman, 1995), the collection and classifying of rocks (Diffily, 1996), bicycles, building construction, newspapers, and even the all-too-familiar neighborhood McDonald's (Helm, 1996) provide the basis for themes that engage and fascinate children and that provide the foundation for a wide range of learning experiences. Projects on ideas initiated by the children and furthered by the teachers make up the heart of the curriculum in an emergent approach.

Documentation

naeyc

documentation
Documentation involves keeping a careful record of the children's involvement in projects; using photographs, samples of children's work, and a record of their words; and arranging these in an aesthetic and informative manner to illustrate the process of learning.

One other aspect of emergent programs, especially in Reggio Emilia, is the careful documentation of the children's work. **Documentation** involves keeping a careful record of the children's learning process in carrying out projects. "An effective piece of documentation tells the story and the purpose of an event, experience, or development" (Seitz, 2008, p. 88). Documentation can take the form of photographs, videotapes, transcriptions of audiotapes of the children's discussions, samples of their work, teacher's reflections on the learning process, and other visual evidence. Typically, documentation shows the progress of a project through several stages. Documentation should illustrate how the children began, carried out, and culminated a project (Katz & Chard, 1997). It is carefully arranged to be aesthetically pleasing as well as informative and is displayed in a prominent place in the school.

Documentation serves several purposes. Children, teachers, families, and the public can be informed through documentation (Forman & Fyfe, 1998;

Seitz, 2008). Children gain a greater depth of understanding of the concepts they are exploring by revisiting the record or documentation of their work. Teachers, through examining and revisiting the learning process shown in the documentation, can extend children's learning by planning follow-up activities that represent a logical next step. Documentation also helps families see in much clearer detail what their children are learning and gives them the opportunity to expand that learning; they see not just the end product but the process involved. Finally, the public can be informed about the abilities and learning process of children, making the school an integral part of the larger society (Rinaldi, 1998).

Final Thoughts on the Emergent Curriculum

An emergent curriculum provides an alternative to a more traditional curriculum. It is based on a strong belief in children's abilities and strength and is implemented in a carefully and beautifully arranged environment. Teachers are co-learners in an emergent classroom, learning from the children through attentive observation and thoughtful dialogue. Projects on wide-ranging topics of interest to the children engage their ideas and zest for learning. The progress of projects is flexible and leisurely, as children explore and teachers provide additional resources based on their observations. Finally, teachers organize materials they collect about each project into some form of documentation, which serves to help children, teachers, families, and even the larger community revisit and learn more about the process of learning. Perhaps the most relevant aspect of this curriculum is that it requires teachers to let go of control and to have faith in children and in their own abilities to develop experiences that are rich and powerful.

FAMILY INVOLVEMENT IN THE CURRICULUM

The curriculum should reflect the backgrounds, needs, and interests of the children. One excellent resource, as you plan a curriculum for your group of children, is their families. Frequent family–teacher communication and an open policy that conveys the school's emphasis on the importance of the family can encourage parents to be part of the early childhood program.

Family expertise and input can greatly enhance the early childhood program. Parents and other family members can provide information about special family, cultural, religious, or ethnic customs, celebrations, foods, or dress. They can visit the classroom to share occupational information or special skills. A family member who makes pottery, weaves baskets, plays an instrument, or knows origami will contribute a fascinating element to the classroom.

Some parents may be particularly interested in the direction and content of the curriculum and may want to offer suggestions or ideas. These should be welcomed and incorporated into the program, as appropriate. If, however, the values of a family seem to be at odds with the program's philosophy, the teacher or director ought to convey that, although she or he respects the family's views, the school has its own approach founded on child development principles and research. As a last resort, a parent who disagrees with the program's direction has the option of placing the child in another school if she is unhappy with the program.

Key Point

Families' values should be reflected in the curriculum; families are also a source of support and resources for the curriculum.

SUMMARY

1. Look at the common components of the daily schedule in an early childhood program.
2. Examine some guidelines for setting an effective schedule.
3. The age of the children, and whether a program operates full-day or part-day, will have an impact on the schedule and what it includes.
4. The schedule should be consistent and predictable, but also flexible when needed.
5. Consideration of the curriculum includes both definition and examination of its elements.
   A. A curriculum needs to be directly related to the development of the children in the program.
   B. A curriculum must include relevant content to be appropriate.
6. Consider the development of written plans, including the overall curriculum, units, daily lesson plans, and activities.
7. An emergent curriculum provides an alternative to a theme-based curriculum, and is based more on the teacher's observations of what interests the children.
   A. The philosophy of emergent programs, such as those of Reggio Emilia, views children as capable and strong.
   B. Projects based on children's interests are the basis of curriculum planning in emergent programs.
   C. Projects often are carried out over a long period of time—weeks, even months—as children and teachers engage in in-depth exploration of a topic of interest.
   D. Children's learning is carefully documented to show the process, not just the end products.

KEY TERMS LIST

activity time	large-group time
curriculum	lesson plans
documentation	project approach
emergent curriculum	self-demand schedule

KEY QUESTIONS

1. Visit an early childhood program and look at its daily schedule. What elements are included? Does the schedule seem developmentally appropriate in that it takes into account the needs of the children? Does it provide the kind of balance discussed in this chapter? Would you change anything in this schedule? Why, or why not?
2. Consider the issue of child-initiated versus teacher-initiated activity. Do you agree that there should be ample time for children to make decisions and exercise independence, or do you think more teacher control is important? Note that not everyone agrees on this question. Discuss this question with others in your class and consider both sides of the issue.
3. You probably know children like Rita, who spend most of their day in a child care center. How are the needs of these children met? How do they differ from a child like David? In what ways can the schedule take the children's needs into consideration?

4. What are your memories of your earliest school experiences? What kinds of activities were involved? Can you glean from your recollections what type of curriculum your preschool, child care, kindergarten, or first-grade teacher might have been following?

5. If there is a school in your community that follows an emergent, project-based curriculum, observe this school to look for elements of such programs, as discussed in this section. Do you see evidence of child-centered activities, projects, documentation, and a carefully arranged, aesthetic environment reflective of the children and teachers?

ADDITIONAL RESOURCES

Select additional books, articles, and websites on topics discussed in Chapter 8.

Copple, C. E., & Bredekamp, S. (2009). *Developmentally appropriate practice in early childhood programs serving children from birth through age 8* (3rd ed.). Washington, DC: NAEYC.

Fraser, S., & Gestwicki, C. (2001). *Authentic childhood: Exploring Reggio Emilia in the classroom.* Clifton Park, NY: Thomson Delmar Learning.

Helm, J. H., & Katz, L. (2011). *Young investigators: The project approach in the early years* (2nd ed.). New York: Teachers College Press.

HELPFUL WEBSITES

Reggio Children:

http://zerosei.comune.re.it

Reggio Children is the Italian-based organization that manages the exchange of information between the Reggio Emilia programs of Italy and interested professionals and programs across the world. This website provides a wealth of information about Reggio programs.

Teaching Strategies, Inc.:

www.teachingstrategies.com

This website for the Creative Curriculum provides a variety of developmentally appropriate information and strategies for early childhood education teachers and parents of young children.

The Center for Best Practices in Early Childhood Education:

www.wiu.edu/thecenter

The Center, at Western Illinois University, aims to develop and promote practices designed to improve educational opportunities for all young children.

Go to **CengageBrain.com** to register your access code for this book's Education CourseMate website, where you will find more resources to help you study. Additional resources for this chapter include TeachSource Videos, glossary flashcards, web links, case studies with critical-thinking questions that apply the concepts presented in this chapter, and more. If your textbook does not include a printed access card, you can go to **CengageBrain.com** to purchase access.

9 *Creative Development through the Curriculum*

 Teachers give children daily opportunities for creative expression and aesthetic appreciation. Children explore and enjoy various forms of dramatic play, music, dance, and visual arts. Whether or not there are specialist teachers for the arts, classroom teachers meaningfully integrate the arts into children's learning experiences.

Developmentally Appropriate Practice, Copple & Bredekamp, 2009, p. 175

In Chapter 9, you will find answers to the following questions about providing for creative development through the curriculum:

▶ Why is creativity so important for young children, and how can you nurture it?
▶ What are appropriate art and music activities for young children of different ages and abilities?
▶ What are some guiding principles that will help you create developmentally appropriate art and music activities for young children?
▶ What elements in young children's social environment can stifle creativity?

NAEYC STANDARDS CONSIDERED IN CHAPTER 9

(See the Standards Correlation Chart on the inside front cover of this book for the titles and description of the standards listed below.)

▶ *Standard 5a:* Understanding the importance of creative development, theories that explain its importance, and the creative activities that promote it (pp. 221–222; 225–228; 237–238).
▶ *Standard 1c:* Providing environments that support creativity (pp. 222–225).
▶ *Standard 5a:* Being familiar with content knowledge related to the arts, including visual arts, music, movement, and dance (pp. 229–236; 238–242).
▶ *Standard 5c:* Using art media and activities to develop meaningful and challenging experiences that are an integral part of curriculum (pp. 228–229).
▶ *Standard 1b:* Promoting creativity through appropriate and meaningful activities for children of different ages and abilities (pp. 242–244).
▶ *Standard 2b:* Partnering with families in valuing activities that foster creativity and in understanding that some activities inhibit creativity (pp. 244–245).

One of the most rewarding joys of working with young children is watching them approach experiences with that spark of freshness and exuberance that opens the door to creativity. Each of us possesses some measure of creativity—some more, some less. This is especially true of young children, for whom creativity increases a sense of competence and well-being (Drew & Rankin (2004).

Unfortunately, there is a danger of their creativity being stifled through increasing pressure to conform to adult expectations (Mayesky, 2012). In this chapter, we will examine creativity in some detail.

WHAT IS CREATIVITY?

Creativity has been defined in a number of ways. Most definitions include such concepts as originality, imagination, divergent thinking (seeing things from different viewpoints), and the ability to create something new or to combine things in novel but meaningful ways. "The goal of engaging in creative arts is to communicate, think, and feel" (Drew & Rankin, 2004). Creativity is more likely to occur when the person possesses traits such as curiosity, flexibility, and interest in investigation and exploration.

Not satisfied with the limited definition of intelligence imposed by tests that measure it by a series of single, "correct" answers, J. P. Guilford (1962) developed a new way of looking at intelligence that includes some of these traits. In Guilford's structure of the intellect, **divergent thinking** is differentiated from **convergent thinking,** both of which are involved in the creative process. Divergence, by one definition, is "the making in the mind of many from one," for instance, by elaborating on a topic as in brainstorming, whereas convergence is defined as "the making of one from many," through narrowing down many ideas to a single, focused point (Hampden-Turner, 1981, p. 104).

One trait often associated with creative thinking is **fluency,** the ability to generate many relevant ideas on a given topic in a limited time. Five-year-old Michelle wonderfully displayed fluency when she was confronted with a sheet of paper containing 20 circles and was asked to draw as many different items from these circles as she could in two minutes. After using some of the circles to make the more conventional face, balloon, ball, sun, orange, and flower, she then created an ashtray, glass, light bulb, and pencil eraser as they would be seen from the top. She had used all but one row of the circles when the teacher told her that she needed to finish in a few seconds. Michelle, after a moment's thought, drew two parallel lines under the remaining row of circles, connected them with crosshatches, then put boxes on top of the circles, creating a quick but recognizable train.

Another measure of creativity is **flexibility,** the capability of adapting readily to change in a positive, productive manner. Three-year-old Ramon showed flexibility when another child accidentally knocked water on the lines that he had carefully painted in different hues of watercolors. After a fleeting look of dismay crossed his face, Ramon surveyed his picture and declared, "Look, the water made new colors!"

A third trait related to creativity is **sensitivity,** a receptivity to external and internal stimuli. Creative people have a heightened awareness of their world, their perceptions, feelings, and images. They often experience through their senses what others miss. The creative child will, most likely, be the one who points out that a cloud looks like a speeding motorboat, appreciatively sniffs the aroma of freshly sawed wood at the woodworking activity, or delights in the softness of the soapy water when blowing bubbles.

naeyc

Key Point ◆

A definition of creativity includes concepts such as originality, imagination, divergent thinking, novelty, fluency, flexibility, and sensitivity to stimuli.

divergent thinking
The act of expanding or elaborating on an idea, for example, brainstorming.

convergent thinking
The act of narrowing many ideas into a single, focused point.

fluency
A measure of creativity involving the ability to generate many relevant ideas on a given topic in a limited time.

flexibility
A measure of creativity involving the capability to adapt readily to change in a positive, productive manner.

sensitivity
As related to creativity, sensitivity refers to a receptivity to external and internal stimuli.

© Cengage Learning

Creative children are more sensitive to the environment, more tuned into its sensations. One trait common to creative people is heightened sensory awareness. What are some other traits of creative children?

multiple intelligences
Howard Gardner's theory that our minds use many types of intelligence, not just those traditionally included in the educational context.

linguistic intelligence
Ability and sensitivity to spoken and written language.

logico-mathematical intelligence
Skills needed for logical, analytical, mathematical, and scientific tasks.

musical intelligence
Skills needed in the performance, composition, and appreciation of music.

bodily kinesthetic intelligence
Effective use of the body to solve problems or create products.

visual-spatial intelligence
The ability to manipulate and portray visual images.

naturalistic intelligence
The ability to see patterns and relationships to nature, also called "nature smarts."

Multiple Intelligences

Children learn and express what they know in many different ways. Through his theory of **multiple intelligences,** Howard Gardner (1983) proposed a view of intelligence that takes into account the many ways in which people express their knowledge. Gardner's theory suggests that there are ways of learning that go beyond those traditionally included in education and those measured in traditional tests of intelligence. Particularly in our educational settings, there is a tendency to focus on linguistic and logico-mathematical intelligence (Gardner, 1999). However, according to Gardner, there are many other, less recognized ways in which our understanding of the world can be shown. Some of these are expressed through creative means rather than through language or mathematics.

What are these multiple intelligences proposed by Gardner? We have already mentioned **linguistic intelligence,** which involves ability with and sensitivity to spoken and written language, and **logico-mathematical intelligence,** which includes skill in analytical, scientific tasks. The next three intelligences are especially related to creativity, notably in the arts. **Musical intelligence** is seen in the performance, composition, and appreciation of music. **Bodily kinesthetic intelligence** involves the potential to use the body effectively to solve problems or create products, as seen in athletes, dancers, surgeons, mechanics, and others. The ability to manipulate and portray visual images is seen through **visual-spatial intelligence.** Gardner also includes interpersonal, intrapersonal, spiritual, and existential intelligences in his list. More recently, Gardner (1999, 2006) added **naturalistic intelligence,** the ability to find patterns and relationships to nature. This intelligence is related to what we discussed in Chapter 7 about the need of children to have contact with the natural environment (Louv, 2008). Gardner also uses the term *nature smarts* to describe naturalistic intelligence (Gardner, 1999).

Viewing intelligence as more than abilities expressed through language and math alone broadens the way we work with young children. Research has shown that children (like adults) have intellectual strengths in some areas and are less capable in others; thus, different types of learning experiences are helpful to children in different ways (Bowman, Donovan, & Burns, 2001). Recognizing that intelligence is expressed in many ways—what Reggio Emilia educators call "the hundred languages of children" (Nelson, 1997)—allows those who work with young children to recognize and value the many ways in which children communicate their ideas. Thus, as we embark on our discussion of creativity in this chapter, thinking of children's expression in art, music, dance, drama, and many other media as alternative forms of intelligence provides a context for nurturing and encouraging the many ways in which children represent their ideas.

AN ENVIRONMENT THAT ENCOURAGES CREATIVITY

naeyc

In our earlier definition of creativity, we examined some traits characteristic of the creative process. The early childhood setting should provide an environment in which these traits are encouraged and valued. Such an environment, however, goes far beyond providing materials for artistic expression. The creative environment is not only made up of the physical arrangement, but is also permeated by an attitude of openness, acceptance, and encouragement. We will examine both of these aspects: the attitudes that promote creativity and the physical parameters of such an environment.

Attitudes That Encourage Creativity

Creativity, as we have seen, is related to flexibility, divergent thinking, and openness to new ideas. Young children's minds strive toward making sense of their world by organizing information and input. Once they become familiar with and master new concepts, they are free to use these in various ways. If we use what we learn in only one way, we are limited and rigid in our approach. Flexible or creative thinking is a mind set that can be encouraged in an open classroom atmosphere. A creative environment promotes new perceptions of and responses to the world.

Creativity has to be nurtured, and the teacher plays an important role in fostering creativity by providing a variety of materials and encouraging imaginative use of them. When children are allowed creative expression, each will produce a different outcome. The teacher's acceptance of all the children's work and unique responses gives them the opportunity to learn that people feel and think differently and that this is all right and valued. Teachers also help children develop awareness of patterns and relationships between what they create and their previous knowledge and experiences (Drew & Rankin, 2004). "Creative acts incorporate previous learning and experiences as well as new expression" (Matlock & Hornstein, 2004, p. 15).

Creativity, however, does not always result in a product, although we traditionally tend to think of the picture, story, or dance as the creative product. But the process, as much as the product, is important for young children. In the process, the child can do the following:

Creativity is nurtured when children have access to a wide variety of materials and are encouraged to use them in their own unique ways.

Key Point ◆◇

An open classroom atmosphere, where flexible and imaginative thinking are valued, will encourage creativity.

- Experiment ("What will happen if I put this block across the top of these two?").
- Enjoy the sensory experience ("Squishing the play dough between my fingers feels nice!").
- Communicate ("I'm a bird!").
- Relive experiences ("I'll tell the 'baby' she has to go to bed because that's what big people always tell me.").
- Work out fears ("I'll be the doctor, and my dolly will be the baby who gets the shot!").

As children mature, as their motor and perceptual skills improve, and as they plan ahead more, their creative efforts may well result in purposeful products. But toddlers and young preschoolers are much more involved in the process of creative experiences. For one-, two-, three-, and many four-year-olds, any end product is usually secondary to the enjoyment of doing the activity.

The teacher, by encouraging children to solve problems, also fosters creativity. By helping children think through different alternatives and find various solutions, the teacher expands their creative capacity. The teacher is a facilitator rather than the one who comes up with answers or solutions, however.

Divergent thinking involves the opportunity to go off in different directions and to explore various strategies. The teacher's acceptance of children's suggestions and willingness to try these tells them that they are capable of having worthwhile ideas.

Another way of accepting and encouraging children's creative work is through uncritical acknowledgment. Well-intentioned praise ("I like your picture.") can stifle creativity because it imposes a value judgment, or becomes meaningless when it is repeated to every child. Rather than evaluating, comparing, or trying to read meaning into nonrepresentational art, a teacher can remark on the process ("You glued the squares on first, then you glued circles over them."); recognize the work that has gone into the picture ("You've really worked hard on this sculpture!"); or comment on its design qualities ("You're using lots of big circles!") (Fox & Schirrmacher, 2012).

In setting an appropriate climate for creativity, it is also important to provide enough time for children to get involved in and complete their projects. Children need to have ample time blocks during the day during which they can explore and try out their ideas. When the time set aside for child-selected activity is short, children tend not to get very involved, thus missing opportunities to engage in creative activity. Children may continue to pursue a creative project over a period of time.

open-ended materials
Early childhood materials that are flexible rather than structured and can be used in a variety of ways rather than in only a single manner.

Key Point ◆◆

A variety of open-ended materials in the environment will encourage creativity.

The early childhood environment promotes creativity by allowing children to explore freely and to select from a variety of accessible materials.

© Cengage Learning

A Physical Environment That Encourages Creativity

The physical setting can support creativity through provision of, and access to, a wide range of **open-ended materials,** ones that lend themselves to various uses. Whenever children are confronted with material that has multiple uses, they have to make choices about how to use the material and have to use imagination because it does not dictate a single outcome. Furthermore, each time they use the materials, they can do so in a unique way. In fact, children do not need a different art activity each day. When a different set of limited materials is provided every day, children never get the chance to explore in depth or experiment with common, basic materials.

A well-stocked early childhood program will be full of open-ended materials. Examples include a wide variety of art materials, manipulatives, blocks, sensory materials, puppets, dramatic play props, musical instruments, and versatile outdoor equipment. (This is not to say that single-purpose materials—for instance, puzzles—are not important, but they meet different developmental needs and are not particularly suited for creative development.) The physical arrangement of the room can also facilitate creativity. Clearly organized classroom areas let children know where they can engage in various creative activities; for instance, where they can build or where they might experiment with messy media. Classroom areas should be set up so that traffic flow does not interfere with or disrupt ongoing activity.

At the same time, children should be able to move freely from one activity to another. When materials are organized and visible on accessible shelves, the children know what is available for them to use independently. These materials should be attractively displayed and uncluttered so that children can see possible new combinations they might try. Such an orderly display also conveys a respect for the materials. Similarly, a safe place to store finished products or an area in which these might be displayed also tells the children that their creative endeavors are valued and respected.

Inclusion of the arts can also increase children's awareness and appreciation of arts from their own culture. Teachers can display prints of artworks and books that show reproductions of such art in the classroom; invite local artists to share their talents; or take the children on excursions to art galleries, museums, or performances to enhance the children's appreciation of their cultural communities (Copple & Bredekamp, 2009).

DIVERSITY

Technology and Creative Arts

A range of technological tools can enhance children's creative experiences, if used appropriately. Drawing tablets such as Sketchboard Studio© from KB Interactive allows children to use the computer for drawing activities. Other tools, such as digital and nondigital cameras, printers, scanners, photocopiers, and the Internet can also support children's experiences (Fox & Schirrmacher, 2012). An example comes from the Reggio Emilia film, "An Amusement Park for the Birds," in which preschool children took photographs of the fountains in the park to study them more carefully. Recall also the photography project described in Chapter 5's "Stories from the Field" box, facilitated by student teacher Amanda with a group of four-year-olds. Another idea comes from DAP, which suggests "using computer software that translates key strokes or mouse clicks into musical notes to gain understanding that symbols can represent ideas" (Copple & Bredekamp, 2009, p. 315).

The remainder of this chapter examines two specific classroom areas in which creativity is likely to flourish: art and music. This discussion is somewhat arbitrary, however, in that creativity can and should occur in every aspect of the early childhood program. One of the difficulties in writing a book such as this one is that some organizational decisions have to be made that place activities into categories that are not nearly as clear in reality as they appear to be in the book. Although art and music foster creativity, they also promote cognition, socialization, language, emotional release, sensory stimulation, and muscle development. Similarly, language, outdoor motor, or manipulative activities can be very creative (as we will point out in the ensuing chapters, where such activities have been placed). As you read on, then, keep in mind that good early childhood activities serve many purposes, meet many needs, and above all contribute to development of the whole child.

ART

Art, in its broadest sense, encompasses the application of creative imagination to a unique product through a wide variety of modes. Art can result in a painting, a sculpture, a collage, a song, a dance, a novel, or a poem. In the context of early childhood education, *art* usually refers to the creative process as applied to two-dimensional graphic arts (painting, drawing, print making) and to three-dimensional modeling arts (using clay or play dough, creating sculptures).

Art has been part of early childhood education since its earliest beginnings. Young children seem to gravitate to art activities through which they can express themselves nonverbally; find satisfying sensory experiences; experiment with a variety of materials; and work in a free, uninhibited way not characteristic of many other aspects of their lives.

Key Point

In its broadest sense, art involves the application of creativity to a unique product through a variety of modes.

Theories of Art Development

You have probably observed a four-year-old boy, crayon in hand, produce a house with a door, windows, and chimney; an adjacent tree with curly, green circles atop a brown stem; and a person next to the house, his stick legs floating slightly above ground level and his head reaching the house's chimney. How did this child come to produce such a picture? What does the picture mean? Where did he learn the skills, since not so long ago his pictures were made up of scribbles? How was he able to translate the image of a house, tree, and person into a recognizable depiction? A number of theories have been proposed to answer such questions and explain how children's art develops.

PSYCHOANALYTIC THEORY. This theory proposes that children's art emerges from emotion and reflects what they feel. Art is an expression of the unconscious and can be interpreted to give insight into a child's personality or emotional state. The use of color, line, size, shape, and space, as well as the complexity of art, convey meaning that a psychoanalyst might read. Although some researchers have found support for a link between art and emotional state, others have found little relationship. A number of common early childhood activities stem from the psychoanalytic theory, particularly the use of fingerpaints, clay, and free-flowing tempera paint. Such activities allow children to release emotion and express themselves freely (Seefeldt, 1999).

PERCEPTUAL THEORY. This theory suggests that children draw what they see. Vision projects an image of the real object on the retina, while perception restructures and interprets the image based on factors such as prior experience, personality, and neurological structure (Fox & Schirrmacher, 2012). Part of the perceptual process involves translating a three-dimensional object into a two-dimensional drawing, a challenge even for adults, let alone young children. Perceptual theory suggests that a drawing will focus on what the child perceives as the most important features of the object because our eyes take in more than we consciously perceive. Practical applications of this theory have led to instructional art programs whose goal is to help children focus on detail and to improve their visual discrimination (Seefeldt, 1999).

COGNITIVE THEORIES. Such theories assume that children draw what they know. The more developed a child's familiarity with a concept or subject, the more detailed or sophisticated the drawing will be. Older children have had a greater number of experiences and more time in which to develop more sophisticated concepts; therefore, their artwork is recognizable.

Piaget discusses the evolution of children's drawings in terms of the developing concept of space (Cox, 1986). In the **scribbling stage,** between the ages of two and four, the child experiments with marks on a page. As the child recognizes that these marks can represent real things, the child begins to give them meaning. Cox tells how her daughter drew a shape, then, in surprise, exclaimed that it was a bird, noting that it needed an eye and adding a dot. In the later **preschematic stage,** from approximately age four to age seven, the child does have a subject in mind when beginning a picture, but the actual product will be an inaccurate, crude representation of the real thing. It isn't until an older age, in the **schematic stage,** that the child's representations become more realistic and accurate. Children's art is also related to Piaget's

Key Point

Psychoanalytic theory holds that art emerges from children's emotions and reflects what they are feeling.

Key Point

Perceptual theory suggests that children draw what they see.

Key Point

Cognitive theory assumes that children draw what they know and that their drawings are reflected in a series of stages.

scribbling stage
The stage in the development of art in which children experiment with marks on a page.

preschematic stage
The stage in the development of art in which children have a subject in mind when they begin a picture, but in which the actual product will be an inaccurate, crude representation of the real thing.

schematic stage
Older children's drawings, which are more realistic and accurate than younger children's in what they depict.

concept of object permanence (Seefeldt, 1999), a recognition that objects continue to exist even when they are out of view. The child, in other words, can evoke a mental image of that object, which is necessary in order to represent the object in a drawing.

DEVELOPMENTAL THEORIES. These theories advocate that children's art ability develops naturally, through a series of universal stages, and that adult intervention or direct teaching can, in fact, adversely affect this development. A view widely accepted by early childhood educators is that the teacher's role is to create a secure environment, make a wide range of materials available, and provide appropriate guidance to facilitate art (Seefeldt, 1999). Howard Gardner (1989) noted an interesting contrast to this approach that he observed during his stay in China, where art techniques are carefully taught to children. The Chinese view would suggest that before people can be creative, they have to achieve competence in using the techniques of the art, techniques that have been developed through long-established traditions that do not need to be reinvented and should not be bypassed.

Researchers have proposed developmental stages of art. Congruent with Piaget's and Vygotsky's theories, children's drawings can be described as evolving in three stages, which are influenced by cognitive development and culture (Davis & Gardner, 1993). From ages 1 to 5, the dominance of universal patterns, and from ages 5 to 7, the flowering of drawing, children move from universal scribbles into unique expressions of artwork. These stages are followed by the height of cultural influence, from ages 7 to 12, when artistic re-creations become much more accurate and realistic and reflect an internalization of the culture.

In her classic book, *Analyzing Children's Art*, Rhoda Kellogg (1969) formulated a series of age-related stages that describe children's artistic development, based on her collection of more than 1 million pictures drawn by two- to eight-year-olds from around the world. In addition, she elaborated on the elements of children's art in each of these stages. Two-year-olds use the **basic scribbles,** 20 kinds of markings that form "the building blocks of art" (p. 15), the elements found in any artistic work. These include various straight and curved line patterns. In addition to examining basic scribbles, pictures can be analyzed in terms of **placement patterns,** 17 ways in which the total picture is framed or placed on the paper. By the age of three, children begin to make six recognizable **diagrams** or shapes, specifically the rectangle, oval, triangle, cross, X, and odd-shaped (but deliberate) line. Kellogg considers that "developmentally, the diagrams indicate an increasing ability to make a controlled use of lines and to employ memory" (p. 45).

In children's art, diagrams are seldom found alone, but rather in **combines** (two diagrams put together) and **aggregates** (combinations of three or more diagrams). Soon diagrams, combines, and aggregates suggest objects, often a face, and thus the transition to **pictorialism** begins, between the ages of four and five. Kellogg characterizes early pictorial efforts as humans, animals, buildings, vegetation, and transportation. Because of her extensive cross-cultural study of young children's art, Kellogg concludes that these stages are universal, occurring naturally in all children. She advises teachers and parents not to

Key Point
Developmental theories advocate that children's art develops naturally, through universal stages seen in children from all parts of the world.

Key Point
Rhoda Kellogg proposes age-related stages in children's art development, each marked by the emergence of unique elements in their art products.

basic scribbles
According to Rhoda Kellogg, the 20 fundamental markings found in all art.

placement patterns
According to Rhoda Kellogg, a way of analyzing children's art by examining the 17 ways in which the total picture or design is framed or placed on the paper.

diagrams
According to Rhoda Kellogg, the stage in children's art when they begin to use the six recognizable shapes—the rectangle, oval, triangle, X, cross, and the deliberate odd-shaped line.

combines
According to Rhoda Kellogg, a step in the development of art in which children combine two simple diagrams.

aggregates
Rhoda Kellogg's term for the step in the development of art in which children combine three or more simple diagrams.

pictorialism
According to Rhoda Kellogg, the stage in the development of art in which children draw recognizable objects.

As children get older, their drawings become more representational, moving from scribbles to recognizable pictures.

Figure **9-1**

Development of Young Children's Art

attempt to judge children's art, nor to provide instruction in how to draw specific objects. Figure 9-1 shows the drawings of children of different ages, illustrating Kellogg's progression in the development of children's art.

Art in Reggio Emilia Programs

The preschool programs of Reggio Emilia in northern Italy (review the discussion of these programs in Chapters 5 and 8) incorporate art into an integrated holistic approach to early education. Their influence has challenged our thinking about art for young children.

The traditional view of allowing children's art to develop naturally without intervention is being reconsidered by some early childhood educators. Observers of the Reggio Emilia schools note the maturity and complexity of the art produced by the children. One reason is that children are introduced to art materials and media at a very young age, during infancy. In this way, children gain an understanding of the uses and effects of various media long before their counterparts in more traditional programs. Observers also note that Reggio teachers take art very seriously and do not consider it a frivolous child's activity; they consider it a strong form of symbolic communication of ideas, feelings, and emotions. Furthermore, children use the same materials and media over and over, taking the time to develop the necessary skills to use them. What changes is the ideas that they are encouraged to express with these media (Seefeldt, 1995).

Art, like all aspects of the curriculum, is not taught as a separate discipline, but is integral to all aspects of the program. The studio teacher, or *atelierista*, guides children's use of art materials in a way that uniquely supports their learning. Art activities complement the projects that children carry out. Children are encouraged to communicate their understanding of concepts through their art, which is considered a symbol-making activity. "Teachers observe children at work, listen to their responses and converse with them about their artwork to plan for their future needs and interests" (Zimmerman & Zimmerman, 2000, p. 90).

There are a number of ways that art education can become more integral to early childhood programs in this country, in a way similar to Reggio Emilia's. Attention to the environment and its aesthetics is very important. A special area in the room should be dedicated to art activities. A variety of materials should be attractively displayed in this area, including artists' brushes, a variety of professional quality paints, clay and sculpting tools, wire for three-dimensional art, and a rich variety of natural materials. Photographs, postcards, colored lights, a prism, and other unusual items can also be included. In addition, other creative activities such as music, drama, dance, and movement can be combined with art to expand its possibilities (Zimmerman & Zimmerman, 2000).

Two-Dimensional Graphic Arts

Young children, as they move from scribbles to gradually more representational depictions, most commonly create these pictures through graphic art media. DAP notes that such graphic art is not only a form of creative expression, which gives teachers insight into children's thinking, but it also "is a child's first step toward writing" (Copple & Bredekamp, 2009, p. 177). We will examine graphic arts in terms of drawing, painting, and printmaking.

DRAWING. Crayons, nontoxic marking pens, pencils, pens, and chalk are the usual media used for drawing. Each produces a different effect and provides satisfaction and enjoyment. Graphic arts are relatively neat—certainly less messy than painting—and may encourage a child who is uncomfortable with messy media or reluctant to participate in more uninhibited art activities to engage in art.

It is important that the drawing tools be appropriate for children. In an art center where children have free access to materials, crayons are often a favorite, partly because most children are already familiar with them. Chunky crayons, especially in small pieces, are easier for toddlers and younger preschoolers to hold because their fine motor coordination is not yet well developed. Crayons lend themselves to experimentation as children become more adept at using them: Colors can be mixed, peeled crayons can be used sideways, and pressure in drawing can produce different color effects. Because crayons can be easily controlled (the colors do not run as they do in painting), they facilitate the emergence of shapes, combines, aggregates, and pictorial representations as children move beyond scribbles.

Key Point ◆◆
Art in Reggio Emilia programs is an integral part of the curriculum, viewed as one important way, through symbolic expression, in which children represent their learning.

DAP

naeyc

Key Point ◆◆
Children's move from scribbling to representational art can be seen in their use of two-dimensional graphic art, which uses a wide range of media.

naeyc

THE PURPLE FLOWER PROJECT

A small group of young four-year-olds was intrigued by a canvas that sat in our classroom. We discussed what they were interested in making, and they indicated they wanted to make something purple. The children had had considerable experience the previous years with drawing flowers and observing closely, so they began by drawing flowers on transparencies. We then projected their collective works through the overhead onto the canvas, but saw that their four pictures wouldn't fit. What to do now? Three of the children wanted to vote on which of the four flowers to use, but one child did not agree: "Mine is the best. We should use mine." I decided to step back and told the children we would not continue until we had resolved our problem.

After about three weeks, the girl who had wanted her flower used came up with the idea for the group to draw one flower together. It was a big step for her to come to this conclusion and everyone agreed. At the next group meeting, we used transparencies again. There was a lot of conversation, and each child decided to draw a different part, flower petals and stem, using pens. We again put this picture on the projector, and they were all satisfied. But a new problem arose. Two of the children were intimidated by their own shadows as these were thrown by the projector lens. A lengthy discussion about shadows followed and the children soon became comfortable enough to learn

Theresa Danna Douglas

Heike, Head Teacher of Four-Year-Olds

to avoid their shadows by ducking down or bending out of the way.

Once the pen drawings were finished, a new discussion developed about how to paint the flower. First, we had to decide how to put their drawing on the canvas, which was a new art surface for them. Using the projector, the children traced their flower onto the canvas with pens. We also realized that there was more than one shade of purple, so the children each mixed blue, red, and white to come up with their own shades. We asked the parents to contribute anything purple they had at home, and soon fabric scraps, yarn, glass pebbles, and other materials were added.

It was intriguing to see how slowly the children worked, how engaged they were, and how carefully they chose their materials. Each child painted and then added different three-dimensional materials to the flower petals. Each child had a different way of doing this. One child carefully measured

yarn and then cut it to the right size; another wove beads into one petal; and a third carefully glued glass pebbles into the flower center. I was impressed by how particular they were about the media they chose and used. Each petal was unique as the children added their own touch to the work.

The final question was about what background to give the picture. I made copies of their original paintings and asked them to try their own color for the background. Each came up with a very different color, from aqua to red, but they voted and agreed that they liked the yellow background best.

Altogether, the purple flower project took about three months. What did the children gain from this experience? They learned how to make choices, how to voice an opinion, how to negotiate, how to work together. They took their time and were able to delay gratification to reach their goals. Their motor skills improved and they became comfortable with using a variety of media. Later in the year, they were often heard to say, "I know how to do it," or "I can show you." I also learned how important it is to listen carefully to the children, determine what their needs and interests are, and incorporate that into a project. This project could have gotten lost if the goal was just to paint something quick.

The purple flower still hangs in the library of our classroom, a reminder of how much all of us learned in the process of this project.

Children also enjoy marking pens because of their vibrant colors and because they are easy to use. It is not necessary to press hard to get a result. Markers come with fine and large tips, allowing children to experiment with different effects. It is important to provide only markers with nontoxic, washable ink because marking pens tend to mark more than the paper; children's tongues, fingers, and clothing are often colored as well. Thinner gel pens provide a different experience, especially if children use these to draw their understanding of an idea or concept.

Pencils and chalk provide additional graphic art alternatives. Pencils with soft lead are easier to use because they leave a strong mark on the paper. Chalk offers a novel experience because the colors are soft, smearing and blending easily. Light-colored chalk shows up well on dark paper. Children enjoy drawing with chalk on paper spread with various liquids such as water, buttermilk, or liquid starch; the effect intensifies and seals the colors. A squirt of hair spray can "fix" the picture more permanently. Chalk can also be used on sidewalks to draw easily removable pictures.

Children most often draw on paper, but a variety of other surfaces make for interesting variations. Cardboard, corrugated cardboard, sandpaper, wallpaper samples, wood, and fabric are some of the alternatives to butcher paper, newsprint, manila paper, and construction paper. Even varying the shape and size of the paper can encourage children to try different approaches in their artwork.

Early childhood educators advise against providing children with dittoes or coloring books because they inhibit creative expression, are not developmentally appropriate because "coloring within the lines" requires fine motor control beyond the abilities of many young children, and serve as poor aesthetic models because the pictures are usually inferior artistic renditions. They also convey the message that children's art is inadequate (Mayesky, 2012).

PAINTING. Painting, with its fluid outpouring of bright colors, is an activity that delights young children, including infants. Because it is rather messy, painting is something most children do primarily at school. We will survey tempera, watercolor, and fingerpainting as three common applications of this art form.

naeyc

Good-quality tempera paints should be a staple in an early childhood program. Such paints come in premixed liquid, in dried blocks that are used like watercolors, or in less-expensive powder form. Adding a small amount of liquid detergent to tempera paints makes cleanup of brushes and accidental spills much easier. A pinch of salt keeps the paint from spoiling and growing mold. Because tempera paints are fairly thick, they are best suited for painting on large surfaces with large brushes or other tools. Children can paint on the slanted surface of an easel, on a flat surface, such as the floor or a table, or on an upright surface,—for instance, against an outdoor fence. Painting with tempera paints involves the use of large muscles (especially shoulders, arms, and back) as well as the small muscles of the hands.

Painting with good-quality tempera paints is a satisfying activity for young children. This child is painting at the easel, a favorite spot for such an activity. In what other ways could this teacher set up a painting activity?

© Courtesy of author

For the youngest children, provide two or three colors at a time, preferably primary colors that the children can then mix to create additional shades. As children get older, variations and new shades of color can revitalize their interest in painting. Although paint is provided in separate containers, each with its own brush, children will invariably mix colors. Keeping small amounts of clean, premixed paints and paper easily accessible promotes independence and allows children to paint when their interest is aroused. It is always a good idea to have a supply of aprons or smocks near paint areas to protect children's clothing. Plastic aprons that slip easily over the head will encourage independence.

Watercolors are often given to children once they have had some experience with painting, because they require finer control. It is again important to provide good-quality materials; inexpensive watercolors are often weak and yield unsatisfactory results. Children who have begun making representational pictures enjoy using this medium because they can manipulate the materials fairly easily to create people, trees, houses, and other objects.

Watercolors usually come in a tray containing 10 or more individual cakes of color. An accompanying small container of water into which the brush is dipped is needed to wet the colors. When children first use watercolors, they tend to use too much water, swamping and diluting the colors. You might demonstrate to children how to dip the brush in the water and then roll it on the paint, as they begin to use this medium. Give each child a paper towel to wipe the previous color off the brush after it has been rinsed. When children have finished using the watercolors, wipe off the excess water and mixed colors.

Fingerpainting is a multisensory activity that encourages uninhibited use of materials and emotional release. It can be done on large sheets of paper or directly on a clean table surface. Tabletop fingerpaint creations can be saved by lifting the print on a piece of superimposed paper. Thickly mixed tempera paints are a good fingerpainting medium, but a wide variety of other media lend themselves to this activity. Liquid starch and wallpaper paste mixed with tempera provide two different consistencies. Whipped soap flakes makes another excellent fingerpaint base to which color can be added. Although many teachers and programs object to the use of food as an art medium for ethical reasons (Fox & Schirrmacher, 2012), items such as pudding are also widely used. Another food-based fingerpainting activity is corn syrup and food coloring, which results in an acrylic-like picture.

Quality is important when purchasing paint brushes because inferior products quickly frustrate and discourage young artists. Good bristles, when carefully cleaned and allowed to air dry after each use, will retain their shape and won't begin to fall out. Provide a variety of brush sizes. Fine-point brushes are good for watercolors. Half-inch to 2-inch widths for tempera painting will allow children to experiment with different-sized brush strokes. Even wider sizes can be used, for instance, if children "paint" the outside of the school building with water. Foam brushes provide a different experience. Alternative utensils such as toothbrushes, empty deodorant containers, cotton swabs, sponges, kitchen utensils, feather dusters, or string are often used.

Watercolors provide children a different experience than tempera paint, allowing for finer, more detailed work when used with thin brushes.

PRINTMAKING. The final graphic art form we will discuss is printmaking, in which children dip into thick paint an object that will leave an imprint when pressed on a piece of paper. Printmaking is different from painting in that the utensil is not moved over the paper but instead leaves a single imprint with each application. Of course, many children mix painting with printmaking, moving the printing utensil over the paper like a brush or, alternatively, leaving single imprints of a brush on the paper. A variety of printmaking objects can be used, such as sponges cut into shapes, cookie cutters, corks, different kitchen utensils, natural materials, and even body parts.

Three-Dimensional Modeling Arts

When children use three-dimensional media, they produce artwork that has depth, height, and solidity in addition to color and shape. Just like graphic arts, three-dimensional projects can be abstract or representational. Play dough and clay, collage, and woodworking are three examples of modeling art that we will examine more closely.

PLAY DOUGH AND CLAY. Teacher-made (and child-made) play dough that contains flour, salt, water, and a few drops of oil is a favorite of children and teachers. Well-made play dough that is stored in an airtight container is soft and can be easily manipulated by small hands to provide a satisfying manual and sensory experience or to create shapes and sculptures. Children can punch, squeeze, roll, pull, stretch, and otherwise manipulate play dough; they can roll balls, pull out long snakes, twist snakes into coiled bird nests, and make human or animal figures.

After children have had ample experience in using play dough with their fingers, tools such as rolling pins, cookie cutters, plastic knives, and other implements that shape the dough or leave interesting imprints in it can be added. Play dough can be used directly on a table surface or on an oilcloth table covering, but individual, smooth-surfaced boards make cleanup much easier.

Potter's clay, which is commercially purchased, should be used in addition to, rather than instead of, play dough because it offers a different experience. Adults use this natural clay to create sculptures and utensils, which are fired, glazed, or painted; children's creations can also be preserved. Some teachers prefer the use of clay to play dough and keep only clay on hand in the art area of their classrooms. As with play dough, it is very important to store clay in airtight containers. It will be necessary to add water periodically to keep the clay pliable. Sculpting can also be done with sand and water or with mud from a nearby river or lake bank.

Fox and Schirrmacher (2012) propose four stages, not unlike the stages that typify the development of drawing, that children pass through in their experiences with clay and dough. Two-year-olds, in the "What is clay?" stage, explore the properties of clay in a multisensory way. They quickly move into the "What can I do with clay?" stage, in which three-year-olds start processing the material manually—rolling, pulling, and patting it. In the "Look what I made!" stage, four-year-olds creatively combine their clay forms into crude representations, though these happen accidentally as often as they do purposefully. Finally, five-year-olds move into the "Know what I'm going to make out of my clay?" stage, in which they begin with a finished product in mind.

COLLAGE. Collages are a creative combination of materials, kept together by glue or some other binding material. Because they contain varied materials,

Key Point
Stages in the development of children's art can also be seen in three-dimensional modeling art, which uses a wide range of media, such as clay, collage, and woodworking.

Clay, combined with a variety of other materials, allows children to manipulate and experiment with shapes, textures, combination, and transformation of a very versatile medium.

© Courtesy of author

collages can reinforce shape, texture, and color awareness. An almost infinite variety of materials and techniques can be used in making collages. Some, especially those in which paper is glued to paper, may be almost two-dimensional, whereas others combine components into a three-dimensional sculpture.

Collages need a base, collage materials, and some kind of binding to hold these together. The base can range from various types of paper used to make lightweight collages to cardboard, mat board, Styrofoam sheets, or wood for heavier concoctions. It can be made of paper or plastic plates, meat or TV dinner trays, various commercial plastic packaging containers, milk cartons, or almost any other suitable material. Collage materials can include torn scraps of foil, tissue, construction, crepe, newspaper, wallpaper, or other types of paper; various fabric scraps and fabric trims such as rickrack and bias tape; yarn, string, and heavy thread; buttons, beads, and toothpicks; hardware items such as nuts, bolts, screws, or washers; leaves, twigs, shells, rocks, and other natural collectibles; and almost any nontoxic, small item that lends itself to the art activity. The binding materials used to keep the collage together is usually white glue, but cellophane or masking tape, staples, pipe cleaners, string, wire, toothpicks, straws, or any other material that ties or tacks items to the base and to each other might be suitable for some collages.

Various techniques can be used for collages. The selection of materials can be provided by the teacher, who may have a specific project-related product in mind, or by the children from available collage materials stored in the art area. If you encourage children to create collages freely, then it is important to provide a good variety of appealing and neatly organized materials. Boxes with dividers can help keep materials separated. The number of materials can be increased as children become more proficient at using materials, and items should be rotated or changed to stimulate new ideas and interest.

Children can change the shape of collage materials by tearing or cutting paper or fabric. Most young children learn to use scissors through exposure and repeated practice. Appropriate preschool scissors that are both safe but not blunt provide excellent fine motor experience. Children usually begin scissors use by snipping sturdy paper, move on to cutting straight lines, and progress to cutting along curved and angular lines. Cutting out drawn shapes is an advanced skill that does not emerge until children have had many, many experiences manipulating and controlling scissors.

Scissors designed especially for left-handed children should be available. In addition, for children who have particular difficulty with fine motor control, double-handled scissors are available, which allow teachers to place their fingers in a second set of holes to guide the child's hand in cutting.

WOODWORKING. One of the most satisfying experiences for young children is to successfully saw a piece of wood in two, pound a nail into a tree stump, or combine two pieces of wood with a nail and hammer. Once children have experimented with and achieved some mastery in the use of tools, they use woodworking as the basis for three-dimensional creations as well. How often we hear a child, who has just combined two crossed pieces of wood with a nail, enthusiastically declare, "See my airplane!" School-age children, who have more highly developed fine motor control and greater skill in planning and implementing more complex projects, find woodworking opportunities particularly gratifying.

Successful and safe woodworking requires high-quality tools, appropriate instruction in using the tools, reasonable rules, and careful supervision. Woodworking tools for children, which can be obtained through various early

Figure **9-2**

Basic Woodworking Tools for Early Childhood

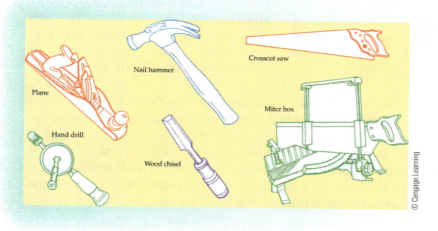

childhood equipment companies, are not toys. Basic tools should include well-balanced, small claw hammers weighing 8 to 12 ounces; crosscut saws, up to about 18 inches long; and well-made vises into which the wood can be securely clamped while children saw. Additional tools, once children have had plenty of practice with hammers and saws, can include braces and bits for drilling holes and rasps and planes for shaving the wood. Screwdrivers are generally too difficult for young children to master, and they end up being more frustrating than satisfying. Figure 9-2 shows some of the basic woodworking tools commonly included in early childhood programs.

In addition to the tools, it is important to provide a selection of soft wood, such as pine, which can usually be obtained from the scrap pile of a local lumber wholesaler or carpenter. Nails with fairly large heads in a variety of lengths should also be made available. The teacher can guide children through the problem-solving process of selecting an appropriate nail length for the sizes of the pieces of wood being nailed together.

It is very important to help children learn how to use tools appropriately, both for reasons of safety and to minimize frustration. To provide good leverage, hammers are best held with a firm grip toward the end of the handle rather than near the head; in this position, however, the swing of the hammer needs to be more accurate, because it takes greater eye–hand coordination to aim at the nail head from the further distance of the end of the handle. Before a piece of wood is sawed, it should be firmly clamped into the vise to allow the child to use both hands to manage the saw. For those inexperienced with a saw, the teacher might want to begin the process by making a small notch as a starting point for sawing. For very young children, wood can be replaced by thick Styrofoam packing material, which is much softer and easier to saw.

Logical rules should be established and reinforced for woodworking activities to ensure safety and success. Such rules might include an understanding that the tools remain in the woodworking area, that only three or four children are allowed in the area at a time, and that the area can be used only if an adult is in attendance. Similarly, it is important that teachers provide attentive and appropriate guidance. This includes helping children learn how to use the tools, providing appropriate physical guidance as needed, reminding children of the rules, verbalizing the process, and encouraging problem solving.

Older preschoolers and primary school children, who have gained proficiency in using the tools and have purposefully made objects from wood, will be interested in added props. These should include round objects that suggest wheels, such as wooden spools, slices of large dowels, bottle caps, the metal ends from 6-ounce frozen juice containers, film canister lids, and a variety of other items. In addition, dowel lengths, knobs, handles, glue and collage materials, and paint and brushes can extend the woodworking activity in many ways.

Wood can also be used with glue rather than with tools. A separate wood center allows children to create sculptures with wood scraps and knobs as well as twigs and other natural items. Bases of corrugated cardboard or larger scraps of wood and wood glue should also become part of such a wood center. Children enjoy creating individual or group sculptures; these can often become long-term projects that last weeks or even months, as did the construction of the White House described in one article (Bisgaier, Samaras, & Russo, 2004).

Visual Literacy

visual literacy
The ability of children to talk about their art and understand the message conveyed in others' artwork.

Margaret Johnson (2008) suggests that attaining **visual literacy** is an important goal for young children. "Visual literacy is the ability to create visual messages and to 'read' messages contained in visual communication. . . . [It] includes being able to talk about art in addition to making it" (p. 74). The author notes that it is important to talk and ask questions about children's artwork to help them reflect on their work. Johnson further suggests that appropriate questions about children's art experiences fall into five categories:

Key Point ◆◆
Visual literacy and aesthetics are important aspects of early childhood education, fostering children's ability to discuss their art as well as appreciate beauty in art and the environment.

aesthetics
Enjoyment and appreciation of beauty, particularly related to all forms of art.

1. *Ideas,* inviting the child to tell the teacher more
2. *Process,* asking the child how the artwork was made
3. *Materials,* discussing the materials or tools used
4. *Knowledge,* linking the child's work to concepts, vocabulary, or artist studies
5. *The future,* wondering about what the child will make next or wants to learn more about

Aesthetic Appreciation

Some museums have programs for young children that focus on aesthetic appreciation of fine art. Preschoolers enjoy seeing works of art and, through an age-appropriate program, can be helped to describe, analyze, interpret, and judge art as well.

Aesthetics, an enjoyment and appreciation of beauty, is related to art in all its forms. We feel a sense of wonder and enjoyment when we are touched by beauty. Aesthetics includes sensitivity and appreciation for both natural beauty and human creations. A teacher who is sensitive to beauty can help children find it in their surroundings. Children can be exposed in age-appropriate ways to fine art; for instance, by displaying reproductions of artwork in the classroom and taking children on trips to local museums and galleries.

Some local museums have specialized staff to provide an age-appropriate introduction to the artworks of the museum. If such a person is not available, you can still take children to a local art museum to view select works. Encourage the children to observe and focus on the elements of the work, describing what they see, both in the subject of the work and elements such as color, lines, shapes, and other qualities, and how it makes them feel. Back in the classroom, children can be invited to create their own art based on what they observed at the museum.

MUSIC

Music is a powerful means of communication. It can be boisterous and joyful, wistful and sad, exuberant and exciting, or soothing and relaxing. Music can match, as well as affect, our moods. Children have an innate, spontaneous affinity to music, which makes this a natural element to incorporate into the early childhood curriculum, appropriate for infants as well as older children. We will look at the development of music during children's early years, then turn to a more careful examination of appropriate activities related to four components of music in the early childhood curriculum: listening to music, singing, playing instruments, and moving to music.

Music and Child Development

From earliest infancy, children are aware of, and respond to, music in their environment. Music has a powerful influence; advanced brain-scan technology shows that when children participate in music, their brains "light up like a Christmas tree" (Shore & Strasser, 2006). Honig (1995) encourages caregivers to sing, croon, and hum formal as well as spontaneous, made-up songs to babies as early as possible. "From birth, the human baby is biologically primed to respond with pleasure to the human voice" (p. 73). Music is an important vehicle for cognitive, social, and physical development in very young children (Stellaccio & McCarthy, 1999).

By the time children enter an early childhood program, they have already had numerous musical and rhythmic experiences. Two-year-olds begin to gain some control over their singing voices and enjoy simple songs and fingerplays, moving to music, and experimenting with simple rhythm instruments; songs with simple physical actions are favorites of this age group. By age three, because of their increasing motor control, attention span, memory, conceptual abilities, and independence, children develop a larger repertoire of songs, begin to note similarities and differences in sounds, and associate special music for special movement.

Four-year-olds appreciate slightly more complex melodies and enjoy creating words and songs and experimenting with musical instruments. By ages five and six, with continual refinement of their abilities in all developmental areas, children begin to appreciate songs and dances that have rules, can follow specific rhythmic patterns, and may pick out simple familiar tunes on musical instruments. Seven- and eight-year-olds may be taking music lessons, often are able to read the words of songs, particularly enjoy music with rules, begin to compare sounds and pitches, and like more complex group activities that incorporate music (Mayesky, 2012). In recent years, the tendency has been to eliminate activities such as art and music from the elementary school curriculum. DAP, however, strongly affirms that the arts need to be integral parts of children's primary school experiences. "The joy of music is central in the experiences teachers share with children" (Copple & Bredekamp, 2009, p. 320).

We are all aware that people have varying musical abilities. Mozart was writing musical scores and playing instruments brilliantly at a very early age; however, we also find individuals who seem to be totally tone deaf. Some children may have a special musical gift while others have talents in other areas. However, inclusion of music in the early childhood curriculum is not a matter of identifying and training special musical talent. Rather, it should promote appreciation and enjoyment of music in all its forms.

Key Point ◆

Children develop an awareness of, and response to, music from a very early age, and the early childhood program should include many music activities to promote music appreciation and enjoyment.

Music that has cultural relevance to children is particularly enjoyable and affirming for young children.

DIVERSITY

naeyc

Key Point ◆

Music activities help sharpen children's listening skills.

Music is also a way of supporting and learning about different cultural and ethnic groups represented in a group of children and teachers. In fact, music is often one of the most powerful ways that a group expresses its uniqueness. Honoring this in the early childhood classroom gives children a sense of pride and pleasure.

Music should be seen as part of children's everyday play and exploration, not only as an activity to be carried out during a special music time in the curriculum. Kemple and her colleagues (2004) provide several suggestions for creating music centers that encourage such play and exploration. One example of such a center focuses on identification of musical instruments. A variety of instruments are put on a shelf, where children can explore them and the sounds they make. Once children have had ample time to familiarize themselves with these, they can try to identify sounds. Two children stand on opposite sides of a screen; one plays an instrument while the other one identifies it from its unique sound or timbre.

Listening

Listening is a prerequisite to understanding and using music. Children would not be able to identify environmental sounds, learn new songs, or move to the rhythm of music if they did not first listen. Children can be helped to develop attentiveness and sensitivity to all kinds of sounds, including music. Listening can be promoted in informal ways and through more formal listening activities.

The environment is full of sounds, which can be brought to children's attention. Periodically direct children's attention to the sounds that surround them—the bird song, car horn, airplane drone, slamming door, or flushing toilet. This practice can begin in infancy. By pointing out sounds, you are focusing children's attention on what often has become just background noise.

In the midst of an activity (for instance, during circle time) you might occasionally suggest that the children close their eyes, listen carefully, and share what they hear. It is amazing how much sound there is in the silence! Listening should not be relegated to a once-a-year topic, when you discuss hearing as one of the senses; it should be a frequent focus of activities. You can also provide good music as an integral part of every day by playing a record or tape during activity time or outdoor time.

In planned, formal listening activities, the primary objectives will be to encourage and sharpen children's skills in listening to music. To help children understand the beat of the music, you can have them clap along with it. You might play very slow music and ask the children to listen to the tempo or speed and then move their bodies in the same tempo; repeat with a musical selection that has a fast tempo, then one that changes speeds, and discuss the difference with the children. Using a selection whose pitch ranges from high to low notes, you can ask the children to stand on tiptoe when the pitch is high and crouch close to the floor when it is low.

You can also discuss the mood of music by asking children to describe how different selections make them feel. The same music can have different tone color, depending on which instrument plays the piece; let children hear the same melody played by a piano, a xylophone, and a guitar, for instance, and discuss the differences. Children should be introduced to music from a wide variety of **genres,** including classical, popular, jazz, folk, country, and spiritual. Musical selections should certainly include those from the children's cultures.

Singing

Children usually join readily in song. Many young children are not yet able to carry a tune, although a sense of pitch seems to come more easily to some youngsters. However, the main purpose of singing with young children should not be musical accuracy but rather enjoyment and building a foundation for music appreciation. The early childhood program should encourage spontaneous singing and teach a repertoire of new songs.

When children feel relaxed and comfortable in an accepting climate, they will readily engage in spontaneous singing. A child may, for instance, sing a lullaby as he puts a doll in a cradle, expanding his play with a familiar element from his home life. Or a child may verbalize what she is doing, as four-year-old Katrina did, chanting a made-up song identifying the items on the lotto cards she was laying out on the table. Some teachers, who do not feel self-conscious about their voices, model spontaneous singing throughout the day. In one unusual program I observed, I had a sense of witnessing a fun-filled opera as teachers and children sang rather than talked almost every communication!

Teaching new songs to children is probably the most common music activity in early childhood programs. Children enjoy learning new songs and developing a growing repertoire of music. Early childhood songs generally have a distinctive rhythm and understandable lyrics, are often repetitive, emphasize enjoyment, and use a limited range of notes. When selecting a new song, be sure the lyrics are appropriate for young children, because many songs have words that rely on themes or humor suited more for adults than for preschoolers. Learning a new song is complex, involving learning of the words, rhythm, melody, pitch, and tone. These skills are gradually acquired through the preschool years (Stellaccio & McCarthy, 1999).

Some appropriate guidelines can make group singing enjoyable for both adults and children (Mayesky, 2012).

- If you are going to teach a new song to children, know the song well first. Listen to and practice a new song until you are comfortable with the melody and lyrics.
- Do not teach the words and music of a new song separately.
- Short, simple songs with repetitive themes can be taught by presenting the entire song at once. Longer, more complex songs can be taught in shorter segments. Let children enjoy listening and let them join in when they can.
- Musical accompaniment on a piano, autoharp, or guitar or with a record or tape can help reinforce the words and melody when a new song is being taught. It is difficult, however, to sing, play an instrument, and observe the reactions of the children simultaneously.

genres
Categories or types of music, such as classical, jazz, or country.

Key Point
Children enjoy learning new songs and singing spontaneously in a relaxed and accepting atmosphere.

Children enjoy all aspects of music, listening to it, singing, playing instruments, and moving to it. Such activities can be both planned and spontaneous.

- When you teach a song on a specific topic because it relates to a curriculum theme, do not abandon that song once you have finished the topic. The song has become part of the class repertoire, and it should continue to be sung.
- Some children are reluctant to join in singing. Encourage but never force a child to participate.
- Rhythm instruments, particularly when they have cultural relevance, provide an enjoyable music activity for young children.
- Singing should be an enjoyable experience. If the children seem disinterested, bored, or distracted with singing activities, carefully examine what is happening. You may need to teach some new songs, use varying techniques, add action elements to some of the songs, add props suggested by the words, or use rhythm instruments as an accompaniment.

BRAIN STORM
THE POWER OF MUSIC

"Music exerts a powerful effect on the brain through intellectual and emotional stimulation" (Sousa, 2006, p. 221). Research has identified the specific parts of the brain that respond to different aspects of music. There have also been a number of studies that have linked music to academic achievement. Several studies have found a relationship between children who play musical instruments and academic performance; for instance, spatial-temporal reasoning, memory, and math (Jensen, 2001; Sousa, 2006). Math achievement, in particular, benefits from instrumental instruction, and recent studies using magnetic resonance imaging (MRI) show that musical training activates the same areas of the brain as those used in math processing (Schmithorst & Holland, 2004). Other studies have concluded that there is a relationship between music skills, phonological awareness, and reading development in young children (Sousa, 2006).

Playing Musical Instruments

naeyc

Key Point ◆

Rhythm and melodic instruments provide another means of promoting music appreciation and enjoyment, and they should be part of any early childhood program.

From their earliest pot-banging days, young children enjoy opportunities to make music. Children often use their body parts, especially hands and feet, to keep rhythm. Instruments appropriate for the early childhood program fall into three categories: rhythm instruments, which have no pitch and are used for striking or scraping; melodic instruments, which present specific pitches; and accompanying instruments, which produce several tones together, particularly chords that accompany a melody. Opportunities to use good instruments, as well as to make rhythm instruments, should be made available.

Rhythm instruments are the most common musical tools to which young children are exposed. Commercial sets of rhythm instruments may include several types of drums, rhythm sticks, pairs of wooden blocks, sand blocks that are rubbed against each other, tambourines, triangles, variously mounted bells, castanets, maracas, and cymbals. Each produces a distinctive sound, but, when played together with no ground rules, they can result in a rather deafening din. It is important, therefore, to introduce rhythm activities properly.

Rhythm instruments need to be handled with respect and care. One way of familiarizing children with instruments is by introducing them, one at a time, and demonstrating how they should be used in a small-group activity. Each instrument can be played so that children are able to hear its distinctive sound and then passed around so all the children have the chance to handle it, examine it, and make sounds with it. It is often best to start small groups of children playing rhythm instruments to an appropriate record or song (one with a strong beat), calling their attention to the rhythm of the music and the unique sound that each instrument makes. Children should have the opportunity to select the instrument they prefer, trade instruments among the players, and try all of them.

Rhythm instruments provide an enjoyable activity that promotes creative, physical, social, cognitive, and language development.

Children can also use assorted materials to make a variety of rhythm instruments. Coffee cans and oatmeal cartons, for instance, can be transformed into drums. Film canisters and egg-shaped plastic hosiery containers can be filled with beans, rice, or small pebbles and taped shut to make shakers or maracas. Such craft activities can help children become more familiar with what makes the sound in instruments, but they should not be considered "art" activities, which allow much more latitude and involve much less instruction in how to use the materials.

Some simple melodic instruments, such as xylophones and bells, can be included in the early childhood program. These allow children to experiment with different tones, discover ascending and descending notes, and begin to pick out simple tunes. Some schools have a piano in the classroom as well, a good addition if one of the teachers is skilled in playing this instrument. Children can make similar discoveries using a piano, but specific rules should be established to ensure that the piano is handled with care and respect. Color-coded bells or piano keys and simple songs with color-coded notes encourage children to play songs.

Accompanying instruments include the autoharp, guitar, and ukelele. Teachers usually play these instruments during music activities, and then they may be stored in an out-of-the-way place until needed. If children are encouraged to try strumming, they should be familiar with the appropriate rules for the instruments' use.

Movement and Music

Small children seem to be in constant motion. Movement activities are a good way of combining this natural inclination with activities that stretch their imaginations, exercise muscles, contribute to formation of spatial and temporal concepts, and build respect for the uniqueness and ideas of others. As with all other aspects of music in the early childhood curriculum, movement activities occur spontaneously as well as in more planned ways.

Because young children still learn very much in a sensorimotor mode, they often use body movements that imitate and are representative of elements of their environment to reinforce what they experience. For instance, children at the edge of a lake will unconsciously squat down in imitation of the birds on the water, seemingly assimilating through active movement what they are observing. Similarly, a child's head might turn in a circular motion as she or he intently watches a spinning top.

Movement reinforces musical beats. Movement progresses from the spontaneous swaying and bouncing to music seen in infants to the more deliberate dancelike moves, accompanied by hand gestures, that emerge by the time children reach ages four to six (Stellaccio & McCarthy, 1999). Children learn to keep time to music with ample practice. Clapping to music, marching in time to its beat, and taking small steps with short beats and long ones with long beats all reinforce children's emerging synchrony with music.

CREATIVE MOVEMENT ACTIVITIES. Children can also move with the mood of the music. Many lyric pieces invoke feelings of joy or sadness or reflectiveness or whimsy; they invite swaying, bending, rolling, swinging, twirling, or stretching. Asking children to move as the music makes them feel can result in a variety of creative dances. After children have had many opportunities to move their bodies to music, you can add various props—such as scarves, ribbons, balloons, hoops, and streamers—to extend this experience.

Another way that children can move creatively is by representing aspects of their environment that they have had an opportunity to observe. Nature provides many fascinating examples: Sway like the trees in our play yard, fly like the butterfly we watched outside, walk like the pigs we saw at the farm, or grow and open like the tulips on the windowsill that we planted and watered. Children can also be the popcorn they watched pop before snack time, the fire engine they saw extend its ladder on the field trip, or the washing machine in which their parents do the laundry. They can make themselves into a ball or a long, long string. Wall mirrors can help children see what they are visualizing. What makes such activities creative is that all children have the opportunity to express themselves in their own unique fashion, not in a way modeled by a teacher. No one rendition of a "tree" or "popcorn" is better than another; each represents a child's own feelings and concepts.

SUPPORTING CREATIVITY IN INFANTS AND TODDLERS

Creativity comes naturally to infants and toddlers. Given an environment that has rich possibilities for exploration and the freedom to discover these, babies will find unique ways to use toys and materials (Gonzalez-Mena & Eyer, 2012). Their curiosity, as they examine and explore new materials, has to be valued and nurtured. Much of the earliest years are spent in *creating* understanding about the world. Creativity is, in fact, a part of cognitive development. As they explore and manipulate things, young children try out new combinations of the things they already know about. By putting together what they know in new ways, they are being creative. The exploration of infants and toddlers is the prelude to creativity (Gonzalez-Mena & Eyer, 2012). Infants are creative in the ways they interact with the world. As they get older, children begin to use materials to create their own products. Such products may be seen in early art and music endeavors as well as in the make-believe play that gradually emerges during toddlerhood.

Babies are not too young for art activities. They can gradually be introduced to a variety of art materials, but they need to be given time and space to explore them in their own way, with the support and interest of caring adults. Messy activities can be especially enjoyable to many babies, for instance, those involving water, sand, and fingerpaints. Certainly with this age group, the

naeyc

Key Point ◆

Creative movement activities, with or without the accompaniment of music, provide a way to reinforce many concepts.

naeyc

▶❚❚ **TeachSource Video Activity**
WATCH • REFLECT • RESPOND

This video reinforces the interrelatedness of developmental domains by examining cognition and imaginative play. Go to CengageBrain.com and view the video entitled, "Infants and Toddlers: Cognitive Development and Imaginative Play," and answer the following questions:

1. How does representational thinking support creativity?

2. How do the activities presented by the teacher in the video support creative thinking?

process of engaging in art activities is more important than the end product (Watson & Swim, 2011). In the infant and toddler programs of Reggio Emilia, each facility includes a well-stocked art studio and art teacher. In addition, each classroom incorporates an art center with a range of materials for exploration and creative construction (Gandini, 2005). Babies have opportunities to interact with paints and a variety of drawing media, clay, different types of paper, different colors, and varied textures.

Music in the infant and toddler program is a must. But be aware that adults must show respect for children's responses to music, including its volume and tempo. You should certainly make singing a part of your infant and toddler program, as you frequently use songs to soothe, create an interest in sounds in, and interact with babies. Music as a daily part of infant care can help them learn to listen. Among the materials that you can provide for babies' exploration can be ones that make different sounds, for instance, rhythm instruments. Babies are also in perpetual motion. Providing music to which they can move and dance promotes both large motor development and creativity.

Music is a must in infant and toddler programs, since it promotes many aspects of development.

SUPPORTING CREATIVITY IN SCHOOL-AGE CHILDREN

We tend to think of the preschool years as being an optimal time for creative expression and think of creative capacity as waning during the school years. In part this is because once children begin formal schooling, the focus often shifts away from play and creative endeavors to more didactic and teacher-directed activity aimed at teaching academic skills. The fact that many children are put into a climate that devalues creativity does not mean, however, that primary school children lose their interest in or inclination for creative activities. To the contrary, children during the primary school years continue to develop in their creative ways, something that is supported by their growing cognitive skills. They often combine their newly acquired skills in reading, writing, math, and science with their creative work (Koralek, Newman, & Colker, 1996).

You can foster creativity for school-age children by providing a variety of open-ended materials; arranging the environment so that there is enough room for exploration and messy activities; providing enough time, both on a daily basis and for longer periods of time, to work on creative projects; surrounding children with examples of creative works, such as reproductions of paintings, award-winning children's literature, pictures of beautiful architecture, a variety of music, and biographies of inventors, scientists, and artists; storing materials where children can easily access them; and providing additional materials to support children's special interests. Children enjoy activities such as word games, dramatic play with costumes and props, a range of art media, using musical instruments, dancing, and writing stories and plays. By this age, products are generally more important than the process. Projects that last days, weeks, or even months are also very appealing to primary school children (Koralek et al., 1996).

Some school-age children find great satisfaction and enjoyment in learning to play a musical instrument.

SUPPORTING CREATIVITY IN CHILDREN WITH DISABILITIES

Because creative activities are individualized and do not rely on reaching some kind of common standard, they are an important part of the inclusive early childhood curriculum for all children. For children with physical disabilities, access to materials is important. A child in a wheelchair may need to have the easel and paint tray lowered to reach these. Some children may need adaptive equipment to help them hold paintbrushes or other drawing implements; putting thin brushes or crayons through a hole in a foam ball or rubber tubing can be a relatively easy solution. Paper may need to be taped to a table surface to keep it from sliding (Allen & Cowdery, 2012). Clay and play dough can be made with differing amounts of water added to make it easier for children with a weak grasp to manipulate. Music activities can help children with physical impairments become more aware of their bodies.

> **Key Point** ◆◆
>
> Creative activities have great value for children of all ages and abilities, and should be supported through careful planning.

Children with visual impairments enjoy the tactile sensations that are part of many art activities. They often enjoy clay, play dough, and fingerpainting activities, especially if these include added textures. If a child has limited sight, bringing the art project closer allows her to engage in the same activity as the other children. Background color and room lighting also need to be considered carefully. Music can be particularly rewarding to a child with little or no vision because of its pleasant auditory qualities.

Creative activities can be particularly rewarding for children with social, emotional, or behavioral disorders. Art can provide acceptable ways of expressing feelings. "Strong feelings can be expressed through the use of bold colors, pounding clay, and tearing paper" (Deiner, 2010, p. 243). Music can be relaxing or can help release feelings, and movement activities can also provide a legitimate outlet for emotional release.

For children with cognitive delays, creative arts offer a chance to participate in their own way, since there is no right or wrong outcome for creative activities. The focus should be on the process rather than on the product of art, much as it is for younger children. Repetition in music will help children learn the words to songs. Music can be an excellent medium for teaching basic concepts such as colors, numbers, or body parts (Deiner, 2010).

FAMILY VALUES FOR CREATIVITY

Some families consider their children's creative development an important goal; others focus more on concerns about their children's preacademic success. It is, therefore, important to share with families the school's philosophy about creativity, particularly in its broad sense of encouraging flexible, open thinking and problem-solving skills. Such information should be part of a philosophy statement that is given to families when they enroll their children in the program. On an ongoing basis, you can let families know which activities are planned and what you expect the children to gain from them. Similarly, a focus on creativity can continue to be reinforced individually, as you share with families information about their child's interests and accomplishments.

> **Key Point** ◆◆
>
> Families can be helped to value children's creative development in the broadest sense of the term.

Families also enjoy seeing tangible evidence that their children are involved and productive at school. It is most often art products, which children bring home in great stacks, that provide them with such confirmation. As the teacher, you can help families appreciate their children's art in relation to the age-appropriateness of the work. It may be easy to dismiss children's scribbles as non-art and to value only representational art products. Information on the development of children's art and the importance and sequence of all the stages can provide families with insight into their children's work. Appropriate handouts, an article in the school's newsletter, an explanatory bulletin-board display, or books on children's art in the school's library can all be good vehicles for conveying such information. The documentation of children's projects used by Reggio Emilia schools is another way to share the children's work and learning with the families. Such documentation often uses the children's artwork and other creative products as a way of illustrating the process of learning in documentation displays.

FACTORS THAT DECREASE CREATIVITY

A discussion about creative development should include a few words about the all-too-present factors in our society that often blunt children's creative impulses. Such information should also be shared with parents. As we have discussed, creativity depends on flexible, open, divergent thinking, which is encouraged in children through a flexible and open environment.

In the same way, however, creativity can also be diminished by socializing factors that narrow, stereotype, or limit ideas. An atmosphere that promotes racial, cultural, or gender stereotypes, for instance, imposes a narrow view of people, which restricts potential. An environment in which the adult is always right and children are expected to do what they are told without asking questions is not conducive to creativity. When children are given coloring books or ditto sheets so that each child has an identical end product, they will not develop creativity. In addition, when children are shown a model to replicate, it deters them from expressing their own creative impressions. When children are always shown how to do tasks, they will not have the opportunity to engage in problem solving and creative thinking. When adults laugh at a child's unique or unusual response, that child is discouraged from expressing other creative ideas.

Researchers have also expressed concern about the toys available to young children, many of which can serve to decrease creativity. Many of the traditional open-ended toys that have been staples in young children's lives for many years have disappeared from toy stores, replaced by electronic substitutes. Classic toys are not competing well with the newer, technologically driven products. "Much of the technology added to toys threatens to change the way children play in fundamental ways. Often electronic toys are less creative, do not involve much imagination, and encourage more passive reactions than older toys" (Barnes, 2000).

Electronic Media and Creativity

One pervasive factor in children's lives that can stifle creativity is the electronic media available to children today, including television. Young children spend considerable time watching television; however, they spend nearly an equal amount of time with all media combined, including videos, video games, and computers (Roberts & Foehr, 2008). What children see—program content—as well as how much time they spend in front of the set can decrease creative thinking. Television viewing is a passive activity that generally does not engage children's creative thinking. See the "Take a Closer Look" box in this chapter for a discussion in greater depth of the effects of media on young children.

Key Point
Creativity can be stifled when stereotypes are imposed, when children are given few choices, and when they are always shown what to do.

Key Point
Television viewing can decrease creativity. Both the content of television programs and the amount of time children spend watching television can have a negative impact.

CHILDREN AND THE MEDIA

THERE IS no question that today's children grow up in an ever-changing environment in which "many of their experiences are mediated by screen technologies" (Wilson, 2008, p. 88). The impact of television and other media has been the focus of considerable research for more than half a century. On average, children ages two to seven watch about two hours of television a day, but spend about three and a half hours with all forms of media, including videos and computers. More than 60 percent of infants and toddlers spend two hours or more per day with media. Nearly a third of children live in homes where the television is on all day long, and about that same number of children have media accessible in their own bedrooms (Roberts & Foehr, 2008). Research has found that background television has a negative impact on parent–child interactions (Kirkorian, Pempek, Murphy, Schmidt, & Anderson, 2009).

Children under the age of two seem particularly vulnerable to media exposure, and some research suggests that such early exposure may be associated with poorer cognitive development and possibly poorer attention skills. "Studies on infants and toddlers suggest that these young children may better understand and learn from real-life experiences than from video" (Kirkorian, Wartella, & Anderson, 2008, p. 39). In fact, the American Academy of Pediatrics (AAP; 2005a) strongly recommends that children not be exposed to media until they are two, and then only in moderation.

What do children learn from television? Research has shown that age-appropriate content is positively related to young children's cognitive skills and academic achievement. Educational programming has been researched in relation to literacy, mathematics, science, and social skills and has shown both short- and long-term improvements. One study, for instance, found a positive relationship between early exposure to *Sesame Street* and school readiness. "Television programs designed with a specific goal to teach academic or social skills can be effective with potentially long-lasting effects" (Kirkorian et al., 2008, p. 47). Children also can learn about emotions and positive social behaviors from age-appropriate programs. Regularly watching a children's program that focuses on prosocial skills can increase such behaviors in young children (Wilson, 2008).

On the other hand, inappropriate programming can result in negative learning and outcomes. Considerable research has shown that children are especially vulnerable to programs depicting violence. Frequent viewing of such programs can result in children who are aggressive and who rationalize that their aggression is an appropriate response. Another potential negative effect is that children can develop anxieties and fears from what they watch.

In fact, research shows that most preschoolers have had some fright reaction to something they saw in the media. For some children, this may even result in long-term fears and phobias (Wilson, 2008). As an example, six-year-old Gene, whose parents closely monitored what he watched, was traumatized by an advertisement for a smoke detector and had nightmares for months about the possibility of a fire in his home.

The position statement from NAEYC and Fred Rogers Center for Early Learning and Children's Media on use of technology and interactive media (2012) provides suggestions for those who work with young children. Teachers are encouraged to evaluate technology in "intentional and developmentally appropriate ways, giving careful attention to . . . the quality of the content . . . and the opportunities for co-engagement" (p. 11). They are also encouraged to provide a balance of activities, particularly those that are hands-on and active; discourage passive use of media; and limit screen time for young children, following the recommendations from public health organizations. In addition, teachers can encourage family members to:

- watch television with their children.
- encourage critical viewing by discussing content with their children.
- keep children's developmental level in mind when making viewing decisions.
- become informed about the potential risks of media violence.

There has been an enormous amount of research done about children and television but relatively little about the impact of other media on young children's development. For this reason, we will consider television in more detail. Programs on this medium tend to convey a very stereotyped view of people, one in which recognition and respect are accorded primarily to those who are white, male, young, and good looking (Liebert & Sprafkin, 1988). Television also generally promotes the view that an effective way of solving problems is through violence, another narrow attitude that often does not model a variety of constructive problem-solving strategies.

Even more disturbing are the results from a number of studies that have shown that frequent and consistent viewing of violent television programming is strongly related to aggressive behavior (Strasburger & Wilson, 2002). As one author of a number of important studies concluded, "Aggressive habits seem to be learned early in life, and once established, are resistant to change and predictive of serious adult antisocial behavior" (Huesmann, 1986, p. 129).

The amount of viewing time can also affect creativity. Creative learning is an active process, dependent on ample time spent exploring, investigating, manipulating, and reflecting. The more a child sits in front of the TV, the less time is available for active, self-directed play.

Furthermore, research has shown that when children watch violent programs, they tend simply to imitate the aggression of these programs and their play becomes more stereotyped and less imaginative (NIMH, 1982). If, in addition to home television viewing, children spend hours in front of a TV or VCR at school, cumulative time in passive viewing can be considerable. A statement by the American Academy of Pediatrics (2005a) clearly addresses the maximum amount of television that children should watch. They recommend that children over the age of two watch no more than one or two hours per day. Even more important, however, is their unprecedented stand that children under the age of two should not watch television at all. One reason for this recommendation is the rapid growth of the brain during the earliest years. The AAP also stresses the great importance of numerous positive interactions between the very young child and adults and other children, something that can suffer if the child sits passively in front of the television. There are, certainly, worthwhile children's programs on television, ones that model and teach children positive, **prosocial behaviors,** especially children's programs on public channels; for instance, *Sesame Street* and *Dragon Tales*, or *Dora the Explorer* on Nickelodeon. These programs provide high-quality, age-appropriate, sensitive fare for young children. Other programs, some of which are appropriate for preschoolers, are designed to promote appreciation of nature, aesthetics, and culture.

prosocial behaviors
Positive, commonly valued social behaviors such as sharing, empathy, and understanding.

SUMMARY

1. Consider the definition and discussion of some of the characteristics of creativity. Howard Gardner's theory of multiple intelligences acknowledges that various forms of creativity are integral parts of our cognitive makeup.
2. Both the teacher's attitude and the physical environment are important in encouraging creativity in young children.
3. One of the early childhood curriculum areas in which creativity can especially flourish is art.
   A. There are several theoretical views of the process of art.
   B. Many types of art activities and materials are appropriate in the early childhood classroom.

4. A second broad curriculum area that fosters creativity is music. Consider listening to music, singing, playing musical instruments, and creative movement as they relate to children.
5. The age and ability level of children need to be taken into consideration when providing activities for the development of creativity.
6. Some factors discourage and decrease creativity, including television.

KEY TERMS LIST

aesthetics

aggregates

basic scribbles

bodily kinesthetic intelligence

combines

convergent thinking

diagrams

divergent thinking

flexibility

fluency

genres

linguistic intelligence

logico-mathematical intelligence

multiple intelligences

musical intelligence

naturalistic intelligence

open-ended materials

pictorialism

placement patterns

preschematic stage

prosocial behaviors

schematic stage

scribbling stage

sensitivity

visual literacy

visual-spatial intelligence

KEY QUESTIONS

1. Which of your friends or acquaintances do you consider to be creative? What creative characteristics do they possess? Do they fit the definition of creativity presented in this chapter? How do they use creativity in ways other than the conventional sense (for instance, art or music expression)?
2. Observe a group of children. What expressions of creativity do you observe? What factors in the environment or in the teachers' behavior encourage or discourage creativity? Does any child in this group stand out as particularly creative? What characteristics does this child possess? Are your criteria for identifying a creative child different from those used to identify a creative adult?
3. Look at children's artwork. Do you see an age progression from scribbles to shapes to representational pictures?
4. Make a fingerpainting or collage with materials typically found in an early childhood program. How does this activity make you feel? What benefits can children gain from such activities? Do the same with a music activity (for instance, using rhythm instruments or dancing freely to music) and answer the same questions.
5. Watch a children's television program; for instance, a cartoon. What messages does this program convey to children? Does it promote stereotypes? If a child watches programs such as this one frequently, how might such viewing affect creativity?

ADDITIONAL RESOURCES

Select additional books, articles, and websites on topics discussed in Chapter 9.

Fromberg, D. P. (2002). *Play and meaning in early childhood education*. Boston: Allyn & Bacon.

Pica, R. (2007). *Moving and learning across the curriculum: More than 300 activities and games to make learning fun* (2nd ed.). Clifton Park, NY: Thomson Delmar Learning.

Fox, J. E., & Schirrmacher, R. (2012). *Art and creative development for young children* (6th ed.). Belmont, CA: Wadsworth, Cengage Learning.

HELPFUL WEBSITES

Howard Gardner's Theory of Multiple Intelligences:

www.thomasarmstrong.com/multiple_intelligences.htm

This website provides further information about Howard Gardner's theory of multiple intelligences and its implications for teaching and learning.

Art Activities:

www.ooeygooey.com

This website provides a variety of ideas for creative activities and materials for young children.

Music Activities:

www.childrensmusic.org

This website has ideas for music activities directed at children, teachers, parents, and performers.

Go to **CengageBrain.com** to register your access code for this book's Education CourseMate website, where you will find more resources to help you study. Additional resources for this chapter include TeachSource Videos, glossary flashcards, web links, case studies with critical-thinking questions that apply the concepts presented in this chapter, and more. If your textbook does not include a printed access card, you can go to **CengageBrain.com** to purchase access.

10 Physical Development through the Curriculum

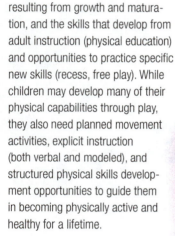

DAP Becoming more adept, coordinated, and skillful involves an interplay between children's emerging physical capacities, resulting from growth and maturation, and the skills that develop from adult instruction (physical education) and opportunities to practice specific new skills (recess, free play). While children may develop many of their physical capabilities through play, they also need planned movement activities, explicit instruction (both verbal and modeled), and structured physical skills development opportunities to guide them in becoming physically active and healthy for a lifetime.

Developmentally Appropriate Practice, Copple & Bredekamp, 2009, p. 117

In Chapter 10, you will find answers to the following questions about providing for physical development through the curriculum:

❱ What are the components of gross and fine motor development and sensory-perceptual development, and how do these develop?
❱ How can you best promote healthy physical development in young children of different ages and abilities through the curriculum?
❱ What can you do to promote a healthy lifestyle for the children in your care?
❱ How do you incorporate nutrition and health concepts into the curriculum?

NAEYC STANDARDS CONSIDERED IN CHAPTER 10

(See the Standards Correlation Chart on the inside front cover of this book for the titles and description of the standards listed below.)

❱ *Standard 1a:* Understanding the processes and progression of motor and sensory development as well as theories and research that help explain these (pp. 251–257).
❱ *Standard 5b:* Knowing and applying central concepts and strategies related to support children's motor and sensory development (pp. 257–267; 269–272).
❱ *Standard 1b:* Supporting physical development in children of different ages and abilities (pp. 267–269).
❱ *Standard 5c:* Implementing appropriate learning experiences related to nutrition, health and safety for young children (pp. 272–275).
❱ *Standard 2b:* Engaging and supporting parents in promoting children's physical development (pp. 275–276).

One of the major tasks of the early years is physical growth and development. At no other time in life is there such a rapid rate of change in size, weight, and body proportions as well as in increased control and refinement in the use of body parts (Allen & Marotz, 2010). Physical changes, which are readily observable, profoundly affect and are affected by all areas of development. As we have emphasized before, a child is a whole, not divisible into components such as physical, social, or cognitive areas—although to be able to manage the information, we do discuss development in such categories. This chapter will examine aspects of physical development and the activities that enhance it.

A DEVELOPMENTAL FRAMEWORK FOR MOTOR DEVELOPMENT

Before we begin discussing theories, we should clarify some terms commonly used in considering physical development. These include **gross motor development**—the skills involved in control of the large muscles of the legs, arms, back, and shoulders needed for large body movements such as crawling, running, jumping, and climbing; **fine motor development**—the skills involved in the use of the small muscles of the fingers and hands necessary for such tasks as picking up objects, writing, drawing, and buttoning; and **sensory-perceptual development**—which is involved in conveying information that comes through the senses and the meaning that it is given. This chapter will include all three aspects of physical development.

Traditionally, physical development has been considered from a **maturational theory** perspective. This viewpoint is based on information about when children reach development milestones in functions such as sitting, standing, and walking—tasks that are largely determined by the maturation of the nervous system (Shonkoff & Phillips, 2000). One of the earliest researchers to carefully observe and record the sequence of motor skill development was Arnold Gesell, whose pioneering work is still used extensively. Most early research on motor development was descriptive, using observations and films to establish the average age at which children achieve various motor skills. Such information, however, does not explain the underlying process of motor development.

In more recent years, Piaget's theory (as discussed in Chapter 5) has led to the **perceptual motor model** of physical development, a more integrative view proposing that motor behaviors are a prerequisite for and lead to cognitive abilities (Williams & Monsma, 2006). As you will remember from the discussion of Piaget's theory, the first level of development is the sensorimotor stage, in which the infant moves through a series of accomplishments, going from primitive reflexes to purposeful manipulation of the environment. In this early stage, covering approximately the first two years of life, the child learns through sensory input and body movement.

Repetition of certain motor patterns leads the child to form schemas, or representations of experiences. In early infancy, children use their own body movement to create different schemas. At approximately six months, they begin to explore the effect of their actions on the environment. During the second year, they become active explorers, engaging in rudimentary problem solving to reach their goals. As they enter the third year of life, children move into Piaget's second level of development, the preoperational stage. They can now mentally represent or think about objects and events that are not present in the immediate environment. This emerging ability for symbolic representations is based on a foundation of the sensory and motor learning of the first two years.

Because young children learn through physical movement and interaction with the environment, they must be provided with numerous movement opportunities and experiences. Furthermore, this viewpoint also assumes that a child's academic performance can be improved by increasing the amount of motor activity, because cognition is predicated on motor experience

gross motor development
Development of skills involving the large muscles of the legs, arms, back, and shoulders, necessary for such tasks as running, jumping, and climbing.

fine motor development
Development of skills involving the small muscles of the fingers and hands necessary for such tasks as writing, drawing, and buttoning.

sensory-perceptual development
Giving meaning to information that comes through the senses.

maturational theory
Explanation of human development dependent on information about when children achieve specific skills.

Key Point

Physical development involves gross motor, fine motor, and sensory-perceptual development and has been viewed from several theoretical perspectives.

perceptual motor model
A theoretical view of physical development that holds that motor behaviors are a prerequisite for and lead to cognitive abilities.

(Williams & Abernathy, 2007). The evidence for this second assumption is still being debated, as we will see later in this chapter.

COMPONENTS OF MOTOR DEVELOPMENT

naeyc

The movement of newborns is primarily reflexive but rapidly becomes more purposeful and controlled as babies learn to grasp objects, move around, and eventually walk. Toddlers and young preschoolers still have rudimentary movement ability and control; but by the time they reach the primary grades, their motions have become much more refined and competent (Gagen, Getchell, & Payne, 2009).

Body Control

naeyc

The foundation of the skills that result in increasingly greater control of the body is laid from the very beginning of life. The earliest movements are jerky and large, often controlled by reflexes rather than being voluntary, but they become smoother and more purposeful with age. In the very earliest months of life, upper body parts, such as the arms, are more active. By two months, the baby raises herself by the arms, gradually learns to change position from front to back and, by the middle of the first year, begins crawling motions. Many eight-month-olds are able to pull themselves up on furniture and by 11 months, may be able to stand alone. The first solo step, unsteady as it is, generally appears around the first birthday, although there is great variation in the age at which this achievement occurs (Allen & Marotz, 2010; Gagen et al., 2009; Gonzalez-Mena & Eyer, 2012).

Key Point ◆◆

In development of body control, young children gain mastery in walking, running, jumping, hopping, throwing, and balancing. Each requires complex skills.

Six important elements of body control—walking, running, jumping, hopping, throwing, and balancing—develop during the next few years (Gagen et al., 2009). Walking is the basic means of **locomotion,** self-movement from place to place; running, jumping, hopping, and throwing are fundamental play skills; and balancing provides one way of assessing postural control. All of these important skills become more accurate, controlled, and efficient during the early years.

locomotion
Self-movement from place to place, such as in walking.

Subtle changes in walking transform the toddler, whose concern is balance rather than efficiency, to the much more graceful preschooler. As the child gets older, legs and arms alternate, toeing-out decreases, stride becomes more consistent, heels and toes rather than the flat foot are used for landing and takeoff of each step, and feet are placed so that they are more parallel. Mastery of stair climbing involves increasing skill in several factors, such as moving from supported walking to walking alone, walking up before coming down, and stepping with both feet on each step to alternating feet (Gagen et al., 2009). By the time children are four years old, most are able to walk up and down stairs independently using alternating feet (Allen & Marotz, 2010).

Running is not just a faster version of walking; running at times makes the child airborne, with both feet off the ground. The earliest form of running is the hurried walk of the 18-month-old, but by age two, most children run, and by ages four to six they are quite skilled, with increased speed and control. Some of the changes involve a longer stride, a shift in the center of gravity as the angle of the legs increases, increased flexion of the knees, and better synchrony between arms and legs (Gagen et al., 2009; Gallahue & Ozmun, 1998). By age four, many preschoolers can start, stop, and move around objects with ease while running (Allen & Marotz, 2010).

© Cengage Learning

During the early years, children quickly master a variety of gross motor skills. This two-year-old is more secure with a hand to hold as he walks up and down the stairs. Within a couple of years he will negotiate stairs with little problem.

Jumping, during which both feet leave the ground simultaneously, seems to follow a consistent pattern in its development. The earliest form of jumping occurs when a toddler steps off a step to be briefly airborne. It is not until the third year that the child leaves a step with both feet, executing a more accurate jump. Another way to view jumping is to observe children jumping vertically off the ground, a feat usually achieved by their second birthday. The broad jump evolves around age three, with the length of the jump increasing with age (Gallahue & Ozmun, 1998). By three, children jump in place with both feet; by four, most can jump over objects five to six inches high; and by five, they can jump forward on both feet 10 times in a row (Allen & Marotz, 2010).

Achievement of one-legged jumping, or hopping, generally emerges between ages three and four, beginning with one hop and then increasing the number of hops. Early attempts at hopping usually end with both feet coming back to the ground for support, because children tend to propel their bodies too high by pushing too hard off the ground. Children are better able to hop forward than in place because the forward momentum helps them maintain their balance. Hopping becomes part of other movements such as galloping and skipping, tasks that appear between the ages of four and five and reach mature skill level by six. Skipping appears to be mastered much more easily by girls than by boys (Gallahue & Ozmun, 1998).

The objective of **ballistic skills,** or throwing, is to propel an object forward with accuracy and enough force so that it reaches the target. Before age two, many toddlers execute an overhand throw, but with poor control and speed. By age three, children become more accurate in throwing in a specific direction, and they can usually propel an object 5 to 10 feet. As they get older, children also become more efficient by rotating the body, stepping forward on one foot, and swinging the throwing arm to improve their throwing skills. Boys are generally more skilled at throwing; some children may, with appropriate encouragement and practice, achieve a mature throwing pattern by age six or seven (Gagen et al., 2009).

Development of balance is essential for children to acquire smooth coordination, which, in turn, leads to self-assurance and success in a variety of activities. By age two, children can stand briefly on one foot, but it is not until after their third birthday that they can maintain this posture for at least five seconds. Two-year-old children can walk, with steps astride, on a line on the floor; a few months later, they can walk backward in the same way. It is not until about age four or five that they can walk heel-to-toe forward, then backward. These same steps on a balance beam are more demanding and are mastered at later ages (Gagen et al., 2009).

Hopping on one foot becomes easy as children move toward the end of the preschool years.

ballistic skills

Applying a force to an object in order to project it, as in throwing.

Manual Control

The infant develops basic grasping and manipulation skills, which are refined during the ensuing years. At a very early age, the infant reflexively grasps and holds onto objects placed in his or her palm but cannot let go at will. During the first three months, hand and arm movement become more voluntary and, by three to four months, he can generally reach for and grasp a nearby object, using the entire hand to do so. By about nine months, the infant has perfected the **pincer grasp,** using the thumb and forefinger adeptly. Toward the end of the first year, fine motor skills have developed enough for the baby to begin taking off clothes, placing objects inside each other, moving a spoon to his mouth, and scribbling spontaneously with a crayon held in his hand. These early skills are gradually refined so that during the next several years children become quite adept in self-help, construction, and holding grips (Allen & Marotz, 2010).

pincer grasp

The use of thumb and forefinger to pick up small objects; this skill develops at around nine months of age.

Key Point ◆◆

Manual and hand control are evident from early infancy; through the early childhood years, increasing competence can be seen in self-help skills, construction ability, and holding grips.

naeyc

self-help skills
Tasks involving caring for oneself, such as dressing, feeding, toileting, and grooming.

holding grip
Placement of the hands in using a tool for drawing or writing.

palmar grasp
A way of holding tools in which the pencil or crayon lies across the palm of the hand with the fingers curled around it, and the arm, rather than the wrist, moves the tool.

tripod grasp
A way of holding tools in which the pencil or crayon is held by the fingers, and the wrist, rather than the whole arm, moves the tool.

Self-help skills such as feeding, dressing, and grooming involve a variety of manual movements that are mastered during the early years. Between ages two and four, children gain dressing skills of increasing difficulty, pulling on simple garments at the earlier age and learning most of the necessary skills by the later age. Most four-year-olds can bathe, wash hands and face, and brush teeth quite competently, although some supervision is helpful. Two-year-olds have some basic self-feeding skills, threes use utensils with increasing competence, fours can use a spoon and fork with dexterity, and fives are mastering the use of the knife to spread or cut soft foods. By age eight, the child uses all utensils with skill and ease (Allen & Marotz, 2010).

Many early childhood manipulative materials are designed to encourage emerging construction skills. One-year-olds begin to stack two to four objects, and by age two, children can build a tower of four to six small blocks, place pegs in a pegboard, and turn doorknobs. Three-year-olds can make a bridge with blocks, discriminate between and correctly place round and square pegs in a pegboard, and build a tower of 9 to 10 blocks (Allen & Marotz, 2010). "Handedness is fairly well established around age four, although the wrist contains some cartilage that will not harden into bone until about age six, placing some constraint on fine motor capacity" (Copple & Bredekamp, 2009, p. 117). As children reach ages four and five, their constructions become more intricate and require more delicate manual dexterity and spatial relations. In the primary grades, children continue to refine their construction skills and often begin assembling models that need detailed attention and control.

The most common task that requires a **holding grip** for a tool is writing or drawing. By age one and a half, children know how to hold a pencil or crayon, and by four they have a large repertoire of holding grips. Early grips include a **palmar grasp,** in which the pencil lies across the palm of the hand with the fingers curled around it and the arm, rather than the wrist, moves the pencil. Later developments involve variations of the **tripod grasp,** in which the fingers hold

Another accomplishment during the early years is the gradual acquisition of self-help skills. Younger children may still require help with zipping and buttoning coats or putting on shoes, but by the end of the preschool period, most children are quite independent in such tasks.

the pencil and the wrist and fingers move it. Children will spend varying amounts of time in each of these stages (Allen & Marotz, 2010).

Although we consider the development of holding grips to be age-related, it also seems to be affected by culture. In one study (Saida & Miyashita, 1979), researchers found that Japanese children achieve the most sophisticated grasp several months before British children do, a result partly attributed to the early mastery of chopstick use in eating. In addition, these researchers found that girls' grasp development is about six months ahead of that of boys.

Toddlers and young preschoolers use a palmar grasp with pencils or crayons.

Sensory-Perceptual Development

Closely intertwined with motor development are sensory and perceptual functioning. Sensory input involves the collection of information through the senses of sight, hearing, taste, smell, touch, and the kinesthetic sense; perceptual input involves attention to, recognition of, and interpretation of that information to give it personal meaning. Thus, perception is a cognitive process.

THE SENSES. Much of what infants learn about their environment is conveyed through the senses. Because children first learn about their world through the senses, it is important to include activities in the early childhood curriculum that involve all sensory modalities. Traditionally, education tends to encourage visual and auditory learning, often to the exclusion of the other senses, but the world, about which children are continually learning, is made up of more than sights and sounds. It has smells, tastes, and textures as well.

Early in life, children begin to discriminate with their visual sense, learning to recognize the familiar, forming preferences for increasingly more complex stimuli, and anticipating events from visual cues. Young children continue to delight in exploring with their eyes. A rich and aesthetic early childhood environment should provide a wealth of opportunities that not only develop visual acuity but also encourage concept formation through exploration. An important integrative development is **eye–hand coordination,** the increasingly accurate use of the hands as guided by information from the eyes. Many early childhood materials, particularly manipulatives such as puzzles or Legos, encourage, exercise, and refine eye–hand coordination.

Hearing is one of the earliest functioning systems, present even before birth. By the time children reach the preschool years, they have achieved a highly sophisticated auditory skill in understanding language and using that understanding to communicate. Of course, the development of language is not a function only of hearing but also involves the perceptual ability to discriminate between discrete sounds and to focus on the relevant sounds to the exclusion of irrelevant ones, as we will discuss in more detail in Chapter 12. The infant, toddler, and early childhood environment provides a variety of auditory stimuli, but it should also provide many opportunities to focus on, discriminate among, and identify various sounds.

The sense of taste is most identified with eating. To a great extent, it reflects learned preferences and socialization, although newborns appear to discriminate among and prefer certain tastes, such as sweet ones, to others—for

naeyc

Key Point ◆◆

Children's earliest learning about the world is through the senses by seeing, hearing, tasting, touching, smelling, feeling, and using the kinesthetic sense; this learning continues to be important throughout the early years.

naeyc

eye–hand coordination
Integrative ability to use the hands as guided by information from the eyes.

As they mature, children develop the tripod grip, which is a more efficient way to hold writing tools.

instance, those that are bitter (Bornstein & Lamb, 2010). But taste is also instrumental in exploration, especially during the first year of life, when children put objects in their mouths. Some young preschoolers continue to mouth some things, especially thumbs or other personally comforting objects, although not as indiscriminately as they did during infancy.

A variety of opportunities to explore new tastes through food experiences should be provided in the early childhood setting. In addition, a safe environment will ensure that anything that goes into children's mouths will not be harmful. At the same time, children will learn to discriminate between what is appropriate and what is inappropriate for putting in the mouth.

Smell, a sense in many ways tied to taste, is also present very early in life; newborns, in fact, have been shown to react favorably to the smell of bananas and with disgust to the smell of rotten eggs (Bornstein & Lamb, 2010). Children continue to show olfactory preferences, and they may reject a new food simply because of its smell or dislike a person because "he smells funny." Smell is an important sensory modality in learning to identify and discriminate among various common and uncommon odors, something the early childhood program can encourage and facilitate. Children enjoy matching familiar smells.

Whereas vision involves the eyes, hearing the ears, taste the mouth, and smell the nose, the sense of touch entails our largest organ, the skin. Touch can be soothing or irritating, pleasant or unpleasant, calming or exciting, and it can project a message of safety or danger. Sensitivity to tactile stimulation develops rapidly during infancy (Bornstein & Lamb, 2010), and by early childhood, children gain a wealth of information through this sense. Children enjoy stroking different fabrics, mounding wet sand with their hands, or feeling tree bark. A variety of tactile experiences, along with opportunities to verbally discriminate among different textures, should be part of the early childhood program.

Key Point ◆◆

The kinesthetic sense provides knowledge about the movement of the body.

kinesthetic sense
Information from the body's system that provides knowledge about the body, its parts, and its movement; involves the "feel" of movement without reference to visual or verbal cues.

Key Point ◆◆

Perception involves being able to select and pay attention to sensory information that is important and relevant.

multisensory
Referring to information that depends on input from several of the senses.

THE KINESTHETIC SENSE. The body's **kinesthetic sense** provides knowledge about the body, its parts, and its movements. All movement experiences add to children's growing understanding of what their bodies can do, their increasing control over their bodies, and their sense of self-confidence in their physical abilities. A child working with hammer and nail in the woodworking center has to make kinesthetic judgments that go beyond visual perception of the location of and the distance between the nail and the hammer; for instance, the child has to know how best to hold the hammer for an effective swing, how to position the body, how hard to swing the hammer, and how to hit the nail head rather than the fingers.

PERCEPTUAL DEVELOPMENT. As children gain information about the world through the senses of sight, hearing, taste, smell, touch, and the kinesthetic sense, they become increasingly skilled in using this information. Perception involves selecting the important features of a complex environment, focusing on the salient aspects of those features, identifying those features, and discriminating them from others. All of these processes entail cognition, again pointing out the interrelatedness of all aspects of development.

Most often, perceptual information does not come from just one sensory mode but is **multisensory** (Allen & Marotz, 2010). If, for instance, you bring a lamb onto the playground, the children will learn about it by seeing it and watching it move, listening to it say "baaaa," smelling its distinctive odor, and feeling its curly fur. Even very young infants demonstrate multimodal abilities. All of this information, coming from the various sensory modalities, contributes to the children's concept of a lamb. From many sensory-perceptual experiences comes **sensory integration,** the translation of sensory information into intelligent behavior. Consider the five-year-old who sees and hears a car coming and waits on the curb for it to pass.

We have briefly examined some developmental and theoretical issues related to gross motor, fine motor, and sensory-perceptual functions in young children. The rest of this chapter will look at some early childhood activities that enhance skill development in these areas. Again, keep in mind that this selection is somewhat forced because almost all preschool activities involve motor and sensory-perceptual elements. Similarly, the activities we will review also promote creativity, cognition, language, and socioemotional development.

sensory integration
The ability to translate sensory information into intelligent behavior.

GROSS MOTOR ACTIVITIES

This section examines gross motor activities, those that involve the large muscles of the body, in three areas. We will examine these activities in relation to physical fitness, consider gross motor activities in outdoor play, and look at them in block usage.

naeyc

BRAIN STORM
TIME TO GO OUTSIDE

The fact that physical activity promotes good health is not new. But more recent research has established that there is a relationship between physical activity and brain functioning in children. Studies have begun to explore that relationship and conclude that exercise can improve brain function. In part this is because "physical activity increases the number of capillaries in the brain thus facilitating blood transport" (Sousa, 2006, p. 233). Researchers have been examining the relationship between physical activity, memory, and the ability to pay attention. Using magnetic resonance imaging (MRI), researchers found that children who were physically fit, as compared with out-of-shape children, appeared to have a larger hippocampus—a part of the brain that is important to memory and other cognitive tasks (University of Illinois at Urbana-Champaign, 2010). In another study, researchers tested a group of children on a series of cognitive tests after they rested for 20 minutes on one day and after they walked for 20 minutes the next day. They found that after walking, as compared with after resting, children performed better in reading comprehension, accuracy, and attention, as measured through electroencephalographic (EEG) activity (University of Illinois at Urbana-Champaign, 2009). Further studies are underway in this intriguing inquiry.

Such research is at odds with the current practice in elementary schools of decreasing or eliminating physical education and recess time. The percentage of elementary schools in the United States that provide daily physical education is 3.8 (Trost, 2007). Several studies have shown that children show more on-task behavior if recess is part of their day (Bjorklund, 2012). Programs for preschoolers typically include many opportunities for physical activity, but once children enter elementary school, they may no longer have such opportunities built into their day.

Physical Fitness

Gross motor exercise occurs in many early childhood activities. It should be emphasized that vigorous, active play is important not only for muscle development but also for the establishment of lifelong healthy habits. In fact, DAP indicates that children must have opportunities throughout the day to move about freely, use their large muscles, and engage in vigorous movement (Copple & Bredekamp, 2009). Yet, there is increasing alarm about the lack of exercise and poor eating habits of young children, resulting in declining levels of fitness. Recent headlines label this state of children's health as an "epidemic" and a "public health crisis" (Sorte & Daeschel, 2006). Close to half of today's children show at least one risk for later heart disease, the leading killer of American adults. Many young children have overall low activity levels and simply do not get enough exercise (Pica, 2006). The sizable number of overweight American preschool-age children further attests to a need for physical education (see the "Take a Closer Look" box).

Key Point ◆

Research has found that most young children do not engage in adequate physical activity; therefore, it is recommended that physical fitness activities regularly be included in the early childhood program.

DAP

Teachers of young children often neglect gross motor development, and instead emphasize fine motor, cognitive, and social areas in the curriculum. "As early childhood professionals we have a duty to educate the whole ... child" (Pica, 2006, p. 12). A number of physical educators further express the concern that free play, which often includes various motor experiences, does not adequately meet the motor development needs of young children. They advocate that structured physical fitness programs (*not* organized sports) be part of the early childhood curriculum. The term *physical fitness* often conjures up our own childhood experiences involving games and sports. Play, games, and sports have characteristics that are tied to developmental readiness and appropriateness. Play is free from time, space, and rule constraints, and reward is inherent in the play rather than dependent on winning. Play involves such activities as running, crawling, climbing, and throwing. Games are more structured than play, although time limitations and rules can be altered to meet the needs of the players involved. Examples of games include chase, tag, jumping rope, and hopscotch.

Sports (for instance, football, track, or gymnastics) are much more structured and are based on external rewards. Preschoolers do not have the physical, social, emotional, and cognitive skills to participate in sports and in many organized games. Instead, young children need to develop physical capabilities through many play experiences in which they can explore their outside world. Children in the primary grades begin to acquire the developmental maturity needed for participation in more organized activities. Keep in mind, however, that competitive activities have no place in early childhood programs. Because one child usually wins at the expense of the other participants, the self-concepts of those who do not win are affected negatively, and hostility and ill will are created. Cooperative games are much more appropriate, and will be discussed in more detail in Chapter 13.

The challenge to early childhood educators is to develop appropriate gross motor and physical fitness activities. Motor skills that emerge during the early years, as discussed previously in this chapter, should be the focus of such activities. In particular, aerobic and muscle-strengthening activities are important to combat body fat. Rae Pica (2006) provides suggestions for encouraging active movement in young children and making it part of the curriculum:

▹ **Environment**—The indoor environment should provide enough room to engage in movement activities. The outdoor area should include opportunities for children to engage in a range of gross motor activities.

THE RISE IN OBESITY IN CHILDREN

SINCE THE early 1960s, the government has been collecting information about the nutritional status of America's children. The National Health and Nutrition Examination Surveys (NHANES) thus provide a unique opportunity to examine trends and changes in children's weight. Thousands of children participate in this research to provide a representative group of the country's youth. The picture that has emerged shows that the percentage of overweight children had steadily increased through 2004, but then decreased by 2008. The data from the NHANES 2004 study shows that 13.9 percent of preschoolers were identified as being obese, but by 2008, that number decreased to 10.4 percent. For school-age children, however, this number is at an all-time high, at 19.6 percent (Centers for Disease Control and Prevention, 2011). It is particularly disturbing that obesity is seen more in children from minority families, especially Hispanic American and African American children (Huettig, Sanborn, DiMarco, Popejoy, & Rich, 2004). This is especially disturbing because of the clear links between obesity and a multitude of health problems, particularly in adulthood. Such problems include coronary heart disease, certain types of cancer, stroke, and diabetes. One especially alarming trend is the increase in what had previously been known as adult-onset diabetes in children. Obese children also suffer from the social isolation of being different from their peers. "The epidemic of childhood obesity in the United States is *the* health issue of this decade" (Huettig et al., 2004).

What are some of the reasons for this alarming trend? Body weight represents a balance between food intake and energy output. The increase in the number of overweight children is a factor of both of these elements—an increase in food intake and a decrease in activity level. Dietary patterns have changed over the past decade, and fast foods and snacks, replete with high-calorie fats and sugars, have become a more regular part of children's daily fare. At the same time, children engage in more sedentary activities, watching more TV and playing more video games than ever before. Families may also fear for the safety of their children and thus not send them outside to play as much as would have happened in the past. Nonetheless, physical inactivity is considered a major public health problem in the United States, according to the Surgeon General (Staley & Portman, 2000).

The Institute of Medicine (2011) released a report that outlines a number of practical steps to fight obesity in young children. The report, *Early Childhood Obesity Prevention Policies*, makes suggestions that early childhood educators as well as families will find helpful in combating obesity. These are:

- Assess, monitor, and track growth, from birth to age 5.
- Increase physical activity in young children.
- Decrease sedentary behavior in young children.
- Promote the consumption of a variety of nutritious foods, and encourage and support breast-feeding during infancy.
- Limit young children's screen time and exposure to food and beverage marketing.
- Promote age-appropriate sleep durations among young children.

What can you, as an early childhood teacher, do to help prevent obesity in children? While your influence extends over only part of the children's day, your contribution to their health and well-being can be significant. The foods you serve for snacks and meals, the example you set in your own eating habits, the exercises and activities you plan and encourage, and your reinforcement of healthy eating and physical activity all contribute to the children's developing acceptance of a healthy lifestyle.

"Simon says, everybody get on your hands and knees! Now Simon says, everybody crawl like a dog!" A variety of group games can be structured to incorporate an exercise component.

❯ **Equipment**—Items such as parachutes, hoops, jump ropes, and balls encourage movement.

❯ **Enthusiasm**—As the teacher, be a role model by being an active person.

❯ **Attitude**—Help children understand why movement is important and help them develop positive attitudes about fitness.

The trends about children's health status imply that early childhood teachers need to be more concerned with providing physical fitness as part of the daily program. Vigorous daily activities that are fun and enjoyable contribute to establishing a foundation for lifelong health habits and attitudes.

Outdoor Play

Uninhibited gross motor activity is most likely to occur during outdoor play. Children are not expected to control their voice and activity level, and space is not constrained, as it often is indoors. As a result, children feel freer to run, jump, crawl, climb, hang, swing, and shout. A variety of interesting and versatile equipment should be available in the outdoor play yard, as we discussed in Chapter 7. The outdoor area and the time children spend outdoors should be integral parts of the early childhood program because of their many inherent values. Outdoor play is not just a time for children to expend excess energy while teachers take a break. Well-planned outdoor activities can meet a range of developmental and educational objectives.

OUTDOOR ACTIVITIES. Although children enjoy the freedom of self-selected ventures while outside, the teacher should also provide and be actively involved in planned activities that enhance motor development. As children get older, they enjoy some noncompetitive games such as "Statues," "Red Light–Green Light," or "Mother May I," which involve both movement and control. Keep in mind, however, that races pitting children against each other, or girls against boys, are inappropriate. Setting up an outdoor obstacle course, which takes advantage of existing places to climb over, crawl through, or jump across, can be enjoyable and provide exercise. A parachute, with children grasping the edges, can be used to reinforce concepts such as up and down and over and under as well as to encourage cooperative effort. The teacher's and the children's creativity are the only limits to how the outdoor play area is used to enhance children's learning and development.

Outdoor play in a separated area should be available for infants and toddlers. Such an area should provide activities and equipment that add opportunities for different movement and sensory experiences. Gentle swings and slides, safe places to crawl and feel new surfaces, places to push, pull, and roll small toys, and the opportunity for messy activities should be available outside for this age group.

Blocks

Blocks are one of the most versatile and enjoyable materials found in early childhood classrooms. Blocks come in many shapes and sizes, are made of various materials, can be used alone or in combination with other items, and lend themselves to an almost infinite variety of play possibilities.

BENEFITS OF BLOCK PLAY. Blocks support all domains of development, though we will particularly focus on how they provide many opportunities for motor development. Children use both their large and small muscles during block play as they lift, bend, stretch, reach, turn, and manipulate and balance various types of blocks. In addition, blocks promote concept learning (big and little, tall and short, over and under); are a natural vehicle for learning about matching, similarities and differences, and classification; entail math and science concepts related to quantity, addition and subtraction, weight, and balance; develop vocabulary and visual memory related to shapes, sizes, and patterns; elicit creativity, problem solving, and role-playing; encourage cooperative play; and are satisfying, giving a sense of accomplishment and self-worth. Blocks are certainly a versatile medium that meets many needs and provides many opportunities for development!

STAGES OF BLOCK PLAY. As you observe young children using blocks, you will note differences in the type and complexity of such play among children. Children go through stages in their development of block play, stages related to age and experience, but certainly showing considerable individual variation. Toddlers often spend considerable time carrying blocks around, perhaps banging them together, and exploring their feel and weight. In the next stage, children's earliest constructions are either vertically stacked or horizontally laid-out blocks. The flat structure suggests a road, and often the earliest dramatic play with blocks involves small cars driving over such a road.

By three to four years, children begin putting blocks together into more deliberate constructions; for instance, enclosures, bridges, or decorative patterns. Enclosures can lead to dramatic play with animal, people, or furniture accessories as children make houses, farms, or zoos. Bridges often become a challenge for cars driving through, as children gauge and compare size, width, height, distance, and balance. Use of decorative patterns shows children's interest in symmetry, repetition of configurations, and exploration of various designs.

In the final stage, reached between four and six years, children engage in more representational constructions, naming their structures, building to create props for dramatic play, and making quite complex and elaborate edifices (Wilburn, 2000).

Young children need vigorous exercise each day for fitness. In addition to providing blocks of time for outside play, how can you, as the early childhood teacher, promote physical fitness for children?

naeyc

Key Point ◆◆
Outdoor play provides one of the best opportunities for physical development, through both self-selected play and specific activities provided by the teacher.

naeyc

Key Point ◆◆
Block play provides excellent opportunities for physical development, through both self-selected play and specific activities provided by the teacher.

Key Point ◆◆
Children's block play evolves through specific, age-related stages.

Young preschoolers enjoy stacking blocks vertically. Reaching as high as possible is often a self-selected challenge for children.

unit blocks
The most common type of blocks, they are precision-made of hardwood in standardized sizes and shapes.

Each of these stages reflects children's increasing understanding of spatial concepts. Well before the age of four, children have mastered basic spatial relationships such as on, by, and in. In the later stages of building with blocks, they demonstrate more advanced spatial concepts as they manipulate space in symbolic representations of structures such as houses, farms, and other enclosures.

Chalufour and Worth (2004) suggest that children need time for open exploration with building materials, such as blocks, and that such exploration can then transition into more focused investigations. Open exploration allows children to notice the properties and relationships among the materials, for instance, concepts such as stability and balance. Focused exploration, on the other hand, revolves around a central question, which challenges the children to think about or solve a problem. You might ask, "Which blocks do you think will be best for making a tall tower?" or "How will you get the roof to stay on top of your house?" During focused exploration, children have opportunities to revisit, represent, and discuss their structures. The evidence of their building tasks allows them to develop and reflect on theories about stability in construction.

TYPES OF BLOCKS. The most common type of blocks is the **unit block,** which is made of hardwood in standardized sizes and shapes. The basic unit is 5½ inches long, 2¾ inches wide, and 1⅜ inches high (Wilburn, 2000). Variations include the square or half unit, double unit, and quadruple unit, and there are a variety of triangular, cylindrical, arched, and curved units. (See Figure 10-1 for some examples of common unit block shapes.) Unit blocks are made with precision to ensure mathematically exact relationships among the various units.

Large, hollow blocks, 11 inches square by 5½ inches high, have one open side and a slit for carrying. Other size variations include a half square and a double square. Hollow blocks are often accompanied by other equipment, such as boards, ramps, sawhorses, ladders, and packing crates. Because of their size, hollow blocks encourage a different kind of dramatic play, one in which children can climb into the structures they build to drive the "car," pilot the "boat," or live in the "house." A variety of accessories can extend their play as well. Hollow blocks are used as easily inside as they are outside. They are particularly good for large muscle development because of their bulk and weight (Wilburn, 2000).

Cardboard blocks, made of heavy corrugated cardboard resembling large bricks, are very useful with toddlers and young preschoolers. These sturdy blocks are lightweight and manageable for very young children, whose motor skills and balance are not yet well developed. They are easily carried around by children in the first stage of block building, are readily stacked by children entering the second stage, and are generally not harmful if knocked over. These blocks are not particularly versatile for more complex block structures, however, because all the blocks are the same size and shape.

A variety of homemade blocks can also be added to your selection of construction materials. Relatively sturdy blocks, for instance, can be made of cylindrical oatmeal boxes and milk cartons. Wooden blocks can also be constructed by someone who enjoys carpentry, uses high-grade hardwood, is exact in cutting shapes, and sands and varnishes carefully.

TEACHERS' ROLE IN BLOCK PLAY. Teachers have to gauge their involvement in block play according to cues from the children. Observation may tell teachers that some children avoid the block area, while others frequently use blocks readily and creatively. Thus, teachers may need to encourage reluctant children to try block play and help the ones who often use blocks to extend

Figure **10-1**

Examples of Common Unit Blocks

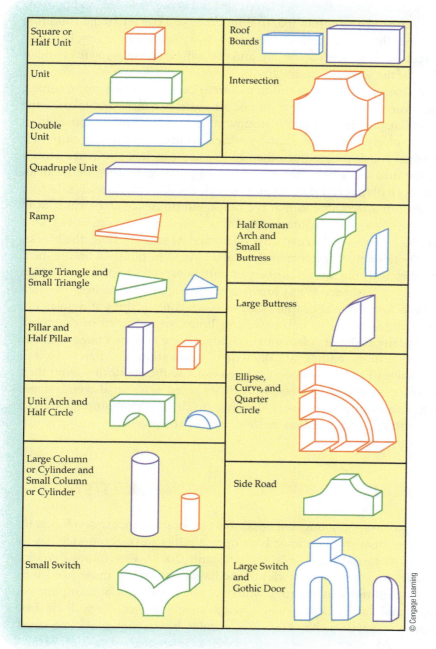

Square or Half Unit	Roof Boards
Unit	Intersection
Double Unit	
Quadruple Unit	
Ramp	Half Roman Arch and Small Buttress
Large Triangle and Small Triangle	Large Buttress
Pillar and Half Pillar	Ellipse, Curve, and Quarter Circle
Unit Arch and Half Circle	
Large Column or Cylinder and Small Column or Cylinder	Side Road
Small Switch	Large Switch and Gothic Door

© Cengage Learning

their play. In some classes, blocks tend to be a boys' activity, and girls may be unwilling to engage in block play for this reason. In such cases, teachers need to support and encourage girls in trying play with blocks, convey that girls can be as effective as boys in constructions, value all the children's structures, and promote individuality rather than stereotyped views of people (Wilburn, 2000).

In talking with children about their block constructions, it is better to use descriptive rather than evaluative comments. As we discussed in Chapter 9 in relation to children's art, judgmental statements tend to discourage and stifle

naeyc

Teachers can help children expand their block play through their interaction and suggestions.

children's creative efforts, because they convey an expectation about what the artwork should be like. Examples of what might be discussed include the names of the blocks used, where they are placed, how many are included, and how the blocks are balanced and connected. In doing this, you convey to the child that you have carefully looked at the construction, you may be promoting language development by using new vocabulary, and you will be encouraging the child to look closely at the work (Wilburn, 2000).

Teachers can also encourage children's extension of block play into dramatic play. Blocks can help children re-create or act out experiences and take on the role of familiar people in their environment. A variety of props can encourage dramatic play. Wooden or plastic vehicles, animals, and figures of people are traditional block props, but other accessories can include items usually found in the dramatic play, woodworking, manipulative, sensory, or art areas. To extend block play, it could be combined with the dramatic play area. In fact, practitioners often recommend that the block and housekeeping areas should be located side by side to facilitate combining activities (Mayesky, 2012). One aspect of block play is its relative impermanence. At cleanup time, the blocks, which are "nonexpendable materials," usually have to be put back on the shelf. Yet, ownership and permanence are very important aspects of activities in which children engage. Kushner (1989) provides some suggestions to help children achieve these. Photographs can be taken of block constructions and posted in the class or on a classroom web page, sent home, or mounted in classroom albums. Similarly, slides or videotapes of children's work can be shared at family events. Sending home enthusiastically written notes about children's play can give importance to a block activity. Children can also dictate stories about their block structures to verbally preserve what they created. Kushner also encourages teachers to rethink attitudes about cleanup, considering the appropriateness of preserving some block structures beyond the limited play time during which they were constructed.

FINE MOTOR ACTIVITIES—MANIPULATIVES

In addition to promoting ongoing opportunities for gross motor development, DAP also notes that children must have opportunities throughout each day to develop fine motor skills (Copple & Bredekamp, 2009). Fine motor development primarily involves the muscles of the hands and wrists, those needed in precise and small movements. Toys, which require some kind of manipulation with fingers and hands, can be categorized as manipulatives. We will consider manipulative materials such as table toys, puzzles, beads, pegboards, and small blocks as they contribute to fine motor as well as other areas of development.

Benefits of Manipulatives

manipulatives
Toys and materials that require the use of the fingers and hands; for instance, puzzles, beads, and pegboards.

Manipulative toys are important for children of all ages, ranging from safe, interesting small objects for infants to handle and manipulate to the multipart, interlocking construction toys that older children enjoy. Manipulative toys enhance fine motor development because they require controlled use of hand and finger muscles. However, they contribute much more. **Manipulatives** are sensory materials, involving visual and tactile discrimination; they require skill in coordinating the eyes with what the hands do. Manipulatives can reinforce a variety of concepts such as color, shape, number, and size, as well as encourage one-to-one correspondence, matching, patterning, sequencing, and grouping.

Some manipulative toys such as puzzles are self-correcting, fitting together in only one specific way. Such toys allow children to work independently and know when they have achieved success. This helps build their sense of self-confidence. Because some manipulative materials have a definite closure point when the child completes the task, they also can contribute to children's growing attention span and the satisfaction of staying at a task until it is completed. One notable feature of Montessori materials (see Chapter 5) is their self-correcting nature, because many are designed with built-in feedback.

Other manipulatives such as Legos and Lincoln Logs are more open-ended, allowing children to work creatively. In a way similar to the development of art, children use open-ended manipulatives in stages, starting by fitting together and pulling apart pieces to explore their properties, moving on to more purposeful pattern and shape constructions, and finally creating specific, representational objects or structures.

Types of Manipulatives

Many materials and games could be classified as manipulatives, including commercial and homemade items. It is not easy to group manipulatives because different combinations of such toys share some properties, but they also have various differences.

PUZZLES. These are among the most popular manipulative materials. Wooden or rubber puzzles are the most durable, but sturdy cardboard puzzles can extend the puzzle selection relatively inexpensively. Children find that puzzles appropriate for their developmental level are very satisfying. First puzzles for toddlers and very young preschoolers should have only three to six pieces, either with each piece as a discrete inset or making a simple fit-together picture. When young children still have difficulty with manual control, pieces with knobs can help them avoid frustration.

Puzzles with an increasing number of pieces and complexity should be available as children's skill level improves. Many five- to eight-year-olds have greater dexterity and enjoy interlocking puzzles with 25 to 100 pieces. These lend themselves well to cooperative work. Puzzle pieces are easy to lose or intermingle, however, and some schools have found it helpful to write an identifying name on the back of each individual piece.

GAMES. A variety of games require manipulative skills and reinforce various concepts. Lotto, bingo, and picture dominoes, for instance, can encourage matching, sorting, and classifying by specific topics. Some board games such as Candy Land™ and Hi-Ho! Cherry-O™ are appropriate for older preschoolers and primary children, if the rules are simple and flexible and the game is played in a cooperative rather than competitive atmosphere.

CONSTRUCTION TOYS. The selection and variety of commercial construction toys have increased considerably so that a wide assortment of choices is now available. Duplos™, Bristle Blocks™, magnetic blocks, and snap blocks are good beginning manipulatives for young children, allowing for easy grip and assembly. Many more complex materials with smaller pieces are available to

Key Point ◆

Fine motor development is enhanced by manipulative materials such as puzzles, pegs, and small construction toys; in addition, such materials further other aspects of children's development.

Children enjoy the challenge of fine motor activities such as stringing beads. What additional benefits do you see as a result of this activity?

parquetry blocks
Variously shaped flat blocks, including diamonds and parallelograms, that can be assembled into different patterns on a form board.

provide a range of construction possibilities. Some come with different accessories, such as small people, wheels, or vehicle bases, which can enhance play. It is best to avoid manipulative sets, such as a helicopter or car, that result in a single outcome. Children quickly lose interest after assembling the pieces a few times, whereas more open-ended materials can be used over and over in an endless variety of ways. Simple toys, such as snap beads and large-sized Legos, are available for toddlers. Teachers of very young children who still enjoy mouthing items should be alert, however, to toys that have pieces small enough to be swallowed.

SMALL BLOCKS. It is possible to find a continuum of open-ended to structured small blocks. Wooden table blocks come in a variety of shapes, similar to the larger unit blocks, and lend themselves to many creative uses. Somewhat more structured are the variety of small block sets that are made up of houses, buildings, and accessories and with which children can build towns, farms, or cities. Play mats and carpets are available that provide the background settings on which such blocks can be used. Because of their angled shapes, **parquetry blocks** are more challenging to assemble into the form board, but they provide a unique perspective and some different pattern possibilities not achievable with the right angles of rectangles or cubes.

MISCELLANEOUS MANIPULATIVES. Many other kinds of manipulatives have value for young children. Children can string beads of different sizes and shapes, assembling them in an arbitrary order or following a preset pattern to reinforce matching and sequencing skills. Pegboards with various colored pegs can be used to create designs or follow patterns. Pegboards can be made or purchased in a variety of sizes, with large holes and pegs for toddlers and very young preschoolers and smaller sizes for older children who have refined eye–hand coordination and manual dexterity. Lacing cards help children master a host of motor, perceptual, and cognitive skills.

SUPPORTING PHYSICAL DEVELOPMENT IN INFANTS AND TODDLERS

The first two years of life are a period of learning through motor activity and movement. An infant and toddler program needs to pay careful attention to opportunities to promote gross motor development through the environment, activities, and teacher involvement. It is important to keep infants in positions where they have the most freedom and least restriction to move while they are awake. Gonzalez-Mena and Eyer (2012) advise teachers to avoid contraptions that confine infants. It is through the practice of developing skills that babies strengthen and coordinate their muscles and nervous system and learn to control their bodies. Just as infants need opportunities to move and explore in a variety of safe places, they also need opportunities to help them develop fine motor skills. Materials and activities that encourage infants to grasp, drop, pull, push, throw, finger, and mouth items support such development (Watson & Swim, 2011).

Similarly, toddlers need freedom to move about and use their skills. Toddlers are constantly on the go, using large muscles, both indoors and outside. Movement has to be the central feature of a curriculum for toddlers. As a teacher of toddlers, you should expect that they will climb; your role then is to support this skill by providing safe, sturdy, low places for them to practice. There should be climbers, steps, low climbing platforms, gently sloping ramps, boxes, and other items that facilitate safe climbing, both inside and outside. Gestwicki (2011) also cautions teachers to avoid being overprotective of toddlers lest they get the message that they are not competent. A carefully designed environment that promotes appropriate challenges for the practice of emerging skills, but one in which safety is a prime consideration, is the best way to help children gain autonomy and self-confidence. Toddlers also practice motor skills by picking up and dropping as well as dumping items. These should not be seen as negative traits but should, in fact, be accommodated in the environment and curriculum. Gonzalez-Mena and Eyer (2012) tell of one program in which a bucket containing small items is suspended from the ceiling for the express purpose of allowing children to dump and refill. Toddlers' fine motor development is facilitated through emerging self-help skills such as eating and undressing. A variety of toys and materials help children refine these skills, including dress-up clothes, dolls, manipulatives, art materials, books, small figures, and small vehicles. One teacher of one-year-olds provided a range of beads of different shapes, colors, and sizes that had come from disassembled jewelry. The children spent several weeks sorting these beads in different ways, but became even more engaged when the teacher provided fishing line on which to string the beads. She was amazed that some of the children spent up to three-quarters of an hour carefully stringing small beads onto the fishing line.

Toddlers are beginning to master new gross motor skills, such as scooting on a small tricycle. The guiding hands of the teacher help these little ones maintain balance.

© Cengage Learning

SUPPORTING PHYSICAL DEVELOPMENT IN SCHOOL-AGE CHILDREN

During the primary years, children continue to refine and coordinate the physical skills that evolved during their earlier years. "Children learn to control their body muscles and to refine the physical skills they will use for the rest of their lives. Although these skills are retained during adolescence and adulthood, new skills are not usually acquired. Therefore, it is crucial for children to have many opportunities to learn and practice basic physical skills" (Koralek, Newman, & Colker, 1996, p. 229). Children are generally drawn to physical activity and are eager to engage in vigorous play after a day in school. On the other hand, we have learned that many American children do not have optimal health because of inappropriate diet and lack of exercise, so providing a wide variety of physical activities that appeal not only to those who are athletically inclined but also to children who are not so inclined becomes all the more important. School-age children can learn that physical fitness is an important lifelong goal. They can be helped to tune in to and become aware of the effect of physical activity, such as increased heart rate and breathing, on their bodies (Hatch, 2005).

naeyc

Older children enjoy games that require considerable coordination, such as jump rope.

© Cengage Learning

MEETING THE PHYSICAL NEEDS OF CHILDREN IN THE PRIMARY GRADES

I am a coach; I was a physical education teacher; I was a three-sport college athlete; I have degrees in early childhood education and human development and family studies; and I student teach in first grade. Because of my background and actively being involved in athletics, my principal, who is well aware of the need for physical activity in the early years, asked me to teach physical education. This was a wonderful opportunity for the children and for me, since P.E. is not required in elementary school. In fact, about half of the children had never participated in P.E., so physical activity was not only a new and exciting adventure but a bit of a challenge as well.

I also had to face some challenges. One had to do with getting to know the children, since I work with several classes for about 45 minutes each once a week. One way that I got to know my students and assess their abilities was by doing stations with them. Stations consist of subgroups that each do a wide variety of activities, such as hula hoops, skipping, jumping in and out of circles on one foot or two feet, bouncing a ball to a partner, and swinging on the swings. Stations enabled me to see which types of games I could introduce.

P.E. does not have to be filled with rules and a difficult playing level. I keep activities

Courtney, Physical Education Teacher and First Grade Student Teacher

© Theresa Danna Douglas

child-driven by incorporating things that the children are learning about in class. For example, I found out that the kindergarteners were learning about transportation, so I made large laminated pictures of a helicopter, airplane, hot air balloon, and jet. We discussed how these sound and fly. After that the students spread out and as I held up a picture, they would have to sound and move like that particular picture once the music started. When I turned off the music, the students knew to look at me for the next picture.

Safety plays an important role during P.E., and I have to be constantly aware of it when teaching. Related to the importance of safety is class management. This is the case because even a small group of children can quickly get carried away. One way to manage a physically active group

of children is by letting them decide on and incorporate their own guidelines and instruction, whether they are involved in games, relays, stations, or group challenges. I believe that children should have opportunities to be engaged as well as learn. Having a sense of ownership in the game is just as important during P.E. time as for any other aspect of the curriculum. For instance, I gave the kindergarteners and first-grade students the chance to develop their own guidelines for playing a simple game of tag. Later, the students played this on their own, even outside of P.E. class.

In addition to working with the children, I also work with the teachers on what activities they can do with their students when they are not having P.E. For instance, one time I provided musical movement CDs to the teachers, with songs that ranged from the Hokie Pokie to animal movements and sound. I also suggested some funny ways the students could dance to the music.

There are many ways to increase young children's physical activity. I have found that the practices I have described here have helped me develop an integrated curriculum for my students, whether they are outside during P.E. or inside my first-grade classroom.

Similar to the development of gross motor skills in the primary years, fine motor skills also continue to become refined and coordinated. Newly acquired academic skill as well as leisure activities challenge and encourage children to further develop fine motor proficiency. There are many opportunities for school-age children to use their small muscles, most of which are secondary to the activity itself. For instance, they exercise small muscles when they draw and write with a variety of implements, use a computer or calculator, make puppets and other props for dramatic play, thread needles, mold clay, use tools to take apart items such as clocks or watches, use tools in the woodworking area, learn to play a variety of musical instruments, or play table games like pick-up sticks (Koralek et al., 1996).

SUPPORTING PHYSICAL DEVELOPMENT IN CHILDREN WITH DISABILITIES

Inclusive early childhood programs must ensure that children with disabilities are involved as much as possible in the physical components of the program. This may mean using special adaptive devices for children with physical limitations or ensuring that materials and activities are low enough for a child in a wheelchair to reach. On the other hand, it may mean that teachers need to look carefully for alternative opportunities for participation. Miller (1996) suggests that a child in a wheelchair may, for instance, be able to kick or throw a ball or hold one end of a jump rope for another child who is jumping.

A child with visual impairments will need to be oriented to the space and equipment to access it safely. "Children with visual impairments enjoy the stimulation of physical activity using large motor skills. As long as they feel safe, they will participate fully" (Miller, 1996, p. 224). Using the large muscles of their body helps children with visual impairments to learn more about their own bodies as well as about the environment (Deiner, 2010). Some children with social, emotional, or behavioral disorders may need help in motor activities. Large motor activity may be one way for children to burn off excess energy or frustration (Deiner, 2010). A child who is emotionally withdrawn may be physically inactive as well. Your gentle and consistent reassurance that the child is safe can help in such a situation. A classroom with a child with out-of-control behaviors can benefit from large cardboard rather than wooden blocks.

Children with cognitive disabilities or developmental delays may well be behind other children of the same age in motor development. Through large motor activities, children can be helped to develop stamina, coordination, and bodily awareness. You can emphasize basic skills and variations, such as walking forward, backward, and sideways, creeping, and running; ensure participation in physical activities, which will build stamina; and provide opportunities to stretch and balance to develop stability. Similarly, opportunities for small motor skill development, including grasping and manipulation, will help develop more adept use of the hands and fingers (Deiner, 2010).

SENSORY ACTIVITIES

Any activity involves a sensory component because we use sight, hearing, or touch almost all the time. But some activities are specifically geared to enhance sensory awareness. Most young children seem to thoroughly enjoy and get immersed in such activities. We will briefly examine activities that are primarily for tactile enjoyment—specifically, water and sand play—and activities that sharpen sensory acuity.

Sensory activities are important for young children, from infancy through the primary years. Much of infants' learning comes through their senses. Just watch a baby explore an object by holding it, turning it this way and that while looking at it and listening to its sounds, exploring its feel with her fingers, and putting it in her mouth. Such exploration is learning. Toddlers continue to be

naeyc

DIVERSITY

Key Point ◆◆

Physical activities and development of fine motor skills are vital for children of all ages and abilities and should be valued and carefully included in programs for infants, toddlers, preschoolers, school-age children, and children with disabilities.

naeyc

sensory explorers, reveling in experiments that test the properties and limits of objects. They drop, throw, strike against different surfaces, push, pull, mouth, stand up, and knock down many objects. Throughout the preschool years, sensory activities continue to be great favorites because children still learn much about the world through their senses. School-age children also get immersed in the sensations afforded by many activities, often using their senses to reinforce and test new learning. Sensory activities are also very important for children with disabilities, since children may rely on alternative senses or need to sharpen their senses to maximize their abilities.

The importance of sensory activities for infants, toddlers, preschoolers, and even school-age children cannot be emphasized enough. Such activities are crucial for brain development because it is through exploration with the body and the senses that children's earliest learning takes place. Cognitive structures in young children are initially built through movement and the senses. This means that children need hands-on experiences with materials they can manipulate and explore with all the senses. Such activities are often messy, which may be disturbing to some parents, who do not like their children's clothing to get dirty at school. One of your roles as a teacher is to help parents understand just how important sensory exploration is and that true sensory exploration often is—and should be—messy!

Water and Sand Play

naeyc

Key Point ◆

Water and sand play, which promote tactile enjoyment, provide sensory stimulation and can promote learning of a variety of concepts.

Water acts like a magnet to young children, who are drawn to this soothing and enjoyable medium. Water play should be considered a requisite activity not only because it is so appealing to children but also because of its many other values. It is as appropriate for infants as it is for school-age children. Water play can take place indoors, at a water table or plastic bins placed on a table, or outdoors during warm weather. Water can be used with squeeze bottles, funnels, flexible tubes, and pouring containers; to wash dolls, doll clothes, or dishes; or to create bubbles with added liquid soap, straws to blow through, and various-sized bubble-making forms. Children enjoy the sensory stimulation of water but also learn about properties of water such as volume, buoyancy, and evaporation. They learn to appreciate its importance as they provide water for plants and animals and are exposed to mathematical concepts through pouring activities.

Sand play is another multipurpose sensory activity that fascinates and entices children. Many schools provide an outdoor sand play area, but sand can also be provided indoors in a sand table. When available by itself, fine-grained sand lends itself to being manipulated, molded, and smoothed. Added props such as containers, shovels, spoons, sifters, cars, and trucks expand the creative potential of sand play. Some simple rules about both water and sand play let the children know that these materials need to stay in specified areas to protect the children, the classroom, and classroom materials.

© Cengage Learning

Sand provides multiple sensory opportunities for young children as they explore it, place it in buckets, empty it out again, and use it for dramatic play possibilities.

Sensory Concepts

Sensory experiences are the foundation of infant learning. The infant and toddler program needs to provide a variety of pleasurable sensory experiences for young children, including colorful, interesting objects to look at and play with; pleasant sounds, including music; a variety of textures to enjoy and contrast; tactile experiences, such as fingerpainting; and varied taste and smell experiences as part of feeding and special activities.

For older children, sensory experiences can be pleasurable for their own sake, but they also provide many opportunities for concept development. Each sense is assailed by a range of stimuli, which children gradually learn to identify and discriminate among. Specific sensory activities can provide experiences and reinforcement for these tasks.

We tend to be most adept at identifying objects in our environment through visual cues, because we gather the majority of our information through our eyes. But it is also important to be able to use the other senses. Consider the following examples of activities that help children in the task of object identification using a single sensory modality.

naeyc

Key Point ◆

Activities aimed at identifying an object by using a single sense (for instance, touch or smell) help children develop the use of all their senses.

Key Point ◆

Sensory discrimination involves making distinctions among stimuli; for instance, distinguishing among sounds, or matching a food smell with the picture of the food.

▸ **Touch identification**—Children use only the sense of touch when they put a hand into a feely bag or box and identify an object.
▸ **Hearing identification**—Children listen to a tape or record of common environmental or animal sounds and identify them, using only the sense of hearing. Similarly, during a walk children can be encouraged to listen for and identify the sounds they hear.
▸ **Smell identification**—Children identify common objects or foods (for instance, a flower or a cotton ball saturated with mint extract) using only the sense of smell. When an actual object is used, the child should not be able to see it so that smell is the only identifying criterion.
▸ **Taste identification**—While blindfolded, children are given a spoonful of common foods, which they identify using only the sense of taste.

In addition to using the various senses to identify objects, children also use sensory information to discriminate as they match, seriate, or classify sensory stimuli. The following are some examples of activities that encourage refinement of sensory concepts.

▸ **Matching**—Children can match like objects using information from primarily one sense. Visual matching can involve color, shape, or size, as well as pairs of objects or pictures that children match on the basis of appearance. A collection of fabrics and sandpaper can provide opportunities for tactile matching. Pairs of sound cans (for instance, film canisters with a variety of objects such as rice, beans, or pebbles) can be matched using the sense of hearing, whereas small jars containing various distinctive smells can encourage smell discrimination.
▸ **Seriation**—A variety of objects can be seriated (placed in order along a dimension such as height, width, or color) using cues from one sensory modality such as vision or hearing. Children can organize a collection of sticks from longest to shortest, seashells from smallest to largest, or color paint chips from lightest to darkest. Similarly, sound cans can be placed in order from loudest to softest.
▸ **Classification**—Children can classify sensory stimuli in a variety of ways. They can group foods into categories such as sweet, sour, and salty; organize

sounds as soft or loud, high or low, or into those made by household pets or farm animals; and classify objects by such visual cues as color, hue, shape, size, sex, or any of a wide variety of dimensions.

The use and integration of more than one sense can also be promoted in a **cross-modal intersensory activity.** For instance, children can look at an object and then be asked to feel inside a box and pull out the object that matches the one viewed.

cross-modal intersensory activity
Use and integration of more than one sensory modality; for instance, matching an object that is seen visually to an identical object selected through touch only.

CARING FOR THE BODY

The early childhood program should help lay the foundation for good health habits. In addition to establishing routines and activities that emphasize the importance of physical exercise, children can learn about appropriate nutrition, health, and safety concepts. Keep in mind, however, that the adults in young children's lives ultimately are responsible for their health, safety, and well-being. We can begin to educate children on these topics, but we should never assume that such education is enough. Children need our continued guidance because they do not have the maturity necessary for the enormous responsibility of self-care.

Nutrition Education and Cooking

Because food is a basic human need and so often provides great pleasure, nutrition education and cooking experiences should be an integral part of the curriculum. Nutrition concepts can be presented to children in an understandable manner, and they can be reinforced by hands-on cooking activities. The topic of nutrition could have been included in several places in this book; nutrition education, although it contributes toward understanding of a basic physical need, equally involves cognitive, language, creative, and social areas of development as well.

Key Point ◆
Young children can learn specific concepts about their need for nutritious foods and the development of good eating habits.

NUTRITION EDUCATION. A variety of concepts about food can be presented to young children through appropriate activities to help them understand the importance of good nutrition. They begin to take into account the complexity of this topic while exploring realistically appropriate concepts. You will need to tailor nutrition concepts to the ages and ability levels of the children, your own knowledge about nutrition, and the depth with which you plan to approach the subject.

Keep in mind that nutrition should be an integral part of the ongoing curriculum, not something that is covered in a once-a-year weekly theme. The following are some basic concepts about nutrition that should be integrated into early childhood programs (Marotz, 2012):

- Children need food to grow and be healthy.
- Many different foods are good for us.
- Nutrients come from food, and these nutrients allow children to grow and be healthy.
- Nutrients work inside our bodies in different ways to make us healthy.
- Food provides all the nutrients we need.
- Different foods provide different nutrients; therefore, we need to eat a variety of foods every day.

- Foods must be handled carefully before they are eaten to ensure that they are healthy and safe.
- It is important that food and anyone who handles it maintain standards of cleanliness, including handwashing.
- Foods come in many shapes, sizes, colors, textures, tastes, and smells.
- Food can be categorized in different ways, such as grains and bread, fruits, vegetables, meats, and milk and dairy products.

COOKING EXPERIENCES. Among the most enjoyable activities for young children are those that involve food preparation. Such activities are multisensory; involve children in a process they have observed but in which they may not have participated; teach and reinforce a variety of concepts related to nutrition, mathematics, science, language and literacy, and social studies; and are very satisfying because they result in a tangible (and delicious) end product.

Some cooking activities are more appropriate than others, and activities should be carefully selected to meet specific criteria and objectives. The following are guidelines to keep in mind when planning food activities.

- **The activity should be matched to the children.** For very young preschoolers, select recipes that do not involve heat or sharp utensils and do not require precise fine motor control. Examples include tearing lettuce for a salad, plucking grapes from the stem for fruit salad, mixing yogurt and fruit in individual cups, or spreading tuna salad on crackers with a spoon. Older preschoolers and primary children have more refined muscle control and can follow more complex instructions. More involved recipes that might require the use of knives or electrical appliances can be planned.
- **Safety is of utmost importance.** Many cooking tools are potentially dangerous, and careful adult supervision is required. Some steps in cooking require that only one child at a time be involved with a teacher; for instance, flipping pancakes in an electric skillet or griddle. Other cooking activities may well require that the number of children be limited, for instance, to five or six at a time, so that the adult can supervise and observe all of the children adequately. The process can then be repeated with additional groups of children so that everyone who is interested has the opportunity to participate. Limiting the number of children who can be involved at one time must be thought out before the activity is presented to the children, however.
- **The recipe should involve enough steps so that all of the children in the group make a significant contribution.** Some recipes can be prepared individually by each child in single-serving sizes. Other recipes will require group cooperation. An appealing activity such as cooking should have enough ingredients and steps (for instance, five or six) so that each child in a group is an involved participant. If children are making muffins, for instance, one child can break and stir the eggs while others add and stir in the butter, flour, milk, honey, nuts and raisins, and flavorings and leavening; then they can take turns stirring the dough.

Well-planned cooking activities can be a wonderful language experience that provides opportunities for physical, cognitive, language, and social development.

© Cengage Learning

Figure **10-2**

Pictorial Recipe Chart for Banana Bread

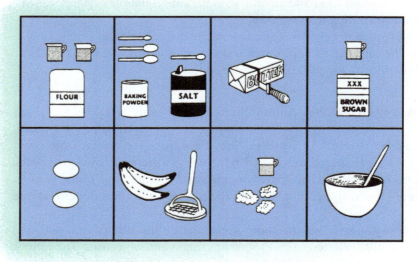

Source: From Essa. Early Childhood Curriculum, 1E. © 1992 Wadsworth, a part of Cengage Learning, Inc. Reproduced by permission. www.cengage.com/permissions

▶ **Children can be helped to understand the entire process.** It is helpful to prepare a pictorial recipe chart (or use one that is commercially made) that shows ingredients and amounts, allowing children to experience measuring as well as mixing (see Figure 10-2 for an example). School-age children who have learned how to read may be able to follow recipes with simple words. Help the children note the changes in ingredients as they are mixed with others; for instance, that the flour loses its dry powderiness as it joins the liquids. Discuss the effect of heat, which solidifies the semiliquid dough into firm muffins, for instance.

▶ **The activity should focus on wholesome, nutritious foods.** It is important to set a good example with the planned cooking activities to reinforce nutritional concepts. There are numerous cookbooks available that focus on healthy recipes.

▶ **The importance of hygiene and cleanliness must be stressed.** Require that children as well as adults wash their hands before participating in cooking experiences. Make sure that cooking surfaces and tools are clean. It contributes to multisensory learning if you allow children to taste at various points during the cooking process; however, instead of letting children use their fingers for tasting, provide individual spoons.

▶ **Cooking activities provide a good cultural link.** One of the most distinctive features of many cultures is their special foods. Dishes that reflect the culture of children in the classroom are a good way of involving families and helping children feel special. Parents, who may feel shy about participating in their child's classroom otherwise, may be delighted to be asked if they would facilitate a cooking activity with the children to make something from their culture, be it tacos or potato pancakes or egg rolls or piroshki.

DIVERSITY

Health

naeyc   Young children get many messages about health needs and practices from what is expected of them, what they are told, and what adults model. School routines (discussed in Chapter 14) will set many expectations and structure the schedule to encourage and facilitate increasing self-care in toileting, cleanliness, and eating. But health information should also be conveyed as part of the curriculum. Discussions and activities can heighten children's awareness of topics such as the relationship between health and growth, the body's need for both activity and rest, temperature regulation through appropriate clothing, hygiene practices as part of disease prevention, the importance of medical and dental care, and health professionals and facilities that care for children in the community. In addition, if a child in the class has a specific allergy or a chronic illness, all of the children can be helped to better understand this condition by including the topic in the curriculum in a sensitive way.

It was helpful in one preschool program, for instance, when the teacher discussed why Jessica could not eat certain foods. The children became more sensitive to Jessica's diabetes and the restrictions it caused, and they saw that her special snacks were not a privilege but a necessity.

Safety

Young children begin to acquire safety information and precautions, although it is important to remember that adults must be responsible for ensuring children's safety by providing a safe environment and preventing accidents. Because very young children may not process safety information accurately, it should be conveyed with a great deal of caution. Some two-year-olds, or young three-year-olds, may fail to understand the negative message in "don't do …" or may get ideas from well-intentioned cautions. Through curriculum topics, older children can gradually acquire information and learn some preventive precautions related to fire, electricity, tools, traffic, potential poisons, and strangers, as well as learn about community safety personnel and resources, and what to do in case of an accident.

FAMILY VALUES RELATED TO PHYSICAL DEVELOPMENT AND CARE

Early childhood teachers and families share responsibility for the development and care of young children in many areas that once were in the domain of the home. Today, children acquire many personal life skills and habits related to exercise, nutrition, health, hygiene, and safety through their early childhood program. Yet, these areas are also very personal to families, representing their own lifelong habits and practices. It is important, therefore, to share with families the school's philosophy about helping children to develop healthy patterns that include daily exercise, good nutrition, appropriate care for the body, and safety precautions. It is equally important to be open to the families' ideas and values on these topics.

Teachers of young children note that one difference between home and school expectations is the desire of some families to have children sit quietly, learn academic skills, listen to the teacher, and do worksheets. In such an instance, it is particularly important that you, as an early childhood professional, provide

Key Point ◆◆
Young children begin to learn many concepts about health, caring for their bodies, and safety, topics that should be integrated into the early childhood curriculum.

naeyc

Key Point ◆◆
Communication between home and school will help in mutual understanding about values related to physical development and self-care.

naeyc

Through repeated experiences, children gradually learn community safety rules, for instance, those related to crossing the street or parking lot safely.

© Cengage Learning

appropriate developmental information and make readings available that clearly demonstrate that young children learn through an active, not a passive, process. You may need to help families share your concern and recognition that all aspects of children's development need to be furthered. Physical development is an integral part of the whole child; thus, all activities that promote fine motor, gross motor, and perceptual skills deserve prominence in the early childhood program.

SUMMARY

1. Consider the theories that explain physical development.
2. Physical development is complex, involving a number of interrelated components.
   A. Body control involves mastering a number of skills important for movement and balance.
   B. Young children gain increasing manual control, the ability to use the hands effectively.
   C. Sensory-perceptual development involves children's increasing accuracy in interpreting information they gain through their senses.
3. Many early childhood activities encourage and promote the use of the large muscles of the body.
   A. Physical fitness activities and outdoor play provide excellent opportunities for large muscle development.
   B. Consider the value of blocks and block play for young children.
4. Many manipulative materials and activities promote the use and development of the small muscles of the hands and fingers.
5. Plan activities that meet the physical needs of children of different ages and abilities.
6. Because of the importance of learning through the senses for young children, consider activities that promote sensory exploration and discrimination.
7. A major aspect of physical development includes learning to care for the body in terms of nutrition, health, and safety.

KEY TERMS LIST

ballistic skills

cross-modal intersensory activity

eye–hand coordination

fine motor development

gross motor development

holding grip

kinesthetic sense

locomotion

manipulatives

maturational theory

multisensory

palmar grasp

parquetry blocks

perceptual motor model

pincer grasp

self-help skills

sensory integration

sensory-perceptual development

tripod grasp

unit blocks

KEY QUESTIONS

1. Observe preschoolers of various ages at play. What differences in physical development do you see as a function of age? What do these abilities tell you about appropriate activities and expectations?

2. If you were asked to plan a physical fitness program for a group of preschoolers, what would you include? Would you plan different activities for three-year-olds than for five-year-olds?

3. Select two different manipulative materials. What do you think children can potentially learn from each of them? Now spend 10 minutes using each manipulative. Would you add any items to your list of what children can learn?

4. Adults generally use their senses of sight and hearing far more than their other senses. Think about how and when you use information from the various senses. Does this suggest activities for young children that could enhance their sensory learning?

5. Plan a cooking activity for preschoolers. How can this activity reinforce concepts of nutrition education?

ADDITIONAL RESOURCES

Select additional books, articles, and websites on topics discussed in Chapter 10.

Gagen, L. M., Getchell, N., & Payne, V. G. (2009). Motor development in young children: Implications and applications. In E. Essa & M. Burnham (Eds.), *Informing our practice: Useful research on young children's development* (pp. 145–161). Washington, DC: NAEYC.

Wellhousen, K. (2002). *Outdoor play everyday: Innovative play concepts for early childhood.* Clifton Park, NY: Thomson Delmar Learning.

Wellhousen, K., & Kief, J. (2001). *A constructivist approach to block play in early childhood.* Clifton Park, NY: Thomson Delmar Learning.

HELPFUL WEBSITES

Kid-Fit Physical Education Classes for Preschoolers:

www.kid-fit.com

Kid-Fit's website provides a physical fitness curriculum for young children and their teachers. The curriculum promotes healthy lifestyle habits, including physical education and fitness and sound nutrition.

Nutrition Resources:

http://www.choosemyplate.gov

This government website provides nutrition information and ideas for nutrition education for young children.

Nutrition Explorations:

http://school.fueluptoplay60.com/tools/nutrition-education/school-nutrition.php

Here you will find a variety of resources and ideas for nutrition education for young children. This website is sponsored by Fuel Up to Play for Education Professionals and the National Dairy Council.

Go to **CengageBrain.com** to register your access code for this book's Education CourseMate website, where you will find more resources to help you study. Additional resources for this chapter include TeachSource Videos, glossary flashcards, web links, case studies with critical-thinking questions that apply the concepts presented in this chapter, and more. If your textbook does not include a printed access card, you can go to **CengageBrain.com** to purchase access.

Cognitive Development through the Curriculum

DAP
Recognizing children's natural curiosity and desire to make sense of their world and gain new skills, teachers consistently plan learning experiences that children find highly interesting, engaging, and comfortable.

Developmentally Appropriate Practice, Copple & Bredekamp, 2009, p. 158

In Chapter 11, you will find answers to the following questions about providing for cognitive development through the curriculum:

▶ How do different theories explain children's cognitive development, and what are their implications for working with young children?
▶ What cognitive abilities do children gain during their early years, and how can these be supported through the curriculum?
▶ What are developmentally appropriate math and science concepts for young children, and how can you best facilitate these for children of different ages and abilities?

NAEYC STANDARDS CONSIDERED IN CHAPTER 11

(See the Standards Correlation Chart on the inside front cover of this book for the titles and description of the standards listed below.)

▶ *Standard 1a:* Familiarity with the theoretical and research foundations on which understanding of cognitive development is based (pp. 279–285).
▶ *Standard 5a:* Knowing and applying cognitive concepts that young children master as a foundation for promoting math and science (pp. 286–291).
▶ *Standard 5c:* Fostering goals such as self-regulation, problem-solving, and academic and social competence in young children (p. 285).
▶ *Standard 5b:* Knowing and using the central concepts of math and science (pp. 291–299).
▶ *Standard 1b:* Supporting cognitive development for children of different ages and abilities (pp. 299–303).
▶ *Standard 2b:* Engaging families in supporting their children's cognitive development (pp. 303–304).

Young children's thinking ability is quite amazing. Within just a few years of their birth, they have acquired an immense repertoire of information and cognitive skills. A child who—two or three or four years before—was a helpless baby responding to the environment mainly through reflexes, is now a competent, thinking, communicating, reasoning, problem-solving, exploratory person.

In studying children's **cognition,** we are more concerned with the process of knowing than with the content of what specifically children know (*how* rather than *what*). In particular, we are interested in how children acquire, organize, and apply knowledge.

As in each of these chapters that focus on a specific area of development, we will consider some activities that are, by necessity, chosen somewhat arbitrarily. Although we will be highlighting science and math, keep in mind that virtually every activity involves cognition. Children actively learn, use problem-solving strategies, and construct new knowledge from all activities—science and math, art, music, movement, manipulatives, story telling, or dramatic play. In no way does this choice imply that such development does not occur in other activities as well.

THEORETICAL FOUNDATIONS OF COGNITIVE DEVELOPMENT

Particularly in the twentieth century, a number of theories have attempted to explain the development of the intellect. The most influential theory on early childhood education is the cognitive developmental theory of Jean Piaget. Another theory that has left its mark on American education through much of the twentieth century is behaviorism. Also noteworthy is the more recent theoretical framework, information processing, which is modeled to some extent on the functioning and operation of computers. Also see the discussion of the impact of recent brain research on views of learning and teaching in the "Take a Closer Look" box.

Piaget's Theory of Cognitive Development

Piaget offers a view of cognitive development that is based on allowing children to build concepts actively rather than on providing those concepts through direct teaching. He has given us a way to understand how children think, pointing out that their minds work in a way that is different from those of adults, and describing how their thinking develops. Taking Piaget's extensive research and writings, others have developed specific applications of his theory, particularly to educational settings. Over the past several decades, many early childhood educators have incorporated Piagetian principles into their programs, to the point at which today many of these are often considered common practice. We shall examine these later in this chapter when we review cognitive tasks.

Chapter 5 stated that one function of the mind is to categorize information into schemata. This is an active process by which the young child continually finds relationships among objects (Goldhaber, 2000). By physically manipulating and changing objects, the child constructs knowledge about the objects and their relationships. This is an important point: Knowledge is not something that is "poured" into children by some external source, such as the teacher, but something that the children have to construct for themselves.

This is why Piaget's theory is also called a **constructivist theory.** For example, a child trying to place a square block on the top point of a triangular one will, after some trials, construct an understanding of the relationship of these two blocks and which block will or will not support the other. By transforming the blocks into a new position, the child acquires knowledge. Because of this need to manipulate and transform materials in the environment, learning has to be an active, not a passive, process.

---

cognition
The process of mental development, concerned more with how children learn than with the content of what they know.

naeyc

naeyc

Key Point ◆
Piaget's theory of cognitive development, which holds that children construct their own knowledge out of direct experiences, has been the most influential theory in early childhood education.

constructivist theory
A theory, such as that of Jean Piaget, based on the belief that children construct knowledge for themselves rather than having it conveyed to them by some external source.

BRAIN RESEARCH: WHAT HAVE WE LEARNED ABOUT LEARNING?

The nature of the mind has been a subject of speculation and mystery for centuries. Over the past few decades, however, scientists have applied new technologies to unravel and give insight into this mystery as a wealth of research provides new information about the workings of the brain. Neurocognitive research shows that children's brains are structurally altered during learning. *How People Learn: Brain, Mind, Experience, and School* (Bransford, Brown, & Cocking, 2000) reshapes our views of learning in a way that implies new ways to design curriculum, to teach, and to assess outcomes that differ from our current practices.

"One of the hallmarks of the new science of learning is its emphasis on learning with understanding" (p. 8). Understanding implies depth of knowledge, not a collection of facts. Deep understanding is more than being able to remember, though this is often how teachers expect children to demonstrate what they have learned. Knowledge is connected by important concepts, and such concepts can be transferred to other contexts.

In addition, children bring what they already know and apply it to new learning. "There is a great deal of evidence that learning is enhanced when teachers pay attention to the knowledge and beliefs that learners bring to a learning task, use this knowledge as a starting point for new instruction, and monitor students' changing conceptions as instruction proceeds" (p. 11). In addition, research confirms the importance of active learning, encouraging children to recognize and evaluate what they learn. This is called **metacognition,** the ability of individuals to predict how they will do on various tasks and monitor their mastery and understanding; it implies thinking about their own thinking.

What does all this mean for you, as a teacher? Children should not be seen as "empty vessels" to be filled by the teacher. Instead, your role is to recognize the viewpoint and understanding that children already have and build on that; to cover topics in depth rather than superficially; and to help children actively evaluate their own thinking. In addition, learning should take place in a community-centered context, in which children help each other, problem solving is a cooperative endeavor, and disagreements lead to genuine consideration of others' viewpoints.

The authors note that "a major goal of schooling is to prepare students for flexible adaptation to new problems and settings" (p. 235). Because of the rapid change in society, what children learn in their early years may not be relevant when they reach adulthood; but they should have the ability to adapt what is familiar to them to new issues they encounter because they have acquired skills for engaging in in-depth learning and analysis.

Such concepts about teaching have a lot in common with emergent curricula, such as the Reggio Emilia and project approaches, which we discussed in earlier chapters. These approaches encourage in-depth explorations of topics of interest to the children. Such explorations are carried out over a lengthy period of time, allowing children to learn a great deal about the topic. Depth of learning is also fostered because children are encouraged to express their understanding of a topic through multiple modes of learning, uncovering new perspectives in the process. In addition, emergent curriculum focuses on collaborative learning, what is called co-construction of knowledge.

The authors of *How People Learn: Brain, Mind, Experience, and School* strongly advocate for a new approach to teaching children based on new knowledge about the workings of the brain. "Developmental processes involve interactions between children's early competencies and their environmental and interpersonal supports. . . . The brain of a developing child is a product, at the molecular level, of interactions between biological and ecological factors. Mind is created in this process" (p. 234).

This process is evident at all stages of development. We will now examine in somewhat more depth three of Piaget's stages of cognitive development.

THE SENSORIMOTOR PERIOD. Piaget labeled the period covering the first two years of life the sensorimotor period; as the term implies, learning in infancy is dependent on the senses and on movement. The sensorimotor period is further divided into six stages, which chart the rapid development of the young child.

1. In the first stage, during the first month of life, babies use the reflexes with which they were born to suck, cry, grasp, hear, and see.
2. By the second stage, between one and four months, learning begins to replace reflexes; repeated experiences teach infants that there are some predictable occurrences. They become more active participants in the social world, engaging in communication with the people around them, and in the physical world, as they look and listen more attentively to stimuli in the environment.
3. From four to eight months, in the third stage, babies come to recognize that they can cause things to happen. They gleefully repeat actions such as hitting objects to again get that interesting sound, kicking at a mobile to make it turn some more, and throwing a rattle off the high chair because someone will again retrieve it. In other words, they learn that they can affect their environment.
4. In the next stage, from eight to twelve months, children use "tools" to achieve goals. They might use a stick to retrieve an object out of reach, showing rudimentary problem-solving ability. Object permanence appears, as babies know that something out of sight continues to exist; but this milestone also means that they realize when mom is leaving and may cry as she puts on her coat.
5. In the fifth stage, twelve- to eighteen-month-olds, whom Piaget termed "little scientists," are characterized by experimentation. They try to find new ways of using familiar objects. Whereas a couple of months ago they may have been content to bang the pot with a fist, now they experiment with banging it with a spoon, a stick, a cup, and other objects to see what effect these might have.
6. The final stage, from eighteen to twenty-four months, marks the shift from dependence on actual objects to mental representations of these. Toddlers begin to develop mental pictures of familiar objects, people, and actions; they can now start working out problems and pursuing ideas in their heads. This landmark achievement parallels the growth of language, which is a major form of representation. Children in this stage also begin to use this skill to pretend to substitute objects in play. A block pushed along the floor, accompanied by chugging sounds, now may represent a train (Goldhaber, 2000).

THE PREOPERATIONAL PERIOD. This newly acquired mental ability of **symbolic representation** marks the beginning of the second period, which lasts from about age two to age seven. Symbolic representation is evident when children use symbols such as words, and in make-believe play, imitation, and drawing or sculpting to represent something they have experienced or seen. Play is particularly important as children learn

metacognition
Thinking about one's own thinking; being able to think about and predict how one might do on various tasks and self-monitor mastery and understanding.

Key Point ◆

The infant in the sensorimotor period, which is divided into six substages, learns through the senses and movement.

symbolic representation
The ability acquired by young children to use mental images to stand for something else.

Key Point ◆◆

The preschooler, in the preoperational period, employs symbolic representation (the ability to use mental images to stand for something else), is egocentric, and relies on perception rather than on logic.

reflective abstraction
According to Jean Piaget, part of a child's self-directed activity that allows the child to think about and reflect on what he or she is doing, leading to the development of new mental abilities.

Key Point ◆◆

School-age children are in the concrete operations period, which is marked by increasingly logical thought and the acquisition of conservation.

Key Point ◆◆

Children in elementary school acquire an essential concept, conservation—the recognition that objects remain the same even if they look different. Grasping the concept of conservation is based on numerous early childhood experiences in manipulating concrete objects.

conservation
Ability to recognize that objects remain the same in amount or number despite perceptual changes; usually acquired during the period of concrete operations.

about the world, because it gives them the opportunity to assimilate experiences without actually having to adapt to the reality of the world. Recall from Chapter 5 that assimilation is a process through which an experience is made to fit a child's schemata, rather than the child changing to accommodate to reality (Crain, 2005; Goldhaber, 2000).

Preoperational children have a limited view of reality, one that comes from their own perceptions, which they rely on to understand what they see. As we all know, our eyes can fool us. As adults, however, we recognize the illusion of appearance—for instance, knowing through logic that although the ball of clay has been stretched out into a long sausage before our eyes, it contains no more or no less clay than it did before. But young children do not yet have that logical ability and rely on their perception, which tells them that it looks as if there is more (or less) clay now. This reliance on their own viewpoints contributes to children's egocentricity, the assumption that everyone experiences and sees the world as they do. Young children assume that other people can understand them and what they think because they believe these people's viewpoints must match theirs; there is no other point of view as far as they are concerned.

For preschool-age children to begin to see experiences from a less egocentric point of view, they must have many opportunities to examine, manipulate, modify, transform, experiment, and reflect on objects. Piaget stressed the importance of **reflective abstraction** for children, the opportunity to think about and reflect on what they are doing, which is part of spontaneous, self-directed activity. Through reflective abstraction, new mental abilities can grow because children are actively engaged in the construction of their knowledge. With active control over materials, children gradually learn to differentiate between what they perceive and reality.

THE CONCRETE OPERATIONS PERIOD. From about 7 to 11 years of age, young children continue to build thinking skills, becoming much more reliant on logic than on external appearances. While their thinking abilities are considerably more logical than they had been during the preoperational period, they still rely very much on the concrete presence of objects for understanding. It is not until the final, formal operational period that adolescents and adults can think abstractly and hypothetically. Through many of the firsthand experiences in which children acted on objects during the preoperational period, concrete operational children move toward a more logical mode of thinking. They refine the ability to classify and seriate objects (processes we will discuss later in this chapter), which allows them to organize information in increasingly logical ways.

In addition, they integrate the various properties of objects and don't focus only on the most obvious one. This skill helps them achieve **conservation,** recognizing that objects remain the same in amount or number despite perceptual changes. So, while it may look as if there is more liquid when the glass of juice is poured from a short, wide glass into a tall, thin one, concrete operational children know that logically the amount is the same because nothing was added or taken away.

During this middle childhood period, children also become much more capable of seeing the viewpoint of another person. The egocentricity of early childhood becomes replaced by an increasing ability to see things from the other perspectives (Crain, 2005; Goldhaber, 2000).

Thus, from Piaget's theory we gain insight into the growing abilities of young children to think logically. Through this insight comes methods of working with young children that suggest that a well-structured environment, ample activities and materials from which children can actively learn, and understanding adults who encourage without interfering will facilitate cognitive growth. Much of this approach is incorporated into many early childhood programs and accepted as developmentally appropriate practice today (Copple & Bredekamp, 2009).

Behaviorism

In our Chapter 5 examination of the influence of B. F. Skinner, we noted the foundation of behaviorism as the belief that learning is controlled by the consequences of behavior. When those consequences are pleasant, a child is likely to repeat the behavior, whereas a disagreeable consequence is more apt to result in the child discontinuing the behavior. By careful control of the learning environment through appropriate reinforcement of selected behaviors or responses, behaviorists believe that they can affect children's learning.

Behavioral theory is applied to teaching children through programmed or direct instruction. In a direct instruction program, the teacher predetermines exactly what children need to know, sets goals accordingly, devises a sequence of learning activities that teach specific information to meet each goal, and directly teaches the children by controlling the information according to their responses. When children respond correctly, the responses are reinforced; if their responses are incorrect, reinforcement is withheld. In this way, children acquire the specific information prescribed in the goals that the teacher considers to be appropriate for them (Crain, 2005).

Information Processing

The term **information processing** literally defines itself because it is concerned primarily with how human beings process information. Although information processing provides an alternative view of how children's thinking abilities develop, it shares a number of features with Piaget's cognitive developmental theory. Both approaches try to identify children's cognitive abilities and limitations at different points in their development. Both also acknowledge that later cognitive abilities build on and grow out of earlier, more primitive ones. In addition, both theories consider that existing concepts have a great impact on the acquisition of new knowledge (Siegler & Alibali, 2004).

But, as is true with behavioral theory, information processing does not focus on stages of cognitive development. Instead, it identifies the exact processes children use to transform information and relate it to other information stored in their memories. As a computer does, the mind relies not only on the information (input) fed into it, but also on its capacity and the strategies (programs) it uses to process the information. The computer analogy has its limits, of course, because the human mind is so much more complex than any computer!

AN INFORMATION PROCESSING MODEL. Information processing is often depicted as a flow chart or model with several interconnected features (Figure 11-1). In the process of cognition, information first comes to us through a **sensory register,** being perceived by one of the senses. The second typical part of this model is memory, where the incoming information moves next.

Preschoolers learn from concrete, hands-on experiences. Their environment should be full of objects they can manipulate and explore.

DAP

naeyc

Key Point ◆

The influence of behaviorism on early childhood education has been particularly strong in direct instruction programs, in which the teacher controls most aspects of learning.

naeyc

information processing
A model of cognitive development that is somewhat analogous to how a computer functions; it is concerned primarily with how human beings take in and store information.

Key Point ◆

Understanding children's thinking processes and limitations helps early childhood educators provide an appropriate environment for cognitive development.

sensory register
In information processing theory, that part of the model describing how information initially comes to our awareness when perceived by the senses.

Figure **11-1**

A Simplified Information Processing Model

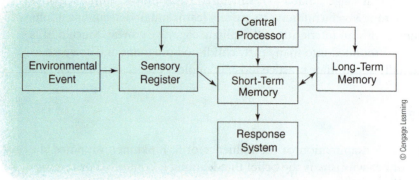

© Cengage Learning

Key Point ◆

Information processing attempts to identify the processes children use to take in information and relate it to other information already stored in their memories.

short-term memory
In information processing theory, limited capacity for temporarily remembering information such as a telephone number.

long-term memory
In information processing theory, the vast store of information and knowledge that is held for a long time.

central processor
That aspect of the information processing model that governs and coordinates other functions such as sensory input and memory.

memory strategies
Various approaches used, especially by older children and adults, to help them remember information.

Key Point ◆

Young children's memories are not as efficient as those of older children and adults.

metamemory
The ability to think about one's own memory.

Memory is divided into short-term and long-term components. **Short-term memory** provides limited capacity for remembering information temporarily; for instance, a telephone number. **Long-term memory** refers to the vast store of information and knowledge that we hold for a long time. This stored information is organized so it can be readily retrieved and linked to new information. A final aspect of the information processing model is the **central processor** that governs and coordinates the other components; for instance, deciding what information should be acknowledged by the sensory register, whether it should remain briefly in short-term memory, or whether it should be stored in long-term memory (Crain, 2005; Goldhaber, 2000).

MEMORY. Children's ability to remember improves over the first years of life, but preschool children do not yet use memory as efficiently as do older children and adults. A number of **memory strategies** are used to remember information; for instance, rehearsal (mentally repeating information over and over), organization (placing items to be remembered into logical categories), and elaboration (making up imaginary connections when there is no logical link among items). Memory strategies, according to DAP, "are deliberate mental activities that allow us to hold information first in working memory and then to transfer it to long-term memory" (Copple & Bredekamp, 2009, p. 132).

Although preschoolers can learn to use such strategies, they are not very adept at this skill, partly because they have fewer schemata to call up in attempts to organize or elaborate on information. Another reason is that familiarity improves memory, and young children have not had as much opportunity as older children to develop this familiarity. It also takes preschoolers longer than older children or adults to retrieve information from both short-term and long-term memory stores. In addition, young children hold considerably fewer pieces of information in their working memories at one time than do older children (Siegler & Alibali, 2004).

One aspect of memory that distinguishes older from younger children's thinking is **metamemory,** the ability to think about one's own memory. For instance, older children are more realistic in answering the question, "Do you forget?" Younger children often deny that they do forget. Young children are also not very good at estimating how many items they think they will be able to remember, unrealistically predicting that they can remember all of a large number of items. Also, the instruction "Remember what I tell you" does not improve preschoolers' memory when they are later asked to recall, whereas the word "remember" gives older children the cue to use some memory strategies (Siegler & Alibali, 2004).

Information processing theory provides some concepts useful in learning how children's cognitive development progresses. Specific consideration of how information is taken in, memory strategies, and metamemory helps us recognize young children's abilities and limitations. The activities planned for young children should be congruent with what we know about their abilities.

TOOLS OF THE MIND

Lev Vygotsky's sociocultural theory, to which you were introduced in Chapter 5, provides the rationale for Elena Bodrova and Deborah Leong's (2007) program and book, *Tools of the Mind: The Vygotskian Approach to Early Childhood Education.* Tools of the Mind is used in many schools across the country. Its purpose is to promote self-regulation in young children. Self-regulation is a good predictor of later school success. In particular, these authors provide concrete strategies for scaffolding children's learning and development. They note the importance of play in early childhood programs; however, they say that play needs to be planned and structured, what they call "mature play," something that sensitive teachers scaffold and support. Mature play includes symbolic representation, language to create pretend scenarios, complex interwoven themes, multifaceted roles, and an extended time frame. Research has found that children who participated in the Tools of the Mind program did significantly better than a control group on basic measures of literacy ability (Tough, 2009). See the "Brain Storm" box below for more insight into such research and brain development.

In her book, *Mind in the Making: The Seven Essential Life Skills Every Child Needs*, Ellen Galinski (2010) proposes that children need some very specific skills to be successful in the twenty-first-century world. The seven skills she discusses are ones that researchers describe as executive functions: (1) focus and self-control, (2) perspective taking, (3) communicating, (4) making connections, (5) critical thinking, (6) taking on challenges, and (7) self-directed, engaged learning. Many early childhood approaches today, such as Tools of the Mind, focus on helping children attain such essential skills because they will help children face the future successfully.

BRAIN STORM
EXECUTIVE FUNCTIONS

Researcher Adele Diamond studies developmental cognitive neuroscience, a field that seeks to understand how children's minds change as they mature and what factors influence these changes. She notes that school success is the result of a combination of cognitive and noncognitive skills. The latter include the ability to be focused, to remember and use new information, to plan actions and revise plans as needed, and to inhibit impulsive behavior. Such skills are called executive functions and are controlled by an area at the front of the brain—the prefrontal cortex. This part of the brain is quite immature in young children and continues to develop into early adulthood. Diamond's research shows that certain activities, such as ones used in Tools of the Mind, can enhance these skills. The study also found that children who improved in executive function skills also made improvements in other measures of academic performance (Diamond, Barnett, Thomas, & Munro, 2007).

executive functions
Noncognitive functions that are, nonetheless, important to school success, including skills such as the ability to focus, to retain and use information, to plan and revise action plans as needed, and to self-regulate.

COGNITIVE TASKS

In addition to helping us understand how children think, theories of cognition also provide some insights into what cognitive skills children acquire or begin to acquire during the early years. Most of these tasks have been derived from Piaget's theory, particularly what he tells us about thinking and learning abilities in the preoperational and concrete operational periods—in other words, preschool and primary children. This provides a basis for curriculum planning to enhance cognitive development. In this section, we will review classification; seriation; number, temporal, and spatial concepts; and acquisition of information.

Classification

classification
The ability to sort and group objects by some common attribute or property; for instance, color or size.

Key Point ◆◆

Young children begin to learn classification, the ability to sort and group objects by some similar characteristic.

Classification is the ability to sort and group objects by some common attribute or property. One of the most important goals of development for young children, according to DAP, is to make sense of the world by organizing it into meaningful categories (Copple & Bredekamp, 2009). To classify, a child has to note similarities and differences among objects. Classification involves two simultaneous processes, sorting (separating) objects and grouping (joining) objects (Charlesworth & Lind, 2010). For instance, in classifying beads, Liam groups the red beads at the same time that he sorts out the blue and yellow ones; Shanda groups the largest beads and sorts out all other sizes.

If we did not have the ability to classify, every object and experience would represent a separate, isolated piece of information in our minds. Classification allows us to deal economically with the environment so that we do not have to go through the process of adaptation each time a new object or experience is encountered. Although preoperational children use perceptual judgment to classify (for instance, grouping items that *look* the same), true classification is a mental operation that goes beyond such sensory cues. True classification appears later in the concrete operations period, but innumerable early childhood classification experiences contribute to its emergence.

Children classify spontaneously and usually have no problems in finding categories. They frequently use themselves as a basis for social classification, grouping the boys and the girls, the older children and the "babies," or those who get to play with the blocks and those who do not. One teacher, responding to one child's dismay at being excluded from a group of four-year-olds, found that the children's basis for group inclusion was whether their shoes were fastened with Velcro. This child's shoes were tied with more conventional laces.

Of course, children can classify a group of objects in many ways. Features such as color, shape, size, material, pattern, and texture provide concrete attributes by which to group. As children get older, they begin to classify by more abstract commonalities such as the function of items (objects that are used in cooking, things that make music); a common feature among an odd assortment of items (things that have four legs, things that have doors); or association (money, paper bags, and milk are associated with the supermarket; galoshes and rain go together) (Charlesworth & Lind, 2010).

Because young children sort and group items naturally, the early childhood environment should provide a rich variety of objects and experiences that can be used for such activities.

▸ Many early childhood materials such as manipulatives, blocks, and science materials lend themselves to being classified.

© Cengage Learning

A variety of early childhood materials lend themselves to grouping and sorting items in different ways. How is this child seriating these manipulatives? What other classroom materials contribute to an understanding of classification and seriation?

- Less obvious items in the art, book, dramatic play, and sensory areas also have inherent properties that children will group and sort.
- In addition, teacher feedback should reinforce the value of children's spontaneous classification activities. ("You put all of the green chairs around the round table and the blue chairs at the rectangular table!") Structured classification activities can also be part of the early childhood program. In large and small groups, and individually, children can be encouraged to find commonalities among people, objects, and experiences.
- Similarly, children can explore objects and describe their attributes, and articulate similarities and differences.
- Older preschoolers and primary school children can be encouraged to group items by two attributes. ("Put together the things that are round *and* hard.")
- Children can also be helped to compare subclasses by distinguishing between "all" and "some" (*all* of these are flowers, but *some* of these are daisies).

Seriation

Seriation concerns the relationship among objects and the ability to place them in a logical sequence or order. Simple seriation involves concrete objects; for instance, arranging objects from longest to shortest or widest to narrowest. Sensory seriation can include ordering sounds from loudest to softest, tastes from sweetest to sourest, or colors from darkest to lightest. Seriation can also relate to time sequences; for example, what happened first, second, third, and so forth. As children engage in seriation activities, they acquire and use a vocabulary of comparative words ("this is the longest," "he is older," "I have more pudding," "your hair is lighter than mine," "my blocks are taller").

The early childhood environment should include many materials and experiences to encourage seriation.

- Unit blocks and a number of manipulatives such as nesting toys offer many opportunities for children to seriate because they are made in graduated sizes.
- Other materials—for instance, dolls, dishes, props for sand and water play, books, woodworking equipment, and nature collections—should be provided in a variety of sizes to prompt spontaneous ordering and comparison.
- Teachers can also encourage children to note and verbalize comparisons among each other, among objects, and among sets of objects.
- Instructions in group activities such as "Simon Says" and "Red Rover" can be worded to encourage comparisons.

Number Concepts

A number denotes an understanding of quantity, an awareness that entails increasingly more complex concepts. In its earliest form, number understanding involves gross comparison of quantity, identifying *more* and *less*. The young preschooler then begins to make more exact comparisons through **one-to-one correspondence,** pairing socks with shoes or plates with napkins. Preschoolers also acquire a large store of words to label their quantitative understanding; for instance, words such as *big, small, more, less, tall, short, lots,* and *few.* By age four, children understand that adding or taking away objects from a group changes

naeyc

seriation
A relationship among objects in which they are placed in a logical order, such as from longest to shortest.

Key Point
Seriation helps children focus on the relationship among objects, as they place them in a logical order or sequence.

naeyc

one-to-one correspondence
A way in which young preschoolers begin to acquire an understanding of number concepts by matching items to each other; for instance, one napkin beside each plate.

Key Point ◆

An understanding of quantity or number concepts involves more than rote counting; it concerns rational counting as well, the ability to correctly attach a numeral name to each item in a group of objects.

rote counting
Reciting numbers from memory without attaching meaning to them in the context of objects in a series.

rational counting
Distinguished from rote counting, in rational counting the child accurately attaches a numeral name to a series of objects being counted.

the number. Not until the primary grades, however, are children able to distinguish the absolute number from arrangement, realizing that despite perceptual changes, the number is still the same even if a group of objects is rearranged (Hohmann, Weikart, & Epstein, 2008).

One aspect of acquiring number concepts is counting. Young preschoolers often learn **rote counting,** reciting numbers as they have been memorized. Rote counting should be distinguished from **rational counting,** which is present when the child attaches a numeral name to a series of objects in a group (Charlesworth & Lind, 2010). Be aware, however, that children do not necessarily have to apply the conventional number names to actually count rationally. Children seem to understand the principle of counting and that number names are attached to each object in a group, even if they count "one, two, three, five, eleven, nine" (Copley, 2000).

The good early childhood environment contains many opportunities to encourage the use of number concepts.

▶ Materials such as Unifix cubes, Cuisenaire rods, dominoes, number bingo, and other specific counting and math games can help children acquire number concepts.

▶ Children will also compare, count, match, add, subtract, and otherwise deal with quantities spontaneously with a wide variety of objects and experiences when they are able to manipulate items actively.

▶ Being able to move objects around is essential to acquiring an understanding of numbers. This requirement for hands-on involvement is one reason that workbooks are an inappropriate way for children to gain number concepts (Charlesworth & Lind, 2010).

Although children must acquire number concepts through their own efforts, the teacher's role in facilitating this learning is very important. Teachers can encourage children to quantify objects logically through a careful choice of words; for instance, asking a child to "put a plate at the table for each of her friends" rather than to "bring six plates." Everyday experiences, such as distribution of snack food, fair division of game pieces, cleanup time, or collection of permission slips for a field trip, can be used as a basis for using number concepts. In addition, group games can be used to encourage numerical concepts, as children count people or objects, use game board counters, and learn about logical rules.

Temporal Concepts

Temporal concepts are concerned with the child's gradual awareness of time as a continuum. Infants in the sensorimotor period, not yet able to mentally represent events and experiences, live only in the *now* time frame, in which *before* now and *after* now do not exist. During the preschool years, children become increasingly aware of temporal relations, such as the order of events and the time relationship between cause and effect ("I hurt my knee because I fell off the climber," rather than "I fell off the climber because I hurt my knee"). Not until early adolescence, however, do children have a true idea of temporal relations (Hohmann, Weikart, & Epstein, 2008).

Preschoolers' sense of time is still quite arbitrary and linked to concrete experiences. It would be meaningless to use conventional time measures (clock or calendar) to answer Mark's concern about how long until lunch or Serafina's question about when the field trip to the museum will be. Thus, saying "we

This child's use of standard measuring tools provides her with opportunities to learn number concepts.

© Cengage Learning

will have lunch in a half hour" or "the field trip is tomorrow" conveys very abstract information to young children. It makes much more sense to answer such questions in relation to concrete events; for instance, "we will have lunch after reading this story and washing hands, Mark" or "after school you will go home, Serafina, have dinner, and go to sleep; when you wake up tomorrow and come back to school, we will go on the field trip."

Older preschoolers and young school-age children begin to recognize that clocks and calendars help us mark time, although this understanding is still very imperfect. Nonetheless, adults should use conventional time measures in their conversations with children to begin exposing them to time-related vocabulary. In addition, concrete experiences with clocks and calendars should be provided. An actual clock alongside a pictorial clock on which key daily events are shown can help children make the connection between the hands on the clock and when snack, outside play time, group time, and other key activities occur. Similarly, a calendar on which the days of the week are accompanied by pictures representing school, interspersed with pictures of a child sleeping in bed, can help make the passage of day and night or weekdays and weekends understandable. By age seven or eight, many children begin to understand the more abstract representations of time and can learn to use clocks and calendars as adults do.

In everyday experiences and conversations, temporal concepts can be strengthened.

> The daily routine reinforces a consistent time sequence (first comes group time, then activity time, next snack, and so forth) as well as intervals of varying lengths (group time is shorter than activity time).

> Children also need to be exposed to and frequently use temporal words such as before, after, start, stop, first, second, last, next, earlier, and later.

> Discussing past occurrences and anticipating future ones gives children the opportunity to use **temporal sequencing,** placing a series of events into their order of occurrence. As an example, children might discuss the steps involved in coming to school in the morning.

Spatial Concepts

Spatial concepts relate to objects and people as they occupy, move in, and use space. Spatial concepts also concern the spatial relationship among people and objects; for instance, standing *behind* the chair, running *toward* the teacher, or putting the triangular block *on top of* the rectangular one. Actually, children are constantly experiencing spatial concepts through their own body movement, activities, and physical proximity to others. Their earliest learning, during infancy, was based to a great extent on their motor activity, and this mode of learning continues through the preschool and primary years.

A wide variety of experiences and equipment strengthen children's growing awareness of spatial concepts and relationships.

> Equipment that invites children to explore spatial possibilities is essential in an early childhood setting. Children need to position their bodies in many possible ways in relation to equipment; for example, they should be able to go over, under, around, through, into, out of, and across.

> Such experiences can also be structured through obstacle courses and group games such as "Simon Says" or "Mother May I."

naeyc

temporal concepts
Cognitive ability concerned with the child's gradual awareness of time as a continuum.

Key Point

Young children begin to acquire temporal concepts, the sense of time as a continuum that includes the past, present, and future.

temporal sequencing
The ability to place a series of events in the order of their occurrence.

naeyc

spatial concepts
A cognitive ability involving an understanding of how objects and people occupy, move in, and use space.

Key Point

Spatial concepts are concerned with how objects and people occupy or relate to each other in space.

Children have many opportunities to use spatial concepts. What concepts might this child be learning as she tries to balance her block structure?

▶ Active manipulation of objects, such as fitting things together or disassembling them, also strengthens children's spatial understanding. For one thing, children can explore manipulative items from all angles, seeing them from different points of view—from the front, back, side, bottom, or top.

▶ Puzzles, shape boxes, nuts and bolts, Tinkertoys, nesting blocks, pegboards with pegs, pots and pans with lids, dress-up clothes, and woodworking and collage materials are examples of common early childhood materials and activities that reinforce spatial concepts (Charlesworth & Lind, 2010; Hohmann, Weikart, & Epstein, 2008).

As is the case with their concept of time, young children's concept of space is viewed from a very subjective perspective. They rely on their perceptions of where, in what position, how close, how far away, or near an object might be. Space is purely visual to young children, and conventional measures such as inches, yards, and miles are meaningless. Space has to be something concrete, within children's experience. To say that it is three miles to the dairy means nothing; instead, saying, "we will be able to sing four or five songs in the bus, and then we'll be at the dairy" is much more concrete. Be aware also that space and time are often closely related, particularly as children move through space at different speeds. Young children see the distance between the building and the fence as closer if they run than if they walk, because they get to the fence more quickly.

Although young children do not yet understand conventional measuring devices and units of measurement, they nonetheless measure space frequently. They gauge the relative sizes of blocks as they build structures, estimate how much more sand is needed to fill the bucket, or judge whether their bodies will fit through the tunnel in the obstacle course.

▶ Teachers can help children verbalize measurement concepts by using words such as more, less, short(er), long(er), full, empty, double, or half.

▶ Activities such as making play dough, woodworking, and cooking can help children recognize the importance of accurate measurement and relative proportions.

mapping
A map-making activity involving spatial relations in which space is represented creatively through media such as marking pens or blocks.

▶ Older preschoolers and primary children also enjoy **mapping,** representing space through media such as marking pens or blocks. For instance, ask children to draw a picture of the route they took to get to school, make a map with unit blocks of their walk around the neighborhood, or fill in special features on an outline map you have drawn of the classroom.

Acquisition of Information

naeyc

Key Point ◆

The early childhood program can help children acquire relevant information through an appropriate curriculum.

While young children learn about the properties of objects, compare objects to discover what makes them similar and different, begin to understand quantity and number concepts, and start to develop a sense of time and space, they also learn a wide variety of facts and information. Some of this information emerges from repeated daily experiences; other items seem to peak children's interest and stick in their memories.

The day after she found an old innersole on a walk with her parents, four-year-old Julie, for instance, told her teacher that she had a "pet paramecium." She made the connection between seeing a picture of a paramecium, an elongated one-celled organism, and the shape of the innersole. Five-year-old Ron is able to recognize pictures of dinosaurs and to name more than a dozen kinds.

Elise, aged three, tells the teacher, "I need an ice bucket to keep my milk cold at lunch." She had watched a movie on television the night before and was impressed by the ice bucket into which a bottle of wine was placed! Young children generally do not discriminate between esoteric and practical facts, collecting and storing much information. It may be charming to hear a young child bring up the subjects of paramecia or ice buckets; however, it makes more sense to help children acquire information that they can connect to existing schemata and that can help them form an increasingly more thorough concept of the world.

Acquisition of information, as well as of the concepts related to classification, seriation, numbers, time, and space, occurs in many ways in the early childhood program. Just about any activity in which young children engage involves one or several of these concepts. Although acquisition of information and concepts is often associated with specific curriculum areas, especially math and science, it is not that easy to place them into discrete categories. Children's thinking is ongoing and involves a constant taking in, sifting, connecting, and storing of experiences, concepts, and information.

One way to help children make meaningful connections among pieces of information is the See/Think/Wonder routine (Salmon, 2010). By using such a thinking routine, a teacher encourages critical thinking to help children understand where their ideas come from. For example, during a field trip, photos are taken of things of interest to the children. Reviewing the pictures back in the classroom, the teacher asks the children, "What do you see?" This is followed by a discussion of "What do you think?" and finally, "What do you wonder?" When children routinely are encouraged to think about their experiences, their minds are opened to inquiry and more acute observation.

The following sections will examine math and science as separate curriculum areas. This is done to reinforce the importance of these subjects as vital parts of the early childhood curriculum, not to imply in any way that these are the only or primary ways in which cognitive development is fostered. Remember also that math and science are part of other activities, such as blocks, cooking, woodworking, manipulatives, dramatic play, and art. It is also important to note that the cognitive tasks we discussed earlier are an inherent part of both math and science. It is easy to see that the acquisition of number concepts is central to math. Classification, seriation, and temporal and spatial concepts are equally integral to both math and science. In addition, these concepts supply some of the tools required to carry out math and science endeavors; for instance, measuring, grouping, and comparing.

Many early childhood materials help children gradually understand a variety of cognitive concepts, including classification, seriation, and number, temporal, and spatial concepts.

MATH CONCEPTS IN THE EARLY CHILDHOOD CURRICULUM

Adults often think of mathematics as an abstract discipline involving complex algebraic formulas and geometric calculations. Yet, DAP notes that young children begin to understand the meaning of whole numbers, begin to use geometry through identifying shapes and relationships in space, and use measurement

Key Point

The foundation of more abstract math concepts is formed in early childhood, as children explore concrete objects and understand their properties and relationships.

Activities such as exploring, comparing, combining, scooping, and measuring at the sensory table reinforce math concepts.

as a way to identify and compare objects (Copple & Bredekamp, 2009). The foundations of math are grounded in concrete experience, such as the exploration of objects and gradual understanding of their properties and relationships. Geist (2003) notes that learning math concepts begins in infancy, as babies begin to notice relationships and classify, seriate, and compare objects. The cognitive concepts we have just discussed—classification, seriation, numbers, time, and space—are all an integral part of the development of mathematical knowledge. Young children are continually involved in mathematical learning, which the early childhood environment and teachers must encourage. The suggested activities listed in the discussion of classification, seriation, numbers, time, and space all contribute to the gradual acquisition of math concepts.

Much of the previous discussion on cognitive tasks reflects what should be part of a math focus in the early childhood curriculum. Math for young children is not abstract. It is, rather, concrete—the provision of many materials invites the child to handle, explore, compare, measure, combine, take apart, reconstruct, and transform in an infinite variety of ways. By acting on materials, children actively construct knowledge and gradually come to understand mathematical principles.

Central to this gradual understanding is the ability to conserve, or recognize that objects remain the same in amount or number despite perceptual changes. As we have discussed before, preschoolers rely very much on their perceptions and think that because materials are rearranged or changed in form, their amount is also changed. Thus, Lisa may think there are more blocks when they are arranged on the floor in a "road" than there were when they were stacked on the shelf; Sylvester will tell you that now that the play dough ball has been made into three snakes, there is more play dough.

This reliance on the observable rather than on an internal understanding that materials do not change unless something is added or taken away is a characteristic of children in the preoperational period. It is through many experiences in arranging and transforming materials that children gradually move to the concrete operational period, in which they are able to conserve. Thus, preschool-age children usually are not conservers, but they need many concrete experiences on which to build the foundation to acquire this ability during their elementary school years.

Mathematics in the early childhood curriculum involves a variety of principles. In the NAEYC's publication, *The Young Child and Mathematics* (2000), Juanita Copley includes concepts such as number and operations; patterns, functions, and algebra; geometry and spatial sense; measurement; and data analysis and probability. Terms such as "algebra" and "geometry," for instance, may seem inappropriate for young children at first glance. Yet the basic principles of more abstract mathematical concepts have their roots in concrete, understandable experiences that young children can readily grasp.

The National Council of Teachers of Mathematics (NCTM) suggest the following research-based math standards for children from prekindergarten to second grade (Cutler, Gilkerson, Parrott, & Bowne, 2003):

▶ **Number and operations**—Recognizing how many objects are in a set, understanding one-to-one correspondence, and arranging objects in increasing order.

- **Algebra**—Understanding patterns and relationships and being able to repeat these.
- **Geometry**—Recognizing attributes of shapes and describing spatial relations.
- **Measurement**—Comparing and seriating objects; beginning to measure objects, using either standard or nonstandard units of measure.
- **Problem solving**—Providing an environment that encourages problem solving and verbalizing children's methods as they solve problems.
- **Data analysis and probability**—Asking meaningful questions and then charting answers.

The early childhood classroom should contain many materials that lend themselves to acquiring math concepts. These include blocks, sand and water implements, dramatic play props such as dishes and cooking utensils, a variety of manipulatives, art and woodworking materials, natural materials such as rocks or pinecones, and a variety of other items that can be compared, grouped, counted, matched, or placed in a logical order. The class may also contain a specific math learning center, in which materials designed to encourage and enhance math concepts are collected.

SCIENCE CONCEPTS IN THE EARLY CHILDHOOD CURRICULUM

Science is a natural endeavor for young children, who are constantly exploring, asking questions, wondering why or why not, observing, touching, and tasting. It involves a growing awareness of self, other living things, and the environment through the senses and through exploration. Science is not so much a body of specific knowledge as it is a way of thinking and acting, of developing hypotheses and theories—an approach to solving problems (Charlesworth & Lind, 2010). In fact, young children have been described as "scientists at play" (Ross, 2000, p. 6). Children playfully explore many elements of their environment and, in the process, learn about their world.

"Young children must be able to co-construct their knowledge about science by imagining possible worlds and then inventing, criticizing, and modifying those worlds as they participate in hands-on exploration" (Conezio & French, 2002, p. 14). As children explore their world, they come up with questions, which lead to possible theories about why something works as it does. The next step—part of the scientific process—is for the children to investigate their theories within the classroom context. Teachers, then, must provide ample time and opportunity for such learning to occur, something that can take many weeks. Science involves the scientific method: observing, classifying, experimenting, predicting, drawing conclusions, and communicating ideas (Neill, 2009). Children should also be encouraged to use appropriate scientific terms, thereby building scientific literacy. "Model the use of terms such as *estimate, predict, atmosphere,* and *habitat* in day-to-day conversation and encourage children to use the vocabulary themselves" (Bosse, Jacobs, & Anderson, 2009, p. 15).

In fact, DAP underscores children's need to be active participants in developing and testing their own ideas or theories about how the world works. "A good science program provides children with opportunities to share their ideas in multiple ways through both actions and words. Rather than being designed to correct early ideas, teach information, or provide explanations, new experiences provide children with opportunities to broaden their thinking and build new understanding" (Copple & Bredekamp, 2009, p. 140).

▶❚❚ **TeachSource Video Activity**
WATCH•REFLECT•RESPOND

This video shows how math concepts are a part of many activities. Go to CengageBrain.com and view the video titled, "Learning Math through Movement and Music Activities in Early Childhood," and answer the following questions:

1. Which math concepts were children able to gain through music and movement activities in this video?

2. How are foundations for addition and subtraction conveyed through music and movement activities?

naeyc

Key Point ◆

Science activities must be based on concrete, observable elements; children's environments provide many opportunities for such learning.

Science should be incorporated into many other classroom activities that are already part of the early childhood program. Science is not separable from activities such as cooking, water and sand play, blocks, or literacy, for example, but should be integrated into a coherent curriculum (Conezio & French, 2002). Keep this in mind as we next examine science within two categories: biological sciences, which deal with living things, and physical sciences, which concern nonliving materials.

Biological Sciences

People, animals, and plant life provide fascinating subjects to discover and explore. Children have a natural interest in their own bodies and bodily functions; they also enjoy learning about and caring for animals and plants. In addition, there is the important interrelation between plant and animal life involved in food. Each of these subjects provides a selection of appropriate topics to include in the early childhood curriculum.

Key Point ◆◆

The biological sciences provide many fascinating topics for young children related to the study of the people, animals, and plants in their environment.

THE HUMAN BODY. Toddlers and young preschoolers are still learning the labels of various parts of their bodies, discovering the body's capabilities, and mastering skills in movement and dexterity. Older preschoolers and primary children, however, have a burgeoning awareness of the less visible parts of the body and want to know why a knee bleeds when someone falls down, where the food goes after it is eaten, or why the heart thumps after a person runs fast.

Children also become increasingly aware of their own growth, relishing the idea of being bigger than they were when they were babies. They are cognizant of each other's characteristics and note that children differ from each other in height, hair length, eye color, and other ways. The following topics can be incorporated into the curriculum to help children increase awareness of their bodies.

▸ Parts of the body and what they can and cannot do make an intriguing topic for movement activities. "Can you touch your knee with your fingers . . . your ear with your elbow? Can you balance on your bottom … on your little fingers?"

▸ The senses deserve exploration. Every action and activity involves the senses, although we are not always consciously aware of it. Specific activities that encourage children to attend to sensory messages, discriminate between various sensory stimuli, or enjoy sensory stimulation for its own sake should be planned. (See Chapter 9 for more discussion on this topic.)

▸ The concepts of growth and change captivate children. Baby pictures, growth charts, and visits from children's younger siblings can help strengthen these concepts.

▸ Comparison among children reinforces that each person is unique and that there are many differences among people.

▸ Care for the body through everyday self-help skills, as well as through activities that focus on the relationship of cleanliness and grooming to health, can be incorporated.

"Can you touch your ear with your elbow?" Such activities may bring on giggles, but they help children learn what their bodies can and cannot do.

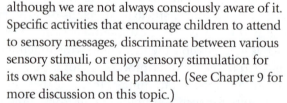

© Cengage Learning

▸ Older preschoolers and primary school children enjoy learning about the inner workings of their respiratory, heart, or digestive systems as long as such information is presented concretely. For instance, a "visit" from a skeleton can help teach the difference between bones and joints. Children can move as the skeleton "moves."

ANIMALS. Any environment contains a variety of animals; for instance, domestic dogs and cats, the classroom gerbil, the sparrows and pigeons that hop in the trees or nest in the eaves of buildings, the horses and cows on nearby farms, the tigers and walruses in the city zoo, the starfish and sea cucumbers in the tide pools, the ants on the playground, the butterflies that flit outside the windows, or the snails that come out after the rain. Children can observe and learn about a wide range of animals in their immediate environment.

These children are searching in the soil to find hidden earthworms. What other types of science activities can help children explore and learn about the natural world around them?

The animals that are part of your ecological system provide a rich variety of topics that can be included in the curriculum. If you live in Nevada, why discuss whales when you have not taken time to observe the animals in your desert surroundings? Animals can be included in the curriculum in some of the following ways:

naeyc

▶ Classroom pets provide a natural way for children to learn about, observe, and care for animals. Small animals such as guinea pigs, hamsters, rabbits, gerbils, mice, aquarium fish, parakeets, earthworms, or hermit crabs are often part of early childhood classrooms. It is important to ensure that the animals are in a suitable enclosure, with appropriate food, water, places for rest and privacy, and protection. Be familiar with the needs, characteristics, and care requirements of animals before they become members of your classroom. Although children can participate in caring for the animals, the teachers are ultimately responsible for classroom pets. Also, be aware of any restrictions or limitations spelled out in your local licensing regulations.

▶ Take time to observe the animals around the school and neighborhood. On the playground or on walks, encourage the children to look or listen for birds, insects, butterflies, squirrels, ducks, and other creatures.

▶ Animals can be temporary guests in the classroom. Such animals might include a visiting calf or pony on the playground, a child's cat and her new kittens, or caterpillars.

▶ Plan field trips to nearby animal habitats such as a zoo, farm, aquarium, fish hatchery, or nature preserve. Visit more than one time because there will be much more to see than can be observed on one trip.

▶ Children's observations about animals should be discussed, both spontaneously and in planned activities.

▶ Document the children's interactions with animals through photographs, children's pictures, and their stories.

▶ Through your modeling and through discussion and reminders, help children develop a respect for all animal life. "In a violent society, learning to love living things in general is a first step in evolving a greater life ethic" (Ross, 2000, p. 11).

A common garden snail, brought into the classroom, has piqued the curiosity of these girls. Children are encouraged to be gentle as they observe the snail.

- Children's exposure to animals through classroom pets, animals that visit the class, neighborhood walks, or field trips should always precede representational activities. Once the children have had ample opportunity to become acquainted with an animal firsthand, they can imitate, discuss, or represent that animal. Thus, the following activities should come after concrete experiences with animals.

    - Through movement activities, children can imitate the walk or characteristic stance of some animals. They can also imitate the animals' sounds.
    - The teacher can make various matching games using pictures of animals, or they can be purchased through commercial sources. Once they have observed and learned about specific animals, children might match animals to their habitats (bird to nest, squirrel to tree hole), with their babies, or with their food.
    - Children can classify animals by those that fly, those that live in water, or those that live on land. Animals can also be classified by other characteristics such as color, size, or number of feet.
    - Children can draw pictures, make sculptures, and dictate or write stories of their experiences with animals.

PLANTS. Plant life surrounds us, whether through the vase of flowers in the classroom, the salad at lunch, or the tree in the play yard. Children can expand their understanding of the world by learning about plants, their function, needs, aesthetic value, and variety. As is the case when helping children learn about animals, children's increasing understanding about plants should focus on the plants in your environment. The following activities can help children increase their awareness of plants:

- Call attention to and encourage children to describe plants in the environment— the classroom fern, the maple outside the window, the pyracantha across the street. Your enjoyment of plants can help children develop an appreciation for the beauty and variety of plant life.
- Help children to observe, take photographs of, and draw evidence of seasonal changes. Compare the photos and drawings and discuss the seasons in the context of the children's concrete observations and recollections.
- Help children understand that plants need water, light, and soil. Note that the leaves droop if a plant does not get enough water, and celebrate as it perks up after an adequate watering. Compare the growth of similar plants on the windowsill and in a shady corner.
- Involve children in observing the growth of plants. Plant seeds in window boxes, pots, an outdoor garden plot, or individual containers that children can take home. (Grass and bean seeds grow very quickly.) Help the children keep a daily record of changes through photographs, measurements, or written records of observations.
- Provide opportunities for children to see the hidden parts of plants. Take a plant out of its pot so that children can explore the roots. Cut open the bulb or stem of a plant. Encourage children to observe, describe, represent, and hypothesize about the functions of the plant's components.
- If possible, observe a plant through a growth cycle from seed to blossom to vegetable, fruit, or flower. Plant tomato or zucchini seeds in the spring, care for the plants throughout the summer, and harvest and eat the vegetables in the fall.
- Consider the plants we eat. Visit commercial farms and orchards or a neighborhood garden to see how plants produce the foods we eat.

- Include frequent cooking activities in the curriculum to introduce children to new foods and to learn more about familiar ones.
- Through concrete activities, convey the idea that food helps meet nutritional needs. (See Chapter 9 for a more detailed discussion of cooking and nutrition as part of the curriculum.)

Physical Sciences

Children are in constant contact with, and take in information about, the inanimate, physical elements of their world, and they acquire many scientific concepts. Patti finds the right length of block to create a bridge, applying an elementary law of physics, for example. Chip mixes water with soil and through basic chemistry, creates a new substance, mud. Kumalo notices that the black rock he found on the field trip is the same color as the dark band along the face of the mountain. Through such experiences, children begin to construct knowledge about the world and the laws that govern it. We will consider how young children acquire knowledge and develop theories about physics, chemistry, and meteorology, three examples of physical sciences.

PHYSICS. Children encounter elements of physics—the relationship of matter and energy—through numerous materials and activities. Blocks, outdoor equipment, water and sand, and manipulatives often present phenomena to be noted and problems to be solved. Children learn about force (throwing the ball hard makes it go further), gravity (cars roll faster down a steep incline), or inertia (a heavy object resists being moved but will move more readily when placed on rollers). Help children label some of the laws of physics involved in their actions by acquiring scientific vocabulary, such as the swing is a "pendulum" or the slide is an "inclined plane" (Bosse et al., 2009).

Provide children with many experiences in which their actions on objects create movement; for instance, rolling on rollers, jumping, tilting, dropping, blowing, sucking, pulling, and swinging. Children thus experience how their actions affect objects, how they can vary their actions to vary the effect, and how different objects react to their actions.

For instance, Sharmila notes that when she kicks a ball, it travels farther away than when she kicks a block; that the lightweight beach ball does not travel as far as the heavier rubber ball; and that she can kick with varying degrees of force to move objects different distances. Through repeated experiences, Sharmila begins to develop some generalizations about force and momentum, aided by appropriate questions posed at the right moment by a teacher.

CHEMISTRY. Chemistry deals with the properties, composition, and changes in substances—phenomena that children observe in everyday life. Sensory experiences help children learn about the properties of things around them. Children make intuitive comparisons that tell them that wood is different from metal, which is different from glass, which is different from plastic. They also learn that soap and water result

naeyc

Key Point ◆

There are many concrete possibilities for learning about the physical sciences, including physics, chemistry, and meteorology.

naeyc

Children have many opportunities to notice the laws governing stability and balance as they work with blocks and other common early childhood materials.

© Cengage Learning

in bubbles, water added to sand makes the sand moldable, and chocolate mixed into milk makes chocolate milk.

Cooking activities are filled with examples of chemistry. Through many cooking experiences, children begin to generalize about how different foods react and are transformed through cutting, mixing, blending, heating, and cooling. For instance, when grapes, banana slices, and orange segments are mixed, they still look like grapes, bananas, and oranges; but when eggs, milk, and flour are mixed, they take on a totally new appearance as batter. When batter is baked, it becomes solid; when potatoes are boiled, they become soft; when eggs are boiled, they become hard. Water can be transformed from a liquid to solid ice after freezing and to elusive steam after boiling. Sugar or salt becomes invisible when stirred into water.

METEOROLOGY. Children are certainly aware of and interested in the weather, making it an appropriate topic for discussion with young children. Mr. Jenkins encouraged the children in his class to listen to the morning weather forecast and discuss it during the first group time. Throughout the day, then, the children validated what they heard through their own activities and observations. For instance, the children discovered that the wind can blow from different directions. The west wind predicted on the radio made their hair fly in their eyes when they faced the building, whereas an east wind blew their hair out behind them. Kites and streamers further reinforced the idea that the wind can blow from different directions. Storm predictions could be verified by noticing the clouds; they usually meant that the children would plan some alternative, indoor, large motor activities. The children decided what kind of outer clothing they needed. They checked the large outdoor thermometer and compared the level of the temperature line with the adjacent picture of a thermometer on which pictures of a shirt, sweater, jacket, and hat with mittens were pasted at appropriate temperature intervals. Experiments, stories, and poems related to various weather phenomena such as rain, rainbows, the sun, the wind, snow, ice, clouds, and storms can be readily incorporated into the curriculum (Huffman, 1996).

Environmental Education and Recycling

Children are not too young to learn about protecting the world around them, although the environment is a complex topic to learn about (Lewin-Benham, 2006). Through environmental education, children learn about our natural environment, how it supports our survival, and what we can do to protect it (Torquati, Gabriel, Jones-Branch, & Leeper-Miller, 2010). They can learn to be responsible for the environment in several ways: through the materials offered in the classroom, through discussion, through the example of teachers who are mindful of the importance of conservation, and through active involvement in recycling activities. Children are enthusiastic participants when asked to reuse, through recycling, the resources we have.

Teachers and parents can facilitate recycling efforts by using a variety of discarded items. Mary Mayesky (2012) offers many suggestions for useful recyclables. Empty plastic containers can be trimmed to become scoops, funnels, carrying baskets, and trays. Buttons are excellent for classification and math activities. Many other items that may otherwise be discarded can be put to good use, including empty cans with plastic lids, egg cartons, scraps of fabric and fabric trim, bottles with sprinkler tops, Styrofoam, and boxes of all sorts.

Children in one early childhood program participated in their community's Earth Day by developing a variety of projects made completely out of recycled materials; their projects became part of a local exhibit. One group made the city in which they lived, making landmark buildings out of boxes, egg cartons, and other items. Another group created a robot out of boxes, plastic milk cartons, old wires, and nuts and bolts. Yet another group made three-dimensional "self-portraits" using a creative array of materials. This activity greatly heightened the children's awareness of their environment and of what they can do to help protect it.

SUPPORTING COGNITIVE DEVELOPMENT IN INFANTS AND TODDLERS

The major task of the first few years of life is to make "sense of the world on many levels, such as language, human interactions, counting and quantification, spatial reasoning, physical causality, problem solving, and categorization. Indeed, even preverbal infants show surprisingly sophisticated understanding in each of these areas" (Shonkoff & Phillips, 2000, p. 147). How do babies begin to acquire these skills?

Infants' cognitive development is best promoted when they are in a safe, loving environment where their basic needs are met. Furthermore, this environment must be rich in appropriate stimuli and sensory experiences that help them explore and learn about their world. In fact, recent research about the development of infants' brains has underscored the importance of a safe, nurturing environment peopled by consistent, familiar caregivers for optimal cognitive development. The importance of continuity of care, which enables infants to form a relationship with a consistent caregiver is also emphasized by DAP (Copple & Bredekamp, 2009). When babies are cared for by unfamiliar adults with whom they do not have an established relationship, they are in a state of unease and stress and are simply not free to use their cognitive powers (Perry, 2000). In a positive environment, cared for by familiar, nurturing adults, children are intensely engaged in intellectual pursuits.

The experiences you provide should also be congruent with infants' particular stages of cognitive development; thus, for babies in Piaget's first and second stages of the sensorimotor period, the awakening awareness of their surroundings should be promoted by frequent interaction with the primary caregiver, loving conversation, gentle sounds, interesting colors and patterns, and the opportunity to view the world from different vantage points.

In the third stage, babies begin to make the connection between their actions and resulting movement, sounds, and sights. You can support this stage by providing appropriate toys that allow trial and error and give infants feedback. When babies begin to acquire object permanence in stage four, they relish games in which you, as the teacher, hide objects while they watch and encourage them to actively search for these. Babies begin to anticipate reactions, and toys and games that provide an expected outcome help them begin to learn about cause and effect.

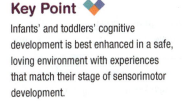

Key Point ◆

Infants' and toddlers' cognitive development is best enhanced in a safe, loving environment with experiences that match their stage of sensorimotor development.

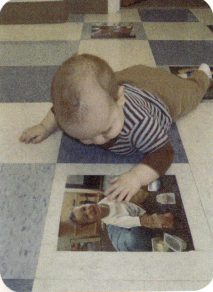

A variety of interesting objects that infants can explore helps them learn about their world.

LEARNING WITH BUBBLES

When we introduced bubbles in water in the sensory bin in our classroom, our 4- to 12-month-olds were very interested in exploring this new medium. A few weeks later, I decided to provide an additional bubble experience by blowing bubble solution through bubble wands. Children who were not yet mobile enjoyed tracking the bubbles with their eyes and reaching toward them. The older children tried to touch them.

Twelve-month-old Nevaeh immediately showed great interest in the bubbles. Whenever I would stop blowing bubbles, she made a sound as if she wanted more bubbles. I asked her, "Do you want more bubbles?" while also using the sign for "more." She imitated the sign and continued asking for bubbles with the sign.

Within a month, she started to point at the bubble container on the counter to show that she wanted to play with it. She did this almost every day. When I intentionally asked her what she wanted from the counter, she signed, "more." She also nodded in response to my questions when I asked her, "Do you want to play with bubbles?" Then she created her own sign for "bubbles"— which was as if she were blowing bubbles with her finger in front of her mouth. She had a huge smile on her face when I understood what she meant, and then she started to blow bubbles. Not long after, Nevaeh produced the sound "ba" for bubbles, using

© Theresa Danna Douglas

Natsumi, Infant Teacher

it along with her invented sign for bubbles, and soon she said the word "bubble" as clearly as she could. Since then, she has been using the word "bubble" with the sign for "please" when she wants bubbles.

While her communication skills were developing, Nevaeh also explored the art of blowing bubbles. She placed her mouth on the wand when I brought it to her face, but at first she licked the bubble instead of blowing. After a while, she wanted to control the wand by herself. At first, she tried to put it in her mouth without dipping it in the bubble solution. No bubbles came out, but she kept blowing. It didn't take long for her to dip the wand as she had seen me do, without being told that this was what she needed to do. After three months of practicing blowing bubbles, she finally was able to blow bubbles by herself. I cannot forget how excited she was when she saw bubbles coming out of the wand. What a big smile!

She has been successful in blowing bubbles since then.

Our curriculum is derived from the children's interests, and the children, including Nevaeh, loved bubbles. So we included them often. Along with the bubbles, I introduced relevant words. In addition to the word "bubble," I emphasized the words "more," "done," and "pop" while I was blowing bubbles. I asked yes/no questions such as "Are you ready?" "Do you want more?" and "Can you pop the bubbles?" I also asked open-ended questions, like "Where are the bubbles?" "How do you feel when you touch the bubbles?" and "How does it taste?" In addition, I described what was happening, for instance, saying "The bubble is coming down on your head!" "It popped on your arm!" or "It is going up into the sky." I know it is important to pay attention to gestures, facial expressions, signs, and any sounds, not just to the language that Nevaeh produced.

I also made sure that there were lots of opportunities for Nevaeh to explore bubbles. I could tell she was observing my mouth while I was blowing. She tried to blow air when we were not blowing bubbles. We blew bubbles in water, tissue paper, and paper towels. She also learned to control the wand to blow bubbles. There was so much that Nevaeh learned from the bubbles!

Toddlers, with the added ability to move about, need many appropriate experiences to help promote cognitive development. They need a variety of materials that can be explored, combined in different ways, put together and taken apart, and in many other ways allow for experimentation. Since object permanence continues to develop, games in which objects are hidden and found are still very appropriate. In addition, games and toys that help children recognize what causes things to happen and that identify them as the causal agent should also be provided. Simple dramatic play props will encourage toddlers' burgeoning ability to pretend (Gestwicki, 2011; Gonzalez-Mena & Eyer, 2012). Much of what very young children do is inquiry. "Science is what young children do. More than just watch, they engage. They are exhilarated by small observations. They experiment and discover" (Shaffer, Hall, & Lynch, 2009).

SUPPORTING MATH AND SCIENCE LEARNING IN SCHOOL-AGE CHILDREN

Much of what we discussed in relation to young children's cognitive development, including cognitive tasks as these relate to math and science, continue to be relevant during the school years. Be aware also of the importance of providing engaging and meaningful math and science activities that attract all children, including young girls. Janice Koch (2010) notes that the prevalent image of a scientist is that of a white male. "It is not surprising that girls and students of minority ethnic and cultural groups all too often distance themselves during science lessons" (p. 299). During the primary years, children begin the gradual shift from Piaget's stage of preoperational to concrete operational thinking. This shift allows them to think in more abstract terms and figure out answers without needing concrete objects in front of them. But they are still a long way from being able to think in purely symbolic and abstract ways and require concrete examples as a reference point. Children continue to need physical actions to help make mental connections. They benefit from active, firsthand experiences and from the chance to manipulate real objects, and they work with things that are relevant, interesting, and meaningful to them (Gestwicki, 2011).

School-age children's budding ability to recognize that objects can change from one form to another—an aspect of conservation—contributes to their understanding of the world. Concrete math and science activities, grounded in the children's everyday experiences, will help reinforce mathematical and science concepts much more effectively than worksheets, with numbers or symbols that are not part of any real context.

You will find many occasions in school-age programs to further math concepts. DAP notes some important math learning during the primary grades; for instance, developing an understanding of addition and subtraction; whole number relationships such as grouping in tens and ones; composing and decomposing geometric shapes; and understanding the principles of measurement (Copple & Bredekamp, 2009). Different types of scales, including balance, electronic, spring, and bathroom scales, can be available for children to weigh different objects and record their weight. This activity

naeyc

Key Point ◆◆

Primary children are in transition to Piaget's period of concrete operations; they are beginning to view concepts more abstractly, but they continue to need many concrete experiences to learn about and reinforce these concepts.

School-age children have attained many of the skills needed to engage in board games. Such games are well-suited to foster the cognitive development of this age group in an enjoyable way.

© Cengage Learning

can lead to conclusions about relative weight and size; for instance, is the smallest object also the lightest? The classification activities that children enjoyed during their preschool years can continue to be extended in complexity during the school years. In particular, children at this age are able to recognize that objects can belong to more than one category and that combinations of categories can lead to new subgroupings. For instance, leaves can be categorized by tree type and by color, but they can also be classified in subgroups such as yellow elm, yellow oak, yellow birch, green elm, green oak, green birch, and so forth. Incorporate the concept of money into dramatic play, for example, the grocery store, pet store, or restaurant. When children help you cut sandwiches and other snacks into halves, fourths, or eighths, reinforce the concept of fractions, and encourage the children to see the relationship of the whole, the parts, and the sum of the parts.

There are also many table games appropriate for primary children that involve counting skills; for instance, Monopoly (Click & Parker, 2012).

Science continues to be fascinating to children as they enter the school years. Children's natural curiosity and drive to construct knowledge makes them want to learn about the world around them. Their growing cognitive skills, combined with an enthusiasm for learning, make them natural scientists. Children at this age are better able to observe and track changes in biological and physical sciences. Encourage them, for instance, to observe and chart the life cycle of frogs, learn about endangered species and what can be done to prevent their extinction, or experiment with and document different growing conditions for plants. They can keep track of the weather, and chart changes in temperature, the sunrise and sunset, rain, or other meteorological features over a period of time. To learn more about chemical reactions, suggest to children that they observe and chart changes in various foods when liquid, heat, cold, yeast, or another agent is added (Click & Parker, 2012).

SUPPORTING MATH AND SCIENCE LEARNING IN CHILDREN WITH DISABILITIES

naeyc

DIVERSITY

Key Point ◆◆

Children with disabilities can benefit from math and science activities, particularly because they promote a discovery approach to learning about the world.

In the inclusive classroom, you as the teacher adapt math and science activities as appropriate for all of the children in the group. For all children, especially children with disabilities, it is important to start with familiar and concrete concepts. Particularly for children with physical disabilities, provide opportunities to learn the problem-solving skills inherent in math and science activities. Consider that activities that help children learn about measurement, weight, and the relationship between speed and distance, can have special relevance to a child who is slowed down because of his disability or who has to have new braces because he has outgrown the old ones. Science activities, such as learning about wheels and pulleys, can provide a way of moving objects for a child who has limited mobility. Gravity is also a relevant topic, since children with physical limitations often struggle against gravity as they sit or stand.

Children with visual impairments can particularly benefit from understanding their world and its logical order. Examples of beneficial math activities that you can include are ones that promote tactile discrimination, matching, number concepts, measurement, and patterns. Gestwicki (2011) suggests that science activities can help children learn about the way the eyes work. Different kinds of lenses, especially ones that magnify objects, are also appropriate, and can be discussed in terms of how they help us see objects in greater detail.

Children with social, emotional, and behavioral disorders benefit from successful learning experiences. Math and science activities, especially those with an emphasis on exploration and discovery, can provide such success. Classification activities can be used to point out similarities among children and to promote a sense of belonging. Math concepts can also be incorporated into taking turns and sharing, for instance, "You can ride the tricycle around the track three times, then it will be Ginny's turn." Science activities provide opportunities for children to observe cause and effect in their physical world. Children can also be encouraged to make predictions about experiments. Opportunities for sharing, understanding cause and effect, and making predictions can help children apply these to social experiences.

A discovery approach, using concrete objects, is important for children with cognitive or development delays as well. When you plan math or science activities, ensure that children can engage in these at different levels of difficulty. Appropriate math activities, depending on the child's ability, can include counting with real objects, grouping objects, and one-to-one correspondence. All the children will also benefit from field trips that help them learn about their natural world. When you focus on the weather and seasons as part of science, you can help the child learn about predictable changes that occur with time, and how these impact people's behavior, for instance, decisions about the clothing they wear (Deiner, 2010).

FAMILY VALUES FOR COGNITIVE DEVELOPMENT

As with all areas of the early childhood curriculum, it is very important to share with families a clear statement of the school's philosophy about how to support and further children's cognitive development. Families should be aware, for instance, that the program is built on the conviction that children learn best through concrete, hands-on activity; that children are able to select meaningful activities on their own; and that play and learning go together. Conversely, such a philosophy means that the program does not engage in abstract and developmentally inappropriate teaching practices that require the child to sit quietly and inactively.

Today's parents are bombarded by pressures to succeed, which includes having successful children as well. Thus, many well-intentioned families feel a need to see evidence that their children are indeed learning in their early childhood program. For instance, they may say to you, "But Marcia does nothing but play all day; when will she learn something?" or "Ron starts kindergarten next year; shouldn't he be learning to read?" or "I want Singh to learn to sit quietly and work on his numbers" or "I'm thinking of enrolling Betsy in the school where my neighbor's son goes; he comes home with dittoes every day and Betsy only brings home paintings." How do you respond in a way that respects the family's concerns but maintains the integrity of your program?

Conveying your philosophy of how children best learn involves frequent explanation and supportive information. First, it requires that you, as the teacher, are secure in your understanding of how young children learn and acquire concepts so that you can answer the families' questions and address their concerns. It is also important to make available information from experts that supports your approach. This might be done through a family library, well-written articles to be distributed to families, short quotes by experts placed on the bulletin board, speakers at family meetings, or family discussion groups with a knowledgeable

Key Point
The school's philosophy about how young children learn has to be shared with families.

facilitator. Let each family know that your profession has a position statement, *Developmentally Appropriate Practice in Early Childhood Programs Serving Children from Birth through Age 8* (Copple & Bredekamp, 2009), and articulated standards that support your approach. In other words, let families know that your work with children is founded on and backed by research and theory.

DIVERSITY

It is also important to remember that families have ideas about how best to facilitate their children's learning because their cultural background provides a framework for such beliefs. In many cultures, for instance, direct instruction and imitation are traditionally how children are expected to learn. In some cultures, the belief is that children learn best by observing, and in others, that adults verbally explain while children are expected to listen. Understanding and acknowledgment of cultural beliefs need to be part of the conversation between teachers and families about how children gain cognitive competence (Klein & Chen, 2001).

SUMMARY

1. There are three influential theoretical views of cognitive development: Piaget's cognitive developmental theory, behaviorism, and information processing.
2. Cognition begins to develop in earliest infancy, through movement and sensory experiences.
3. During the preschool years, children begin to acquire some specific cognitive skills.
   A. Consider five cognitive tasks—classification, seriation, number concepts, temporal concepts, and spatial concepts—and activities that can help children master them.
   B. Children also acquire a considerable amount of information during their early years.
4. Two important early childhood curriculum areas to consider are math and science.
5. The age and ability level of the children need to be taken into consideration in planning math and science activities for young children.

KEY TERMS LIST

central processor

classification

cognition

conservation

constructivist theory

executive functions

information processing

long-term memory

mapping

memory strategies

metacognition

metamemory

one-to-one correspondence

rational counting

reflective abstraction

rote counting

sensory register

seriation

short-term memory

spatial concepts

symbolic representation

temporal concepts

temporal sequencing

KEY QUESTIONS

1. Consider the people in the class for which you are reading this book. In how many different ways can you classify these individuals? Think of as many categories as possible. What does this exercise tell you about cognitive skill development in young children?

2. Observe a young child for about 20 minutes. How does this child use cognitive skills? Note the many ways in which this child uses her or his thinking abilities, including evidence of problem solving, symbolic representation, memory, classification, seriation, time and space concepts, and number concepts.

3. In this chapter, we have considered only math and science as activities in which children use cognitive processes. How is cognition a part of other areas in the early childhood curriculum?

4. Think of a science class you have taken. What topics or concepts from this class might engage young children's interest? How do you modify information that you, as an adult, have learned to be appropriate for young children?

5. What do children learn from the study of animals and plants?

ADDITIONAL RESOURCES

Select additional books, articles, and websites on topics discussed in Chapter 11.

Charlesworth, R., & Lind, K. (2010). *Math and science for young children* (6th ed.). Belmont, CA: Wadsworth, Cengage Learning.

Hohmann, M., & Weikart, D. P. (2008). *Educating young children: Active learning practices for preschool and child care programs* (2nd ed.). Belmont, CA: Wadsworth, Cengage Learning.

Okagaki, L., & Diamond, K. E. (2009). Cultural and linguistic differences in families with young children: Implications for early childhood teachers. In E. L. Essa & M. M. Burnham (Eds.), *Informing our practice: Useful research on young children's development* (pp. 216–226). Washington, DC: National Association for the Education of Young Children.

Shonkoff, J. P., & Phillips, D. A. (Eds.) (2000). *From neurons to neighborhoods: The science of early childhood development.* Washington, DC: National Academy Press.

HELPFUL WEBSITES

Promoting Children's Readiness to Learn:

http://futureofchildren.org/futureofchildren/publications/docs/ 15_01_FullJournal.pdf

The Future of Children, a publication of Princeton University and the Brookings Institution, offers in-depth information about topics of importance. This particular issue is titled, "School Readiness: Closing Racial and Ethnic Gaps."

Early Childhood: Where Learning Begins—Mathematics:

www.ed.gov/pubs/EarlyMath/index.html

This U.S. Department of Education website provides suggestions for everyday activities that build on children's growing understanding of math. It focuses on the presence of math in the everyday environment.

Project Construct:

www.projectconstruct.org

In the Project Construct approach, focus is on how children learn through hands-on exploration. This website provides numerous resources on using a constructivist approach to working with preschool through early-elementary-age children.

 Go to **CengageBrain.com** to register your access code for this book's Education CourseMate website, where you will find more resources to help you study. Additional resources for this chapter include TeachSource Videos, glossary flashcards, web links, case studies with critical-thinking questions that apply the concepts presented in this chapter, and more. If your textbook does not include a printed access card, you can go to **CengageBrain.com** to purchase access.

Innatist View of Language Development

At the opposite end of the spectrum of language theories is the innatist view, which considers the capacity for language to be inborn. Noam Chomsky (1972), one of the leading proponents of this view, hypothesizes that children are born with a linguistic structure that makes it possible for them to acquire language as quickly as they do during the preschool years.

Chomsky believes that every person starts life with an innate **deep structure,** the underlying rules of grammar and meaning that are universal across all languages. As a result, children are "wired" to know without being taught that communication has meaning or that it can affirm, negate, question, and command. Beyond this deep structure, then, children have to learn the specific vocabulary and grammar of their language, what Chomsky calls the **surface structure.** The deep structure includes the common features of all languages, whereas the surface structure involves the specifics that vary from language to language.

Because language is innate, it is linked to biological maturation and follows an internal clock, needing to emerge during the "critical age" for language acquisition. Children who do not learn language in early childhood have a much more difficult time later, just as learning a second language later in life is not nearly as easy as acquiring it in the early years. Language, however, does not emerge automatically; rather, it is triggered by exposure to verbal communication in the environment (Owens, 2011).

Interactionist View of Language Development

A compromise between the behaviorist view, in which the external environment is all important, and the innatist view, in which inborn factors are the key, is the interactionist view, which takes important elements from the two theoretical extremes. Children are seen as neither passive recipients of language training from their parents nor the active language processors whose internal structures are the primary determinants of language acquisition. Interactionists see many factors—such as the social environment, maturation, biology, and cognition— at play in the development of language. These elements interact with and modify each other (Owens, 2011).

There are two major approaches to this view— the **cognitive interactionist view of language development** and the **social interactionist view of language development.** Piaget (1926) and other cognitive theorists, as proponents of the cognitive interactionist view, in which the ability to mentally represent objects is required, considered that children's understanding of language is rooted in their cognitive development. Language is one way of expressing representational or symbolic thought.

Social interactionist theorists deem that language is intimately tied to social processes. Children's language development is guided by internal factors, but the critical fact is that it must emerge within the social environment provided by the parents. Furthermore, the social interaction that triggers language is a two-way operation, in which children cue their parents and parents, in turn, supply appropriate language experiences

Key Point

The innatist view, voiced by theorists such as Chomsky, holds that children are born with an inherent linguistic structure.

deep structure
According to Noam Chomsky, inborn understanding or underlying rules of grammar and meaning that are universal across all languages.

surface structure
According to Noam Chomsky, specific aspects of language that vary from one language to another.

Key Point

The interactionist view suggests that there is interplay between inborn and environmental factors in children's language learning.

cognitive interactionist view of language development
The view that children's language is rooted in cognitive development, requiring, for instance, the ability to represent objects mentally.

social interactionist view of language development
Theoretical view that considers language to be closely tied to and dependent on social processes.

Language, according to the interactionist view, develops from a combination of inborn and environmental factors.

(Owens, 2011). Vygotsky (1962), one of the leading proponents of the social interactionist view, considers that the young child's primary social tool is language. (See Chapter 5.)

COMPONENTS OF LANGUAGE

Language is a complex system involving a variety of components. Included are learning as well as understanding words, knowing the rules for using words accurately, learning the rules for putting words together meaningfully, and obtaining a grasp, always growing, of the appropriateness of what is being communicated. As each theory of language development indicates, children's early years are particularly crucial in the evolution of language skills. To better grasp the complexity of this task, we will take a closer look at early language development as well as at some of these components related to meaning and rules of language.

Early Language Development

Language does not begin when babies speak their first words around the end of the first year. It has been developing from their earliest days. A newborn prefers the human voice over other sounds and can even distinguish his or her mother's voice from another woman's at a very early age. Research has underscored the importance of the earliest months to language development. The amount of talk mothers and other caregivers direct to very young children is strongly linked with the children's vocabulary growth and the later emergence of their reading and writing skills (Shonkoff & Phillips, 2000). Early communication takes the form of **cooing,** throaty vowel sounds, which are later combined with laughter. This combination delights adults as they "converse" with babies. Remember from Chapter 11 that infants discover their own power to make interesting things happen again; the same holds true for language. Babies gradually recognize that they can repeat interesting sounds to their own delight and amusement.

In the second half of the first year, cooing is replaced by **babbling,** strings of consonants and vowels that are repeated in a form of play with sounds. Babies also begin to imitate sounds and participate in give-and-take conversation, taking turns talking and listening. Toward the end of the first year, words like mama, dada, and a few other familiar labels appear. Intonation, tone, and pitch become more varied and expressive.

During the second year, more and more recognizable words become part of, and eventually replace, babbling. At first, one word may communicate an entire thought; later, toddlers put two words together (for instance, "more juice" or "truck bye-bye"), effectively conveying what they mean. Children learn the labels for familiar objects, begin to use negatives (no) and possessives (mine), and learn some action words. By the end of the second year, many toddlers have a vocabulary of 25 to 50 words (Allen & Marotz, 2010; Dyson & Genishi, 1993).

Language Meaning

VOCABULARY. One way of studying children's language development is to examine the rapid acquisition of vocabulary. For instance, one early study reported that between the ages of two and a half and four and a half, children

---

cooing
The language of babies in the first half of the first year, consisting primarily of strings of throaty vowels sounds.

babbling
The language of babies in the second half of the first year, consisting of strings of vowels and consonants that are often repeated over and over.

Key Point ◆◆

Babies' language moves from cooing to babbling to the emergence of recognizable words in the first year; toddlers become increasingly adept, acquiring both more words and some rudimentary grammatical rules.

acquire two to four new words per day on the average (Pease & Gleason, 1985); another report estimates that young children learn about 10 words every day (Miller & Gildea, 1987). A three-year-old has a vocabulary of 900 to 1,000 words, a four-year-old's vocabulary typically contains 1,500 to 1,600 words, and a five-year-old has acquired a vocabulary of 2,100 to 2,200 words (Owens, 2011). Vocabulary continues to grow rapidly beyond the preschool years. A six-year-old learns as many as 5 to 10 new words a day and has a vocabulary of 10,000 to 14,000 words (Allen & Marotz, 2010). Estimates of vocabulary size vary, but they are impressive when you consider that a young child has picked up such a large amount of information in such a short time.

Although vocabulary counts provide interesting figures, their use in understanding language development is limited. For one thing, it is difficult to determine whether a child really understands the words he uses. When Colin says, "We're going to Disneyland, and we're going to stay there a million days," does he really understand the word *million*? While he clearly does not have a grasp of *million* as an absolute amount, he nonetheless knows that it has quantitative meaning. This is a case in which the study of semantics is relevant.

SEMANTICS. Children learn the meanings of words in the context of their experiences. The study of **semantics** examines the understanding of word meanings. One significant part of semantics is a scrutiny of emotion-laden words; the most common examples are those connected to racism. In addition, name calling depends on the negative impact of certain words. For instance, an "unloaded" word such as *pill* simply refers to a form of medication, whereas labeling a child as "a pill" makes this fairly straightforward word derogatory. The importance of this aspect of semantics in the handling of children is that children tend to hurt one another through verbal attacks such as name calling.

In addition, word meaning is related to the **semantic network,** the interrelationship among words (Gleason, 2008). Fourteen-month-old Monica calls the family pet by its name, "Lucky." She then applies the same word to other dogs and even some other four-legged animals she comes across. This **overextension** is typical of toddlers learning their first words, and it reflects their vocabulary limitations (Clark, 1978b).

As they get older, however, children narrow the meanings of words until they become closer to adults' meanings. Monica will gradually learn that Lucky is a dog, that dogs are animals, and that other creatures can also be called animals. Thus, the semantic network includes an increasing understanding of classification (see Chapter 11) through this relationship among the various words (Gleason, 2008).

The meanings of some words, which adults take for granted, pose some problems for young children. For instance, they acquire an understanding of prepositions only gradually. It is not until their third year that preschoolers comprehend the word *in*, followed by *on* and *under*.

More complex prepositions (for instance, *between* or *beside*) are not grasped until ages four to five (Clark, 1978a; Johnston & Slobin, 1979). Therefore, when a teacher tells a group to "wait beside the sink to wash your hands," and three-year-old Jimmy is under a table, the teacher must recognize that it is not that Jimmy

Key Point ◆

Young children's vocabulary expansion is quite astounding, estimated to average between two and four new words every day.

naeyc

semantics
Understanding and study of word meaning.

Key Point ◆

Children's growing understanding of word meanings, including those that have an added emotional context, is called "semantics."

semantic network
The interrelationship among words, particularly related to word meaning.

overextension
Application of a word to a variety of related objects, especially used by toddlers.

Children learn the meaning of words in the context of experience. How might this teacher help these toddlers expand their language learning from the water play experience and their social interaction?

© Cengage Learning

is "not listening" but rather that he is "not understanding." Young children also have difficulty understanding a sentence in which a sequence is not in its logical order (Goodz, 1982). Therefore, it is harder for preschoolers to understand "before you go outside, put on your coat" than "put on your coat before you go outside."

Language Rules

morphology
The study of word rules; for instance, tense, plurals, and possessives.

Key Point

Morphology refers to children's learning of rules about words; for instance, how to make a verb into the past tense or how to make the plural form.

syntax
Involves the grammatical rules that govern the structure of sentences.

MORPHOLOGY. As children acquire words and understand their meanings, they also learn rules that apply to these words; the study of such word rules is called **morphology.** Some examples of morphological word rules include verb tense, plurals, and the possessive form. Researchers have identified a fairly predictable sequence in which children learn specific morphemes (Brown, 1973; deVilliers & deVilliers, 1973). Among the first such rules that children learn are the present progressive form (-*ing* ending), the words *in* and *on*, and the regular plural (-*s* ending). Irregular verb forms and contractions (*isn't, we're*) are learned later.

SYNTAX. Rules also apply to combinations of words. **Syntax** involves the grammatical rules that govern the structure of sentences. Even very young children show a grasp of such rules in their construction of two-word sentences. A toddler is much more likely to say "my car" than "car my" or "more juice" than "juice more," indicating a sensitivity to conventional word order in sentences.

Whereas very young children often use simple nouns and verbs to convey meaning, older children elaborate on these to create increasingly more complex noun phrases and verb phrases as parts of longer sentences. In addition, somewhere between the ages of two and four, children begin to combine more than one idea in one complex sentence rather than saying two simple sentences (Genishi & Fassler, 1999). Children also become progressively more adept at asking questions and stating negatives (deVilliers & deVilliers, 1979). As a result, children's language, though limited in vocabulary, can take on infinite variety in its forms of expression. Careful analysis of how children learn grammatical rules indicates that they are not merely imitating what they have heard from adults, but that they are constructing a cohesive language system of their own (Gleason, 2008).

pragmatics
Rules that govern language use in social contexts.

Key Point

Learning the social rules of conversation is called pragmatics.

PRAGMATICS. One additional set of rules governs our system of language. The aspect of communication governed by the social context is called **pragmatics.** Children gradually learn the give-and-take rules of becoming a conversationalist. They learn that during certain times it is appropriate to remain quiet (for instance, when the teacher is reading a story), whereas at other times their verbal input is desired. They also come to understand that different forms of communication are expected in different situations. Depending on the conversational partner, children learn to use different words, apply different levels of formality, and give different types of responses to questions. Accordingly, they modify how they speak when they talk to a younger child, a friend, a visitor at school, or the teacher; or when they assume the role of Superman, a parent, or a fireman in role-playing (Shatz & Gelman, 1973). A child may say to a neighbor at snack, "Gimme the milk," but say to the teacher, "May I have the milk, please?" (Owens, 2011).

ENGLISH-LANGUAGE LEARNERS

Nearly 20 percent of Americans speak a language other than English at home, according to the Census Bureau's American Community Survey. About two-thirds of those speak Spanish at home (U.S. Bureau of the Census, 2009). Early childhood programs increasingly include children from other linguistic and cultural backgrounds: children who may only speak a language other than English, children who are in the process of acquiring English as a second language, and children who have grown up acquiring more than one language simultaneously. **Bilingualism,** although it is often considered primarily a matter of language learning, also needs to be viewed as intricately tied to cultural and social dimensions. Awareness of and sensitivity to family values is particularly important in working with children learning English as a second language (Maschinot, 2008; Okagaki & Diamond, 2009).

In general, young children have little difficulty acquiring more than one language and eventually speaking each of them with no interference from the other. In learning a second language, children follow a process similar to that used to acquire the first language. In fact, common principles of learning are seen as the foundation for acquiring both languages (Shonkoff & Phillips, 2000). To function effectively in their multilanguage environment, bilingual children have to be able to switch from one language system to the other. As a result, bilingual children are at an advantage because they often develop a deeper awareness of how language works. In fact, bilingualism generally enhances cognitive development (Genishi, 2002). On the other hand, children's cognitive and socioemotional skills can be negatively affected if they learn a language and then lose it because the environment does not support its use (Maschinot, 2008).

Some children are exposed to two languages from birth. At first, such children are a little slower in acquiring vocabulary because each object or event has two words attached to it, but they soon catch up with children who are learning only one language (deVilliers & deVilliers, 1979). In general, research has shown that learning two languages simultaneously does not lead to delays in the speech or language development of young children (Maschinot, 2008). However, many other young children are not exposed to two languages from birth; instead, they are exposed first to their family's language and later to English, when they enter a school setting.

In programs that serve children whose first language is not English, the acquisition of English proficiency is essential. At the same time, support also must be provided for developing and maintaining the child's home language while she learns English (Tabors, 2008). According to DAP, "Well implemented bilingual preschool programs are most effective in reducing the achievement gap between English-language learners and English speakers, and these gains have long-term implications" (Copple & Bredekamp, 2009, p. 146).

The following examples of Nina and Hoang illustrate why more than language has to be considered. When Nina came to the United States from San Salvador with her family, she was enrolled in a daily preschool program to help her learn English. Nina, an outgoing, friendly four-year-old, found little problem interacting with the other children and the teachers. She quickly acquired a basic English vocabulary and, combined with nonverbal cues, soon communicated very effectively. Hoang, on the other hand, entered the United States as a refugee and experienced considerable hardships as well as a series of unsettling changes, including the recent death of his mother. He seemed to find his kindergarten bewildering and rarely participated in activities, instead standing at the sidelines in somber silence.

DIVERSITY

bilingualism
Ability to use two languages.

Key Point
Children generally have little difficulty learning more than one language.

Early childhood programs increasingly enroll children from other cultures whose primary language is not English.

Although the approach to helping Nina acquire English involved the encouragement of peer interactions, exposure to stimulating activities, and a language-rich environment, Hoang's needs were clearly different. Before language learning could be addressed, his emotional needs had to be considered. After almost two months, Hoang began to establish a relationship with one of the teachers and gradually became involved in activities. Throughout this time of silence, Hoang had nonetheless been surrounded by language, and eventually it became clear that he had attended to much of what he heard. Once Hoang felt stability in his home and school life, his mastery of English progressed significantly.

Second-Language Teaching Strategies

DIVERSITY

The following specific strategies provide some guidelines to help young children learn a second language. As you read this list, notice that many of these suggestions are equally important for all young children, not only those learning a new language.

- A new experience such as school can be bewildering to any young child, particularly if the child cannot understand the language. A friendly, consistent, supportive atmosphere can help make the child feel welcome and comfortable, which, in turn, will facilitate learning English.
- If someone who speaks the child's first language is available, enlist that person to help the child learn the routines and expectations, as well as the new language. If another child in the class speaks the child's first language, interaction between the two should be encouraged, although certainly not forced.
- Encourage all of the children to talk to and include the child in activities.
- Use the child's name frequently, being sure to pronounce it properly when talking to the child.
- A non–English-speaking child should not be forced to speak, because the natural process of learning a second language usually entails a time of silent assimilation. Even if he is not yet actively speaking it, the child is still acquiring the language.

The teacher can encourage the children in the class to invite their non-English-speaking classmates to join in their activities. What are some ways you might help this child become an integral part of his new class?

- Involve the child in the classroom through non–language activities (for instance, helping to set the table for snack) to help the child become part of the group.
- Language should be presented in a natural, meaningful way, in the context of the child's experiences and interests.
- Concrete objects or demonstration of actions should be paired with new words. Say the word "milk" when helping the child pour it at snack; pair the word "cut" with a demonstration using scissors.
- Repetition of new language learning is important, provided it is done naturally. Meaningless drills do not help. Consistently using the same wording each day (for instance, to signal classroom transitions) will help the child connect words and meaning more easily.
- When a child shares feelings or an idea verbally, such communication should be encouraged through uncritical acceptance. Correcting grammar or pronunciation tends to inhibit rather than foster language.

▸ Particularly if your class includes a number of children who speak a language other than English, make their language a natural part of the program. A teacher who speaks the children's native language can use that language as a means for facilitating learning. In this way, language is not an end in itself, but rather a tool for many kinds of learning.

LANGUAGE AND THE EARLY CHILDHOOD CURRICULUM

The following sections will examine several important aspects of language. First, we will discuss the informal, ongoing use of language that should be a natural accompaniment to whatever children are doing. Next we will look at some specific activities that teachers plan to enhance language development. Finally, we will examine children's emerging literacy and their awareness that language extends to reading and writing, and how this is supported through integrated language experiences.

Spontaneous Language

Because language is so pervasive in almost everything children do, it must be central to the early childhood program. Children are constantly involved in communication—listening, hearing, talking, interpreting, writing, and reading. All forms of language surround them as they interact with each other, with adults, with media, with activities, and with varied materials. Language activities do not need to be structured to teach language because by preschool age children have already acquired an elaborate and complex language system. Rather, early childhood language experiences should emerge from natural and meaningful conversations and experiences between adults and children, as well as among children. Such talk is used to inform, tell stories, pretend, plan, argue, discuss, express humor, and so on. Classrooms for young children, therefore, are not quiet. They are abuzz with language almost all of the time.

Almost every aspect of the early childhood environment and program facilitates language. For instance, the knowledgeable teacher, who values what children have to say and listens to them carefully, promotes language development. Similarly, a daily schedule (as we discussed in Chapter 8) that provides large blocks of time in which children can become immersed in activities and interactions fosters language usage. In addition, language growth is encouraged by a curriculum that introduces interesting and stimulating objects, experiences, and concepts, just as a classroom environment that is set up to invite small groups of children to work together promotes language.

CONVERSATIONS. A natural way of using language is through conversation. This begins in earliest infancy. In good early childhood programs, there is an almost constant, ongoing buzz of conversations between children and teachers and among children. For children, conversation is an art

▶❚❚ **TeachSource Video Activity**
WATCH • REFLECT • RESPOND

This video deals with supporting English language learners by working with their families. Go to CengageBrain.com and view the video titled, "English Language Learners: Partnering with Parents to Promote Oral Language and Literacy," and answer the following questions:

1. How does Teacher Mona convey her respect for the child's first language and culture?

2. What strategies does Teacher Mona provide for parents to encourage language and literacy in their children?

naeyc

naeyc

Key Point ◆◆

Because language is so integral to all parts of the early childhood program, much language learning occurs spontaneously.

Language is used and reinforced countless times in the early childhood program, as teachers and children, as well as children and children, interact and converse informally.

© Cengage Learning

that takes time to develop, since it involves learning a number of elements, such as how to initiate and end conversations, maintain coherent dialogue, take turns, and restore a failed conversation. It is important, therefore, that there be many, many opportunities for children to practice their emerging conversational skills.

The teachers' ability to engage in effective conversations with children is also an art. Dialogue between adults and small groups or individual children is essential (Cadwell & Fyfe, 2004). DAP suggests that "conversations should include discussion of events, experiences, or people that are beyond the here and now—events from the past, the future, or the imagination. Such interaction requires children and adults to use more explanations, descriptions, narratives, and pretend talk" (Copple & Bredekamp, 2009, pp. 144–145).

Lessons from the Reggio Emilia approach also underscore the importance of meaningful conversations with young children. One of the key components in the work of Reggio Emilia programs is the dialogue between teachers and small groups of children. Teachers help children strengthen and deepen their understanding of various concepts through such conversations. Teachers ask questions that provoke the children to think critically and creatively and to be astute observers. Cadwell and Fyfe (2004) relate one such conversation between a teacher and a small group of children about leaves. From the conversation, which was also used as a basis for emergent curriculum planning, they found a number of interesting themes raised by the children. For instance, the children compared the leaves to humans, noting that they had spines and curled up when they were tired. They also commented on how leaves move, comparing the leaves' flight to a human's walking. Finally, the conversation also revealed that, when the children were faced with difficult-to-explain phenomena, such as why leaves change color, they resorted to magic explanations. This lively conversation occurred because a sensitive teacher asked good questions, listened carefully, and gave the children the respect and opportunity to express their ideas.

PLAYING WITH LANGUAGE. Another facet of language that teachers can use to enrich its use in the early childhood setting is children's language play. Infants delight in physical humor such as tickling. However, once children have a good grasp of the principles of language and the correctness of a concept, they delight in confirming this by expressing the opposite, usually accompanied by much laughter and giggling. Expressions of humor through silliness, nonsense words or rhymes, and "dirty" words particularly enthrall young children. Children enjoy humor, and teachers can use it to capture and maintain children's attention, both in the stories they read or tell and in their conversations with children.

One basis for humor is children's increasing ability to recognize incongruity (Honig, 1988). For preschoolers, this can involve changing the words of their favorite rhymes ("Mary had a little bleep"), putting an absurd element into a picture (a cat's head on a goldfish's body), or calling a known object by an obviously inappropriate name.

Most riddles and jokes that depend on the double meaning of a word are too sophisticated for preschoolers, who do not yet have the cognitive skills to comprehend this level of linguistic incongruity, although such jokes are grasped by many primary school children. Seven-year-old Caleb asks his family at dinner, "What did the dog say when he saw the top of the house?" His parents and four-year-old sister Nancy laugh when he tells them, "Roof, roof!" Then Nancy decides to relate a riddle as well. "What did the kitty say when he saw the top of the house?" Nancy's answer—"Meow, meow!"—and her accompanying laughter indicate that she does not yet understand that words sometimes have double

Key Point ◆
Effective conversations between teachers and children are responsive to the child rather than being controlled by the teacher.

Key Point ◆
Once children have a good grasp of the principles of language, they begin to play with it through humor, nonsense words, rhymes, or "dirty" words.

meanings, although she does understand that a joke is something funny that people enjoy sharing.

Children usually know when they are using a naughty word, and this is also a source of humor for them. "Bathroom language" is a particular favorite of many four-year-olds, who can dissolve into paroxysms of laughter as they recite a litany such as "poo-poo poo-poo." Usually, such language is best ignored. If it seems unduly disruptive, you might tell the children involved that bathroom language is restricted to the bathroom. Children also enjoy repeating adult swear words; they are usually unaware of their meaning but know that such words are somehow inappropriate. Let children know that swear words are not acceptable at school. This is particularly important if children use words that are intended to hurt others; for instance, racial or ethnic slurs.

The teacher can structure activities that tickle the children's funny bones, or as is often the case, children will find their own ways to play with language. Silly words, nonsense words, bathroom terms, and rhyming words are favorites.

Language Activities

In addition to the ongoing use of language in the early childhood program, specific activities based on language use and elaboration are also incorporated. Such activities are often presented at large- or small-group times, enhancing not just language but also listening skills, group social skills, creative thinking, concept formation, and other areas of development.

Stories, in their various forms, are the most popular vehicle for such activities. Stories can be told or read by teachers, children, or both together; they can be enacted by children or with flannelboard pieces, puppets, or play dough; or they can come from the rich store of children's literature or be made up out of the fabric of the children's experiences. We will briefly look at some of the ways in which stories can be used and presented.

BOOKS. The most popular story activity in most early childhood programs is book reading. Very young children enjoy book reading, and teachers should certainly incorporate reading into the routines of infants and toddlers. Because so many excellent books are available for young children, they provide a wealth of ways to contribute to language experience, reinforce concepts, entertain, stimulate thought, and offer emotional support.

Key Point

Book reading is one of the most popular language activities; good children's books on a variety of topics are available.

Many children have had happy experiences with books all of their lives. They anticipate enjoyment from book reading activities; they also have developed the concentration and attention required for full involvement. Others may not have had many such opportunities and may need some individual, more intimate story reading time to help them acquire a greater appreciation for books.

Some techniques help engage children in the book reading process. For one thing, teachers play a vital role in how children respond to story reading. In a sense, they endorse the story through their enthusiasm, interest in the story, animation, and the use of their voices as tools in making the characters and action come alive. In addition, book reading—whether with a large group, a small group, or an individual child—should be interactive rather than a one-way endeavor. Children should have opportunities to comment on and discuss the story and illustrations, speculate on what might

Book reading remains a perennial favorite among language activities for young children. The teacher makes the book come alive through her voice inflection and animation.

happen next, and relate the story to their personal experiences. When children only listen passively, learning is less likely to be taking place, and many children may well tune out. It is important to keep in mind that it is not the words themselves, but the relevance of those words to the children's lives that make books meaningful; that relevance is explored through discussion between the children and teacher.

Many wonderful books are available for young children, spanning a wide range of appropriate and relevant topics. Among these are storybooks on familiar topics, fairy tales and fables, informational nonfiction books, wordless books, alphabet books, and therapeutic books (see the discussion on bibliotherapy in Chapter 16) (Machado, 2013). A school should have a good selection of children's books in its own library, rotating them as curriculum topics and the children's interests change. In addition, the local community library can expand the available supply. Figure 12-1 lists guidelines for selecting children's books.

DIVERSITY

Books also are a wonderful way to support and validate the cultures of the children in your classroom. "Literature from authors and illustrators who authentically depict various cultures and backgrounds is an important part of building classroom community" (Hall, 2008, p. 80). In addition, books such as *Something Beautiful* (Wyeth, 2005), *Homemade Love* (Hooks, 2002), and *Nappy Hair* (Herron, 1997), encourage self-worth, inspiration, and pride, especially in girls, since these books' heroines are African American female characters (Brinson, 2009).

naeyc

POETRY. In many early childhood programs, poetry is a sadly neglected aspect of literature, perhaps because teachers have not had much exposure to poetry themselves. This is unfortunate because appropriate poems can broaden children's experiences and add a magical aspect to language activities. The cadence of well-rhymed words, as is true with music, invites attention and involvement. Poetry's strongest appeal is its "singing quality" (Sutherland & Arbuthnot, 1997). Poems, like any literature, must interest children, speaking to a familiar experience or delighting with their nonsense and humor. For instance, children can relate to Robert Louis Stevenson's poem, "Bed in Summer" (1985), a child's complaint about having to go to bed when the sky outside is still blue—just as they enjoy the silly image of the "Mother Goose" cow jumping over the moon or Shel Silverstein's humorous poems. Poetry, with its play on sounds, also supports children's developing phonological awareness (Yopp & Yopp, 2009) and awareness of the many possible uses of language (Elster, 2010).

Key Point ◆

Poetry, storytelling, flannelboard stories, story enactment, and puppets are variations of language activities that children enjoy.

STORYTELLING. Telling a story, rather than reading one from a book, can be a more direct, intimate experience (Machado, 2013) and can stimulate children's imaginations as they visualize the story line and characters. The story can be original, pulled from a proficient teacher's imagination, or it can be a paraphrased version of a book or folktale. Of course, the teacher's skill in holding the children's attention through eye contact, voice variation, and dramatic pauses contributes considerably to storytelling.

naeyc

Stories can also be told by children, either individually or as a group activity. "One of the greatest outcomes of storytelling is that it inspires children to create their own stories. This experience adds new dimensions to language and literacy learning" (Isbell, 2002, p. 30). In particular, older children, who have well-developed language fluency and vocabulary, enjoy making up original stories, which can be recorded in writing by an adult or tape recorded if you wish to

Figure **12-1**

Criteria for Selecting Children's Books

The books you select for children should meet the best standards, both for literary and artistic quality. Just because a book is in print does not necessarily ensure that it is a good book. There are some published guides to selecting high-quality children's books (for instance, the monthly *Bulletin of the Center for Children's Books,* the bimonthly *Horn Book Magazine,* or the American Library Association's *Notable Children's Books*), and resource persons such as children's librarians can prove extremely helpful. But it is also important to develop a sense of what constitutes a good book. As you review books to read to children, apply the following guidelines (Glazer, 2000; Goodman, Smith, Meredith, & Goodman, 1987; Machado, 2013).

Overall Impression
- The length of the book should be appropriate to the ages of the children. Although engrossing stories of increasing length should be presented as children get older, 5 to 10 minutes (not including discussion) is generally a good time limit for preschoolers. Primary children will listen to an engrossing story for longer periods.
- The amount of text per page should also be considered. Young preschoolers especially will find long text with few pictures difficult.
- The size of the book is important, particularly when you read to a group of children. Very small books should be kept for one-on-one reading sessions. Children also enjoy oversized books.
- The binding of a book is important if you are planning to buy it for the school library. Sturdy binding will ensure durability. Some schools prefer buying less expensive books such as paperbacks; these will not last as long, but the cost is considerably less than that of hardbound books. Sturdy cardboard and cloth books are available for infants and toddlers.

Text Elements
- Read the book carefully and consider whether the plot or story line is coherent and interesting. The plot doesn't have to be complex, but it should be plausible and logical. The adventure of Max in Maurice Sendak's *Where the Wild Things Are* is a good example of a well-written plot that appeals to young children.
- The characters of the book should be distinctive and memorable, should not be stereotyped, and should provide children something with which they can identify. For instance, many excellent books break gender role stereotypes (see a suggested list of such books from Roberts and Hill (2003, pp. 40–41). Children have no trouble remembering mischievous Curious George or spunky Madeline from their books.
- Characters in many books represent diversity; for example, racial, gender, age, and ability diversity. Ensure that such portrayals are sensitive and accurate, promote inclusion, and help strengthen children's value of differences.

DIVERSITY

- Many books revolve around a theme; for instance, friendship, emotional reactions, or exploration. If there is a theme, it should not sound like a sermon. A theme should be relevant to young children's lives and worth sharing with them. Ann Scott's *On Mother's Lap* contains the common theme of jealousy over a new sibling, an experience with which many children can relate.
- As you review a book, pay close attention to the style of writing. Language should be simple but vivid and evoke the appropriate mood and images. Because children delight in repetition and humor, look for some books that incorporate these elements. Children love to chime in the refrain of Wanda Gag's *Millions of Cats* as the old couple's acquisition of cats reaches the ludicrous stage with "hundreds of cats, thousands of cats, millions, and billions, and trillions of cats!"

Illustrations
- Above all, pictures should be aesthetic and should complement and enliven the words of the story. Many skilled artists' talents enrich children's books. Illustrators use numerous, effective ways to convey the story in pictures. As you browse through some children's classics, compare the whimsical characters of Dr. Seuss, the humorous pen-and-ink drawings of Maurice Sendak, and the vivid characters of Eric Carle.

Pictures should be placed adjacent to the text so that the story and illustrations work in harmony.

preserve them. In fact, research links beginning reading skills and the development of literacy to opportunities for telling as well as listening to stories.

Groups of children can also participate in storytelling. Whalen (2002) suggests several approaches to group stories:

▶ **Round-robin or sentence stories**—Start a story on a familiar topic, and then ask each child to add a sentence to the story.

▶ **Theme stories**—Ask children to select a theme, and then develop the story from there.

▶ **Descriptive stories**—As children develop a story, encourage them to add new descriptive words with each addition.

▶ **Picture stories**—After children select pictures from various sources, have them use the pictures to describe what is happening; then they can use their imagination to flesh out the plot.

▶ **Grab-bag stories**—Have children select an item out of a bag, and then tell a story about the object; the teacher can encourage a group story involving all the items.

▶ **Finish-story stories**—Have one child briefly start a story, and then have the group fill in its development and ending; conversely, a child can tell the ending of a story after which the group describes the beginning of the plot.

Storytelling promotes a more sophisticated engagement in language activities, particularly because it encourages children's participation, such as in role playing and performance of the story (Berkowitz, 2011).

FLANNELBOARD STORIES. A version of storytelling with props, flannelboard stories easily capture children's attention as they look forward to seeing what will be put on the board next (Machado, 2013). A flannel- or felt-covered board serves as a background, while cutouts of characters made of felt, fabric, or construction paper backed with Velcro are used to relay the story. A selection of favorite stories can be available for the teachers' and children's use through a flannelboard story file (see the discussion of teacher-made materials in Chapter 7).

Flannelboard stories can be derived from a variety of sources, including favorite books and poems, nursery rhymes, teacher-made stories, and stories based on the children's experiences such as field trips. A new flannelboard story can be presented during a group time, and then the props left out so the children can retell the story in their own way later. In addition, a selection of familiar flannelboard stories can be placed in the language arts area of the classroom for children's everyday use.

STORY ENACTMENT. Children respond with great enthusiasm to opportunities to enact their favorite stories. Story enactment involves both language and social skills as children cooperate and share the roles of a given story. Stories such as "The Three Little Pigs," "Goldilocks and the Three Bears," "Caps for Sale," and "Stone Soup" provide important elements such as repetitive dialogue, strong action lines, and familiarity. These stories can and should be adapted as needed to incorporate the children's interests, increase repetitive elements, elaborate on what is most familiar to the children, simplify the plot if it is too complex, or challenge sex-role stereotypes. For instance, several children can play the role of Cinderella while the teacher takes on the other roles, Papa Bear can cook the porridge, or a female hunter can save Little Red Riding Hood.

PUPPETS. Another way to enact stories is to use puppets as the actors. A make-shift stage made from a table set on its side, or a more elaborate one with curtains, can provide the backdrop; alternatively, puppets can be used to enact a story without such a setting. A variety of commercial, teacher-made, or child-made puppets can help enact the story. Teachers can use puppets to convey a story during group time because children enjoy watching a lively puppet show. The puppets can be left out for the children to reenact the story or to make up a different one later. Puppets can be an ongoing part of the language arts center, inviting children to engage in puppetry at other times. Puppets allow children to project onto another character ideas and feelings that they might hesitate to express as their own. Puppets can also help a shy child by allowing that child to speak through an intermediary.

Puppets, as an ongoing part of the language center, encourage conversation and story reenactment and can provide shy children with an intermediary through whom they can speak.

Emergent Literacy

As we have seen, children learn to understand and express language in a natural way, through a process that begins very early in life. Similarly, children also begin to form an understanding of reading and writing, something that has come to interest researchers and educators only relatively recently. The term **emergent literacy** acknowledges that learning to read and write (in other words, becoming literate) is a dynamic, ongoing, emerging process. In fact, all aspects of language—listening, speaking, writing, and reading—are intertwined and develop concurrently, not sequentially. Review the report of the National Early Literacy Panel (2008), *Developing Early Literacy*, in the "Take a Closer Look" box.

In their position statement on children's emergent literacy, NAEYC (2005) and the International Reading Association (IRA) identify the following phases in children's development of reading and writing, pointing out that the ages and grade levels are approximations:

emergent literacy
The ongoing, dynamic process of learning to read and write, which starts in the early years.

▸ Phase 1, Infancy through preschool: Awareness and exploration
▸ Phase 2, Kindergarten: Experimental reading and writing
▸ Phase 3, Grade 1: Early reading and writing
▸ Phase 4, Grade 2: Transitional reading and writing
▸ Phase 5, Grade 3: Independent and productive reading and writing

Children develop an understanding of reading and writing through a supportive literate environment that is started at home and furthered in the early childhood program. Catherine Snow concludes that when parents read to their young children, these children's language is more complex during reading time than it is during other times of play (Snow & Ninio, 1986). Both home and school experiences with books provide children with further insights; for example, that print should make sense, that print and speech are related, that book language is different from speech, and that books are enjoyable. Out of many experiences with the verbal and printed forms of the language come the foundations for writing and reading. This has been supported by the Home-School Study of Language and Literacy Development, which concluded that literacy success in school is related to early exposure to a varied vocabulary, opportunities to be part of extended conversations, and an environment that is cognitively and linguistically stimulating (Dickinson & Tabors, 2002).

In the past few years, there has been an increasing focus on literacy and the importance of its development during the earliest years of a child's life, when the foundations for literacy emerge. A variety of research efforts, such as the

Key Point ◆
Emergent literacy acknowledges that reading and writing are ongoing processes that begin early in life.

WHAT DOES IT TAKE TO DEVELOP LITERATE CHILDREN?

W̲E̲ ̲K̲N̲O̲W̲ that a majority of American children spend some time in an early childhood program. We also know that by fourth grade, more than one-third of children do not achieve basic reading levels. What needs to be done to better prepare children to learn to read and write? This question is at the heart of the report *Developing Early Literacy* (National Early Literacy Panel, 2008). The National Early Literacy Panel, made up of eminent scholars, reviewed and synthesized hundreds of studies to determine what skills and abilities in young children predict later literacy success and what kinds of approaches and teaching methods are linked to successful reading and writing.

The panel identified a number of early skills that were related to later literacy development. Most of those that were seen in the preschool years were precursor or emergent skills that contribute to later literacy. There was a particularly strong relationship between skills such as alphabet knowledge, phonological awareness, and ability to write letters or one's name and later success in reading and writing. Another group of skills, including an understanding of what print is, awareness of environmental print (discussed below), and a good command of spoken language, also were found to contribute to reading and writing, though less strongly than was found for the earlier-mentioned

skills. "These findings highlight the fact that the origins of well-developed conventional literacy skills are found very early in children's educational experience, and these findings are consistent with studies showing that the consequences of falling seriously behind in the development of conventional literacy skills are likely to be long-lasting in the absence of substantial remedial efforts" (Lonigan, Schatschneider, Westberg, & National Early Literacy Panel, 2008a, p. 68).

Given these findings about which early skills are important to later literacy achievement, the National Early Literacy Panel also sought to identify what kinds of instructional strategies were most effective in preparing children for later success as readers and writers. Interestingly, they found that nearly all the studies they reviewed described programs that included some form of phonetic awareness training. Activities encouraged children to identify sounds in words, for instance, matching words with the same initial sound. Even more common were activities in which children were asked to manipulate sounds in words, for example, combining sounds to form words. Another frequently used activity was to help children learn the names and sounds of the letters of the alphabet.

Another set of studies reviewed by the National Early Literacy Panel had to do with shared reading—when adults read books with

children. "Shared-reading activities are often recommended as the single most important thing adults can do to promote the emergent literacy skills of young children" (Lonigan, Shanahan, Cunningham, & National Early Literacy Panel, 2008b, p. 153). Yet surprisingly, the Panel found few studies that examined the linkage between shared reading and later literacy success. The Panel did find some positive effects of shared reading on children's print knowledge and oral language skills.

What do the results of the National Early Literacy Panel's report tell us? DAP summarizes the findings well:

> Compelling evidence has shown that young children's alphabet knowledge and phonological awareness are significant predictors of their later proficiency in reading and writing. A decade ago, many preschool teachers did not perceive it as their role—or even see it as appropriate—to launch young children on early steps toward literacy, including familiarizing them with the world of print and the sounds of language. The early childhood profession now recognizes that gaining a foundation in literacy is an important facet of children's experience before kindergarten, although the early literacy component still needs substantial improvement in many classrooms. (Copple & Bredekamp, 2009, p. 7)

322

following, have identified key components of emergent literacy and essential elements of literacy instruction (Halle, Calkins, Berry, & Johnson, 2003; Roscos, Christie, & Richgels, 2003):

▶ **Rich teacher talk**—Engaging children in rich conversations, introducing new vocabulary, extending children's comments to be more descriptive or grammatically mature, discussing cognitively challenging topics, and listening and responding respectfully to children.

▶ **Reading**—At least once or twice a day, using pleasurable material and including conversation about the topic; making distinctions between paper and print.

▶ **Phonological awareness**—Understanding that speech is made up of units, such as words, syllables, and sounds; having the ability to use these when speaking; acquiring increasing awareness of the sounds of language, including activities that involve rhyme, alliteration, and sound matching.

▶ **Letter recognition**—Association of letters with appropriate sounds through alphabet books, blocks, puzzles, and charts; focus on letters with personal meaning, such as the first letter of the child's name.

▶ **Awareness of print and support for emergent reading**—Understanding that words in print convey a message, that we read from left to right and top to bottom, and that printed words have corresponding spoken words; providing a library center, reading favorite books often, and using print in play and functional class activities.

▶ **Early writing development**—Attempts to imitate writing, such as with scribbles or invented spelling (discussed below); support through a well-stocked writing center; and writing opportunities through play and functional class activities.

Mock writing is distinct from children's scribbling or drawing and appears at a relatively early age. A three-year-old, for instance, may tell you he is "writing a letter," using mock writing in a deliberate imitation of adult writing. Look at samples of children's artwork and see if you can find examples of mock writing.

LEARNING TO WRITE. The beginnings of writing emerge early in life through a number of antecedent steps. Vygotsky (1978) (recall the discussion of his theory in Chapter 5) traces the roots of writing to the earliest infant gestures, described as "writing in the air." During the preschool years, children become aware of the differences between drawing and writing, a distinction that is evident in their

naeyc

BRAIN STORM
LEARNING TO READ

Using imaging scans, neuroscientists have been exploring what brain areas are involved in reading. Interestingly, they have found that the areas of the brain involved in reading depend on whether the child is a novice reader or a skilled reader. When a child is just learning to read, she has to analyze each new word, pull it apart, and match letters to sounds. "When, for example, the child's brain first sees the word *dog* in print, the word analysis area records the three alphabetic symbols and matches the *duh-awh-guh* sounds to their appropriate letters. . . . Eventually, a mental image of a furry animal is conceptualized in the mind's eye, adding meaning to the symbolic representation" (Sousa, 2005, p. 55). The experienced reader, however, has read many words on numerous occasions and has created a neural model that includes spelling, pronunciation, and meaning of each word. This model allows the child to read the word much more quickly because it is stored in a region of the brain not yet used by the novice reader (Hoff, 2009; Sousa, 2005).

mock writing
Young children's imitation of writing through wavy, circular, or vertical lines, which can be seen as distinct from drawing or scribbling.

Key Point ◆◆

Antecedents of writing begin early in life, including use of mock writing, which is distinctly different from drawing, scribbling, and invented spelling.

invented spelling
Used by young children in their early attempts to write by finding the speech sound that most clearly fits what they want to convey.

environmental print
Print and other graphic symbols that are found in the physical environment, such as signs, billboards, TV commercials, and common containers.

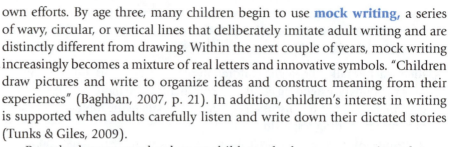

Key Point ◆◆

The ability to read also emerges gradually, as children increasingly make sense out of print.

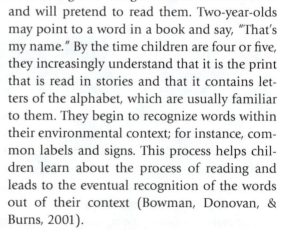

Commonly seen words that appear on labels and signs are among the first that children "read." This four-year-old recognizes the word milk *on the carton.*

own efforts. By age three, many children begin to use **mock writing,** a series of wavy, circular, or vertical lines that deliberately imitate adult writing and are distinctly different from drawing. Within the next couple of years, mock writing increasingly becomes a mixture of real letters and innovative symbols. "Children draw pictures and write to organize ideas and construct meaning from their experiences" (Baghban, 2007, p. 21). In addition, children's interest in writing is supported when adults carefully listen and write down their dictated stories (Tunks & Giles, 2009).

By early elementary school, most children who have grown up in a pleasurable, literate environment and who recognize most or all of the letters of the alphabet begin to use **invented spelling** by finding the speech sound that most closely fits what they want to convey (McBride-Chang 1998). Many kindergarten classes incorporate writing activities, including journals, stories, messages to friends, and writing as part of everyday activities (Mayer, 2009). In one class, five-year-old Abby wrote, "I M GNG TO DRV MI KAR AT HOM" (I am going to drive my car at home) in one of her stories, accompanied by a picture of Abby atop a blue vehicle. Analysis of the errors seen in invented spelling indicates that children are trying to work out a system of rules, just as they did when, as toddlers, they were acquiring oral language. Because reading and writing are intertwined processes, such early attempts at phonemic spelling are soon replaced with more conventional forms as children repeatedly come across the same words in their reading.

LEARNING TO READ. When children read and write, they have gained an understanding of the consistent relationship between the letters of the alphabet and their use in the written form. This understanding develops gradually, through many experiences. Early literacy includes a growing awareness of **environmental print,** for instance, that a stop sign indicates "step on the brake." Many of children's first encounters with print and other graphic symbols, in fact, come from their environment (Xu & Rutledge, 2003).

Children who, from an early age, engage in pleasurable book reading activities with their families and caregivers begin to learn about the functions and uses of books and print. Toddlers begin to recognize their favorite books and will pretend to read them. Two-year-olds may point to a word in a book and say, "That's my name." By the time children are four or five, they increasingly understand that it is the print that is read in stories and that it contains letters of the alphabet, which are usually familiar to them. They begin to recognize words within their environmental context; for instance, common labels and signs. This process helps children learn about the process of reading and leads to the eventual recognition of the words out of their context (Bowman, Donovan, & Burns, 2001).

Children actively seek to make sense of print in their environment by using a variety of strategies that they themselves invent. Younger preschoolers' strategies focus on such clues as the first letter of a word ("That's my name," says Paul, "because it's got a 'P' "); the shape of the word, such as its length or spacing if there is more than one word in a configuration; and pictures, which are used as clues to help decipher accompanying words. As children get older and more experienced in acquiring reading skills, they use some additional strategies. Such strategies include looking for familiar letters or combinations of letters in words; spontaneously and repeatedly practicing the spelling and copying of words; and inventing a phonological system to sound out words, similar to that used in inventive spelling. Gradually, they internalize the conventional rules of reading, as they become proficient readers in the early grades.

IMPLICATIONS. As the preceding discussions suggest, young children have a natural interest in the print environment around them, an interest most of them express through their own inventive attempts at writing and reading. This view of how children learn to read and write is far removed from some of the stereotyped notions of reading and writing as formal subjects best begun in first grade.

Yet all too often, young children are placed into high-powered, rigid, formalized programs that focus on isolated skills involved in the reading process, rather than on the integration of all aspects of language. The majority of early childhood professionals express great concern over this developmentally inappropriate practice. Reading and writing emerge from many successful and enjoyable experiences with language, both oral and written. According to research, literacy develops best through meaningful context in an informal, supportive environment. As Judith Schickedanz (1982), one of the leading authorities in children's emergent literacy, writes:

> We need to abandon ideas and practices that assume early literacy development to be simply a matter of teaching children a few basic skills such as alphabet recognition or letter–sound associations. Much more is involved. Limiting children's reading experiences to contacts with bits and pieces of print isolated from meaningful contexts may actually prevent them from developing broader and more complex insights that are the key to understanding what written language is all about. (p. 259)

PROMOTING LITERACY DEVELOPMENT. Literacy, like oral language, emerges in a natural way that does not require formal teaching to prompt interest. What it does need is a language-rich environment to encourage its development. Literacy is best promoted when high-quality oral and print language surrounds children, children can observe others using literacy skills, and they are encouraged to experiment with all forms of language. Such an approach integrates all forms of communication, including speaking, listening, writing, reading, art, music, and math (Koralek, 2007). It is also dependent on the support, modeling, and mediation of adults and more experienced peers within the zone of proximal development, as described by Vygotsky (Manson & Sinha, 1993). Recall from Chapter 5 that, according to Vygotsky, children can acquire new skills that are too difficult for them to complete alone but which they can accomplish with some guiding help from someone more experienced. Such an approach should be combined with other methods that can help children develop literacy and acquire reading and writing skills. NAEYC and the IRA (2005), for instance, note the importance of alphabet knowledge and connections between letters and sounds. In particular as they get older, children need

Children enjoy looking through books on their own as well as having adults read to them. A wide range of appropriate books should be attractively displayed and available for children at all times.

© Cengage Learning

Key Point

The development of literacy in young children is promoted through a variety of activities, techniques, and environmental accommodations.

more explicit emphasis on phonics. The following suggestions for supporting literacy development come from a variety of sources:

▶ The aim of supporting literacy development in young children should be to enhance their desire to read and write by building on their intrinsic motivation to learn these skills (NAEYC & IRA, 2005).

▶ A language-rich environment must contain many materials, opportunities, and experiences for planned and spontaneous interaction with language, both oral and written. This means providing appropriate materials and scheduled time blocks for children to pursue language activities (Machado, 2013).

▶ A carefully selected library of high-quality children's books must be available. Good books attract children's interest so that they often seek them out to browse through or to ask a teacher to read.

▶ Children can be exposed to a variety of text types, not just storybooks; for instance, newspapers, magazines, nonfiction books, and letters to the editor (Donovan, Milewicz, & Smolkin, 2003). Information books and nonfiction reference materials can hold special interest for children, as they seek answers to a variety of questions (Duke, 2007).

▶ Stories should not just be read but should also be discussed. Children understand stories better when they have opportunities to ask and answer questions about the plot and characters of a story and relate the story to their own lives.

▶ One important skill for early reading is story awareness. Children need many story reading experiences to acquire a sense of what a story is and how it is organized. Knowing, for instance, how a story begins and ends and the story's sequence of events is important for literacy development (Schickedanz, 1999).

▶ Books should be read more than one time. Children are more likely to reenact a book on their own if they have heard it at least three times (Schickedanz, 1999).

▶ Children should be encouraged to "read" to each other, whether or not they actually know how to read.

▶ If some children in the class seem to have had few one-on-one reading experiences at home, time should be set aside for story reading; for instance, during self-selected activity blocks when a teacher can spend time reading to just one or two children.

▶ Print awareness can be supported through books as well as through other forms of print in the school environment. Charts, lists, labels, and bulletin boards that surround children in the environment contribute to print awareness, as does a teacher who interprets, calls attention to, and gets the children's input when creating print (Schickedanz, 1999).

▶ Children gradually learn that there is a relationship between written and spoken words. When children are read certain books frequently, they often become so familiar with the stories that they know which words correspond with which pages. Such experiences contribute to making the connection between speech and print (Schickedanz, 1999).

▶ Children should be provided with a variety of reading and writing materials to incorporate into their play. For example, paper, pencils, markers, and other implements in the art, language arts, dramatic play, science, and math areas should be included to suggest a link between the activities that go on in those areas and reading/writing.

▶ Given a supportive atmosphere, children will engage in story writing. Although children may not be using conventional letters and words, their stories (as well as the writing process) are still full of meaning. The sensitive teacher must carefully attend to what children are trying to convey to understand that meaning (Schickedanz, 1999).

▶ Some children show little interest in reading and writing, perhaps because they have had little access to materials that promote these activities. One successful strategy to stimulate this interest is to provide a "writing suitcase" that the children can take home overnight or over a weekend. This suitcase can include such materials as various sizes and shapes of paper and notebooks; chalk and chalkboard, pencils, crayons, and markers; magnet, cardboard, or plastic letters and stencils; favorite picture books; scissors; and tape, glue, stapler, hole punch, and ruler (Rich, 1985).

The information we have considered so far in relation to language in the early childhood curriculum, including the acquisition of literacy, is particularly geared to preschool-age children. Some of the principles and activities we have discussed are, however, relevant to children across the ages from birth through eight. In the next sections, we will consider some more specific elements involved in the support of the language and literacy development of infants and toddlers, school-age children, and children with disabilities.

SUPPORTING LANGUAGE AND LITERACY DEVELOPMENT IN INFANTS AND TODDLERS

At the start of this chapter we noted that "the odyssey of children's early development is particularly astounding when we consider the acquisition of language." The ability to communicate is a complex process that begins very early in life. Children are born with "communication intent" but not with language (Gonzalez-Mena & Eyer, 2012). Acquiring language depends on the two-way interchanges provided by nurturing adults.

There are so many ways that you, as a teacher, can support babies' language development. The daily conversations discussed above are extremely important for infants and toddlers. Talk about what they are doing during routine activities; engage in give-and-take conversations in response to babies' verbalizations;

naeyc

Key Point ◆

Infants and toddler teachers nurture language through their frequent, loving interactions with the babies in their care, reading books to even the youngest children, and recognizing that literacy has its roots in these early years.

The seeds of literacy are planted early in life. Toddlers who have access to age-appropriate books will be more likely to develop a love for reading because of this early exposure.

expand children's early language attempts; label and discuss familiar objects and experiences; and use a variety of songs, fingerplays, books, stories, poems, and games to encourage language. Talk to, not about babies. Babies need to be acknowledged by name and given the opportunity to communicate (Kovach & De Ros-Voseles, 2011). Listen attentively to try to understand a toddler's meaning; don't rush or interrupt attempts at communication.

You should read books to children from earliest infancy. Book reading should not be a scheduled group activity but, rather, a pleasurable, intimate activity you share with one child or a small interested group (Birckmayer, Kennedy, & Stonehouse, 2009). Book reading should happen frequently and spontaneously, a time to cuddle and enjoy the shared experience of reading a book. Many appropriate books are available for very young children and should be a part of infant and toddler programs. Babies enjoy interacting with books, seeing bright visual images, hearing the repetition of familiar words, and savoring pleasing rhythmic sounds. Cloth, soft vinyl, or cardboard books allow babies to "explore" the books with all their senses. Older infants enjoy books showing familiar objects, and toddlers love simple stories about familiar events, routines, experiences, and feelings. Repetition and rhyme delight toddlers as well. Books with simple pictures and few words are appropriate. A separate book area or "book nook" for older babies can be a wonderful addition to an infant room (Schickedanz, 2003).

Keep in mind that literacy has its roots in the infant and toddler years, since the continual exposure to literacy at home and at school lays the foundation. In addition to reading favorite books and connecting words and images, babies enjoy making marks on large sheets of paper with various media, a foundation for writing.

SUPPORTING LANGUAGE AND LITERACY DEVELOPMENT IN SCHOOL-AGE CHILDREN

naeyc

Primary children's language and literacy development is considered to be on a continuum of earlier experiences (Gestwicki, 2011). Many things contribute to this development, including the acquisition of more advanced cognitive, motor, and social skills; many early experiences; consistent modeling of communication skills by important adults; and the new expectations set by entry into elementary school. Children continue to hone the skills that make them effective communicators, including listening, speaking, reading, and writing. Keep in mind that the key components of emergent literacy that we discussed earlier are as relevant to young primary school children as they are to preschoolers. In particular, children will be enthusiastic about writing when they write about a topic of importance and relevance to them (Stonier & Dickerson, 2009).

Communication skills are encouraged through the environment, interactions, activities, and time made available to the children. An environment that includes places for children to work, talk, and play in small groups fosters good communication. Reading and writing materials can be incorporated into all classroom areas. In addition, audio- and video-recording equipment can add value to children's storytelling and other creations. The early childhood reading area for primary children should include a variety of books, magazines and reference materials to augment the youngsters' interests. Classic books, perhaps ones that were your favorites when you were growing up, can be added to the classroom reading area. Many such materials and activities can help children recognize that reading and writing are pleasurable activities, not just tasks to be completed because they have been assigned.

Key Point ◆◆

School-age children are learning new skills related to literacy, which expand the opportunities and scope of many of their activities.

EMERGING LITERACY SKILLS

I always start off the year by focusing on building children's confidence when it comes to reading and writing. I conduct the necessary assessments to see where each child is developmentally and begin his or her instruction from there. My students do journal writing every day. When they start their first journal I encourage them to write whatever they wish. This could be working on learning to write their first or last name, the alphabet, etc. I want them to feel confident in their writing, regardless of their ability level. Because the children have a wide range of skills, I am soon working with them on a wide range of activities. I have children who are still working on learning letter–sound relationships, children who are already learning how to write a sentence, and children who are even beginning to write stories.

The most important thing to focus on with the children and their writing once they understand letter–sound relationships is their use of invented spelling. I administer a spelling inventory to each child, where I might give him or her five words to spell—and from looking at the child's spelling I can generally determine what he or she needs to focus on, whether it be initial consonants, final consonants, or short vowels. I will then do word study, which mainly consists of picture sorts, with each child focusing on

© Theresa Danna Douglas

Shari, Kindergarten Teacher

whichever of these parts of spelling he or she needs to master next, until it begins to transfer over to the child's everyday writing.

I focus heavily on reading in my classroom as well. I have a word wall where the children learn a new high-frequency word each week. I also write a morning message to the children each day that we use to practice reading and recognizing the words from our word wall. Along with reading to the children several times a day, I have the parents involved on a daily basis by doing an at-home reading program with the children. I send home a leveled book each day so parents can support their child in his or her reading of the book, and work on things such as learning the concepts of words by pointing to each word as they read, using pictures as visual cues, and decoding words.

Besides providing direct teaching of reading and writing to the children, I encourage them to read and write on their own as well. I have writing tools, paper, and books available in several areas of the classroom. I have children who, when they want to build a city out of Legos, will, on their own, go and get clipboards, paper, and writing utensils to make a list of all of the items they want to include in their city. I have children who use large blocks as dramatic play and often use their writing to name their store and label items. Children will often ask for specific books to help support their work as well. They also enjoy writing letters to one another.

Overall, I feel that there has to be a balance between direct teaching and having the children discover learning on their own. Over the years, as I have begun to give the children some power over their own learning, I have begun to see them show much more interest in reading and writing. When given the necessary tools, the children are constantly developing reading and writing skills without even being aware that they are doing it—for example, while building, cooking, participating in dramatic play, etc. Learning to read and write is definitely a process, but because of the children's interest in doing it on their own and my direct teaching of specific skills, the children make great leaps in their progress over the course of the year.

A quiet corner where school-age children can enjoy a variety of books is a must in any program for this age group.

DIVERSITY

Key Point

Teachers in inclusive classrooms particularly should focus on language and literacy activities for children with disabilities.

Koralek and colleagues (1996) provide some excellent suggestions for furthering literacy skills in primary children. School-age children enjoy forming groups around common interests, which often develop into more formal clubs. Children can be encouraged to publish a newsletter or magazine for their club. Another way for children to engage in literacy activities is for them to write journals, recounting their daily activities and experiences. Message boards provide an alternative means for children to communicate with each other. Teachers also can extend communication beyond the classrooms, by helping children to engage in correspondence with pen pals in other countries; e-mail can provide an interesting way for children to share with age-mates from around the world. Trips to the library to check out books can extend the enjoyment of reading, particularly if children are allowed to check out books that match their interests. Beth McCarry (McCarry & Greenwood, 2009) shares her experience in setting up a "Writers' Lunch Club" for her first-grade students, noting that this club helped the children become confident writers and readers.

SUPPORTING LANGUAGE AND LITERACY DEVELOPMENT IN CHILDREN WITH DISABILITIES

Language is critical to learning and, as we have seen, most children develop language skills naturally, without any deliberate "teaching" from adults. A rich language environment, in which people talk and listen to each other and in which books and other literacy materials are present and used with pleasure, facilitates language and literacy development. Some children, however, do not follow this natural pattern of language development because of a disability. For such children, the early childhood program can use many appropriate strategies to help them develop language and literacy skills or learn alternative ways of communicating.

Children with hearing impairments often have difficulty in learning language, since learning to speak is intertwined with being able to hear language. Children need to be helped to maximize whatever limited hearing they have, something that may be facilitated by a hearing aid or other device. Often, other senses, such as vision, develop more keenly. (Deiner, 2010). As a teacher of such a child, you will need to provide many hands-on experiences, coupled with simple words, and use as many visual aids and gestures as you can to help children understand concepts. Literacy skills become very important for children with hearing impairments, so frequent, enjoyable activities with books and other reading materials should be a part of the program. Fine visual discrimination, a skill related to emergent reading, can be promoted through various Lotto and matching games (Allen & Cowdery, 2012; Deiner, 2010).

Another group of children experience difficulty in learning to speak or some aspect of speaking. Children with speech or language impairments should be differentiated from youngsters who are shy. As the teacher, you need to provide simple, concrete language that contains a lot of repetition when communicating with children who have language impairments. Children may have had negative experiences when they have tried to talk, such as others making fun of them, so they may well need a lot of encouragement to talk. Provide many one-on-one opportunities to communicate, use puppets as language intermediaries for the child, or use play telephones to encourage talking. If a child has difficulty with a specific sound, reading books that feature this sound can be helpful. "Children with hearing impairments need to replace some of the auditory skills they lack with visual skills" (Deiner, 2010, p. 450). A variety of games and activities can be helpful, for instance, finding pictures with specified beginning sounds, identifying one item out of four that is in some way different from the other three, or playing Letter Lotto (Deiner, 2010).

Another group of children who will need added help with language and literacy development are children with cognitive disabilities. In general, children with cognitive delays have a smaller vocabulary, use less complex sentence structure, and may speak less than other children in the class. As the teacher, you should use simple communication, focusing on concrete, firsthand experiences to which the child with a cognitive disability can relate. Rhymes and fingerplays provide enjoyable language experiences as well. Children with cognitive delays also will attain literacy skills later than other children. Reading frequently and helping children make the basic connections between written words and reading are important.

FAMILY VALUES FOR LANGUAGE AND LITERACY DEVELOPMENT

Families and teachers share the task of providing the experiences that will best promote language acquisition in young children. Language learning is furthered when teachers and families share goals, insights, and information through regular communication. By the very fact that parents do not set out to "teach" their young children oral language, they consciously or unconsciously appreciate that language learning is a natural process that they promote through modeling and interaction. It is assumed that children will learn language.

Yet families often do not have the same intuitive understanding of children's literacy learning, although they may well be providing many high-quality language experiences that will lead to competent, literate children. Some families assume that learning to read and write begins in elementary school and is best left until the child reaches the appropriate age. Others, anxious that their children succeed in school, may seek formal reading and writing training in the preschool years to give their children a head start. It is important, therefore, that as an early childhood teacher you convey to families your philosophy of providing a language-rich environment and many opportunities to engage in and enjoy language and literacy activities.

Share with families information through articles and books that point out the early beginnings of literacy development. You might, for instance, provide a copy of the NAEYC and International Reading Association's position statement, *Learning to Read and Write: Developmentally Appropriate Practices for Young Children* (http://www.naeyc.org/files/naeyc/file/positions/PSREAD98.PDF), which considers relevant research and addresses appropriate reading practices for children of different ages. Help families recognize the many ways in which their children engage in reading and writing every day and how they, as parents, facilitate this. Also reinforce that the many activities they already engage in with their children—book reading, talking, shared time, outings, matching and sorting games, identifying food labels and road signs—contribute immensely to language and literacy development. The following suggestions for enhancing this development can be shared with families (Mavrogenes, 1990):

▶ Provide an environment that conveys the value of literacy. Let children see their parents reading and writing. Make books, magazines, and newspapers

naeyc

Key Point ◆

Working closely with families ensures support for language and emergent literacy development.

an important part of the home. A literate environment need not be expensive when the community library or a lending library from the early childhood program is used.

▶ Make reading time with the child a special daily occasion. Read as well as discuss books.

▶ Give books as presents for birthdays and holidays.

▶ Make writing materials available to children. A special writing area with paper, pencils, markers, envelopes, memo pads, and forms from school, restaurants, or the doctor's office will encourage writing as well as incorporation of writing into pretend play.

▶ Help children write letters to friends and relatives or to the author of a favorite book.

▶ Write special word or picture notes to children and put these in their lunch boxes.

▶ Write out grocery lists and recipes with children to illustrate the usefulness of writing.

▶ Share the titles of favorite school books that their children particularly enjoy.

It is reassuring to families when teachers frequently reinforce the point that children are enthusiastic and active learners in all areas, including language and literacy. It is particularly important that teachers find ways to communicate this message to parents whose children are learning English as a new language. Usually, in such a case, there is also a language barrier between teachers and families. Teachers can meet this challenge by finding an interpreter to help in communication, by learning some words and phrases in the family's primary language and using these in combination with nonverbal messages, and by recommending English instruction for the parents, if this is appropriate.

DIVERSITY

Finally, teachers of infants and toddlers can reinforce the importance of reading to very young children by encouraging families to use simple picture books with their little ones. When parents see sturdy books included in infant and toddler rooms, or note teachers routinely reading to babies, they may be encouraged to engage in this activity at home as well.

SUMMARY

1. There are several divergent theoretical views of language development.
2. Some components of language can help us understand the complexity of all that children attain during their early years.
3. Because many early childhood programs include children who are English-language learners, consider bilingualism and effective strategies for teaching children a second language.
4. Many components of the early childhood program support and reinforce language learning:
   A. Conversations and language play offer many spontaneous opportunities for language learning.
   B. Also consider some of the many types of planned activities aimed at enhancing language.
   C. Emergent literacy is children's ongoing process of learning reading and writing.
5. Language and literacy activities are important for children of different ages and abilities.

KEY TERMS LIST

babbling	invented spelling
behaviorist view of language development	mock writing
bilingualism	morphology
cognitive interactionist view of language development	overextension
	pragmatics
cooing	semantic network
deep structure	semantics
emergent literacy	social interactionist view of language development
environmental print	surface structure
innatist view of language development	syntax
interactionist view of language development	

KEY QUESTIONS

1. Listen to a young child's spontaneous language usage. What components of language do you note? Consider the child's understanding of the meaning of language as well as the child's grasp of language rules.
2. Talk to someone you know who learned English as a second language. What are this person's recollections about this learning process? What was most difficult and what was easiest? What strategies or techniques were most helpful in this learning process? Talk with others in your class and compare the findings of those whose friends learned English at an early age and of those who learned it later in life.
3. Observe a teacher of young children engage in spontaneous conversation with children. What techniques does she or he use? How are the children encouraged to interact with each other as well as with the teacher? Did you hear examples of language play or humor?
4. Read a book written for preschool-age children. Does this book appeal to you? Do you think it will appeal to children? Evaluate this book using the criteria outlined in Figure 12-1.
5. Examine some samples of children's artwork. Do you see examples of mock writing? Are there letters included? Are there any recognizable words written in invented spelling by the child?

ADDITIONAL RESOURCES

Select additional books, articles, and websites on topics discussed in Chapter 12.

Okagaki, L., & Diamond, K. E. (2009). Cultural and linguistic differences in families with young children: Implications for early childhood teachers. In E. L. Essa & M. M. Burnham (Eds.), *Informing our practice: Useful research on young children's development* (pp. 216–226). Washington, DC: National Association for the Education of Young Children.

Sawyer, W. E. (2012). *Growing up with literature* (6th ed.). Belmont, CA: Wadsworth, Cengage Learning.

Schickedanz, J. A. (1999). *Much more than the ABCs*: *The early stages of reading and writing*. Washington, DC: NAEYC.

HELPFUL WEBSITES

National Center for Family Literacy:

www.famlit.org

The National Center for Family Literacy works to create educational and economic opportunity for the most at-risk children and parents. Information about the organization's work is available on this website.

International Reading Association (IRA):

www.reading.org

IRA is a professional organization dedicated to promoting high levels of literacy by improving reading instruction, disseminating research and information about reading, and encouraging good lifetime reading habits.

Caldecott Medal Winners:

www.ala.org

The Caldecott Medal is given every year to the artist of the most distinguished American picture book for children. Some of the most engaging books of the past century have been Caldecott Medal winners, and a list of titles can be found on this web page.

 Go to **CengageBrain.com** to register your access code for this book's Education CourseMate website, where you will find more resources to help you study. Additional resources for this chapter include TeachSource Videos, glossary flashcards, web links, case studies with critical-thinking questions that apply the concepts presented in this chapter, and more. If your textbook does not include a printed access card, you can go to **CengageBrain.com** to purchase access.

Social Development through the Curriculum

13

In Chapter 13, you will find answers to the following questions about providing for social development through the curriculum:

- How do different theories explain children's social development and their acquisition of social competence?
- How can you help to encourage children's relationships with peers?
- How can you help children develop sensitivity and understanding toward those who are of a different culture, ethnicity, linguistic background, gender, and ability?
- How does children's sense of what is moral develop, and how can you help them develop prosocial skills?
- How can you support social development in children of different ages and abilities?

DAP Teachers help children learn how to establish positive, constructive relationships with others. They support children's forming of friendships and provide opportunities for children to play and work together.

Developmentally Appropriate Practice, Copple & Bredekamp, 2009, p. 150

NAEYC STANDARDS CONSIDERED IN CHAPTER 13

(See the Standards Correlation Chart on the inside front cover of this book for the titles and description of the standards listed below.)

- *Standard 1a:* Knowing the theoretical and research foundations on which understanding of social development, socialization, and emotional intelligence are based (pp. 336–339).
- *Standard 5a:* Understanding foundational concepts related to peer interactions, including friendships, on which to base appropriate experiences for children (pp. 339–341).
- *Standard 4b:* Supporting positive relations and interactions in children by implementing nonbias concepts related to gender, ethnicity and culture, and ability and by promoting moral development (pp. 341–350).
- *Standard 5a:* Providing opportunities to develop prosocial behaviors through dramatic play and cooperative games (pp. 351–353).
- *Standard 1b:* Appropriately supporting development of prosocial skills for children of different ages and abilities (pp. 353–358).
- *Standard 2b:* Engaging families in supporting their children's social development (p. 358).

socialization
The process through which children become a functioning part of society and learn society's rules and values.

One major function of the early childhood program is to facilitate the process of **socialization,** the means through which children become a functioning part of society and learn society's rules and values. Socialization is a lifelong process that begins from the first day of life; during the early years, the foundation for later attitudes, values, and behaviors is laid.

Unquestionably, socialization begins with the parent–child relationship in infancy, where patterns of response, need fulfillment, and give-and-take have their roots. When children come to the early childhood program, they have already had a lifetime of socializing experiences. They may have learned to trust or be wary of others, to meet new experiences enthusiastically or with caution, to care about others' feelings because their needs have always been considered, or to think of others as competitors for affection or resources.

Because socialization is such an important responsibility of the early childhood teacher, we will consider some of its facets in more than one chapter. This chapter will focus primarily on the development of social competence as it is facilitated and supported through the curriculum; the following chapters discuss guidance techniques that facilitate the development of positive social skills. The term *curriculum* as it is used in this chapter does not refer solely to the planned activities of the day, but also includes all the elements in the environment that lead to conversations and activities that promote socialization.

THEORETICAL VIEWS OF THE SOCIALIZATION PROCESS

Recall that in Chapter 5 we considered the work of Erik Erikson, whose psychosocial theory of young children's stages of development has had tremendous influence on early childhood education. Although we will not review this theory in detail here, keep in mind Erikson's emphasis on the importance of providing for children a social environment in which people can be trusted, children can safely exercise their growing independence, and many opportunities to explore and experience competence are available. A good early childhood program is built on the premise that children's needs for trust, autonomy, initiative, and industry must be met.

Key Point ◆

An understanding of Erikson's theory is important for developing an appropriate social environment for young children.

We will consider three theoretical views that are pertinent to our discussion of socialization. One important view of how children become socialized has stemmed from the work of Jean Piaget. This approach centers on the idea that children construct all knowledge, including social knowledge. This contrasts with the behaviorist idea that social knowledge is transmitted through environmental and cultural means. A third view, the sociocultural theory of Lev Vygotsky, focuses on the role of adults and more experienced peers in the transmission of social values (Saracho & Spodek, 2007).

The Constructivist View of Socialization

social cognition
Organization of knowledge and information about people and relationships.

In the Piagetian view of social development, social knowledge is acquired in much the same way as other knowledge (refer to Chapter 11). Children use their evolving **social cognition,** or understanding of other people's problems and how they feel, to organize and structure information about people and relationships in a way similar to the one used in organizing and structuring information about the physical properties of their world (Kohlberg, 1966). For instance, children classify the people they meet in relation to themselves and their own existing schema, which have, of course, been shaped by their culture.

As with all other learning, such understanding comes from the child's active involvement, not from passive transmission of information. As part of a complex world, children need to make sense of themselves and others. "Simply by being born into the human family, then, young children are challenged to understand self, others, social and moral relations, and societal institutions" (Edwards, 1986, p. 3).

The Behaviorist View of Socialization

In contrast to Piagetian theory, the traditional behavioral assumption is that children are taught about the social world when their responses are reinforced by the adults who shape their behavior. **Social learning theory,** which is derived from but goes beyond traditional behaviorism, does not consider reinforcement as always necessary for social learning. From the social learning perspective, children also learn social behaviors through **observational learning,** by observing, noting the behavior of, and imitating or **modeling** their behavior on that of a **model.** Adults and peers can be models. Research has shown that particularly nurturing and warm adult models influence children's social behaviors (Shonkoff & Phillips, 2000). It is possible that children imitate those they are fond of because they want to be like them. In addition, children are more likely to imitate models they observe being rewarded (Bandura, 1977).

The Vygotskyan View of Socialization

In Chapter 5 you were introduced to Lev Vygotsky, whose sociocultural theory is particularly pertinent to a consideration of social development. Social development is inseparable from cognitive and language development. It is through language that the child's mind is "joined" with the minds of others to gain insight into the world. "A basic premise of Vygotsky's theory is that all uniquely human, higher forms of mental activity are jointly constructed and transferred to children through dialogues with other people" (Berk, 1994, p. 30). Vygotsky dwells on the role of adults and more experienced peers in transmitting information about the culture and about social skills and expectations. The role of teachers is particularly meaningful in the context of this theory, which underscores their contribution to children's socialization into the larger society. Within the zone of proximal development, the range of tasks that a child is not yet able to do alone but can accomplish with help, teachers are available to children as they learn a variety of skills. In Vygotsky's terms, adults provide **scaffolding,** an evocative term when we think about the type of support and guidance teachers offer children to help them learn socially relevant skills.

EMOTIONAL INTELLIGENCE

Closely entwined with development of socialization skills are the perception, understanding, and management of emotions, skills that begin early in life. The term **emotional intelligence** was popularized in 1990 with publication of Peter Salovey and John Mayer's influential article on this topic. These authors define emotional intelligence as "the subset of social intelligence that involves the ability to monitor one's own and others' feelings and emotions, to discriminate among them, and to use this information to guide one's thinking and actions" (p. 189).

Key Point ◆

The constructivist view of socialization holds that children gain social knowledge through the same process used in gaining other knowledge, by constructing it from their experiences.

social learning theory
Theoretical view derived from but going beyond behaviorism, which considers that children learn not just from reinforcement but from observing and imitating others.

observational learning
In social learning theory, the process of learning that comes from watching, noting the behavior of, and imitating models.

modeling
In social learning theory, the process of imitating a model.

model
In social learning theory, those whom children imitate, particularly because of some desirable feature or attribute.

Key Point ◆

Social learning theory suggests that children learn social behaviors through observation and imitation.

scaffolding
In Vygotsky's sociocultural theory, the support provided by adults and older peers to help children learn the new tasks they are not yet able to accomplish on their own.

Key Point ◆

Vygotsky helps explain how the development of language is intricately tied to socialization as adults and more experienced peers help transmit culturally and socially relevant information to young children.

Key Point ◆

Emotional intelligence is the ability to perceive, control, and evaluate emotions and use this information to manage our emotions effectively.

emotional intelligence
The ability to perceive, control, and evaluate emotions and use this information to manage our emotions effectively.

SOCIAL COMPETENCE AND EMOTIONAL WELL-BEING: IMPORTANT INGREDIENTS FOR LEARNING

"WHEN WE invest wisely in children and families, the next generation will pay that back through a lifetime of productivity and responsible citizenship. When we fail to provide children with what they need to build a strong foundation for healthy and productive lives, we put our future prosperity and security at risk" (National Scientific Council on the Developing Child, 2007a, p. 1). Thus states the council's report, *The Science of Early Childhood Development: Closing the Gap between What We Know and What We Do.* This report, prepared by a team of neurobiologists, developmental psychologists, and economists, provides a scientifically grounded framework for ensuring that we do invest wisely in our next generation.

The authors of the report present a set of core principles, with implications for policy and practice. While these principles reinforce what we know about the importance of children's early development, it also links this information to descriptions of how the basic architecture of the brain is constructed. One of the most important aspects of this report is the continual reinforcement of the interrelationship between cognitive and socioemotional development. "The brain is a highly integrated organ and its multiple functions operate in a richly coordinated fashion. Emotional well-being and social competence provide a strong

foundation for emerging cognitive abilities, and together they are the bricks and mortar that comprise the foundations of human development" (p. 8).

The implication of such a holistic approach is that parents and professionals who work with young children must pay attention to the children's emotional and social needs as well as their cognitive and literacy skills to have maximum impact on the development of the brain architecture. "Preschool policies and programs . . . that embed the promotion of literacy and numeracy in a rich environment of age-appropriate social interaction" (p. 9) are most likely to help children succeed in school. Education of young children should focus on the "whole child."

The architecture of the brain is made up of a complex network of neural circuits that connect brain cells and are continually influenced by both genetics and the environment. From the beginning, stable, responsive social relationships with family and caregivers are integral to laying a strong foundation for learning, behavior, and health throughout life. "Decades of research tell us that mutually rewarding interactions are essential prerequisites for the development of healthy brain circuits and increasingly complex skills" (p. 6). The report also warns that lack of consistent, nurturing relationships in the face of persistent stress will result in

an altered physiological state that "disrupts the architecture of the developing brain" (p. 10), likely with negative outcomes for the rest of the child's life. Intervention may help stave off some of these negative outcomes, but prevention is much more efficient and effective.

The authors of the report make a strong case that we need to pay close attention to child development research when setting policies that govern both the services provided to young children and the practices of professionals who work with children and families. Higher school achievement and more productive adults will result from policies that promote supportive relationships and appropriate learning environments for young children. The report suggests a range of programs and services that address issues such as parent and family support and education, early care and education, health, and intervention. The authors also recommend that early education staff be well trained since "the essence of quality in early childhood services is embodied in the expertise and skills of the staff and in their capacity to build positive relationships with young children" (p. 2). In summary, the authors advise that creating appropriate conditions for children's early development will be more effective and less costly than current practices and will ultimately benefit society.

These authors propose that emotional intelligence involves four distinct elements: (1) *perceiving emotions*, which is the ability to perceive them accurately, for instance, appropriately reading nonverbal cues such as facial expressions; (2) *reasoning with emotions*, which is the ability to use emotions to promote thinking and prioritize what we pay attention to; (3) *understanding emotions*, which involves interpreting perceived emotions accurately; and (4) *managing emotions*, which includes self-regulation and responding appropriately to one's own and others' emotions.

As an early childhood professional, you have multiple opportunities to help young children develop emotional intelligence. Keep in mind that positive early experiences are important for brain development in all areas—physical, cognitive, social, and emotional. Furthermore, research suggests that children's cognitive and physical potential cannot be reached unless the brain is appropriately wired to support healthy social and emotional development; in fact, children's social and emotional skills are strongly linked to school readiness (Willis & Schiller, 2011). Many of the strategies discussed in this chapter, as well as in other chapters of this book, are appropriate for supporting the development of healthy social and emotional skills.

More specifically, Clarissa Willis and Pam Schiller (2011) suggest important ways to support social skills and emotional intelligence.

Teachers can support development of young children's emotional intelligence by providing opportunities to solve problems with confidence and success.

▶ First, help children develop *confidence* by providing many opportunities to solve problems, encounter new experiences successfully, and receive positive feedback and challenges to expand their thinking further. Confident children have a positive outlook, show persistence and determination, and listen attentively to others.

▶ Second, encourage *self-control* by involving children in setting class rules, discussing strong emotions and how they make one feel, and reading books that have themes related to self-control. Children who demonstrate self-control express emotions appropriately, control impulses, are able to delay gratification, and respect the boundaries of others.

▶ Finally, the authors underscore the importance of *communication*. Foster the capacity to communicate effectively by modeling good communication skills, talking about communication, and providing an environment in which effective communication skills are practiced and celebrated. Children who are good communicators express their ideas clearly, use words to resolve conflicts, discuss emotions appropriately, and are able to read and respond effectively to social cues.

DEVELOPMENT OF SOCIAL COMPETENCE

As increasing numbers of young children enter group care, they experience increasingly intimate peer contact. By age three or four, most children are part of a social world that is truly egalitarian, a world of peers who are equals. In this world, children are expected to share and cooperate, to learn the rules and expectations. As young children go through this process of becoming socialized to the peer society, they gain skill and competence in peer interaction, enter into friendships, develop gender identity, adopt racial and cultural attitudes, form a sense of morals and values, and acquire a host of prosocial behaviors.

The opportunity to develop multicultural, multiracial, and multieconomic acceptance will, to a large extent, depend on the integrative nature of the early childhood program. Although programs can help children learn about people

A good early childhood program is an ideal setting for children to gain skills in positive peer socialization. Sensitive adult guidance and an appropriate environment and program are important in this process.

naeyc

Key Point ◆

The early childhood teacher facilitates development of positive peer relationships from infancy on through guidance and by setting an appropriate environment.

from diverse backgrounds, early childhood programs tend to be rather homogeneous, joining children from a common racial, cultural, and economic milieu.

Peer Interaction

Peer interaction is an essential ingredient in the process of childhood socialization (in fact, in the total development of the child). Such interactions begin in infancy, when as early as two months of age, babies show an interest in peers. By the middle of the first year, they direct smiles and vocalizations toward other infants. The imitation that becomes a part of babies' repertoire is also integrated into peer play; very young children often develop games based on imitation that they play with each other (Ladd, 2007).

The early childhood setting offers an ideal opportunity for young children to develop social skills with peers. As with any skill, it is through practice in real situations that children develop competence in peer interaction. The many naturally occurring opportunities of day-to-day life allow children to be sympathetic and helpful to peers. These social skills include the many strategies children learn to help them initiate and continue social interactions, negotiate, and settle conflicts (Miller, 2010).

For young children who are just entering peer relationships, adult guidance—not interference—is important; as children get older and less egocentric, the presence of an adult becomes less necessary (Howes & Lee, 2007). The teacher, in facilitating social development, first must provide children with ample time and space and appropriate materials to facilitate social interaction. A child who has difficulty engaging in social play can be helped through sensitive teacher guidance; for instance, directing that child to a group with similar play interests or pairing the child with a more socially competent peer (Miller, 2010).

Friendship

naeyc

One special type of peer relationship is friendship, that close link between people typified by mutual concern, sharing, and companionship. Research points to the importance of early friendship to later emotional well-being (Goldman & Buysse, 2007). Young children's concept of friendship is limited, primarily revolving around the immediate situation with little thought given to the enduring nature of friendship. As children grow older, their friendships typically become more stable.

Nonetheless, there is growing research evidence that toddlers form early friendships, showing preference for and affection toward specific peers. Such early friendships, which sometimes continue for many years, also have strong affective ties and show characteristics similar to the attachment behavior seen between young children and adults (Goldman & Buysse, 2007).

Preschoolers view friends in terms of their accessibility, physical attributes, and actions rather than their personality traits. In other words, a friend is "someone you play with a lot," "someone who wears a Batman T-shirt," "someone who invites you to her birthday party," or "someone who isn't mean." Another insight into early friendship can be found in the often-heard question, "Are you my friend?" which can be translated to mean, "Will you play with me?" (Rogers & Evans, 2008).

Preschoolers expect friendships to maximize their enjoyment, entertainment, and satisfaction in play. Young children are focused on themselves, as well as their own feelings and needs; not until later in childhood do they shift to a greater awareness of the needs and feelings of others. Yet, as many observers have noted, young children are also surprisingly capable of caring about and giving emotional support to each other; for instance, observe the concern of onlookers when a child cries because he is hurt or distressed.

By the time children enter elementary school, their peer group has become a much more important source of support. Peers are influential in determining many aspects of primary school children's lives, including what to wear, how to behave, and how to speak. Children's self-esteem is more strongly affected by peers than in earlier years. Children also become more selective in their choice of "best friends," almost always of the same sex, the one or few other children to whom they have a strong attachment (Click & Parker, 2012).

Trust is the basic foundation on which friendship is built. Children who are trustworthy, who share and cooperate, are more likely to be considered as friends by their peers. Trust in the peer relationship, however, does not simply emerge, but is built on the sense of trust that children established early in life (as described by Erikson), when nurturing adults met their needs consistently. Teachers can help children develop a sense of trust, which can enhance friendships, through their support and guidance. More specifically, they can help children recognize their own needs and goals and those of others, develop more effective social skills (strategies will be discussed in more detail in the next chapter), recognize how their behavior affects others, and become aware of their own social successes so that they can be repeated (Rogers & Evans, 2008).

Gender-Role Development

Research has shown that one of the most powerful determinants of peer interaction and friendship is the children's gender. If you work with young children, you will have observed that the majority of their playmates are of the same sex. This holds true in all cultural settings, not just in America (Cranley Gallager, Dadisman, Farmer, Huss, & Hutchins, 2007; Maccoby, 1990). Cross-sex friends are not uncommon; however, as they get older, girls increasingly choose to play with other girls and boys seek out other boys as play partners.

This distinct separation based on gender begins to be evident before children reach age three. Four-year-olds play with same-sex peers nearly three times as often as with children of the opposite sex; two years later, this preference has increased elevenfold (Maccoby & Jacklin, 1987). Children choose same-sex friends spontaneously, and attempts to change or influence their choices to encourage more cross-sex interaction have generally not been very successful (Cranley Gallagher et al., 2007).

Much speculation exists about the reasons for this separation by sex. Eleanor Maccoby (1990), who was involved in research on gender differences for many years, hypothesizes that girls avoid boys because they find it aversive to interact with unresponsive play partners. She speculates that girls generally dislike boys' competitive, rough-and-tumble play styles and, more importantly, find that they seem to have little influence over boys. The issue of influence becomes increasingly important during early childhood, as children learn to integrate and

These friends enjoy a special reunion each morning when they get to their school. Many young children begin to form friendships, forging a unique and close bond with a peer.

© Cengage Learning

Key Point ◆◆

Toddlers begin to develop friendships, although early friendships are more concerned with the immediate situation than with long-term commitments.

Key Point ◆◆

Children tend to choose playmates of the same sex, a tendency that increases with age.

Key Point ◆◆

At a very young age, children identify themselves as boys or girls, although they do not realize until between the ages of five and seven that gender is permanent and cannot be changed.

It is most common for children to seek out same-sex playmates. Boys tend to play with typically male toys; girls usually find typical female toys.

gender identity
Identification with the same sex.

gender stability
Children's recognition that sex is constant and cannot be changed; occurs by age five to seven, but not earlier.

Key Point ◆
When teachers are sensitive to providing a nonsexist, nonstereotyped atmosphere, children will more likely develop attitudes based on respect for each person as an individual.

coordinate their activities with those of playmates. In attempts to influence others, girls typically are more polite, whereas boys are much more direct; over the span of the preschool years, boys increasingly disregard girls, and girls, in turn, increasingly avoid boys because their efforts to influence them are not successful.

How does this awareness of sex differences develop? Lawrence Kohlberg (1966) discusses a developmental process in the formation of sex-role attitudes. It begins with **gender identity,** when even very young children, often before their second birthdays, accurately identify and label themselves and others as boys or girls based on observable physical cues. Between the ages of five and seven, children acquire **gender stability.** Younger children do not yet realize that they will always remain the same sex; this sense of constancy emerges in middle childhood at about the same time as the development of such cognitive concepts as conservation, for instance, that the amount of clay in a ball does not change even if its shape is changed.

Another development in this process, evolving during the preschool years and becoming very pronounced by the time the child enters elementary school, is value of the same sex and whatever pertains to it. Children value the concrete symbols of their gender that confirm their maleness or femaleness, and they construct and adopt a rigid set of rules and stereotypes about what is gender-appropriate. This rigidity is consistent with a similar approach to other cognitive concepts. In acquiring same-sex values, children also form an identity with like-sex persons.

GUIDELINES FOR NONSEXIST TEACHING. This rigidity, children's gravitation toward same-sex peers, and their engagement in gender-stereotyped activities is often troublesome to adults, who want children to be broad-minded and tolerant of others. Despite many families' and teachers' efforts to present nonsexist models to the children in their lives, these same children will often display highly sex-stereotyped behaviors and attitudes. In fact, by the end of the primary school years, children often become quite antagonistic toward peers of the opposite sex, engaging in teasing and quarreling (Click & Parker, 2012). Some guidelines, such as the following, can help the early childhood teacher lay the foundation for nonbiased attitudes based on respect for each person as an individual.

▶ **Value each child as an individual.** Focus on the strengths and abilities of each child as a person, and help children recognize and value these characteristics.
▶ **Help children learn that gender identity is biologically determined.** Before they develop gender constancy, children may feel that it is their preference for boy or girl activities that makes them boys or girls. Reassure them that their bodies, not their activities, determine their sex.
▶ **Be aware of possible gender biases in your own behavior.** Studies have shown, for instance, that adults tend to protect girls more, react to boys' misbehaviors more, encourage independence more in boys, and expect girls to be more fearful (Honig, 1983; Rogers & Evans, 2008).

- **Listen carefully to all children.** Adults tend to interrupt or speak simultaneously more with girls than with boys, suggesting that what girls have to say is less important (Honig, 1983).
- **Help children find the words to get their nurturance needs met.** Little boys are not as likely to ask for a hug or a lap to sit on as girls are. Teachers can help all children find the right words to communicate their needs for affection (Honig, 1983).
- **Use language carefully, avoiding bias toward male identity.** The English language tends to assume male identity when sex is not clear. We generally say "he" when we don't know whether an animal, person, or storybook character is male or female, and this tricks children into thinking that a "he" is more important and more pervasive than a "she."

Boys are less likely to ask for a hug than girls are. It is important, therefore, to help children find the right words to express their needs for nurturance.

- **Provide materials that show males and females in a variety of roles.** Puzzles, Lotto games, posters, and photographs can portray males and females in nontraditional roles. Dramatic play props can draw children into a variety of roles sometimes stereotyped as male or female.
- **Select children's books that portray nonsexist models.** Characters in children's literature run the gamut from the very sex-stereotyped to the very nonsexist. A study of widely read children's books, including award-winning ones, showed that male and female roles are often distorted and stereotyped. Males appear far more often; females, when they are portrayed, tend to be shown as passive and dependent (McDaniel & Davis, 1999; Nodelman, 1999).
- **Plan a wide range of activities and encourage all children to participate.** Children will participate in and enjoy a variety of activities—cooking, woodworking, blocks, housekeeping, book browsing, sewing, sand and water, art—if they are well planned and the teacher's words or attitudes do not promote sex stereotyping.
- **Provide gender-neutral toys for infants and toddlers.** Avoid giving the blue rattles and car-shaped teething rings to the boys and the pink, feminine toys to the girls. Similarly, avoid offering gender-specific toys to toddlers; they will quickly pick up the message that dolls are for girls while trucks are for boys.
- **Discuss blatant sex stereotyping with children.** Older preschoolers and primary children, especially if they have been around adults who are sensitive to using nonbiased concepts and vocabulary, can engage in discussions about sex stereotypes in books, favorite television programs, or movies.

Racial and Cultural Awareness and Attitudes

Similar to their early recognition of gender differences, children also develop an awareness of racial variations at an early age. Although little research has been conducted to document this with children under the age of three, many three-year-olds and most four-year-olds not only recognize racial cues, but also show racial preferences (Nesdale, 2007). Thus, children at a very young age already have a sense of racial difference. Preschoolers use the most readily visible physical differences as cues; skin color in particular, as well as hair and eye color, provide a basis for comparison and classification.

naeyc

DIVERSITY

Key Point

Children develop an awareness of racial differences at an early age.

Positive relations with peers from different racial, ethnic, and cultural backgrounds are fostered by sensitive and knowledgeable teachers. What guidelines will help you, as a teacher, promote positive relations in a class of children from diverse backgrounds?

In a way similar to the process of acquiring gender identity, young children also do not seem to understand fully the permanence of race until they reach the stage of concrete operations in middle childhood. It may be somewhat more difficult for children to develop a sense of racial permanence because many youngsters have limited contact with people of other races, growing up in fairly homogeneous environments. For many children, the primary encounter with people of other races is through television, movies, and books rather than in real life. In addition, children witness contradictory evidence when they see that skin color can be changed by the sun. A rather subtle variation in learning about different people arises when children begin to discover cultural differences. Family, neighborhood, school, church, books, and mass media can introduce children to the fact that people meet their daily needs in different ways. All people need to communicate, but they may do so in different languages; all people need to eat, but they don't all eat the same types of foods; all people require clothing, shelter, and transportation, but they meet these needs in unique ways. A focus on the similarities among people should be the basis of multicultural programming for young children.

Although children's cognitive development steers them toward noting differences and classifying accordingly, society applies the comparative values that lead to stereotypes and prejudice. Children are bombarded with subtle and not-so-subtle messages about the worth of people. Parents, as the primary socializers of their children, seem the obvious transmitters of racial and cultural attitudes; yet, research has shown little relationship between children and their parents in this respect (Nesdale, 2007). A more plausible source of racial and cultural information may be television, movies, and books that, by their portrayals or by their omissions, imply superiority of some groups and inferiority of others.

GUIDELINES FOR TEACHING ABOUT RACE AND CULTURE. DAP "calls for teachers to pay attention to the social and cultural contexts in which their children live and to take these into account when shaping the learning environment and their interactions with children and families" (Copple & Bredekamp, 2009, p. 331). The early childhood program is an ideal place to help children learn about themselves and others, learn to value and have pride in themselves, and learn to respect others. This involves conveying accurate knowledge about and pride in children's own racial and cultural groups, accurate knowledge about and appreciation of other racial and cultural groups, and an understanding of racism and how to counter it. There are a number of excellent resources for helping teachers of young children in this task; for instance, Louise Derman-Sparks's *Anti-Bias Curriculum: Tools for Empowering Young Children* (1989) and Patricia Ramsey and Sonia Nieto's *Teaching and Learning in a Diverse World: Multicultural Education for Young Children* (2004). These books sensitively and succinctly discuss and suggest strategies for helping children learn about and respect racial, gender, cultural, and physical differences; strategies for promoting antidiscrimination and activism are also explored.

The following guidelines are gleaned from various sources (Derman-Sparks, 1989; Ramsey & Nieto, 2004; Robles de Melendez & Beck, 2010). They can help

DIVERSITY

naeyc

Key Point ◆

The early childhood curriculum should provide many opportunities for children to learn about themselves and others, value their own and others' races and cultures, and develop appreciation and acceptance of diversity.

you provide children with a developmentally appropriate understanding of other races and cultures.

▶ **When children bring up racial/cultural differences, discuss them honestly.** Help children recognize that there are differences among people, but that these differences do not make them superior or inferior to others. Stress the unique personality of each individual.

▶ **Help children develop pride by encouraging positive attitudes about their racial/cultural identity.** Children's self-concepts are tied to feeling good about all aspects of their beings. Acknowledgment and positive comments about the beauty of different types of skin, hair, and eye color is important to developing feelings about self-worth.

▶ **Help children develop positive attitudes about other races.** Children need accurate information about other races and must be guided to appreciate others. Modeling acceptance and appreciation of all races is an important factor.

▶ **Help children see skin-color variations as a continuum rather than as extremes.** Color charts to which children can match their own skin color can help them recognize that everyone is a shade of brown.

▶ **Post photographs of children and their families.** This can help children begin to acquire the concept of racial constancy as teachers point out similarities (as well as differences) among family members. Help dispel misconceptions about racial constancy as these come up spontaneously. Be prepared for questions if a child in your class was adopted by parents of a different race.

▶ **Ensure that the environment contains materials representing many races and cultures.** Books, dolls, pictures, posters, dramatic play props, manipulatives, puzzles, and other materials should portray people of all colors and cultures in very positive ways. This is particularly important if your class is racially/culturally mixed; it is also important, however, to expose children in homogeneous classes to different racial and cultural groups through the environment. Include such materials in infant and toddler rooms as well.

▶ **Discuss incidents of racism and racial stereotypes with the children.** Model antiracist behaviors by challenging incidents of racism or racial stereotyping. Help children find alternative words if they use racial slurs in arguments with each other.

▶ **Focus curriculum material about cultures on similarities among people rather than on differences.** Children can identify with shared experiences engaged in by people of other cultures. All people eat, wear clothes, need shelter, share special occasions, and value family activities. Focusing on "exotic" aspects of a culture only points out how different those aspects are and robs them of the shared human factor. Focusing on differences develops stereotypes, whereas focusing on similarities builds understanding.

▶ **Avoid a "tourist" approach to teaching about cultures.** Do not teach children about other cultures out of context. For instance, avoid using only the holidays celebrated by other cultures or a one-shot "cultures" week to focus on this topic (Monday—Mexico, Tuesday—Japan, Wednesday—Africa, Thursday—Germany, and Friday—France). Also avoid using an ethnic cooking activity and a display of ceremonial clothing as the main components of these occasions. Such an approach is disconnected from everyday life, trivializes cultural diversity, and merely represents

DIVERSITY

Key Point

The early childhood curriculum should help children develop sensitivity toward those with disabilities.

multiculturalism as a token gesture rather than as a genuine reflection of life around the world.

▸ **Make cultural diversity part of daily classroom activity.** Integrate aspects of the children's cultures into the everyday routine of your class to emphasize that culture is pervasive in all groups.

▸ **Ensure that the classroom reflects many ways of life.** Consider that the typical housekeeping corner in many early childhood classrooms conveys a single culture: a white, middle-class model. Many ways of life should be reflected throughout the classroom. For instance, you can include dolls of different races, post pictures showing different ethnic groups, introduce food packages in the housekeeping cupboard that reflect cultural preferences, or include home or cooking implements used by the cultures of some of the children.

▸ **Convey the diversity of cultures through their common themes.** Read about different cultures to find out how various cultural groups meet their physical needs, engage in celebrations, and adapt to their environment. For instance, Americans carve pumpkins into jack-o'-lanterns at Halloween, while other cultures also commonly carve fruits and vegetables on certain occasions.

▸ **Consider the complexity involved in celebrating holidays when their observance might contradict, or even be offensive to, some families' beliefs or cultures.** The celebration of Christmas could offend the non-Christian families who have children in your program. Thanksgiving as a holiday might be an occasion of loss rather than celebration for Native American families. The celebration of holidays should not be avoided but should be considered carefully, taking into account the attitudes, needs, and feelings of the children, families, and staff. Holiday celebrations should focus on the respect and understanding of cultural observances.

▸ **Do not single out a minority child in a way that would make that child feel "different."** Learning about a child's culture should be done in the context of learning about all of the children's cultures. Help such a child and the others in the class recognize that a particular culture is shared by many other people in the world.

▸ **Involve children's families.** Families are a prime source of information about cultural diversity. Invite families to participate in the class and share ideas about how all of the children can learn more about their unique backgrounds. Particularly in child care centers, families may not have the time to join the class, but they should always feel welcome.

Sensitivity toward People with Disabilities

Children can also learn to develop understanding, acceptance, and an attitude of helpfulness toward those who have special needs. As we discussed in Chapter 2, many children with disabilities are included in early childhood programs. But integrating nondisabled children and children with special needs in and of itself does not ensure interaction and acceptance.

Children need accurate information about why a peer (or a teacher) looks, moves, sounds, or behaves differently. Children need the chance to express fears or misgivings and to ask questions. It is not unusual for children to be apprehensive about things that are unfamiliar and different or to worry that the disability could happen to them as well. Offering a simple, honest explanation will answer the child's concern and respect the person with the disability (Derman-Sparks, 1989).

When a child with cerebral palsy was enrolled at one school, Martin called her "a baby." The teacher explained, "Roberta cannot walk because there is something wrong with the muscles in her legs. She can get around on this scooter board by using her arm muscles. Would you like to ask Roberta if you can try her scooter board so you can see what it feels like?"

In addition to helping children accept and include peers with special needs, the early childhood program can also incorporate activities in the curriculum that are specifically aimed at dispelling stereotypes and helping to build an accepting atmosphere.

Moral Development

One primary aim of socialization is for children to learn and internalize standards of what is right and wrong; in other words, to develop a conscience. **Moral development** is a long-term process to which many factors contribute. Children are surrounded by a social climate in which the actions of others convey degrees of fairness, consistency, respect, and concern for others. Children's observations of how others behave, how others are treated, and their own cognitive maturation contribute to their emerging sense of morality.

Children adopt a more mature set of standards if they are raised in an atmosphere of clearly set and enforced standards, support and nurturance, open communication in which the child's viewpoint is valued, and other-oriented reasons for expected behavior. There is also evidence that the onset of the distinction between right and wrong may be an inborn trait, emerging by children's second birthday (Johansson, 2006; Killen & Smetana, 2006).

Certainly, the transition from infancy to the preschool years is an important time for laying the foundation for understanding right and wrong. Such learning occurs most effectively when, as Erik Erikson (see Chapter 5) points out, infants have developed a strong sense of trust through loving, caring relationships with significant adults. On this foundation of trust, toddlers' growing assertion of independence can develop in a healthy way, facilitated by nurturing, encouraging adults who set appropriate limits on behavior; for instance, helping toddlers to curb aggressive impulses and learn alternative, socially acceptable behaviors. These conclusions are supported by a study (Howes & Hamilton, 1993) that found that when toddlers lost a teacher with whom they had developed a secure and trusting relationship, they tended to become more aggressive, a trait that was seen at age four.

Another factor with which children have to contend, especially in a pluralistic society such as ours, is that moral standards vary in different cultures. Some universal **interpersonal moral rules**—ones prohibiting harm to others, murder, incest, theft, and family responsibility—are found across cultures. Other **conventional moral rules** are arrived at by general consensus and are more culture-specific, for example, being expected to wear clothes in public or chew with your

moral development
The long-term process of learning and internalizing the rules and standards of right and wrong.

Key Point ◆

Moral development is concerned with children's development of conscience through the internalization of society's rules and standards.

interpersonal moral rules
Considered as universal, including prohibitions against harm to others, murder, incest, and theft.

conventional moral rules
Standards, which are generally culture-specific, arrived at by general consensus.

Moral development evolves over time as children begin to internalize standards of fairness, respect and concern for others, and right and wrong.

mouth closed. In addition, each society specifies some regulations that ensure orderly and safe functioning; for instance, being required to stop at red lights. Implied in this differentiation is that some rules are more important than others. This is usually reflected in the classroom, where some transgressions (for instance, harm to others) are considered more serious than others. DAP also emphasizes the importance of helping children in conscience development by talking about feelings, values, and the consequences of behavior (Copple & Bredekamp, 2009).

PIAGET'S VIEW OF MORAL DEVELOPMENT. Much of today's theoretical writing about moral development is derived from Piaget's work on children's developing understanding of rules (Piaget, 1932). From his observations of children at play, Piaget formulated a stage theory of moral development that moves from a higher authority (for instance, God or parents) to the more mature perspective that rules are made by and can be changed through mutual consent of the players. Interestingly, even though young children see rules as inflexible, they also change them to suit their own interests; this is not a contradiction, but rather a reflection of their limited understanding of the nature and purpose of rules as reciprocal. Piaget also described young children as unconcerned with intentions, because they focus on the concrete and observable outcome. Thus, a preschooler will think that a child who breaks one plate while trying to get a forbidden cookie is less at fault than a child who accidentally breaks several plates while helping his mother set the table. During middle childhood, children gradually move toward a more flexible view and take into account intention when judging moral behaviors.

KOHLBERG'S STAGES OF MORAL DEVELOPMENT. Lawrence Kohlberg (1969) took Piaget's stage theory and developed a more elaborate framework for considering moral development based on why people make certain choices rather than on what those choices are (Killen & Smetana, 2006). He describes three levels, each divided into two substages, which relate to the person's view of social conventions.

> ▸ The **preconventional level of moral development** coincides roughly with Piaget's preoperational stage, and moral decisions are based on personal preference or avoidance of punishment.
> ▸ The **conventional level of moral development** coincides approximately with Piaget's concrete operations stage. Children are mostly concerned with group approval and consensus.
> ▸ The **postconventional level of moral development,** coinciding with Piaget's stage of formal operations, represents independent choices, based on moral principles.

preconventional level of moral development
According to Lawrence Kohlberg, the stage during which moral decisions are made based on personal preference or avoidance of punishment.

conventional level of moral development
According to Lawrence Kohlberg, the stage concerned with the pleasing of others and respect for authority.

postconventional level of moral development
According to Lawrence Kohlberg, the stage in which moral decisions are made according to universal considerations of what is right.

There has, however, been considerable criticism of Kohlberg's theory. In particular, concern has been expressed that Kohlberg's theory was based solely on interviews with white, middle-class American males and is not representative of women or of people of other races, economic classes, or cultures. One of the most vocal critics of Kohlberg's theory is Carol Gilligan (1993), whose research indicates that women base moral decisions on different criteria than men do, focusing on relationships rather than on abstract notions of justice.

WILLIAM DAMON'S STAGES OF YOUNG CHILDREN'S MORAL DEVELOPMENT. William Damon's research (1977, 1983) further delineates young children's thought processes as they move through the stages of moral development, especially as they relate to concepts of authority and fairness. His studies are based on interviews with children aged four or older.

▸ Four-year-olds base decisions on self-interest, not really differentiating their own perspective from that of adults. Justification for a choice is simply, "I should get it because I want it."

▸ By age five, children recognize the potential conflict between what they want and external rules, and they obey to avoid the consequences. They also begin to view authority as an obstruction to their own desires. Justification for their choices is based on visible external cues such as size or sex; for instance, "We should get more because we're girls."

Four-year-olds generally understand the concept that if they do something nice for someone, that person may well do something nice in exchange.

▸ Over the next year, children show respect for authority because of the authority figure's social or physical power, which is considered almost as omnipotent. They also progress to a view of strict equality, where everyone gets the same amount when resources are distributed.

▸ Subsequent stages show more complex thinking, as children see authority figures in terms of their special attributes that give them leadership qualities. Their view of fair distribution of resources increasingly considers more factors; for instance, looking at competing claims and at compromising.

Key Point ◆

To a greater extent, young children's moral development is based on personal preference, but gradually evolves to consider the need for rules and the role of authority figures.

naeyc

GUIDELINES FOR PROMOTING MORAL DEVELOPMENT. As a teacher of young children, you will be primarily concerned with children who are still developing morally. It is important to recognize their abilities and limits in terms of moral reasoning and to guide children on the road to moral understanding. The following guidelines will help in this task (Buzzelli, 1992; Sunal, 1993):

▸ **Use other-oriented reasoning with children.** When giving children reasons for doing or not doing something, help them understand this in terms of the impact their action will have on others. Rather than stating, "Our rule is that we don't run inside," use wording that implies potential consequences to others: "We don't run inside because we could hurt other children by bumping into them." Adults reasoning with children and encouraging them to be concerned about the welfare and feelings of others leads to higher levels of moral development.

▸ **Set clear and appropriate expectations and standards for children's behavior.** In particular, ensure that your rules protect children from hurting each other, either physically or emotionally.

▸ **Use stories to promote thinking and discussion about moral issues.** Favorite children's stories often pose interesting moral dilemmas that, with teacher guidance, can help children articulate their thinking. The teacher's role is not to judge or seek consensus but to encourage discussion by asking appropriate questions.

▸ **Provide ample time for child-selected play and materials that promote cooperation.** Dramatic play allows children to take the viewpoints of others; equipment that requires more than one child to operate encourages cooperation; and group games promote turn taking and social coordination.

Any group activity in which the children work toward a common goal will invite cooperation.

▶ **Provide activities that help children become more aware of how the face conveys emotions.** Collages, masks, photos, acting out feelings, and "emotion puzzles" can strengthen this awareness.

▶ **Initiate thinking games that encourage children to seek multiple alternatives for social problems.** Flannelboard characters or puppets can enact a common social dilemma (for instance, one dealing with sharing), and children can generate as many alternative solutions to the situation as possible.

▶ **Plan thinking games that deal with moral intentionality.** Children over the age of four can begin to differentiate between intended naughtiness and an accident that happened while a child was trying to help. Discuss the context of consequences in each instance.

▶ **Realize that not all cultures share the same values.** Communication with parents can help teachers find which values are important to families and help to reinforce these as appropriate with the children.

DIVERSITY

naeyc

Key Point ◆◆

Prosocial behaviors are best promoted in an early childhood program that stresses caring and kindness.

DEVELOPMENT OF PROSOCIAL BEHAVIORS

Peer relations, friendship, gender role acquisition, racial and cultural awareness, and moral development are all part of intertwined processes that involve the emergence of a number of other related traits. Researchers have looked at how such social characteristics as nurturance, empathy, altruism, generosity, sharing, and tolerance evolve in young children. Children's social cognition will affect how they respond to others. With age comes greater comprehension, although a

mirror neurons
Recent discovery of cells in the brain that respond both when a person acts and when he simply watches the same action, "mirroring" movement and emotion, as though the observer himself were acting or feeling.

BRAIN STORM
MIRROR, MIRROR

Why do very young children cry or show distress when they see another child fall and hurt herself? Recent neurological research has led to an intriguing explanation—the discovery of what are called mirror neurons, in the brain. "Some scientists speculate that a mirror system in people forms the basis for social behavior, for our ability to imitate, acquire language, and show empathy and understanding" (Society for Neuroscience, 2007). Some researchers have concluded that mirror neurons seem to allow us to determine not only other people's actions but also their intentions. The mirror neuron system also appears to allow us to interpret facial expressions. Whether we are observing a specific expression or making it ourselves, the same regions of our brain become activated. In essence, "mirror neurons allow us, without thinking, to mimic the feelings and movements of people around us" (Bruno, 2011, p. 23). Such findings suggest that the mirror neuron system plays a major role in our ability to empathize and socialize with others, since we communicate our emotions mostly through facial expressions. So, do mirror neurons help us understand the roots of empathy? Research has not yet determined this, but it is providing fascinating new insight into the ways we acquire social skills and communicate our deepest feelings and intentions to others (Society for Neuroscience, 2007, 2008).

higher level of understanding will not ensure that children's responses will necessarily be appropriate. Other factors contributing to the emergence of prosocial behaviors include the modeling of the significant people in children's lives as well as the kinds of other-oriented values that have been stressed (Schickedanz, Hansen, & Forsyth, 1990). An early childhood program in which adults model, emphasize, and value prosocial behaviors will facilitate the development of such traits in children.

Previous sections of this chapter presented activities and strategies that can help encourage developmentally appropriate and positive social attitudes and behaviors. In the context of supportive atmosphere, understanding of child development, concern for children's needs, respect for their opinions, encouragement of their autonomy, support for their individuality, and provision of a stimulating program and environment, such activities will help promote positive socialization.

SOCIODRAMATIC PLAY

Although the development of positive social traits is fostered in a variety of preschool activities and learning centers, it is perhaps most naturally facilitated in dramatic and **sociodramatic play.** Recall from Chapter 2 that one of Sara Smilansky's stages of play is dramatic play. In dramatic play, children use symbols such as words, actions, or other objects to represent the real world; in sociodramatic play, they expand this symbolic play to include other children (Rogers & Evans, 2008).

Theorists and researchers have postulated a relationship between sociodramatic play and the development of social competencies. For instance, through such play children have many opportunities to learn about social rules by taking on someone else's identity and enacting common situations, as well as by negotiating with peers when conflicts arise. Most, though not all, children engage in sociodramatic play. If children have very limited skills, the teacher can facilitate such play by directly participating in or helping the child enter into the play of an ongoing group. Vygotsky's theory has relevance to such a teacher role, since it suggests that teachers adapt their level of support to the skill level of the child. DAP notes that children's engagement in such play is declining. "Active scaffolding of imaginative play is needed in early childhood settings if children are to develop the sustained, mature dramatic play that contributes significantly to their self-regulation and other cognitive, linguistic, social, and emotional benefits" (Copple & Bredekamp, 2009, p. 15).

In many cases, children assist peers who are not as skilled in entering sociodramatic play. For instance, four-year-old Felix most often engaged in onlooker behavior during child-selected activity times, usually by standing on the outskirts of social groups. On one day in November, Yasmine, just five, deftly included Felix, who stood at the edge of the housekeeping corner observing a "family" group prepare dinner. The participants had assumed all the obvious roles, including that of family dog.

sociodramatic play
Children's dramatic or symbolic play that involves more than one child in social interaction.

Key Point
Sociodramatic play takes place when children are jointly involved in symbolic or pretend play; it provides children with valuable opportunities to learn about themselves in peer relationships and to take on someone else's identity.

Key Point
An appropriate classroom environment and the teacher's guidance will facilitate children's involvement in sociodramatic play.

A dramatic play area is a must for an early childhood program. Such play allows children to try on different roles, learn social skills, and work through feelings.

© Cengage Learning

The "mother," Yasmine, took Felix by the hand, led him to the play oven, and declared, "You can be the turkey." She helped Felix fit himself into the oven and closed its door. A few seconds later she opened the door, checked Felix's doneness by squeezing his thigh, and declared, "Turkey's done!" Everyone gathered around as the turkey was helped out of the oven. Felix's big grin testified to his delight at being assigned such an important role!

Most young children engage in dramatic pretend play naturally; however, such play should also be purposefully encouraged and enhanced in the early childhood setting. Every early childhood classroom, including toddler classes, should have an area set aside and equipped for dramatic play. Most commonly, dramatic play props and children's engagement in dramatic play will center on housekeeping because home-related roles and activities are most familiar to young children. Children re-create and enact what happens at home: meal preparation and consumption, bedtime routines, visitors, child-rearing, even arguments. Home-related kitchen, living room, and bedroom items, as well as a selection of dolls, dress-up clothes, and mirrors, stimulate children's creative and social engagement in housekeeping play. Be sure to include props that appeal to boys as well as to girls. Materials for toddlers and younger preschoolers should be realistic, whereas they should be more abstract for older preschoolers and primary children, to encourage pretending. Children can be further encouraged to broaden their concepts and dramatic play through displays and pictures of people of all ages and different ethnic groups engaged in common household activities.

Dramatic play can also revolve around any other theme familiar to the children—health care, shopping, and recreation are usually particularly relevant to young children because they invariably have visited the doctor, grocery store, and park. Children will also enact their favorite book, television, or movie roles and stories. It is important, however, that children be thoroughly familiar with a topic through concrete, firsthand experience before they engage in dramatic play. Following a field trip, for instance, appropriate props in the dramatic play area can help children assimilate and integrate information from the trip.

COOPERATIVE GAMES

naeyc

Key Point ◆

Cooperation can be promoted in the early childhood environment through activities and games that join the children in working together toward a common goal; there is no place in the early childhood program for competition.

One prosocial goal that early childhood educators cite for young children is cooperation, the force that unites people in working together toward a common objective. In an effort to promote cooperation, there should be no place in the early childhood program for competitive activities in which all but one child end up as losers, even if they are called "second winners." Races, board games, musical chairs, and similar activities in which one child emerges as the winner only promote feelings of resentment, anger, failure, and lack of confidence. Yet, often such games can be easily adapted to keep the element of fun while eliminating competition. For instance, the game of musical chairs can be changed so that all the children share the decreasing number of chairs, until everyone is piled on (and around) the last chair, usually dissolved in gales of laughter!

Writers such as Terry Orlick (2006) have expressed concern over the destructive outcome of competitive games and have proposed as an alternative cooperative games in which no one is a loser and everyone is a winner. Research has, in fact, supported Orlick's approach. In one study, aggressive and cooperative behaviors of preschool children were measured during and after games that were either cooperative or competitive in nature. Results showed that aggressive behaviors increased during free play periods following competitive games, while cooperative behaviors increased following cooperative games (Bay-Hinitz, Peterson, & Quilitch, 1994). The rationale for cooperative games is not just the avoidance of situations in which most of the participants lose, but is much broader, extending to a general concern for the quality of life, emphasis on peace and harmony, and decrease in societal aggressiveness. Although Orlick recommends organized group games as a vehicle for promoting cooperation, this trait can be encouraged in more indirect and less structured ways as well.

Classroom space can be organized to encourage interactions, and ample time blocks can be allocated for child-selected play. Cooperative endeavors may well require more space and more time than activities in which children act alone. In addition, materials should be selected for their cooperative properties. Open-ended materials such as dramatic play props, blocks, water and sand, and puppets particularly promote cooperation. Teachers can also set up activities so that more than one child is involved. Instead of simply putting out beads and yarn as a fine motor activity, try laying long pieces of yarn across the table, with beads at each end, so that two children can work cooperatively on one yarn piece.

SUPPORTING SOCIAL DEVELOPMENT IN INFANTS AND TODDLERS

From birth, babies seek social contact. They are predisposed to interacting with the people around them. We have always known how vital these earliest social interactions are, but recent research about the developing brain has provided us with considerable insight into the importance of providing this early socioemotional support, and the consequences for later development when this support is not provided. A warm and responsive early caregiving environment is crucial to healthy development. Babies whose experiences have been with caring and respectful adults are much more likely to be prosocial babies than their peers whose early experiences were not positive (McMullen et al., 2009). During the

early years, a solid foundation is laid for how children will function for the rest of their lives. While this early period is one of unparalleled and remarkable development, it is also a period of great vulnerability. In your teaching career, you will undoubtedly meet some children who are highly competent, sociable, and eager to learn, and others who are fearful, unable to accomplish seemingly simple tasks, or lacking in rudimentary social skills. It may well be that their earliest experiences, where they did or did not find nurture and security, made all the difference. "Early child development can be seriously compromised. . . . The causes ... are multiple but often revolve around disturbances in close relationships" (Shonkoff & Phillips, 2000, p. 387). Your role as a teacher of young children is, therefore, extremely important. You are one of the forces that help to develop competent children.

naeyc

Key Point

Brain research underscores the importance of the need for a warm, nurturing, and consistent caregiving environment during the earliest years for the development of social competence.

DIVERSITY

Teachers of toddlers facilitate social interactions among the children by modeling words and actions and offering appropriate guidance.

© Cengage Learning

THE MANY LANGUAGES OF MUSIC

Every year a new infant classroom is formed within our center. During the initial weeks of care, families gather together to introduce their infants into a new environment; teachers and children spend time together and routines are established. After discovering that our newly formed infant classroom included the English, Turkish, Lithuanian, Spanish, and Mandarin Chinese languages, our desire to incorporate the diversity in my classroom was undeniable. Doing it in a valuable and interesting way was the challenging part. In addition, the children had an unusually deep interest in, and excitement about, music and movement. Their enjoyment became strikingly apparent in their everyday activities, into which they incorporated singing and dancing. Through the collaborative efforts of the teachers and families a cultural event ensued, bringing music and culture together.

During our typical morning routine of music time with the infants, a ritual of incorporating the languages into the classroom began with a Mandarin Chinese song of hide and seek. This song required me to learn to count to seven in Chinese, a big challenge to say the least. Initially the song was quite difficult for me to learn and remember. Recalling the different sounds and rhythm of the song was no easy feat, but the practice of singing it over and over eventually proved

© Theresa Danna Douglas

Arryell, Infant/Toddler Teacher

to work out well. In addition, observing the children shake, sway, bounce, and totter reinforced my desire to continue learning and practicing the song. One of our fathers also turned the already interesting activity of singing our new song into a ritualistic activity for drop-off time with his son that continued as a transitional point between home and school. Now, the entire class accompanies the child and his father in singing their song.

Through the musical contributions of parents, various other songs were also added, for instance, "Ali Baba," a Turkish version of "Old McDonald." In this song, the labeling of animals provided a unique way of introducing and expanding the children's rhyming and literacy skills. "Tortilla," our Spanish song about making tortillas with your hands, and "Katu Les," our Lithuanian song about making buns, included movement and the use of fine motor skills. "Twinkle, Twinkle,

Little Star," "Itsy Bitsy Spider," "Wheels on the Bus," and "Bubbles in the Air" rounded out the English songs for our last language.

The musical and cultural components of the classroom were used as a unique tool to bring the families and teachers together. Learning and singing these very different songs within my classroom provided a new medium for sharing cultural differences. The fingerplays and hand or arm movements during music time have now become a consistent routine in my class. The way the children often request that we sing certain songs is by moving in time to the beat, for example, patting legs in a steady rhythm. The children in my class also now imitate the various musical tones through humming and speech sounds, signifying their request to sing one of the many songs they have learned.

Throughout this multicultural experience of learning new songs, the children and I have become aware and appreciative of the individual differences within our classroom. The enjoyment stems from learning about and gaining knowledge or experience with others. The skill of collaborating and sharing our cultures with others has been an invaluable experience. I know that these skills offer the children, and me, tools we can use later on in life when meeting and working with individuals from different cultures or linguistic backgrounds.

A major part of your role in promoting social development in infants comes from providing the kind of sensitive caregiving that results in secure, trusting babies. This means getting to know each child's unique style of interaction and response, responding appropriately to their social gestures and vocalizations, and making frequent eye contact. Games such as "peek-a-boo" or rolling a ball back and forth set the stage for rewarding relationships through give-and-take activities. As babies become older and more mobile, your role includes facilitation of social interactions with other young children. It is important to structure times for social interaction with other children, while remaining available to protect, comfort, or facilitate, but not interfere unless necessary (Gestwicki, 2011; Gonzalez-Mena & Eyer, 2012; Watson & Swim, 2011).

One task that teachers of infants and toddlers undertake is to facilitate self-regulation, an emerging process in young children through which they learn to monitor and control their own behavior. Caregivers help by providing predictability; helping in development of awareness and acceptance of their feelings; encouraging focus and attention; allowing children to learn that they can solve their own problems; helping children understand others' perspectives; and supporting them to handle prohibitions (Elliot & Gonzalez-Mena, 2011).

From the rather agreeable infant emerges the toddler, a little person who has much stronger opinions about what she does and does not want to do. This newly independent being may be self-assured and mature at one moment and clinging and crying the next. Toddlers are just beginning to learn who they are, what their bodies are capable of, what the limits of their environment are, and how to engage others in social exchanges. This is also the age at which children begin to learn such prosocial behaviors as empathy, generosity, and the inclination to help others. You foster such behaviors by modeling them in your treatment of other people, your acknowledgment of cooperation and thoughtfulness in the children, and through the books you read that promote themes of being helpful and being a friend. At the same time, you also must recognize that sharing, taking turns, and playing with others is hard for toddlers. These behaviors take time and encouraging adults to develop. The nature of play also changes during toddlerhood. Children begin to engage in symbolic play, something you will notice in their emerging interest in dramatic play scenarios of familiar events. Offer simple props, such as dolls, dishes and spoons, and hats. Also use dramatic play to help children express their feelings, for instance, in dealing with the sadness of losing Mommy when she leaves at the start of the day. Remember also, from Chapter 2, that young children's early play is usually parallel rather than interactive, and that cooperative play takes time and guidance to develop (Gestwicki, 2011; Gonzalez-Mena & Eyer, 2012; Watson & Swim, 2011).

SUPPORTING SOCIAL DEVELOPMENT IN SCHOOL-AGE CHILDREN

Friendships become increasingly important to children during the primary school years. The sphere of influence on school-age children shifts increasingly from the family to the peer group, and acceptance by peers is extremely important for children's social and emotional well-being. Good social skills built during the infant, toddler, and preschool years result in children who function comfortably in their social world, enjoy close friendships, deal in more mature ways with social and emotional issues, and have a sense of group belonging. They are gradually moving away from the egocentric view they held during the preschool years and are much more capable of understanding the perspectives of other people.

It is important that you, as the teacher, set the stage for building a positive sense of community, one where children and adults feel accepted and respected. Deliberate, carefully planned attention to the socioemotional needs and learning of children in primary grade programs is very important (Mindess, Chen, & Brenner, 2008). Allow ample time for children to work on self-initiated projects in small groups that include friends. Encourage children to participate in program planning, whether it is forming a new club, selecting new classroom materials, or deciding where to go on a field trip. Children's growing sense of initiative leads many of them to develop special skills, for instance, in crafts, science, art, or other areas. Provide materials to encourage these special interests. Involve children in real jobs that will be helpful in running the program more smoothly. The children themselves can help identify what jobs need to be done. During the primary years, children also become more aware of their membership in the larger community. You can encourage involvement in appropriate community activities, take advantage of community resources, or encourage the children to take on a civic project that will enhance their community. You can contribute to children's growing prosocial repertoire through such activities as regular visits to a nursing home, making tapes of favorite books for a local Head Start program, helping stuff envelopes for a community fund-raiser, or knitting hats for a local homeless shelter.

Play continues to be an important vehicle for school-age children's social development. Sociodramatic play becomes more sophisticated, but continues to provide an important means for social exploration. Play may revolve around fantasy themes or may replay real-life experiences. Sociodramatic play provides many opportunities for children to learn to get along, to resolve problems, share information, and offer suggestions to each other. An extension of such activity can be dramatic plays that children themselves plan and produce. As the teacher, you can support such efforts by providing writing materials, relevant props, and a venue for showing the play to an audience. Primary school children also enjoy more structured play—for instance, organized games with rules. These might be board games, sports, computer games, or games that the children themselves develop. If children get too caught up in games that result in winners and losers, you can discuss with them that there are other ways of playing games and suggest some cooperative games. Most children at this age thoroughly enjoy such alternatives (Click & Parker, 2012; Gestwicki, 2011).

SUPPORTING SOCIAL DEVELOPMENT IN CHILDREN WITH DISABILITIES

naeyc

DIVERSITY

Like all children, youngsters with disabilities must learn to get along with other people. To achieve this goal, they need to learn appropriate social skills, but learning such skills may pose difficulties that children without disabilities usually do not face. The role of adults, both at home and at school, will help set expectations and provide guidelines for children so they can function in social situations (Allen & Cowdery, 2012).

Learning to get along with others is extremely important for children with social, emotional, or behavioral disorders. Some children may not be well tuned in to the people around them, or they may be unwilling to reach out to others. Some may display behaviors that are not socially acceptable and may even pose a risk to other children. You can use a variety of techniques to help include a child with such disabilities in your class. Help a child with social or behavioral disabilities join others in play. This may require your coaching and participation, as you help the child enter into the play of the other children by providing a desirable prop (for instance, a length of garden hose to become part of the fire station dramatic play) or finding words to be part of a game ("Tell Tatiana that you will push her on the swing and then she can push you."). Talk with the children about what makes them similar to each other as well as what makes them unique. Use children's names often, in songs, fingerplays, and stories and on their artwork. Ask children to think about a time when they felt or acted aggressively or were withdrawn. They can be encouraged to role-play such behavior, and then discuss how they felt. Help the child with the social or behavioral disorder to identify what she really is feeling when she acts out, and help her verbalize genuine feelings.

Children with physical disabilities also may need help to feel that they are part of the group. Do not exclude children from activities because of physical limitations but, rather, make necessary adjustments through equipment or a helper to ensure that they can participate. You can also change some activities so that the other children participate in a way that allows the child with the disability to engage in the activity. The author recalls Sherman, a child with severe limitations, sitting in a circle of standing children doing the Hokey-Pokey. He put his feet, hands, and other body parts "in" from his sitting position. One of the other children noticed this, grinned at Sherman, then sat down and started to do the Hokey-Pokey from a sitting position as well. Soon others joined in until the entire group, laughing as they were singing and moving body parts, all did a seated Hokey-Pokey. Sherman was delighted and when his mother came to pick him up at the end of the day, he proudly told her, "I got to be the leader of everyone today!"

Social skills are also very important for children with visual impairments. If a child with very limited or no vision is in your class, teach the other children to verbally identify themselves before talking to this child. Provide role models who wear glasses if a child also wears these or has some other optical device to correct vision. A visually impaired child may seem unresponsive when others approach her. Explain to the other children the impact of limited or no vision and why the child may respond as she does. Encourage other children to include the child in their play and to help her find tactile or auditory components of the play.

Children with cognitive disabilities also need to learn social skills that will serve them well as they get older. Help children learn about themselves, their body parts, and characteristics to support positive self-esteem. Focus on the child's accomplishments and encourage the other children in the class to be proud of these as well. You can encourage other children to include the child in play, providing support and participation as needed. Help the child find simple words for what he and the other children are doing. If you give children tasks to carry out as classroom helpers, don't exclude a child because of a cognitive

Key Point ◆

Social skills are especially important for children with disabilities, and the inclusive early childhood program can help them, as well as the other children in the class, develop the skills to get along with all their peers.

Inclusion of children with disabilities in classroom activities promotes positive socialization for all the children in the class.

© Cengage Learning

disability. All children can contribute and should be acknowledged for their part in classroom functioning (Allen & Cowdery, 2012; Deiner, 2010).

DIVERSITY

REFLECTING THE FAMILY'S CULTURE AND VALUES

Key Point ◆◆

Communication with families about values as well as about cultural and racial identity are very important.

Communicating with families is particularly important for clarifying home and school values concerning socialization and children's cultural and racial identities. Although the school is responsible for conveying to families what values it tries to instill in the children through its curriculum and guidance techniques, the school also is responsible for obtaining similar information from families about what they value for their children.

Teachers need to be sensitive to the many variations among families of different cultures, and they must be particularly aware of their own attitudes and biases. It is easier to convey positive messages to a family whose parenting style and values you are familiar with and agree with than it is to understand and accept an approach different from your own. Furthermore, it is important not to make assumptions about children's home life based on cultural generalizations; such stereotypes can best be avoided through thoughtful and ongoing family–teacher communication.

Derman-Sparks (1989), in her book *Anti-Bias Curriculum: Tools for Empowering Young Children*, suggests that in addition to open communication in which values and ideas can be shared by families and teachers, the school can provide accurate information to parents about the development of children's sexual, racial, and ethnic identities and attitudes. A series of family meetings can inform and invite discussion about such topics as gender identity and sexism, the creation of nonsexist environments, the development of racial identity and awareness, the creation of antiracist environments, and evaluation of children's books for sexist and racial stereotypes. Such groups can help parents gain information about the school's philosophy, help teachers attain insight into family values and attitudes, and provide families with strategies for antibiased socialization of children.

SUMMARY

1. Consider the theoretical views of how socialization takes place.
2. Consider the development of social competence.
   A. An important element in the development of social competence is peer interaction and friendships.
   B. Children also develop gender role identity; consider nonsexist teaching strategies that promote positive gender attitudes.
   C. Racial and cultural attitudes, and attitudes toward those with disabilities, are formed early in life; review guidelines that can help promote accepting attitudes toward others.
   D. The foundations for moral development and positive social skills and behaviors are also formed during the early years.
3. Many activities promote positive social interaction, including sociodramatic play and cooperative games.
4. Social development needs to be facilitated for all children, though the process may differ for children of different ages and abilities.

KEY TERMS LIST

conventional level of moral development	moral development
conventional moral rules	observational learning
emotional intelligence	postconventional level of moral development
gender identity	preconventional level of moral development
gender stability	scaffolding
interpersonal moral rules	social cognition
mirror neurons	social learning theory
model	socialization
modeling	sociodramatic play

KEY QUESTIONS

1. As we discuss in this chapter, becoming socialized into society is a complex process. Which early childhood activities and teacher behaviors do you think contribute to this goal?
2. What is your earliest recollection of a friendship? Can you recall why this friendship developed? How long did it last? What was special about this particular friend? What feelings does your recollection of this friendship evoke right now?
3. Observe a group of young children during a time when they can self-select activities. Note with whom they interact. How many of the children interact primarily with peers of the same sex? How many interact with peers of the opposite sex? Estimate the proportion of same-sex and cross-sex interactions.
4. Look around an early childhood classroom to assess how it promotes positive (or negative) attitudes toward other people in relation to sex, race, culture, or disability. What recommendations can you make for setting up a nonbiased classroom?
5. Observe a group of children engaged in sociodramatic play. What characteristics of this type of play do you see? What skills do children gain from sociodramatic play? How does such play support social competence in children?

ADDITIONAL RESOURCES

Select additional books, articles, and websites on topics discussed in Chapter 13.

Derman-Sparks, L. (1989). *The anti-bias curriculum: Tools for empowering young children*. Washington, DC: NAEYC.

Orlick, T. (2006). *Cooperative games and sports: Joyful games for everyone*. Champaign, IL: Human Kinetics.

Robles de Melendez, W., & Beck, V. (2010). *Teaching young children in multicultural classrooms: Issues, concepts, and strategies* (3rd ed.). Belmont, CA: Wadsworth, Cengage Learning.

HELPFUL WEBSITES

Power Play: The Good, the Bad and the Ugly:

www.preschooleducation.com

This website provides information for teachers whose young children engage in power play, suggests reasons why such aggressive play is appealing to some youngsters, and offers some guidelines for dealing with such play.

The Anti-Bias Curriculum:

www.ericdigests.com

This website consists of ERIC digests (educational articles).

There are several articles that relate to the topics discussed in Louise Derman-Sparks's 1989 book, *Anti-Bias Curriculum: Tools for Empowering Young Children* (Washington, DC: NAYEC).

Go to **CengageBrain.com** to register your access code for this book's Education CourseMate website, where you will find more resources to help you study. Additional resources for this chapter include TeachSource Videos, glossary flashcards, web links, case studies with critical-thinking questions that apply the concepts presented in this chapter, and more. If your textbook does not include a printed access card, you can go to **CengageBrain.com** to purchase access.

VI

The *How* of Early Childhood Education— Guidance

Another important part of the *how* of early childhood education is guidance, the principles that teachers use in directing the social behavior of young children.

14 | Guiding Routines and Group Activities

DAP Teachers set clear and reasonable limits on children's behavior and apply those limits consistently. Teachers help children be accountable to themselves and to others for their behavior. In the case of preschool and older children, teachers engage children in developing their own community rules for behavior.

Developmentally Appropriate Practice, Copple & Bredekamp, 2009, p. 17

In Chapter 14, you will find answers to the following questions about guiding routines and group activities:

▸ How do you help children deal with routine times that may have emotional significance, for instance, arrival and departure from school?

▸ How can you provide appropriate nutrition for young children, and what can you do to help them develop healthy eating habits?

▸ How can you best meet the needs of infants, toddlers, and young children in relation to diapering and toileting?

▸ How can you plan a relaxing and restful nap or rest time for young children?

▸ What factors affect group behavior, and how do you work with these to ensure, through your guidance, that group routines and activities function smoothly?

▸ How can you plan for effective transitions and for both planned and unplanned unusual occurrences?

NAEYC STANDARDS CONSIDERED IN CHAPTER 14

(See the Standards Correlation Chart on the inside front cover of this book for the titles and description of the standards listed below.)

▸ *Standard 4a:* Understanding effective daily routines (e.g., arrival at school, nap, meals) as centered on supportive relationships and interactions (pp. 363–378).

▸ *Standard 1c:* Using and applying developmental knowledge about the nutritional needs of infants, toddlers, and young children (pp. 365–373).

▸ *Standard 2b:* Supporting and coordinating with families about routines such as eating, toileting, and sleeping (pp. 378–379).

▸ *Standard 4c:* Using developmentally appropriate strategies to guide children's group activities and help children become members of the group (pp. 379–389).

In a well-managed classroom, children and teachers are involved, busy, happy, organized, and smoothly functioning, working within a flexible schedule and curriculum. Children know what is expected and behave according to those expectations. The classroom atmosphere is one in which the children are continually learning to be responsible for their own and the group's behavior. Such a classroom does not just happen, however. Teachers set the stage through their guidance techniques.

GUIDING ROUTINES

Two guidance aspects of the early childhood program deserve special consideration. The first of these is routines, such as meals or naps, which, by necessity, are a part of all programs. In infant programs, such routines take up the major part of the day and are determined by individual needs; in toddler, preschool, and before- and after-school programs, increasingly many of these elements become more scheduled for the group as a whole. The other guidance aspect of early childhood programs has to do with the times when all of the children or groups of children participate in the same activity at one time. This chapter will consider some strategies to facilitate both routines and group guidance.

Arrival Time

The first order of the day, the transition from home to school, has to be considered carefully, because leaving their parents can be very difficult for children. One factor affecting the ease of arrival at preschool or child care is children's general enjoyment of school. Another consideration is the security of children's **attachment** to their mothers, which is related to the quality of the mother–child relationship; the young children who are most distressed at separation often also show signs of anxious attachment (Thompson, 2000). When babies have established a secure attachment to a familiar caregiver, this relationship can help ease and cushion separation from the parent (Balaban, 2006). Feelings of **separation anxiety** are normal and common in older infants and toddlers and also often are exhibited by preschoolers (Thyssen, 2000). Other factors, particularly what happened at home as a child was getting ready that morning, also have an impact.

Arrival procedures need special thought in infant and toddler programs. It is the time when families share relevant information with caregivers. In general, young infants do not react adversely when left by the parent, but at around six months of age, babies begin to exhibit **stranger anxiety.** They are now well able to distinguish the familiar face of the parent from other faces. By nine months and often continuing well into the next year, many babies display more active separation anxiety, crying and clinging, whereas before they may have had no trouble going to a familiar caregiver. This behavior is usually as hard on the parent as it is on the child. A gentle, unrushed transition, during which the parent and the teacher can spend a few moments focused on the child, often helps children adjust. A security object from home, such as a favorite toy or blanket, can also help (Gonzalez-Mena & Eyer, 2012; Watson & Swim, 2011).

In classrooms for preschoolers and primary school children, it is important also to think through the arrival procedure and individual children's reactions and needs. Especially in a child care setting in which many children will be spending a large portion of their waking hours and where they arrive at different times of the morning, it is best to provide a low-key opening for the day. A few quiet activities, some soft music, and available teachers to ease anxiety or welcome enthusiastic children can help the day get off to a good start. This allows Jesse to sit quietly in a teacher's lap with his thumb in his mouth until he feels fully awake; lets Katrina take her father to check on the guinea pig babies

naeyc

attachment
The child's bond with the mother, established during the first year of life.

separation anxiety
Emotional difficulty experienced by some young children when leaving their parents.

Key Point ◆◆
Some young children experience separation anxiety on leaving their parent. This is especially characteristic of older infants and toddlers.

stranger anxiety
Displays of fear and withdrawal by many infants beginning around six months of age, when babies are well able to distinguish their mother's face from the faces of other people.

Key Point ◆◆
A well-thought-out procedure for arrival, particularly when children don't all arrive at the same time, will help get the day off to a good start.

When they are dropped off at school, children are not always ready for their parents to leave. Particularly for a child who is new to the school, a gentle and gradual transition is important.

naeyc

Key Point ◆

A number of strategies can help the new child adjust to the early childhood program.

she has been talking about since their birth last week; provides time for Thui's mother to spend a few minutes with Thui until he gets involved in an activity; or gives Larry's mother a chance to tell the teacher that her husband was in an auto accident the previous day and that Larry might be upset.

In any program, whether infant, toddler, preschool, or before- and after-school, provisions must be made for a teacher to welcome each child and family individually. It is reassuring to a family member on parting from his or her child to know that someone is aware of and pleased about the child's presence at school. Similarly, children need to know that the teacher is glad to see them and is looking forward to mutual enjoyment during the day. This time also provides a chance for the family to share with the teacher pertinent information that might affect the child's behavior that day. Morning is not, however, a time for the teacher to bring up concerns with the family.

THE NEW CHILD. A special example of arrival at school, which often causes great anxiety for children, is the initial entry into an early childhood program. This experience can be traumatic and fraught with the unknown. It is difficult for a child, who thinks in concrete terms, to conjure up a mental image of what school is; without such an image, the idea of school can be very frightening. Therefore, it is helpful if the child can have the chance to gradually become familiar with school, with the security of a familiar family member nearby, rather than being thrust into a first day with no introduction or transition.

Ideally, a new child should visit the school with a family member before his or her first day. After this visit, the child can stay for a short period while the familiar adult leaves briefly, which can help the child realize that she has not been abandoned. After that, the family member can be encouraged to stay a few minutes at the beginning of the first few days, as the child needs additional reassurance. If such an arrangement cannot be made because of family's work schedule, ask if a family can allocate a little extra time at the beginning of those first few days.

It is important to help the family, as well as the child, say goodbye when it is time for Dad, Mom, or another family member to leave. Families should be encouraged to establish a routine that maintains trust (for instance, always waving good-bye from the door) rather than one that undermines trust (such as sneaking out when the child is not looking).

One designated teacher should be available to welcome and spend some time with a new child. It is good for the child to have a reliable adult to turn to with questions or concerns. This teacher also should be prepared to deal with the child's fears, anger, or tears, if necessary.

Other children, those who are veterans of the program, often help ease the new child into the center. You might facilitate this by introducing the newcomer to another child who can show the new child the classroom. As children get older, peers become increasingly more important in supporting separation from one's mother. A classroom pet may also ease the anxiety of the new school experience. Support from a caring adult when children begin to explore new options and activities also helps ease children into the new experience. Before the new child arrives, the teacher can share some basic information with the other children, for instance, the new child's name, interests, and commonalities with the other children in the classroom.

The first few days at school can be difficult for the new child, the family, and the teachers. This experience can be even more disconcerting, however, when not just one new child but many or all of the children, starting a new school year, find themselves in unfamiliar surroundings. In such a case, it is best to encourage a family member to stay with anxious children. Another approach is to plan a phased-in start to school, with only a few new children beginning at a time.

Departure Time

The end of the school day can bring challenges to early childhood teachers as well as to children and families. This time may provide an opportunity for teachers and families to exchange information when they are not as rushed as they may be in the morning. However, the latter part of the day is also the time when everyone is tired and, perhaps, stressed after a long day. It is, therefore, important for teachers to give some thought to what is the most important positive aspect of the child's day to share with the family; an accomplishment, an exciting discovery, or a painting could help send the family and child on their way home with an affirmative message about the day. Such information sharing is especially important for families of infants and toddlers, who cannot verbally share what happened during their day.

A young child who shows no interest in the arrival of the parent or even actively resists leaving school may make the parent feel insecure and guilty. The teacher can reassure the parent of the normalcy of such behavior. Preparing the child for the imminent arrival of the families (for instance, saying, "It is almost time for Mom or Dad to pick you up") can provide the cue needed to get ready for the end-of-day transition.

Meals and Eating Behavior

Meals are an important element of the early childhood program because they fulfill a vital physiological need, as well as social and emotional needs. Care and thought must be given to feeding routines and menu planning—whether children will be eating a single, daily snack in a part-day program or breakfast,

Key Point ◆

Departure time, at the end of the day, can be stressful for children, families, and teachers, but is a time that provides an opportunity to share something positive with the family about the child's day.

BRAIN STORM

FEEDING THE BRAIN

The brain is most sensitive to the quality of nutrition during a baby's first two years of life. Breast milk has the ideal mix of nutrients for promoting brain growth. As we discussed in Chapter 2, rapid myelination takes places during the first few years of life. To facilitate myelination during the first two years, children should have a high level—about 50 percent—of fat in their diets, most of which comes from breast milk or formula during the first year and from whole cow's milk or breast milk during the second year. Recall that myelin is the fatty substance that coats the nerve cells and speeds up transmission among cells.

Children who do not get adequate calories or protein in their diets early in life suffer from malnutrition, and their physical and mental growth is affected. One outcome from the lack of needed nutrients early in life is reduced myelination. As a result, malnourished children have smaller-than-normal brain size; the neurons in their brains are not developing as they should. Malnourished children can suffer lasting consequences, including lower IQ, slower language and fine motor development, and poor school performance (Zero to Three, 2011).

When children spend the bulk of their day in an early childhood program, it is important that the meals and snacks they eat at school contribute to their overall nutritional intake.

naeyc

DAP

Key Point ◆◆

It is challenging but important to provide nutritious, healthy foods for meals and snacks eaten at school because these must be considered part of the child's daily intake of nutrients.

Key Point ◆◆

Infants subsist on breast milk or formula for the first several months, after which semisolid foods are gradually added. Feeding babies provides an opportunity to establish and affirm a sense of trust.

naeyc

lunch, and two snacks in a child care program. Young children take in relatively few calories, yet they need a wide range of nutrients; thus, foods that maximize nutritional value should be selected. Meeting children's nutritional needs is particularly important because many of today's families do not do so as reliably as did families of past generations (Simontacchi, 2007).

FEEDING INFANTS. Infants up to four to six months of age can obtain all of their nutrient needs from milk. Mother's milk is ideally suited to provide for all the nutritional needs of the baby, as well as to provide immune protection against some infections. Mothers who wish to breast-feed should be encouraged and accommodated by the program. Some mothers who cannot come to the school to feed their babies may express their breast milk and make a day's supply available in bottles. Other infants are fed formula milk, one of many commercially available products that are fortified with nutrients in amounts similar to those found in human milk. When babies are fed by bottle, they should be held by a caregiver, who provides full and nurturing attention. This is also reinforced by DAP, which further notes that infants should "always be held, their bodies at an angle" when being fed from a bottle (Copple & Bredekamp, 2009, p. 84). Feeding is one of the most important times for babies to establish a sense of trust. Mealtimes for babies should be unhurried and pleasant, providing opportunities for social interaction and closeness with a caregiver (Branscomb & Goble, 2008).

Babies must be allowed to set their own schedule for feeding. How much food they require varies according to the child; whether they receive the required amount depends on the sensitivity of adults to the child's cues about hunger and satiety. According to the Food and Nutrition Information Center (U.S. Department of Agriculture [USDA], 2009), milk provides enough nutrients for an infant up to about four to six months of life, and other foods should not be introduced until that time. Babies' digestive systems are not able to properly break down many of the components of solid foods until they are at least four months old; giving such food to very young babies can make them susceptible to food allergies (USDA, 2009).

Between four and eight months, the first solid food should be iron-fortified rice cereal. This can be followed with some fruits, additional cereals, vegetables, and diluted noncitrus juices for infants between the ages of six and eight months. From 7 to 10 months, strained or mashed fruits and vegetables, egg yolk, and finely chopped meat or poultry can be added. Soft combination foods such as casseroles, yogurt, cheese, and beans can be added from 9 to 12 months. Some guidelines from the Food and Nutrition Information Center (USDA, 2009) can help in the introduction of solid foods:

▶ Provide small servings of one or two teaspoons at first, and gradually increase to three or four teaspoons. Solid foods should not replace milk.
▶ New foods should be introduced one at a time, and given for two to three days.
▶ Provide the solid foods first, then follow with the bottle. Solids should not be added to the bottle.

The American Academy of Pediatrics (1999) warns that children, up to age two, need whole milk. Thus, reduced fat milk or skim milk should not be given to babies and toddlers until they have passed their second birthday.

NUTRITIONAL NEEDS OF YOUNG CHILDREN. How much older children of the same age and sex will eat varies widely, with boys generally taking in somewhat more than girls (Holden & MacDonald, 2001). Even with this variation, the relative percentages of protein, fat, and carbohydrate consumed remain

Figure **14-1**

MyPlate

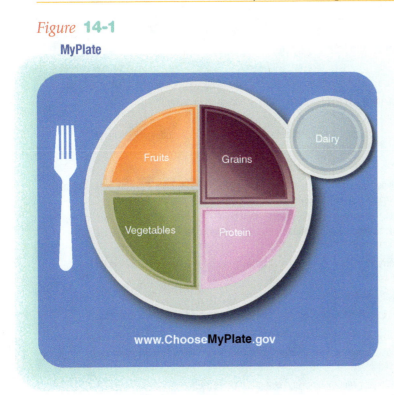

www.ChooseMyPlate.gov

similar. In June 2011, First Lady Michelle Obama, introduced the U.S. Department of Agriculture's new *MyPlate* icon (see Figure 14.1). This icon, which is accompanied by a long-range media campaign, serves as a guide and reminder about making healthy food choices. You will notice that the icon is made up of fruits, vegetables, grains, proteins, and dairy portions. More specifically, the recommendation is that half of the plate of a meal should include fruits and vegetables, complemented by whole grains, low-fat proteins, and fat-free or low-fat milk. The *MyPlate* symbol can be downloaded free of cost from ChooseMyPlate.gov and posted in your classroom as a reminder and a prompt for conversations with children about eating healthy and balanced meals.

Minimum daily nutritional requirements have been established for the nutrients that children of different ages need for growth, health, and well-being. Nutrients include proteins, fats, specific vitamins, and specific minerals (Figure 14.2). Using this information, you can provide carefully thought-out meals that meet all of these nutritional needs.

PROVIDING NUTRITIOUS MEALS THAT CHILDREN WILL EAT. It is challenging to meet children's nutritional needs, not only in terms of including the needed nutrients in their diets but also because children often are picky eaters. Let's look at some guidelines that can be helpful for providing nutritious foods that children will eat.

▶ **Provide variety.** A long-range menu (for instance, for a month at a time) can help ensure that children are not repeatedly being offered the same food items. One useful tool that ensures variety but helps avoid the need for constant meal planning is a cycle menu. Each cycle contains a set of three to four weekly menus for a particular season, and these menus can be repeated for a three-month period.

▶ **Take advantage of fresh seasonal fruits and vegetables.** Children enjoy watermelon in the summer or grapes in the fall, when these foods are

Key Point ◆

Some specific mealtime guidelines can help encourage children, including finicky eaters or those who are overweight, to form good eating habits.

Figure **14.2**

Guide to Nutrients and What They Do

Protein	Essential for growth and lifelong body maintenance. Builds resistance to disease.
Sources:	Animal foods and plant foods such as dry peas or beans.
Minerals	
Calcium	Forms healthy bones and teeth. Aids in normal blood clotting. Helps nerves and muscles react normally.
Sources:	Milk and other dairy products.
Iron	Helps blood cells carry oxygen from the lungs to body cells. Protects against some forms of nutritional anemia.
Sources:	Liver, meat, egg yolks, dry beans, dark greens. Other minerals are important too, such as **zinc, iodine, phosphorus, and magnesium**. Eating a wide variety of nutritious foods will provide them.
Fats	Carry vitamins A, D, E, and K. Source of energy (calories); best used in limited amounts.
Sources:	Meat group and milk group.
Carbohydrates	Inexpensive source of energy. Best when consumed as fruit sugar or starch.
Sources:	Whole-grain bread, cereal, rice, pasta, or potatoes.
Vitamin A	Protects eyes and night vision. Helps keep skin healthy. Builds resistance to disease.
Sources:	Deep yellow/orange or very dark green vegetables.
B-complex vitamins	Protects the nervous system. Keeps appetite and digestion in working order. Aids body cells in using carbohydrates, fat, and protein for energy. (The more important B-complex vitamins include **thiamine, riboflavin, folic acid, niacin, B_6, and B_{12}.**)
Sources:	Whole-grain products, enriched rice, wheat germ, beans, peas, nuts, peanut butter, fish, and leafy green vegetables.
Vitamin C	Keeps body cells and tissues strong and healthy. Aids in healing wounds and broken bones.
Sources:	Citrus fruit, melon, strawberries, broccoli, tomatoes, raw cabbage.
Vitamin D	Aids in absorption and use of calcium and phosphorus by body cells. Helps build strong bones and teeth.
Source:	Vitamin D–fortified milk.

Source: Adapted from Rothlein, L. (1989). Nutrition tips revisited: On a daily basis, do we implement what we know? *Young Children, 44*(6), 30–36.

available and inexpensive. Fruit, as part of a snack or as dessert, will provide some important nutrients in children's diets. Similarly, fresh vegetables can add enjoyment as well as a learning experience. Not all children have had the chance to see that peas do not grow in freezer packages or cans but come in pods!

▶ **Offer simple foods.** Most young children prefer unmixed foods; thus, noodles, hamburger, and broccoli as three separate dishes are preferable to a beef-noodle-broccoli casserole. In general, young children are suspicious of foods that are not readily recognizable.

▶ **Introduce children to new foods carefully.** Children often reject foods they are not familiar with, so plan with care when you present something new. In fact, young children do not readily accept new foods unless they are sweet (Ventura, Johnson, & Birch, 2009). Introduce only one new food at a time, and serve it with familiar foods; talk about the color, texture, shape, and taste of the food; encourage but do not force tasting; introduce the food in a cooking activity; and be a good model for good eating habits.

▶ **Limit sugar in the foods you provide.** Too much sugar leads to dental caries and provides too many empty calories, quickly satiating children's small appetites without contributing to their nutritional needs. Avoid foods with added refined sugar, such as processed desserts, canned fruits packed in sugary syrup, soft drinks, and punch; read food labels to help you avoid the hidden sugars in many foods (for instance, peanut butter is manufactured both with or without added sugar); use alternative natural sweeteners such as fresh fruits or fruit juices; and reduce the amount of sweetener called for in recipes.

▶ **Keep in mind that water is an indispensable nutrient.** Water is essential for life, making up about 70 percent of our bodies. While water is an ingredient in many foods such as juices and fruits, children also should be encouraged to drink water on a regular basis. Water should be available to the children when they are outdoors, during vigorous physical activity, and when the weather is warm. "Children who learn to drink water at an early age are more likely to turn to water to quench their thirst instead of sugary drinks" (Robertson, 2010, p. 246).

In planning meals for young children, it is important to include a variety of healthy foods, take advantage of seasonal fruits and vegetables, and keep foods tasty but simple.

© Cengage Learning

▶ **Provide healthy snacks that contribute to the daily nutrient intake.** Cheese, whole-grain crackers or toast, fresh fruit, unsweetened fruit juices, milk, vegetables and dip, yogurt popsicles, and unsweetened peanut butter are a few simple, yet nutritious snack ingredients that children enjoy.

▶ **Time meals carefully.** Children should not feel hungry between meals, yet they should have enough appetite to eat an adequate amount. Children's capacity is small, so meals should be relatively frequent, with small servings. Plan snacks so that they are served at least two hours before the next meal.

▶ **Giving special names to dishes sometimes adds to the fun of eating.** "Ants-on-a-log," celery sticks with peanut butter and raisins, are a favorite at many schools.

▶ **Vary the location of meals now and then.** Most meals and snacks will be eaten inside the school, but an occasional picnic on blankets on the playground or at a nearby park, a bag lunch or snack taken on field trips, or a meal shared with another class at the school can add to the enjoyment of eating. Even a picnic eaten on a blanket inside the classroom can provide a change from routine. Similarly, a holiday buffet or cafeteria-style meal can add variety.

▶ **Be sensitive to children's cultural food preferences as you plan meals.** Such awareness helps you establish rapport with children and families in your program. If the majority of children at your center come from the same cultural or ethnic background, daily meals should incorporate foods from that culture. If one or two children in your class are from a different background, periodically plan to include foods with which they are familiar. Families and ethnic cookbooks can help provide appropriate recipes.

DIVERSITY

▶ **Some foods are not allowed in some cultures or religions.** Be aware of food restrictions based on culture or religion. For instance, Muslim and some Jewish families never eat pork. Some families do not eat meat. Discuss special dietary requirements with the families and assure them that you will respect their wishes, whether you provide alternative food or ask the families to do so.

NUTRITION FOR THE WHOLE FAMILY

In our program, parents are scheduled one day a month to bring snacks to the classroom. I noticed right from the beginning that the parents did not know what to bring. They would bring chips, sugary cookies, punch, and sometimes even candy or soda. Because these were not healthy choices, I provided a list of healthy snacks for parents to bring. One day a mom brought a big tray of fresh vegetables (carrots, celery, broccoli, and ranch dressing). The children were not pleased to see that snack, and they certainly made their opinions known:

"Yuck, that is a disgusting snack!"
"I am not going to eat that!"
"I don't like vegetables!"

So I came up with a weekly plan. I thought it was a great opportunity for me to teach healthy eating habits to the children. I started my plan the first week by making a vegetable soup with the children. I asked the children to bring one or two vegetables from home. Their activity was to wash, cut, and pour the vegetables into the pot so we could make the vegetable soup. At the end of the day, all of the children had eaten a bowl of their soup and were very interested in making it again. They said the best part of it was the cutting of the vegetables! That whole week the children explored fresh vegetables in many different ways. They played with vegetables in the sensory bin, they used carrots, potatoes, and celery to paint with at the easel, and they played with

© Theresa Danna Douglas

Gloria, Bilingual Preschool Teacher, School District "COW Bus" (Classroom On Wheels)

the vegetables in the dramatic play area. They also drew and wrote stories about the vegetables at the writing table, and at the math center they sorted them and counted them. In addition, they grew carrots from seeds in the classroom. While we were doing activities with the vegetables we were also reading books about how vegetables and fruits help get you strong and healthy. I realized from the soup project that when the children themselves handle the preparation and cooking of food, they are more likely to eat what they have cooked.

The following week I started using fruits to teach about healthy habits. Each child brought fruit from home. They prepared everything and made fruit salad. They also squeezed oranges in the sensory bin and painted with apples, oranges, grapes, and pears. They made a graph showing which fruit was their favorite. They drew fruits and vegetables and dictated stories inspired from their drawings. They recognized

letters in the song "I Like to Eat Apples and Bananas," and loved singing it over and over.

The "fruit and soup" projects were successful because they helped reverse the children's negative attitudes toward fruits and vegetables, which means that now the children will allow themselves to be more exposed to those foods. And the more exposed children are to fruits and vegetables, the more likely they will be to try them.

I also helped the parents learn about healthier eating habits by inviting them to a nutrition workshop that I put together. In the workshop, we talked about the food pyramid for children and adults. I also explained the importance of eating different kinds of fruits and vegetables daily to get the right nutrients for a healthy diet. As an illustration, I provided fruits and vegetables for snacks at the workshop. I explained that children need smaller portions of food and more meals a day in order for their metabolism to stay healthy. I also discussed the fact that eating healthy snacks is very important for the healthy development of your body and mind. At the workshop I showed the video, "Fun with Fruits and Vegetables." After the video, I gave the parents a take-home activity to do with their children: to prepare one of the fun recipes shown in the video. Now, we have healthy snacks in our classroom every day. The children are anxious to prepare snacks and are very pleased to enjoy them.

- **Be aware that some children have allergies, sometimes severe ones, to certain foods.** Dairy products, nuts, wheat, and corn products are some of the common foods to which many children have allergic reactions. A list of children and their allergies should be prominently posted in the kitchen and the classroom, and all teachers who work with a group of children should be aware of both the specific foods that should be avoided and the reaction of the child if given such food.

ENCOURAGING HEALTHY EATING HABITS. In any given class, you will find children who are vigorous eaters, enjoying whatever is served, and others who are picky and selective. Even individual children will vary considerably in appetite from day to day or meal to meal. Let's look at some suggestions for encouraging the formation of good eating habits and for dealing with some eating problems.

- **A relaxed, comfortable atmosphere is important to good eating.** Mealtimes should be an important part of the social and learning experiences of the program. The focus should be on enjoying the food and on pleasing mealtime conversations, not on nagging children to "eat up." An aesthetic table setting, with child-sized plates and utensils, will also contribute to pleasant mealtimes.
- **Teachers should sit and eat with the children during all meals.** In doing so, they are partners, not supervisors, of the experience and can model good eating habits.
- **Children should never be forced to eat a food against their will, but they should be encouraged to taste all menu items.** Forcing will generally have the opposite of the desired effect, and children may become all the more adamant in insisting that they hate this food, even if they have never tasted it!
- **Food preferences and aversions are formed at an early age.** The early years are a particularly sensitive period in the formation of food likes and dislikes; thus, the infant, toddler, preschool, and primary years are important for helping children acquire healthy eating patterns (Endres, Rockwell, & Mense, 2004). Innate as well as cultural factors affect which foods will appeal to an individual, but learning and exposure to different foods can modify this.
- **Children should be allowed to be as independent as possible at mealtimes.** Provide finger foods and foods that are easy to scoop in a spoon or spear with a fork, especially for toddlers and younger preschoolers whose fine motor control is still developing. Let children serve themselves in a family-style approach to help them develop decision-making skills about how much they can eat.
- **It is important to be aware of foods that put young children, especially those under the age of three, at risk of choking.** Especially problematic are foods that are hard, slippery, or of a size that can plug up the throat, such as raisins, nuts, popcorn, seeds, carrots, and grapes (American Academy of Pediatrics, 2010).

PROBLEM-EATING BEHAVIORS. Some children are finicky eaters. Innate as well as learned preferences seem to play a role in developing food habits. In some cases, children are picky eaters because they have learned that such behavior gets them attention (Essa, 2007). By not focusing on children's eating behavior in your conversations, you take away that attention while directing it to something more pleasant. You are, in essence, giving children responsibility for their eating behavior. As you converse with the children, you might talk about how crunchy the orange carrot sticks are, but not focus on the child who refuses to eat those carrots. Peers can also influence children's food choices as can repeated exposure to a new food (Ventura et al., 2009).

Overweight children pose a special concern because of long-range social and health problems associated with obesity. It is very likely that obese children will become obese adults, so early intervention is crucial. A variety of reasons has been suggested as the cause for obesity, but regardless of the underlying cause, obesity results when more calories are taken in than are expended. As a result, overweight children need to reduce their food intake while increasing their activity level. All children, not just obese ones, will benefit from a healthy, low-sugar, low-salt menu. You can monitor the food intake of overweight children and help them serve themselves reasonably sized portions. Also encourage children to eat slowly, perhaps by putting their forks down between bites. Encouragement to increase activity levels is also important for overweight children (USDA, 2009).

For all children, healthy development depends on a diet that includes an appropriate number of calories and the right nutrients. Some children in the United States suffer from **malnutrition,** insufficient food intake to support growth and development. However, more American children, from all types of families, suffer from **misnourishment,** a serious nutritional problem. They eat the wrong kinds of high-fat foods, ones that do not meet their nutritional needs, and generally eat too much of these. While 27 percent of preschoolers' nutritional intake is rated as "good," only 9 percent of primary school children eat appropriately. When children's food intake does not meet their developmental needs, both cognitive and social development can be noticeably affected (Marcon, 2009).

FOOD ASSISTANCE PROGRAMS. Because the nutritional status of children is of national concern, a number of public assistance programs are available for families and early childhood programs. Your school may already avail itself of one or more of these programs or may be eligible for assistance. Similarly, families with low incomes may be able to get food assistance through local, state, and federal programs. Your familiarity with such programs can help improve the nutritional status of the children in your care.

Availability of such programs depends on local resources and your state's participation in federal programs. The Child and Adult Care Food Program (CACFP) is a federal program that reimburses the cost of meals and snacks for infants and children, up to age 12, who come from low-income families. CACFP programs are administered by agencies in individual states, and reimbursement is made to child care centers and licensed family child care homes for eligible children. Nearly 3 million children receive service under this program, including not-for-profit early childhood programs such as Head Start. Cost is provided for up to two meals and a snack each day (www.fns.usda.gov). The After School Snack Program provides similar services for after-school programs operated within schools (www.fns.usda.gov). Low-income families who are nutritionally at risk can avail themselves of food stamps (www.fns.usda.gov) and WIC (the Special Supplemental Food Program for Women, Infants, and Children). WIC covers women during pregnancy and while breast-feeding, and also covers infants and children up to age five (www.fns.usda.gov/wic).

malnutrition
Children do not have sufficient food to support growth and development.

misnourishment
Children do not eat the right kinds of foods needed for healthy development, but overeat the wrong kinds of foods.

Key Point

Public assistance programs are available to families with low incomes and to some early childhood programs.

These programs are administered through different agencies, depending on where you live. A call to the local education, welfare, health, or social services agencies can provide a starting point for information about such programs if your school is eligible or if you are concerned about the nutritional status of one of your center's families.

Diapering and Toileting

Infants and toddlers are dependent on responsive adults to make them comfortable when their diapers are wet or soiled. Diapering routines are important parts of the day not only because of babies' comfort but because they afford many opportunities for quality interaction and communication. The diapering routine has to be carefully considered to ensure the safety of the children being changed, convenience for the caregiver, and hygiene. The area should be sanitized after every use and soiled diapers appropriately disposed of; the caregiver must thoroughly wash her or his hands with warm water and soap before and after the baby is changed (Gonzalez-Mena & Eyer, 2012; Watson & Swim, 2011). In addition, caregivers can wash toddlers' hands to establish a foundation for handwashing as part of the toileting routine.

Toileting is also important because it helps children become more independent and establishes habits of good hygiene. Toileting takes on particular significance in groups of toddlers, who are in the process of toilet training, and young preschoolers, who are in the process of mastering or have recently mastered bowel and bladder control. Even with older preschoolers, it is good to remind ourselves that these children were still in diapers just a couple of years ago!

Teachers in toddler programs are often required to guide their young charges in toilet training. Children between the ages of two and three (and sometimes later) usually signal their readiness to be toilet trained, often by telling the teacher they have wet or soiled their diaper, staying dry for several hours, or watching with interest as older children use the bathroom. Early pressures to use the potty are usually futile and result in resistance rather than compliance. Toilet training should be pleasant, never a stressed or punitive experience. Accomplishments should be acknowledged and praised and accidents handled in a matter-of-fact manner. It is particularly important that parents and teachers communicate during toilet training, so they are on the same schedule, use the same methods, and are aware of progress while the child is not with them (Gonzalez-Mena & Eyer, 2012; Watson & Swim, 2011).

Before toileting becomes a matter-of-fact routine of life, young children may go through a period when they are especially interested in the acts of urinating and defecating as well as everything that surrounds them. Toddlers and young preschoolers may enjoy flushing the toilet repeatedly, watching others sit on the toilet, or talking about their accomplishments. It is best to react in a matter-of-fact way that acknowledges the child's interest but does not convey shame or self-consciousness about these natural bodily functions.

With young children who are just mastering bladder control, you may need to provide reminders or periodically ask children if they need to go to the bathroom. Be particularly aware of signs such as wiggling or holding, which indicate a need to urinate. Some young children are reluctant to go to the bathroom because they fear losing the activity in which they are involved. If this seems to be the case, reassure them that you will keep their place at the play dough table or protect their block structure until they return.

Key Point

Diapering of infants and toilet training of toddlers are important parts of the daily routine.

It is an exciting day when a toddler is successful in using the toilet!

© Cengage Learning

Many preschools have a common bathroom for all children, not separating boys from girls. This provides a setting in which children can observe and note sex differences without any attending mystery or fuss. School-age children, however, require more privacy.

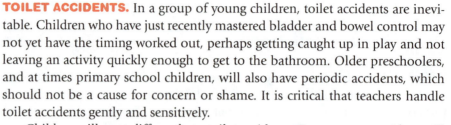

TOILET ACCIDENTS. In a group of young children, toilet accidents are inevitable. Children who have just recently mastered bladder and bowel control may not yet have the timing worked out, perhaps getting caught up in play and not leaving an activity quickly enough to get to the bathroom. Older preschoolers, and at times primary school children, will also have periodic accidents, which should not be a cause for concern or shame. It is critical that teachers handle toilet accidents gently and sensitively.

Children will react differently to toilet accidents. For some, an accident will be embarrassing and upsetting, whereas for others it will be, at most, a minor irritant. In neither instance should a child ever be lectured, shamed, or chastised for a mishap. Accidents should be handled in a matter-of-fact manner that does not call attention to the child and conveys acceptance of the accident as "no big deal."

Any school should have a supply of extra underwear, pants, and socks available in case of accidents. For a group of younger children, families might be asked to bring a change of clothing for possible mishaps. When children have an accident, the teacher should furnish the needed change of clothes and encourage them to change themselves. Make sure a child has privacy to avoid embarrassment or ridicule by others. Also keep a stock of plastic bags for storing soiled clothes.

One contributing factor to accidents may be the clothing that children wear. For young children to be independent, they have to be able to get their clothes off easily and quickly. Small buttons, overalls, belts, and back fasteners can frustrate a child trying to undress to use the toilet. Simple clothes with elastic waistbands are the easiest for children to handle.

Sometimes children will suddenly have repeated accidents long after they have achieved toileting independence. If this is the case, it would be wise to try to determine the reason for this behavior. Could the child have a bladder infection that is affecting control? Is the child reverting to a younger behavior to regain an earlier status; for instance, after the birth of a new sibling? Is the child using accidents to get attention? Each of these reasons will require a different approach.

BATHROOM FACILITIES. It is beneficial to children if toilets and sinks are child-sized and easy to reach. If only adult facilities are available, sturdy, wide steps should be placed in front of toilets and sinks to promote independence. Children should also be able to reach toilet paper, soap, and towels with ease. Having to overreach can cause accidents.

Bathrooms should be adjacent to the classroom and easy to supervise. Children are more likely to have an accident when they have to ask for permission to go to the bathroom than when they can go on their own when they need to. Some schools have one large bathroom that all of the classrooms share, rather than a bathroom for each class. If so, teachers need to think through an arrangement that promotes independence but still lets them know where each child is at all times. Children should not be taken

Key Point ◆

Occasional toileting accidents should be expected in a group of young children and should never be considered a cause for punishment or shame.

Key Point ◆

Child-sized toilets and sinks can help decrease toileting accidents and facilitate independence.

© Cengage Learning

Child-sized bathroom fixtures facilitate independent self-help skills. Learning about going to the toilet and washing hands is easier for young children because the toilets and sinks are just the right size for them.

to the bathroom in large groups. Such a procedure, in which children have to wait unnecessarily, only promotes pushing, shoving, frustration, and even toilet accidents if a child just can't wait.

TOOTHBRUSHING. Especially in child care centers, toothbrushing supplies are often located in the bathroom. Wet toothbrushes should not be stored in a closed cabinet, but in an out-of-the-way place where they can air out after each use. Each child should have an individual, clearly marked brush; disposable paper cups can be used for rinsing. The teacher can dispense the toothpaste, preferably from a pump. It is important to the establishment of good hygiene habits that, from an early age, children be allowed to brush their teeth after meals.

Sleep and Rest Times

Newborns spend a majority of their time sleeping, but sleep needs decrease as children get older. When older children spend all day at a child care center, a rest or nap time should be an integral part of the day. Not all children need a nap, especially as they get older, but for children who are on the go all day, a time to slow down is important. Until about age three, most children take a daytime nap or naps. By four to five, children generally outgrow the need for a nap and, often, bedtime at night comes a little earlier (Pritchard, 2000).

INFANT SLEEP PATTERNS AND NEEDS. Infants' sleep must follow each individual child's schedule rather than being imposed for the group. Some babies have a fairly consistent sleep–wake cycle, while others are more unpredictable in their schedules. In the first couple of months of life, babies will sleep most of the time. Babies should be positioned to sleep on their backs rather than their stomachs during the first year of life to reduce the risk of **sudden infant death syndrome (SIDS).** SIDS, also called "crib death," involves the unexplained death of an infant during sleep. Sleeping on the back has reduced the incidence of SIDS by half, according to the American Academy of Pediatrics (2005b). As they reach the middle of the first year, their sleep needs continue to decrease and sleep patterns become more predictable, including two or three naps during the day. By the age of one, most children take only one nap a day.

Especially in child care centers, the availability of individual toothbrushes reinforces good habits of hygiene.

sudden infant death syndrome (SIDS) Also called "crib death," this is the unexplained death of an infant during sleep; sleeping on the back reduces the incidence of SIDS.

Key Point

Infants set their own sleep patterns, spending much of the earliest months sleeping. Around the end of the first year, they generally take one nap per day.

Many children, especially young preschoolers, need a nap during the early afternoon hours. A soothing, low-key environment and a predictable routine will facilitate children's sleep.

SLEEP IN YOUNG CHILDREN

ONE OF THE most common problems reported by parents of young children has to do with sleep disturbance. In particular, babies and toddlers who have difficulty falling asleep or who wake up frequently during the night are of concern to their parents (Burnham & Gaylor, 2008). Early childhood teachers also often report concern over such problems. On the other hand, many children have no problems sleeping and follow a predictable daily sleep schedule. Why are there such differences in children's sleep patterns?

One factor has to do with normal development. Babies gradually develop a fairly predictable sleep–wake pattern in which the proportion of time spent sleeping as well as the day's distribution of time spent in sleep and waking change. By about three months, "sleep becomes consolidated to the nighttime hours" for most babies (Burnham, Gaylor, & Anders, 2006, p. 188). In addition, during the day most three- to six-month-olds take three naps. Infants and toddlers continue to wake at night, but many develop the ability to soothe themselves back to sleep (Montgomery-Downs, 2008). The need for naps decreases with age; while nearly 100 percent of two-year-olds sleep during the day, fewer than 10 percent of six-year-olds take naps (Giannotti, Cortesi, Sebastiani, & Vagnoni, 2008).

DIVERSITY

Another factor contributing to differences in sleep patterns among young children is culture. "The ways in which culture and biology interact play a major role in the establishment of sleep patterns, developmental norms and expectations regarding normal and problematic children's sleep development" (Giannotti et al., 2008, p. 37). In Chapter 4, we introduced the concepts of individualistic and collectivistic societies, with the former encouraging independence and autonomy and the latter emphasizing strong interpersonal connections and greater concern for the group than for the individual. These categories also affect children's sleep. For instance, in collectivistic societies, children are much more likely to sleep with their mother or other adults.

Factors within the family also contribute to variations in children's sleep patterns. A mother who is depressed or in poor health, tired parents, and general disruptions to family life all can impact a child's sleep. At the same time, a child with sleep problems contributes to family distress. Unfortunately, the full impact of disrupted sleep on children has not been researched. Better understanding through research of sleep problems among infants and toddlers is important "because optimal sleep may provide the foundation for neurocognitive development

and growth" (Burnham & Gaylor, 2008, p. 29).

Children's development, culture, and family factors, therefore, all may impact the sleep of young children. In addition, some children suffer from diagnosed sleep disorders. About 30 percent of young children have some kind of problem with sleep; some of these problems are mild, while others are much more serious. An example of more serious problems involves sleep-disordered breathing, including sleep apnea, a temporary cessation of breathing during sleep. Snoring and prolonged mouth-breathing during sleep are signs of this sleep disorder. Some children, after age three, are awakened by nightmares and anxiety dreams (Burnham et al., 2006). It should also be noted that sleep disorders often accompany a host of other childhood problems (many of which were discussed in Chapter 2), including attention deficit–hyperactivity disorder, autism spectrum disorder, and anxiety disorder.

Appropriate amounts and quality of sleep are important for children's development and learning. Chances are that the majority of the young children in your program will have healthy, normal sleep patterns. For those children whose sleep is problematic, however, communicate and work together with parents to find ways to help the child get the restful sleep she or he needs.

Babies signal tiredness by yawning, rubbing their eyes, fussing, crying, or falling asleep toward the end of feeding. Some children will fall asleep readily when put in their cribs, while others need to be held and gently rocked to encourage sleep. Sleep space for babies should be away from active areas, and not contain stimulating toys, bright colors, or other distracters. Each baby should have an individual crib (Gonzalez-Mena & Eyer, 2012; Watson & Swim, 2011).

CHILDREN WHO DON'T NEED TO SLEEP. A variety of arrangements can be made for older children who do not take a nap in the middle of the day. In some programs, children are asked to lie on a cot quietly for a period of relaxation; if this is not handled punitively, children can enjoy a short period of rest and quiet. In other centers, children who do not sleep engage in a quiet activity, such as book browsing, while they are on their cots. Nonsleepers are usually placed apart, so as not to disturb those who are expected to fall asleep. Some children, when they lie down in a relaxed atmosphere, will eventually fall asleep. Those who do not can get up after about a half hour and move into an activity apart from the sleepers. Another alternative is to have a quiet time, when nonnappers, rather than lying down, participate in a period of individual, restful activity; for instance, book browsing or playing quietly with manipulatives.

NAP GUIDELINES. Sleep, which is a natural part of the body's daily rhythm, requires that the body and mind be relaxed and at ease. If children are anxious or wound up, they will have a difficult time falling asleep. Thus, the way you prepare for nap time and set up the environment will either facilitate or hinder sleep.

Children should not be expected to move directly from a high-energy activity, such as outdoor play, into nap; rather, a transition is needed to let children slow down gradually. A predictable prenap routine that is followed every day is as important as the nap itself. For instance, a leisurely 10-minute period is set aside for children to go to the bathroom, get a drink of water, take off shoes and tight clothing, get a favorite stuffed animal and blanket, and settle down on cots. The lights are dimmed, and drapes or shades are drawn. Cots are spaced far enough apart, and friends who enjoy talking are separated, to facilitate sleeping. Once all the children are settled down, a teacher may read a story or play a story record, sing softly, or lead the children in relaxation exercises.

After these preliminaries, the teachers move from child to child, gently rubbing backs, whispering a soothing word, or stroking children's hair. Children who need a midday nap will fall asleep in a conducive atmosphere in which lighting is dim, the temperature is comfortable, the room is relatively quiet, and the teachers convey a gentle, soft mood. Some research has found that playing soft classical music in the background helps toddlers and preschool children fall asleep more quickly (Field, 1999).

If the policy of the center dictates that all children lie down for a nap, special provisions may need to be made for children who do not sleep during this time. At one center, teachers have found "rest packs" to be effective for nonsleepers. Rest packs contain two to four items for quiet play, which children can use while on their cots. Teachers can prepare several rest packs to be distributed generally or can make individual packs for each child.

Key Point ◆◆
A nap or rest is important for children who spend all day in a child care center.

Key Point ◆◆
A consistent prenap routine and a relaxing atmosphere facilitate sleep.

© Cengage Learning

Some children have more difficulty in falling asleep at nap time than others. What strategies can the teacher use to help a child fall asleep?

The contents of rest packs (for instance, books, crayons, paper, small puzzles, or manipulatives) should be changed frequently.

Because sleeping children would need extra help to move out of the building in case of an emergency, it is especially important that teachers be aware of exits and alternative escape routes.

Children should not sleep for too long; an average of an hour to two suffices for most children. Some children need time to wake up gradually, so an unstructured transition in which children can join the class at their own pace is helpful. An afternoon snack, to which children can move as they are ready, often helps provide that transition.

CHILDREN WHO HAVE PROBLEMS SLEEPING. Occasionally you will encounter children who consistently resist sleep, even though they need the rest. A few children have genuine sleep problems, stemming from such conditions as chronic middle ear infection, the use of certain medications, and some cases of brain damage. For other children, falling asleep represents a letting go, where anxieties and fears can surface, and their sleep reluctance comes from a need to avoid such scary thoughts. Most children's difficulty in falling asleep, however, results from poorly established sleep habits and routines.

Three-year-old Becky had a very hard time going to sleep, both at home and at school, and engaged in a variety of disruptive stalling techniques to avoid nap time. Often, by late afternoon she was grumpy and tired, and she invariably fell asleep in the car on the way home or "crashed" in the classroom around 4:00 P.M. Her teachers eventually decided that it was not worth trying to put Becky down for nap with the other children because she prevented everyone from sleeping when she was in the nap room. Instead, once the other children had fallen asleep, one teacher would sit with Becky in the rocking chair and read a quiet story to her. This seemed to work about three days out of the week, when Becky would fall asleep on the teacher's lap and then be put down on her cot.

Family Concerns about Routines

Key Point

Regular exchange of information between families and teachers about routines will help provide consistency regarding expectations and experiences for children.

DIVERSITY

As with all aspects of the early childhood program, the school's philosophy about meals, toileting, nap or rest, and group guidance should be shared with families. An exchange of information between teachers and families helps provide a consistent set of expectations for children.

To help children achieve a balanced diet, families and teachers need to cooperate. One way to further this goal is for the school to post a detailed menu of all meals and snacks served. The school may also compile and distribute a "cookbook" of healthy alternatives for snacks and lunches.

Some families have particular restrictions or preferences in their dietary habits, and these need to be honored. Muslims and some Jewish families do not eat pork, for instance, so children from these religious backgrounds should not be served luncheon meats or hot dogs made from pork. Some families are vegetarian because of religious, ethical, or health reasons; the school will need to make special provisions to furnish appropriate meals for vegetarian children or make arrangements with the family to provide alternative foods.

Families may convey concerns about their children's eating patterns, and the teachers' advice and informed responses can be very reassuring. One frequent family concern involves lunch box meals, particularly if food items remain uneaten. Teachers can share the school's philosophy about meals, suggest alternative menu items, and discuss appropriate serving sizes for preschoolers, depending on the circumstances.

Toileting, especially if children take home plastic bags with wet or soiled clothing, can be a cause of concern for families. If toilet mishaps seem to be happening too frequently in relation to the child's age, explore potential causes with the family. Check with them about possible stressful events in the child's life and assure them that toilet accidents are not uncommon among young children. Share the school's nonpunitive philosophy toward accidents. Your matter-of-fact perspective can be reassuring.

Families may also feel concern over naps, particularly if they affect evening bedtime. Some children, if they sleep too long during the day, are not ready for sleep at night until quite late. This puts a burden on families who want their children in bed at a reasonable time. It may take some coordination to meet the needs of the child, the family, and the school, but effective family–teacher communication is the important ingredient to reaching such a goal. Families may also seek your advice in dealing with their children's nighttime sleep problems. Your advice or recommendations for further readings can help parents establish a consistent and pleasant bedtime routine and recognize factors that can disrupt sleep patterns.

Families of infants and toddlers especially need consistent and thorough information about their children's routines. A special form, on which information about the child's eating, sleeping, elimination, play, and developmental progress are briefly noted, should be available for families at the end of each day.

FACTORS THAT AFFECT GROUP BEHAVIOR

Each of the previously discussed routine elements of the young child's day is important and needs careful consideration as you decide how best to guide the group of children in your care. We will now turn to another aspect of guidance, those times of the day when all the children participate together in a common activity. Although it is important to consider each child as an individual within that group, some factors can facilitate group guidance.

The Physical Environment

For one thing, it is important to examine the physical environment in relation to group behavior. Are several children running in the classroom, for instance, although the rule is "walk inside, run outside"? Perhaps too much open space invites children to run. Critically examine the room arrangement in relation to group behaviors. Reggio Emilia programs in Italy and programs in the United States that have adopted many Reggio principles have found that when an environment is thoughtfully and aesthetically prepared in a way that respects the children's interests and needs, children will use such an environment productively and appropriately (Gandini, 2004). (See Chapters 5 and 7 for more details on this topic.)

Developmentally Appropriate Expectations

Another important factor in setting expectations for the group is the developmental level of the children. Carefully examine activities, the daily schedule,

naeyc

naeyc

naeyc

▶❚❚ TeachSource Video Activity
WATCH • REFLECT • RESPOND

This video provides ideas for promoting positive behavior. Go to CengageBrain .com and view the video titled, "Guidance for Young Children: Teacher Techniques for Encouraging Positive Social Behavior," and answer the following questions:

1. What is the relationship between curriculum and children's behavior?

2. What techniques does this teacher use to promote prosocial behavior?

and materials to be sure they are appropriate to the ages of the children. Keep in mind the attention span, social ability, activity level, muscle control, and cognitive skills of your group and plan accordingly (look back at Chapter 2). Realistic expectations are essential to good group guidance and have to be aligned with the children's developmental level so that you do not have either underexpectations or overexpectations. Frequently refer to NAEYC's *Developmentally Appropriate Practice in Early Childhood Programs Serving Children from Birth through Age 8* as a guide (Copple & Bredekamp, 2009).

DAP

Key Point ◆◆

Group guidance can be facilitated by such factors as a well-set-up environment, schedule, activities, materials, and expectations that are appropriate for the developmental level of the children. When expectations are inappropriate, frustration or boredom are likely to result.

Children who are expected to behave beyond their capability will become frustrated, and frustration results in misbehavior. Similarly, if the expectations are too simple for the children's abilities, the children will easily get bored; this can also lead to misbehavior.

An example in which the need for understanding of child development provides the teacher with guidance is in the pacing of activities. Avoid situations in which a group of children must wait for more than a minute or two. For instance, it is *generally unrealistic to make children wait until everyone is seated to start, or until everyone is finished to move on to the next activity. Also, standing in line to wait for a turn to get a drink, go outside, go to the bathroom, go to lunch, or wash hands is difficult for active preschoolers.* By the time children are in the primary grades, they have a better capacity for waiting a few minutes, although waits should not be excessive. There are other methods of moving children from one place to another without chaos, which we will discuss later in this chapter.

Also keep in mind that although developmental guidelines help you identify appropriate expectations for the age of the children, each child is an individual and will conform to some but not to other developmental milestones. You may also have children in your class who have disabilities and in some ways do not fit the profile for their age group. Be sensitive to their unique needs and characteristics, make alternative arrangements if they cannot be expected to participate in the same way as the other children in some activities, but help them fit into the group as smoothly as possible.

naeyc

Active young children should not be expected to wait in lines to go outside, go to the bathrooms, get a drink, go to lunch, or for any other reason. What alternatives to lining up could you suggest to the teacher of these children to get them outside?

© Cengage Learning

Conveying Expectations

Young children are exuberant and active, so you may find times when their voices or activity levels get too high. Shouting instructions to "quiet down!" or "settle down!" will only add to the confusion. A more effective way of controlling children's voice levels is to whisper softly. Move from small group to small group and speak in a soft, slow voice. Children will quiet down so that they can hear you. You will find the noise level quickly reduced by your modeling.

You might want to let the children know that it will be "shout time when we go outside." Similarly, an elevated activity level, if it seems unproductive, also can be reduced by a quiet voice, dimmed lights, or soft music that induces relaxation rather than agitation.

As individual children quiet or settle down, let them know with a smile or nod that you appreciate how they are speaking or behaving, rather than calling attention to inappropriate behavior; appropriate behavior can be contagious. Teachers will frequently praise the behavior of one compliant child publicly in the hopes that others will behave similarly because they also want to be acknowledged. Research shows, however, that praise given in this manner can lead to resentment and anger because it is manipulative rather than sincere (Kohn, 2001).

Rules

Another way of encouraging good behavior from the group is by letting the children know just what is expected. This can be done through a few simple, established rules. Children should know what the limits are and why they are set. Like adults, children are much more likely to follow rules if they understand the reasons behind them. Children can be involved in setting rules as well. Their involvement can help in their budding understanding of fairness and concern for others. It is also easier to remind children of the rules if they have a sense of ownership because they helped establish them. In addition, when teachers respond to children sensitively and "talk to them with a playful voice, the rules are implicit and no reprimands are necessary" (Emilson, 2007, p. 11).

Group behavior, as indicated in the previous discussion, can be affected by factors such as room arrangement, developmental level of the children, and clearly spelled out expectations and rules. These factors are, in a sense, constants that do not change from day to day, although they do change over longer periods of time as the children change. They provide a framework for the group guidance techniques that relate to specific parts of the daily schedule and that a teacher uses in the minute-by-minute functioning of the class.

Key Point ◆◆

Children are most apt to follow rules if there are few of them and if they understand the reasons for these rules.

GROUP GUIDANCE AND THE DAILY SCHEDULE

In Chapter 8, we discussed some guidelines for planning the daily schedule. Many have a direct effect on group guidance because the schedule is a very important element in successful guidance of group behavior and needs to be thought through carefully. The actual sequence and timing of the daily schedule, as well as the length of activities, will have a bearing on group guidance.

There must be a logical rhythm and flow to the sequence of daily activities that relates to the developmental level of the children. If children are expected to sit quietly for several activities in a row, they will tend to find unacceptable ways to release some of the energy that is pent up during this overly long period; if too many boisterous activities are scheduled one after another, the children may tire or get too keyed up. All elements of the schedule should be carefully timed to avoid boredom (because activities last too long) or frustration (when activities are not long enough).

Let's look at some specific aspects of the daily routine in relation to group guidance techniques. At certain times in the schedule, careful forethought and planning can make the difference between a chaotic and a well-ordered classroom.

The Start and End of the Day

Morning arrival can be a difficult time because much is going on. Children, families, and staff are starting a new day for which information needs to be shared. If families bring the children to school individually (rather than children

arriving in a group by bus), one teacher needs to be available near the door to
exchange greetings and a few words with arriving children and families. To free
this teacher from classroom chores, it is helpful to have a few, simple activities
available for children who arrive early. These activities should be relatively self-
directed, easy for the children to disengage from, and easy to clean up. Puzzles
and other manipulative materials serve well for this purpose.

If the children arrive in a group for an after-school program, you can move
into your first scheduled activity immediately. A good starting point might be a
large group activity to orient the children to what will happen that day.

Departure at the end of the day should be similarly handled. If all families
come for their children at about the same time or if the children go home by bus,
a cleanup period followed by a group activity works well. If children are picked
up over a period of time, some selected activities that are easy to clean up and
disengage from should be made available. Manipulative materials, book browsing, table games, or outdoor play are examples of appropriate activities. When a
parent arrives, the child can finish and put away the activity while a teacher chats
for a few moments with the family. The transition from school to home, as well
as from home to school, will be much smoother if you plan carefully.

Activity Time

A good part of the day will be scheduled for activities that children select from
several planned by the teachers or from the classroom learning centers. Children have the opportunity to engage in a decision-making process at these times
(Hohmann, Weikart, & Epstein, 2008). Some group guidance principles can
help keep activity time blocks running smoothly.

One of the main guidance problems during activity time can arise from the
grouping and distribution of children among activities. What if 10 children want
to participate in the water-play activity, 8 more are in the housekeeping area,
and only 1 chooses to do the art project you planned so carefully? Chances are
that problems will develop at the water table and in dramatic play. How can you
avoid such a situation?

One way to establish limits is to post happy faces in a conspicuous place at
the entrance to each learning center. The number of happy faces corresponds
with the number of children who can be in a given area at one time. Thus, four
happy faces above the water table mean that only four children at one time may
be in that area. The teacher can help the child count the number of happy faces
and match it to the number of children in the area. In this concrete way, a child
can be helped to understand why there is no more room. The child can then be
redirected to another area with an assurance that he will be informed if a child
leaves the desired area and there is room for one more.

The number of children can also be limited by the availability of materials and equipment in an area. Thus, five chairs around the art table indicates
how many artists can work at one time; six play dough boards tells how many
youngsters can engage in that activity; four hard hats set the limits in the block
area, and so forth. Your imagination and ingenuity as a teacher will help you
determine how such controls can best be set.

*It is best to make some activities that are
simple and easy to clean up available
during the early and later parts of the day,
when children are arriving and leaving.*

Children can also be involved in determining the number that can comfortably be accommodated in an area. The teacher's assistance in problem solving
a situation when an area is too crowded can help the children be participants
in making logical choices. In one class, for instance, the teacher used skillful

listening and negotiation with six children who wanted to participate in a dramatic play activity, a reenactment of a trip to the airport, for which there was limited space and materials. She helped the children decide to expand the available space by annexing the adjoining science area and adding some unusual props that creatively expanded and enhanced play opportunities.

Meals

Breakfast, lunch, dinner, or snack can pose group guidance problems if these times are not carefully planned. What happens before, during, and after a meal will directly affect group behavior, not to mention digestion.

Before the children sit down to eat, tables should be set and the food prepared. Children should be involved in this process. It provides an excellent opportunity for young children to be engaged in a practical activity that builds self-concept, self-confidence, social competence, eye–hand coordination, and cognitive skills. Special helpers can assist in setting the table by putting out a plate, napkin, and silverware for each child.

Once the children have washed their hands and are ready to sit down, waiting should be kept to a minimum. Young children especially should not have to wait for everyone to be seated. Older preschoolers and primary school children, in whom patience is beginning to develop, can wait a few minutes until all the children at their table are seated. If, for some reason, the children are at the table and have to wait for more than a minute, initiate a song or fingerplay to keep the youngsters occupied until they can eat. Waiting for any prolonged period, especially quietly with hands folded in their laps, only frustrates children and is an invitation to behavior problems.

During the meal, establishing a few simple rules about eating (as discussed earlier in this chapter) and a pleasant, relaxed atmosphere are important. Conversation with peers and adults should be encouraged; silence does not inspire a pleasant mealtime. After the meal, children can help to clear their dishes and clean their area at the table. Children should not have to wait until everyone is finished eating. They should be able to engage in a self-directed, quiet activity such as book browsing, or move individually to the next activity. The staff should be distributed according to where the children are. As more children finish eating and move to another area, so should more of the staff move. One staff member should stay with the eaters until all are finished and then clear away all food and utensils (unless there is a separate kitchen staff who do this).

Group Activity Times

One of the most rewarding, as well as most difficult, parts of the early childhood day occurs when children participate in teacher-initiated group activities. Good guidance is particularly important at group times because the success of such activities may well depend on your ability to keep the group attentive. This is

A good part of the daily schedule will be devoted to time blocks in which children can select from a variety of available activities and materials.

naeyc

Key Point

Pleasant mealtimes result when children help set up, when they are not required to wait, when there is relaxing conversation, and when they know that cleanup is expected after they finish eating.

naeyc

Both children and teachers find mealtimes more enjoyable in a comfortable and relaxed atmosphere. Pleasant conversation is an asset to meals and should be facilitated by the teacher.

In large-group activities, teachers need to pay attention to how children are seated so that all can see visual props, such as books.

Key Point

Effective group activities require careful planning and preparation, as well as forethought to the seating arrangement.

no simple task because you are trying to move children gradually from their egocentric focus toward some specific social behaviors, ones that are particularly important in primary school. The control you maintain over the group will, to a great extent, be a function of the environment and activities you provide for group times.

THE ENVIRONMENT. The physical environment within which group activities are conducted has to be carefully thought out. It should be relatively free from distractions so that the children focus on the activity. If, for instance, a shelf of attractive materials competes for the children's attention, a simple covering of butcher paper or fabric can be used during group activities.

Also, if children cannot see you or are crowded, they will respond with frustration or lose interest in the activity. Therefore, arrange the group seating with thought. A carpeted area works best; children should be physically comfortable. Depending on the activity, a circle or semicircle around which children sit works well. If the activity is basically verbal with no visual props, such as group discussion, use a circle. If there is something to look at, such as a book or flannelboard, a semicircle works better, because in a circle the children next to the teacher will not be able to see the visuals very well. The visual prop should be held at or slightly above the children's eye level; if it is too high, the children will have to tilt their heads back at an uncomfortable angle. Get down on the floor with the children to see what they see or how they see it.

Sometimes, however, as much as you try to delineate an outer edge for the group, the children gradually creep closer and closer until you have a knot of little people sitting in no designated order. This may happen particularly with a group of toddlers and younger preschoolers. Some things can help children stay on the periphery of the group area. You might simply outline the area with masking tape and mark Xs or dots at intervals where children sit. You may also use carpet samples from a local carpet or interior design business; carpet squares can provide a colorful and appealing outline for your group area. You can set out the squares yourself, or you can have the children select a color and place the square in the circle to sit on.

Keep in mind that several smaller groups, rather than one large group, can be much more effective in reaching your goals. You can plan simultaneous group activities, each with a separate teacher, or have group activities with different children at different times of the day. When there are fewer children in a group, they can more easily be drawn into discussions, do not have to compete for attention, and will engage in more meaningful conversations and activities.

THE LENGTH OF GROUP TIME. The timing of group activities is also important. Be aware of the developmental abilities of your group to sit quietly and pay attention. Begin the year with relatively short group times and lengthen these as the children are able to sit for increasingly longer times. You may plan several short group times at the beginning of the year and fewer longer ones later in the year. Although the ability to sit and listen will vary depending on the children in the group, there are some rough guidelines for the length of group time. For groups of one- and two-year-olds, 5 minutes of group time is plenty;

toddlers should not, however, be required to sit for group but should be invited to join and free to leave if they wish. Three-year-olds should be able to manage a 10-minute group, whereas four- and five-year-olds can handle 15 to 20 minutes. School-age children can sit longer for an interesting activity. Keep in mind, however, that children in an after-school program have spent the day in fairly structured activities. They will be more responsive to activities they can self-select.

A stimulating, longer group activity is sometimes fine, but as a rule do not expect children to sit quietly and attend for extended periods. It may also happen that, although the group as a whole can pay attention for a certain period of time, one child lacks the maturity of the rest. In such a case, provide that child with a quiet alternative away from the group, rather than punishment for something that the child is developmentally not capable of.

GROUP TIME ACTIVITIES. What happens during group times is very important to group guidance. Your activities must be age-appropriate to hold the children's interest. A wide variety of appropriate activities can be included during group time. Most popular among early childhood teachers are books, stories, and music activities, but there are many other possibilities, as we discussed in Chapter 8.

It is also important to be prepared for whatever you plan to cover during group time; you should have read the stories, have all props prepared and at hand, and know songs and fingerplays by heart. If you try to "wing it," you may well lose the all-important sense of pacing. Several group guidance techniques help keep the children's attention while you are reading or telling a story.

If you see a child's attention wavering, you might try saying, "And do you know what happened next, Amy?" to gently bring Amy back to the group. To involve children in the story process, plan enough time to stop every so often to ask the children questions or to have them find something in a picture. Another way to heighten interest in a story is to periodically substitute the names of some of the children in the group for those of the characters in the story.

When you are using fingerplays and song during group activity, keep in mind that some of these excite children and others quiet them. Have a repertoire of songs and fingerplays on hand to use as a stimulant or a relaxant, as needed. Children should learn an increasingly larger number of songs and fingerplays as the year goes on. Remember, young children enjoy and need repetition, so when you introduce a new song, give the children enough time to learn it thoroughly, then continue to use it periodically thereafter.

Songs and fingerplays serve an excellent group guidance function at the beginning and end of group time. At the beginning, they provide a good transition from the previous activity; start a familiar song as soon as a couple of children are seated in the group area, or even before children arrive—as a signal that the group is starting.

Do not wait for everyone to be seated before you start. You can also end your group with a familiar song or fingerplay, particularly if you need a good transitional device to move children to the next activity. (This will be discussed in more detail in the upcoming section on transitions.)

One more group activity, a favorite of many teachers, is **show-and-tell** or "sharing time," which is often used to allow children to share something special and personal with their classmates. Such an activity can be tiresome and difficult, or it can provide a rich learning experience for all of the children.

Show-and-tell gives children a chance to be in the limelight as well as to practice talking before a group. But show-and-tell has to be planned and carried

show-and-tell
A common group activity in which children can share something special and personal with their classmates.

out carefully. As with other early childhood activities, you should keep in mind the attention span of the group. It is not necessary for all of the children to participate on the same day. The ages of the children will determine how many youngsters should share on one day.

Another favorite group activity for many teachers is a daily **calendar activity,** which focuses on reviewing the days of the week, the months, and the date. Teachers have expectations that children will begin to develop a sense of time as well as reinforce math concepts and other skills and knowledge. Often, however, the act of naming the next day or putting a number on a calendar chart does not help children gain such concepts. "If we look at the development of children's understanding of time . . . , there is little evidence that calendar activities that mark extended periods of time (a month, a week) are meaningful for children below first grade" (Beneke, Ostrosky, & Katz, 2008, pp. 12–13). Helping children gain an understanding of temporal concepts can be better accomplished through some of the activities described in Chapter 11 rather than through a daily calendar review.

Transitions

A very important, though often unplanned for or neglected, part of the day's schedule is not the daily activities but what happens in the gaps or transitions between them. Transitions really have to be thought of as part of the routine, a part that provides many opportunities for children to learn. Learning certainly takes place as children have to cooperate and be considerate of each other during toileting before lunch; classify, seriate, match, and organize during cleanup; or bend, lift, stretch, and pull in putting outdoor toys into storage before coming back inside.

A beautifully planned day can fall apart if no thought is given to transitions between activities. "Challenging behavior is more likely to occur when there are too many transitions, when all the children transition at the same time in the same way, when transitions are too long and children spend too much time waiting with nothing to do, and when there are not clear instructions" (Hemmeter, Ostrosky, Artman, & Kinder, 2008, p. 18). Carefully think through what has to happen at the beginning of an activity, at the end of an activity, and between activities. In fact, to help you plan transitions, role-play with the rest of the staff what occurs during transition times. Fix in your mind the sequence and steps of various transitions to ensure that your guidance and expectations of the children are appropriate.

Children should always be aware of upcoming transitions, and you can make them aware in a variety of ways. For instance, you might use a cue or signal to let children know a change is coming. A song, chant, record, bell, flick of the lights, or specific clapped or drummed beat can be used regularly as a transitional signal. For instance, such cues can announce cleanup time, group time, or outside time.

Even before you announce the end of an activity, however, and the transition to the next, give children a warning. Do this to help children finish activities they may still be involved in. For older preschoolers and primary school children who are more product-oriented with projects or who are concerned about completing a game, a longer warning will be needed. As a rough guide, allow 1 minute of warning for each year of age (2 minutes for two-year-olds, 3 minutes for threes). Tell children, "In a few minutes, I will ask you to put your blocks

calendar activity
A common group activity that focuses on a daily review of the days of the week, the months, and the date.

naeyc

Key Point ◆◆
Children best respond to upcoming transitions, such as cleanup time, if they know what to expect; therefore, a warning a few minutes before the change will help them be prepared for it.

Key Point ◆◆
Teachers need to think through how children will move through activities and where the adults should be stationed to provide appropriate assistance when it is needed.

away so we can get ready for snack." This is the first warning, to be followed within a few minutes by the cue that signals cleanup time.

As you give the warning, and later as you encourage cleanup, do not make a megaphoned announcement to the class as a whole. Rather, move from small group to small group with your message. In supervising cleanup, remember that the children are cleaning up with some help from the teachers, not vice versa. Your role is that of teacher and guide. Be as specific in your verbal instructions as you can. Rather than telling children, "Put everything away," say, "Jimmy, you get to put the shoes on the shelf and the purses and hats on the hat rack; Lesley, please stack the dishes in the cupboard on the top shelf; Tom, you can put all the long blocks on top of the red rectangle on the block shelf."

Cleanup will, of course, be facilitated by an orderly, well-thought-out environment (also see Chapter 7), where every item has a logical place. Sometimes you may have to devise games to encourage cleanup, especially for reluctant helpers, until they accept it as part of the routine. Suggestions to "drive your truck into the garage" or "swim like a fish to the sink and get the sponge to wash this table" can help encourage cleanup participation.

Sometimes a transition needs to be used to limit the flow of children to the next activity. For instance, you may have snack following group activity, with handwashing between the two. Sending 20 children at one time to a bathroom with two sinks is asking for problems. Think through ahead of time how many children can be in the bathroom comfortably at one time, and plan accordingly. A familiar song or fingerplay is a good device for such controlled flow. For instance, sing "Five Little Monkeys" using five children as participants at one time, and send each "monkey" to the bathroom as it "falls off the bed."

The position of teachers, as in the previous example of moving children from group to bathroom to snack, is an important factor in smooth transitions. The teachers should be positioned in key places (in the bathroom, in the group area, at the snack table). As the bulk of the group moves to the next area, so should the adults.

OUT-OF-THE-ORDINARY OR UNEXPECTED SITUATIONS

A regular schedule and routine are essential for helping young children work comfortably in their environment; they need the security and regularity. But sometimes the unusual or unexpected comes along. It is important that children be able to handle deviations from the usual since life is full of the unexpected. Some guidance techniques will help you give the children in your group the coping skills to deal with unusual situations if and when they come up. It should be noted, by the way, that if children are allowed to make choices frequently, they will not panic when the unexpected happens. Unusual situations can be grouped into two categories—the planned and the unplanned.

Planned Unusual Events

These include changes from the regular routine such as special events, special circumstances that you know about ahead of time, and field trips. Children can be prepared for expected changes, although it is advisable not to prepare them too far in advance to avoid undue anxiety or disappointment if they become ill. Also keep in mind that children's time sense is not the same as adults'; a week can seem like an eternity! When you prepare children, tell them exactly what will happen during the special event. If Santa Claus is coming tomorrow, tell the children that they will sing some songs for Santa and then they will each have a chance to sit on Santa's lap if they would like. A calendar that refers to the special coming event can help older preschoolers and primary children "see" the time span in a concrete way.

If you can anticipate a special circumstance that will involve a change—for instance, if you will be away from school for a few days next week and a substitute teacher will be taking your place—prepare the children. Discuss your upcoming absence and reassure the group that you will still be their teacher, even if you are gone for a few days. If possible, have the substitute teacher visit your class so the children have a concrete idea of who that person is.

 **FIELD TRIPS.** This is probably the most common example of a planned unusual event, and some of the principles we just discussed also apply here. Children should be well prepared ahead of time so they know what to expect. Review with them what the schedule for the field trip will be, what the rules are, when they will be returning ("we'll get back just before lunch"), the transportation arrangements, and the transportation rules. It is particularly important to review safety rules with the children. If necessary, role-play or present a flannelboard story to cover key points that the children need to know before leaving. Before leaving, also put a name tag on each child's outer garment with the child's name and the school's name and phone number. Even before you go on the field trip, careful preplanning is essential. Ensuring that the trip provides developmentally appropriate experiences, with plenty of time for hands-on exploration, is essential to a good field trip for young children.

Key Point ◆

Careful planning and forethought are important to ensure safety and enjoyment on field trips and walks.

If you are going by car, assign children and adults to a specific car in which they must go and return. This avoids a child being left behind accidentally because everyone assumes she is in the other car. In the car, be strict about safety rules and expectations. If the children do not comply with the rules (and in the excitement of the trip this could well happen), pull the car to the nearest curb and tell the children that the trip will continue when everyone obeys the safety rules again. Be familiar with the child safety restraint laws of your state and follow these carefully on car trips. Before and frequently during the trip, count noses. It is also advisable to get extra adult supervision for field trips (family members are often willing to go along and help) because any environment outside the school will be less familiar and less controlled, and therefore less safe.

WALKS. Similar to field trips but with some different guidelines are walks. When you take the group on a walk, you again need to inform the children of expectations and safety rules. A buddy system works well. Children are paired off, and each partner is responsible for the other by holding hands. It's a good idea to establish an engine and a caboose if the children have to walk in a line (such as along a sidewalk). An adult at the beginning and end of the line are essential on a walk. Any additional adults can walk in between or act as rovers.

An alternative arrangement is to have each adult in charge of a small group of children, but enough adults must be available for this to work. Especially with a group of toddlers and young preschoolers, there may be some strayers in the group. If you know who they are, be sure an adult is holding their hands. If there are too many strayers in the group, it is probably better not to leave the building at all or to use a group stroller that can seat six children. One thing that works with some children who tend to run off is a rope. Take a sturdy, smooth, long rope and have the children hold onto it at intervals; knots tied in the rope can indicate handholds. Often a strayer will hang onto a piece of rope but not a hand.

Unplanned Unusual Situations

There are times when the really unexpected occurs. A fire drill or a real fire, a serious accident involving a child, or any other emergency can throw the class into an agitated state or even panic. Although you cannot foretell unplanned unusual events, you can prepare the children for these situations with some discussion and practice. As with planned unusual happenings, you can role-play, present a flannelboard story, use puppets, or otherwise pose hypothetical problem situations so children know what may happen and what they are to do. Also, children will be more likely to handle emergency situations well in a classroom where they are routinely trusted as competent and are viewed as partners with the teachers in the learning process. If, on a day-to-day basis, children are expected and trusted to make good decisions, they will be able to think about the consequences of the emergency and behave more independently and responsibly.

One way to ensure that no stragglers are lost when taking children on a walk is to use a buddy system—children hold the hand of a partner or the teacher.

Key Point ◆

Children cannot be prepared for all unexpected or emergency situations, whether these may be fire drills, a broken window, or an injury; but some specific teacher strategies can help them respond calmly.

Emergency procedures should be thought through so that teachers as well as children know what to do. A written policy for handling emergencies should be visibly posted. Such a policy statement can be written in another language if some of the parents or staff are not native English speakers. One example of a carefully planned emergency procedure is a fire drill. These should be part of any early childhood program. It can also be helpful to have an "emergency pack" available by the exit, which might include a class list, phone numbers, a flashlight, and a couple of favorite children's books in case there is a wait.

Another type of emergency situation that is helped by forethought occurs if a child is seriously injured. One teacher should stay with the child while another moves the rest of the group away. It should be agreed on ahead of time who is responsible for which tasks; a teacher who has had first aid training should, of course, stay with the hurt child. If necessary, a responsible child can be sent to get additional help—the director, secretary, cook, janitor—so arrangements for needed medical care can be made. Once the emergency is settled, review with the children what happened so they can express their concerns and feelings and be reassured.

The unexpected does not always have to be a dire emergency. Less serious occurrences such as broken glass, spilled paint, or a minor injury can still be disconcerting to children. If children realize that the teacher's attention must be focused temporarily on the calamity, they can take responsibility for being self-directed if they have been prepared to do so.

The teacher should set the stage by verbalizing what is happening: "Usually we get ready for snack at this time. But because this window was broken, we will have to take care of the broken glass first. So instead of snack right now, we get to do something else. Jenny, get the 'Goldilocks' flannelboard pieces and all of you help Jenny tell the story. Bobby, please get the broom and dustpan from the bathroom. Anita and Todd, go to the office and tell Mrs. Arnold we have a broken window." When adults are organized—even in unexpected situations—know what to do, and do not panic, children will respond in a similarly calm manner, particularly if they have been prepared for unexpected events.

SUMMARY

1. Consider four routine times: arrival and departure, meals, toileting, and sleep. All four have strong emotional significance for the child and need sensitive handling by the teachers.
2. Some important factors affect group behavior, particularly the developmental appropriateness of expectations and activities.
3. Forethought and planning can help ensure an orderly classroom during specific time blocks within the daily schedule.
4. Transitions, those times when children move from one activity to the next, deserve special attention.
5. Consider occasions when the out-of-the-ordinary happens, either planned— such as a field trip—or unplanned—for instance, an accident.

KEY TERMS LIST

attachment	separation anxiety
calendar activity	show-and-tell
malnutrition	stranger anxiety
misnourishment	sudden infant death syndrome (SIDS)

KEY QUESTIONS

1. Observe children arriving at school with their families. What differences in the way they leave their parents do you note?
2. A three-year-old in your class consistently refuses to go to sleep during nap, but then almost always falls asleep later in the afternoon. What strategies might you use in such a situation?
3. Ask three teachers what rules they set for the young children in their class. Are there commonalities among the rules listed by the different teachers? Are there differences? Which rules seem reasonable and understandable to preschoolers? Do any of the rules seem inappropriate?
4. Observe a preschool class during transitions between activities. What strategies does the teacher use? Do these strategies reflect a sense of preparedness and forethought? Did the transitions go smoothly or were there some problems? How could these transitions be improved?
5. You are going to take a group of children on the first field trip of the year. How will you and the other staff members prepare for this trip? How will you prepare the children?

ADDITIONAL RESOURCES

Select additional books, articles, and websites on topics discussed in Chapter 14.

Carter, D., & Curtis, M. (1996). *Reflecting children's lives: A handbook for planning a child-centered curriculum*. St. Paul, MN: Redleaf Press.

Gonzalez-Mena, J., & Eyer, D. W., (2012). *Infants, toddlers, and caregivers* (9th ed.). New York: McGraw-Hill.

Honig, A. S. (2002). *Secure relationships: Nurturing infant-toddler attachment in early care settings*. Washington, DC: National Association for the Education of Young Children.

Marotz, L. (2012). *Health, safety, and nutrition for the young child* (8th ed.). Belmont, CA: Wadsworth, Cengage Learning.

HELPFUL WEBSITES

National Resource Center for Health and Safety in Child Care:

http://nrckids.org

This website provides many useful links to numerous websites on topics that are relevant to issues of health and safety in child care.

Preschool Nutrition:

www.keepkidshealthy.com

This informative article on good preschool nutrition provides concrete information about the nutritional needs, serving sizes, and balance of nutrients that children need each day for optimal growth and development.

National Safe Kids Campaign:

http://safekids.org

The mission of the National Safe Kids Campaign is to prevent unintentional childhood injuries, the number-one killer of children under age 14. This is a good website to share with parents as well.

Go to **CengageBrain.com** to register your access code for this book's Education CourseMate website, where you will find more resources to help you study. Additional resources for this chapter include TeachSource Videos, glossary flashcards, web links, case studies with critical-thinking questions that apply the concepts presented in this chapter, and more. If your textbook does not include a printed access card, you can go to **CengageBrain.com** to purchase access.

Guidance is effective when teachers help children learn how to make better decisions the next time. Excellent early childhood teachers recognize children's conflicts and "misbehavior" as learning opportunities. Hence, they listen carefully to what children say, model problem solving, and give patient reminders of rules (and reasons for them)—this too, is effective guidance. A caring community of learners provides young children with a foundation that they will carry with them into their future lives in and out of school.

Developmentally Appropriate Practice, Copple & Bredekamp, 2009, pp. 35, 36

In Chapter 15, you will find answers to the following questions about guiding social behaviors:

▶ What are some philosophies of guidance, and how do you select one that works well for you and the children in your care?
▶ What techniques of guidance are available, and how and when should these be used?
▶ How do you differentiate between behaviors that fall within the range of "normal" and ones that are so problematic that you should seek help?
▶ What factors affect children's behavior?
▶ How can you help children deal with and learn alternative behaviors to aggression, biting, and shyness?

NAEYC STANDARDS CONSIDERED IN CHAPTER 15

(See the Standards Correlation Chart on the inside front cover of this book for the titles and description of the standards listed below.)

▶ *Standard 4d:* Reflecting on the characteristics that are desirable in children, how these relate to guidance practices, and which guidance techniques to use (pp. 393–394; 399–400).
▶ *Standard 4a:* Understanding the underlying research and theories of guidance that lead to positive outcomes for children (pp. 394–399).
▶ *Standard 4c:* Knowing and using effective strategies of guidance (pp. 400–407).
▶ *Standard 1b:* Understanding the multiple influences on children's behavior and development and using appropriate strategies to support children (pp. 409–413).
▶ *Standard 2b:* Supporting families in solving children's behavioral issues (pp. 416–417).

When we discuss the guidance of children's behaviors, we are not considering just what we expect of them today, but we are looking at the beginning of a lifelong process. It may sound like a cliché, but today's children *are* tomorrow's adults. In that context, guiding the behavior of young children takes on an important and delicate meaning. Every time you give children direction, ask for their help, mediate an argument, step in before a fight starts, respond to a misbehavior, or convey your expectations to them, you are not affecting just their immediate behavior, but you are also shaping future behavior. You are, in essence, contributing another grain to the growing hill of such grains that is becoming the child's character. In this chapter, then, we will discuss the guidance of children's behavior.

WHAT BEHAVIORS DO WE EXPECT OF YOUNG CHILDREN?

Families and early childhood educators in general hope to help children develop into people who are friendly, sociable, responsible, helpful, cooperative, considerate, and have a conscience. Such a repertoire of behaviors, however, does not emerge without thoughtful and consistent guidance from families and teachers. Reflect on your own expectations of young children as you read this chapter and consider how your experiences as a child affect your guidance strategies and whether your actions now, as an adult, will lead to those expectations.

Among the qualities of children that families and teachers often value is an ability to care about others, to share willingly, to be altruistic and empathetic, and to be understanding of the needs of others. Such prosocial behaviors are most likely to appear in children who live in a nurturing environment, where understanding and caring are modeled, where responsibility is expected, and where **inductive reasoning** is used (Eisenberg, 1992). Induction involves an approach in which adults use logic and reasoning to help children see the consequences of their behavior for other people.

One characteristic that is often seen in children who possess prosocial qualities is self-control. This, in turn, leads to self-regulation, in which the child's judgment about the situation dictates the response (Bronson, 2009). Internal rather than external control is critical, for it means the child does what is right, not because she or he might be rewarded (or punished), but because she or he knows this action is the morally responsible thing to do. Development of inner control, a long process tied to the gradual evolution of ego strength and moral judgment, is fostered through many opportunities for the child to make decisions and to experience the consequences of those decisions.

A climate in which such opportunities are offered is child-centered and nurturing, based on trust, and respectful of the child's growing autonomy. Adults in the child's world are careful to use inductive reasoning, focusing on explanations that stress the rights and feelings of others rather than on punitive admonitions or restrictions. The child is told, "It really makes Ingrid feel unhappy and hurt when you tell her nobody likes her," rather than "Don't you say that, you selfish brat!" In an article titled, "Obedience Is Not Enough," Constance Kamii (1984) differentiates between morality of autonomy—based on an inner sense of integrity—and morality of obedience—based on doing what one is told to do. To achieve morality of autonomy, children need, from an early age, many opportunities to develop a sense of personal values (for instance, recognizing that honesty is important because it is the foundation for trust from another person); Kamii notes that children can be motivated to tell the truth if they are made aware that adults don't believe or trust them (p. 12). Development of values comes from the chance to exchange viewpoints with others and from opportunities to make decisions.

Thoughtful and respectfully guidance practices result in children who are socially competent and responsible.

naeyc

Key Point ◆

Prosocial behaviors have to be nurtured in an atmosphere of acceptance, in which inductive reasoning is used and children are helped to take the rights and feelings of others into consideration.

inductive reasoning
A guidance approach in which the adult uses logic and reasoning to help the child see the consequences of a behavior for other people.

Diana Baumrind (Baumrind, 1967; Baumrind & Black, 1967), in her classic studies of parenting styles, concluded that an interaction style between adult and child, in which the child is given a reason for what the adult expects, has also been shown to produce children who are socially competent; have positive interactions with peers; and are self-controlled, assertive, self-reliant, generally happy, and explorative. The adult engages in verbal give-and-take with the child, provides opportunities for decision making, and is consistent in setting and enforcing rules and expectations.

Research supports the fact that the process of child-rearing and child care-giving is tied to the characteristics that the child displays. A consistent, loving, firm, reasonable, inductive environment helps lead to children who are morally responsible, considerate of others, independent, and assertive. These findings give direction to early childhood settings, which are partners with families in the process of child rearing.

IMPORTANT DEFINITIONS

We have and will continue to use the word *guidance* throughout this chapter. Before continuing, let's briefly examine this word and differentiate it from some other related ones. One definition of **guidance** in *Webster's Dictionary* is "the act of directing . . . to a particular end." This implies, as we discussed earlier, that guidance is an ongoing process and that techniques must be congruent with the kind of people you want children to grow up to be. Guidance is also related to **discipline,** which, for many adults, connotes a reaction to a misbehavior by the child who did not follow the rules. **Positive discipline** helps children achieve self-discipline and can be considered interchangeably with guidance.

One form of discipline is punishment, which implies inflicting a painful consequence for a misbehavior and which relies on retribution rather than correction (Gartrell, 2011). Early childhood experts discourage punishment because of its long-term ineffectiveness in changing behavior. Numerous studies have shown that physical punishment increases undesirable behaviors such as aggression because it models the very behavior it is intended to discourage (Gershoff, 2008).

Punishment emphasizes what the child should not do, without giving any indication of what the desired behavior is; it is a one-time rather than an ongoing occurrence; it focuses on obedience rather than on development of self-control; it undermines self-esteem; and it makes a decision for the child rather than allowing the child to think through a solution. Children will also learn to dislike and avoid those who punish them. See the "Take a Closer Look" box, in which research about the use of physical punishment is discussed.

PHILOSOPHIES OF GUIDANCE

A number of philosophies and approaches deal with children's behaviors. These are, quite often, addressed to parents but have relevance to teachers as well. The common aim of these approaches is to contribute positively to the development of productive and responsible youngsters by giving families and teachers a consistent method and workable strategies. Like the theories we have previously

Key Point

Although the word *discipline* often has negative connotations, the terms *guidance* and *positive discipline* are more concerned with the ongoing process involved in socializing children.

guidance
Ongoing process of directing children's behavior based on the types of adults children are expected to become.

discipline
Generally considered a response to children's misbehavior.

positive discipline
Synonymous with guidance, an approach that allows the child to develop self-discipline gradually.

Key Point ◆

Punishment as a technique is discouraged because it is ineffective in the long run.

Guidance is an ongoing process through which adults help children develop self-discipline and learn the socially acceptable rules of society.

WHAT RESEARCH TELLS US ABOUT THE USE OF PHYSICAL PUNISHMENT

OVER THE past century, hundreds of studies have been published about the effects of physical punishment on children. The recent report of the Center for Effective Discipline, *Report on Physical Punishment in the United States: What Research Tells Us about Its Effects on Children* (Gershoff, 2008), synthesized the outcomes of this work, stating, "There is little research evidence that physical punishment improves children's behavior in the long term" (p. 7).

The term **physical punishment** is defined as the use of physical force with the intent of causing bodily pain or discomfort to a child for the purpose of correcting or punishing the child's behavior. It can include both light force, such as a slap on the bottom, or more severe force, such as hitting a child with a hard object. In addition, it includes such practices as washing out a child's mouth with soap or making the child stand or sit in a painful position for extended periods of time. The terms *corporal punishment* and *physical discipline* can also be used to denote physical punishment. Researchers have found that a majority of American parents physically punish their children, with nearly two-thirds of parents of one- and two-year-olds reporting using such punishment. When adolescents are asked whether they have experienced physical punishment, 85 percent report that they have and more than half say that

they have been hit with a belt or similar object.

What are the effects of physical punishment on children? Are they better behaved as a result? There is some evidence that physical punishment has some immediate results on children's compliance. Yet other studies have found the opposite, that children are less likely to comply after being physically punished. More concerning is the finding that such punishment does not promote long-term, internalized compliance. Almost all of the studies reviewed concluded "physical punishment to be associated with less moral internalization of norms for appropriate behavior and long-term compliance. Similarly, the more children receive physical punishment, the more defiant they are and the less likely they are to empathize with others" (p. 13). As part of this report, Gershoff also reviewed studies from many parts of the world, all of which concluded that physical punishment led to more aggression, fighting, bullying, and antisocial behavior rather than decreasing such behaviors. In addition, research has shown that the greater the use of physical punishment by parents, the higher the levels of aggression in their children over time.

There are additional risks for children who are physically punished. Frequent and severe punishment is strongly associated with children's mental health problems such as anxiety, depression, substance abuse, general maladjustment, and

high levels of stress. Physically punished children also tend to have poor relations with their parents, which interferes with the development of trust and attachment. Furthermore, punished children grow up to become abusive parents and spouses, according to research.

There are, therefore, a number of reasons why physical punishment is not effective as a child-rearing technique: It does not teach why behavior is wrong or suggest alternative behaviors; it interferes with the parent's intended message and the internalization of that message by the child; it teaches that the reason to behave is to avoid punishment rather than to understand the positive reasons for appropriate behavior; it models that aggression is acceptable; it sets children up to expect hostile intentions in others; it may lead children to be afraid of their parents, resulting in poor parent–child relations; and it may convey to children that violence is linked with loving relationships.

The results of the numerous studies reviewed in this report reinforce the ineffectiveness of physical punishment as a discipline technique. They also raise concern about the abuse of children who are subject to severe and persistent physical punishment. As a knowledgeable early childhood professional, you can help inform parents about the research on such abuse and provide information on more effective, alternative guidance methods.

discussed that are relevant to other topics covered in this text, similar approaches also have something to say about how adults can best guide children's behaviors. We will discuss three such programs—those of Rudolf Dreikurs, Thomas Gordon, and the behaviorists—each stemming from a very different underlying theory and philosophy and with a different thrust, but also sharing some commonalities.

Dreikurs's Child Guidance Centers

Key Point ◆◆

According to Dreikurs, all children's misbehaviors stem from one of four underlying goals: attention, power, revenge, and inadequacy; the use of logical consequences is one of Dreikurs's most widely used techniques.

Psychiatrist Rudolf Dreikurs, through his Child Guidance Centers, promoted a program based on the work of Alfred Adler (an associate of Sigmund Freud in his early career). Adler's theory that people are goal-seeking organisms led Dreikurs to identify four underlying goals of all misbehavior—attention, power, revenge, and inadequacy (Dreikurs & Soltz, 1964). Thus, in keeping with the psychoanalytic underpinnings of his approach, Dreikurs felt that one cannot effectively change a child's misbehavior without analyzing and understanding which goal motivates the child. All goals, according to Dreikurs, result from feelings of discouragement.

Appropriate reaction to the child's behavior will depend on the child's goal (Dreikurs & Cassel, 1972). For instance, it is best to deal with the child who seeks attention, the usual first step in misbehavior, by ignoring the bid for attention. This is not to say that attention should not be given to the child; on the contrary, attention for positive behavior should be given freely and frequently. But inappropriate bids for attention need to be ignored.

The child who feels that bids for attention are still not providing what is needed will often escalate the behavior pattern and turn to power seeking. To respond to the child whose goal is power, it is best to disengage from any power struggle; a power contest is no contest if you, as the opponent, refuse to participate. Children need to feel important, but the way to establish their importance is not through disobedience, tantrums, and arguments. You can help the child find legitimate and productive ways of asserting that power—not through power plays.

The next step, if the child continues to feel discouraged in attempting to assert those needs, is revenge. The aim at this stage is to get even for feelings of hurt and rejection by hurting others. It is important to recognize that the child's attempts to hurt you reflect the child's own pain; do not let the child see your feelings of hurt, since this will only reinforce the child's actions. Above all, do not retaliate. Instead, work on making the child feel accepted, enlisting another child if appropriate, and be as encouraging as possible.

The fourth goal, inadequacy, is perhaps the easiest to identify as stemming from discouragement. People around the child have often suggested to that child that he is inept, or the child misinterprets environmental cues and comes to such a conclusion (Dreikurs, 1972). To help the child shed such helplessness, you cannot accept these expressions of inadequacy. You continually need to convey encouragement, faith in the child's ability, praise, and support.

Dreikurs suggests that instead of reward and punishment, parents and teachers should use encouragement and logical consequences. Encouragement focuses on increasing children's confidence by accepting them as they are rather than as they might be (Dreikurs & Cassel, 1972). It builds on children's strengths, thus boosting self-esteem. Encouragement is also differentiated from praise; praise focuses on your perception and approval of the child ("I'm so proud of you for helping clean the class!"), whereas encouragement centers on the child's accomplishment and ability ("How nice our classroom looks now!"). Praise rewards the child's action and makes it dependent on your approval; encouragement puts the action in the context of the child's contribution to the total group.

One of the most widely used tools suggested by Dreikurs is **logical consequences.** By allowing children to experience the natural outcome of their actions, you provide a real learning experience. If they do not come to the table for snack, they miss snack; if they do not stay with the group on a walk, they cannot go on the next outing; if children consistently put their shoes on the wrong feet, they will feel uncomfortable. As the teacher, you are not inflicting a punishment in any of these instances; it is within the child's control to change the consequence of the behavior. Logical consequences also follow positive actions and provide natural reinforcement for a variety of prosocial behaviors.

Gordon's Teacher Effectiveness Training

The second guidance approach was developed by Thomas Gordon, a humanistic psychologist. In humanistic psychology, the basic, underlying tenet is mutual respect and acceptance between adult and child (Gordon, 1974, 1976). His books, *P.E.T. [Parent Effectiveness Training] in Action* and *T.E.T.: Teacher Effectiveness Training,* have been used widely. The foundation for mutual respect is laid in early infancy, as adults handle and respond to babies in a way that conveys respect for what they are communicating. According to Gordon, it is important that you, as the adult, identify which behaviors are acceptable and which are not. Then, when a problem arises, you can examine the situation and decide who "owns" the problem; some problems are owned by children, some by adults, and some by the relationship between the two. The method of dealing with the issue will depend on "ownership."

When the child owns the problem, she is sending a cue that something is wrong. In this case, you use **active listening,** a technique in which you reflect on what the child is saying to help the child find his or her own resolution. You respect the child's right to solve his or her own problem and do not solve it for him or her through more standard reactions such as giving advice, moralizing, or distracting. Active listening conveys acceptance and thus encourages the child to reveal the true, underlying cause of his or her distress.

For example, if Carol reacts with an angry outburst when asked to clean up the blocks she has been playing with, your active listening response might be, "You sound awfully angry" rather than, "Carol, I need you to clean up the blocks *now.*" Carol, seeing that you accept her feelings rather than focusing on your own, can respond more openly by acknowledging her anger or by shifting to another cause of her reaction, for instance, "Nobody likes to play with me any more." By listening and reflecting her feelings, you help Carol acknowledge and find her own solutions to her problems.

However, when you, the adult, own the problem, a different technique is called for. If, for instance, Carol does not want to help pick up the blocks because she is more excited about joining the story another teacher is reading to two of her friends in the library area, the problem of the blocks on the floor is yours. In this case, you respond with an **I-message,** telling Carol how you feel, rather than a **you-message,** which focuses on her character. Thus, you might say, "When I find the blocks all over the floor, I'm afraid someone will trip and get hurt, and that really upsets me," rather than, "You are being very irresponsible."

logical consequences
Rudolf Dreikurs's technique of allowing children to experience the natural outcome of their actions.

Key Point ◆
Gordon's approach focuses on building mutual respect and acceptance between child and adult; the type of technique the adult uses depends on whether the problem is "owned" by the child, the adult, or their relationship.

active listening
Thomas Gordon's term for the technique of reflecting back to children what they have said as a way to help them find their own solutions to problems.

I-message
Thomas Gordon's term for a response to a child's behavior that focuses on how the adult feels rather than on the child's character.

you-message
Thomas Gordon's term for a response to a child's behavior that focuses on the child's character (usually in negative terms) rather than on how the adult feels.

Active listening, a technique suggested by Thomas Gordon, is used to help children find solutions to their problems.

When the ownership of the problem is a joint one, belonging to both adult and child, Thomas suggests a third strategy. A process of no-lose problem solving, in which those involved discuss and negotiate until they find a mutually satisfactory resolution, is used.

Behavior Management

naeyc

behavior management
Behavioral approach to guidance holding that the child's behavior is under the control of the environment, which includes space, objects, and people.

Key Point ◆◆

Behavior management is based on the notion that children's behavior can be changed by changing the environment; techniques such as positive reinforcement for desirable behaviors and ignoring for undesirable behaviors are used.

The **behavior management** approach is derived from behavioral theory. The underlying philosophy is that the child's behavior is under the control of the environment (which includes space, objects, and people), which can be changed by the adult through some kind of environmental manipulation. It is based on the notion that the consequences of behavior are vital and that children engage in behaviors that are reinforced and cease behaviors that are not reinforced. A number of techniques have been developed as part of behavior management; some are used frequently in early childhood settings, and we will concentrate our discussion on these. (Recall our discussion of the principles of behaviorism in Chapter 5.)

Behavior management focuses on observable traits that can be noted and measured, such as crying, hitting, or whining, as opposed to unobservable qualities, such as jealousy, insecurity, or separation anxiety. The observable can be defined and is objective rather than relying on subjective interpretation.

When a misbehavior is to be changed, it is carefully measured (for instance, the number of occurrences are counted or the duration is timed) and quantified, as in a graph. If, for instance, Edward has been hitting other children frequently, it is more accurate to know that after two weeks of a behavior management program he has decreased his rate of hitting from an average of five times a day to two times a day than to conclude that the program is not working because Edward is still hitting.

Positive reinforcement is perhaps the most widely used application of behavior management. You use it every time you smile at the children who are playing cooperatively in the dramatic play area, gently touch the head of the child who is engrossed in putting together a puzzle, or say thank you to the children for helping to clean up after snack; such subtle social reinforcers come naturally to most teachers. Your reaction is conveying approval of these behaviors. The principle applied in behavior management is that children will continue to display behaviors for which they get acknowledgment or attention. In behavior management, reinforcers are often used systematically to encourage specified behaviors. If Julio gets positive attention every time he hangs up his coat, he is more likely to repeat the behavior.

To be effective, it is important that reinforcement immediately follow the behavior, although the frequency of reinforcement will vary. When you first attempt to help a child acquire a new behavior (for instance, Julio hanging up his coat when he comes inside), the reinforcement must be applied every time the behavior appears; however, once the child is on the way to remembering to hang up his coat, the reinforcement schedule can be decreased gradually, until eventually Julio is reinforced for this behavior about as frequently as the other children.

ignoring
A principle of behavior management that involves removing all reinforcement for a given behavior to eliminate that behavior.

Positive reinforcement, whether it comes in the form of a hug, a smile, or a thank you, is an effective way to encourage children to continue desirable behaviors.

Just as positive reinforcement strengthens behaviors, withdrawing it, through **ignoring,** or extinction, can weaken and eliminate behaviors. We often inadvertently reinforce a negative behavior by our reactions: frowning when a child shouts in the classroom; repeatedly saying, "Stop shouting, you are disturbing everyone"; or taking the child aside and sitting with her until she promises to stop making noise. Each of these reactions tells children that they have successfully gotten our attention. Ignoring, if it is persistent and complete, can extinguish the behavior. But ignoring is not always the best method to use, particularly if aggression is involved. Aggressive behavior must be dealt with more firmly and quickly for the safety of all involved (Walker, Shea, & Bauer, 2007).

One variant of ignoring is **time-out,** when the child is given time away from both the reinforcement and the stimulation of the classroom. Consistent time-out can be effective in eliminating undesirable behaviors, but it should be used sparingly and only for situations in which the removal of the child is the best response, such as following an angry, aggressive outburst. Time-out, however, should never be used to get rid of the child. Its purpose, according to behaviorist theory, should be to remove the child from the reinforcement of the classroom to decrease the negative behavior.

time-out
Technique in which the child is removed from the reinforcement and stimulation of the classroom.

Modeling, advocated by social learning theorists, is effective because research has told us that children are likely to imitate those they admire and like. Observational learning occurs frequently in the classroom, and we use it when we, as teachers, model politeness, friendliness, and caring, although modeling is not a simple cause-and-effect phenomenon. Certain conditions (for instance, children seeing a model being reinforced) will be more likely to result in imitation of the behavior (Bandura, 1977).

Factors in Selecting a Guidance Technique

Where do you begin? What approach to guidance should you use? The examples we cited are only three of a number of approaches that professionals advocate. Some guidelines may help you select an approach to working with young children.

First, try to think through your own values and expectations as they relate to the care of young children. Do this in the context in which you were reared, because your own background will affect your views. If you were raised in a family that used firmness and fairness, you will most likely bring your own experiences to the task of guiding young children. If your family was authoritarian—you were expected to follow rules because someone bigger than you said these were the rules—then you will need to examine whether you carry this attitude into your work. Self-understanding is very important in working with young children; if you acknowledge your strengths and identify areas you might want to change, you will emerge with a more solid foundation.

As you examine your own values, keep in mind your aim in working with the children whose families have entrusted them to your care. As was stated at the beginning of this chapter, guidance is a long-term process, contributing to the evolution of children into adults. If the aim is to help children develop into caring, competent, self-directed adults, this process begins early in life. What matters is that the guidance principles applied are congruent with the desired outcome.

It is also important to be aware of the philosophy of the early childhood program in which you work. Some follow a specific guidance

Key Point ◆◆

An eclectic approach to guidance allows teachers to select those features of various approaches that work best for them.

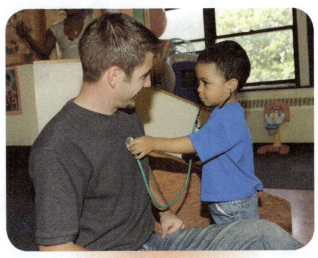

Teachers' own values and background will affect their philosophy of guidance and the way they interact with children.

philosophy for which training is often provided and which all employees are expected to use. If you are comfortable with the philosophy, there is no problem; if you do not agree with the approach, then you have the choice of discussing your reservations with the director or finding another position. Many programs, however, do not have a firmly stated philosophy and rely on the good judgment of the staff.

As we reviewed Dreikurs's, Gordon's, and the behaviorists' approaches to guidance, we discussed the main features of these three divergent philosophies. Good early childhood educators use many of these techniques. When you select the salient features from different programs that you think will work, you are using an **eclectic approach.** Being eclectic, for instance, allows you to use logical consequences, positive reinforcement, and active listening, consciously aware that these are features of different philosophical methods; in so doing, you are developing an approach that works best for you.

Developing a personal style of guidance takes time, and it may well change over the years of your professional involvement and development. What is important is that you are comfortable with the guidance approach you use because it is effective and supports children's development in a positive, nurturing manner.

> **eclectic approach**
> Describing an approach in which various desirable features from different theories or methods are selected; drawing elements from different sources.

SOME TECHNIQUES OF GUIDANCE

Keep in mind that your attitude toward your job and toward children, your skill as a teacher, your ability to be consistent as well as flexible, and a good sense of humor all contribute to setting the tone for the classroom. A respect for all children and a willingness to get to know each child as an individual are basic ingredients in positive guidance. So is a sense of partnership with the children. There is no doubt that you, the teacher, are central to establishing a productive, lively, happy environment for children and adults.

In addition, when children are engrossed in meaningful activities that they find rewarding and interesting, they are much less likely to misbehave. A good curriculum is integrally tied to your guidance approach and will in itself provide a key technique for preventing misbehavior. Similarly, an environment that is stimulating and interesting to children will engross them in constructive ways. Children find satisfaction in meaningful activity.

We have discussed guidance from the viewpoint of what kinds of adults we would like children to grow up to be, within the context of some different philosophical approaches, and as it is related to and distinguished from some other terms. Let us now turn to some specific techniques that can help you better deal with children's behavior.

How Do You Handle Infants?

Babies do not require discipline. It is the responsibility of adults to meet their needs in a way that contributes trust, the underlying prerequisite in the process of socialization. Sometimes infants lose control, reflecting some kind of discomfort or distress rather than a problem behavior. Gonzalez-Mena and Eyer (2012) recommend that babies may need to be held close and tight to help them regain control.

Toddlers, because they are mobile and verbal, require guidance to help them develop control over their impulses. Developing internal control over behavior is a slow, long-term process. It is important to set clear limits for toddlers to ensure their safety and provide a sense of security. DAP confirms this process, stating, "Caregivers patiently redirect toddlers to help guide them toward controlling their own impulses and behaviors" (Copple & Bredekamp, 2009, p. 95). Toddlers are notorious for testing the limits adults impose; without stretching these limits, they cannot find out exactly where the boundaries are (Gonzalez-Mena & Eyer, 2012; Watson & Swim, 2011).

Reinforcement

We examined positive reinforcement from the viewpoint of behavior management as a way to maintain desired behavior. Reinforcement can be a powerful tool for guiding children by attending to them when they are engaged in positive rather than negative behaviors. Be aware, however, that ineffective praise (for example, general or gratuitous statements such as "Good job!" or "Good boy!") can actually be counterproductive to the intended goal (Gartrell, 2011).

Alfie Kohn (2001) argues that phrases like "Good job!" are damaging to children in a number of ways. Such words are manipulative because they are really intended to get the child to conform to the teacher's expectations; they are, in essence, a form of control, benefiting the teacher rather than the child. Kohn also feels that excessive praise can make "praise junkies" of children, increasing their dependence on adults rather than bolstering their self-esteem. In addition, praise takes away the pleasure a child can take in his successes; praise tells the child how to feel rather than allowing the child to experience her own joy in her accomplishments. Praise can also cause children to lose interest in an activity because they begin to do the activity for the praise rather than the enjoyment of the activity itself. Finally, Kohn cites research that tells us that praise actually reduces rather than raises children's achievement, motivating them to get praise rather than accomplish a task. He summarizes his point by underscoring the need of children for unconditional support—"love with no strings attached" (p. 27)—rather than the conditions that praise puts on getting adult attention.

Instead, it is recommended that you use **effective praise,** or encouragement, which focuses on the activity and process, allows children to evaluate their own work, and discourages competition. Following are some examples of encouragement, as proposed by Hitz and Driscoll (1988, p. 12):

> Denise played with Jimmy at the sand table. They experimented with funnels for more than 20 minutes.
> *Encouraging statement:* "You and Jimmy played together for a long time at the sand table."

> Sue seldom talks in the group, but today she told a short story about Halloween.
> *Encouraging statement:* "That was a very scary story you told. When you told that story, I could just picture ghosts in our classroom. It gave me goosebumps."

> Daniel just finished a painting. He comes to you, the teacher, and says, "Look at my painting, isn't it beautiful?"
> *Encouraging statement:* "You look happy about your painting. Look at all the colors you used."

naeyc

Key Point ◆◆
Reinforcement should never be given gratuitously or thoughtlessly. Rather, for praise to be effective it must be personalized to what the child is doing in a way that is encouraging.

effective praise
A form of encouragement that focuses on children's activities rather than on teacher evaluation of their work; praise that is meaningful to children rather than general or gratuitous.

Effective praise focuses on the child's activity and accomplishment. Thus, the teacher may comment on the combination of colors or shapes, or the techniques used in the activity rather than give a gratuitous statement of praise.

© Cengage Learning

Attention

unconditional attention
A way of conveying acceptance to children by letting them know they are valued and liked; attention that is not given in response to a specific behavior.

Key Point ◆

Whereas positive reinforcement is given as a consequence for a desirable behavior, unconditional attention is not linked to any particular behavior. It conveys to children that they are valued as people in their own right.

Reinforcement is a form of attention, but attention is more than reinforcement. Reinforcement is conditional on the child responding in a specific way; but children also need **unconditional attention.** Such attention makes an enormous difference to a child. Unconditional acceptance and response begin in earliest infancy and lay the foundation for feelings of trust. As a result, many children, receiving such attention in ample supply at home, have strong, trusting relationships in their lives. These children usually come to school full of independence and openness to new experiences. Other children, whose foundation for trust is not as firmly established or has been shaken by a disruptive experience such as divorce, may seem unduly demanding; they may constantly seek your attention, possibly through misbehavior.

Most often, a child who engages in a lot of attention-getting behavior is expressing a need for attention. It is not wise to provide attention when a child expresses that need through some form of misbehavior; that only reinforces the child's mistaken notion that the main way to get attention is to do something unacceptable. Such attention is generally negative and will not help the child feel good about himself. Two kinds of attention should be provided instead. One is reinforcement of appropriate behavior, as we have already discussed. The other is unconditional attention.

Unconditional attention tells the child that you value *her*, as a person in her own right, not just because she behaves as you want her to behave. You can give unconditional attention in a number of ways. Many teachers express it as they greet children at the beginning of the day with genuine statements such as, "Good morning, Jenny! I'm so glad to see you!" During the day, teachers also provide such attention when they smile at, hug, cuddle, or soothe a child or when they respond to the child who requests help or attention.

special time
A method for spending a few minutes a day with just one child as a way of providing unconditional attention.

One mechanism for providing unconditional attention to a child who particularly seems to need extra attention is **special time** (Essa, 2007). The teacher sets aside just a few minutes a day, or even two or three times a week, just for the child. This one-on-one time is *not* conditional on the child behaving in a particular way (for instance, "If you _____, then we will spend special time") but is unconditional, not at all tied to the child's behavior. Special time should be planned just for the child alone with the teacher. The teacher conveys the message, "I want to spend time with just you because you are you." The teacher can ask what the child would like to do for special time and then follow up on that suggestion, whether it is going for a short walk, reading a book, or playing a game; the specific activity is less important than the teacher's undivided attention during this time together.

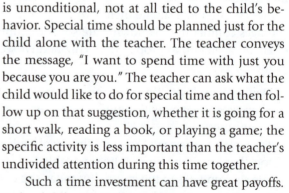

Such a time investment can have great payoffs. Early childhood teachers who have used special time with children who seem to be seeking extra attention have found that these children seem to feel better about themselves and greatly decrease their acting-out behavior. Some schools also recommend this method to families, with the result that children whose parents regularly spend a few minutes in one-on-one interaction with them seem much more self-assured and secure.

Special time, during which an adult spends a few minutes giving undivided attention to one child, can have great payoffs.

Ignoring

Another behavioral technique that early childhood teachers use frequently is ignoring, although it is always important to pay attention to the removal of the behavior, especially to a behavior that is opposite to the one you are trying to remove. For instance, if you ignore Lily's whining, be sure to provide appropriate attention when she speaks without whining. The principle of extinguishing a behavior by removing all reinforcement works well in many instances in which the behavior can safely be ignored, when all adults consistently and totally ignore the behavior, and when the child is not getting reinforcement for the behavior from other sources.

You need to think carefully about whether ignoring is the best tactic to use when you are examining a behavior of concern. Ignoring works well for annoying behaviors that are clearly a bid for your attention. Such behaviors, however, should not harm or potentially harm the child or other children. Persistent and repeated instances of whining, pouting, baby talk, crying as a means of getting attention, tantrums (for younger preschoolers), and deliberately creating annoying noises are some examples of behaviors that can be changed through ignoring.

In all of these instances, let the child know clearly that you will not respond to the attention-getting behavior, but also tell the child clearly how to get your attention. It is important to provide attention when the child asks you a question without whining or requests your interaction without pouting, particularly at first, to show the child that appropriate behavior can be rewarding.

For ignoring to be effective, attention needs to be totally removed. This means that all teachers in the class have to agree to use ignoring. It is counterproductive if you remove attention from the child who throws a tantrum and another teacher goes to the child and attends in the old ways. Before using this technique then, all teachers should discuss the behavior thoroughly, agree on an approach, and help each other stick to implementing it. A caution about ignoring: one problem that makes this technique difficult to use is that the child, who has been used to getting attention for a given behavior, will often redouble his efforts and increase the behavior to regain the old response, so the behavior gets worse before it gets better. Ignoring, therefore, should not be tried for a day or two and then deemed a failure.

Ignoring works only if your attention, as the teacher, is the main source of reinforcement for the behavior. If the child is getting reinforcement from other sources (for instance, the other children) ignoring will probably not work. Before using it, check what the child seems to expect as a result of the behavior. Does David look at you or another adult before he throws the blocks across the room? If he does, your attention is what he is most likely expecting for his efforts. If, however, other children laugh every time he engages in the behavior, and this brings out a little smile on his face, ignoring probably will not be very effective.

Time-Out

Although consistent ignoring should gradually eliminate an undesirable behavior, behaviorists recommend time-out as a method for speeding up the removal of reinforcement that maintains the behavior. Time-out should be used only

naeyc

Key Point ◆
Particularly for attention-seeking and annoying behavior, ignoring can be an effective technique; however, any time a behavior is ignored, the attention that is withdrawn through the ignoring has to be given at other times in a positive way.

naeyc

when a child engages in a behavior consistently, not for one-time occurrences. It is also most effective when used infrequently and for short durations, two to three minutes. Time-out has been shown to be most effective when paired with ample attention for appropriate social interactions.

Many early childhood educators feel that time-out is not an effective method of discipline because it does not help children learn positive alternatives to inappropriate behavior. Gartrel (2011) suggests using social problem solving as an alternative. The adult guides the child in learning the skills he needs to learn from his mistakes. Central to this approach is mediation, in which the affected parties brainstorm solutions.

Time-out is usually carried out in an identified location, such as a chair placed in an area of the classroom with the least amount of stimulation and chance for reinforcement. If the child engages in a behavior such as hitting, the teacher matter-of-factly takes the child to the time-out area, calmly explains the reason for being removed, then leaves the child there for a few minutes. The teacher tells the child, "You hit Arthur. Hitting is not allowed in our class, so you will have to sit here until I tell you that you may get up." After a few minutes, the teacher gets the child from the time-out area and helps that child find an activity in which to engage.

It should be reemphasized that time-out should not be overused. It should also never be considered the primary method of disciplining children, although it seems to be the most prevalent disciplinary method used in many child care centers. In one study (Essa, 2000), teachers of young children were asked to discuss the discipline methods they regularly use. Time-out was the most frequently mentioned method, although many of the teachers seemed to be very ambivalent about whether it is an appropriate or effective technique.

self-selected time-out
A technique in which children are given the responsibility for removing themselves from the classroom if they feel they are about to lose control.

One variation of this is **self-selected time-out** (Essa, 2007), in which children are given the responsibility of removing themselves from the class if they sense that they are about to lose control. In one center, a child who seemed to be overly affected by the stimulation of a busy, active preschool classroom was given the option to remove himself from the class whenever he felt upset. He was able to go to a nearby office, which was equipped with a small table and some low-key toys. It was made clear to him that coming to this room was not a punishment but an aid to help him regain control. The opportunity to remove himself from the class when he felt the need made all the difference for this three-year-old, whose frequent tantrums and disruptive behaviors decreased dramatically. Gartrell (2011) also suggests self-removal as a way of dealing with repeated behaviors. He cites an example of a "peace island," where children can go when they need a few calm minutes. He emphasizes that this approach is not a punishment.

naeyc

Prevention

It is much easier on you, as the teacher, as well as on children to prevent problems before they occur. Prevention is an excellent guidance technique because you step in to stop a potential problem before tempers flare. One way to use preventive guidance is to keep an eye on as much of the group as possible; both inside and on the playground, position yourself with your back to a wall or fence where you can watch the majority of the children, even though in general you are with an individual child

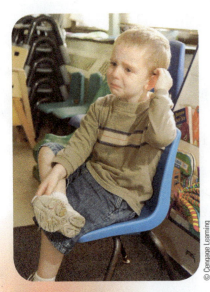

Time-out is a technique, recommend by behaviorists, in which the child is removed for a few minutes from the stimulation and reinforcement of the class. If used at all, it should be used very sparingly.

© Cengage Learning

or a small group. Prevention is particularly important at the beginning of the school year, when you set expectations for the rest of the year. It is an especially effective technique to use with toddlers and young preschoolers, who are just beginning to acquire self-control and learn about social expectations.

Also know what triggers certain children's problem behaviors. If Shane tends to hit others when he gets frustrated, be available when you see him trying a difficult puzzle; if Rhonda cries when she does not get to be "Mommy" in housekeeping play, be available to guide children's role selection if needed; if Susannah has a difficult time sharing, keep a close eye on the block area when you see Andy approaching Susannah to join her construction project. You are not stepping in to solve the children's problems but are being available to guide them if needed in learning problem-solving skills.

Key Point ◆
Prevention is an excellent guidance technique in which the teacher steps in when noting a potential problem situation before the problem actually occurs.

Redirection

One way to prevent potential problems is by redirection. For instance, if Sylvia is about to kick over the block tower, distract her by steering her to the water table, or provide Yusuf with an alternative toy to replace the one he is about to snatch from Richie. Redirection works particularly well with toddlers and very young preschoolers, whose self-control is just emerging and who do not yet have the verbal and social skills required for sharing. Sensitive teachers can help one- and two-year-olds develop these attributes over time and through many positive interactions. Redirection should not be used routinely with older children, however, who need guidance and practice in handling social situations effectively (Essa, 2007).

Distraction through humor is used very effectively by some teachers. Many potential "me-against-you" situations can be avoided by using the light touch—distraction to something interesting and fun, directions in the form of a jingle or song, or a joke (not at the child's expense, of course).

Humor helps avoid power struggles because the teacher and children are joint participants in a fun-filled friendship. Telling a child, "Now . . . let . . . me . . . see . . . you . . . walk . . . slow . . . slow . . . like . . . a . . . turtle" will be more effective than saying, "How many times do I have to tell you not to run in the classroom?"

Key Point ◆
Toddlers and younger preschoolers can sometimes be distracted from a potential problem situation, although this should not be used at the expense of helping children learn problem-solving techniques.

Key Point ◆
Some older children respond well to talking about their problem behavior, particularly if they feel motivated to change this behavior with help from the teacher.

Discussion

Talking about behavior can be effective with some children. A teacher can often enlist the child's help in changing an undesirable behavior by discussing it with the child. Older preschoolers and primary children often respond well to such discussion, particularly if they have adequate verbal skills, the budding ability to look at themselves, and the motivation to change a behavior that makes them unhappy. In essence, the teacher and child form a partnership: the child agrees to try to make some behavioral changes, while the teacher promises to support the child and be there to help or remind.

Sometimes children are ready to discuss a specific behavior because they are motivated to change it. The child and the teacher, in essence, become partners in their attempt to help the child change the behavior.

BECOMING A GROUP MEMBER

With the regular kindergarten teacher on maternity leave, this was truly our first opportunity as solo teachers. I (Jenna) was completing my internship for my early childhood education degree and working alongside Colin, a fourth-year student who was working on his elementary education degree. The majority of the teaching experiences shared by the two of us involved a recycled art-learning project designed by Jenna. The goal of the project was to allow young children an opportunity to manipulate unusual and unwanted materials into unique, personally engaging artistic creations. With the introduction of the recycled objects, the children excitedly envisioned a project that would be the focus of many weeks in the classroom. This new direction brought with it many challenges—not only for the children, but also for us, as teachers.

One project involved five children working collaboratively to create a model of our city. Within this group, a focus on teamwork quickly emerged as we planned to begin the city. Almost immediately, one child found it difficult to engage in the group work. Her participation in group planning was positive; however, the focus of her interest tended to be on her own ideas rather than on participating in a collaborative group

Jenna and Colin, Kindergarten Student Teachers

© Theresa Danna Douglas

effort. We knew that recent family changes were affecting her behavior. It became evident while working on the project that she needed beneficial redirection.

She struggled to find a focus on tasks while creating the city. In her desire to please herself and the teachers, she placed things constantly on the project without concern for the final result or the goals of her peers. As teachers, we strived to give the children daily opportunities in which they could make open-ended choices. This resulted in directly influencing their work. In this child's case, Jenna decided to meet with her and discuss the problematic situation that was now affecting the creation of the city.

As we worked with her, we began to realize that the most effective tools we had

as teachers were discussions in which we detailed our expectations. Simply by verbalizing our concerns and allowing the other group members to share their feelings, the child responded almost immediately with positive results. We explained the importance of taking time in the work, setting mutual goals as a group, and collaborating as a whole. The child soon found a focus in acting as the foreman for the city construction project; she even displayed a newfound desire to maintain the project checklist describing the daily completion of construction.

This experience truly helped us, as first-year teachers, put into actual practice the idea that all children learn in varying and unique ways. In the case of this child, taking into account her social background and behavior in the class—while simultaneously developing a suitable role and direction for her in the recycled art project—was key. We both agreed that we had to step beyond our initial assessments of child behavior and realize the profound effect our expectations have on individual as well as group work. By using the vital techniques of redirection and the stating of expectations, we were able to successfully support this child's positive contribution to her collaborative project.

Problem Solving

Our goal for children is that they eventually learn constructive ways of dealing with and resolving conflicts, whether among themselves or with adults. Teachers can help children develop creative problem-solving skills and strategies. Earlier in this chapter, we reviewed Thomas Gordon's approach to guidance. One of Gordon's strategies involves a no-lose method of conflict resolution in which the outcome ensures that both parties are winners and no one is a loser.

The teacher's role in implementing this method begins with helping children identify and clarify the problem, which is done best through active listening. Children are then enlisted in brainstorming some possible ways of dealing with the problem, evaluating these possibilities, selecting the one that best satisfies both parties, and finding ways of implementing and affirming the solution. The key to this approach is to avoid having one person, child or adult, impose his or her position on the other person. This method conveys a sense of mutual respect based on the equality of both rather than on the power of one over the other.

This teacher is helping these girls develop effective problem-solving skills by encouraging them to identify their concerns and find a mutually agreeable resolution.

naeyc

Key Point ◆◆

The long-range goal, which is that children learn constructive ways of solving problems, can involve a no-lose method of conflict resolution.

naeyc

WHAT IS THE DIFFERENCE BETWEEN NORMAL AND PROBLEM BEHAVIOR?

When you view guidance as an ongoing process that contributes to the socialization of the child, it is easier to consider a solution to a problem behavior as a change that has a far-reaching impact, rather than as a stopgap measure to make your class run more smoothly. Although many children go through temporary periods in their early years that can be difficult for the adults around them, children pass through these without too many residual effects. The challenging stage of many twos, for instance, often dissolves within a few months into a period of cooperation. But some behaviors persist and become more problematic as children get older. It is such behaviors that we will discuss in this section.

Problem behaviors are one of the greatest challenges facing teachers of young children. Remember that all children test the limits at times. Some children, although they misbehave, can easily be rerouted by the adults around them. Other children have identifiable challenges (for instance, diagnosed attention deficit–hyperactivity disorder) that give direction as to the handling of problem behaviors. Some children, however, totally frustrate all their teachers' attempts to deal with them. Teachers can go through a series of up-and-down feelings about their own competence as they try to cope with such children in the classroom.

But which behaviors are normal, and which should send up a red flag? Some guidelines follow that can help you make that distinction.

Key Point ◆◆

All children misbehave at times; the early childhood educator, using child development knowledge and exploring available information, distinguishes between normal behaviors and those that merit concern and intervention.

▶❙❙ **TeachSource Video Activity**
WATCH • REFLECT • RESPOND

This video discusses positive guidance approaches. Go to CengageBrain.com and view the video titled, "Preschool: Emotional Development," and answer the following questions:

1. Why is it important to help children understand their emotions?

2. What techniques to prevent problems did the teacher in the video use?

▪ Know the developmental stages of the children in your class, particularly as they relate to social, emotional, and moral development. Many children of a given age go through a phase that will most likely pass. Many toddlers go through a stage in which they assert their growing autonomy by throwing spectacular tantrums, which gradually taper off and disappear as children

All young children misbehave at times. It is important, however, to recognize signs that distinguish the normal testing of limits from behavior problems that signal a more serious difficulty. As you have interacted with young children, have you felt that some behaviors go beyond the limits of normal behavior?

gain better inner control. Similarly, four-year-olds, with their ingenious imaginations and elaborate world of fantasy, often have the propensity to blur the line between truth and nontruth; but this certainly does not predict a life of dishonesty and pathological lying.

- Realistic expectations for the age group, tempered by recognition of individual variations among children, are important. However, if a child appears extremely immature in relation to her peers—for instance, a four-year-old who acts more like a two- to three-year-old in social behavior—the child may be developmentally delayed, particularly if other areas of development also are delayed.

- Be aware that young boys often have a harder time meeting the expectations of the early childhood classrooms than girls do. According to King and Gartrell (2003), boys often need more physical activity and "may be developmentally younger by 6 to 18 months than girls" (p. 33). The authors suggest making allowances in the environment and curriculum for ample large motor engagement, building and construction activities, and sensory exploration.

- Look for signs of possible medical causes for problem behaviors. As we will discuss later in this chapter, a chronic infection, allergy, nutritional deficiency, or sensory deficit can profoundly affect behavior. If, in addition to disruptive social behavior, the child frequently rubs the eyes, winces when urinating, or appears unduly clumsy, consider a possible link between the social behavior and an underlying health problem.

- When the behavior of a child in your class is out of hand so frequently that you feel there is a preponderance of negative experiences between you and the child, it is probably time to bring in professional assistance to help you deal with the situation. This holds particularly true if other teachers who are generally very effective in dealing with children share your experience and feel as baffled and frustrated by this child as you do. If a child is so frequently disruptive and not able to get along in the early childhood program without continuous help, that child needs professional, one-to-one help that cannot be given in a group school setting.

- We generally notice children who are acting out because they force our attention to their behavior. But also be alert to the extremely withdrawn child who stays away from social interactions, is reluctant to participate in activities, avoids eye contact, or refuses to talk. Many children are shy and exhibit reluctance in social situations; however, extreme withdrawal might signal a deeper problem for which help should be sought.

- A child whose behavior changes suddenly and drastically may be signaling a problem requiring attention. You should feel concerned about the generally happy, outgoing child who suddenly becomes antisocial, or the active, assertive child who inexplicably becomes withdrawn and passive, particularly if the changed behavior persists for more than a few days and is not a sign of illness. Your first source of information, of course, is the child's family. But if they too are baffled, a more thorough search for the cause of the change is in order.

Finally, if you notice unexplainable bruises, abrasions, cuts, or burns on a child, consider the possibility of child abuse. Other forms of abuse do not leave physical scars but are just as damaging. Unfortunately, far too many children are subject to physical, verbal, and sexual abuse and neglect. An abused child usually also exhibits behavioral symptoms of the problem. If you have reason to suspect child abuse, speak to your director so the concern can be followed up by notifying the appropriate authorities. (We will discuss this issue further in the next chapter.)

When competent teachers find that a particular child's behavior is just beyond their coping capacity, it is time to look to outside resources. It is wise to remember that many community professionals, in addition to early childhood teachers, share responsibility for the care and guidance of young children. Medical, mental health, special education, and social work professionals provide an expanded network of resource persons to call on in any community.

BRAIN STORM
FEELING GOOD

The emotional climate of the classroom, which is controlled by the teachers, has a great deal to do with children's behavior and learning. If children feel safe and relaxed in the environment, they are more likely to behave in positive ways than if they feel threatened or unnoticed in the class. When children's feelings about their school environment are positive, endorphins are released into the brain, making learning more enjoyable. They are more likely to experience success and behave in ways that the teacher, whom they regard in a positive way, expects. On the other hand, when children feel stressed about their school environment, the hormone, cortisol, is released into the blood and brain, resulting in defensive and negative behaviors and little attention to learning (Sousa, 2006). Your role, as a teacher of young children, includes the responsibility of ensuring the emotional well-being of all the children.

FACTORS THAT AFFECT CHILDREN'S BEHAVIOR

In dealing with a child's misbehavior, it is important to examine all potential factors that might be affecting that behavior. All kinds of subtle influences, some internal and others external, undoubtedly contribute to behavior. Particularly when you are concerned about a repeated misbehavior, it is wise to give careful thought to what might be triggering the problem. It is easy to blame children for challenging behaviors—"he is aggressive" or "she is disruptive"—and look no further for reasons before working to eliminate the problem. But the approach to changing a problem behavior is often in the control of the adult rather than the child. A number of factors can cause some children to act out, as discussed below.

Clear-Cut Guidelines

According to DAP, it is important for teachers to set clear limits about unacceptable behavior, enforce such limits with explanations about their underlying rationale, and enforce them in a climate of respect and caring (Copple &

Key Point ◆◆

Many times the causes of misbehavior are not within the control of the child but come from some source beyond the child's ability to change.

Key Point ❖

Children need to understand what is expected of them; a few clear-cut and logical rules will help children comply with such expectations.

Key Point ❖

When children are not feeling well, they may respond with unacceptable behaviors; other physiological factors that can affect behavior include allergies, sensory deficits, and poor nutrition.

allergies
Physiological reactions to environmental or food substances that can affect or alter behavior.

sensory deficit
A problem, particularly of sight or hearing.

Bredekamp, 2009). Children generally abide by rules if they are logical, simple, and not too numerous. There is no need to overwhelm children with too many rules. Four to six simple rules, focused on personal safety and respect for the rights of others, can be set with the help of the children, posted in the classroom, and discussed periodically. Chapter 14 discusses rules in the context of group guidance in more detail.

Sometimes children's behavior is a function of not understanding what is expected. When a child engages in a new misbehavior, do not jump to the conclusion that the child is misbehaving deliberately. The child may simply be acting out of ignorance or misunderstanding of the expectations of the setting. Make sure that the child understands the expectations.

Health and Related Problems

Children often react in unacceptable ways because their bodies are not functioning well or are sending messages of discomfort or pain. When children do not feel well, they cannot be expected to behave normally. Think how you feel when your stomach is upset, your head hurts, or your nose is stuffy. Most of us become very irritable under such circumstances, and children are no different. In fact, children have fewer resources for controlling their behavior when they do not feel well (Essa, 2007).

When infants are unduly fussy or children are misbehaving, consider whether they might be feeling unwell. Ill children should not be at school where they can infect others; but many children have debilitating, chronic health problems such as asthma or low-grade infections, and in spite of them, they continue to attend school. It is important to know what health limitations children might have and to understand emergency medical procedures, if these are called for.

Many children are also affected by environmental or food **allergies,** which can change their behavior in unpredictable ways. "Young children are particularly susceptible to food allergies and intolerances because their digestive and immune systems are immature" (Holland, 2004, p. 42). It is not uncommon for children to be allergic to dust, animal hair, milk, eggs, peanuts, wheat, or other food products, and if exposed to these, children may respond by being cranky or overactive, or by having a short attention span. Be aware of children's allergies, their reactions if inadvertently exposed to an allergen, and measures that should be taken in such a case.

Some children have an undetected **sensory deficit** that may be affecting their behavior. Could the clumsy child who is unwilling to try anything new have a vision deficit? Might the child who is often distractible and seems to ignore what you tell him have trouble hearing? If you suspect a vision or hearing problem, discuss your concerns with the director and the child's parents. Some children's behavior may be related to exposure to any of a variety of substances during their prenatal development. Children exposed prenatally to alcohol, nicotine, some prescription drugs, and many illicit drugs may suffer permanent effects. Restlessness, poor ability to attend to tasks, short attention span, lack of impulse control, and other symptoms may appear to be behavior problems that the child can control but are, in reality, side effects of a circumstance they inherited at birth. Nutrition, both the quality and the quantity of food, is another factor that can affect children's behavior (Simontacchi, 2007). A child who comes to school hungry will be irritable or listless; a basic physiological need must be met before that child can be expected to participate effectively. A child

A child's inattention to what the teachers say may be a result of a sensory defect (for instance, inability to hear well or distinguish sounds), not a sign of deliberate misbehavior.

© Cengage Learning

whose diet is imbalanced and lacks certain nutrients may not work to his or her potential or may misbehave. Studies have linked nutrition to behavior and learning. In our society, children from all social strata are at risk for malnutrition and undernutrition. Although children from low-income families may not get proper nutrients because of the cost factor, middle-class children often subsist on a diet high in sugar, fats, additives and preservatives, and empty calories, putting them at risk also (American Academy of Pediatrics, 1999).

Individual Temperament

To a large degree, children's personalities are molded by their environment, but research has also shown that children are born with a certain temperament, which persists and affects them as they grow up (Thomas & Chess, 1969). Behavior is often a by-product of the child's inborn temperamental disposition, further shaped by how people have reacted to the child. More recently, different temperaments have been found to show different brain activity. Children displaying more negative temperaments showed higher levels of activity in parts of the right side of the brain, while those exhibiting more positive traits had greater activity on the left side of the brain (Bates, 2000).

In their classic study, Thomas, Chess, and Birch (1968), after extensive and in-depth observations and interviews of children beginning in their infancy, classified children into three general categories: easy, slow to warm up, and difficult. They concluded that the largest group in their sample—40 percent—were classified as easy children, whereas 15 percent belonged to the slow-to-warm-up category and 10 percent to the difficult category; 35 percent of the children did not fit neatly into any of these categories.

Easy children, from their earliest days, follow a regular cycle in sleeping, eating, and eliminating; are readily adaptable to change and are open to new experiences; have a reasonable attention span; are easily distractible; display a moderate level of activity; are not overly sensitive to stimuli in their environment; and have a generally happy disposition. Difficult children, however, show opposite traits such as irregularity, intensity in reactions, an inability to adapt, a high activity level, and they are often out of sorts. Slow-to-warm-up children fall in between these two extremes.

It is not easy to deal with difficult children because they often defy all attempts to pacify or engage them. "Children with a bold or impulsive temperament often find it difficult to adjust to the self-control needed in the school setting" (Watson, 2003, p. 14). As you pursue your early childhood teaching career, you likely will be entrusted with one or more temperamentally difficult children. Many beginning (as well as veteran) teachers have found this to be a real test of their self-confidence. Keep in mind that consistent, positive guidance skills and ingenuity can help channel the child's energy, perhaps into a leadership role, rather than into that of an unhappy outcast. Rely on your teaching strengths, examine and acknowledge your own feelings, and then continue to view each child—whether easy or difficult—as an individual worthy of your respect and support.

The Child's Family

A child's behavior may be a reaction to stress or change at home. A large number of young children experience their parents' divorce, enter a single-parent family where there will most likely be financial as well as emotional stresses, or

naeyc

Key Point ◆

Children are born with individual temperaments—some basically easy, others difficult—that affect how they respond to the world around them. Difficult children generally have a harder time complying with expectations; in turn, adults find it more challenging to deal with such children.

naeyc

Children are born with different temperaments. Some have an easygoing, even disposition; others have a more difficult temperament with more extreme reactions.

© Cengage Learning

Key Point ◆

Children's misbehavior may be a reaction to stress they are experiencing at home. A variety of family changes, including divorce, a new sibling, or a parent's job loss, can upset children because they sense their parents' distress.

experience reconstitution of a family as one of their natural parents remarries. Such major changes, even when parents are very sensitive to and mindful of the needs and feelings of their youngsters, are invariably upsetting to children who cannot fully understand what is happening. Other changes, such as a new baby in the family, a visit from grandparents, a parent away on a business trip, the death of a family member or pet, or moving to a new house, can also trigger behavioral responses. (These topics are discussed further in Chapter 16, in which we will examine stress and young children.)

It is important to maintain frequent and open communication with families to find out what is happening at home. If you know that Eddie's parents are heading toward a divorce, you can better understand his sudden angry outbursts; or you can see why Lisa is suddenly sucking her thumb and clinging to you since her baby brother was born. You cannot put Eddie's family back together or make Lisa's brother disappear, but you can convey to the children that you understand their distress and are there for them. If Eddie hits out at other children, you can let him know that you do not condone his behavior and will take measures to stop it, but that you do acknowledge his pain.

DIVERSITY

It is also important to be mindful of diverse perspectives on guidance, especially in families from a culture that is different from yours. The values of different cultural groups are reflected in guidance and discipline strategies. Some groups value independence while others value interdependence, some value compliance while others value assertiveness, and some believe in physical punishment for infractions while others are very indulgent of children's behaviors (Klein & Chen, 2001). Janet Gonzalez-Mena and Intisar Shareef (2005) suggest that teachers need to recognize that "multiple realities exist and that opposing perspectives can all be valid, understand that context affects truth, see beyond perspectives to a larger unifying picture, have faith that it is possible to come together across differences ..., work on relationships, and have patience" (p. 38).

Attachment Disorders

naeyc

One of the most important tasks for a young child is to develop a secure attachment to a stable, significant adult, usually the mother. Children's quality of attachment can fall anywhere on a continuum from securely attached to totally unattached. Children who form particularly negative attachments, or no attachment, generally do so as the result of early trauma, such as abuse or neglect, excessive punishment, hostile or rejecting parents, or parents who suffer from depression (Watson & Swim, 2011). Such children are often diagnosed as having an **attachment disorder,** which is marked by disturbed and inappropriate social relations. Their behavior may show one of two extremes—some children show extreme withdrawal and resistance to any kind of approach or comfort from adults; others show complete lack of selectivity in attachment and inappropriate and excessive familiarity with any adults who may be nearby. Both types have trouble forming meaningful relationships with adults or other children (Keith & Campbell, 2000).

attachment disorders
Problems in establishing a secure attachment can result in later disturbed and inappropriate social relations.

Based on their history, children with insecure attachment seem to expect little from adults. Early childhood teachers, however, can have a positive influence on children with problematic attachment. Carollee Howes (1999) considers that children form attachment networks because of the many contexts in which children are placed, including child care. Teachers serve as attachment figures, providing consistent physical and emotional care (Bowman, Donovan,

Key Point ◆

Children's behavior may be affected by an attachment disorder, when children fail to accomplish one of the important tasks of earliest childhood, the formation of a secure attachment with a significant adult, usually the mother.

& Burns, 2001), and can even ameliorate a negative attachment relationship between the child and mother. When faced with challenging behavior from a child with insecure attachment, teachers need to find minimally coercive ways of helping the child find alternative behaviors. A child who is already mistrustful of adults needs to be helped to learn acceptable behaviors through gentle, not punitive, guidance (Watson & Swim, 2011).

DEALING WITH SPECIFIC BEHAVIOR CHALLENGES

As an early childhood teacher, you will encounter many behavior challenges in your career. We will examine two such concerns in this chapter. We will first discuss children who are aggressive, because such behavior is probably the one that most concerns and ignites adults' emotions, and then we will discuss children who are shy or uninvolved.

naeyc

Aggressive Children

naeyc

Children who exhibit **aggression** deliberately hurt others. It is their intent to hurt that makes the act aggressive, not just the fact that someone was hurt, although the unobservable "intent" is difficult to assign. Because of this difficulty, intention is generally just one criterion in the definition of aggression; others include the antecedents of the act, its form and intensity, the extent of injury, and the role of both victim and perpetrator.

aggression
Behavior deliberately intended to hurt others.

One thing that makes dealing with aggression so difficult is an ethical dilemma, the potentially conflicting needs of the total group for a reasonably safe and peaceful environment and the child's need for appropriate guidance (Feeney, 1988). Countless teachers who cope with aggressive behaviors each day have used many approaches to decrease it; these methods often prove effective, although equally often they do not. Some guidelines for dealing with aggressive behaviors follow.

Key Point ◆

Aggressive children deliberately hurt others; aggression should never be acceptable and teachers can use a variety of strategies to change aggressive behavior.

▶ **Under no circumstances should aggression be acceptable.** A classroom rule should ensure each child's right not to be hurt, spell out a child's responsibility not to hurt others, and underline the teachers' obligation to make aggression unacceptable. Stating such a rule lets everyone know that if a child hurts another, the behavior is not condoned and will be dealt with.

▶ **Aggression should never be ignored.** It is equally important to recognize that simply ignoring aggression will not make it go away. When an adult does not respond to an aggressive act, the child is given the subtle message that the adult approves of the behavior.

▶ **Prevention through vigilance is important in handling aggression.** If you know that a child engages in frequent aggression, it makes sense to keep an eye on that child. Be prepared to avert trouble if you see it brewing. You may be able to mediate an argument, or you may have to restrain the child who is raising a fist to hit out.

Providing frequent and consistent positive attention to children is one way to discourage aggressive behaviors. Children tend to repeat behaviors that are reinforced.

❯ **When the child is not being aggressive, it is important to take time to work on acceptable alternative behaviors.** Some children who engage in aggressive behaviors also exhibit good prosocial skills, indicating that they perhaps participate in more social interactions of all kinds. Such children will need careful guidance to channel them toward using the more positive skills they already have mastered in their interpersonal behavior. Other children, however, have a limited repertoire of social skills and need to be taught more systematically how to play with others, how to share, or how to be gentle. This can be done both through modeling and coaching of appropriate social responses. Careful observation will tell you whether an aggressive child has adequate social skills or whether that child needs your help to learn them.

❯ **The aggressive child should be provided with positive attention.** A child who uses excessive aggression often needs to unlearn the idea that the main way to gain teacher attention is to hurt someone else. It is important to reinforce appropriate social behaviors systematically as well as to provide a message of acceptance through unconditional attention; for instance, through special time. Furthermore, DAP notes that children who exhibit behavior problems "may be especially affected by the quality of the teacher–child relationship, benefiting tremendously from teachers who promote both closeness and independence" (Copple & Bredekamp, 2009, p. 265).

❯ **Environmental factors that may contribute to aggression should be minimized.** Many children's aggression seems to be heightened when they are in a crowded situation. Think through ahead of time how group size can be controlled (for instance, only four children at a time at the woodworking table), position an adult next to a child who seems sensitive to the proximity of others during circle time, or plan circle time with smaller groups rather than all the children at once. Adequate amounts of equipment and materials can also help minimize frustration and potential aggression. Finally, another environmental problem that can lead to aggression is an inappropriate schedule, particularly if children are not given enough opportunity to expend physical energy or if they are expected to sit passively for too long.

bullying
Behavior intended to harm the victim, which occurs repeatedly over time and involves a more powerful person attacking a less powerful person.

BULLYING. Aggressive behavior can turn into **bullying,** a serious problem that has gained increasing attention in recent years, and has been researched in depth through a large-scale study by the National Institute of Child Health and Human Development (Nansel, Overpeck, Pilla, Ruan, Simons-Morton, & Scheidt, 2001). Bullying is defined as "a type of behavior intended to harm or disturb the victim . . . . behavior that occurs repeatedly over time and involves an imbalance of power, with the more powerful person or group attacking the less powerful one" (NIH News Release, 2006).

naeyc

While bullying is particularly prevalent in elementary and secondary schools, it is also found in early childhood programs. It has become the most common type of violence experienced by children (Gartrell, 2011). However, researcher Richard Tremblay argues that "high quality preschool programs are more likely the cure for, not the cause of, bullying behavior (NIEER, 2003). Tremblay considers that during the early years, as their neurological structures mature, children learn to control their natural aggressive impulses. Teachers in high-quality early childhood programs help children learn self-control by channeling aggression into more constructive solutions, for instance, using words and negotiating with peers (Tremblay, 2006).

Teachers should have a zero tolerance policy toward bullying (Tips to Stop Bullying, 2011). Darla Miller (2010) suggests the following to prevent bullying: create a positive, calm environment; provide positive role models; support nurturing peer relationships; help children recognize and understand emotions, whether their own or others'; find ways to strengthen children's self-esteem; help children accurately perceive social situations so they can respond appropriately; help children learn to understand the consequences of their actions, especially aggressive ones; and help children learn to use group processes to resolve social problems (pp. 301–302). In addition, "clear boundaries and consistent expectations are prime ingredients" for working with children who are bullies (Kostelnik, Gregory, Soderman, & Whiren, 2012, p. 383).

TODDLERS WHO BITE. One especially difficult form of aggression common among toddlers is biting. Some young children whose teeth are still erupting may bite out of discomfort. A teething ring or other toy on which they can safely bite can provide an appropriate alternative. Toddlers may also bite in the process of exploration, out of curiosity; because they are bidding for attention and know that an adult will quickly attend to them if they sink their teeth into another child; in anger; out of frustration because of their limited verbal ability in conveying their needs; or as an expression of power, since their sharp little teeth can be a potent tool with which to inflict damage (Gonzalez-Mena & Eyer, 2012). Toddlers are just beginning to learn the rules of socially acceptable behaviors, so reactions like biting should be expected. Because of their limited language ability, apologies should not be expected.

Biting should not be condoned. Toddlers need to hear adults verbalize that biting hurts, thus modeling empathy for the victim's feelings. For very young children, probably the best deterrent to biting is prevention. Careful vigilance, especially of children who have bitten before, is important. Written observation of the child can provide clues to what happens just before a child bites, time of day when the child bites, or what activities tend to be associated with biting. Such clues will facilitate prevention.

A group of researchers have posed a different perspective on biting by linking it to children's oral motor development (Ramming, Kyger, & Thompson, 2006). "Viewing biting behavior as a toddler's developmental need for oral sensory stimulation is beneficial because it means that families and educators can address problem behavior by adjusting food choices and offering appropriate objects on which to chew" (p. 22). They suggest providing crunchy foods such as crackers, raw vegetables, and apple slices as part of a program of intervention.

Shy Children

Most children experience shyness at some times in their lives, although some children can be characterized as basically shy whereas others are generally outgoing. Evidence suggests that shyness is perhaps more influenced by hereditary factors than any other personality trait, and physiological differences have been found between children who are shy and those who are outgoing (Moehler et al., 2008).

Key Point
Biting is a common toddler behavior that may stem from a variety of causes; biting should not be allowed.

Key Point
Shy children may need the teacher's assistance to help them become assimilated into the social environment of the early childhood classroom.

Shy children often engage in solitary activities because they have a more difficult time approaching and interacting with peers. It is important for the teacher to be aware of quiet, withdrawn children and help them become more integrated into the class if this is warranted.

DIVERSITY

Key Point ◆

When families ask for help in dealing with children's behavior problems, it is important to build on an atmosphere of trust and mutual understanding.

These findings do not, however, preclude environmental factors, because children of shy parents also tend to be shy, whether or not they were adopted. A cultural effect is also indicated, evidenced in one study in which young Chinese children were consistently rated as more inhibited whether they attended full-time child care or were at home with their mothers full time (Kagan & Reznick, 1986). Thus, the reasons for shyness are not easy to pinpoint. It is important, however, to identify shy children and provide assistance in social assimilation if this is called for.

Shy children, because they feel inhibited and fearful in social situations, often have less opportunity to learn and practice social skills. Their self-concepts suffer because they are ignored, and this reinforces their feelings of isolation. Honig (1987) proposes many excellent suggestions for helping shy children.

▶ Observing the shy child trying to join others in play can provide insight into ineffective social strategies. From this, the teacher might identify some social skill words and phrases that he can teach the child as an entree into social situations. The teacher can also role-play how to join others in their play with the child.

▶ Small social groups, rather than large ones, are easier for the shy child to handle, and there is also evidence that shy children may play more effectively with younger playmates. Activities should be cooperative, not competitive. The teacher should be a facilitator for situations in which the shy child can experience success.

▶ The teacher's consistency, nurturance, and acceptance will help the shy child feel more secure. In such an environment, the child can feel safe enough to take some social risks.

You can read several case studies of children who are very shy, as well as of children who are persistently aggressive, and how their teachers handled them, in the Education CourseMate at www.CengageBrain.com.

FAMILY SUPPORT: WORKING WITH FAMILIES TO SOLVE BEHAVIOR CHALLENGES

Perhaps the topic most frequently brought up by families when they talk with teachers is child behavior. Similarly, a child's behavior often prompts a teacher to want to consult with the family. Because families and early childhood teachers share responsibility in the socialization of young children, it is important that effective communication, based on mutual understanding, take place.

It is critical to recognize that a child cannot be viewed in isolation, solely within the context of the hours spent at school. What happens during the other hours, the people with whom the child interacts, the quality of these interactions, the cultural background of the family, and the overall quality of the lives of these other people all affect the child. Thus, to understand the child well, you must also get to know the other important people in the child's life; the most basic way to do this is through frequent, informal, positive contact (Gestwicki, 2010). Then if a problem behavior becomes a concern to the family, the teachers, or both, a trusting relationship that facilitates communication has already been established.

When parents bring up concerns about their child's behavior, it is helpful for you, as the teacher, to keep certain points in mind. For instance, never forget the depth of the emotional investment parents have in their children and acknowledge underlying feelings such as anger, defensiveness, or frustration. One underlying message may be a parent's need for reassurance that she is a good parent; whenever appropriate, provide sincere feedback. Also recognize that families may have different values and beliefs about appropriate guidance; for instance, in relation to spanking. Acknowledge the parent's view nonjudgmentally, while stating your philosophy. If suitable, you may use such an opportunity to help the parent explore an alternative method of guidance. In some instances, clarifying the parent's misconception about child development can be reassuring and can help parents see a child's behavior in better perspective.

While helping parents deal with behavior concerns, it is also important to keep in focus the concept of guidance as an ongoing, positive process and to convey this philosophy. Let families know that your approach to guiding children is primarily concerned with helping them develop inner control and self-direction rather than merely a matter of dealing with problems. Many adults think of working with children in terms of discipline; however, you can help families see guidance more broadly by framing your philosophy in terms of laying a foundation for lifelong patterns of creative problem solving, positive interactions, and concern for the needs of others.

SUMMARY

1. Consider the kinds of behaviors we expect of children.
2. Examine workable philosophies of guidance.
   A. These include the approaches of Rudolf Dreikurs, Thomas Gordon, and the behaviorists.
   B. Look at how to select a personal guidance approach.
3. Consider definitions and distinctions among words related to guidance and discipline.
4. Look at a variety of guidance techniques and when these are used most effectively.
5. Consider where to draw the line between behaviors that fall within the normal range and behaviors for which professional help should be sought.
6. Consider the underlying causes of misbehavior, factors that in both subtle and direct ways affect the way children behave.
7. Two specific behavioral concerns, aggression and shyness, are of particular concern to many teachers.

KEY TERMS LIST

active listening

aggression

allergies

attachment disorders

behavior management

bullying

discipline

eclectic approach

effective praise

guidance

ignoring

I-message

inductive reasoning

logical consequences

physical punishment

positive discipline

self-selected time-out

sensory deficit

special time

time-out

unconditional attention

you-message

KEY QUESTIONS

1. List the behaviors you think are desirable in young children. Then make a list of the characteristics you like to see in adults. Now compare the two lists. Are the qualities on your two lists similar? Do you see a link between your expectations of children's behaviors and the outcomes you find desirable in adults?

2. Consider the three philosophies of guidance discussed in this chapter. Does one appeal to you more than the others? Why? Are there specific features in the approaches that you think would be effective as you work with children?

3. Observe a teacher at work with young children. What guidance techniques do you see this teacher using? Can you relate these techniques to any particular theory? Is this teacher's approach based on one theory, or does it seem to be eclectic?

4. Why is it important to consider the underlying cause of a child's misbehavior? Consider the consequences for a child who is continually berated or punished for a behavior that he or she is not able to control.

5. Observe a group of children and note any aggressive behavior. What was the nature of the aggression? How did the aggressive child act? How did the victim of the aggression react? What did the teacher do? Was the teacher's action or reaction effective? Why, or why not?

ADDITIONAL RESOURCES

Select additional books, articles, and websites on topics discussed in Chapter 15.

Carlsson-Paige, N., & Levin, D. E. (1998). *Before push comes to shove: Building conflict resolution skills with children*. St. Paul, MN: Redleaf Press.

Essa, E. L. (2007). *What to do when: Practical guidance strategies for challenging behaviors in the preschool* (6th ed.). Clifton Park, NY: Thomson Delmar Learning.

Gartrell, D. (2011). *A guidance approach for the encouraging classroom* (4th ed.). Clifton Park, NY: Thomson Delmar Learning.

Howes, C., & Ritchie, S. (2002). *A matter of trust: Connecting teachers and learners in the early childhood classroom*. New York: Teachers College Press.

HELPFUL WEBSITES

Young Children with Challenging Behavior:

www.challengingbehavior.org

This website from the Center for Social and Emotional Foundations for Early Learning provides suggestions for addressing concerns about children who have or are at risk of having problem behavior; suggestions include Positive Behavior Support (PBS).

Guidance and Discipline:

www.nncc.org

The website of the National Network for Child Care provides a variety of resources, including articles for dealing with aggressive behavior and other challenging behaviors.

The Center on the Social and Emotional Foundations for Early Learning:

http://cfs.cbcs.usf.edu/projects-research/detail.cfm?id=372

The mission of CSEFEL is to help child care and Head Start programs strengthen and improve the social and emotional outcomes in young children. Practical preventive strategies and techniques for dealing with problem behaviors are offered through training modules from CSEFEL.

Go to **CengageBrain.com** to register your access code for this book's Education CourseMate website, where you will find more resources to help you study. Additional resources for this chapter include TeachSource Videos, glossary flashcards, web links, case studies with critical-thinking questions that apply the concepts presented in this chapter, and more. If your textbook does not include a printed access card, you can go to **CengageBrain.com** to purchase access.

16 Helping Children Cope with Stress

DAP Teachers . . . need to help children build coping skills and resilience in the face of a range of stressful events. Yet again, one of the best ways to help children cope is to give them the benefit of a close, nurturing relationship. Especially when children do not have such a relationship at home, teacher–child relationships can help "buffer" the negative effects of stress.

Developmentally Appropriate Practice, Copple & Bredekamp, 2009, p. 129

In Chapter 16, you will find answers to the following questions about helping children cope with stress:

▶ What is stress and what are common sources of stress in the lives of young children?
▶ What are some reactions to stress that you might see in young children?
▶ Why do some children seem to be resilient in spite of considerable stress in their lives?
▶ What can you do to help children and families cope with the stress in their lives?

NAEYC STANDARDS CONSIDERED IN CHAPTER 16

(See the Standards Correlation Chart on the inside front cover of this book for the titles and description of the standards listed below.)

▶ *Standard 1b:* Understanding the potential sources of stress on young children and its influence on early development and learning (pp. 421–434).
▶ *Standard 6e:* Recognizing the need for advocacy through familiarity with the multiple sources of stress affecting young children (pp. 421–434).
▶ *Standard 4a:* Being sensitive to the needs of children experiencing stress and using a variety of appropriate strategies to help children cope (pp. 434–439).
▶ *Standard 2b:* Using effective methods to help families cope with stress (pp. 439–440).

Stress is inevitably a part of life. Stress causes disequilibrium, for which we have to make some kind of adjustment. Undoubtedly, you know exactly what the word *stress* means and can define it in terms of your own experiences. We all experience stress.

A variety of internal and external causes of stress are an inevitable part of life for young children as well. In this chapter, we will examine stress and young children.

DEFINING STRESS AND COPING

Stress has proven a difficult term to define because researchers who study stress use the word in different ways. Hans Selye, the "father" of stress research, considered stress to be any demand on our ability to adapt (Selye, 1980). Stress is triggered by a threat to physical or psychological well-being and, as a result, causes changes in the body and the brain (Shonkoff & Phillips, 2000). These changes, in turn, interfere with normal functioning. "Toxic stress in early childhood is associated with persistent effects on the nervous system and stress hormone system that can damage developing brain architecture and lead to lifelong problems in learning, behavior, and both physical and mental health" (National Scientific Council on the Developing Child, 2007a, p. 9).

Stress is not in itself a negative force and, in fact, often provides the challenge and motivation to improve, grow, and mature. However, many stressful experiences are negative, requiring the child to deal with an emotional or physical situation that is unsettling, frustrating, painful, or harmful. More often than not, the child does not have the resources to cope with this kind of stress. This is particularly true of infants, who are totally dependent on adults to relieve the cause of their stress. From our own experience, we are aware that stress causes emotional reactions; for instance, anxiety, fear, guilt, anger, and frustration in some cases, or joy, euphoria, and happiness in others. Behind these emotional responses are physiological, neurochemical reactions involving many bodily changes, such as in hormones, heart rate, blood flow, skin, and muscles. Brain research has shed additional light on some of the physiological factors involved in stressful experiences. Stress "produces a shift in the body's priorities" (Shonkoff & Phillips, 2000, p. 213) because the body's resources are diverted to managing or dealing with the stress. Other functions of the body (including the capacity to learn) are, in essence, put on hold while the body copes with the stress (LeDoux & Phelps, 2000). Thus, it is important to recognize that stress is as much a physical as an emotional phenomenon because children often respond to stress in physical ways. The complexity of responses to stress has made its study a challenge to researchers and those who work with young children.

In response to stress, we use different **coping strategies** to ease the tension. Coping always involves mental and/or physical action and can take such forms as denial, regression, withdrawal, impulsive acting out, or suppression, as well as humor and creative problem solving. Coping reactions vary according to the stressful situation, and they depend on such innate factors as temperament, the age and cognitive functioning of the child, and a variety of learned responses and social factors (Honig, 2009). Children also begin to develop certain patterns of coping with specific stressors through habituation and adaptation. Some coping strategies are more effective and more socially acceptable than others; when a child uses aggression as a coping reaction to rejection by peers, we view such behavior as less acceptable than if the child uses a problem-solving approach. Later in this chapter, we will discuss in more detail how to help children cope with stress.

SOURCES OF STRESS IN CHILDREN'S LIVES

Today's children grow up in a complex world that contains a host of potential and actual stressors. A helpful framework for viewing sources of tension for children is the ecological systems theory developed by such researchers as

naeyc

stress
Internal or external demand on a person's ability to adapt.

Key Point ◆

Stress has been defined in a variety of ways, but a definition usually includes the concept of an environmental change that brings about a response that interferes with normal functioning.

Key Point ◆

Stress is not necessarily negative; but if it makes demands on children beyond their ability to cope, it can be harmful.

coping strategies
Mental or physical reactions, which can be effective or ineffective, to help deal with stress.

naeyc

Stress involves both physical and emotional reactions. Young children have limited resources to help them deal with their stress and may, in fact, feel a total sense of powerlessness.

© Cengage Learning

Urie Bronfenbrenner (1979). This approach takes into account the various interconnected ecological contexts within which children live. (This model was discussed in more detail in Chapter 3.) Stress sources as well as potential moderating influences within the social system can come from any of the interacting and overlapping systems. These systems can include the microsystem—the family, friends, school, and extended family; the mesosystem—interactions among the communities that make up the microsystem; the exosystem—programs or agencies that affect the child indirectly, such as the school board or the parents' employer; and the macrosystem—the larger society, with its values and beliefs. Read the "Take a Closer Look" box, which provides insight into factors from the macrosystem that contribute to stress.

Because stress is an individual's unique reaction to a specific event or circumstance, there is an infinite variety of possible stressors. "The circumstances that provoke stress responses vary a great deal for different children and their responses also differ markedly" (Honig, 2009, p. 71). Young children's stressors most often have their roots in the microsystem and mesosystem, and to some extent the exosystem; however, the larger macrosystem also affects young children, as social forces and policies have an impact on their families. For purposes of discussion, we will focus on some common contemporary sources of stress, many of which have received the attention of researchers and theorists.

Family Stressors

Children's security is anchored in their families. Ideally, this security is created by a caring family that provides a protected, predictable, consistent environment in which challenges and new experiences occur as the child is able to handle them successfully. But families do not have such control over the environment and increasingly are caught up as victims of forces that produce enormous stress. Today's families face innumerable struggles—such as family violence, hostile divorces, custody battles, poverty, homelessness, unemployment, hunger, slum environments, neighborhood gang wars, serious chronic illness, and drug and alcohol abuse—that can shatter their control and sense of security.

DIVORCE. One of the most pervasive stressors that today's children face is divorce. A substantial number of children in our society experience their parents' divorce at some point in their lives. The expectation of many professionals has been that children are resilient and that they will overcome the temporary stress of the crisis that takes place when parents are in the process of a divorce. Research by Judith Wallerstein and her colleagues (Wallerstein, Lewis, & Blakeslee, 2001) has questioned this conclusion. After following a group of children of divorce for 25 years, these researchers have concluded that the effects of divorce are long lasting and profound; they continue to have an impact well into adulthood. Thus, both the experience of an ongoing divorce and the years after the divorce affect children.

Young children in the midst of a divorce see what is happening from an egocentric viewpoint. They tend to attribute the departure of one parent to their own "bad" behavior, in essence a punishment for something they did wrong. Accompanying this anxiety is the worry that the other parent may also abandon them. After a divorce, young children are likely to regress behaviorally; for instance, experience sleep disturbances and be tearful, irritable, and more aggressive (Wallerstein et al., 2001).

naeyc

Key Point ◆◆

Many young children experience the divorce of their parents, one of the major sources of stress for today's youngsters.

naeyc

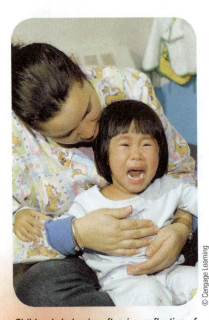

Children's behavior often is a reflection of the stress in their lives. It is particularly important to maintain close contact with each child's family so you, as the teacher, have a better understanding of unexpected or uncharacteristic behaviors.

© Cengage Learning

GEOGRAPHY MATTERS

THE ORGANIZATION Every Child Matters has published a report entitled, *Geography Matters: Child Well-Being in the States* (2008). "All states provide a basic network of social programs to assist vulnerable children and families [but] children do much better in some states than in others" (p. 1). The report shows that there is an enormous gap among states in how children are cared for. In fact, children are twice as likely to die in some states as in others, a very dire statistic. Children's life chances as well as their opportunities to receive adequate care and protection are at the mercy of geography—the state in which they live.

Infants, for instance, have more than twice the chance to survive in Montana and Vermont as they do in Louisiana, where infant mortality is the highest in the country. Children between the ages of 1 and 14 have more than three times greater odds of dying in South Dakota than in Rhode Island. The highest statistic of deaths from child abuse came from Oklahoma, while no child abuse fatalities were reported in Delaware, Idaho, Vermont, and North Dakota. Children born in the 10 lowest-ranking states are 70 percent more likely to die in their first year than children born in the 10 top-ranked states.

Some of these statistics are tied to concern about the mothers and the care that they receive. In some

states the great majority of women receive prenatal care, while in other states far more women receive late or no prenatal care. In Vermont and Rhode Island, a very small percentage of women go without such care; yet in New Mexico, five times as many mothers-to-be forgo care during pregnancy. There is also great variation by state in terms of the number of teen mothers. Nearly three times as many babies were born to mothers aged 15 to 19 in Texas than in New Hampshire.

Health care for children and mothers is tied to insurance and ability to pay. In Texas, more than 21 percent of children are uninsured, as compared with just over 4 percent in Rhode Island. Some states fill the gap for families in poverty through the provision of welfare. There is, however, huge disparity in child welfare expenditures among states. South Carolina spends one-twelfth of what Rhode Island spends on child welfare.

Why is there such a discrepancy among states in how children's well-being is considered? *Geography Matters* notes a number of related factors. The bottom-ranked states have much higher poverty rates than the top-ranked states. There is also a higher proportion of minority children living in low-ranking states. Citizens in low-ranking states have lower levels of education than in the top-ranked states.

In addition, taxes are higher in the top-ranked states, providing a larger pool of funding for the children of those states. In addition, "federal initiatives to address the well-documented needs of children across the country . . . have [recently] been scant. Historically, federal initiatives in social programs have improved the lives of millions of children" (p. 7). The level of investment in the well-being of children declined sharply as a percentage of the federal budget over the first decade of the twenty-first century.

The country needs to place priority on investment in the future of children, including closing the disparities among states. As the report asks:

> Are Maine children, for example, Maine children first? Or are they American children first? Does every child in the U.S. deserve an equal opportunity to succeed? Is there a floor below which no American child should fall which trumps an accident of geography—i.e., living in a state with poor outcomes for its most vulnerable children? Or does it remain politically acceptable to permit vast differences in life chances for children?" (p. 8)

The answers to such questions will have an impact on the country as a whole, on all of us.

423

▶❙❙ **TeachSource Video Activity**
WATCH • REFLECT • RESPOND

This BBC News Video considers research on the effects of divorce on children. Go to CengageBrain.com and view the video entitled, "Divorce and Children," and answer the following questions:

1. What are some of the stresses that children of divorce feel?

2. How might you, as a teacher, support children whose parents are divorced?

naeyc

Key Point ◆◆

A sizable number of American families live in poverty; this includes a rapidly increasing number of homeless families. Poverty and homelessness are grave sources of stress for young children.

naeyc

Divorce is usually accompanied by a range of other occurrences that can have a profound effect on young children. Before the divorce there is often parental anger, discord, and open fighting, which can be very frightening to children. After the divorce, about 90 percent of children end up living with the custodial mother (Hetherington, Stanley-Hagan, & Anderson, 1989), not only experiencing a shift from a two-parent to a single-parent arrangement but also undergoing a shift to a lower income bracket, having fewer resources, possibly living in less expensive housing or with a transitional family (for instance, grandparents or mother's new boyfriend), living with a parent who is stressed in new ways, and perhaps entering or spending more hours in child care. All these changes, on top of the loss of one parent, can be very traumatic.

POVERTY. Another area of stress on which increasing attention has been focused recently is the plight of children whose families lack adequate resources to meet basic needs. The National Center for Children in Poverty (www.nccp.org) reports that more than 15 million children in America live in a family with an income below the federal poverty level. Between the years 2000 and 2009, the number of children living in poverty increased by 33 percent. Minority children and nearly one-fourth of immigrant children are disproportionately poor. A larger percentage of children under the age of six live in poor families than do older children. But, the Center explains, these figures tell only half the story. The official poverty level (in 2011 it was $21,200 for a family of four) "is widely viewed as a flawed metric of economic hardship. … Research consistently shows that, on average, families need an income of about twice the federal poverty level to make ends meet" (National Center for Children in Poverty, 2011). Therefore, an amended estimate, based on $44,100 per year for a family of four, would place 42 percent of American children into low-income families.

Living in a poor family can affect children's cognitive development, impact their ability to learn, contribute to behavioral, social, and emotional problems, and affect health. Very young children living in poor families are at greatest risk for poor outcomes later in life. Stable, nurturing, and enriching environments in the early years help create a sturdy foundation for later school achievement, economic productivity, and responsible citizenship (National Center for Children in Poverty, 2011).

HOMELESSNESS. Homelessness presents another serious stressor for many families and children in the United States. The National Center for Family Homelessness, in its report, *America's Youngest Outcasts* (2009), reports that more than one and a half million American children go to sleep without a home. Considered in a different way, this number indicates that 1 out of every 50 American children, living in the richest country in the world, is homeless. "These children also endure a lack of safety, comfort, privacy, reassuring routines, adequate health care, interrupted schooling, sustaining relationships, and a sense of community" (National Center for Family Homelessness, 2009, p. 1). Homeless children are also twice as likely as other children to experience hunger and to worry about not having enough to eat. They are also twice as likely as middle-class children to have moderate-to-severe health problems. Nor do these children do well in school, having a high school graduation rate of 25 percent, which narrows their opportunity to improve their lives.

As discussed previously in relation to children who live in poverty, homeless children need the same kinds of things as other children do to grow up healthy and happy. They need stable and safe homes, good schools, affordable and consistent health care, appropriate nutrition, the opportunity to play in safe neighborhoods, and qualified, sensitive caregivers with whom they form strong attachments.

CULTURAL DIFFERENCES AND FAMILY STRESS. There is an increasing number of families and children who immigrate to the United States from many parts of the world. Many come from cultures that are very different from American culture, know little or nothing of the English language, and have customs that differ from those of Americans. The isolation of being away from one's cultural support system and the struggle to understand the society in which they find themselves can be highly stressful. Working with families from diverse backgrounds can also be challenging for teachers. According to DAP, it is, therefore, very important that teachers "strive to understand in order to ensure that learning experiences in the program or school are meaningful, relevant, and respectful for each child and family" (Copple & Bredekamp, 2009, p. 10).

OTHER FAMILY STRESSORS. We can easily recognize that experiences such as divorce, poverty, and homelessness can be grave sources of stress for young children. Children may also experience stress from family occurrences that to adults may not appear on the surface to be as stressful. For some children, for instance, the birth of a new sibling triggers regression to earlier behaviors, increased crying, and sleep problems (Honig, 2009). Other stressors can include any event that causes a change, such as the death of a pet, relatives who are visiting, or a parent's prolonged business trip. An abusive marital relationship or a parent's struggle with substance abuse also places great stress on families and children. Read about Sam's experiences in "Stories from the Field."

FAST-PACED FAMILY LIFE. Some children, who at first glance might appear to be privileged, actually experience a great deal of stress. Some dual-income professional families, in which both parents work 60 or more hours a week to keep up with their medical, law, or executive jobs, may produce a different kind of stress for themselves and their children. Families are frequently rushed and beset by the constant need to make quick and important decisions. Their children may be in the care of nannies, be enrolled in special schools, and attend ballet or tennis classes for tots.

Leisure time is spent at special resorts that are often more oriented toward adults than children, a fact brought home to the author by five-year-old Nina, who was overheard discussing her recent vacation at Club Med. When looking at the child from a high-power family, surrounded by abundant material possessions, keep in mind that this child may be involved in a fast-paced and stressed lifestyle, which can take its toll.

Child Abuse and Neglect

Stress is certainly an issue for children who are victims of abuse or neglect, although the more pervasive danger is that serious harm can befall them. The earliest years are when children are most at risk for child abuse (Child Welfare Information Gateway, 2008). Because young children are inexperienced and

Key Point ◆◆

Becoming part of a different culture is often a source of stress for children and families.

naeyc

DIVERSITY

DAP

naeyc

naeyc

Key Point ◆◆

Children from affluent families, whose parents have a fast-paced, hectic lifestyle, can also experience stress.

naeyc

HELPING SAM
COPE WITH STRESS

When Sam's mom was pregnant with him she drank regularly and was involved in an abusive marriage. Because of her drinking and the unstable home life, Sam was taken at birth and placed in foster care, where he lived with a very loving family for the first 11 months of his life. After the birth of her son, Sam's mother entered an intense in-patient drug and alcohol recovery program. During her recovery she was granted limited visitation with Sam. Nearly a year later she was reunited with Sam, and together they now live in a small cottage on the campus of the recovery program. Sam entered child care at that time, and I became his teacher. Sam and I have been together now for a year and a half.

Throughout this difficult transition to being with his mother full-time, Sam showed signs of stress which displayed itself in numerous ways. It began as frustration; he would often scream or yell when he was having difficulty completing a task. Soon after, anger would set in and Sam would become aggressive with his friends, pushing, hitting, or biting them. We also saw sad emotional outbursts that seemed to be for little reason. Naptime was no longer a peaceful time of rest; he had difficulty relaxing enough to fall asleep.

As Sam became more and more unhappy I began to speculate about what

© Theresa Danna Douglas

Wendi, Infant-Toddler Teacher, Residential Rehabilitation Program for Mothers and Their Children

I could do to help him through this difficult time. First and foremost I knew I needed to be extremely patient; this situation was not going to correct itself overnight. Consistency was critical, as were guidelines and boundaries. I met with Sam's mother and we discussed how we could work together to keep the consistency between home and school. Sam's mother was very open about the challenges she was facing and her concerns for Sam's well-being. We both agreed that consistency and boundaries were important to help Sam feel safe and secure; we also acknowledged the comfort that comes with predictability.

Sam is a very active child: jumping, running, throwing balls, and climbing are activities that Sam often engages in. I decided to provide more opportunities than usual for gross motor activities. I introduced

Sam to something I call "heavy work." Two empty liter bottles were filled with water and placed near tote bags; Sam was then encouraged to place the water bottles into the bag and carry the bag from one place to another. Milk crates were also added to the classroom; Sam's friends would climb into the crates and he would push them around the class taking them for a ride. Baskets of rocks were loaded and unloaded and even carried with us outside to play. With the addition of these gross motor activities I began to see a reduction in Sam's stress level.

Naptime was the next hurdle; we decided to make some changes to our regular routine. We slowed down the transition from lunch to nap, giving Sam more time to unwind from the morning's activities. We now also ask Sam to choose a book and then lay on his cot to read. When he is accepting of it, we will hold his hands or give him a gentle massage. We freely give Sam praise when he relaxes on his bed, reading and "resting his body." He now falls asleep on his own with little difficulty and wakes up happy.

The outcome of these changes has been remarkably positive. His interactions and relationships with his peers are more gentle and friendly than before. Sam now spends many cheerful hours engaging in daily activities and exploring with his teachers and friends.

because they depend on adults to care for their needs, they are particularly vulnerable to abuse. Often **child abuse and neglect** occur within the family.

"Children are suffering from a hidden epidemic of child abuse and neglect. While 3 million reports of child abuse are made every year in the United States, experts estimate that the actual number of incidents of abuse and neglect is three times greater than reported" (Childhelp, 2006). Some experts consider that official statistics are "just the tip of the iceberg," since numerous cases go unreported or are unsubstantiated (Hopper, 2008).

Child maltreatment includes any act that deliberately or potentially harms or fails to protect a child. In defining whether child abuse has actually occurred, researchers agree that five factors need to be taken into consideration. These are the severity or intensity of the maltreatment, the type of maltreatment, the duration of the abuse, the age at which maltreatment first began, and the frequency or number of reports about the abuse (Hirschy & Wilkinson, 2010).

Child maltreatement is classified into six major types of abuse, including the following (Child Welfare Information Gateway, 2008):

▶ **Physical abuse** includes nonaccidental physical injuries that result from punching, beating, kicking, biting, shaking, throwing, hitting, burning, or otherwise harming a child.
▶ **Neglect** is characterized by failure of the parent, guardian, or other caregiver to provide for children's basic physical, medical, emotional, or educational needs.
▶ **Sexual abuse** includes activities by a parent or caregiver that involve fondling a child's genitals, penetration, incest, rape, sodomy, indecent exposure, and sexual exploitation.
▶ **Emotional or psychological abuse** occurs when the child's emotional development or sense of self-worth are impaired through constant criticism, threats, rejections, or withholding of love or support.
▶ **Abandonment**, when a child is left alone and the parents' identity or whereabouts are not known, is defined as a form of neglect.
▶ **Substance abuse** includes prenatal exposure of the child to the mother's use of illegal substances, the manufacture of illegal substances in the child's presence, the giving of illegal drugs or alcohol to a child, and use of a controlled substance by a caregiver that impairs that person's ability to adequately care for the child.

Physical marks or unusual behavior may tell you that a child has been, or is at risk of being, abused or neglected, although it is not always easy to read such signs. Cigarette burns on a child's body are more recognizable as abuse, for instance, than a child's inability to sit for any length of time because of sexual molestation. Emotional abuse and neglect are particularly difficult to read because the behavioral symptoms could have any number of causes. Figure 16.1 lists some physical signs of child abuse, whereas Figure 16.2 outlines some behavioral indicators of physical and emotional abuse that can help identify children who are being victimized. It is your skill as a careful observer, combined with your knowledge of child development, that can best provide clues about abnormal or unusual evidence that could indicate abuse or neglect.

Another source of information about whether a child has been or is at risk of being abused or neglected is the cues you might pick up from the child's family. As you interact with families informally, you might note whether they convey unrealistic expectations for the child, seem to rely on the child to meet their own social or emotional needs, lack basic knowledge and skills related

child abuse and neglect
Any action or inaction that harms a child or puts that child at risk.

Key Point

Children who are abused or neglected are beset by multiple sources of stress.

Key Point

Early childhood educators need to be able to recognize potential signs of abuse. It is their ethical and legal responsibility to report suspected child abuse or neglect.

Child abuse and neglect are a source of stress for many young children. The support of nurturing teachers can make a difference in children's lives.

Figure **16.1**

Physical Signs of Child Abuse and Neglect

Physical abuse: unexplained bruises or wounds on various parts of the body; wounds of unusual shapes suggesting that an instrument such as a belt buckle was used; wounds in various states of healing

Sexual abuse: torn, stained, or bloody underclothes; frequent unexplained yeast or urinary infections; complaints about pain in the genital area

Emotional abuse: developmental delays; speech disorders such as stuttering; weight or height level substantially below norm; nervous disorders such as rashes, hives, tics, or stomachaches

Neglect: poor hygiene, such as the presence of lice, scabies, untreated diaper rash, or body odor; unsuitable clothing for weather; weight or height level substantially below norm; lack of immunizations; indicators of prolonged exposure to the elements, such as excessive sunburn, insect bites, or colds

Source: Adapted from *Indications of Child Abuse & Maltreatment* (2008), Childabuse.com. Available online at http://childabuse.com/help.htm.

Figure **16.2**

Behavioral Indicators of Abuse and Neglect

Physical abuse: behavioral extremes such as withdrawal, aggression, regression, or depression; inappropriate or excessive fear of parent or caretaker; unbelievable or inconsistent explanation for injuries; unusual shyness and wariness of physical contact; infants lie unusually still while surveying surroundings

Sexual abuse: regressive behavior such as thumb-sucking, bedwetting; sexually seductive behaviors; disturbed sleep patterns; age-inappropriate interest in sexual matters; avoidance of undressing; difficulty walking or sitting

Emotional abuse: habit disorders such as biting, rocking, or head-banging; cruel behavior, such as getting pleasure from hurting others; age-inappropriate behavior such as wetting or soiling; behavioral extremes, such as being overly compliant or demanding, withdrawn or aggressive, or listless or excitable

Neglect: inconsistent school attendance; chronic hunger, tiredness, or lethargy; begging for food or collecting leftovers; assuming adult responsibilities; reporting no caretaker at home

Source: Adapted from *Indications of Child Abuse & Maltreatment* (2008), Childabuse.com. Available online at http://childabuse.com/help.htm.

to child-rearing, or show signs of substance abuse. Chronic family problems and frustrations stemming from unemployment, illness, and poverty often also result in child abuse and neglect. The majority of parents who abuse or neglect their children can be helped through intervention (Guterman, 2001).

It is important to stress that it is your ethical as well as legal responsibility as a professional to report suspected child abuse or neglect to an appropriate child welfare or protection agency. Every state mandates that professionals report suspected cases, and specific laws protect them from any liability for that report (Child Welfare Information Gateway, 2008). It is not easy to make the decision to report a family for suspected child abuse or neglect. You may be aware of stress afflicting the family and be reluctant to add to it through your report; the evidence of abuse may not be clear-cut or the child may tell you that he or she fell rather than he or she was hit. But it is your responsibility as an early childhood educator and caregiver to act on your concern and speak for and protect young children.

BRAIN STORM
HANDLE WITH CARE

Critical structure and organization of the brain takes place in early childhood. "Childhood experiences define the adult by shaping the developing brain" (Perry & Pollard, 1998, p. 35). What the child experiences during the first year of life actually lays the pattern for all subsequent development. "The more a certain neural system is activated, the more it will 'build-in' this neural state; what occurs in this process is the creation of an 'internal representation' of the experience corresponding to the neural activation" (Perry & Marcellus, 2011). In essence, this internal representation becomes the basis for learning and memory. When a child is born into a loving family and experiences positive interactions, the brain develops in a healthy way, but when the child experiences abuse and neglect early in life, this can have a devastating impact on his neurodevelopment. In other words, early traumatic experiences become internalized and create memories that affect how the child functions and views the world in the future.

Health Stressors

Another source of childhood stress derives from health-related problems. Children suffering from chronic asthma, facing a tonsillectomy, undergoing chemotherapy for cancer, or enduring the aftermath of a serious automobile accident experience stress. This stress is a combination of factors surrounding the physical problem—pain and discomfort—as well as of related elements such as fear of the unknown, limited understanding of what is happening, a strange environment populated by strangers, an exotic medical vocabulary that can conjure up terrifying images, and, perhaps most frightening, fear of being abandoned by the parents. This last factor causes particular distress for very young children facing hospitalization, because attachment and separation are important issues at this age. In addition, children who are seriously ill or face surgery are also aware of their parents' anxiety, and this adds further to their own stress.

A parent's serious health problem, whether physical or mental, is also a source of stress for children. If a parent is hospitalized, the child's familiar routine is disrupted and the remaining parent or another adult fulfills some of the absent parent's functions. These changes produce stress, particularly if a new caretaker is involved. During the parent's convalescence, the child may also have to adapt to changes in the ill parent's personality, energy level, and preoccupation with health.

Death

Inevitably, as a teacher of young children, you will find a need to discuss and explain death, perhaps because the classroom parakeet was lying stiffly on the floor of the birdcage when the children arrived in the morning, or because one of the children's relatives died. Most young children encounter death, whether it is the death of a grandparent, a friend, a sibling, a parent, a family or classroom pet, or a dead worm found in the backyard.

naeyc

Key Point

Children who suffer from chronic illness or experience a serious illness or accident are faced with many health-related stressors.

naeyc

Key Point

Although young children have a limited view of death, they nonetheless experience bereavement after the loss of a significant person in their lives.

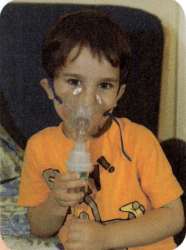

Health problems, whether the child is ill or distressed over a parent's illness, can be a source of great stress.

© Cengage Learning

PRESCHOOLERS' UNDERSTANDING OF DEATH. Young children's understanding of death is a function of their cognitive development. Children in the preoperational stage of cognitive development do not yet have the mental ability to grasp fully the concepts involved in understanding death; nonetheless, anecdotes as well as research show that even toddlers have some cognitive awareness of death. Nonetheless, young children's limited understanding can lead to misconceptions when they come face to face with death (Essa & Murray, 1994).

Death is not a single concept, but involves several subcomponents. Finality is an understanding that death cannot be reversed by magic, medicine, or other means, which is something preschoolers often believe can happen. Inevitability involves an understanding that death eventually comes to all living things, though preschoolers consider death to happen only to others. Recognizing that death involves the cessation of all bodily functions, including movement, thought, and feeling, is another concept difficult for preschoolers to grasp. Between the ages of five and seven, children generally gain an understanding of these three concepts. In addition, the concept of causality, that death is caused by internal factors such as illness, injury, or old age, rather than external factors, seems the most difficult one for children to grasp; most do not gain this understanding until a somewhat later age (Essa & Murray, 1994).

BEREAVEMENT. Young children's limited understanding of death does not mean that they do not experience genuine grief at the loss of someone who was important in their lives. **Bereavement** is a natural process, an essential reaction to loss, which needs to be worked out and supported. Children's reactions to death will vary. Although some children will show no overt signs of mourning or may even seem indifferent to the death, others may react with anger, tantrums, and destructive rages. "Grieving children react differently from grieving adults. Some young children withdraw from friends and family while others play more aggressively" (Wood, 2008, p. 28).

It is important that teachers provide strong support and help in the mourning process of young children who have experienced the death of someone close. The early childhood teacher can offer such support by being willing to discuss the death, recognize and accept the child's feelings, and answer questions. Children have different ways of responding to and expressing their feelings about death that teachers should respect and accept. Adults have to provide a safe environment in which discussion of death is accepted and give children permission to act out, talk about, and interpret what they think and feel in relation to death (Hopkins, 2002).

A special example of death occurs when a young child in your class battles cancer unsuccessfully or is killed in an accident. Almost a year after the death of five-year-old Robbie, there was still considerable discussion and expressions of grief by peers in his class. During his 10 months of illness, chemotherapy, and hospitalizations, Robbie continued to see his friends and visited his class a few times. When Robbie died, the grief process involved the children, their families, and the center staff. Frequent discussions, prompted by questions or angry outbursts, continued. Some of the older children expressed anger that they had lost a good friend whom they would never see again, while the younger children sought frequent affirmation of the finality of Robbie's death ("Robbie won't be back because he is dead, right?"). Underlying many of the children's comments was a sense of their own vulnerability, the fear that they too might die. The staff and some of the parents also engaged in discussions, both to deal with their own fears and grief and to consider how best to help the children. Robbie's death was

bereavement
The grief over a loss, such as after the death of a loved one.

a painful experience, but also one that brought growth and understanding for everyone involved.

Children's Fears

Lisl's mother had gone to the apartment next door, when the thunderstorm broke. Lisl was five years old, and the remembered boom of that thunderclap, while she was all alone, continued to frighten her for many years. Even long after Lisl learned about the physical workings of storms, thunder had the power to cause stress, to accelerate her heartbeat and make her mouth feel dry.

This early experience is not uncommon, and you can undoubtedly recall some generalized feeling of unease or a precise incident that caused a specific fear for you. Everyone experiences fear at some time since fear is a normal response to a threat, whether that threat is real or imagined. Fear is an important self-protective response because it alerts us to danger. Children facing an unknown situation for the first time (for example, a visit to the dentist) will experience natural apprehension. In other instances, a fear can turn into a **phobia,** which is intense, irrational, and stems directly from a specific event such as the thunderstorm just mentioned. A more generalized, vague feeling of uneasiness that cannot be traced to any specific source is labeled **anxiety,** and it is the most difficult form of fear to deal with. Overcoming phobias and anxieties often requires professional help, although teachers can support children as they struggle to understand the source of the fears and their feelings.

Young children's cognitive characteristics influence the types of fears they experience. They are not yet able to classify their fears realistically, thus they may assign them to a "mysterious" category, which is not based on logical thinking. Young children also do not differentiate well between reality and fantasy, nor do they understand cause-and-effect relationships. As we discussed in relation to children's understanding of death, their tendency to think of events as irreversible can also contribute to fears; a child may fear abandonment when left by his mother at school, and cannot think of the reverse—mom returning to pick him up. Finally, children's egocentric thinking gives them a single view, their own, which makes it difficult for them to view an object or situation from more than one perspective (Muris, 2007). Such characteristics, reflecting incomplete and inaccurate understanding, contribute to children's fears.

Although all people develop fears based on their unique experiences, some common fears of young children can be identified. Pervasive fears include the unknown and abandonment, apprehensions that commonly emerge when children deal with divorce, hospitalization, and death. Other frequent sources of fears are animals, the dark, doctors, heights, school, monsters, nightmares, storms, and water (Muris, 2007). Children have experienced such fears throughout time; in addition, modern society has created the source of some unique fears for children. Today's children worry not just about the dark or the "boogie man"; they are also victims of feelings of powerlessness and helplessness in an age of nuclear war, meltdown, and sophisticated missiles. Fears are powerful stressors for young children.

Key Point ◆

Almost all young children experience some common fears; for instance, the unknown, abandonment, animals, the dark, or monsters.

phobia
An intense, irrational fear.

anxiety
A general sense of uneasiness that cannot be traced to a specific cause.

Many children experience feelings of fear, whether from a real threat or an imagined one.

As a teacher, you can help children face their fears by listening carefully, providing reassurance and comfort, letting the child know that all people, including you, are afraid at times, and conveying to the child your confidence in the child's ability to confront his fears in the future. DAP further suggests that you might "give a fearful child a chance to draw or write about her fears. Other coping strategies can include dramatic play, getting information from books or from teachers, talking about the stressful event, seeking comfort from an adult, learning ways to calm down, and learning to 'reframe' (think differently about) a stressful situation" (Copple & Bredekamp, 2009, p. 129).

Community Violence

Increasingly, focus has been placed on children who grow up in violence-riddled inner cities, which have been likened to "war zones" (Garbarino, Dubrow, Kostelny, & Pardo, 1992). Every day, young children witness or fall victim to violent acts, assaults, and death in their communities. The United States has the dubious distinction of being labeled as the most violent country, with far larger numbers of murders, assaults, and rapes than any other industrialized nation (Dodd, 1993). Often an early childhood program is the only safe haven in young children's lives; thus, early childhood educators have taken the plight of children from violent neighborhoods seriously.

In 1993, the NAEYC, concerned about the escalation of violence in the communities in which increasing numbers of young children live, adopted a position statement on *Violence in the Lives of Children* (NAEYC, 1993a). This statement articulates two goals. The first is to decrease violence in children's lives through advocacy; the second aims to enhance educators' ability to help children and families cope with violence through improved professional practice in early childhood programs.

Key Point ◆◆

Increasing numbers of children grow up in violent communities; early childhood programs can serve as one stable, supportive environment in their lives.

Child Care

We may not think of children's experiences in child care as stressful, but research has provided some fascinating insight into this topic. Researchers have examined children's physiological responses under various conditions, including child care, and have come up with some provocative results. All of us have a specific hormone called **cortisol,** known as one of the stress hormones, which is elevated when we are under stress. This is a protective hormone that helps us deal with dangerous or threatening situations. When cortisol is chronically elevated, however, it can become problematic because it can interfere with normal functioning. "Cortisol increases when demands exceed the individual's coping resources" (Dettling, Parker, Lane, Sebanc, & Gunnar, 2000, p. 820). The cortisol level can be measured from a sample of the child's saliva.

Researchers have examined the effects of child care on cortisol levels in young children. They have concluded that, especially for toddlers and younger preschoolers, cortisol is elevated when the children are in child care (Dettling, Gunnar, & Donzella, 1999; Gunnar, Kryzer, Van Ryzin, & Phillips, 2010; Tout, deHaan, Campbell, & Gunnar, 1998). Measures were also taken at the same time of day when children were home, at which time the cortisol levels were found to be normal. Even more telling is a follow-up study that examined the relationship of child care and cortisol levels in the context of child care quality. "In lower-quality settings, defined by the quality of focused attention and stimulation the

cortisol

A stress hormone that is elevated when the person is under some form of stress and when external demands exceed the person's ability to cope.

Key Point ◆◆

Recent physiological research is showing that child care, especially poor-quality care, is stressful to children; such stress is measured by increased levels of the stress hormone, cortisol.

child received from the child care provider, children tend to exhibit a rising pattern of cortisol over the day, while in higher-quality settings this was not the case" (Dettling et al., 2000, p. 832). Poor-quality care seems to put an undue demand on young children's ability to cope, resulting in higher levels of cortisol.

This finding supports several other studies that have looked at children's overt signs of stress, such as nail biting or tremors, in relation to the developmental appropriateness of their early childhood program. More stress signs such as these were found in children in developmentally inappropriate programs than in programs that were appropriate (Burts, Hart, Charlesworth, & Kirk, 1990; Charlesworth, Hart, Burts, & DeWolf, 1993; Hyson, Hirsh-Pasek, & Rescorla, 1990). Therefore, you can see that child care can be a source of stress for young children, especially if the expectations and activities do not properly support children's development. Since such a large proportion of American children participate in child care for much of their day, it is all the more important that we provide experiences that are developmentally appropriate and not unduly stressful.

As we have reviewed, a variety of risk factors can result in stress in children's lives. Some of these factors may prove to be a positive challenge to some children, result in short-term distress for others, or turn into chronic, long-lasting issues in the case of severe, toxic stress. Today's society adds many sources of stress over which children and families have little or no control, including children's exposure to news and information through the media. Your role as a teacher can be to provide a safe environment in which children are nurtured and accepted, as we will discuss. For some children, this may provide the security they are missing in their lives outside the classroom.

RESILIENT CHILDREN

It is important to be aware of what factors cause stress and that stress can result in a variety of undesirable or harmful outcomes. Yet, such a focus on the negative effects of stress should be balanced by considering that not all children respond adversely to stress. Some researchers have focused their attention on children who appear to be stable, healthy, outgoing, and optimistic in spite of incredibly stressful lives. The term commonly used for children who seem to be able to deal effectively with vulnerabilities is **resilient children.**

Resilient children have some shared characteristics identified by various research studies. In an early study, Emily Werner (Werner & Smith, 1982), studying high-risk children in Hawaii and following them for over 30 years, found that one-third grew up to become competent adults. Subsequent studies have found that emotionally responsive parents are important for helping children deal effectively with multiple risk factors in their lives. Other studies have identified heightened sensory awareness, high positive expectations, a clear understanding of one's strengths and accomplishments, and a heightened sense of humor (Pizzolongo & Hunter, 2011). The protective mechanism that promotes resilience includes personality, family, and social characteristics (Werner & Essa, 2009).

Resilient children tend to have an inborn temperament or character that elicits positive responses from adults: being cuddly, affectionate, good-natured, and easy to deal with as infants. They have established a close bond with at least one caregiver, enabling them to establish a basic sense of trust. As preschoolers, they have been shown to have a marked independence—playing vigorously, seeking

DAP

naeyc

Key Point ◆
Some children, despite incredible stress, are stable and optimistic; such youngsters are called "resilient children."

resilient children
Children who, despite extremely stressful lives, appear to be stable, outgoing, and optimistic.

Resilient children seem to be able to establish a close bond with a caregiver. Their inborn temperament or character tends to elicit positive responses from adults.

out novel experiences, showing fearlessness, and being self-reliant. They are highly sociable and often develop a close bond with a favorite teacher. In fact, they have been described as being adept at actively recruiting surrogate parents. In spite of poverty, abuse, a broken home life, and other chronic distress, resilient children grow up to feel in control of their destinies and to be loving and compassionate (Werner & Essa, 2009).

Teachers can play an important role in the lives of children at risk in a number of ways. It is important to help children build a healthy and positive sense of self-esteem and to help them feel that their contributions are important and needed, as a way of building a sense of commitment. It is also important to provide a place where children are valued and where their individual interests can bloom. Resilient children seem to have a strong sense of independence and sociability, which should be valued and encouraged. In retrospect, most resilient children have been found to form a close bond with a responsive caregiver, a role that early childhood teachers can certainly assume. Definitely, a high-quality early childhood program can provide support to children and families at risk from multiple stressors.

TECHNIQUES TO HELP CHILDREN COPE WITH STRESS

As an early childhood educator, you have the power to help children cope with some of the stresses in their lives, although you do not have the ability to change the source of most of their stressors. You cannot reconcile divorcing parents, make the new baby sister go away, move the child away from a dangerous neighborhood, or disperse the monsters in the closet. But you can help children develop some of the skills that will enable them to handle stress more effectively. As we will discuss, the kind of atmosphere you establish and your skills as a good communicator are part of a stress-reducing approach. We will also examine bibliotherapy, relaxation techniques, and play as they contribute to stress reduction in young children.

A Consistent, Supportive Atmosphere

A good early childhood program—one that is child-oriented, supports children's development, is consistent and predictable, provides experiences that are not boring or overly demanding, affords appropriately paced challenges, and is staffed by knowledgeable and nurturing teachers—is one important element in reducing children's stress. Establishing such a program allows you to provide direct help to stressed children. According to DAP, "Teachers' first responsibility is to protect children from the kind of stress that can cause long-term damage" (Copple & Bredekamp, 2009, p. 129). Also keep in mind our earlier discussion of social and physiological research showing that a developmentally appropriate early childhood program does not contribute to children's stress, while inappropriate programs do. One underlying component of stress is that it results from something unknown and potentially scary over which the child

One way in which the early childhood teacher can reduce stress in young children is to provide a supportive, developmentally appropriate classroom environment.

© Cengage Learning

has little control. Thus, a safe and predictable school environment, in which children can experience success and their actions are valued, will contribute to reduced stress.

Communication

One of the most important ways that you, as a teacher of young children, can help mitigate stress is by how and what you communicate. The process (how you communicate) as well as the content (what you say) of communication are important. Thus, it is important that someone share the child's concern, acknowledge how the child feels, and provide reassurance by hugging, holding, or rocking. Such responses are particularly important for very young children and for older children who are extremely distressed. Listening carefully to what children say and encouraging them to ask questions, express feelings, and discuss their perceptions are important techniques for helping children deal with stress in their lives.

In addition to such responses, it is also important to give accurate and developmentally appropriate explanations and information to children old enough to understand. Vague reassurances such as "don't worry about the doctor" do not help the child develop control and alternative coping skills. However, information about what the doctor will do and what instruments will be used will help reduce the child's sense of helplessness. Four-year-old Percy, whose parents were in the process of getting a divorce, spent most of his time at the child care center involved in activities and play. But when he was confronted with minor frustrations, he would fly into angry outbursts, using abusive language and exhibiting unmanageable behavior. Such conduct was quite different from Percy's former competent approach to life. His teacher, Ann, had been in close contact with Percy's mother and recognized his behavior as resulting from stress. Ann did several things for Percy. She spent extra time with him, encouraging him to talk about his father, his fears, and his anxieties. She also tried to give Percy accurate information about the divorce, based on what she had learned from his mother. When Percy flew into one of his rages, Ann would quickly pick him up, move with him away from centers of activity in the class, and hold him in her lap and rock him. This calmed him, and within 5 or 10 minutes he was usually ready to return to an activity or sit quietly looking at a book.

DAP

Key Point

When children are stressed, it is particularly important to provide a supportive, stable, predictable, developmentally appropriate environment.

Key Point

The teacher's communication, through understanding and acknowledgment of the child's feelings, can help a child cope with stress.

Bibliotherapy

bibliotherapy
The use of books that help children deal with emotionally sensitive topics in a developmentally appropriate way.

The term **bibliotherapy** refers to the use of books that deal with emotionally sensitive topics in a developmentally appropriate way that helps children gain accurate information and learn coping strategies. "Many kinds of literature can help support children as they confront emotional challenges in their daily lives" (Roberts & Crawford, 2008, p. 13). Many books are available that deal with issues such as death, divorce, new siblings, separation, sexuality, disabilities, hospitalization, and fears. Bibliotherapy can help children cope with varying fears, anxieties, and concerns that are associated with everyday life. Through exposure to appropriate books, children can identify with a character who experiences a problem similar to theirs; experience emotional release, which is a part of confronting the problem; and gain insight into the problem by developing a better understanding of the character's (and therefore their own) motives and emotions (Sawyer, 2012). Sawyer (2012) outlines some decided advantages of bibliotherapy:

Key Point ◆

Some excellent children's books that deal with sensitive topics can help children gain accurate information and learn coping strategies.

- ▶ **Information**—The use of books can help children gain accurate and reliable information about a topic of concern to them.
- ▶ **Comfort**—A well-selected book can convey such information in a nonthreatening, indirect manner and can help children gain perspective and destroy misconceptions.
- ▶ **Mutuality**—The experience of sharing a problem helps children not feel so alone in facing their difficulties. Sometimes children feel frightened because they feel alone in their distress. Sharing through books can dispel some of this feeling of isolation.
- ▶ **Empathy**—Books can help children understand and appreciate peers who may be different from them by allowing them to enter into the thoughts and feelings of others.
- ▶ **Options for action**—Books can help children see a different way of solving a problem they face, a way they may not have thought of on their own.
- ▶ **Reaffirmation of life**—Difficult and stressful situations can make the world seem frightening and cold. Good books can help children affirm positive aspects of the world.

Just because a book deals with a sensitive topic, however, does not necessarily make it a good book for young children. In addition to meeting the general guidelines for the selection of good children's literature presented in Chapter 12, children's books that deal with challenging topics also need to have settings and characters with which children can identify, accurately depict and explain the situation, examine the origins of emotional reactions, consider individual differences, model good coping strategies, and display optimism. Figure 16.3 lists selected books for bibliotherapeutic use with young children.

Relaxation Techniques

Children can be helped to reduce some of the physical tension associated with stress through guided relaxation exercises. Relaxation routines can easily be incorporated into the early childhood program, for instance, as part of movement activities or during rest or prenap time.

Key Point ◆

Relaxation techniques and imagery can help children reduce some of the tension associated with stress.

One approach to relaxation is to experience muscle tension followed by muscle relaxation. For instance, children can be instructed to make themselves

Figure **16.3**

Suggested Bibliotherapeutic Books

Loss, Death, and Dying
▶ Brown, M. W. (1935). The dead bird. New York: Morrow. **Ages 4–8.**
▶ Buscaglia, L. (1982). *The fall of Freddie the Leaf: A story of life for all ages.* Thorofare, NJ: Slack. **Ages 4 and up.**
▶ Clifton, L. (1983). *Everett Anderson's goodbye.* New York: Holt, Rinehart and Winston. **Ages 4–8.**
▶ DePaola, T. (1981). *Now one foot, now the other.* New York: Putnam. **Ages 4–8.**
▶ Hickman, M. W. (1984). *Last week my brother Anthony died.* Nashville: Abingdon. **Ages 3–8.**
▶ Taback, S. (2007). *I miss you every day.* New York: Viking. **Ages 3–8.**
▶ Viorst, J. (1987). *The tenth good thing about Barney.* New York: Aladdin. **Ages 4–8.**
▶ Wilhelm, H. (1985). *I'll always love you.* New York: Crown. **Ages 3–8.**

Family-Related Matters
▶ Brown, M. T. (1998). *Arthur's baby.* Boston: Little, Brown. **Ages 2–5.**
▶ Casely, J. (1994). *Mama, coming and going.* New York: Greenwillow. **Ages 3–6.**
▶ Drescher, J. (1986). *My mother is getting married.* New York: Dial Press Books. **Ages 4–8.**
▶ Galloway, P. (1985). *Jennifer has two daddies.* Toronto: Women's Educational Press. **Ages 3–8.**
▶ Girard, L. W. (1987). *At daddy's on Saturday.* Niles, IL: Whitman. **Ages 3–8.**
▶ Johnson, A. (1991). *When I am old with you.* New York: Orchard. **Ages 4–8.**
▶ Lapsley, S. (1975). *I am adopted.* New York: Bradburg. **Ages 2½–6.**
▶ Lasky, J., & Knight, M. B. (1984). *A baby for Max.* New York: Scribner. **Ages 4–7.**
▶ McElroy, L. T. (2005). *Love Lizzie: Letters to a military mom.* Morton Grove, IL: Whitman. **Ages 4–8.**
▶ Perry, A. M. (2005). *Just like always.* New York: Children's Press. **Ages 4–8.**
▶ Perry, P., & Lynch, M. (1978). *Mommy and daddy are divorced.* New York: Dial Press Books. **Ages 4–8.**
▶ Ransom, J. F. (2000). *I don't want to talk about it.* Washington, DC: Magination. **Ages 4–8.**
▶ Smith, P. (1981). *Jenny's baby brother.* New York: Viking Press. **Ages 3½–7.**
▶ Stinson, K., & Reynolds, N. L. (1985). *Mom and dad don't live together anymore.* Toronto: Annick Press. **Ages 3–5.**
▶ Thomas, P. (2000). *My family's changing: A first look at family breakup.* Hauppauge, NY: Barron's. **Ages 5–8.**
▶ Vigna, J. (1988). *I wish daddy didn't drink so much.* Niles, IL: Whitman. **Ages 3–7.**

Fears
▶ Aylesworth, J. (1985). *The bad dream.* New York: Whitman. **Ages 4–8.**
▶ Bunting, E. (1987). *Ghost's hour, spook's hour.* New York: Clarion. **Ages 3–7.**
▶ Emberly, E. (1999). *Go away, big green monster!* Boston: Little, Brown. **Ages 4–8.**
▶ Harter, D. (1997). *Walking through the jungle.* New York: Orchard. **Ages 4–8.**
▶ Howe, J. (1986). *There's a monster under my bed.* New York: Atheneum. **Ages 4–8.**
▶ Jonas, A. (1984). *Holes and peeks.* New York: Greenwillow. **Ages 2–5.**
▶ Jones, R. (1982). *The biggest, meanest, ugliest dog in the whole wide world.* New York: Macmillan. **Ages 3–7.**
▶ Matthews, J., & Robinson, F. (1999). *Nathaniel Willy, scared silly.* New York: Bradbury. **Ages 4–8.**
▶ Mayer, M. (1969). *There's a nightmare in my closet.* New York: Dial Press Books. **Ages 4–7.**
▶ Sendak, M. (1988). *Where the wild things are.* New York: HarperCollins. **Ages 3–8.**
▶ Szilagyi, M. (1985). *Thunderstorm.* New York: Bradbury Press. **Ages 3–6.**
▶ Viorst, J. (1972). *Alexander and the terrible, horrible, no good, very bad day.* New York: Atheneum Press. **Ages 3–6.**
▶ Viorst, J. (1988). *The good-bye book.* New York: Atheneum Press. **Ages 3–7.**

Bullying
▶ Berenstain, S., & Berenstain, J. (1993). *The Berenstain Bears and the bully.* New York: Random House. **Ages 4–8.**
▶ Brown, M. (1985). *Arthur's April fool.* New York: Little Brown. **Ages 4–8.**
▶ Henkes, K. (1996). *Chrysanthemum.* Bel Air, CA: Mulberry Books. **Ages 3–8.**

Illness and Hospitalization
▶ Hautzig, D. (1985). *A visit to the Sesame Street hospital.* New York: Random/Children's Television Workshop. **Ages 2–7.**
▶ Krementz, J. (1986). *Taryn goes to the dentist.* New York: Crown. **Ages 3–4.**
▶ Rockwell, A., & Rockwell, H. (1982). *Sick in bed.* New York: Macmillan. **Ages 3–6.**
▶ Rockwell, A., & Rockwell, H. (1985). *The emergency room.* New York: Macmillan. **Ages 2–5.**
▶ Rockwell, H. (1973). *My doctor.* New York: Macmillan. **Ages 2–6.**
▶ Rogers, F. (1986). *Going to the doctor.* New York: Putnam. **Ages 3–6.**
▶ Wolde, G. (1976). *Betsy and the chicken pox.* New York: Random House. **Ages 3–6.**

"First we'll make our bodies very stiff. Then we'll make them as floppy as a Raggedy Ann or Andy doll." Relaxation exercises are an enjoyable way to reduce tension.

progressive relaxation
A technique in which various specified muscle groups are tensed, then relaxed systematically.

imagery
A relaxation technique in which a mental image such as "float like a feather" or "melt like ice" is invoked.

Key Point ◆

Play is one important outlet for children as they attempt to assimilate and cope with stressful events.

stiff as a board, then to become as floppy as a Raggedy Ann or Andy doll. A more systematic approach, called **progressive relaxation,** asks children to tense and then relax various specified muscle groups. For instance, squeeze your eyes shut tightly, then relax; make fists with both hands, then relax; push your knees together hard, then relax. A game such as Simon Says can be used to promote relaxation activities.

Imagery, a mental image that helps in the process of relaxation, can also be used effectively with young children. After children are lying in a comfortable position, they can be asked to "float like a feather" or "melt like ice." A poem or story, read very slowly and softly (for instance, a poem about snowflakes falling), can help children visualize an image in their own way.

Play and Coping with Stress

Play provides a natural outlet for children to cope with and work out stressors in their lives because it "allows the child to relive past experiences and express subjective feelings" (Benham & Slotnick, 2006, p. 339). Play provides a safe setting in which children can confront fears and anxieties, express anger, and find solutions to problems. In particular, role-playing and sociodramatic play allow children to reenact frightening experiences, feel what it is like to take on the perspective or role of others, and make reality more acceptable. Taking on the role of the doctor by using a stethoscope or giving a doll an injection with an empty syringe can help children dispel some of the fears associated with an upcoming visit to the doctor's office.

Another effective approach to decreasing fear is to increase understanding about something unknown. For instance, one study reported that children who used the game Hospital Windows—a medically oriented Lotto game that helps children gain accurate information—increased their knowledge of health care concepts significantly while decreasing their fear of medical equipment and procedures (Henkens-Matzke & Abbott, 1990).

Play is one of the most important ways for children to deal with stress, because it allows children to experience their feelings in a safe setting. Children often gravitate to dramatic play when medical props are available.

SELF-PROTECTION PROGRAMS

With increased social awareness and concern about child sexual abuse has come a proliferation of programs aimed at teaching children some self-protection techniques. Specially designed programs such as Child Assault Prevention, Safe and Drug Free, Who Do You Tell? and "Bubbylonian Encounter" are usually presented to groups of young children by volunteer, law enforcement, or social agencies. They address such topics as the difference between "good" and "bad" touching and the child's right to say "no," and they present some specific protective techniques, including running away from a potential assailant and rudimentary karate moves.

Although such programs are well-intentioned, their effectiveness has been questioned. A number of studies have concluded that such programs are more effective for older children, and that younger children have difficulty in grasping the concepts—which often are abstract—that these programs convey (Miltenberger & Roberts, 1999; Tutty, 1997). A critical review of research evaluating child sexual-abuse prevention programs found little evidence that such programs for preoperational children actually meet their goals (Reppucci & Haugaard, 1989). These authors raise serious questions about the developmental readiness of young children for meaningful understanding of the concepts these programs teach. It is a fundamentally important point that adults, not children, are responsible for providing protection against abuse (Jordan, 1993). Young children are too inexperienced to be given such a serious responsibility. We need to protect them through our consistent and constant supervision, through our modeling of appropriate interactions with strangers, and by teaching respect and ownership of the body through nurturing care.

HELPING FAMILIES COPE WITH STRESS

A stressed child most likely comes from a stressed family. Although all families experience stress, the circumstances and their available resources for coping with stress will differ. Early childhood programs can function as important family-support systems for parents of young children, although traditionally they have focused more on the child than on the family system. Certainly from an ecological perspective, the child cannot be separated from the family; therefore, a good early childhood program includes a family-support component. As an early childhood educator, you can help families cope with life stressors, whether through your support, modeling, education, or referrals. Carol Gestwicki, in her book Home, School, and Community Relations: A Guide to Working with Parents (2010), provides some helpful guidelines for teachers interacting and working with stressed families.

▶ **Reassure parents**—Through empathy and caring, teachers can encourage parents and reassure them about such things as the amount of time needed to readjust after a divorce or the grief process. Suggested books for both children and adults can also provide reassurance.

▶ **Know available community resources**—Teachers' expertise is in working with children rather than in professional counseling. Their role with highly stressed parents is to provide emotional support, information, and a listening ear. Beyond that, they should refer the parents to appropriate community agencies. It is important that early childhood teachers be aware of what is available in their own areas. Different communities have different services, such as family and children's services or United Way agencies. There

Key Point ◆
A number of programs designed to help children protect themselves against abuse have been developed; however, research has found little evidence that such programs actually meet their goals for young children.

Key Point ◆
Usually a stressed child comes from a stressed family; teachers may be able to help families cope with stress.

are also mutual support groups such as Parents Without Partners, organizations for parents who have abused their children, and associations for parents of children with disabilities. The yellow pages section of the telephone directory often has appropriate listings under the heading "Social Services."

▸ **Be aware of legal agreements**—It is important to know both legal and informal agreements between parents, particularly when custody battles are involved. A written statement from every family listing persons who are authorized to pick up the child should be on file.

▸ **Keep requests light**—It is important to be sensitive to the stress level of families and not to ask an overwhelmed, single parent to bake two dozen cookies for tomorrow's snack.

▸ **Be aware of your own attitudes and feelings**—It is sometimes easy to lay blame, be judgmental, or get angry at parents, especially when the teacher perceives them as inadequate. Teachers should examine their own attitudes and work especially hard to get to know the families and their special circumstances so that true empathy can develop.

In addition to these suggestions, teachers can also assist families through modeling positive guidance techniques, respect for children's ideas, and enforcement of reasonable limits. For some families, it may be necessary to accompany modeling with verbal explanations and a discussion of alternatives.

It is also important to differentiate between a family that is coping adequately and continuing to carry out its family functions in the face of stress and a family that is in trouble and may require intervention. Some signs of parents who may be at the breaking point include the following:

▸ **Disorganized behavior**—Parents frequently forget vital things (for instance, the child's jacket on subzero days, or the child's lunch).

▸ **Frustration**—Parents have perpetually worried expressions, are unduly impatient with a slow child, threaten punishment, express a lack of confidence in their parenting ability, or appear confused about how to handle the child.

▸ **Inability to accept help**—Parents get defensive and become verbally aggressive or walk away from a teacher who tries to discuss the child, perhaps in response to their own sense of guilt, failure, or inadequacy.

▸ **Concern more for themselves than for their child**—Parents seem more focused on their own problems and bring them up any time the teacher tries to talk about the child.

If you suspect that a parent is under so much stress that she or he is temporarily unable to cope, discuss your concerns with other teachers who interact with the parent, as well as with the director or principal. A poorly functioning parent puts the child at risk. Your school's decision may be to contact a social service agency, which, in turn, may recommend that the child be temporarily removed from the home, require parental counseling, or offer some other form of support for the parent.

SUMMARY

1. A variety of possible sources of stress exist in young children's lives.
   A. Family stressors, including divorce, poverty and homelessness, fast-paced family life, and cultural differences can have a serious effect on children.
   B. Child abuse and neglect, in addition to the potential for severe harm, is a serious source of stress for young children.

C. Health problems and dealing with death are other stressful occurrences for children.

D. Children may also be stressed by their fears and the violence in their environment.

E. Participation in child care, particularly if it is developmentally inappropriate, can also be a source of stress for children.

2. Some children, who seem to share some common characteristics, are considered resilient in spite of stressful events.

3. The early childhood teacher can use a number of effective techniques to help children cope with the stress in their lives.

4. Some programs are designed to teach young children self-protection from potentially harmful encounters.

KEY TERMS LIST

anxiety

bereavement

bibliotherapy

child abuse and neglect

coping strategies

cortisol

ecological systems theory

imagery

phobia

progressive relaxation

resilient children

stress

KEY QUESTIONS

1. What have been the most stressful events in your life? What were your reactions? How did you cope? What support systems did you have during these stressful events? What feelings did you experience? Can you think of a stressor in your life that has had a positive effect on you?

2. Talk to a teacher of young children and ask that teacher what types of family stressors are experienced by the children in his or her class. How do these stressors affect the children? How does the teacher help the children deal with their stress?

3. Check what the procedures are for reporting suspected child abuse and neglect in your local community. Which agency or agencies should be contacted? What procedure will be set in motion by such a report? What is the involvement of the person who makes the report?

4. Review several children's books, such as those listed in Figure 16.3, that deal with sensitive issues. How do these books address such topics as loss, divorce, or fear? Could a young child identify with the characters? Do the books offer alternatives to the child who is experiencing a similar stressor?

5. Observe a self-protection program presentation for young children. What concepts are being presented? Are these concepts appropriate for the cognitive and emotional abilities of young children? What do you think young children might learn from this program? Do you see any drawbacks or potential problems with this program?

ADDITIONAL RESOURCES

Select additional books, articles, and websites on topics discussed in Chapter 16.

Crosson-Tower, C. (2007). *Understanding child abuse and neglect* (7th ed.). New York: Allyn & Bacon.

Honig, A. S. (2009). Stress and young children. In E. Essa & M. Burnham (Eds.), *Informing our practice: Useful research on young children's development* (pp. 71–88). Washington, DC: NAEYC.

Werner, E. E., & Smith, R. S. (2001). *Journeys from childhood to midlife: Risks, resilience, and recovery.* Ithaca: Cornell University Press.

HELPFUL WEBSITES

The ChildTrauma Academy:

www.ChildTrauma.org

The mission of the ChildTrauma Academy is to improve the lives of children who have been traumatized and maltreated. A wide range of resources and additional links are available through this website.

Child Welfare Information Gateway: Protecting Children, Strengthening Families:

www.childwelfare.gov

This government website provides a wealth of information about issues and policies related to the welfare of American children.

National Coalition for the Homeless:

www.nationalhomeless.org

The mission of the National Coalition for the Homeless is simply to end homelessness. The website provides information and statistics about homelessness in the United States and strategies for grassroots action to help end homelessness.

Helping Children Cope with Stress:

www.athealth.com/Consumer/disorders/childstress.html

A valuable article on stress in children, its symptoms, and potential causes; the article offers strategies for helping children cope with stress.

Go to **CengageBrain.com** to register your access code for this book's Education CourseMate website, where you will find more resources to help you study. Additional resources for this chapter include TeachSource Videos, glossary flashcards, web links, case studies with critical-thinking questions that apply the concepts presented in this chapter, and more. If your textbook does not include a printed access card, you can go to **CengageBrain.com** to purchase access.

PULLING IT ALL TOGETHER:
An Early Childhood Classroom Observation

In this epilogue, we will apply what we have learned in this course by visiting an early childhood classroom. We will observe a group of children and teachers and follow them through a typical day. Much of what goes on in this classroom reflects topics we have discussed in various chapters of this text, as you will be reminded by the chapter numbers that appear throughout the epilogue. Now that you know so much more about early childhood education, you can recognize many of its features as we take our tour. Ready to begin our visit?

MEET THE "PANDAS"

Welcome to the Children's Center and the "Panda" class. The class has 18 children, ages three to almost six, and three teachers (Chapter 1). A few children in this class have special needs (Chapter 2). Let's go see what's happening in the class now. The early arrivers are already at the center. Teacher Kathy, who works in one of the other classrooms, is in charge of the early-morning shift, which includes some of the children from the Panda class. This early time is relatively low-key; children can choose from several easy-to-clean-up and safe activities, such as story reading and manipulative games (Chapter 8). Jane, the head teacher for the Panda group, usually arrives by 8:30 A.M. and spends some time readying the activities that are planned for the day. Richard and Yvonne, the other two teachers, get to the center by 9:00 A.M. (Chapter 4). Let's observe now.

MORNING ARRIVAL

Teacher Jane stays near the door and greets the arriving children and their parents. Nicholas's mother briefly tells Jane about his fall over the weekend, which is how he cut his lip. After a quick kiss from Nicholas, his mother is off to work.

Nicholas goes into the room and spots Joel in the reading area with Zachary and Amanda.

"My tooth went into my lip," Nicholas tells Joel. "See!"

Joel checks out Nicholas's lip.

"I fell and hurt my knee," Joel tells Nicholas.

"I hurt my knee too … and my arm … and my head … and my bottom … and my booboo!" Nicholas adds. The two of them laugh uproariously.

Notice the use of typical four-year-old humor by Joel and Nicholas.

"My Daddy is bringing a snake to school today," Zachary tells the others. Nicholas and Joel stop their conversation for a moment to look at Zachary, then continue to discuss their various "wounds."

Pause and Reflect:
Consider the role of child care in the lives of contemporary families. (Review Chapter 3.)

Pause and Reflect:
What did you learn in Chapter 11 about children's humor? Did you notice how the boys seem to congregate together? You'll see the same pattern from some of the girls in a few minutes.

ACTIVITY TIME

All of the children and teachers are here now. Notice that several additional activities are now available to the children, like the paints at the easel. Children can select their own activities, and you will see children finding things to do with friends or alone.

Pause and Reflect:
Discuss likely reasons for this gender segregation, as discussed in Chapter 13.

Pause and Reflect:

Why does Teacher Jane provide a variety of activities for the children during Activity Time? (Check Chapter 8.)

Pause and Reflect:

How did Teacher Jane set up the dramatic play area to foster the kind of play you see in Jillian and Christine? What do you think these girls are learning from engagement in sociodramatic play? (See Chapters 7 and 13.)

Pause and Reflect:

What principles about choosing appropriate computer software for young children do you think Teacher Jane applied as she made "Facemaker" available to the children today? (See Chapter 7.)

Pause and Reflect:

What other activities might you provide for Sheena to help her improve fine motor skills? (Check Chapters 2 and 10.)

Pause and Reflect:

Is Teacher Jane's choice of snack and this "smorgasbord snack" arrangement appropriate for this group of children? If so, why? If not, why not? (See Chapter 10 and 14.)

Pause and Reflect:

What concept or concepts, as discussed in Chapter 11, do you see in Christopher's reasoning?

Jillian and Christine head for the dramatic play area. Jillian pulls a skirt on over her clothes, then joins Christine to look for shoes to go with her outfit.

"OK, we'll go shopping. I have to get some food and some new dresses and some other stuff," she announces. Within a few minutes, they are dressed and ready to go shopping.

Christine sees a blanket over the dolls in the cradle and spreads it out on the floor. "We'll have a picnic first," she tells Jillian. The two of them fill a basket with plastic foods from the dramatic play cupboard and set out their picnic.

In the meantime, Alex has turned on the computer and is playing "Face-maker." Nicholas joins Alex and sits in the second computer chair, first watching, then participating.

"Put that nose on the man," Nicholas suggests. "Boy, he looks dumb!" They laugh as they try different features and body parts. Shila walks by and watches quietly for a few minutes.

Sheena wanders about the room, then walks by Jillian and Christine's picnic. She sees the cradle and the now-uncovered dolls in it. She checks them out, then picks up one of the dolls, rocking the baby in her arms. She walks to the mirror, where she shows the baby to itself. "Look, look," she tells it softly.

Then she decides to undress the doll. "Take it off," Sheena says, pulling the doll's shirt. She spends several minutes of great concentration working on this task. Teacher Yvonne holds the doll to help Sheena get its shirt off. Once the shirt is off the doll, Sheena works equally hard to get it back on.

Yvonne has been working with Sheena to help her improve her small muscle skills. This self-selected activity provides good practice for Sheena.

SNACK

Notice the snack at the far table. Some of the children who arrive at the center early are ready for a snack because it has been several hours since their breakfast. Others want something a little later. To accommodate the children's varying schedules, the teachers provide a "smorgasbord snack," available until after 10:00 each morning. The snack is usually a "fix-it-yourself" affair.

Several children move to the snack table after washing their hands. Christopher spreads peanut butter on a celery stick; then, with great concentration, he tops it with a handful of raisins. He then places some raisins in a celery stick without peanut butter and watches them fall out. He discusses with Teacher Jane how the raisins stick to the peanut butter but not to the plain celery.

"It sticks because it's sticky!" exclaims Christopher, as he licks his gluey fingers, then crunches down on his snack.

During the next hour, children come and go to the snack table, making and eating "ants-on-a-log" (celery with peanut butter and raisins) and drinking milk. Periodically, Teacher Jane asks children who have not yet had a snack if they would like one.

Patrick tells her, "I'm not hungry yet. Maybe later."

GROUP TIME

It's almost 10:00. At this time, the children and teachers straighten the room and then participate in a short circle activity. This gets the children together for the first time today and helps the teachers concentrate on current class projects. For the past three weeks, the children have been focusing on insects and spiders, a topic of great interest to *Patrick* and *Shila*, who were the first to suggest that they would like to find out more about the very small flying insects that have been busy near a flowering plant by the window. The children have participated in a variety of activities to help them explore and learn more about these specific flying insects and others that live in their part of the country.

Teacher Jane tells the children a flannelboard story, *The Little Green Caterpillar*. "One day the little green caterpillar was looking for something to eat," Jane begins. She goes on to relate the caterpillar's search for a meal and his encounter with other insects. The children listen attentively and laugh delightedly at some of the absurd meal suggestions. At the end of the story, Jane asks the children some questions about the story and helps them recount its sequence.

She then dismisses the children a few at a time to get their coats. One teacher is available to help the children with their zippers and buttons as needed. Most of the children, like Jason, have no problems getting dressed. A few, like Sheena, are helped by a teacher.

OUTDOOR TIME

Outside, the children move to the climbers, tricycles, swings, slides, and other equipment. A few minutes later, Teacher Richard brings out a parachute. There is a shout of glee, and most of the children run toward him.

"Everyone get a hold of the edge of the parachute. Now, let's lift it way, way up high. Good! Now, down, way down!"

The children lift and lower, laughing and giggling as the parachute flutters in the wind. The fact that the children on one side of the parachute are lifting, while several on the other side are trying to lower the parachute, only makes them laugh harder.

"Who wants to get under the parachute?" Richard asks.

"Me, me!" shout several voices.

"All right, Jillian and Alex, you go first. Trade places." The two run under the parachute, while the rest of the group lifts and lowers it.

"Takor and Shila, now you two trade places." Soon most of the children have had a chance to run under the parachute, and the giggling has intensified.

Angela has been watching this activity quietly from the side.

"You can hold it right here," Patrick tells Angela. She takes hold of the edge of the parachute between Patrick and Marusha. Soon Angela is laughing and running under the parachute, too.

After the children go inside and hang up their coats, they reconvene on the rug. Teacher Jane tells the group that they have a special guest today—Zachary's father, a biologist who works with animals.

FAMILY PARTICIPATION

Zachary's father tells the children about the beetles he has brought in a plastic box and then introduces a snake, which he pulls out of a sack. The children watch with reserved fascination as the snake emerges. It wiggles around, coiling and stretching, moving from the middle to the edges of the circle. Laughter erupts each time the snake nears the children.

"Does he sleep with Zachary?" Shila wants to know.

"Will he bite?" asks Christine.

"Only if you're a rat," Zachary's father tells her. "He likes to eat rats."

"I'm not a rat!" exclaims Vincent.

Pause and Reflect:

What is the value for the children of a sustained project focused on one topic, such as this insect and spider project? (Check the discussion of projects in Chapters 5, 6, and 8.)

Pause and Reflect:

Discuss three ways in which this flannelboard activity promotes language development. (Review Chapter 12.)

Pause and Reflect:

What group management techniques, as discussed in Chapter 14, are these teachers using?

Pause and Reflect:

Which developmental domains might be supported through Teacher Richard's parachute activity? (Review Chapters 9 through 13.)

Pause and Reflect:

How does Patrick, as one of the older children in this group, use his more mature social skills to invite Angela to join the group rather than stand on the sidelines? (Consider information in Chapter 13.)

"No rats here. I guess he won't bite anyone," says Zachary's father.

"Why does he stick out his tongue?" Patrick asks.

"Does he bite with his tongue?" Joel chimes in.

"He smells with his tongue," says Zachary's father. "See, he is smelling all of us."

More laughter erupts as the children watch the snake wiggle around the circle, tongue flipping in and out. The snake moves toward Alex, who squeals in delight as it comes near him. B.J., however, moves behind Teacher Yvonne, who reassures him quietly. Zachary pets the snake frequently. Later, Teacher Richard takes the snake and lets it crawl around him. Richard tells the children that he had a pet snake when he was a little boy.

ACTIVITY TIME ... AGAIN

After 15 minutes, Zachary's father and the snake leave. The beetles, however, will stay in the class for the day. "You can look at them at the science table," Jane tells the children. She also places sheets of paper, pencils, gel pens, and crayons nearby in case some of the children want to draw pictures of the beetles. Jane also tells the children which other activities are available. The children are dismissed a few at a time, and they move into the various classroom learning centers.

At the woodworking table, Christine puts on goggles and takes out a block of Styrofoam, a hammer, and nails, and starts to bang away. Jillian watches for a few moments, then gets goggles and a hammer as well. Teacher Jane gives Jillian a piece of Styrofoam, into which the child quickly hammers half a dozen nails.

Other children move to other activities. Takor and Sheena spend some time at the sand table's "Creature World." The moist sand holds a variety of plastic "creatures" as well as sticks, pine cones, and other sensory materials.

"Look, I got a green spider. It's bigger than this yellow spider," Takor says, as he digs in the sand.

Shila moves to the easel, puts a plastic apron over her head, and affixes a sheet of paper onto the easel with clothespins. She works with great concentration on her painting, first using separate colors, then mixing them on the pictures. Teacher Richard comments quietly on the colors she is using.

In the block area, several children are joined by Teacher Richard. At first Joel, Zachary, Chris, and Vincent build an enclosure with the large, hollow blocks. Takor spends a few minutes rolling cars down a ramp-shaped block. By the time he joins the other boys, the block construction has become a house.

"Get a roof," Zachary says. Joel finds two flat pieces of cardboard, which he lays over the top. "See our house!" someone calls out. Several children crawl under the roof, and they have to lie flat to be enclosed inside their house. They take turns getting into it and repairing it each time the roof slips off.

"This is our boat. Let's go fishing. Hop in the boat." Vincent has turned the house into a boat now. Christopher, Takor, and Zachary hop in with Vincent.

"How's the fire doing in there, Zach?" Joel asks, apparently making the boating trip into a camping trip as well.

"OK. Are you hungry now?" Zachary asks.

"Yeah," Joel answers.

Angela walks to the block area and starts to get in the boat. One of the boys pulls her out.

"You can't get in here. This is *our* boat!"

Pause and Reflect:

The visit from Zachary's father and the beetles and snake illustrate a number of early childhood education concepts. Which concepts can you identify? (Hint: Check Chapters 3, 11, 12, and 16 for some ideas.)

Pause and Reflect:

What rules about woodworking do you think have been established in this classroom? (See Chapter 9.)

Pause and Reflect:

What might you say to Shila, as you observe her in this painting activity? (See Chapter 9.)

Pause and Reflect:

Many skills are evident in the play of these boys. Identify and discuss two developmental skills that are supported through this kind of play. (Review Chapters 9 through 13.)

Angela starts to cry, saying, "No! No!" Teacher Yvonne moves over as Angela says, "He hurt me."

"She was getting in our boat," another boy says.

Yvonne spends a few moments helping Angela and the boys tell each other how they feel. The boys eventually agree that they could let a girl join them.

A little before noon, all of the teachers move around the classroom and tell groups of children that it will be time to clean up soon. A few minutes later, Teacher Jane rings a bell, the usual signal, and announces cleanup time.

"I need a couple of people to help put the top on the 'Creature World,'" Teacher Jane says. "Alex, can you help me?" Alex, along with Zachary, Joel, and Nicholas, helps the teacher place the wooden cover on the sand table.

When they are finished, Zachary says, "Hey, Takor, me and Nicholas and Alex, we put the top up. We have muscles!"

Pause and Reflect:
What are some underlying issues in the children's dilemma? How might you have reacted? (Check Chapters 2, 13, 14, and 15.)

GROUP TIME ... AGAIN

The children gather on the rug. They sing, "Head, Shoulders, Knees, and Toes," touching the various named body parts as they sing. After singing the song at a reasonable tempo, they repeat it quickly, to fast movement, fast words, and giggles.

"Today we're going to play a bug game. This will be our bug house here," says Teacher Jane, indicating the center of the circle. "I want you to think of a bug and move how you think that bug might move. And, if you think that bug makes a sound, I want you to make that sound. But don't tell us what the bug is. We'll try to guess. Who can think of a bug they'd like to be?"

"I know one," Jillian says. She moves around the circle, buzzing and flapping her arms.

"A bee! She's a bee!"

Vincent is an ant. Amanda is a fly, and Shila, crawling very quietly and slowly with hands tucked under her face, is a caterpillar.

Nicholas hops around the circle, saying, "Boing, boing, boing, boing."

"Is he a bunny?" asks B.J.

"Is a bunny an insect?" asks Teacher Jane.

"I'm not a bunny, I'm a grasshopper!" explains Nicholas.

"Grasshoppers are good jumpers. But I never heard a grasshopper say 'boing'!" says Jane. Everyone laughs.

All of the children who wanted to be an insect have had a turn.

"How about if we have some grasshoppers wash their hands? Amanda, Zachary, and B.J., will you be grasshoppers and hop to the bathroom to wash your hands, please?" Soon, going a few at a time, all of the children are ready for lunch.

Pause and Reflect:
Consider how well the children are engaged in this group activity. What strategies does Teacher Jane use to get the children involved in this activity? (See Chapters 9 through 14.)

LUNCH TIME

Richard has brought a cart with the children's lunch boxes into the room. Each child picks up her or his box and finds a place at one of the tables. The teachers join them in eating lunch. Children inspect what their parents have packed for their lunches and also see what others have brought. Milk is available for those who did not bring a drink from home. There is a quiet buzz of conversation as everyone eats.

Children finish lunch at different paces. After putting their lunch boxes back into their cubbies, the children move to the reading area to get a book, which they can look at quietly. Zachary and Joel are still eating. Shila, looking behind her as she walks, bumps into Zachary as she moves past him, spilling some of the milk he is drinking. Zachary bursts into tears. Joel, sitting next to him, reaches over and gives him a comforting hug. Shila watches a moment, then quietly gets a sponge and wipes the spilled milk. She also pours a little more milk into Zachary's cup from the pitcher.

"It's OK. It's OK," Joel tells Zachary, as he pats his back. Zachary calms down, rubbing his eyes. Teacher Jane approaches Zachary, saying,

"It's almost nap time, Zachary. We've had a really exciting morning, with your dad and snake visiting, haven't we?" Zachary produces a weak smile, and he and Joel finish their lunches.

You may wonder why Jane did not deal with the milk-spilling accident. Most likely, Jane realizes that Zachary, who is usually very even-tempered, is just overtired at this point, so she's not adding to the overstimulation, but simply trying to calm him.

Pause and Reflect:

A successful lunch period takes thoughtful planning. Which strategies for mealtime, discussed in Chapter 14, help to make lunch a pleasant activity in this classroom? What social skills do the children exhibit as they deal with an unexpected spill of milk?

NAP AND REST TIMES

Teacher Yvonne is placing nap cots around the room for the children who will be sleeping.

In the early afternoon, some of the children sleep, but a number of the older ones do not take daily naps anymore. They will go to one of the other classrooms for quiet activities.

By 1:00, the nappers have gone to the bathroom, taken off their shoes, and snuggled down for their naps. The lights are dimmed, and soft music is playing on the tape recorder. Some children fall asleep quickly, while others wiggle around for a while. Yvonne rubs Vincent's and Amanda's backs to help them sleep.

Children begin waking up around 2:30, some slowly, some with a burst of renewed energy, ready for a snack and afternoon activities. It takes about a half hour before everyone is up.

"Angela, where did you put your shoes before nap?" Teacher Yvonne asks her. Angela shrugs. After a few minutes of looking, the shoes are found amid the dress-up shoes in the dramatic play area.

"Let's put these back on," suggests Yvonne. Angela pulls off her right sock while Yvonne puts on her left shoe. In a few minutes, however, Angela's shoes and socks are back on both her feet.

Amanda is one of the last children to wake from her nap. "I don't feel good," she tells Teacher Richard, rubbing her eyes. Richard feels her forehead and tells Teacher Jane, "She feels like she might have a fever." A check with the thermometer confirms that Amanda does have a high temperature.

This early childhood center has an arrangement for children who do not feel well. While the adults try to reach one of their parents, the children stay with a staff member in the office, where a cot and a few quiet toys are kept for such occasions.

Pause and Reflect:

Which principles related to effective nap or rest times, as discussed in Chapter 14, do you see exhibited in this classroom?

BACK OUTSIDE

The rest of the group has now had a snack and is ready to go outside.

"Look at me! Look at me!" calls Joel, sitting on a swing and swinging up high.

"Wow," Teacher Jane says. "You're really swinging high. You've worked hard at learning to pump!"

The tricycles are all taken by this time, although Sheena indicates that she wants to ride one, too.

"There are no tricycles right now, Sheena," Teacher Yvonne says. "But maybe Marusha could give you a ride on the back of hers. Marusha, could Sheena ride with you?"

Marusha pulls to the side and waits for Sheena to get into the "passenger seat." Marusha pedals hard to pull the extra weight. Vincent, who has been digging in the sand, watches Marusha struggling with the tricycle, then lays down his shovel and gets behind Sheena to push. They gather speed and take several turns around the cement path.

"Can I ride now?" Vincent asks.

"OK. I'll push," suggests Marusha. Sheena stays in the passenger seat while Marusha and Vincent trade places.

Pause and Reflect:

What techniques, as discussed in Chapter 15, might the teachers have used in the past to help children learn the kinds of negotiation skills shown today in relation to the tricycles?

THE END OF THE DAY

The children go back inside around 4:00. A few parents have begun to pick up their children. In the room, several quiet activities are set out.

The beetles that Zachary's father had brought that morning are on the science table. Christopher and Vincent check them out.

"I want the beetles to come out," Christopher says, poking his finger in the sand.

"You know, the beetles burrow in the sand. That's what they like to do," Teacher Richard tells them. "There is some beetle food on top of the sand. Maybe they'll come up where we can see them when they get hungry."

"Hey, there's one!" Vincent says, as one of the beetles emerges from the sand. The two boys continue to watch.

Christopher says, "I'm going to draw a picture of the beetle so I can show my dad." He examines the beetle a few moments, then picks up a piece of paper, selects a brown crayon, and carefully draws a picture of the beetle that is now sitting atop the sand. Teacher Richard watches a few moments and comments on how Christopher captured the shape and feelers of the beetle in his drawing.

In the meantime, Jillian and Christine move to the game shelf. Christine takes out the counting flowers and Jillian finds the dominoes.

"One, two, three, four, …" Christine accurately matches the 10 flowers and pots, placing the flowers with numerals on top of the flower pots with the corresponding number of dots.

Jillian, meanwhile, lays out a domino with two dots on one side and four on the other. She looks over the remaining dominoes and finds one with four dots, which she lays next to the other four-dotted piece. She continues building a chain of matching dominoes.

Alex wanders to their table and picks up the flower pot with two dots from Christine's game. "That's two," he tells Christine, then moves off elsewhere.

Gradually all of the parents come to pick up their children, some stopping for a few moments to chat with the teachers, others rushing off. A little after 5:30 P.M., the last child has left and another day has ended.

Pause and Reflect:

What science and math principles, discussed in Chapter 11, are the children learning through these activities?

* * *

Now you have had the opportunity to experience a day in the lives of a group of young children and their teachers. Much of what you experienced will be familiar because you have had a chance to read about and study it in the chapters of this book. The synopsis of this day in the Panda room at the Children's Center, and the questions you were asked to consider, provided some specific connections to various chapters in the text. Now see if you can find some additional connections by answering the following questions:

1. Much of what you saw reflects the school's *philosophy*. From what you saw today, what do you think the philosophy of the Children's Center is? What reflections of *quality* components of early childhood programs did you see reflected in the Panda room?

2. You may have noticed that Sheena and Angela are two children with some *special needs*. How did the teachers work to make these two an integral part of the program? Did you see evidence that the teachers respected the individual differences and strengths of other *children*?

3. What behaviors of the three *teachers* reflected their commitment to their jobs?

4. What is the relationship of the teachers and *parents*?

5. A lot went on during this day in the Panda room, some of it planned, other aspects more spontaneous. What can you discern about the kind of *planning* that the teachers engaged in to make this day flow so smoothly? What kinds of goals did they set and how might they have reached these?

6. What evidence did you see that the teachers prepared a child-appropriate *environment*, a developmentally appropriate *curriculum*, and a flexible *schedule*?

7. What opportunities to help children expand their learning did the teachers take advantage of during the day?

8. How did the teachers contribute to the children's *socialization* and guide their behaviors?

9. How did the teachers promote and encourage *creativity, cognitive* learning, *language,* and *physical* activity?

10. How did the teachers help children deal with *stressful* situations?

Code of Ethical Conduct and Statement of Commitment

Revised April 2005.
Reaffirmed and Updated May 2011.

A position statement of the National Association for the Education of Young Children

Preamble

NAEYC recognizes that those who work with young children face many daily decisions that have moral and ethical implications. The **NAEYC Code of Ethical Conduct** offers guidelines for responsible behavior and sets forth a common basis for resolving the principal ethical dilemmas encountered in early childhood care and education. The **Statement of Commitment** is not part of the Code but is a personal acknowledgement of an individual's willingness to embrace the distinctive values and moral obligations of the field of early childhood care and education.

The primary focus of the Code is on daily practice with children and their families in programs for children from birth through 8 years of age, such as infant/toddler programs, preschool and prekindergarten programs, child care centers, hospital and child life settings, family child care homes, kindergartens, and primary classrooms. When the issues involve young children, then these provisions also apply to specialists who do not work directly with children, including program administrators, parent educators, early childhood adult educators, and officials with responsibility for program monitoring and licensing. (Note: See also the "Code of Ethical Conduct: Supplement for Early Childhood Adult Educators," online at www.naeyc.org/about/positions/pdf/ethics04.pdf. and the "Code of Ethical Conduct: Supplement for Early Childhood Program Administrators," online at http://www.naeyc.org/files/naeyc/file/positions/PSETH05_supp.pdf.)

Core values

Standards of ethical behavior in early childhood care and education are based on commitment to the following core values that are deeply rooted in the history of the field of early childhood care and education. We have made a commitment to

- Appreciate childhood as a unique and valuable stage of the human life cycle
- Base our work on knowledge of how children develop and learn
- Appreciate and support the bond between the child and family
- Recognize that children are best understood and supported in the context of family, culture,* community, and society
- Respect the dignity, worth, and uniqueness of each individual (child, family member, and colleague)
- Respect diversity in children, families, and colleagues
- Recognize that children and adults achieve their full potential in the context of relationships that are based on trust and respect

Conceptual framework

The Code sets forth a framework of professional responsibilities in four sections. Each section addresses an area of professional relationships: (1) with children, (2) with families, (3) among colleagues, and (4) with the community and society. Each section includes an introduction to the primary responsibilities of the early childhood practitioner in that context. The introduction is followed by a set of ideals (I) that reflect exemplary professional practice and by a set of principles (P) describing practices that are required, prohibited, or permitted.

The **ideals** reflect the aspirations of practitioners. The **principles** guide conduct and assist practitioners in resolving ethical dilemmas.** Both ideals and principles are intended to direct practitioners to those questions which, when responsibly answered, can provide the basis for conscientious decision making. While the Code provides specific direction for addressing some ethical dilemmas, many others will require the practitioner to combine the guidance of the Code with professional judgment.

---

*The term *culture* includes ethnicity, racial identity, economic level, family structure, language, and religious and political beliefs, which profoundly influence each child's development and relationship to the world.

**There is not necessarily a corresponding principle for each ideal.

Source: Reprinted with permission from the National Association for the Education of Young Children (NAEYC). Copyright © 2011 by NAEYC. Full text of all NAEYC position statements is available at www.naeyc.org/positionstatements.

The ideals and principles in this Code present a shared framework of professional responsibility that affirms our commitment to the core values of our field. The Code publicly acknowledges the responsibilities that we in the field have assumed, and in so doing supports ethical behavior in our work. Practitioners who face situations with ethical dimensions are urged to seek guidance in the applicable parts of this Code and in the spirit that informs the whole.

Often "the right answer"—the best ethical course of action to take—is not obvious. There may be no readily apparent, positive way to handle a situation. When one important value contradicts another, we face an ethical dilemma. When we face a dilemma, it is our professional responsibility to consult the Code and all relevant parties to find the most ethical resolution.

Section I Ethical Responsibilities to Children

Childhood is a unique and valuable stage in the human life cycle. Our paramount responsibility is to provide care and education in settings that are safe, healthy, nurturing, and responsive for each child. We are committed to supporting children's development and learning; respecting individual differences; and helping children learn to live, play, and work cooperatively. We are also committed to promoting children's self-awareness, competence, self-worth, resiliency, and physical well-being.

IDEALS

I-1.1—To be familiar with the knowledge base of early childhood care and education and to stay informed through continuing education and training.

I-1.2—To base program practices upon current knowledge and research in the field of early childhood education, child development, and related disciplines, as well as on particular knowledge of each child.

I-1.3—To recognize and respect the unique qualities, abilities, and potential of each child.

I-1.4—To appreciate the vulnerability of children and their dependence on adults.

I-1.5—To create and maintain safe and healthy settings that foster children's social, emotional, cognitive, and physical development and that respect their dignity and their contributions.

I-1.6—To use assessment instruments and strategies that are appropriate for the children to be assessed, that are used only for the purposes for which they were designed, and that have the potential to benefit children.

I-1.7—To use assessment information to understand and support children's development and learning, to support instruction, and to identify children who may need additional services.

I-1.8—To support the right of each child to play and learn in an inclusive environment that meets the needs of children with and without disabilities.

I-1.9—To advocate for and ensure that all children, including those with special needs, have access to the support services needed to be successful.

I-1.10—To ensure that each child's culture, language, ethnicity, and family structure are recognized and valued in the program.

I-1.11—To provide all children with experiences in a language that they know, as well as support children in maintaining the use of their home language and in learning English.

I-1.12—To work with families to provide a safe and smooth transition as children and families move from one program to the next.

PRINCIPLES

P-1.1—**Above all, we shall not harm children. We shall not participate in practices that are emotionally damaging, physically harmful, disrespectful, degrading, dangerous, exploitative, or intimidating to children.** *This principle has precedence over all others in this Code.*

P-1.2—We shall care for and educate children in positive emotional and social environments that are cognitively stimulating and that support each child's culture, language, ethnicity, and family structure.

P-1.3—We shall not participate in practices that discriminate against children by denying benefits, giving special advantages, or excluding them from programs or activities on the basis of their sex, race, national origin, immigration status, preferred home language, religious beliefs, medical condition, disability, or the marital status/family structure, sexual orientation, or religious beliefs or other affiliations of their families. (Aspects of this principle do not apply in programs that have a lawful mandate to provide services to a particular population of children.)

P-1.4—We shall use two-way communications to involve all those with relevant knowledge (including families and staff) in decisions concerning a child, as appropriate, ensuring confidentiality of sensitive information. (See also P-2.4.)

P-1.5—We shall use appropriate assessment systems, which include multiple sources of information, to provide information on children's learning and development.

P-1.6—We shall strive to ensure that decisions such as those related to enrollment, retention, or assignment to special education services, will be based on multiple sources of information and will never be based on a single assessment, such as a test score or a single observation.

P-1.7—We shall strive to build individual relationships with each child; make individualized adaptations in teaching strategies, learning environments, and curricula; and consult with the family so that each child benefits from the program. If after such efforts have been exhausted, the current placement does not meet a child's needs, or the child is seriously jeopardizing the ability of other children to benefit from the program, we shall collaborate with the child's family and appropriate specialists to determine the additional services needed and/or the placement option(s) most likely to ensure the child's success. (Aspects of this principle may not apply in programs that have a lawful mandate to provide services to a particular population of children.)

P-1.8—We shall be familiar with the risk factors for and symptoms of child abuse and neglect, including physical, sexual, verbal, and emotional abuse and physical, emotional, educational, and medical neglect. We shall know and follow state laws and community procedures that protect children against abuse and neglect.

P-1.9—When we have reasonable cause to suspect child abuse or neglect, we shall report it to the appropriate community agency and follow up to ensure that appropriate action has been taken. When appropriate, parents or guardians will be informed that the referral will be or has been made.

P-1.10—When another person tells us of his or her suspicion that a child is being abused or neglected, we shall assist that person in taking appropriate action in order to protect the child.

P-1.11—When we become aware of a practice or situation that endangers the health, safety, or well-being of children, we have an ethical responsibility to protect children or inform parents and/or others who can.

Section II Ethical Responsibilities to Families

Families* are of primary importance in children's development. Because the family and the early childhood practitioner have a common interest in the child's well-being, we acknowledge a primary responsibility to bring about communication, cooperation, and collaboration between the home and early childhood program in ways that enhance the child's development.

* The term *family* may include those adults, besides parents, with the responsibility of being involved in educating, nurturing, and advocating for the child.

IDEALS

I-2.1—To be familiar with the knowledge base related to working effectively with families and to stay informed through continuing education and training.

I-2.2—To develop relationships of mutual trust and create partnerships with the families we serve.

I-2.3—To welcome all family members and encourage them to participate in the program, including involvement in shared decision making.

I-2.4—To listen to families, acknowledge and build upon their strengths and competencies, and learn from families as we support them in their task of nurturing children.

I-2.5—To respect the dignity and preferences of each family and to make an effort to learn about its structure, culture, language, customs, and beliefs to ensure a culturally consistent environment for all children and families.

I-2.6—To acknowledge families' childrearing values and their right to make decisions for their children.

I-2.7—To share information about each child's education and development with families and to help them understand and appreciate the current knowledge base of the early childhood profession.

I-2.8—To help family members enhance their understanding of their children, as staff are enhancing their understanding of each child through communications with families, and support family members in the continuing development of their skills as parents.

I-2.9—To foster families' efforts to build support networks and, when needed, participate in building networks for families by providing them with opportunities to interact with program staff, other families, community resources, and professional services.

PRINCIPLES

P-2.1—We shall not deny family members access to their child's classroom or program setting unless access is denied by court order or other legal restriction.

P-2.2—We shall inform families of program philosophy, policies, curriculum, assessment system, cultural practices, and personnel qualifications, and explain why we teach as we do—which should be in accordance with our ethical responsibilities to children (see Section I).

P-2.3—We shall inform families of and, when appropriate, involve them in policy decisions. (See also I-2.3.)

P-2.4—We shall ensure that the family is involved in significant decisions affecting their child. (See also P-1.4.)

P-2.5—We shall make every effort to communicate effectively with all families in a language that they understand. We shall use community resources for translation and interpretation when we do not have sufficient resources in our own programs.

P-2.6—As families share information with us about their children and families, we shall ensure that families' input is an important contribution to the planning and implementation of the program.

P-2.7—We shall inform families about the nature and purpose of the program's child assessments and how data about their child will be used.

P-2.8—We shall treat child assessment information confidentially and share this information only when there is a legitimate need for it.

P-2.9—We shall inform the family of injuries and incidents involving their child, of risks such as exposures to communicable diseases that might result in infection, and of occurrences that might result in emotional stress.

P-2.10—Families shall be fully informed of any proposed research projects involving their children and shall have the opportunity to give or withhold consent without penalty. We shall not permit or participate in research that could in any way hinder the education, development, or well-being of children.

P-2.11—We shall not engage in or support exploitation of families. We shall not use our relationship with a family for private advantage or personal gain, or enter into relationships with family members that might impair our effectiveness working with their children.

P-2.12—We shall develop written policies for the protection of confidentiality and the disclosure of children's records. These policy documents shall be made available to all program personnel and families. Disclosure of children's records beyond family members, program personnel, and consultants having an obligation of confidentiality shall require familial consent (except in cases of abuse or neglect).

P-2.13—We shall maintain confidentiality and shall respect the family's right to privacy, refraining from disclosure of confidential information and intrusion into family life. However, when we have reason to believe that a child's welfare is at risk, it is permissible to share confidential information with agencies, as well as with individuals who have legal responsibility for intervening in the child's interest.

P-2.14—In cases where family members are in conflict with one another, we shall work openly, sharing our observations of the child, to help all parties involved make informed decisions. We shall refrain from becoming an advocate for one party.

P-2.15—We shall be familiar with and appropriately refer families to community resources and professional support services. After a referral has been made, we shall follow up to ensure that services have been appropriately provided.

Section III Ethical Responsibilities to Colleagues

In a caring, cooperative workplace, human dignity is respected, professional satisfaction is promoted, and positive relationships are developed and sustained. Based upon our core values, our primary responsibility to colleagues is to establish and maintain settings and relationships that support productive work and meet professional needs. The same ideals that apply to children also apply as we interact with adults in the workplace. (Note: Section III includes responsibilities to co-workers and to employers. See the "Code of Ethical Conduct: Supplement for Early Childhood Program Administrators" for responsibilities to personnel (*employees* in the original 2005 Code revision), online at http://www.naeyc.org/files/naeyc/file/positions/PSETH05_supp.pdf.)

A—Responsibilities to co-workers

IDEALS

I-3A.1—To establish and maintain relationships of respect, trust, confidentiality, collaboration, and cooperation with co-workers.

I-3A.2—To share resources with co-workers, collaborating to ensure that the best possible early childhood care and education program is provided.

I-3A.3—To support co-workers in meeting their professional needs and in their professional development.

I-3A.4—To accord co-workers due recognition of professional achievement.

PRINCIPLES

P-3A.1—We shall recognize the contributions of colleagues to our program and not participate in practices that diminish their reputations or impair their effectiveness in working with children and families.

P-3A.2—When we have concerns about the professional behavior of a co-worker, we shall first let that person know of our concern in a way that shows respect for personal dignity and for the diversity to be found among staff members, and then attempt to resolve the matter collegially and in a confidential manner.

P-3A.3—We shall exercise care in expressing views regarding the personal attributes or professional conduct of co-workers. Statements should be based on firsthand knowledge, not hearsay, and relevant to the interests of children and programs.

P-3A.4—We shall not participate in practices that discriminate against a co-worker because of sex, race, national origin, religious beliefs or other affiliations, age, marital status/family structure, disability, or sexual orientation.

B—Responsibilities to employers

IDEALS

I-3B.1—To assist the program in providing the highest quality of service.

I-3B.2—To do nothing that diminishes the reputation of the program in which we work unless it is violating laws and regulations designed to protect children or is violating the provisions of this Code.

PRINCIPLES

P-3B.1—We shall follow all program policies. When we do not agree with program policies, we shall attempt to effect change through constructive action within the organization.

P-3B.2—We shall speak or act on behalf of an organization only when authorized. We shall take care to acknowledge when we are speaking for the organization and when we are expressing a personal judgment.

P-3B.3—We shall not violate laws or regulations designed to protect children and shall take appropriate action consistent with this Code when aware of such violations.

P-3B.4—If we have concerns about a colleague's behavior, and children's well-being is not at risk, we may address the concern with that individual. If children are at risk or the situation does not improve after it has been brought to the colleague's attention, we shall report the colleague's unethical or incompetent behavior to an appropriate authority.

P-3B.5—When we have a concern about circumstances or conditions that impact the quality of care and education within the program, we shall inform the program's administration or, when necessary, other appropriate authorities.

Section IV Ethical Responsibilities to Community and Society

Early childhood programs operate within the context of their immediate community made up of families and other institutions concerned with children's welfare. Our responsibilities to the community are to provide programs that meet the diverse needs of families, to cooperate with agencies and professions that share the responsibility for children, to assist families in gaining access to those agencies and allied professionals, and to assist in the development of community programs that are needed but not currently available.

As individuals, we acknowledge our responsibility to provide the best possible programs of care and education for children and to conduct ourselves with honesty and integrity. Because of our specialized expertise in early childhood development and education and because the larger society shares responsibility for the welfare and protection of young children, we acknowledge a collective obligation to advocate for the best interests of children within early childhood programs and in the larger community and to serve as a voice for young children everywhere.

The ideals and principles in this section are presented to distinguish between those that pertain to the work of the individual early childhood educator and those that more typically are engaged in collectively on behalf of the best interests of children—with the understanding that individual early childhood educators have a shared responsibility for addressing the ideals and principles that are identified as "collective."

IDEAL (INDIVIDUAL)

I-4.1—To provide the community with high-quality early childhood care and education programs and services.

IDEALS (COLLECTIVE)

I-4.2—To promote cooperation among professionals and agencies and interdisciplinary collaboration among professions concerned with addressing issues in the health, education, and well-being of young children, their families, and their early childhood educators.

I-4.3—To work through education, research, and advocacy toward an environmentally safe world in which all children receive health care, food, and shelter; are nurtured; and live free from violence in their home and their communities.

I-4.4—To work through education, research, and advocacy toward a society in which all young children have access to high-quality early care and education programs.

I-4.5—To work to ensure that appropriate assessment systems, which include multiple sources of information, are used for purposes that benefit children.

I-4.6—To promote knowledge and understanding of young children and their needs. To work toward greater societal acknowledgment of children's rights and greater social acceptance of responsibility for the well-being of all children.

I-4.7—To support policies and laws that promote the well-being of children and families, and to work to change those that impair their well-being. To participate in developing policies and laws that are needed, and to cooperate with families and other individuals and groups in these efforts.

I-4.8—To further the professional development of the field of early childhood care and education and to strengthen its commitment to realizing its core values as reflected in this Code.

PRINCIPLES (INDIVIDUAL)

P-4.1—We shall communicate openly and truthfully about the nature and extent of services that we provide.

P-4.2—We shall apply for, accept, and work in positions for which we are personally well-suited and professionally qualified. We shall not offer services that we do not have the competence, qualifications, or resources to provide.

P-4.3—We shall carefully check references and shall not hire or recommend for employment any person whose competence, qualifications, or character makes him or her unsuited for the position.

P-4.4—We shall be objective and accurate in reporting the knowledge upon which we base our program practices.

P-4.5—We shall be knowledgeable about the appropriate use of assessment strategies and instruments and interpret results accurately to families.

P-4.6—We shall be familiar with laws and regulations that serve to protect the children in our programs and be vigilant in ensuring that these laws and regulations are followed.

P-4.7—When we become aware of a practice or situation that endangers the health, safety, or well-being of children, we have an ethical responsibility to protect children or inform parents and/or others who can.

P-4.8—We shall not participate in practices that are in violation of laws and regulations that protect the children in our programs.

P-4.9—When we have evidence that an early childhood program is violating laws or regulations protecting children, we shall report the violation to appropriate authorities who can be expected to remedy the situation.

P-4.10—When a program violates or requires its employees to violate this Code, it is permissible, after fair assessment of the evidence, to disclose the identity of that program.

PRINCIPLES (COLLECTIVE)

P-4.11—When policies are enacted for purposes that do not benefit children, we have a collective responsibility to work to change these policies.

P-4.12—When we have evidence that an agency that provides services intended to ensure children's well-being is failing to meet its obligations, we acknowledge a collective ethical responsibility to report the problem to appropriate authorities or to the public. We shall be vigilant in our follow-up until the situation is resolved.

P-4.13—When a child protection agency fails to provide adequate protection for abused or neglected children, we acknowledge a collective ethical responsibility to work toward the improvement of these services.

Statement of Commitment*

As an individual who works with young children, I commit myself to furthering the values of early childhood education as they are reflected in the ideals and principles of the NAEYC Code of Ethical Conduct. To the best of my ability I will

- Never harm children.
- Ensure that programs for young children are based on current knowledge and research of child development and early childhood education.
- Respect and support families in their task of nurturing children.
- Respect colleagues in early childhood care and education and support them in maintaining the NAEYC Code of Ethical Conduct.
- Serve as an advocate for children, their families, and their teachers in community and society.
- Stay informed of and maintain high standards of professional conduct.
- Engage in an ongoing process of self-reflection, realizing that personal characteristics, biases, and beliefs have an impact on children and families.
- Be open to new ideas and be willing to learn from the suggestions of others.
- Continue to learn, grow, and contribute as a professional.
- Honor the ideals and principles of the NAEYC Code of Ethical Conduct.

*This Statement of Commitment is not part of the Code but is a personal acknowledgment of the individual's willingness to embrace the distinctive values and moral obligations of the field of early childhood care and education. It is recognition of the moral obligations that lead to an individual becoming part of the profession.

Glossary

A

ABC analysis—An observational technique in which the observer records observations in three columns, identifying antecedent, behavior, and consequence.

absorbent mind—Maria Montessori's term to describe the capacity of young children to learn a great deal during the early years of their lives.

abstract thinking—According to Jean Piaget, the ability to solve a variety of problems abstractly, without a need to manipulate concrete objects.

accommodation—According to Jean Piaget, one form of adaptation, which takes place when an existing concept is modified or a new concept is formed to incorporate new information or a new experience.

accountability—Being answerable to the agency or people who fund a program or initiative, ensuring that the funds were well used to reach the stated goals of the program.

action research—Research carried out by teachers as a way of finding practical solutions to the everyday problems encountered in teaching.

active listening—Thomas Gordon's term for the technique of reflecting back to children what they have said as a way to help them find their own solutions to problems.

activity time—Largest block(s) of time in the early childhood program day during which children can self-select from a variety of activities.

adaptation—Jean Piaget's term for the process that occurs anytime new information or a new experience occurs.

aesthetics—Enjoyment and appreciation of beauty, particularly related to all forms of art.

Ages and Stages Questionnaires (ASQ)—Brief tests designed to screen for developmental delays in children from 4 to 60 months.

aggregates—Rhoda Kellogg's term for the step in the development of art in which children combine three or more simple diagrams.

aggression—Behavior deliberately intended to hurt others.

allergies—Physiological reactions to environmental or food substances that can affect or alter behavior.

anecdotal record—A method of observation involving a written "word picture" of an event or behavior.

anxiety—A general sense of uneasiness that cannot be traced to a specific cause.

assessment—A systematic way of gathering information about children's learning and development, through a variety of methods, including observation, tests, portfolios, and other evaluations.

Assessment, Evaluation, and Programming System (AEPS)—Diane Bricker's evaluation instrument for children ages birth to six, which links assessment, intervention, and evaluation in six developmental areas.

assimilation—According to Jean Piaget, one form of adaptation, which takes place when the person tries to make new information or a new experience fit into an existing concept.

assistant teacher—Also called aide, helper, auxiliary teacher, associate teacher, or small-group leader; works under the guidance of the head teacher in providing a high-quality program for the children and families in the class.

Association for Childhood Education International (ACEI)—Professional organization that focuses on issues related to children from infancy to early adolescence, particularly those issues involving international and intercultural concerns.

at-risk children—Children considered to be at risk for developmental delay because of adverse environmental factors, such as poverty or low birth weight.

attachment—The child's bond with the mother, established during the first year of life.

attachment disorders—Problems in establishing a secure attachment can result in later disturbed and inappropriate social relations.

attention deficit disorder (ADD)—Difficulty in concentrating on an activity or subject for more than a few moments at a time.

attention deficit–hyperactivity disorder (ADHD)—Manifested by short attention span, restlessness, poor impulse control, distractibility, and inability to concentrate.

authentic assessment—A comprehensive approach to assessment, using multiple methods, that takes into account the whole child and focuses on all aspects of development.

autism spectrum disorder—A socioemotional disorder of unknown origin in which the child's social, language, and other behaviors are inappropriate, and often bizarre.

Autonomy vs. Shame and Doubt—The second stage of development described by Erik Erikson, occurring during the second year of life, in which toddlers assert their growing motor, language, and cognitive abilities by trying to become more independent.

B

babbling—The language of babies in the second half of the first year, consisting of strings of vowels and consonants that are often repeated over and over.

ballistic skills—Applying a force to an object in order to project it, as in throwing.

basic scribbles—According to Rhoda Kellogg, the 20 fundamental markings found in all art.

behavior management—Behavioral approach to guidance, holding that the child's behavior is under the control of the environment, which includes space, objects, and people.

behavior modification—The systematic application of principles of reinforcement to modify behavior.

behaviorism—The theoretical viewpoint, espoused by theorists such as B. F. Skinner, that behavior is shaped by environmental forces, specifically in response to reward and punishment.

behaviorist view of language development—The view that children learn language primarily through positive reinforcement from parents.

bereavement—The grief over a loss, such as after the death of a loved one.

bibliotherapy—The use of books that help children deal with emotionally sensitive topics in a developmentally appropriate way.

bilingualism—Ability to use two languages.

board of directors—Policy making or governing board that holds ultimate responsibility, particularly for a not-for-profit program.

bodily kinesthetic intelligence—Effective use of the body to solve problems or create products.

Brigance Diagnostic Inventory of Early Development—Revised—A developmental assessment tool for children from birth to age seven.

bullying—Behavior intended to harm the victim, which occurs repeatedly over time and involves a more powerful person attacking a less powerful person.

burnout syndrome—Condition experienced by professionals as a result of undue job stress; characterized by loss of energy, irritability, and a feeling of being exploited.

C

calendar activity—A common group activity that focuses on a daily review of the days of the week, the months, and the date.

caregiver (or child care worker)—Term traditionally used to describe a person who works in a child care setting.

center-based programs—Programs for young children located in school settings; these programs usually include larger groups of children than are found in home-based programs.

central processor—That aspect of the information processing model that governs and coordinates other functions such as sensory input and memory.

checklist—A method of evaluating children that consists of a list of behaviors, skills, concepts, or attributes that the observer checks off as a child is observed to have mastered the item.

child abuse and neglect—Any action or inaction that harms a child or puts that child at risk.

child–adult ratio—The number of children for whom an adult is responsible, calculated by dividing the total number of adults into the total number of children.

child advocacy—Political and legislative activism by professionals to urge change in social policies affecting children.

Child Development Associate (CDA)—An early childhood teacher who has been assessed and proven competent through the national CDA credentialing program.

child study movement—This movement occurred in the early years of the twentieth century in the United States, when many university preschools were established to develop scientific methods for studying children.

chronosystem—According to family systems theory, this system takes into account the passage of time, both as the individual gets older and in terms of historic changes.

classification—The ability to sort and group objects by some common attribute or property; for instance, color or size.

code of ethics—Agreed-upon professional standards that guide behavior and facilitate decision making in working situations.

cognition—The process of mental development, concerned more with how children learn than with the content of what they know.

cognitive developmental theory—The theory formulated by Jean Piaget that focuses on how children's intelligence and thinking abilities emerge through distinct stages.

cognitive interactionist view of language development—The view that children's language is rooted in cognitive development, requiring, for instance, the ability to represent objects mentally.

collectivism—The general tendency of a cultural group to place greater emphasis on the needs and wants of the group rather than on those of the individual.

combines—According to Rhoda Kellogg, a step in the development of art in which children combine two simple diagrams.

computer literacy—Familiarity with and knowledge about computers.

conceptual—Montessori classroom area that focuses on academic materials related to math, reading, and writing.

concrete operations period—Piaget's period covering the elementary school years.

confidentiality—Requirement that results of evaluations and assessments be shared with only the appropriate family members and school personnel.

conservation—Ability to recognize that objects remain the same in amount or number despite perceptual changes; usually acquired during the period of concrete operations.

constructivist theory—A theory, such as that of Jean Piaget, based on the belief that children construct knowledge for themselves rather than having it conveyed to them by some external source.

content standards—The concepts and skills that children are expected to acquire in relation to their age or grade level and that should be covered in the program or curriculum.

conventional level of moral development—According to Lawrence Kohlberg, the stage concerned with the pleasing of others and respect for authority.

conventional moral rules—Standards, which are generally culture-specific, arrived at by general consensus.

convergent thinking—The act of narrowing many ideas into a single, focused point.

cooing—The language of babies in the first half of the first year, consisting primarily of strings of throaty vowel sounds.

coping strategies—Mental or physical reactions, which can be effective or ineffective, to help deal with stress.

cortisol—A stress hormone that is elevated when the person is under some form of stress and when external demands exceed the person's ability to cope.

criterion-referenced—A characteristic of tests in which children are measured against a predetermined level of mastery rather than against an average score of children of the same age.

cross-modal intersensory activity—Use and integration of more than one sensory modality; for instance, matching an object that is seen visually to an identical object selected through touch only.

cultural scripts—Unspoken, and often unconscious, messages that are rooted in our culture and upbringing and tell us how to behave and respond in different situations.

curriculum—Overall master plan of the early childhood program reflecting its philosophy, into which specific activities are fit.

D

daily living—Montessori classroom area that focuses on practical tasks involved in self-care and environment care.

deep structure—According to Noam Chomsky, inborn understanding or underlying rules of grammar and meaning that are universal across all languages.

deficit (or impairment)—A problem in development, usually organic, resulting in below-normal performance.

Denver II—A quick test for possible developmental delays in children from infancy to age six.

developmental delay—A child's development in one or more areas occurring at an age significantly later than that of peers.

Developmental Indicators for the Assessment of Learning (DIAL III)—A developmental screening test for children ages two to six, assessing motor, concept, and language development.

developmental interactionist model—Foundation of the Bank Street approach, concerned with the interaction among various aspects of each child's development as well as between child and environment.

Developmentally Appropriate Practice (DAP)—Teaching young children by matching practice with what we know about their development.

developmental test—This type of test measures the child's functioning in most or all areas of development, although some such tests are specific to one or two areas.

diagnostic testing—Another term for screening, which might indicate that more thorough testing should be carried out.

diagrams—According to Rhoda Kellogg, the stage in children's art when they begin to use the six recognizable shapes—the rectangle, oval, triangle, X, cross, and the deliberate odd-shaped line.

didactic—A term often applied to teaching materials, indicating a built-in intent to provide specific instruction.

digital citizenship—The need for adults and children to use media in an appropriate, responsible, and ethical way and to understand the uses, abuses, and misuses of technology.

discipline—Generally considered a response to children's misbehavior.

disequilibrium—According to Jean Piaget, the lack of balance experienced when existing mental structures and new experience do not fit exactly.

disposition—The tendency consciously to exhibit a set of behaviors that reflect a pattern of good early childhood practice.

divergent thinking—The act of expanding or elaborating on an idea, for example, brainstorming.

documentation—Documentation involves keeping a careful record of the children's involvement in projects; using photographs, samples of children's work, and a record of their words; and arranging these in an aesthetic and informative manner to illustrate the process of learning.

Down syndrome—A disability in which children have significant developmental, cognitive, and intellectual delays, marked by noticeable physical characteristics such as small head and stature, slanted eyes, and protruding tongue.

E

early childhood education—Term encompassing developmentally appropriate programs that serve children from birth through eight years of age; a field of study that trains students to work effectively with young children.

early childhood education models—Approaches to early childhood education, based on specific theoretical foundations, for instance, the behavioral, Piagetian, or Montessori view.

Early Childhood Environments Rating Scale (ECERS)—A widely used assessment of the early childhood environment, used both for research and for program-evaluation purposes.

early childhood teacher or **educator**—A specifically trained professional who works with children from infancy to age eight.

eclectic approach—Describing an approach in which various desirable features from different theories or methods are selected; drawing elements from different sources.

ecological systems theory—A view of the family as an ever-developing and changing social unit in which members constantly accommodate and adapt to each other's demands as well as to outside demands.

effective praise—A form of encouragement that focuses on children's activities rather than on teacher evaluation of their work; praise that is meaningful to children rather than general or gratuitous.

ego strength—Ability to deal effectively with the environment.

emergent curriculum—An alternative to the theme-based curriculum; topics are developed based on the interests of the children.

emergent literacy—The ongoing, dynamic process of learning to read and write, which starts in the early years.

emotional intelligence—The ability to perceive, control, and evaluate emotions and use this information to manage our emotions effectively.

empowerment—Helping families gain a sense of control over events in their lives.

environmental print—Print and other graphic symbols that are found in the physical environment, such as signs, billboards, TV commercials, and common containers.

equilibrium—According to Jean Piaget, the state of balance each person seeks between existing mental structures and new experiences.

equipment—Large items, such as furniture, that represent a more expensive, long-term investment in an early childhood facility.

event sampling—A method of observation in which the observer records a specific behavior only when it occurs.

executive functions—Noncognitive functions that are, nonetheless, important to school success, including skills such as the ability to focus, to retain and use information, to plan and revise action plans as needed, and to self-regulate.

exosystem—According to family systems theory, that part of the environment that includes the broader components of the community that affect the functioning of the family, such as governmental agencies or mass media.

extended family—Family members beyond the immediate nuclear family, for instance, aunts and uncles, grandparents, and cousins.

extinction—In behavioral theory, a method of eliminating a previously reinforced behavior by taking away all reinforcement, for instance, by totally ignoring the behavior.

eye–hand coordination—Integrative ability to use the hands as guided by information from the eyes.

F

family child care homes—Care for a relatively small number of children in a family home that has been licensed or registered for that purpose.

family education—Programs aimed at enhancing parent family–child relations and improving parenting competence.

family engagement—The commitment of families to the early childhood program through a wide variety of options.

family–teacher conference—A one-on-one interaction between the child's family and the teacher.

fetal alcohol effect (FAE)—Not as serious or noticeable as fetal alcohol syndrome, FAE, nonetheless, can leave children at a disadvantage in their ability to learn and reach optimal development.

fetal alcohol syndrome (FAS)—Irreversible birth abnormalities resulting from the mother's heavy alcohol consumption during pregnancy. Children are usually mentally challenged and hyperactive and may have small head size, small overall size, and various limb or facial abnormalities.

fine motor development—Development of skills involving the small muscles of the fingers and hands necessary for such tasks as writing, drawing, and buttoning.

flexibility—A measure of creativity involving the capability to adapt readily to change in a positive, productive manner.

fluency—A measure of creativity involving the ability to generate many relevant ideas on a given topic in a limited time.

formal operations period—Piaget's period covering adolescence.

fragile X syndrome—A disability in which children have significant developmental, cognitive, and intellectual delays, marked by noticeable physical characteristics such as large head, crossed eyes, and poor muscle tone.

G

gender identity—Identification with the same sex.

gender stability—Children's recognition that sex is constant and cannot be changed; occurs by age five to seven, but not earlier.

generativity—According to Erik Erikson, the stage of human development in which the mature adult focuses on the care and nurture of the young.

genres—Categories or types of music, such as classical, jazz, or country.

gifted children—Children who perform significantly above average in intellectual and creative areas.

gross motor development—Development of skills involving the large muscles of the legs, arms, back, and shoulders, necessary for such tasks as running, jumping, and climbing.

guidance—Ongoing process of directing children's behavior based on the types of adults children are expected to become.

H

Head Start Program Performance Standards—Federal accountability system for all Head Start programs, requiring that children meet specific outcomes in language, literacy, and math competencies.

head teacher—The person in charge of a class who is ultimately responsible for all aspects of class functioning.

High/Scope Child Observational Record (COR)—An alternative method of gathering reliable information about young children; COR uses teachers' notes of observations by classifying them into specific categories.

holding grip—Placement of the hands in using a tool for drawing or writing.

home visit—A one-on-one interaction between the teacher and the child's family that takes place in the child's home.

human development theory—A way to describe what happens as individuals move from infancy through adulthood, identifying significant events that are commonly experienced by all people, and explaining why changes occur as they do.

I

ignoring—A principle of behavior management that involves removing all reinforcement for a given behavior to eliminate that behavior.

imagery—A relaxation technique in which a mental image such as "float like a feather" or "melt like ice" is invoked.

I-message—Thomas Gordon's term for a response to a child's behavior that focuses on how the adult feels rather than on the child's character.

individualism—The general tendency of a cultural group to place greater emphasis on the needs and wants of the individual rather than on those of the group.

Individualized Education Plan (IEP)—Mandated by Public Law 94-142, such a plan must be designed for each child with a disability and must involve parents as well as teachers and other appropriate professionals.

Individualized Family Service Plan (IFSP)—Required by the 1986 Education of the Handicapped Act Amendments for children with disabilities under the age of three and their families; the IFSP, often developed by a transdisciplinary team that includes the teachers, social workers, psychologists, and parents, determines goals and objectives that build on the strengths of the child and family.

inductive reasoning—A guidance approach in which the adult uses logic and reasoning to help the child see the consequences of a behavior for other people.

Industry vs. Inferiority—The fourth stage of development described by Erik Erikson, starting at the end of the preschool years and lasting until puberty, in which the child focuses on the development of competence.

information processing—A model of cognitive development that is somewhat analogous to how a computer functions; it is concerned primarily with how human beings take in and store information.

Initiative vs. Guilt—The third stage of development described by Erik Erikson, occurring during the preschool years, in which the child's curiosity and enthusiasm lead to a need to explore and learn about the world, and in which rules and expectations begin to be established.

innatist view of language development—The view that inborn factors are the most important component of language development.

integrated curriculum—A program that focuses on all aspects of children's development, not just cognitive development.

interactionist view of language development—The view that language develops through a combination of inborn factors and environmental influences.

interpersonal moral rules—Considered as universal, including prohibitions against harm to others, murder, incest, and theft.

invented spelling—Used by young children in their early attempts to write by finding the speech sound that most clearly fits what they want to convey.

K

key experiences—In the cognitively oriented curriculum, the eight cognitive concepts on which activities are built.

kindergarten—German word, literally meaning "garden for children," coined by Friedrich Froebel for his program for young children.

kinesthetic sense—Information from the body's system that provides knowledge about the body, its parts, and its movement; involves the "feel" of movement without reference to visual or verbal cues.

L

large-group time circle, story, or group time)—Time block(s) during the day when all of the children and teachers join together in a common activity.

latch-key (or self-care) children—School-age children who, after school, return to an empty home because their parents are at work.

learning centers (also called interest or activity areas)—Areas where materials and equipment are combined around common activities, for instance, art, science, or language arts.

learning standards—The expectations for the learning and development of young children across all developmental domains, including physical, cognitive, language, and socioemotional, which are generally published in some kind of document.

least restrictive environment—A provision of Public Law 94-142 that children with disabilities be placed in a program as close as possible to a setting designed for children without disabilities, while still being able to meet each child's special needs.

lesson plans—The working documents from which the daily program is run, specifying directions for activities.

linguistic intelligence—Ability and sensitivity to spoken and written language.

locomotion—Self-movement from place to place, such as in walking.

logical consequences—Rudolf Dreikurs's technique of allowing children to experience the natural outcome of their actions.

logical thinking—According to Jean Piaget, the ability that begins to emerge around age seven in which children use mental processes to solve problems rather than relying solely on perceived information.

logico-mathematical intelligence—Skills needed for logical, analytical, mathematical, and scientific tasks.

long-term memory—In information processing theory, the vast store of information and knowledge that is held for a long time.

M

macrosystem—According to family systems theory, the broadest part of the environment, which includes the cultural, political, and economic forces that affect families.

malnutrition—Children do not have sufficient food to support growth and development.

manipulatives—Toys and materials that require the use of the fingers and hands; for instance, puzzles, beads, and pegboards.

mapping—A mapmaking activity involving spatial relations in which space is represented creatively through such media as marking pens or blocks.

materials—The smaller, often expendable, items used in early childhood programs that are replaced and replenished frequently.

maturational theory—Explanation of human development dependent on information about when children achieve specific skills.

memory strategies—Various approaches used, especially by older children and adults, to help them remember information.

mesosystem—According to family systems theory, the linkages between the family and the immediate neighborhood and community.

metacognition—Thinking about one's own thinking; being able to think about and predict how one might do on various tasks and self-monitor mastery and understanding.

metamemory—The ability to think about one's own memory.

Metropolitan Readiness Test—A test to determine whether a child is prepared to enter a program such as kindergarten.

microsystem—According to family systems theory, that part of the environment that most immediately affects a person, such as the family, school, or workplace.

mirror neurons—Cells in the brain that respond both when a person acts and when he simply watches the same action, "mirroring" movement and emotion, as though the observer himself were acting or feeling.

misnourishment—Children do not eat the right kinds of foods needed for healthy development, but overeat the wrong kinds of foods.

mock writing—Young children's imitation of writing through wavy, circular, or vertical lines, which can be seen as distinct from drawing or scribbling.

model—In social learning theory, those whom children imitate, particularly because of some desirable feature or attribute.

modeling—In social learning theory, the process of imitating a model.

Montessori equipment—Early childhood learning materials derived from and part of the Montessori approach.

moral development—The long-term process of learning and internalizing the rules and standards of right and wrong.

morphology—The study of word rules; for instance, tense, plurals, and possessives.

multisensory—Referring to information that depends on input from several of the senses.

multiple intelligences—Howard Gardner's theory that our minds use many types of intelligence, not just those traditionally included in the educational context.

musical intelligence—Skills needed in the performance, composition, and appreciation of music.

myelin—A white, fatty substance that coats nerve fibers in the brain, thereby increasing the speed at which nerve impulses are transmitted from cell to cell.

myelination—The gradual process by which myelin coats brain cells, thus facilitating the development of skills controlled by different parts of the brain as these become myelinated.

N

National Association for the Education of Young Children (NAEYC)—Largest American early childhood professional organization, which deals with issues related to children from birth to age eight and those who work with young children.

natural playscapes—A new playground movement that emphasizes a focus on nature; features of the outdoor space are composed of natural materials.

naturalistic intelligence—The ability to see patterns and relationships to nature, also called "nature smarts."

neurons—The specialized cells of the brain.

norm-referenced—A test in which scores are determined by using a large group of same-age children as the basis for comparison, rather than using a predetermined criterion or standard of performance.

nuclear family—The smallest family unit, made up of a couple or one or two parents with child(ren).

number concepts—One of the cognitive concepts young children begin to acquire, involving an understanding of quantity.

O

object permanence—Part of Jean Piaget's theory, the recognition that objects exist, even when they are out of view; a concept that children begin to develop toward the end of their first year of life.

observable behavior—Actions that can be seen rather than those that are inferred.

observational learning—In social learning theory, the process of learning that comes from watching, noting the behavior of, and imitating models.

one-to-one correspondence—A way in which young preschoolers begin to acquire an understanding of number concepts by matching items to each other; for instance, one napkin beside each plate.

open education—A program that operates on the assumption that children, provided with a well-conceived environment, are capable of selecting and learning from appropriate activities.

open-ended materials—Early childhood materials that are flexible rather than structured and can be used in a variety of ways rather than in only a single manner.

operant conditioning—The principle of behavioral theory whereby a person deliberately attempts to increase or decrease behavior by controlling consequences.

organization—According to Jean Piaget, the mental process by which a person organizes experiences and information in relation to each other.

overextension—Application of a word to a variety of related objects, especially used by toddlers.

P

palmar grasp—A way of holding tools in which the pencil or crayon lies across the palm of the hand with the fingers curled around it, and the arm rather than the wrist moves the tool.

parquetry blocks—Variously shaped flat blocks, including diamonds and parallelograms, that can be assembled into different patterns on a form board.

perceived competence—Children's belief in their ability to succeed in a given task.

perceptual motor model—A theoretical view of physical development that holds that motor behaviors are a prerequisite for and lead to cognitive abilities.

performance standards—The benchmark that describes the level at which children should perform in relation to their age or grade level, measured through some form of test or assessment.

personal control—The feeling that a person has the power to make things happen.

phobia—An intense, irrational fear.

physical punishment—Use of physical force with the intent of causing bodily pain or discomfort to a child for the purpose of correcting or punishing the child's behavior.

pictorialism—According to Rhoda Kellogg, the stage in the development of art in which children draw recognizable objects.

pincer grasp—The use of thumb and forefinger to pick up small objects; this skill develops at around nine months of age.

PK-3 movement—A relatively new approach that stresses the importance of continuity and alignment among early childhood and early elementary programs.

placement patterns—According to Rhoda Kellogg, a way of analyzing children's art by examining the 17 ways in which the total picture or design is framed or placed on the paper.

plan–do–review cycle—The heart of the cognitively oriented curriculum through which children are encouraged to make deliberate, systematic choices with the help of teachers by planning ahead of time, carrying out, then recalling each day's activities.

planning time—In the cognitively oriented curriculum, the time set aside during which children decide what activities they would like to participate in during the ensuing work time.

playscapes—Contemporary, often innovative, playground structures that combine a variety of materials.

positive discipline—Synonymous with guidance, an approach that allows the child to develop self-discipline gradually.

positive reinforcement—Application of a behavioral principle, which includes any immediate feedback (either through tangible or nontangible means) to children that their behavior is valued.

postconventional level of moral development—According to Lawrence Kohlberg, the stage in which moral decisions are made according to universal considerations of what is right.

pragmatics—Rules that govern language use in social contexts.

preconventional level of moral development—According to Lawrence Kohlberg, the stage during which moral decisions are made based on personal preference or avoidance of punishment.

preoperational period—Piaget's period covering the preschool years.

prepared environment—Maria Montessori's term to describe the careful match between appropriate materials and what the child is most ready to learn at any given time.

preschematic stage—The stage in the development of art in which children have a subject in mind when they begin a picture, but in which the actual product will be an inaccurate, crude representation of the real thing.

programmed instruction (or direct instruction)—A method of teaching in which the teacher determines exactly what the children should learn, devises a sequence of learning activities to teach specific information, and teaches it directly by controlling the information according to children's responses.

progressive relaxation—A technique in which various specified muscle groups are tensed, then relaxed systematically.

project approach—A curriculum that expands children's learning through in-depth exploration of topics that are of interest to children and teachers.

prosocial behaviors—Positive, commonly valued social behaviors such as sharing, empathy, and understanding.

psychosocial theory—The branch of psychology founded by Erik Erikson, in which development is described in terms of eight stages that span childhood and adulthood, each offering opportunities for personality growth and development.

punishment—An aversive consequence that follows a behavior for the purpose of decreasing or eliminating the behavior; not recommended as an effective means of changing behavior.

Q

Quality Rating and Improvement System (QRIS)—Rating of quality of child care programs to help parents make informed choices; implemented in a number of states.

R

rating scale—An assessment of specific skills or concepts that are rated on some qualitative dimension of excellence or accomplishment.

rational counting—Distinguished from rote counting, in rational counting the child accurately attaches a numeral name to a series of objects being counted.

recall time—In the cognitively oriented curriculum, the time when children review their work-time activities.

reflection—Being thoughtful and analytical in the act of teaching.

reflective abstraction—According to Jean Piaget, part of a child's self-directed activity that allows the child to think about and reflect on what he or she is doing, leading to the development of new mental abilities.

reinforcement—In behavioral theory, any response that follows a behavior that encourages repetition of that behavior.

reliability—A measure of a test indicating that the test is stable and consistent, to ensure that changes in score are due to the child, not the test.

representation—According to Jean Piaget, the ability to depict an object, person, action, or experience mentally, even if it is not present in the immediate environment.

resilient children—Children who, despite extremely stressful lives, appear to be stable, outgoing, and optimistic.

rote counting—Reciting numbers from memory without attaching meaning to them in the context of objects in a series.

rough-and-tumble play—highly physical play, which should be distinguished from fighting; in such play there is laughter, children's faces reflect enjoyment, and their muscle tone is relaxed.

running record—A type of observation that provides an account of all of the child's behavior over a period of time.

s

scaffolding—In Vygotsky's sociocultural theory, the support provided by adults and older peers to help children learn the new tasks they are not yet able to accomplish on their own.

schemata (singular, schema)—According to Jean Piaget, cognitive structures into which cognitive concepts or mental representations are organized.

schematic stage—Older children's drawings, which are more realistic and accurate than younger children's in what they depict.

screening test—A quick method of identifying children who might exhibit developmental delay; it is only an indicator and must be followed up by more thorough and comprehensive testing.

scribbling stage—The stage in the development of art in which children experiment with marks on a page.

self-concept—Perceptions and feelings children may have about themselves, gathered largely from how the important people in their world respond to them.

self-correcting—Learning materials such as puzzles that give the child immediate feedback on success when the task is completed.

self-demand schedule—Infants' schedules are determined by their individual needs, and adults respond appropriately to these.

self-esteem—Children's evaluation of their worth in positive or negative terms.

self-help skills—Tasks involving caring for oneself, such as dressing, feeding, toileting, and grooming.

self-selected time-out—A technique in which children are given the responsibility for removing themselves from the classroom if they feel they are about to lose control.

semantic network—The interrelationship among words, particularly related to word meaning.

semantics—Understanding and study of word meaning.

sensitive periods—Maria Montessori's term describing the times when children are most receptive to absorbing specific learning.

sensitivity—As related to creativity, sensitivity refers to a receptivity to external and internal stimuli.

sensorial—Montessori classroom area in which materials help children develop, organize, broaden, and refine sensory perceptions of sight, sound, touch, smell, and taste.

sensorimotor period—Piaget's period covering infancy.

sensory deficit—A problem, particularly of sight or hearing.

sensory discrimination—Involvement in an activity in which one of the senses is used to distinguish a specific feature or dimension of similar materials; it might include matching or sorting by size, color, shape, sound, smell, or taste.

sensory integration—The ability to translate sensory information into intelligent behavior.

sensory-perceptual development—Giving meaning to information that comes through the senses.

sensory register—In information processing theory, that part of the model describing how information initially comes to our awareness when perceived by the senses.

separation anxiety—Emotional difficulty experienced by some young children when leaving their parents.

seriation—A relationship among objects in which they are placed in a logical order, such as from longest to shortest.

shaping—In behavioral theory, a method used to teach a child a new behavior by breaking it down into small steps and reinforcing the attainment of each step systematically.

short-term memory—In information processing theory, limited capacity for temporarily remembering information such as a telephone number.

show-and-tell—A common group activity in which children can share something special and personal with their classmates.

social cognition—Organization of knowledge and information about people and relationships.

social interactionist view of language development—Theoretical view that considers language to be closely tied to and dependent on social processes.

social learning theory—Theoretical view derived from but going beyond behaviorism, which considers that children learn not just from reinforcement but from observing and imitating others.

social reinforcer—In behavioral theory, a reward that conveys approval through such responses as a smile, hug, or attention.

socialization—The process through which children become a functioning part of society and learn society's rules and values.

sociocultural theory—Originated by Lev Vygotsky, this theory gives prominence to the social, cultural, and historic context of child development.

sociodramatic play—Children's dramatic or symbolic play that involves more than one child in social interaction.

software—The "instructions" that direct a computer to perform an activity, usually stored on a disk or directly in the computer; many such programs are available for young children.

spatial concepts—A cognitive ability involving an understanding of how objects and people occupy, move in, and use space.

spatial relationship—The relative position to each other of objects and people in space.

special time—A method for spending a few minutes a day with just one child as a way of providing unconditional attention.

stage theorist—Any theory that delineates specific stages in which development is marked by qualitatively different characteristics and accomplishments and in which each stage builds on the previous ones.

Stanford–Binet Intelligence Scale—A widely used test that yields an intelligence quotient (IQ).

stranger anxiety—Displays of fear and withdrawal by many infants beginning around six months of age, when babies are well able to distinguish their mother's face from the faces of other people.

stress—Internal or external demand on a person's ability to adapt.

sudden infant death syndrome (SIDS)—Also called "crib death," this is the unexplained death of an infant during sleep; sleeping on the back reduces the incidence of SIDS.

surface structure—According to Noam Chomsky, specific aspects of language that vary from one language to another.

symbolic representation—The ability acquired by young children to use mental images to stand for something else.

syntax—Involves the grammatical rules that govern the structure of sentences.

T

team teaching—An approach that involves co-teaching in which status and responsibility are equal rather than having a pyramid structure of authority, with one person in charge and others subordinate.

temperament—Children's inborn characteristics—such as regularity, adaptability, and disposition—that affect behavior.

temporal concepts—Cognitive ability concerned with the child's gradual awareness of time as a continuum.

temporal sequencing—The ability to place a series of events in the order of their occurrence.

time-out—Techniques in which the child is removed from the reinforcement and stimulation of the classroom.

time sampling—A quantitative measure or count of how often a specific behavior occurs within a given amount of time.

total communication approach—In children with hearing impairments, using a combination of methods such as sign language, speech reading, and hearing aids.

tripod grasp—A way of holding tools in which the pencil or crayon is held by the fingers, and the wrist, rather than the whole arm, moves the tool.

Trust vs. Mistrust—The first stage of development described by Erik Erikson, occurring during infancy, in which the child's needs should be met consistently and predictably.

U

unconditional attention—A way of conveying acceptance to children by letting them know they are valued and liked; attention that is not given in response to a specific behavior.

unit blocks—The most common type of blocks, they are precision-made of hardwood in standardized sizes and shapes.

V

validity—A characteristic of a test that indicates that the test actually measures what it purports to measure.

visual literacy—The ability of children to talk about their art and understand the message conveyed in others' artwork.

visual-spatial intelligence—The ability to manipulate and portray visual images.

W

work sampling system—An alternative method of gathering reliable information about young children, using a combination of observations, checklists, portfolios, and summary reports.

work time—In the cognitively oriented curriculum, the large block of time during which children engage in self-selected activities.

Y

you-message—Thomas Gordon's term for a response to a child's behavior that focuses on the child's character (usually in negative terms) rather than on how the adult feels.

Z

zone of proximal development (ZPD)—In Vygotsky's theory, this zone represents tasks children cannot yet do by themselves but which they can accomplish with the support of an older child or adult.

References

ACEI. (2008). Association for Childhood Education International. Available online at www.acei.org.

Ackerman, D. J. Barnett, W. S., & Robin, K. B. (2005). *Making the most of kindergarten: Present trends and future issues in the provision of full-day programs.* New Brunswick, NJ: Rutgers University, National Institute for Early Education Research.

Allen, K. E., & Cowdery, G. E. (2012). *The exceptional child: Inclusion in early childhood education* (7th ed.). Belmont, CA: Wadsworth, Cengage Learning.

Allen, K. E., & Marotz, L. (2010). *Developmental profiles: Pre-birth through twelve* (6th ed.). Belmont, CA: Wadsworth, Cengage Learning.

Alliance for Childhood. (2005). *Time for play, every day: It's fun—and fundamental.* Available online at www.allianceforchildhood.org.

American Academy of Pediatrics. (1999). *Guide to your child's nutrition.* New York: Villard.

American Academy of Pediatrics. (2002). *Caring for our children. National Health and Safety Performance Standards: Guidelines for out-of-home child care programs* (2nd ed.). Elk Grove Village, IL: American Academy of Pediatrics.

American Academy of Pediatrics. (2005a). *Television and the family.* Available online at www.aap.org.

American Academy of Pediatrics, Task Force on Sudden Infant Death Syndrome. (2005b). The changing concept of sudden infant death syndrome: Diagnostic coding shifts, controversies regarding the sleeping environment, and new variables to consider in reducing risk. *Pediatrics, 116,* 1245–1255.

American Academy of Pediatrics. (2007). *The importance of play in promoting healthy child development and maintaining strong parent-child bonds.* Available online at www.pediatrics.org/cgi/doi/10.1542/peds.2006-2697.

American Academy of Pediatrics. (2010). *Policy statement: Prevention of choking among children.* Available online at http://pediatrics.aappublications.org/content/early/2010/02/22/peds.2009-2862.

Andersson, B. E. (1989). Effects of public day-care: A longitudinal study. *Child Development, 60,* 857–866.

Andersson, B. E. (1992). Effects of day-care on cognitive and socioemotional competence of thirteen-year-old Swedish school children. *Child Development, 63,* 20–36.

Arnett, J. (1987). *Caregivers in day care centers: Does training matter?* Presented at the biennial meeting of the Society for Research in Child Development, Baltimore, MD.

Association of Waldorf Schools of North America. (2008). What is Waldorf Education? Available online at www.whywaldorfworks.org.

Baghban, M. (2007). Scribbles, labels, and stories: The role of drawing in the development of writing. *Young Children, 62*(1), 20–26.

Bailey, C. T. (2004, with 2006 updates). *The National Survey of Child Development Associates (CDAs).* Available online at http://www.eric.ed.gov/PDFS/ED444713.pdf.

Balaban, N. (1992). The role of child care professionals in caring for infants, toddlers, and their families. *Young Children, 47*(5), 66–71.

Balaban, N. (2006). Easing the separation process for infants, toddlers, and families. *Young Children, 61*(6), 14–20.

Bandura, A. (1977). *Social learning theory.* Englewood Cliffs, NJ: Prentice Hall.

Barnes, J. E. (2000, February 10). Where did you go, Raggedy Ann? *New York Times,* 1, 14.

Barnett, W. S. (1996). *Lives in the balance: Age-27 benefit-cost analysis of the High/Scope Perry Preschool Program.* Ypsilanti, MI: High/Scope Press.

Bates, J. E. (2000). Temperament as an emotion construct: Theoretical and practical issues. In M. Lewis & J. H. Haviland-Jones (Eds.), *Handbook of emotions* (2nd ed., pp. 382–396). New York: Guilford.

Baumrind, D. (1967). Child care practices anteceding three patterns of preschool behavior. *Genetic Psychological Monographs, 75,* 43–88.

Baumrind, D., & Black, A. E. (1967). Socialization practices associated with dimensions of competence in preschool boys and girls. *Child Development, 38,* 291–327.

Bay-Hinitz, A. K., Peterson, R. F., & Quilitch, H. R. (1994). Cooperative games: A way to modify aggressive and cooperative behaviors in young children. *Journal of Applied Behavior Analysis, 27,* 435–446.

Bayman, A. G. (1995). An example of a small project for kindergartners that includes some 3Rs learning. *Young Children, 50*(6), 27–31.

Behrmann, R. E. (2000). Children and computer technology. *The Future of Children, 10*(2).

Belm, D., & Whitebook, M. (2006). *Roots of decline: How government policy has de-educated teachers of young children.* Berkeley, CA: Center for the Study of Child Care Employment Institute of Industrial Relations, University of California at Berkeley.

Belsky, J., Vandell, D. L., Burchinal, M., Clarke-Stewart, A. K., McCartney, K., & Owen, M. T. (2007). Are there long-term effects of early child care? *Child Development, 78*, 681–701.

Beneke, S. J., Ostrosky, M. M., & Katz, L. G. (2008). Calendar time for young children: Good intentions gone awry. *Young Children, 63*(3), 12–16.

Benham, A. L., & Slotnick, C. F. (2006). Play therapy: Integrating clinical and developmental perspectives. In J. L. Luby (Ed.), *Handbook of preschool mental health: Development, disorders, and treatment* (pp. 330–371). New York: Guilford.

Bentzen, W. R. (2009). *Seeing young children: A guide to observing and recording behavior* (6th ed.). Belmont, CA: Wadsworth, Cengage Learning.

Bereiter, C. (1986). Does direct instruction cause delinquency? *Early Childhood Research Quarterly, 1,* 289–292.

Bereiter, C., & Engelmann, S. (1966). *Teaching disadvantaged children in the preschool.* Englewood Cliffs, NJ: Prentice Hall.

Berk, L. E. (1994). Vygotsky's theory: The importance of make-believe play. *Young Children, 50*(1), 30–39.

Berkowitz, D. (2011). Oral storytelling: Building community through dialogue, engagement, and problem solving. *Young Children, 66*(2) 36–40.

Biber, B. (1984). *Early education and psychological development.* New Haven, CT: Yale University Press.

Birckmayer, J., Kennedy, A., & Stonehouse, A. (2009). Using stories effectively with infants and toddlers. *Young Children, 64*(1), 42–47.

Bisgaier, C. S., Samaras, T., & Russo, M. J. (2004). Young children try, try again using wood, glue, and words to enhance learning. *Young Children, 59*(4), 22–29.

Bjorklund, D. F. (2012). *Children's thinking: Cognitive development and individual differences* (5th ed.). Belmont, CA: Wadsworth, Cengage Learning.

Bodrova, E., & Leong, D. J. (2003). The importance of being playful. *Educational Leadership, 60*(7), 50–53.

Bodrova, E., & Leong, D. J. (2007). *Tools of the mind: The Vygotskian approach to early childhood education* (2nd ed.). Upper Saddle River, NJ: Merrill/Pearson.

Bornstein, M. H., & Lamb, M. E. (2010). *Development in infancy: An introduction.* New York: Psychology Press.

Bosse, S., Jacobs, G., & Anderson, T. L. (2009). Science in the air. *Young Children,64*(6), 10–15.

Bowman, B. T. (2006). Standards: At the heart of educational equity. *Young Children, 61*(5), 42–48.

Bowman, B. T., Donovan, M. S., & Burns, M. S. (Eds.). (2001). *Eager to learn: Educating our preschoolers.* Washington, DC: National Academies Press.

Bracey, G. W. (1996). The impact of early intervention research. *Phi Delta Kappan, 77,* 510, 512.

Branscomb, K. R., & Goble, C. B. (2008). Infants and toddlers in group care: Feeding practices that foster emotional health. *Young Children, 63*(6), 28–33.

Bransford, J. D., Brown, A. L., & Cocking, R. R. (2000). *How people learn: Brain, mind, experience, and school.* Washington, DC: National Academies Press.

Braun, S. J., & Edwards, E. P. (1972). *History and theory of early childhood education.* Worthington, OH: Charles A. Jones.

Brazelton, T. B. (1990, September 9). Why is America failing its children? *New York Times Magazine,* pp. 40–43, 50, 90.

Bredekamp, S. (1993). Reflections on Reggio Emilia. *Young Children, 49*(1), 13–17.

Bredekamp, S. (2009). Early learning standards and developmentally appropriate practice: Contradictory or compatible? In S. Feeney, A. Galper, and C. Seefeldt (Eds.), *Continuing issues in early childhood education* (pp. 258–271). Upper Saddle River, NJ: Merrill.

Bredekamp, S., & Copple, C. E. (Eds.). (1997). *Developmentally appropriate practice in early childhood programs serving children from birth through age 8* (Rev. ed.). Washington, DC: National Association for the Education of Young Children.

Bredekamp, S., & Shepard, L. (1989). How best to protect children from inappropriate school expectations, practices, and policies. *Young Children, 44*(3), 14–24.

Bricker, D. (2003). *Assessment, Evaluation, and Programming System for Infants and Children* (2nd ed.). Baltimore: Brookes.

Brigance, A. H. (2004). *Brigance inventory of early development—II.* North Billerica, MA: Curriculum Associates.

Brinson, S. A. (2009). Behold the power of African American female characters! Reading to encourage self-worth, inform/inspire, and bring pleasure. *Young Children, 64*(1), 26–31.

Bronfenbrenner, U. (1979). *The ecology of human development.* Cambridge, MA: Harvard University Press.

Bronfenbrenner, U. (1994). Ecological models of human development. In *International Encyclopedia of Education* (Vol. 3, 2nd ed.). Oxford, United Kingdom: Elsevier. Reprinted in M. Gauvain & M. Cole (Eds.), *Readings on the development of children* (pp. 37–43). New York: Freeman.

Bronfenbrenner, U., & Crouter, A. C. (1983). Ecology of the family as a context for human development research perspectives. In P. H. Mussen (Ed.), *Handbook of child psychology (Vol. 1): History, theory and methods.* New York: Wiley.

Bronfenbrenner, U., & Morris, P. A. (1998). The ecology of developmental processes. In R. M. Lerner (Vol. Ed.), *Handbook of child psychology (Vol. I): Theoretical models of human development* (pp. 993–1028). New York: Wiley.

Bronson, M. B. (2009). Recognizing and supporting the development of self-regulation in young children. In E. Essa & M. Burnham (Eds.), *Informing our practice: Useful research on young children's development* (pp. 50–58). Washington, DC: NAEYC.

Brooks-Gunn, J., Rouse, C. E., & McLanahan, S. (2007). Racial and ethnic gaps in school readiness. In R. C. Pianta, M. J. Cox, & K. L. Snow (Eds.), *School readiness and the transition to kindergarten in the era of accountability* (pp. 283–306). Baltimore: Council of Chief State School Officers Brookes.

Brown, R. (1973). *A first language.* Cambridge, MA: Harvard University Press.

Bruer, J. T. (1997). Education and the brain: A bridge too far. *Educational Researcher, 26,* 4–16.

Bruer, J. T. (2002). *The myth of the first three years: A new understanding of early brain development and lifelong learning.* New York: Free Press.

Bruno, H. E. (2011). The neurobiology of emotional intelligence: Using our brain to stay cool under pressure. *Young Children, 66*(1), 22–26.

Bumgarner, M. A. (1999). *Working with school-age children.* Mountain View, CA: Mayfield.

Burchinal, M., Howes, C., Pianta, R., Bryant, D., Early, D., Cliffort, R., & Barbarin, O. (2008). Predicting child outcomes at the end of kindergarten from the quality of pre-kindergarten teacher-child interactions and instruction. *Applied Developmental Science, 12,* 140–153.

Burchinal, M. R., Roberts, J. E., Nabors, L. A., & Bryant, D. M. (1996). Quality of center child care and infant cognitive and language development. *Child Development, 67,* 606–620.

Burd, L., Cotsonas-Hassler, T. M., Martsolf, J. T., & Kerbeshian, J. (2003). Recognition and management of fetal alcohol syndrome. *Neurotaxicological Teratology, 25,* 681–688.

Burnham, M. M., & Gaylor, E. E. (2008). Behavioral sleep disorders in infants and toddlers. In A. Ivanenko (Ed.), *Sleep and psychiatric disorders in children and adolescents* (pp. 23–35). New York: Informa.

Burnham, M. M., Gaylor, E. E., & Anders, T. F. (2006). Sleep disorders. In J. L. Luby (Ed.), *Handbook of preschool mental health: Development, disorders, and treatment* (pp. 186–208). New York: Guilford Press.

Burts, D. C., Hart, C. H., Charlesworth, R., DeWolf, D. M., Ray, J., Manuel, K., & Fleege, P. O. (1993). Developmental appropriateness of kindergarten programs and academic outcomes in first grade. *Journal of Research in Childhood Education, 8,* 23–31.

Burts, D. C., Hart, C. H., Charlesworth, R., & Kirk, L., (1990). A comparison of frequencies of stress behaviors observed in kindergarten children in classrooms with developmentally appropriate versus developmentally inappropriate instructional practices. *Early Childhood Research Quarterly, 5,* 407–423.

Buzzelli, C. A. (1992). Young children's moral understanding: Learning about right and wrong. *Young Children, 47*(6), 47–53.

Cadwell, L. B., & Fyfe, B. V. (2004). Conversations with children. In J. Hendrick (Ed.), *Next steps toward teaching the Reggio way: Accepting the challenge to change* (pp. 137–150). Upper Saddle River, NJ: Merrill.

Calman, L. J., & Tarr-Whelan, L. (2005). *Early childhood education for all: A wise investment.* Recommendations arising from the conference, The Economic Impacts of Child Care and Early Education: Financing Solutions for the Future (December 2004, Cambridge, MA). New York: Legal Momentum.

Campbell, F. A., & Ramey, C. T. (1994). Effects of early intervention on intellectual and academic achievement: A follow-up study of children from low income families. *Child Development, 65,* 684–698.

Campbell, F. A., & Taylor, K. (1996). Early childhood programs that work for children from economically disadvantaged families. *Young Children, 51*(4), 74–80.

Capizzano, J., Adams, G., & Sonnenstein, F. (2000). *Child care arrangements for children under five: Variations across states.* New federalism: National survey of America's families, Series B (No. B-7). Washington, DC: The Urban Institute.

Carlson, F. M. (2011). *Big body play: why boisterous, vigorous, and very physical play is essential to children's development and learning.* Washington, DC: National Association for the Education of Young Children.

Carter, D. B. (1987). Early childhood education: A historical perspective. In J. L. Roopnarine & J. E. Johnson (Eds.), *Approaches to early childhood education* (pp. 1–14). Columbus, OH: Merrill.

Caulfield, R. (1997). Professionalism in early care and education. *Early Childhood Education Journal, 24,* 261–263.

Centers for Disease Control and Prevention. (2011). *Prevalence of obesity among children and adolescents: United States, Trends 1963–1965 through 2007–2008.* Available online at www.cdc.gov/nchs/data/hestat/obesity_child_07_08/obesity_child_07_08.htm.

Ceppi, G., & Zini, M. (1998). *Children, spaces, relations: Metaproject for an environment for young children.* Reggio Emilia, Italy: Reggio Children.

Chafel, J. A. (1990). Children in poverty: Policy perspectives on a national crisis. *Young Children, 45*(5), 31–37.

Chalufour, I., & Worth, K. (2004). *Building structures with young children.* Washington, DC: National Association for the Education of Young Children.

Charlesworth, R., Hart, C., Burts, D., & DeWolf, M. (1993). The LSU studies: Building a research base for developmentally appropriate practice. *Advances in Early Education and Day Care, 3,* 3–28.

Charlesworth, R., & Lind, K. K. (2010). *Math and science for young children* (6th ed.). Belmont, CA: Wadsworth, Cengage Learning.

Chattin-McNichols, J. P. (1981). The effects of Montessori school experience. *Young Children, 36*(5), 49–66.

Chattin-McNichols, J. P. (1992). *The Montessori controversy.* Clifton Park, NY: Thomson Delmar Learning.

Child Care Services Association. (2008). *The T.E.A.C.H. Early Childhood and Childcare Wage$ projects: Annual program report 2007–2008.* Chapel Hill, NC: CCSA. Available online at www.childcareservices.org.

Childhelp. (2006). *National child abuse statistics.* Available online at http://pages.uoregon.edu/lougee/Dreiling%20Summer%2009/readings/National%2520Child%2520Abuse%2520Statistics%2520-%2520Childhelp.pdf.

Child Trends Data Bank. (2008). America's children: Key national indicators of well-being, 2007. Available online at www.childtrendsdatabank.org.

Child Welfare Information Gateway. (2008). *Child abuse and neglect fatalities: Statistics and intervention.* Available online at www.childwelfare.gov/pubs/factsheets/fatality.cfm#groups.

Children's Defense Fund. (2000). *Yearbook 2000: The state of America's children.* Washington, DC: The Children's Defense Fund.

Children's Defense Fund. (2008). *State of America's children: 2008 report.* Available online at http://www.childrensdefense.org/child-research-data-publications/data/state-of-americas-children-2008-report.html.

Children's Defense Fund. (2011). *Yearbook 2011: The state of America's children.* Washington, DC: The Children's Defense Fund.

Chomsky, N. (1972). *Language and mind.* New York: Harcourt Brace Jovanovich.

Clark, E. V. (1978a). Non-linguistic strategies and the acquisition of word meaning. In L. Bloom (Ed.), *Readings in language development* (pp. 433–451). New York: Wiley.

Clark, E. V. (1978b). Strategies for communicating. *Child Development, 49,* 953–959.

Clarke-Stewart, K. A. (1987a). In search of consistencies in child care research. In D. A. Phillips (Ed.), *Quality in child care: What does research tell us?* (pp. 105–120). Washington, DC: National Association for the Education of Young Children.

Clarke-Stewart, K. A. (1987b). Predicting child development from child care forms and features. Chicago Study. In D. A. Phillips (Ed.), *Quality in child care: What does research tell us?* (pp. 21–41). Washington, DC: National Association for the Education of Young Children.

Classen, A. (Ed.). (2005). *Childhood in the middle ages and the renaissance: The results of a paradigm shift in the history of mentality.* New York: Walter de Gruyter.

Clements, D. H., & Samara, J. (2003). Young children and technology: What does the research say? *Young Children, 58*(6), 34–40.

Click, P. M., & Karkos, K. (2008). *Administration of schools for young children* (7th ed.). Belmont, CA: Wadsworth, Cengage Learning.

Click, P. M., and Parker, J. (2009). *Caring for school age children* (5th ed.). Belmont, CA: Wadsworth, Cengage Learning.

Click, P. M., and Parker, J. (2012). *Caring for school age children* (6th ed.). Belmont, CA: Wadsworth, Cengage Learning.

Click, P. M., & Karkos, K. (2010). *Administration of schools for young children* (8th ed.). Belmont, CA: Wadsworth, Cengage Learning.

Cohen, D. H., & Stern, V. (1978). *Observing and recording the behavior of young children* (2nd ed.). New York: Teachers College Press, Columbia University.

Colker, L. J. (2008). Twelve characteristics of effective early childhood teachers. *Young Children, 63*(2), 68–73.

Conezio, K., & French, L. (2002). Science in the pre-school classroom: Capitalizing on children's fascination with the everyday world to foster language and literacy development. *Young Children, 57*(2), 12–19.

Cook, R. E., Klein, M. D., Chen, D., & Tessier, A., & Klein, M. D. (2011). *Adapting early childhood curricula for children in inclusive settings* (8th ed.). Englewood Cliffs, NJ: Prentice Hall.

Copley, Y. V. (2000). *The young child and mathematics.* Washington, DC: National Association for the Education of Young Children.

Copple, C. E., & Bredekamp, S. (Eds.). (2009). *Developmentally appropriate practice in early childhood programs serving children from birth through age 8* (3rd ed.). Washington, DC: National Association for the Education of Young Children.

Cottrell, E. (2010). The shocking statistic on child poverty. Available online at www.news.change.org/stories/the-shocking-statistics-on-child-poverty.

Couchenor, D., & Chrisman, K. (2011). *Families, schools, and communities: Together for young children* (4th ed.). Belmont, CA: Wadsworth, Cengage Learning.

Council for Early Childhood Professional Recognition. (2009). *National competency standards for CDA credential.* Available online at www.cdacouncil.org.

Council of Chief State School Officers. (2008). Accountability systems. Available online at www.ccsso.org/projects/accountability_systems.

Cox, M. V. (1986). *The child's point of view: The development of cognition and language.* New York: St. Martin's Press.

Crain, W. (2005). *Theories of development* (5th ed.). Upper Saddle River, NJ: Prentice Hall.

Cranley Gallager, K., Dadisman, K., Farmer, T. W., Huss, L., & Hutchins, B. C. (2007). Social dynamics of early childhood classrooms. In O. Saracho & B. Spodek (Eds.), *Contemporary perspectives on social learning in early childhood education* (pp. 17–48). Greenwich, CT: Information Age.

Cuffaro, H. K., Nager, N., & Shapiro, E. K. (2000). The Developmental-Interaction Approach at Bank Street College of Education. In J. L. Roopnarine & J. E. Johnson (Eds.), *Approaches to early childhood education* (3rd ed.). Upper Saddle River, NJ: Merrill.

Cunningham, B., & Watson, L. W. (2002). Recruiting male teachers. *Young Children, 57*(6), 10–15.

Curtis, D., & Carter, M. (1996). *Reflecting children's lives: A handbook for planning child-centered curriculum.* St. Paul, MN: Redleaf Press.

Curtis, D. & Carter, M. (2003). *Designs for living and learning: Transforming early childhood environments.* St. Paul, MN: Redleaf Press.

Curtis, D. & Carter, M. (2008). *Learning together with young children: A curriculum framework for reflective teachers.* St. Paul, MN: Redleaf Press.

Cutler, K. M., Gilkerson, D., Parrott, S., & Bowne, M. T. (2003). Developing math games based on children's literature. *Young Children, 58*(1), 22–27.

Damon, W. (1977). *The social world of the child.* San Francisco: Jossey-Bass.

Damon, W. (1983). The nature of social-cognitive change in the developing child. In W. F. Overton (Ed.), *The relationship between social and cognitive development* (pp. 103–141). Hillsdale, NJ: Erlbaum.

Dancy, R. B. (March/April 2004). The wisdom of Waldorf: Education for the future. *Mothering Magazine, Issue 123.*

Da Ros-Voseles, D., & Moss, L. (2007). The role of dispositions in the education of future teachers. *Young Children, 62*(5), 90–98.

Database Systems Corporation. (2009). Age restrictions for latchkey kids. Available online at www.latchkey-kids.com/latchkey-kids-age-limits.htm.

Davis, J., & Gardner, H. (1993). The arts and early childhood education: A cognitive developmental portrait of the young child as artist. In B. Spodek (Ed.), *Handbook of research on the education of young children* (pp. 191–206). New York: Macmillan.

Deiner, P. L. (2010). *Inclusive early childhood education: Development, resources, and practice* (5th ed.). Belmont, CA: Wadsworth, Cengage Learning.

Derman-Sparks, L. (1989). *Anti-bias curriculum: Tools for empowering young children.* Washington, DC: National Association for the Education of Young Children.

Dettling, A. C., Gunnar, M. R., & Donzella, B. (1999). Cortisol levels of young children in full-day childcare centers: Relations with age and temperament. *Psychoneuroendocrinology, 24,* 519–536.

Dettling, A. C., Parker, S. W., Lane, S., Sebanc, L., & Gunnar, M. R. (2000). Quality of care and temperament determine changes in cortisol concentrations over the day for young children in childcare. *Psychoneuroendocrinology, 25,* 819–836.

deVilliers, J. G., & deVilliers, P. A. (1973). A cross-sectional study of the acquisition of grammatical morphemes in child speech. *Journal of Psycholinguistic Research, 2,* 267–278.

deVilliers, P. A., & deVilliers, J. G. (1979). *Early language.* Cambridge, MA: Harvard University Press.

Diamond, A., Barnett, W. S., Thomas, J., & Munro, S. (2007). Preschool program improves cognitive control. *Science, 318,* 1387–1388.

Dickinson, D. K., & Tabors, P. O. (2002). Fostering language and literacy in classrooms and homes. *Young Children, 57*(2), 10–18.

Diffily, D. (1996). The project approach: A museum exhibit created by kindergartners. *Young Children, 51*(2), 72–75.

Dodd, C. (1993). Testimony before the Joint Senate-House Hearing on *Keeping Every Child Safe: Curbing the Epidemic of Violence.* 103rd Congress, 1st session, March 10.

Dodge, D. T. (2004). *The Creative Curriculum for preschool* (4th ed.). Clifton Park, NY: Thomson Delmar Learning.

Dodge, D. T., Heroman, C., Charles, J., & Maiorca, J. (2004). Beyond outcomes: How ongoing assessment supports children's learning and leads to meaningful curriculum. *Young Children, 59*(1), 20–28.

Donovan, C. A., Milewicz, E. J., & Smolkin, L. B. (2003). Beyond the single text: Nurturing young children's interest in reading and writing for multiple purposes. *Young Children, 58*(2), 30–36.

Dreikurs, R. (1972). *Coping with children's misbehavior: A parent's guide.* New York: Hawthorne Books.

Dreikurs, R., & Cassel, P. (1972). *Discipline without tears.* New York: Hawthorne Books.

Dreikurs, R., & Soltz, V. (1964). *Children: The challenge.* New York: Duell, Sloan and Pearce.

Dresden, J., & Myers, B. K. (1989). Early childhood professionals: Toward self-definition. *Young Children, 44*(2), 62–66.

Drew, W. F., Christie, J., Johnson, J. E., Meckley, A. M., & Nell, M. L. (2008). Constructive play: A value-added strategy for meeting early learning standards. *Young Children, 61*(5), 38–44.

Drew, W. F., & Rankin, B. (2004). Promoting creativity for life using open-ended materials. *Young Children, 59*(4), 38–45.

Duke, N. K. (2007). Let's look in a book: Using nonfiction reference materials with young children. *Young Children, 62*(3), 12–16.

Dunlap, K. (2000). *Family empowerment: An outcome of parental participation in cooperative preschool education.* New York: Garland.

Dunst, C. J., Trivette, C. M., & Hamby, D. W. (2006). *Family support program quality and parent, family and child benefits.* Asheville, NC: Winterberry Press.

Dyson, A. H., & Genishi, C. (1993). Visions of children as language users: Language and languages education in early childhood. In B. Spodek (Ed.), *Handbook of research on education of young children* (pp. 122–136). New York: Macmillan.

ECLK (Early Childhood Learning and Knowledge Center). (2008). Statutory degree and credentialing requirements for Head Start teaching staff. Available online at http://eclkc.ohs.acf.hhs.gov/hslc/Head%20Start%20Program/Program%20Design%20and%20Management/Head%20Start%20Requirements/IMs/2008/resour_ime_012_0081908.html.

Edwards, C. P. (1986). *Promoting social and moral development in young children.* New York: Teachers College Press, Columbia University.

Eisenberg, E. (1997). Meeting adult needs within the classroom. *Child Care Information Exchange, 117,* 53–56.

Eisenberg, N. (1992). *The caring child.* Cambridge, MA: Harvard University Press.

Elkind, D. (1983). Montessori education: Abiding contributions and contemporary challenges. *Young Children, 38*(2), 3–10.

Elkind, D. (1987). *Miseducation: Preschoolers at risk.* New York: Knopf.

Elicker, J. (2002). More men in early childhood education? Why? *Young children, 57*(6), 50–54.

Elliot, E., & Gonzalez-Mena, J. (2011). Babies' self-regulation: Taking a broad perspective. *Young Children, 66*(1), 28–32.

Elster, C. A. (2010). Language awareness through age-appropriate poetry experiences. *Young Children, 65*(5), 48–55.

Emilson, A. (2007). Young children's influence in preschool. *International Journal of Early Childhood, 39,* 22–38.

Endres, J. B., Rockwell, R. E., & Mense, C. G. (2004). *Food, nutrition, and the young child* (5th ed.). Upper Saddle River, NJ: Pearson/Merrill/Prentice Hall.

Erikson, E. H. (1963). *Childhood and society* (2nd ed.). New York: Norton.

Essa, E. L. (2000). Preschool teachers' use of time-out: Is what they say what they do? *Early Child Development and Care, 165,* 85–94.

Essa, E. L. (2007). *What to do when: Practical guidance strategies for challenging behaviors in the preschool* (6th ed.). Clifton Park, NY: Thomson Delmar Learning.

Essa, E. L., Bennett, P. R., Burnham, M. M., Martin, S. S., Bingham, A., & Allred, K. (2008). Do variables associated with quality child care programs predict the inclusion of children with disabilities? *Topics in Early Childhood Special Education, 28,* 171–180.

Essa, E. L., & Burnham, M. (2001). Child care quality: A model for examining relevant variables. In S. Reifel & M. H. Brown (Eds.), *Early education and care, and reconceptualizing play* (Vol. 11, pp. 59–113). Oxford, England: Elsevier Science.

Essa, E. L., Favre, K., Thweatt, G., & Waugh, S. (1999). Continuity of care for infants and toddlers. *Early Child Development and Care, 148,* 11–19.

Essa, E. L., & Murray, C. I. (1994). Research in review: Young children's understanding and experience with death. *Young Children, 49*(4), 74–81.

Essa, E. L., & Rogers, P. R. (1992). *An early childhood curriculum: From developmental model to application.* Clifton Park, NY: Thomson Delmar Learning.

Ethics Commission. (1987). Ethics case studies: The working mother. *Young Children, 43*(1), 16–19.

Evans, E. D. (1982). Curriculum models and early childhood education. In B. Spodek (Ed.), *Handbook of research in early childhood education* (pp. 107–134). New York: The Free Press.

Everts, J., Essa, E. L., Cheney, C., & McKee, D. (1993). Higher education as child care provider. *Initiatives, 55*(4), 9–16.

Every Child Matters. (2008). *Geography matters: Child well-being in the states.* Available online at http://www.everychildmatters.org/storage/documents/pdf/reports/geomatters.pdf.

Every Child Matters. (2009). *Homeland insecurity.* Available online at http://www.everychildmatters.org/resources/reports/homeland-insecurity.

ExchangeEveryDay. (2008, November 15). So much beauty. Available online at www.childcarexchange.com/eed/news_print.php?news_id=2120.

Fair Test (National Center for Fair and Open Testing). (2007). Available online at www.fairtest.org/readiness-tests.

Feeney, S. (1988). Ethics case studies: The aggressive child. *Young Children, 43*(2), 48–51.

Field, T. (1991). Quality infant day-care and grade school behavior and performance. *Child Development, 62,* 863–870.

Field, T. (1999). Music enhances sleep in preschool children. *Early Child Development and Care, 150,* 65–68.

Finkelstein, B. (1988). The revolt against selfishness: Women and the dilemmas of professionalism in early childhood education. In B. Spodek, O. N. Saracho, & D. L. Peters (Eds.), *Professionalism and the early childhood practitioner* (pp. 10–28). New York: Teachers College Press, Columbia University.

Fleege, P. (1997). Assessment in an integrated curriculum. In C. H. Hart, D. C. Burts, & C. Charlesworth (Eds.), *Integrated curriculum and developmentally appropriate practice: Birth to age eight* (pp. 313–334). Albany, NY: SUNY Press.

Flynn, L. L., & Kieff, J. (2002). Including everyone in outdoor play. *Young Children, 57*(3), 20–26.

Forman, G. (1993). The constructivist perspective to early education. In J. L. Roopnarine & J. E. Johnson (Eds.), *Approaches to early childhood education* (2nd ed., pp. 137–155). New York: Merrill.

Forman, G., & Fyfe, B. (1998). Negotiated learning through design, documentation, and discourse. In C. Edwards, L. Gandini, & G. Forman (Eds.), *The hundred languages of children: The Reggio Emilia approach—Advanced reflections* (2nd ed., pp. 239–260). Greenwich, CT: Ablex.

Forman, G., & Gandini, L. (1994). *An amusement park for the birds* (videotape). Amherst, MA: Performanetics Press.

Fox, J. E. & Schirrmacher, R. (2012). *Art and creative development for young children* (7th ed.). Belmont, CA: Wadsworth, Cengage Learning.

Frankenburg, W. K., & Dodd, J. B. (1990). *Denver II screening manual.* Denver: Denver Developmental Materials.

Fraser, S., & Gestwicki, C. (2001). *Authentic childhood: Exploring Reggio Emilia in the classroom.* Clifton Park, NY: Thomson Delmar Learning.

Fronczek, V. (2004). The International Play Association (IPA): Promoting the child's right to play. *Children, Youth, and Environments, 14*(2). Available online at www.colorado.edu/journals/cye/14_2/playassociation.htm.

Frost, J. L. (1992). *Play and playscapes.* Clifton Park, NY: Thomson Delmar Learning.

Gagen, L. M., Getchell, N., & Payne, V. G. (2009). Motor development in young children: Implications and applications. In E. Essa & M. Burnham (Eds.), *Informing our practice: Useful research on young children's development* (pp. 145–161). Washington, DC: NAEYC.

Galinsky, E. (1988). Parents and teacher-caregivers: Sources of tension, sources of support. *Young Children, 43*(3), 4–12.

Galinsky, E. (1989). Update on employer-supported child care. *Young Children, 44*(6), 75–77.

Galinsky, E. (1990). Why are some parent/teacher partnerships clouded with difficulties? *Young Children, 45*(5), 2–3, 38–40.

Galinsky, E. (2010). *Mind in the making: The seven essential life skills every child needs.* New York: HarperCollins.

Galinsky, E., Bond, J. T., & Sakai, K. (2008). *National study of employers.* Available online at http://familiesandwork.org/site/research/reports/2008nse.pdf.

Gallagher, K. C., & Mayer, K. (2008). Research in Review: Enhancing development and learning through teacher-child relationships. *Young Children, 63*(6), 80–87.

Gallahue, D., & Ozmun, J. (1998). *Understanding motor development: Infants, children, adolescents, adults.* Boston: McGraw-Hill.

Gallimore, R., & Tharp, R. (1990). Teaching mind in society: Teaching, schooling, and literate discourse. In L. C. Moll (Ed.), *Vygotsky and education* (pp. 175–205). New York: Cambridge University Press.

Gandini, L. (1993). Fundamentals of the Reggio Emilia approach to early childhood education. *Young Children, 49*(1), 4–8.

Gandini, L. (2004). Foundations of the Reggio Emilia approach. In J. Hendrick (Ed.), *Next steps toward teaching the Reggio way* (pp. 13–26). Upper Saddle River, NJ: Merrill.

Gandini, L. (2005). From the beginning of the *atelier* to materials as language. In L. Gandini, L. Hill, L. Cadwell, & C. Schwall (Eds.), *In the spirit of the studio: Learning from the atelier of Reggio Emilia* (pp. 6–15). New York: Teachers College Press, Columbia University.

Gandini, L., Hill, L., Cadwell, L., & Schwall, C. (2005). *In the spirit of the studio: Learning from the atelier of Reggio Emilia.* New York: Teacher's College Press.

Garbarino, J., Dubrow, N., Kostelny, K., & Pardo, C. (1992). *Children in danger: Coping with the consequences of community violence.* San Francisco: Jossey-Bass.

Gardner, H. (1983). *Frames of mind: The theory of multiple intelligences.* New York: Basic Books.

Gardner, H. (1989). Learning, Chinese-style. *Psychology Today, 23*(12), 54–56.

Gardner, H. (1999). *Intelligence reframed: Multiple intelligences for the 21st century.* New York: Basic Books.

Gardner, H. (2006). *Multiple intelligences.* New Horizons, NY: Basic Books.

Gargiulo, R., & Kilgo, J. (2011). *An introduction to young children with special needs: Birth through age 8.* (3rd ed.). Belmont, CA: Wadsworth, Cengage Learning.

Gartrell, D. J. (2011). *A guidance approach for the encouraging classroom* (5th ed.). Belmont, CA: Wadsworth, Cengage Learning.

Gates, G., Badgett, L. M. V., Macomber J. E., & Chambers, K. (2007). Adoption and foster care by lesbian and gay parents in the United States. Available online at www.urban.org/url.cfm?ID411437.

Geist, E. (2003). Infants and toddlers exploring mathematics. *Young Children, 58*(1), 10–12.

Genishi, C. (2002). Young English language learners: Resourceful in the classroom. *Young Children, 57*(4), 66–71.

Genishi, C., & Fassler, R. (1999). Oral language in the early childhood classroom: Building on diverse foundations. In C. Seefeldt (Ed.), *The early childhood curriculum: Current findings in theory and practice.* New York: Teachers College Press, Columbia University.

Gershoff, E. T. (2008). *Report on physical punishment in the United States: What research tells us about its effects on children.* Columbus, OH: Center for Effective Discipline.

Gersten, R. (1986). Response to "Consequences of three preschool curriculum models through age 15." *Early Childhood Research Quarterly, 1,* 293–302.

Gestwicki, C. (2010). *Home, school, and community relations: A guide to working with parents* (7th ed.). Belmont, CA: Wadsworth, Cengage Learning.

Gestwicki, C. (2011). *Developmentally appropriate practice: Putting theory into practice in early childhood classrooms* (4th ed.). Belmont, CA: Wadsworth, Cengage Learning.

Gettman, D. (1987). *Basic Montessori: Learning activities for under-fives.* New York: St. Martin's Press.

Giannotti, F, Cortesi, F., Sebastiani, T., & Vagnoni, C. (2008). Sleep practices and habits in children across different cultures. In A. Ivanenko (Ed.), *Sleep and psychiatric disorders in children and adolescents* (pp. 37–48). New York: Informa.

Gilligan, C. (1993). *In a different voice.* Cambridge, MA: Harvard University Press.

Ginsburg, H., & Opper, S. (1969). *Piaget's theory of intellectual development: An introduction.* Englewood Cliffs, NJ: Prentice Hall.

Glazer, J. I. (2000). *Literature for young children* (4th ed.). Columbus, OH: Merrill.

Gleason, J. B. (2008). *The development of language* (7th ed.). Boston: Allyn & Bacon.

Goldhaber, D. E. (2000). *Theories of human development: Integrative perspectives.* Mountain View, CA: Mayfield.

Goldman, B. D., & Buysse, V. (2007). Friendships in very young children. In O. Saracho & B. Spodek (Eds.), *Contemporary perspectives on socialization and social development in early childhood education* (pp. 165–192). Greenwich, CT: Information Age.

Gonzalez-Mena, J., & Eyer, D. W. (2012). *Infants, toddlers, and caregivers* (9th ed.). New York: McGraw Hill.

Gonzalez-Mena, J., & Shareef, I. (2005). Discussing diverse perspectives on guidance. *Young Children, 60*(6), 34–38.

Goodman, K. S., Smith, E. B., Meredith, R., & Goodman, Y. M. (1987). *Language and thinking in school: A whole-language curriculum* (3rd ed.). New York: Owen.

Goodz, N. S. (1982). Is before really easier to understand than after? *Child Development, 53,* 822–825.

Gordon, T. (1974). *T.E.T.: Teacher Effectiveness Training.* New York: Wyden.

Gordon, T. (1976). *P.E.T. in action.* New York: Wyden.

Gould, R. L. (1978). *Transformations: Growth and change in adult life.* New York: Simon & Schuster.

Graham, J., & Forstadt, L. A. (2011). *Children and brain development: What we know about how children learn.* University of Maine Cooperative Extension Publications. Available online at http://umaine.edu/publications/4356e.

Gratz, R. R., & Boulton, P. J. (1996). Erikson and early childhood educators: Looking at ourselves and our profession developmentally. *Young Children, 51*(5), 74–78.

Graves, B. (May 2006). PK-3: What it is and how do we know it works? FCD Policy Brief, *Advancing PK-3.* New York: Foundation for Child Development.

Grimsley, R. (1976). Jean-Jacques Rousseau. In P. Edwards (Ed.), *The encyclopedia of philosophy* (Vol. 7–8, pp. 218–225). New York: Macmillan and Free Press.

Gronlund, G. (2008). Standards, standards everywhere. *Young Children, 62*(4), 10–13.

Guilford, J. P. (1962). Creativity: Its measurement and development. In S. Parnes & H. Harding (Eds.), *A sourcebook for creative thinking* (pp. 151–168). New York: Scribner.

Gunnar, M. R., Kryzer, E., Van Ryzin, M. J., & Phillips, D. A. (2010). The rise in cortisol in family day care: Associations with aspects of care quality, child behavior, and child sex. *Child Development, 81,* 851–869.

Guterman, N. B. (2001). *Stopping child maltreatment before it begins: Emerging horizons in early home visitation services.* Thousand Oaks, CA: Sage.

Hale-Jinks, C., Knopf, H., & Kemple, K. (2006). Tackling teacher turnover in child care: Understanding causes and consequences, identifying solutions. *Childhood Education, 82*(4), 219.

Halgunseth, L. (2009). Family engagement, diverse families, and early childhood education programs: An integrated review of the literature. *Young Children, 64*(5), 56–58.

Hall, K. W. (2008). The importance of including culturally authentic literature. *Young Children, 63*(1), 80–86.

Halle, T., Calkins, J., Berry, D., & Johnson, R. (2003). Promoting language and literacy in early childhood care and education settings. Available online at www.childcareresearch.org/location/ccra2796.

Hampden-Turner, C. (1981). *Maps of the mind: Charts and concepts of the mind and its labyrinths.* New York: Collier Books.

Harms, T., & Clifford, R. M. (1989). *Day care environment rating scale.* New York: Teachers College Press, Columbia University.

Harms, T., Clifford, R., & Cryer, D. (1998). *The Early Childhood Environments Rating Scale.* New York: Teachers College Press, Columbia University.

Harms, T., Cryer, D., & Clifford, R. M. (2003). *Infant/toddler environment rating scale.* New York: Teachers College Press, Columbia University.

Harms, T., Jacobs, E. V., Romano, D. (1996). *School-age care environment rating scale.* New York: Teachers College Press, Columbia University.

Harms, W. (2006a). Enriching education throughout childhood pays big dividends for disadvantaged. Chicago: University of Chicago News Office.

Harms, W. (2006b). Pritzker Family Foundation and Professor James Heckman launch Consortium on Early Childhood Development. Chicago: University of Chicago News Office.

Harris, J. D., & Larsen, J. M. (1989). Parent education as a mandatory component of preschool: Effects on middle-class, educationally advantaged parents and children. *Early Childhood Research Quarterly, 4,* 275–287.

Harwood, M., & Kleinfeld, J. S. (2002). Up front in hope: The value of early intervention for children with fetal alcohol syndrome. *Young Children, 47*(4), 86–90.

Hatch, J. A. (2005). *Teaching in the new kindergarten.* Clifton Park, NY: Thomson Delmar Learning.

Haugland, S. W. (1999). What role should technology play in young children's learning? Part I. *Young Children, 54*(6), 26–31.

Haugland, S. W. (2000). What role should technology play in young children's learning? Part II. Early childhood classrooms in the 21st century: Using computers to maximize learning. *Young Children, 55*(1), 12–18.

Haugland, S. W., & Shade, D. D. (1990). *Developmental evaluations of software for young children.* Clifton Park, NY: Thomson Delmar Learning.

Hawley, T., & Gunnar, M. (2000). *Starting smart: How early experiences affect brain development.* Washington, D.C.: Zero to Three. Available online at http://main.zerotothree.org/site/DocServer/startingsmart.pdf?docID=2422.

Head Start: A child development program. (1990). Washington, DC: Government Printing Office, Department of Health and Human Services.

Head Start Program Fact Sheet. (2010). Washington, DC: Head Start Bureau. Available online at http://www.acf.hhs.gov/programs/ohs/about/fy2010.html.

Helburn, S. W. (2003). Thinking BIG: The federal role in building a system of child care and early education. *Young Children, 58*(2), 66–71.

Helburn, S., Culkin, M. L., Howes, C., Bryant, D., Clifford, R., Cryer, D., Peisner-Feinberg, E., & Kagan, S. L. (1995). *Cost, quality, and child care outcomes in child care centers.* Denver: University of Colorado at Denver.

Helburn, S. W., & Howes, C. (1996). Child care cost and quality. *The Future of Children: Financing Child Care, 6*(2), 62–82.

Helm, J. H. (Ed.). (1996). *The project approach catalog.* Urbana, IL: ERIC Clearing House on Elementary and Early Childhood Education.

Helm, J. H. (2008). Got standards? Don't give up on engaged learning. *Young Children, 63*(4), 14–20.

Helm, J. H., & Katz, L. (2011). *Young investigators: The project approach in the early years* (2nd ed.). New York: Teachers College Press, Columbia University.

Hemmeter, M. L., Ostrosky, M. M., Artman, K. M., & Kinder, K. A. (2008). Moving right along . . . planning transitions to prevent challenging behavior. *Young Children, 63*(3), 18–25.

Hendrick, J., & Weissman, P. (2007). *Total learning: Curriculum for the young child* (7th ed.). Columbus, OH: Merrill.

Henkens-Matzke, A., & Abbott, D. A. (1990). Game playing: A method for reducing young children's fear of medical procedures. *Early Childhood Research Quarterly, 5,* 19–26.

Herron, C. (1997). *Nappy hair.* New York: Dragonfly Books.

Hestenes, L. L., Kontos, S., & Bryan, Y. (1993). Children's emotional expression in child care centers varying in quality. *Early Childhood Research Quarterly, 8,* 295–307.

Hetherington, E. M., Stanley-Hagan, M., & Anderson, E. R. (1989). Marital transitions: A child's perspective. *American Psychologist, 44,* 303–312.

High/Scope. (2002). *Child Observation Record for Infants and Toddlers.* Clifton Park, NY: Thomson Delmar Learning.

High/Scope. (2003). *Preschool Child Observation Record (COR)* (2nd ed.). Clifton Park, NY: Thomson Delmar Learning.

Hirschy, S. T., & Wilkinson, E. (2010). *Protecting our children: Understanding and preventing abuse and neglect in early childhood.* Belmont, CA: Wadsworth, Cengage Learning.

Hirsh-Pasek, K., & Bruer, J. T. (2007). The brain/education barrier. *Science, 317.* Available online at www.sciencemag.org.

Hitz, R., & Driscoll, A. (1988). Praise or encouragement? New insights into praise: Implications for early childhood teacher. *Young Children, 44*(5), 6–13.

Hobbs, F., & Stoops, N. (2002). *Demographic trends in the 20th Century: Census 2000 Special Reports.* Washington DC: U.S. Department of Commerce Economics and Statistics Administration.

Hoff, E. (2009). *Language development* (4th ed.). Belmont, CA: Wadsworth, Cengage Learning.

Hofstede, G. (1991). Empirical models of cultural differences. In N. Bleichrodt & P. J. Drenth (Eds.), *Contemporary issues in cross-cultural psychology* (pp. 4–20). Lisse, The Netherlands: Swets & Zeitlinger.

Hohmann, M., & Weikart, D. P. (2002). *Educating young children: Active learning practices for preschool and child care programs.* Clifton Park, NY: Thomson Delmar Learning.

Hohmann, M., Weikart, D. P., & Epstein, A. S. (2008). *Educating young children: Active learning practices for preschool and child care programs* (2nd ed.). Belmont, CA: Wadsworth, Cengage Learning.

Holden, C., & MacDonald, A. (2001). *Nutrition and child health.* New York: Bailliere Tindall.

Holland, M. (2004). "That food makes me SICK!" Managing food allergies and intolerances in early childhood settings. *Young Children, 59*(2), 42–46.

Holloway, S. D., & Reichhart-Erickson, M. (1988). The relationship of day care quality to children's free-play behavior and social problem-solving skills. *Early Childhood Research Quarterly, 3,* 39–53.

Honig, A. S. (1979). *Parent involvement in early childhood education.* Washington, DC: National Association for the Education of Young Children.

Honig, A. S. (1983). Sex role socialization in early childhood. *Young Children, 38*(6), 57–70.

Honig, A. S. (1987). The shy child. *Young Children, 42*(4), 54–64.

Honig, A. S. (1988). Humor development in children. *Young Children, 43*(4), 60–73.

Honig, A. S. (1993). Mental health for babies: What do theory and research tell us? *Young Children, 48*(3), 69–76.

Honig, A. S. (2009). Stress and young children. In E. L. Essa & M. M. Burnham (Eds.), *Informing our practice: Useful research on young children's development* (pp. 71–88). Washington, DC: National Association for the Education of Young Children.

Hooks, B. (2002). *Homemade love.* White Plains, NY: Hyperion Books.

Hooper, F. H. (1987). Epilogue: Deja vu in approaches to early childhood education. In J. L. Roopnarine & J. E. Johnson (Eds.), *Approaches to early childhood education* (pp. 301–314). Columbus, OH: Merrill.

Hopkins, A. R. (2002). Children and grief: The role of the early childhood educator. *Young Children, 57*(1), 40–47.

Hopper, J. (2008). *Child abuse: Statistics, research, and resources.* Available online at www.jimhopper.com/abstats.

Howes, C. (1983). Caregiver behavior in center and family day care. *Journal of Applied Developmental Psychology, 4,* 99–107.

Howes, C. (1988). Relations between early child care and schooling. *Developmental Psychology, 24,* 53–57.

Howes, C. (1990). Can the age of entry into child care and the quality of child care predict adjustment in kindergarten? *Developmental Psychology, 26,* 292–303.

Howes, C. (1997). Children's experiences in center-based child care as a function of teacher background and adult–child ratio. *Merrill-Palmer Quarterly, 43,* 404–425.

Howes, C. (1999). Attachment relationships in the context of multiple caregivers. In J. Cassidy & P. R. Shaver (Eds.), *Handbook of attachment theory and research.* New York: Guilford.

Howes, C., & Hamilton, C. E. (1993). The changing experience of child care: Changes in teachers and in teacher-child relationships and children's social competence with peers. *Early Childhood Research Quarterly, 8,* 15–32.

Howes, C., Hamilton, C. E., & Phillipsen, L. C. (1998). Stability and continuity of child-caregiver and child peer relationships. *Child Development, 69,* 418–426.

Howes, C., & Lee, L. (2007). If you're not like me, can we play? In O. Saracho & B. Spodek (Eds.), *Contemporary perspectives on social learning in early childhood education* (pp. 259–277). Greenwich, CT: Information Age.

Howes, C., & Marx, E. (1992). *Raising questions* about improving the quality of child care: Child care in the United States and France. *Early Childhood Research Quarterly, 7,* 347–366.

Howes, C., Smith, E., & Galinsky, E. (1995). *The Florida child care quality improvement study: Interim report.* New York: Families and Work Institute.

Huesmann, L. R. (1986). Psychological processes promoting the relation between exposure to media violence and aggressive behavior by the viewer. *Journal of Social Issues, 42,* 125–139.

Huettig, C. I., Sanborn, C. F., DiMarco, N., Popejoy, A., & Rich, S. (2004). The O generation: Our youngest children are at risk for obesity. *Young Children, 59*(2), 50–55.

Huffman, A. B. (1996). Beyond the weather chart: Weathering new experiences. *Young Children, 51*(5), 34–37.

Hyson, M. C., Hirsh-Pasek, K., & Rescorla, L. (1990). The Classroom Practices Inventory: An observational instrument based on NAEYC's guidelines for developmentally appropriate practices for 4- and 5-year-old children. *Early Childhood Research Quarterly, 5,* 475–494.

Indications of Child Abuse & Maltreatment (2008), Childabuse.com. Available online at http://childabuse.com/help.htm.

Institute of Medicine. (2011). *Early childhood obesity prevention policies: Goals, recommendations, and potential actions.* Washington, DC: Institute of Medicine. Available online at www.iom.edu/~/media/Files/Report%20Files/2011/Early-Childhood-Obesity-Prevention-Policies/Young%20Child%20Obesity%202011%20Recommendations.pdf.

International Play Association. (2008). *The IPA Declaration of a Child's Right to Play.* Available online at www.ipausa.org/ipadeclaration.html.

International Society for Technology in Education (2007). *NETS for students 2007 profiles.* Available online at www.iste.org/standards/nets-for-students/nets-for-students-2007-profiles.aspx#PK-2.

Isbell, R. T. (2002). Telling and retelling stories: Learning language and literacy. *Young Children, 57*(2), 26–30.

Izard, C. (2004). *The psychology of emotions (emotions, personality, and psychotherapy).* New York: Springer.

Jablon, J. R., Dombro, A. L., & Dichtelmiller, M. (2007). *The power of observation for birth through eight* (2nd ed.). Washington, DC: National Association for the Education of Young Children.

Jackman, H. L. (2009). *Early education curriculum: A child's connection to the world* (4th ed.). Belmont, CA: Wadsworth, Cengage Learning.

Jensen, E. (2001). *Art with the brain in mind.* Alexandria, VA: Association for Supervision and Curriculum Development.

Johansson, E. (2006). Children's morality: Perspectives and research. In B. Spodek & O. Saracho (Eds.), *Handbook of research on the education of young children* (pp. 55–83). Mahwah, NJ: Erlbaum.

Johnson, M. H. (2008). Developing verbal and visual literacy through experiences in the visual arts: 25 tips for teachers. *Young Children, 63*(1), 74–79.

Johnston, J. R., & Slobin, D. I. (1979). The development of locative expressions in English, Italian, Serbo-Croatian, and Turkish. *Journal of Child Language, 6,* 529–545.

Jones, J. (2004). Framing the assessment discussion. *Young Children, 59*(1), 144–18.

Jones, N. P. (2005). Big Jobs: Planning for competence. *Young Children, 60*(2), 86–93.

Jordan, N. H. (1993). Sexual abuse prevention programs in early childhood education: A caveat. *Young Children, 48*(6), 76–79.

Kagan, J., & Reznick, J. S. (1986). Shyness and temperament. In W. H. Jones, J. M. Cheek, & S. R. Briggs (Eds.), *Shyness: Perspectives on research and treatment* (pp. 81–90). New York: Plenum Press.

Kagan, S. L., & Cohen, N. E. (1997). *Not by chance: Creating an early care and education system for America's children.* New Haven, CT: The Bush Center in Child Development and Social Policy.

Kagan, S. L., & Kauzer, K. (2009). Governing American early care and education: Shifting from government to governance and from form to function. In S. Feeney, A. Galper, & C. Seefeldt (Eds.), *Continuing issues in early childhood education* (pp. 12–32). Upper Saddle River, NJ: Merrill.

Kamii, C. (1984). Obedience is not enough. *Young Children, 39*(4), 11–14.

Katz, L. G. (1984). The professional early childhood teacher. *Young Children, 39*(5), 5–10.

Katz, L. G. (1988). Where is early childhood education as a profession? In B. Spodek, O. N. Saracho, & D. L. Peters (Eds.), *Professionalism and the early childhood practitioner* (pp. 75–83). New York: Teachers College Press, Columbia University.

Katz, L. G. (1993). Dispositions as educational goals. ERIC-EDO-PS-93-10. Available online at http://ceep.crc.uiuc.edu/eecearchive/digests/1993/katzdi93.html.

Katz, L. G. (1995). *Talks with teachers of young children: A collection.* Norwood, NJ: Ablex.

Katz, L. G. (2000). *How can we strengthen children's self-esteem?* ERIC Clearinghouse on Elementary and Early Childhood Education. Available online at www.kidsource.com/kidsource/content2/Strengthen_Children_Self.html.

Katz, L. G., & Chard, S. C. (1997). Documentation: The Reggio Emilia approach. *Principal, 77,* 16–17.

Kauerz, K. (2006). Ladders of learning: Fighting fade-out by advancing PK-3 alignment. Available online at http://www.newamerica.net/publications/policy/ladders_of_learning.

Kauerz, K. (Spring 2010). P-3: Getting out of the catch-up business. *Insights,* 5–8.

Kauerz, K. (April 1, 2011). PK-3: What, why, how? Presented at the 2011 annual conference of the Nevada Association for the Education of Young Children.

Keeler, R. (2008). *Natural playscapes: Creating outdoor play environments for the soul.* Redmond, WA: Exchange Press.

Keith, L. K., & Campbell, J. M. (2000). Assessment of social and emotional development in preschool children. In B. A. Bracken (Ed.), *The psychoeducational assessment of preschool children* (3rd ed., pp. 364–382). Boston: Allyn & Bacon.

Kellogg, R. (1969). *Analyzing children's art.* Palo Alto, CA: Mayfield.

Kemple, K. M., Batey, J. J., & Hartle, L. C. (2004). Music play: Creating centers for musical play and exploration. *Young Children, 59*(4), 30–37.

Kersey, K. C., & Masterson, M. L. (2009). Teachers connecting with families—In the best interest of children. *Young Children, 64*(5), 34–38.

Kilburn, M. R., & Karoly, L. A. (2008). *The economics of early childhood policy: What the dismal science has to say about investing in children.* Available online at www.rand.org/pubs/occasional_papers/OP227.

Killen, M., & Smetana, J. S. (2006). *Handbook of moral development.* Mahwah, NJ: Erlbaum.

King, M., & Gartrell, D. (2003). Building an encouraging classroom with boys in mind. *Young Children, 58*(4), 33–36.

Kirkorian, H. L., Wartella, E. A., & Anderson, D. R. (2008). In J. Brooks-Gunn & E. H. Donahue (Eds.), *Children and electronic media* (pp. 39–62). Available online at www.futureofchildren.org.

Kirkorian, H. L., Pempek, T. A., Murphy, L. A., Schmidt, M. E., & Anderson, D. R. (2009). The impact of background television on parent-child interaction. *Child Development, 80,* 1350–1359.

Kirmani, M. H. (2007). Empowering culturally and linguistically diverse children and families. *Young Children, 62*(6), 94–98.

Klein, M. D., & Chen, D. (2001). *Working with children from culturally diverse backgrounds.* Clifton Park, NY: Delmar Thompson Learning.

Koch, J. (2010). *Science stories: Science methods for elementary and middle school teachers* (4th ed.). Belmont, CA: Wadsworth, Cengage Learning.

Kohlberg, L. (1966). A cognitive-developmental analysis of children's sex-role concepts and attitudes. In E. E. Maccoby (Ed.), *The development of sex differences* (pp. 82–173). Stanford, CA: Stanford University Press.

Kohlberg, L. (1969). Stage and sequence: The cognitive developmental approach to socialization. In D. A. Goslin (Ed.), *Handbook of socialization theory and research.* Chicago: Rand McNally.

Kohn, A. (2001). Five reasons to stop saying "good job!" *Young Children, 56*(5), 24–28.

Koralek, D. (2007). Beyond the library corner: Incorporating books throughout the curriculum. *Young Children, 62*(3), 10–11.

Koralek, D. G., Newman, R. L., & Colker, L. J. (1996). *Caring for children in school-age programs: A competency-based training program (Vol. I).* Clifton Park, NY: Thomson Delmar Learning.

Kostelnik, M. J., Gregory, K. M., Soderman, A. K., & Whiren, A. P. (2012). *Guiding children's social development and learning* (7th ed.). Belmont, CA: Wadsworth, Cengage Learning.

Kovach, B., & De Ros-Voseles, D. (2011). Communicating with babies. *Young Children, 66*(2), 48–50.

Kozol, J. (2007). *Letters to a young teacher.* New York: Crown.

Kushner, D. (1989). "Put your name on your painting, but . . . the blocks go back on the shelves." *Young Children, 45*(1), 49–56.

Ladd, G. W. (2007). Social learning in the peer context. In O. Saracho & B. Spodek (Eds.), *Contemporary perspectives on socialization and social development in early childhood education* (pp. 133–164). Greenwich, CT: Information Age.

Lally, J. R., Mangione, P. L., & Honig, A. S. (1988). The Syracuse University Family Development Research Program: Long-range impact on an early intervention with low-income children and their families. In D. R. Powell (Ed.), *Emerging directions in parent-child intervention* (pp. 79–104). Norwood, NJ: Ablex.

Landau, S., & McAnich, C. (1993). Young children with attention deficits. *Young Children, 48*(4), 49–58.

Lascarides, V. C., & Hinitz, B. F. (2000). *History of early childhood education.* New York: Falmar Press.

Lavatelli, C. S. (1970). *Piaget's theory applied to an early childhood curriculum.* Boston: American Science and Engineering.

LeDoux, J. E., & Phelps, E. A. (2000). Emotional networks in the brain. In M. Lewis & J. M. Haviland-Jones (Eds.), *Handbook of emotions* (2nd ed., pp. 157–172). New York: Guilford Press.

Lee, V. E., Brooks-Gunn, J., Schnur, E., & Liaw, F. R. (1990). Are Head Start effects sustained? A longitudinal follow-up comparison of disadvantaged children attending Head Start, no preschool, and other preschool programs. *Child Development, 61,* 495–507.

Legrendre, A. (2003). Environmental features influencing toddlers' bio-emotional reactions in day care centers. *Environment and Behavior, 35,* 523–549.

Lepper, M. R., Greene, D., & Nisbett, R. E. (1973). Undermining children's intrinsic interest with extrinsic reward: A test of the "overjustification" hypothesis. *Journal of Personality and Social Psychology, 28,* 129–137.

Levinson, D. J. (1978). *The seasons of a man's life.* New York: Knopf.

Lewin-Benham, A. (2006). One teacher, 20 preschoolers, and a goldfish. *Young Children, 61*(2), 28–34.

Liebert, R. M., & Sprafkin, J. N. (1988). *The early window: Effects of television on children and youth* (3rd ed.). New York: Pergamon Press.

Lillard, P. P. (1973). *Montessori: A modern approach.* New York: Schocken Books.

Lino, M. (2008). *Expenditure on children by families, 2007.* Washington DC: U.S. Department of Agriculture, Center for Nutrition Policy and Promotion. Miscellaneous Publication #1528-2007.

Lonigan, C. J., Schatscheider, C., Westberg, L., & National Early Literacy Panel (2008a). Identification of children's skills and abilities linked to later outcomes in reading, writing, and spelling. In National Literacy Panel (Eds.), *Developing early literacy* (pp. 55–106). Jessup, MD: National Institute for Literacy.

Lonigan, C. J., Shanahan, T., Cunningham, A., & National Early Literacy Panel (2008b). Impact of shared-reading interventions on young children's early literacy skills. In National Literacy Panel (Eds.), *Developing early literacy* (pp. 153–172). Jessup, MD: National Institute for Literacy.

Louv, R. (2008). *Last child in the woods: Saving our children from nature-deficit disorder.* Chapel Hill, NC: Algonquin Books.

Maccoby, E. E. (1990). Gender and relationships. *American Psychologist, 45*, 513–520.

Maccoby, E. E., & Jacklin, C. N. (1987). Gender segregation in childhood. In H. W. Reese (Ed.), *Advances in child development and behavior* (Vol. 20, pp. 239–288). New York: Academic Press.

Machado, J. M. (2010). *Early childhood experiences in language art* (9th ed.). Belmont, CA: Wadsworth, Cengage Learning.

Machado, J. M. (2013). *Early childhood experiences in language arts: Early literacy* (10th ed.). Belmont, CA: Wadsworth, Cengage Learning.

Magnuson, K. A., Ruhm, C., & Waldfogel, J. (2006). Does prekindergarten improve school preparation and performance? *Economics of Education Review, 26*, 33–61.

Maier, H. W. (1990). Erikson's developmental theory. In R. M. Thomas (Ed.), *The encyclopedia of human development and education: Theory, research, and studies* (pp. 88–93). New York: Pergamon Press.

Magnuson, K. A., Myers, M. K., Ruhm, C. J., & Waldfogel, J. (2005). Inequality in children's school readiness and public funding. *Focus, 24*(1), 12–18.

Malaguzzi, L. (1993). For an education based on relationships. *Young Children, 49*(1), 9–12.

Manson, J. M., & Sinha, S. (1993). Emerging literacy in the early childhood years: Applying a Vygotskian model of learning and development. In B. Spodek (Ed.), *Handbook of research on the education of young children* (pp. 137–150). New York: Macmillan.

Marcon, R. A. (2009). Growing children: The physical side of development. In E. L. Essa & M. M. Burnham (Eds.), *Informing our practice: Useful research on young children's development* (pp. 162–172). Washington, DC: National Association for the Education of Young Children.

Mardell-Czudnowski, C. D., & Goldenberg, D. S. (1998). *Developmental Indicators for the Assessment of Learning* (DIAL-III). Circle Pines, MN: American Guidance Service.

Marotz, L. R. (2012). *Health, safety, and nutrition for the young child* (8th ed.) Belmont, CA: Wadsworth, Cengage Learning.

Marshall, H. H. (2001). Cultural influences on the development of self-concept: Updating our thinking. *Young Children, 56*(6), 19–25.

Marshall, H. H. (2009). The development of self-concept. In E. L. Essa & M. M. Burnham (Eds.), *Informing our practice: Useful research on young children's development* (pp. 59–70). Washington, DC: National Association for the Education of Young Children.

Marshall, K. L. (2003). Research in review: Opportunity deferred or opportunity taken? An updated look at delaying kindergarten entry. *Young Children, 58*(5), 84–93.

Maschinot, B. (2008). *The changing face of the United States: The influence of culture on early child development.* Washington, DC: Zero to Three.

Matlock, R., & Hornstein, J. (2004). Sometimes a smudge is just a smudge, and sometimes it's a saber-toothed tiger: Learning and the arts through the ages. *Young Children, 59*(4), 12–17.

Mavrogenes, N. A. (1990). Helping parents help their children become literate. *Young Children, 45*(4), 4–9.

Maxwell, K. L. & Clifford, R. M., (2004). Research in review: School readiness assessment. *Young Children, 49*(1), 42–46.

Mayer, K. (2009). Emerging knowledge about emergent writing. In E. L. Essa & M. M. Burnham (Eds.), *Informing our practice: Useful research on young children's development* (pp. 111–118). Washington, DC: National Association for the Education of Young Children.

Mayesky, M. (2012). *Creative activities for young children* (10th ed.). Belmont, CA: Wadsworth, Cengage Learning.

Mays, R., & Nordwall, S. (2006). *Waldorf answers on the philosophy and practice of Waldorf education.* Available online at www.waldorfanswers.org.

McBride-Chang, C. (1998). The development of invented spelling. *Early Education and Development, 9*, 147–160.

McCarry, B. S., & Greenwood, S. C. (2009). Practice what you preach: Writer's lunch club in first grade. *Young Children, 64*(1), 37–41.

McCartney, K. (1984), Effect of quality of day care environment on children's language development. *Development Psychology, 20*, 244–260.

McCartney, K., Scarr, S., Rocheleau, A., Phillips, D., Abbott-Shim, M., Eisenberg, M., Keefe, N., Rosenthal, S., & Ruh, J. (1997). Teacher-child interaction and child-care auspices as predictors of social outcomes in infants, toddlers, and preschoolers. *Merrill-Palmer Quarterly, 43*, 436–450.

McDaniel, T. R., & Davis, A. P. (1999). You've come a long way, baby—or have you? Research evaluating gender portrayal in recent Caldecott-winning books. *Reading Teacher, 52*, 532–536.

McGinnis, J. R. (2002). Enriching the outdoor environment. *Young Children, 57*(3), 28–30.

McMullen, M. B., Addleman, J. M., Fulford, A. M., Moore, S. L., Mooney, S. H., Sisk, S. S., &

Zachariah, J. (2009). Learning to be *me* while coming to understand *we*: Encouraging prosocial babies in group settings. *Young Children, 64*(4), 20–28.

Meisels, S. J. (1993). Remaking classroom assessment with the Work Sampling System. *Young Children, 48*(5), 34–40.

Meisels, S. J., & Atkins-Burnett, S. (2004). The Head Start National Reporting System: A critique. *Young Children, 59*(1), 64–66.

Miller, D. F. (2010). *Positive child guidance* (6th ed.). Belmont, CA: Wadsworth, Cengage Learning.

Miller, G. A., & Gildea, P. M. (1987, September). How children learn words. *Scientific American,* 94–99.

Miller, L. B., & Bizzell, R. P. (1983). Long-term effects of four preschool programs: Sixth, seventh, and eighth grade. *Child Development, 54,* 727–741.

Miller, L. B., & Dyer, J. L. (1975). Four preschool programs: Their dimensions and effects. *Monographs of the Society for Research on Child Development* (Serial No. 162), Nos. 5–6.

Miller, R. (1996). *The developmentally appropriate inclusive classroom in early education.* Clifton Park, NY: Thomson Delmar Learning.

Miltenberger, R. G., & Roberts, J. A. (1999). Emerging issues in the research on child sexual abuse prevention. *Education and Treatment of Children, 22,* 84–102.

Mindess, M., Chen, M., & Brenner, R. (2008). Social-emotional learning in the primary curriculum. *Young Children, 63*(6), 56–60.

Moehler, E., Kagan, J., Oelkers-Ax, R., Bruner, R., Paustka, L., Haffner, J., & Resch, F. (2008). Infant predictors of behavioural inhibition. *British Journal of Developmental Psychology, 26,* 145–150.

Montgomery-Downs, H. E. (2008). Normal sleep development in infants and toddlers. In A. Ivanenko (Ed.), *Sleep and psychiatric disorders in children and adolescents* (pp. 11–21). New York: Informa.

Moore, M. R., Campos, D., Collazo, J., Maytum, A. F., Sampayo, V., & Sanchez, M. A. (2010). Inspiration to teach—Reflections on Friedrich Froebel and why he counts in early childhood education. *Young Children, 65*(6), 74–76.

Moravcik, E., & Feeney, S. (2009). Curriculum in early childhood education: Teaching the whole child. In S. Feeney, A. Galper, and C. Seefeldt (Eds.), *Continuing issues in early childhood education* (pp. 219–237). Upper Saddle River, NJ: Merrill.

Morgan, H. (2007). *Early childhood education: History, theory, and practice.* New York: Rowman & Littlefield.

Morissey, T., & Banghart, P. (2007). Family child care in the United States. *Child Care & Early Education Research Connections.* Available online at www.researchconnections.org/childcare/resources/12036/pdf.

Muris, P. (2007). *Normal and abnormal fear and anxiety in children and adolescents.* Oxford, England: Elsevier Science.

NACCP. (2008). An accreditation program committed to excellence. Available online at www.naccp.org/displaycommon.cfm?an=1&subarticlenbr=518#.

NACCRRA. (2008a). Grandparents: A critical child care safety net. Available online at www.naccrra.org/publications/naccrra-publications/grandparents.

NACCRRA. (2008b). *Parents and the high price of child care.* Arlington, VA: National Association of Child Care Resource and Referral Agencies.

NAEYC. (1993a). Position statement: Violence in the lives of children. *Young Children, 48*(6), 80–85.

NAEYC. (1994). Position statement: Media violence in children's lives. *Young Children, 45*(5), 18–21.

NAEYC. (1997). Position Statement: Licensing and public regulation of early childhood programs. Available online at http://www.naeyc.org/files/naeyc/file/positions/PSLIC98.PDF.

NAEYC. (2003). Position statement: *Curriculum, assessment, and program evaluation.* Available online at http://www.naeyc.org/files/naeyc/file/positions/StandCurrAss.pdf.

NAEYC. (2005). Position statement: Screening and assessment of young English-language learners. Available online at http://www.naeyc.org/files/naeyc/file/positions/WWSEnglishLanguageLearnersWeb.pdf.

NAEYC. (2006). *Technology and young children—Ages 3 through 8.* Available online at http://www.naeyc.org/content/technology-and-young-children. NAEYC. (2008a). *Early childhood associate degree preparation.* Available online at www.naeyc.org/faculty/asdeg.asp.

NAEYC. (2008b). History of NAEYC. Available online at http://www.naeyc.org/content/about-naeyc.

NAEYC. (2010). 2010 NAEYC standards for initial and advanced early childhood professional preparation programs. Available online at www.naeyc.org/ncate/files/ncate/NAEYC%20Initial%20and%-20Advanced%20Standards%206_2011-final_2.pdf.

NAEYC. (2011). Position statements on ethical conduct. Available online at www.naeyc.org/positionstatements/ethical_conduct.

NAEYC. (2012). Technology and interactive media as tools in early childhood programs serving children from birth through age 8. Washington, DC: National Association for the Education of Young Children.

Nansel, T. R., Overpeck, M., Pilla, R. S., Ruan, W. J., Simons-Morton, B., & Scheidt, P. (2001). Bullying behaviors among U.S. youth: Prevalence and association with psychosocial adjustment. *Journal of the American Medical Association, 285*(16), 2094–2100.

National Accreditation Commission for Early Care and Education Programs. (2004). Austin, TX: National Association of Child Care Professionals.

National Child Care Information and Technical Assistance Center. (2011). *America's Children: Key National Indicators of Well-Being, 2011.* Available online at http://www.childstats.gov/pdf/ac2011/ac_11.pdf.

National Center for Children in Poverty. (2011). Available online at www.nccp.org.

National Center for Education Statistics. (2008). Initial results from the 2005 NHES early childhood program participation survey. Available online at http://nces.ed.gov/pubsearch/pubsinfo.asp?pubid=2006075.

National Center for Family Homelessness. (2009). America's youngest outcasts. Available online at www.HomelessChildrenAmerica.org.

National Early Literacy Panel. (2008). *Developing early literacy.* Jessup, MD: National Institute for Literacy.

National Scientific Council on the Developing Child. (2007a). The science of early childhood development: Closing the gap between what we know and what we do. Available online at http://developingchild.net/pubs/persp/pdf/Science_Early_Childhood_Development.pdf.

National Scientific Council on the Developing Child. (2007b). *The timing and quality of early experiences combine to shape brain architecture: Working Paper #5.* Available online at http://developingchild.net.

National Television Violence Study: Key findings and recommendations. (1996). *Young Children, 51*(3), 54–55.

NCATE. (2006). *Standards, procedures and policies for the accreditation of professional educational units.* Washington, DC: National Council for Accreditation of Teacher Education.

Neill, P. (2009). *Real science in preschool: Here, there, and everywhere.* Ypsilanti, MI: High/Scope Press.

Nelson, B. G., Carlson, F. M., & West, R. (2006). Men in early childhood: An update. *Young Children, 61*(5), 34–36.

Nelson, J. A. N. (1997). The Reggio Emilia approach: Creativity in 100 languages. *Early Childhood Connections, 3*(1), 25–29.

Nesdale, D. (2007). The development of ethnic prejudice in early childhood. In O. Saracho & B. Spodek (Eds.), *Contemporary perspectives on socialization and social development in early childhood education* (pp. 213–240). Greenwich, CT: Information Age.

Neugebauer, R. (1991, January/February). How's business? Status report #4 on for-profit child care. *Child Care Information Exchange,* 46–50.

New, R. S. (2000). Reggio Emilia: An approach or an attitude? In J. L. Roopnarine & J. E. Johnson, *Approaches to early childhood education* (3rd ed., pp. 341–358). Upper Saddle River, NJ: Merrill.

New, R. S., & Beneke, M. (2009). Negotiating diversity in early childhood education: Rethinking notions of expertise. In S. Feeney, A. Galper, and C. Seefeldt (Eds.), *Continuing issues in early childhood education* (pp. 303–324). Upper Saddle River, NJ: Merrill.

NICHD Early Child Care Research Network. (1999). Child outcomes when child care center classes meet recommended standards for quality. *American Journal of Public Health, 89,* 1072–1077.

NICHD Early Child Care Research Network. (2000a). Characteristics and quality of child care for toddlers and preschoolers. *Applied Developmental Science, 4,* 116–135.

NICHD Early Child Care Research Network. (2000b). The relation of child care to cognitive and language development. *Child Development, 71,* 960–980.

NICHD Early Child Care Research Network. (2006). *The NICHD Study of Early Child Care and Youth Development: Findings for children up to age 4½ years.* Washington, DC: National Institutes of Health.

NIEER (National Institute for Early Education Research). (2007). *The state of preschool 2007: State preschool yearbook.* Available online at http://nieer.org/publications/state-preschool-2007.

NIEER (National Institute for Early Education Research). (2003). Quality preschool—a cure for bullying? *Preschool Matters, 1*(1). Available online at http://www.factsinaction.org/brief/brmar041.htm.

NIH News Release. *Bullying widespread in S.S. schools, study finds.* Washington, DC: National Institute of Child Health and Human Development. Available online at www.nichd.nih.gov/news/releases/bullying.cfm.

NIMH (National Institute of Mental Health). (1982). *Television and behavior: Ten years of scientific progress for the 80s.* Vol. I: Summary report. Washington, DC: Government Printing Office.

Nodelman, P. (1999, Fall). The boys in children's books. *Riverbank Review,* 5–7.

Nurss, J. R., & McGauvran, M. E. (1995). *Metropolitan Readiness Assessment Program* (6th ed.). Orlando, FL: Harcourt Brace Jovanovich.

Nutbrown, C. Clough, P., & Selbvie, P. (2008). *Early childhood education: History, philosophy and experience.* Los Angeles: Sage.

Odom, S. L., Vitztum, J., Wolery, R., Lieber, J., Sandall, S., Hanson, M. J., Beckman, P., Schwartz, I., & Horn, E. (2004). Preschool inclusion in the United States: A review of research from an ecological systems perspective. *Journal of Research in Special Educational Needs, 4,* 17–49.

Okagaki, L., & Diamond, K. E. (2009). Cultural and linguistic differences in families with young children: Implications for early childhood teachers. In E. L. Essa & M. M. Burnham (Eds.), *Informing our practice: Useful research on young children's development* (pp. 216–226). Washington, DC: National Association for the Education of Young Children.

Olfman, S. (Ed.). (2003). *All work and no play: How educational reforms are harming our preschoolers.* Westport: Praeger.

Olson, M. (2007). Strengthening families: Community strategies that work. *Young Children, 62*(2), 26–32.

Orlick, T. (2006). *Cooperative games and sports: Joyful games for everyone.* Champaign, IL: Human Kinetics.

Owens, R. E. (2011). *Language development: An introduction* (8th ed.). Boston: Allyn & Bacon.

Paasche, C. L., Gorrill, L., & Strom, B. (2004). *Children with special needs in early childhood settings: Identification, intervention, inclusion.* Clifton Park, NY: Thomson Delmar Learning.

Parlakin, R. (2001). *Look, listen, and learn: Reflective supervision and relationship-based work.* Washington, DC: Zero to Three.

Parten, M. B. (1932). Social participation among preschool children. *Journal of Abnormal and Social Psychology, 27,* 243–269.

Pease, D., & Gleason, J. B. (1985). Gaining meanings: Semantic development. In J. B. Gleason (Ed.), *The development of language* (pp. 103–138). Columbus, OH: Merrill.

Peisner-Feinberg, E. S., & Burchinal, M. R. (1997). Relations between preschool children's child-care experience and concurrent development: The Cost, Quality, and Outcomes Study. *Merrill-Palmer Quarterly, 43,* 451–477.

Peisner-Feinberg, E. S., Clifford, R. M., Culkin, M. R., Howes, C., & Kagan, S. L. (1999). *The children of the Cost, Quality, and Outcomes Study go to school.* Available online at www.fpg.unc.edu/~ncedl/pdfs/cqo-es.pdf.

Peltzman, B. R. (1998). *Pioneers of early childhood education: A bio-bibliographical guide.* Santa Barbara, CA: Greenwood Press.

Perry, B. (2000). *How we influence brain development in young children: The relationship between early life experiences and emotional, cognitive, social, and physical health.* Presented at the annual conference of the National Association for the Education of Young Children, Atlanta, GA.

Perry, B. (2001). Cited in M. Prensky, *Digital natives, digital immigrants, part II: Do they really think differently?* Available online at http://www.marcprensky.com/writing/Prensky%20-%20Digital%20Natives,%20Digital%20Immigrants%20-%20Part2.pdf.

Perry, B. D., & Marcellus, J. (2011). The impact of abuse and neglect on the developing brain. Available online at http://teachers.scholastic.com/professional/bruceperry/abuse_neglect.htm.

Perry, B. D., & Pollard, R. (1998). Homeostasis, stress, trauma, and adaptation: A neurodevelopmental view of childhood trauma. *Child and Adolescent Psychiatric Clinics of North America, 7,* 33–51.

Perry, B., & Szalavitz, M. (2007). *The boy who was raised as a dog and other stories from a child psychiatrist's notebook: What traumatized children can teach us about loss, love and healing.* New York: Basic Books.

Peters, D. L., Neisworth, J. T., & Yawkey, T. D. (1985). *Early childhood education: From theory to practice.* Monterey, CA: Brooks/Cole.

Petit, M. R. (2009). Preface to Every Child Matters. (2009). *Homeland insecurity.* Available online at www.everychildmatters.org/resources/reports/homeland-insecurity.

Phillips, D. A., Scarr, S., & McCartney, K. (1987). Dimensions and effects of child care quality: The Bermuda Study. In D. A. Phillips (Ed.), *Quality in child care: What does research tell us?* (pp. 43–56). Washington, DC: National Association for the Education of Young Children.

Phillipsen, L. C., Burchinal, M. R., Howes, C., & Cryer, D. (1997). The prediction of process quality from structural features of child care. *Early Childhood Research Quarterly, 12,* 281–303.

Phyfe-Perkins, E. (1980). Children's behavior in preschool settings: A review of research concerning the influence of the physical environment. In L. G. Katz (Ed.), *Current topics in early childhood education* (Vol. 3, pp. 91–125). Norwood, NJ: Ablex.

Piaget, J. (1926). *The language and thought of the child.* London: Routledge & Kegan Paul.

Piaget, J. (1932). *The moral judgment of the child.* New York: Harcourt, Brace & World.

Piaget, J. (1983). Piaget's theory. In P. H. Mussen (Ed.), *Handbook of child psychology* (4th ed.), W. Kessen

(Ed.), *History, theory, and methods* (Vol. 1, pp. 103–128). New York: Wiley.

Pianta, R. C., Belsky, J., Houts, R., & Morrison, F. J., (2007). Opportunities to learn in America's elementary classrooms. *Science, 315*, 1705–1796.

Pica, R. (2006). Physical fitness and the early childhood curriculum. *Young Children, 61*(3), 12–19.

Pomper, K., Blank, H., Campbell, N., & Schulman, K. (2004). Be all that we can be: Lessons from the military for improving our nation's child care system. Washington DC: National Women's Law Center.

Pizzolongo, P. J., & Hunter, A. (2011). I am safe and secure: Promoting resilience in young children. *Young Children, 66*(2), 67–69.

Powell, D. R. (1986). Parent education and support programs. *Young Children, 41*(3), 47–53.

Powell, D. R. (1998). Reweaving parents into the fabric of early childhood programs. *Young Children, 53*(5), 60–67.

Powell, D. R., & O'Leary, P. M. (2009). Strengthening relations between parents and early childhood programs. In E. L. Essa & M. M. Burnham (Eds.), *Informing our practice: Useful research on young children's development* (pp. 193–202). Washington, DC: National Association for the Education of Young Children.

Prensky, M. (2001). Digital natives and digital immigrants, part II: Do they really think differently? Available online at http://www.marcprensky.com/writing/Prensky%20-%20Digital%20Natives,%20Digital%20Immigrants%20-%20Part2.pdf.

Prescott, E. (1997). 3 keys to flexible room arrangement. *Child Care Information Exchange, 117*, 48–50.

Pritchard, P. (2000). Sleep disorders in the pre-school child: How the health professionals can help. In K. Booth & K. A. Luker (Eds.), *A practical handbook for community health nurses: Working with children and their parents* (pp. 176–184). Malden, MA: Blackwell Sciences.

Prior, J., & Gerard, M. R. (2007). *Family involvement in early childhood education: Research into practice*. Clifton Park, NY: Delmar Thompson Learning.

Puckett, M. B., & Black, J. K. (2008). *Meaningful assessments of the young child: Celebrating development and learning* (3rd ed.). Upper Saddle River, NJ: Merrill.

Ramey, C. T., Campbell, F. A., Burchinal, M., Skinner, M. L., Gardner, D. M., & Ramey, S. L. (2000). Persistent effects of early intervention on high-risk children and their mothers. *Applied Developmental Science, 4*, 2–14.

Ramming, P., Kyger, C. S., & Thompson, S. D. (2006). A new bit on toddler biting: The influence of food, oral motor development, and sensory activities. *Young Children, 61*(2), 17–26.

Ramsey, P. G. , & Nieto, S. (2004). *Teaching and learning in a diverse world: Multicultural education for young children*. New York: Teachers College Press, Columbia University.

Raver, C. C., & Zigler, E. F. (2004). Another step back? Assessing readiness in Head Start. *Young Children, 59*(1), 58–63.

Read, M. A. (2007). Sense of place in child care environments. *Early Childhood Education Journal, 34*, 387–392.

Reppucci, N. D., & Haugaard, J. J. (1989). Prevention of child sexual abuse: Myth or reality. *American Psychologist, 44*, 1266–1275.

Reynolds, C. R. & Kamphaus, R. W. (2004). *BASC-2, Behavior assessment system for children* (2nd ed.). Circle Pines, MN: AGS.

Rich, S. J. (1985). The writing suitcase. *Young Children, 40*(5), 42–44.

Rinaldi, C. (2001). Reggio Emilia: The image of the child and the child's environment as a fundamental principle. In L. Gandini & C. Pope Edwards (Eds.), *Bambini: The Italian approach to infant/toddler care* (pp. 49–54). New York: Teachers College Press, Columbia University.

Roberts, D. F., & Foehr, U. G. (2008). In J. Brooks-Gunn & E. H. Donahue (Eds.), Children and electronic media (pp. 11–48). Available online at www.futureofchildren.org.

Roberts, L. C., & Hill, H. T. (2003). Come and listen to a story about a girl named Rex: Using children's literature to debunk gender stereotypes. *Young Children, 58*(2), 39–42.

Roberts, S. K., & Crawford, P. A. (2008). Real life calls for real books: Literature to help children cope with family stressors. *Young Children, 63*(5), 12–17.

Robertson, C. (2010). *Safety, nutrition, and health in early education*. Belmont, CA: Wadsworth, Cengage Learning.

Robinson, B. E. (1988). Vanishing breed: Men in child care programs. *Young Children, 43*(6), 54–57.

Robles de Melendez, W., & Beck, V. (2010). *Teaching young children in multicultural classrooms: Issues, concepts, and strategies* (3rd ed.). Belmont, CA: Wadsworth, Cengage Learning.

Rogers, S., & Evans, J. (2008). *Inside role-play in early childhood education: Researching young children's perspectives*. New York: Routledge.

Roid, G. H. (2003). *Stanford-Binet Intelligence Scale* (5th ed.). Chicago: Riverside.

Roscos, K. A., Christie, J. F., & Richgels, D. J. (2003). The essentials of early literacy instruction. *Young Children, 58*(2), 52–60.

Ross, M. E. (2000). Science their way. *Young Children, 55*(2), 6–13.

Rothbart, M., & Derryberry, D. (2002). Temperament in children. In C. von Hofsten & L. Backman (Eds.), *Psychology at the turn of the millennium, vol. 2: Social, developmental, and clinical perspectives.* Florence, KY: Taylor & Frances/Routledge.

Rothlein, L. (1989). Nutrition tips revisited: On a daily basis, do we implement what we know? *Young Children, 44*(6), 30–36.

Roupp, R., Travers, J., Glantz, F., & Coelen, C. (1979). *Children at the center: Final report of the National Day Care Study.* Cambridge, MA: Abt.

Rowell, E. H. (2007). Missing! Picture books reflecting gay and lesbian families. *Young Children, 62*(3), 24–30.

Royce, J. M., Darlington, R. B., & Murray, H. W. (1983). Pooled analyses: Findings across studies. In *The Consortium for Longitudinal Studies, As the twig is bent. . . . Lasting effects of preschool programs* (pp. 411–459). Hillsdale, NJ: Erlbaum.

RTI Goes to pre-k: An early intervening system called Recognition and Response. (2007). Chapel Hill, NC: Frank Porter Graham Child Development Institute, University of North Carolina.

Saida, Y., & Miyashita, M. (1979). Development of fine motor skills in children: Manipulation of a pencil in young children aged two to six years old. *Journal of Human Movement Studies, 5*, 104–113.

Salkind, N. J. (2004). *Introduction to theories of human development.* Thousand Oaks, CA: Sage.

Salmon, A. K. (2010). Tools to enhance young children's thinking. *Young Children, 65*(5), 26–31.

Saltz, R. (1997). The Reggio Emilia influence at the University of Michigan-Dearborn Child Development Center: Challenges and changes. In J. Hendrick (Ed.), *First steps toward teaching the Reggio way* (pp. 167–180). Upper Saddle River, NJ: Merrill.

Sameroff, A. J. (1983). Developmental systems: Contexts and evolution. In P. H. Mussen (Ed.), *Handbook of child psychology* (4th ed.), *History, theory, and methods* (Vol. 1, pp. 237–294). New York: Wiley.

Samuelsson, I. P., Sheridan, S., Williams, P. (2006). Five preschool curricula—Comparative perspective. *International Journal of Early Childhood, 38*, 11–30.

Saracho, O., & Spodek, B.,(2007). Theories of socialization and social development. In O. Saracho & B. Spodek (Eds.), *Contemporary perspectives on socialization and social development in early childhood education* (pp. 1–17). Greenwich, CT: Information Age.

Sargent, P. (2002). Under the glass: Conversations with men in early childhood education. *Young Children, 57*(6), 22–28.

Satkowski, C. (2009, April 27,). A stimulus for second generation QRIS. *Early Ed Watch Blog.* New America Foundation. Available online at www .newamerica.net/blog/early-ed-watch/2009/ stimulus-second-generation-qris-11274.

Saunders, R., & Bingham-Newman, A. M. (1984). *Piagetian perspectives for preschools: A thinking book for teachers.* Englewood Cliffs, NJ: Prentice Hall.

Salovey, P., & Mayer, J. D. (1990). Emotional intelligence. *Imagination, Cognition and Personality, 9*(3), 185–211.

Sawyer, W. E. (2012). *Growing up with literature* (6th ed.). Belmont, CA: Wadsworth, Cengage Learning.

Schamer, L. A., & Jackson, J. B. (1996). Coping with stress: Common sense about teacher burnout. *Education Canada, 36*(2), 28–31, 49.

Scarr, S., Phillips, D., & McCartney, K. (1990). Facts, fantasies and the future of child care in the United States. *Psychological Science, 1*(1), 26–35.

Schickedanz, J. A. (1982). The acquisition of written language in young children. In B. Spodek (Ed.), *Handbook of research in early childhood education* (pp. 242–263). New York: Free Press.

Schickedanz, J. A. (1999). *Much more than the ABCs: The early stages of reading and writing.* Washington, DC: National Association for the Education of Young Children.

Schickedanz, J. A. (2003). NAEYC resources in focus: Selected excerpts. Creating a book nook for babies and toddlers. *Young Children, 58*(2), 61.

Schickedanz, J. A., Hansen, K., & Forsyth, P. D. (1990). *Understanding children.* Mountain View, CA: Mayfield.

Schiller, P., & Willis, C. A. (2008). Using brain-based teaching strategies to create supportive early childhood environments that address learning standards. *Young Children, 63*(4), 52–55.

Schmithorst, V. J., & Holland, S. K. (2004). The effect of musical training on the neural correlates of math processing: A functional magnetic resonance imaging study in humans. *Neuroscience Letters, 354*, 193–196.

Schumacher, R., Ewen, D., Hart, K., & Lombardi, J. (2005). *All together now: State experiences in using community-based child care to provide pre-kindergarten.* Center for Law and Social Policy, Policy Brief no. 5. Available online at www.clasp.org/admin/site/ publications/files/0225.pdf.

Schweinhart, L. J. (2004). *The High/Scope Perry Preschool Study through age 40: Summary, conclusions, and frequently asked questions.* Ypsilanti, MI: High/Scope Press.

Schweinhart, L. J., Barnes, H. V., & Weikart, D. P. (1993). *Significant benefits: The High/Scope Perry Preschool study through age 27.* Ypsilanti, MI: High/Scope Press.

Schweinhart, L. J., Montie, J., Xiang, Z., Barnett, W. S., Belfield, C. R., & Nores, M. (2005). *Lifetime effects: The High/Scope Perry Preschool study through age 40.* (Monographs of the High/Scope Educational Research Foundation, 14). Ypsilanti, MI: High/Scope Press.

Schweinhart, L. J., & Weikart, D. P. (1985). Evidence that good early childhood programs work. *Phi Delta Kappan, 66,* 545–551.

Schweinhart, L. J., Weikart, D. P., & Larner, M. B. (1986a). Consequences of three preschool models through age 15. *Early Childhood Research Quarterly, 1,* 15–45.

Schweinhart, L. J., Weikart, D. P., & Larner, M. B. (1986b). Child-initiated activities in early childhood programs may help prevent delinquency. *Early Childhood Research Quarterly, 1,* 303–312.

Schweinhart, L. J., & Weikart, D. P. (1997). *Lasting differences: The High/Scope preschool curriculum comparison study through age 23.* Ypsilanti, MI: High/Scope Press.

Sciarra, D. J., & Dorsey, A. G. (2010). *Developing and administering a child care center* (7th ed.). Belmont, CA: Wadsworth, Cengage Learning.

Seefeldt, C. (1999). Art for young children. In C. Seefeldt (Ed.), *The early childhood curriculum: Current findings in theory and practice* (pp. 201–217). New York: Teachers College Press, Columbia University.

Seefeldt, C. (2005). *How to work with standards in the early childhood classroom.* New York: Teachers College Press, Columbia University.

Seifert, K. L. (1993). Cognitive development in early childhood education. In B. Spodek (Ed.), *Handbook of research on the education of young children* (pp. 9–23). New York: Macmillan.

Seitz, H. (2008). The power of documentation in the early childhood classroom. *Young Children, 62*(2), 88–93.

Seitz, V., Rosenbaum, L. K., & Apfel, N. H. (1985). Effects of family support intervention: A ten-year follow-up. *Child Development, 56,* 376–391.

Selye, H. (Ed.) (1980). *Guide to stress research* (Vol. I). New York: Van Nostrand Reinhold.

Shaffer, L. F., Hall, E., & Lynch, M. (2009). Toddlers' scientific explorations: Encounters with insects. *Young Children, 64*(6), 18–23.

Shapiro, E., & Biber, B. (1972). The education of young children: A developmental-interaction approach. *Teachers College Record, 74,* 55–79.

Shatz, M., & Gelman, R. (1973). The development of communication skills: Modifications in the speech of young children as a function of listener. *Monographs of the Society for Research in Child Development, 38*(5, #152).

Sheehy, G. (1976). *Passages: Predictable crises of adult life.* New York: Dutton. (pp. 307–341). Rockville, MD: Aspen.

Shepherd, W., & Eaton, J. (1997). Creating environments that intrigue and delight children and adults. *Child Care Information Exchange, 117,* 42–47.

Shonkoff, J. P., & Phillips, D. A. (Eds.) (2000). *From neurons to neighborhoods: The science of early childhood development.* Washington, DC: National Academies Press.

Shore, R. (1997). *Rethinking the brain: New insights into early development.* New York: Families and Work Institute.

Shore, R. (2009). The case for investing in PreK-3rd education: Challenging myths about school reform. Policy to action brief of the Foundation for Child Development. Available online at http://fcd-us.org/resources/case-investing-prek-3rd-education-challenging-myths-about-school-reform.

Shore, R., & Strasser, J. (2006). Music for their minds. *Young Children, 61*(2), 62–67.

Siegel, A. W., & White, S. H. (1982). The child study movement: Early growth and development of the symbolized child. *Advances in Child Development and Behavior, 17,* 233–285.

Siegler, R. S. & Alibali, M. W. (2004). *Children's thinking* (4th ed.). Englewood Cliffs, NJ: Prentice Hall.

Simons, J. A., & Simons, F. A. (1986). Montessori and regular preschools: A comparison. In L. G. Katz (Ed.), *Current topics in early childhood education* (Vol. 6, pp. 195–223). Norwood, NJ: Ablex.

Simontacchi, C. (2007). *The crazy makers: How the food industry is destroying our brains and harming our children.* New York: Tarcher.

Skiffington, S., Washburn, S., & Elliot, K. (2011). Instructional coaching: Helping preschool teachers reach their full potential. *Young Children, 66*(3), 12–19.

Skinner, B. F. (1957). *Verbal behavior.* New York: Appleton-Century-Crofts.

Skinner, B. F. (1969). *Contingencies of reinforcement: A theoretical analysis.* New York: Appleton-Century-Crofts.

Skinner, B. F. (1974). *About behaviorism.* New York: Knopf.

Sloane, M. W. (2000). Make the most of learning centers. *Dimensions of Early Childhood, 28,* 16–20.

Smilansky, S. (1968). *The effects of sociodramatic play on disadvantaged children.* New York: Wiley.

Snow, C. E., & Ninio, A. (1986). The contracts of literacy: What children learn from learning to read books. In W. H. Teale & E. Sulzby (Eds.), *Emergent literacy: Writing and reading* (pp. 116–138). Norwood, NJ: Ablex.

Society for Neuroscience (2007, November 7). Mirror, mirror in the brain: Mirror neurons, self-understanding and autism research. *ScienceDaily.* Available online at http://www.sciencedaily.com/releases/2007/11/071106123725.htm.

Society for Neuroscience. (2008, November). Mirror neurons. *Brain briefings.* Available online at http://www.sfn.org/index.aspx?pagename=brainBriefings_MirrorNeurons.

Solley, B. A. (2007). On standardized testing: An ACEI Position Paper. *Childhood Education, 84,* 31–37.

Solomon, S. (2005). *American playgrounds: Revitalizing community spaces.* Hanover, NH: University Press of New England.

Sorte, J. M., & Daeschel, I. (2006). Health in action: A program approach to fighting obesity in young children. *Young Children, 61*(3), 40–48.

Sousa, D. A. (2005). *How the brain learns to read.* Thousand Oaks, CA: Corwyn Press.

Sousa, D. A. (2006). *How the brain learns* (3rd. ed.). Thousand Oaks, CA: Corwyn Press.

Squires, J., & Bricker, D. (2009). *Ages and Stages Questionnaires: A parent-completed, child monitoring system.* Towson, MD: Brookes.

Staley, L., & Portman, P. A. (2000). Red rover, red rover, it's time to move over! *Young Children, 55*(1), 67–72.

Steglin, D. A. (2005). Making the case for play policy: Research-based reasons to support play-based environments. *Young Children, 60*(2), 76–85.

Stellaccio, C. K., & McCarthy, M. (1999). Research in early childhood music and movement education. In C. Seefeldt (Ed.), *The early childhood curriculum: Current findings in theory and practice* (pp. 179–200). New York: Teachers College Press, Columbia University.

Stevenson, R. L. (1985). *A child's garden of verse.* M. Forman (Illustrator). New York: Delacorte Press.

Stipek, D. J., Feiler, R., Daniels, D., & Milburn, S. (1995). Effects of different instructional approaches on young children's achievement and motivation. *Child Development, 66,* 209–223.

Stonier, F. W., & Dickerson, D. L. (2009). When children have something to say, writers are born. *Young Children, 64*(1), 32–36.

Stuhlman, M. W., & Pianta, R. C. (2009). Profiles of educational quality in first grade. *The Elementary School Journal, 109*(4), 323, 342.

Strasburger, V. C., & Wilson, B. J. (2002). *Children, adolescents, and the media.* Thousand Oaks, CA: Sage.

Stremmel, A. J. (2002). Teacher research: Nurturing professional and personal growth through inquiry. *Young Children, 57*(5), 62–70.

Sulzby, E., & Teale, W. H. (2003). The development of the young child and the emergence of literacy. In J. Flood (Ed.), *Handbook of research on teaching the English language arts* (2nd ed.). Mahwah, NJ: Erlbaum.

Sumsion, J. (1999). James' story: A decade in the life of a male early childhood professional. *Early Child Development and Care, 149,* 5–15.

Sunal, C. S. (1993). Social studies in early childhood education. In B. Spodek (Ed.), *Handbook of research on the education of young children* (pp. 176–190). New York: Macmillan.

Sutherland, Z., & Arbuthnot, M. H. (1997). *Children and books* (9th ed.). New York: Longman.

Tabors, P. O. (2008). *One child, two languages: A guide for early childhood educators of children learning English as a second language* (2nd ed.). Baltimore: Brooks.

Tarrant, K., Greenberg, E., Kagan, S. L., & Kauerz, K. (2009). The early childhood workforce. In S. Feeney, A. Galper, & C. Seefeldt (Eds.), *Continuing issues in early childhood education* (pp. 134–157). Upper Saddle River, NJ: Merrill.

Tegano, D. W., Moran, J. C., DeLong, A. J., Brickey, J., & Uramassini, K. K. (1996). Designing classroom spaces: Making the most of time. *Early Childhood Education Journal, 23,* 135–141.

Tertell, E. A., Klein, S. M., & Jewett, J. L. (Eds.). (1998). *When teachers reflect: Journeys toward effective, inclusive practice.* Washington, DC: National Association for the Education of Young Children.

Thomas, A., & Chess, S. (1969). *Temperament and development.* New York: New York University Press.

Thomas, A., Chess, S., & Birch, H. G. (1968). *Temperament and behavior disorders in children.* New York: New York University Press.

Thomas, R. M. (1990a). Basic concepts and applications of Piagetian cognitive development theory. In R. M. Thomas (Ed.), *The encyclopedia of human development and education: Theory, research, and studies* (pp. 53–56). New York: Pergamon Press.

Thomas, R. M. (1990b). *The encyclopedia of human development and education: Theory, research, and studies.* New York: Pergamon Press.

Thompson, R. A. (2000). The legacy of early attachments. *Child Development, 71,* 145–152.

Thompson, R. A. (2008). Connecting neurons, concepts, and people: Brain development and its implications. NIEER Policy Brief #17. Available online at http://nieer.org/resources/policybriefs/17.pdf.

Thyssen, S. (2000). The child's start in day care centers. *Early Child Development and Care, 161,* 33–46.

Tips to stop bullying. (2011). Available online at www.livestrong.com/article/96196-tips-stop-bullying.

Torquati, J., Gabriel, M. M., Jones-Branch, J., & Leeper-Miller, J. (2010). Environmental education: A natural way to nurture children's development and learning. *Young Children, 65*(6), 98–104.

Torrence, M., & Chattin-McNichols, J. (2000). Montessori education today. In J. L. Roopnarine & J. E. Johnson (Eds.), *Approaches to early childhood education* (3rd ed.). Upper Saddle River, NJ: Merrill.

Tough, P. (September 25, 2009). Can the right kinds of play teach self-control? *New York Times,* p. MM31.

Tout, K., deHaan, M., Campbell, E. K., & Gunnar, M. (1998). Social behavior correlates of cortisol activity in child care: Gender differences and time-of-day effects. *Child Development, 69,* 1247–1262.

Trawick-Smith, J. (2006). *Early childhood development: A multicultural perspective* (4th ed.). Upper Saddle River, NJ: Merrill.

Tremblay, R. E. (2006). Prevention of youth violence: Why not start at the beginning? *Journal of Abnormal Child Psychology, 34*(4), 481–487.

Tribe, C. (1982). *Profile of three theories: Erikson, Maslow, Piaget.* Dubuque, IA: Kendall/Hunt.

Trost, G. (2007). *Active education: Physical education, physical activity, and academic performance.* Fall 2007 Research Brief. San Diego, CA: San Diego State University.

Tunks, K. W., & Giles, R. M. (2009). Writing their words: Strategies for supporting young authors. *Young Children, 64*(1), 22–25.

Tutty, L. M. (1997). Child sexual abuse prevention programs: Evaluating "who do you tell." *Child Abuse and Neglect: The International Journal, 21,* 869–881.

Ulich, R. (1947). *Three thousand years of educational wisdom.* Cambridge, MA: Harvard University Press.

Ulich, R. (1967). Johann Heinrich Pestalozzi. In P. Edwards (Ed.), *The encyclopedia of philosophy* (Vol. 5–6, pp. 121–122). New York: Macmillan & The Free Press.

University of Illinois at Urbana-Champaign (2009, April 1). Physical activity may strengthen children's ability to pay attention. *ScienceDaily.* Available online at www.sciencedaily.com/releases/2009/03/090331183800.htm.

University of Illinois at Urbana-Champaign (2010, September 16). Children's brain development is linked to physical fitness, research finds. *ScienceDaily.* Available at www.sciencedaily.com/releases/2010/09/100915171536.htm.

U.S. Bureau of Labor Statistics. (2008). Bulletin 2307. Available online at http://www.census.gov/prod/2/gen/96statab/labor.pdf.

U.S. Bureau of Labor Statistics. (2011). *Occupational outlook handbook, 2010–11 edition.* Washington, DC: Government Printing Office.

U. S. Bureau of the Census. (2000). *Percent of households that are married-couple families.* Available online at http://factfinder2.census.gov/faces/tableservices/jsf/pages/productview.xhtml?pid=ACS_10_1YR_GCT1101.US01PR&prodType=table.

U.S. Bureau of the Census. (2007a). *Custodial mothers and fathers and their child support: 2005.* Available online at http://www.census.gov/prod/2007pubs/p60-234.pdf.

U.S. Bureau of the Census. (2007b). Single-parent households showed little variation since 1994, Census Bureau reports. Available online at http://web.docuticker.com/go/docubase/16627

U.S. Bureau of the Census (2009). 2005–2009 American Community Survey. Available online at http://www.census.gov/acs/www/data_documentation/2009_5yr_data.

U.S. Bureau of the Census (2011a). Family groups with children under 18 years old by race and Hispanic Origin: 1990 to 2009. Available online at http://www.census.gov/compendia/statab/2012/tables/12s0067.pdf

U.S. Bureau of the Census (2011b). People below poverty level by selected characteristics: 2008. Available online at www.census.gov/compendia/statab/2011/tables/11s0711.pdf.

U.S. Bureau of the Census (2011c). USA Quick Facts from the US Census Bureau. Available online at www.census.gov/quickfacts.census.gov/qfd/states/00000.html.

U.S. Department of Agriculture (USDA). (2009). Food and nutrition information center. Available online at http://fnic.nal.usda.gov/nal_display/index.php?info_center=4&tax_level=2&tax_subject=358&topic_id=1612.

U.S. Department of Health and Human Services and Head Start. (2003). *The Head Start path to positive child outcomes.* Available online at http://www .ecechicago.org/resources/pdfs/headstart01.pdf.

Vance, E., & Weaver, P. J. (2002). *Class meetings: Young children solving problems together.* Washington, DC: National Association for the Education of Young Children.

Ventura, A., Johnson, S. L., & Birch, L. L. (2009). Children's eating: The development of food acceptance patterns. In E. Essa & M. Burnham (Eds.), *Informing our practice: Useful research on young children's development* (pp. 173–188). Washington, DC: NAEYC.

Vygotsky, L. S. (1962). *Thought and language.* New York: Wiley.

Vygotsky, L. S. (1978). The prehistory of written language. In M. Cole, V. John-Steiner, S. Scribner, & E. Souberman (Eds.), *Mind and society: The development of higher psychological process* (pp. 105–119). Cambridge, MA: Harvard University Press.

Wadsworth, B. J. (1984). *Piaget's theory of cognitive and affective development* (3rd ed.). New York: Longman.

Walker, J. E., Shea, T. M., & Bauer, A. M. (2007). *Behavior management: A practical approach for educators.* Upper Saddle River, NJ: Merrill.

Wallerstein, J., Lewis, J., & Blakeslee, S. (2001). *The unexpected legacy of divorce: A 25 year landmark study.* New York: Hyperion.

Wat, A. (2007). *Dollars and sense: A review of Economic Analyses of Pre-K.* Washington, DC: Pre-K Now.

Watson, M. (2003). Attachment theory and challenging behaviors: Reconstructing the nature of relationships. *Young Children, 58*(4), 12–20.

Watson, L. D., & Swim, T. (2011). *Infants and toddlers: Curriculum and teaching* (7th ed.). Belmont, CA: Wadsworth, Cengage Learning.

Weber, E. (1984). *Ideas influencing early childhood education.* New York: Teachers College Press, Columbia University.

Weikart, D. P., & Schweinhart, L. J. (2000). The High/Scope cognitively oriented curriculum of early education. In J. L. Roopnarine & J. E. Johnson (Eds.), *Approaches to early childhood education* (3rd ed., pp. 253–267). Columbus, OH: Merrill.

Werner, E. E., & Essa, E. L. (2009). Resilient children. In E. Essa & M. Burnham (Eds.), *Informing our practice: Useful research on young children's development* (pp. 89–96). Washington, DC: NAEYC.

Werner, E. E., & Smith, R. S. (1982). *Vulnerable but invincible: A longitudinal study of resilient children and youth.* New York: McGraw-Hill.

Wertsch, J. V. (1985). *Vygotsky and the social formation of mind.* Cambridge, MA: Harvard University Press.

Whalen, C. (2002). Meeting the diverse needs of children through storytelling. *Young Children, 57*(2), 31–34.

Whitebook, M. (1986). The teacher shortage: A professional precipice. *Young Children, 41*(3), 10–11.

Whitebook, M., Howes, C., & Phillips, D. (1989). *Who cares? Child care teachers and the quality of care in America: Executive summary, National Child Care Staffing Study.* Oakland, CA: Child Care Employee Project.

Whitebook, M., Sakai, L., Gerber, E., & Howes, C. (2001). *Then and now: Changes in child care staffing, 1994–2000.* Washington, DC: Center for the Child Care Workforce.

Wilburn, R. E. (2000). *Understanding the preschooler.* New York: Lang.

Willer, B. (1990). Estimating the full cost of quality. In B. Willer (Ed.), *Reaching the full cost of quality in early child-hood programs* (pp. 55–86). Washington, DC: National Association for the Education of Young Children.

Williams, A. E. (2008). Exploring the natural world with infants and toddlers in an urban setting. *Young Children, 63*(1), 22–26.

Williams, H. G., & Abernathy, D. (2007). Assessment of gross motor development. In B. A. Bracken & R. J. Nagle (Eds.), *The psychoeducational assessment of preschool children* (pp. 204–233). Mahwah, NJ: Erlbaum.

Williams, H. G., & Monsma, E. V. (2006). Assessment of gross motor development. In B. A. Bracken & R. J. Nagle (Eds.), *The psychoeducational assessment of preschool children* (4th ed., pp. 397–434). Mahwah, NJ: Erlbaum.

Willis, C. A., & Schiller, P. (2011). Preschoolers' social skills steer life success. *Young Children, 66*(1), 42–49.

Wilson, B. J. (2008). Media and children's aggression, fear, and altruism. In J. Brooks-Gunn & E. H. Donahue (Eds.), *Children and electronic media* (pp. 87–118). Available online at www.futureofchildren.org.

Wilson, L. C. (1999). *Infants and toddlers: Curriculum and teaching* (4th ed.). Clifton Park, NY: Delmar Learning.

Winter, S. M. (2007). *Inclusive early childhood education: A collaborative approach.* Upper Saddle River, NJ: Pearson Prentice Hall.

Wolfe, J. (2000). *Learning from the past: Historical voices in early childhood education.* New York: Piney Branch Press.

Wood, F. B. (2008). Grief: Helping young children cope. *Young Children, 63*(5), 28–31.

Wortham, S. C. (2011). *Assessment in early childhood education* (6th ed.). Upper Saddle River, NJ: Merrill.

Wyeth, S. D. (2005). *Something beautiful.* New York: Firefly.

Xu, S. H., & Rutledge, A. L. (2003). Chicken start with *Ch!* Kindergartners learn through environmental print. *Young Children, 58*(2), 44–51.

Yopp, H. K., & Yopp, R. H. (2009). Phonological awareness is child's play. *Young Children, 64*(1), 12–18, 21.

Zero to Three. (2011). How does nutrition affect the developing brain? Available online at http://main.zerotothree.org/site/PageServer?pagename=ter_key_brainFAQ#nutrition.

Zigler, E., & Berman, W. (1973). Discerning the future of early childhood intervention. *American Psychologist, 38,* 894–906.

Zigler, E. F., & Freedman, J. (1987). Head Start: A pioneer of family support. In S. L. Kagan, D. R. Powell, B. Weissbourd, & E. F. Zigler (Eds.), *America's family support programs* (pp. 57–76). New Haven, CT: Yale University Press.

Zimmerman, E., & Zimmerman, L. (2000). Art education and early childhood education: The young child as creator and meaning maker within a community context. *Young Children, 55*(6), 87–92.

Name Index

Subject Index

Receptionists (support staff), 82
Recommendations, 156–160
Recycling, 298–299
Redirection, 405
"Red Rover" (game), 287
Reflection, 91
Reflective abstraction, 282
Reflective teaching, 91–93
Reggio Children (website), 219
Reggio Emilia approach
  art, 228–229
  environment, 168
  program, 128–129, 208, 214–217
  team teaching, 80, 92
  website, 141
Regulation and licensing, 86
Reinforcement, 119, 398–399, 401
Relaxation techniques, 436–438
Reliability, 152
Religion-sponsored programs, 12
Religious dietary restrictions, 369, 378
Report on Physical Punishment in the United States: What Research Tells Us about Its Effects on Children (Gershoff), 395
Representation, 117
Research support for early childhood education, 132–137
Respect, 19, 79, 397
Rest packs, 377–378
Rest time, 197, 375–378
Rethinking the Brain (Shore), 84
Revenge, 396
Rhymes, 316, 331
Rhythm instruments, musical, 240–241
Rich teacher talk, 323
Riddles, 316
Risk taking, 79
Role play, 108
Room size and shape, 169
Rote counting, 288
Rough-and-tumble play, 40
Round-robin stories, 320
Rousseau, Jean-Jacques, 107, 110
Routines and group activities
  activity time, 382–383
  arrival time, 363–365, 381–382
  bathroom facilities, 374–375
  calendar activity, 386
  daily schedule, 381–387
  departure time, 365, 381–382
  diapering, 373–375
  eating behavior, 365–373
  expectations, 380–381
  family concerns about, 378–379
  feeding infants, 366
  field trips, 388
  food assistance programs, 372–373
  group time, 383–386
  healthy eating habits, 371
  meals, 365–373, 383
  nap guidelines, 377–378
  naps, 197, 379, 426
  new child at school, 364–365
  nutritional needs, 366–371, 372
  physical environment, 384
  planned unusual events, 387–389

problem-eating behaviors, 371–372
problem sleepers, 376, 378
religious dietary restrictions, 369, 378
rest time, 375–378
rules, 381
sharing time, 385
show-and-tell, 385–386
sleep time, 375–378
toilet accidents, 374
toileting, 373–375, 379
toothbrushing, 375
transitions, 386–387
walks, 388–389
Rowell, Elizabeth, 60
Rules
  games with, 39
  group activity, 381
  guidelines for, 410
  moral, 347
Running, 252
Running record, 147, 149

SACERS (School-Age Care Environments Rating Scale), 161
Safety
  health and, 171
  physical development and, 275
  while cooking, 273
Salary, 96–97
Sand play, 270
Scaffolding, 337
Scheduling
  activity level of children, 198
  activity time, 193–194
  alternating active and quiet times, 197–198
  arrival of children, 199
  child-initiated and teacher-initiated activities, 198
  cleanup, 196
  developmental level of children, 198–199
  examples of schedules, 203–205
  flexibility of schedule, 205–206
  group size, 199
  infants, 200–201
  large-group activities, 194–195
  meals, 196–197
  nap time, 197
  outdoor activity, 196
  school-age children, 201–203
  seasonal considerations, 199–200
  small-group activities, 195–196
  toddlers, 200–201
  transitions, 197
  types of schedules, 203–205
Schemata, 117
Schematic stage, 226
School-Age Care Environments Rating Scale (SACERS), 161
School-age children
  creativity, 243
  developmental characteristics, 32–33
  language development, 328–330
  math learning, 301–302
  physical development, 267–269
  physical environment, 178

scheduling, 201–203
science learning, 301–302
social development, 355–356
School handbook, 68
School programs, 69
Science, 293–299, 301–302
Science learning, 302–303
The Science of Early Childhood Development: Closing the Gap between What We Know and What We Do, 338
Scissors, 234
Scott, Ann, 319
Scrap materials, 186
Screening tests, 152–153, 159
Scribbles, basic, 227
Scribbling stage, 226
Sculpting, 233
Seasonal considerations, 199–200
SECA (Southern Early Childhood Association), 91
Second-language teaching strategies, 314–315
Secretary (support staff), 82
Self-care children, 11
Self-care theme play kits, 186
Self-concept, 33–34
Self-control, 339
Self-correcting, 123
Self-demand schedule, 200
Self-esteem, 33–34
Self-help skills, 254
Self-protection programs, 439
Self-selected learning activities, 193
Self-selected time-out, 404
Self-understanding, 210
Semantic network, 311
Semantics, 311–312
Sendak, Maurice, 319
Sense of humor, 79
Senses, 255–256, 294
Sensitive periods, 109
Sensitivity, 221
Sensorial (activities and materials), 123
Sensorimotor period, 118, 281
Sensory activities, 269–272
Sensory concepts, 271–272
Sensory deficit, 410
Sensory discrimination, 109
Sensory integration, 257
Sensory-perceptual development, 251, 255–257
Sensory register, 283
Sentence stories, 320
Separation anxiety, 363
Seriation, 127, 271, 287
Sesame Street (television program), 246, 247
Seven-year-olds, 32–33
Sex stereotyping, 343
Sexual abuse, 427, 428
Sexual-abuse prevention programs, 439
Shame and doubt, 115
Shaping, 120
Shared reading, 322
Sharing time, 385
Shelves, 169